Onshape 2025 for Beginners

Tutorial Books

Onshape for Beginners

For resource files contact us at
Online.books999@gmail.com

Table of Contents

Introduction

Welcome to *Onshape for Beginners* book. This book is written to assist students, designers, and engineering professionals in designing 3D models. It covers the essential features and functionalities of Onshape using relevant tutorials and exercises.

Topics covered in this Book

- Chapter 1, "Getting Started with Onshape," gives an introduction to Onshape. The user interface and terminology are discussed in this chapter.
- Chapter 2, "Sketch Techniques," explores the sketching commands in Onshape. You will learn to create parametric sketches.
- Chapter 3, "Extrude and Revolve features," teaches you to create basic 3D geometry using the Extrude and Revolve commands.
- Chapter 4, "Placed Features," covers the features which can be created without using sketches.
- Chapter 5, "Patterned Geometry," explores the commands to create patterned and mirrored geometry.
- Chapter 6, "Sweep Features," covers the commands to create swept and helical features.
- Chapter 7, "Loft Features," covers the Loft command and its core features.
- Chapter 8, "Additional Features," covers additional commands to create complex geometry.
- Chapter 9, "Modifying Parts," explores the commands and techniques to modify the part geometry.
- Chapter 10, "Assemblies," helps you to create assemblies using the bottom-up and top-down design approaches.
- Chapter 11, "Drawings," covers how to create 2D drawings from 3D parts and assemblies.

Chapter 1: Getting Started with Onshape

Introduction to Onshape

Onshape is a cloud-based CAD application. It is a parametric and feature-based system that allows you to create 3D parts, assemblies, and 2D drawings. The design process in Onshape is shown below.

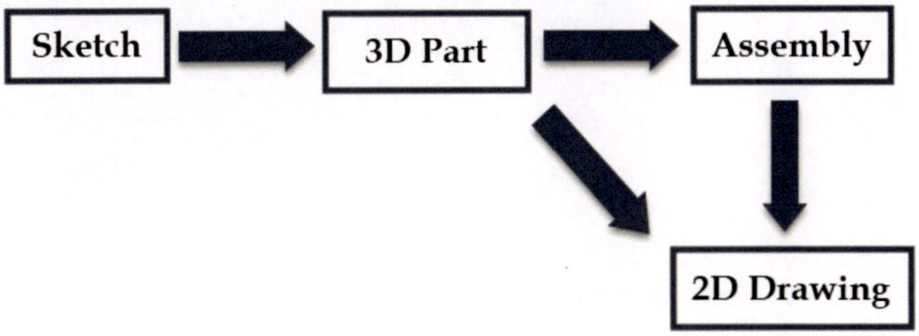

In Onshape, everything is controlled by parameters, dimensions, or constraints. For example, if you want to change the position of the hole shown in the figure, you need to change the dimension or relation that controls its position.

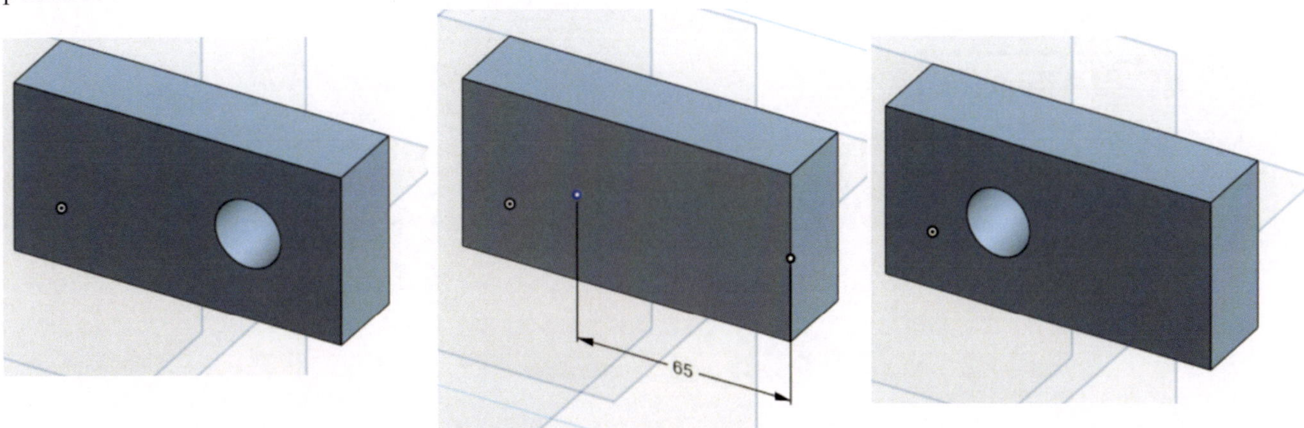

The parameters and constraints that you set up allow you to have control over the design intent. The design intent describes the way your 3D model will behave when you apply dimensions and constraints to it. For example, if you want to position the hole at the center of the block, one way is to add dimensions between the hole and the adjacent edges. However, when you change the size of the block, the hole will not be at the center.

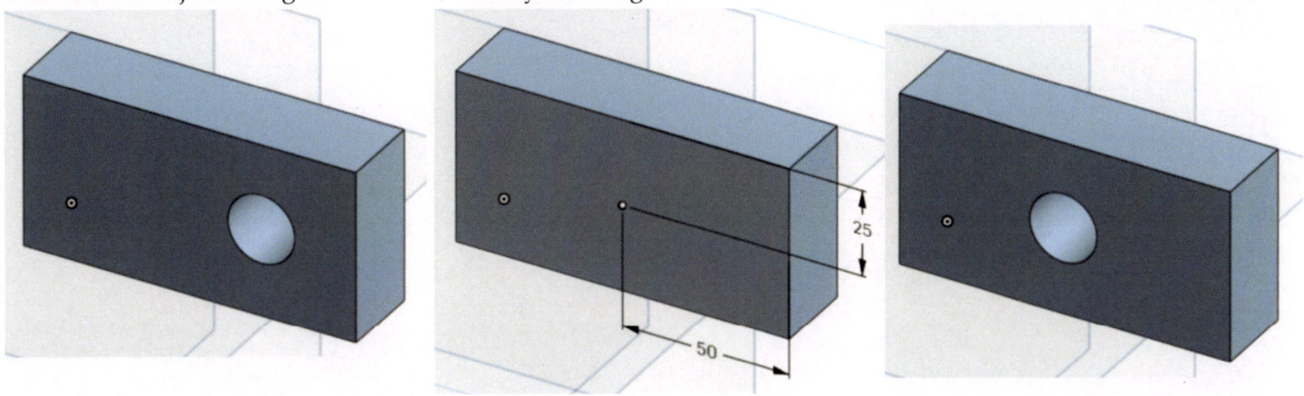

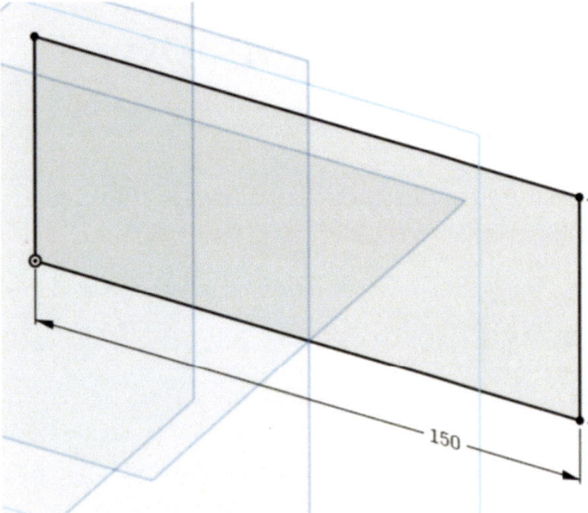

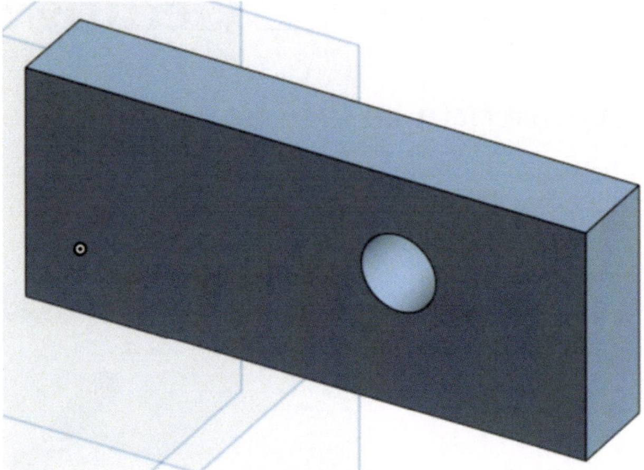

You can make the hole to be at the center, even if the size of the block changes. To do this, right click on the sketch used to create the hole and select **Edit**. Next, delete the dimensions and create a diagonal construction line. Apply the Midpoint constraint between the hole point and the diagonal construction line. Next, click the green check on the Sketch dialog.

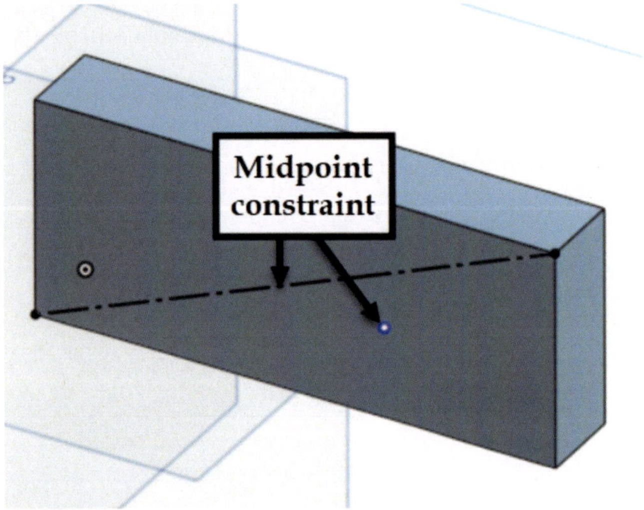

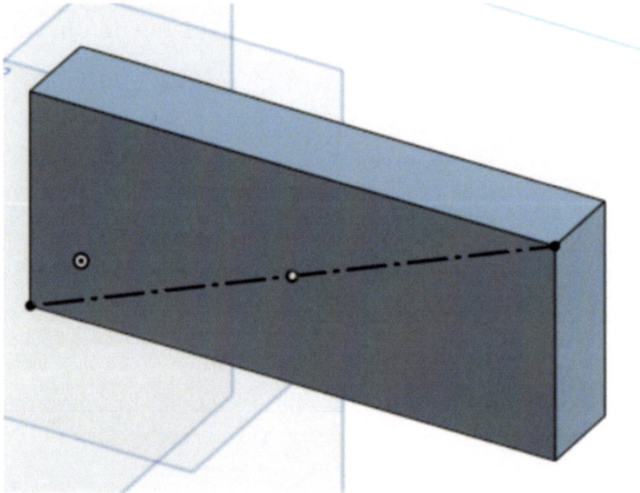

Now, even if you change the size of the block, the hole will always remain at the center.

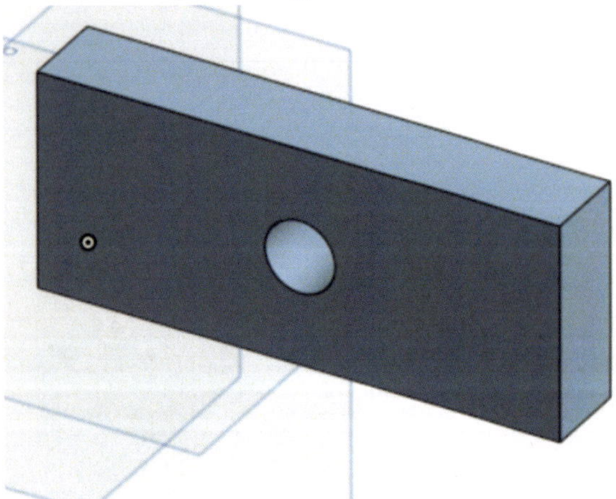

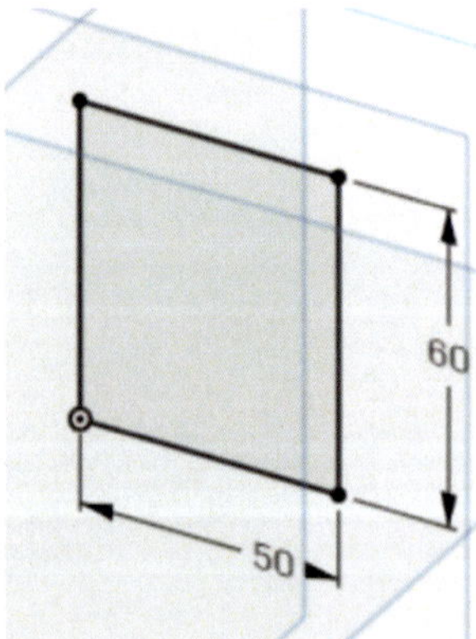

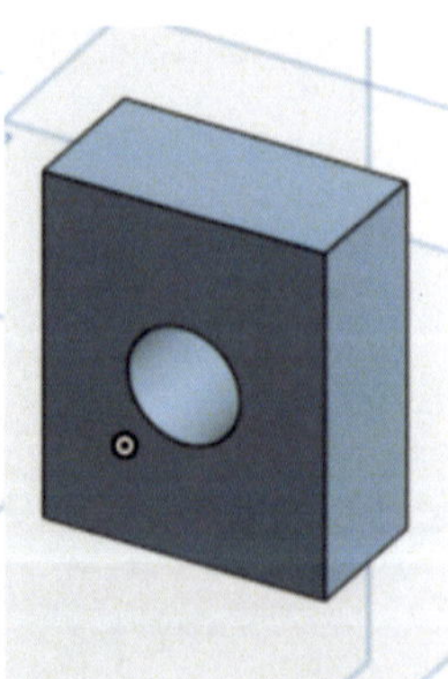

Starting Onshape

To start **Onshape**, open your internet browser and type www.onshape.com in the address bar. Next, click the **SIGN IN** button located at the top right corner. Next, enter your registered email ID and password, and then click the **Sign in** button. On the Documents page, click the **Create** button located at the top left corner, and then select **Document**. Next, enter the name of the document in the **Document name** box and click **OK**; a new design file will appear on the screen. You can change the working units of the file. To do this, click the **Document menu** located at the top left corner. Next, click the **Workspace units** option and set the **Default unit type** and click the green check.

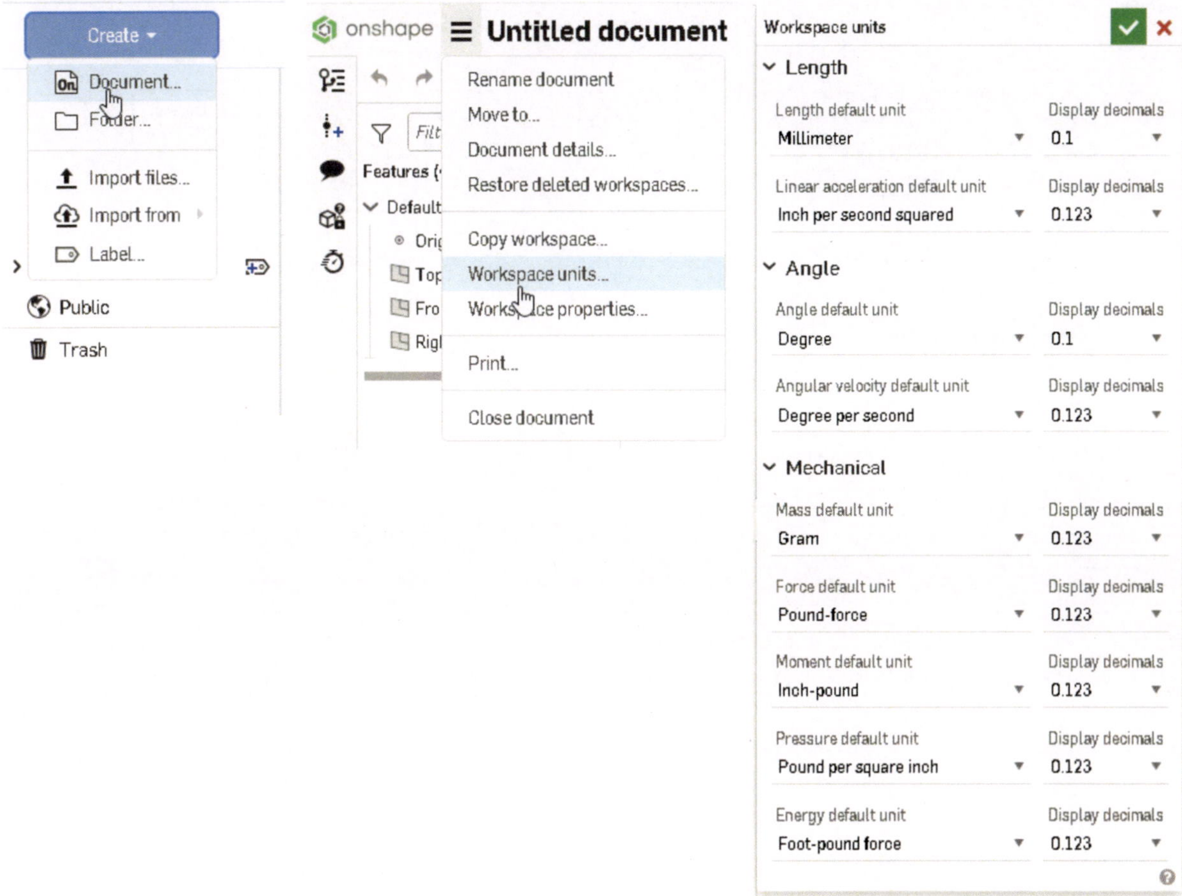

User Interface

The following image shows the **Onshape** application window.

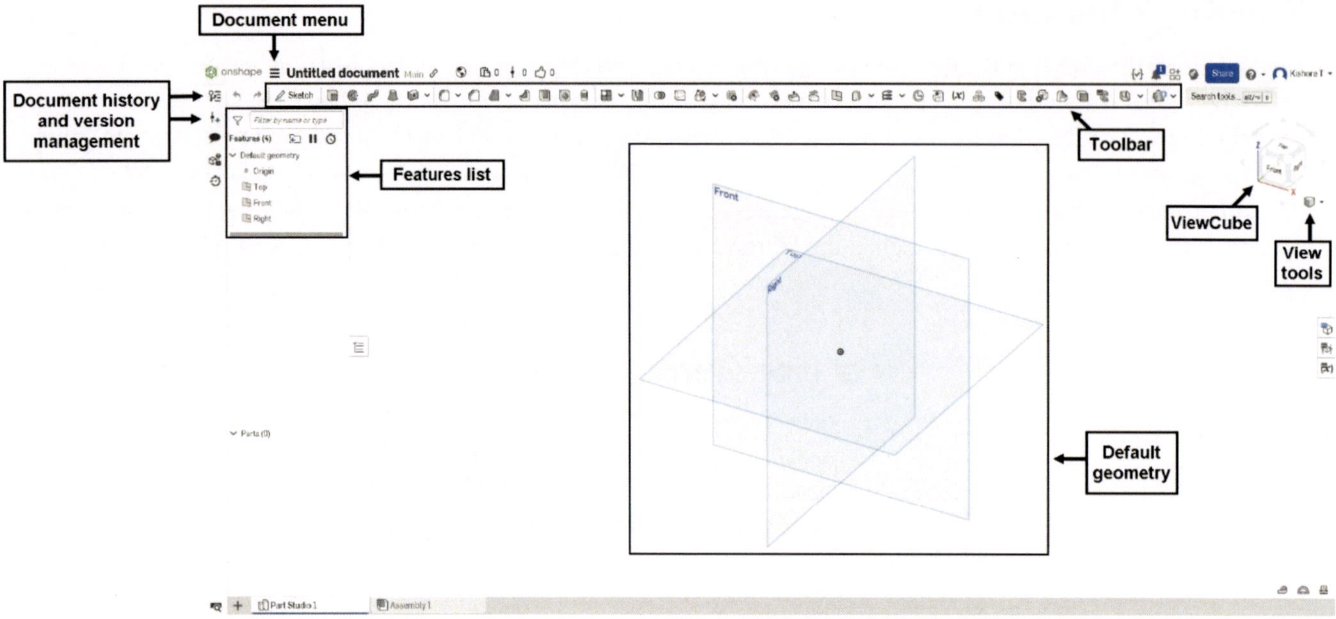

Toolbars in Onshape

There are five toolbars available in Onshape: **Document**, **Feature**, **Assembly**, **Sketch**, and **Drawing**.

The **Document** toolbar has commands to create documents, document versions, add comments, share documents, and so on.

The **Feature** toolbar has all the commands to create solid models.

This **Sketch** toolbar has commands to create sketches.

The **Assembly** toolbar has commands to assemble the parts.

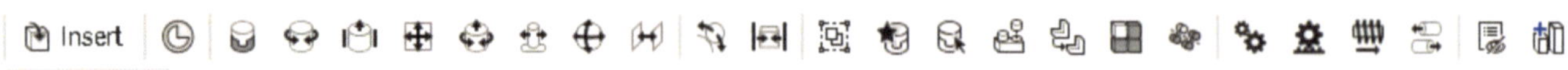

The **Drawing** toolbar has all the commands to generate 2D drawings of parts and assemblies.

The other components of the user interface are discussed next.

Document menu

This is located at the top left corner of the window. It consists of commonly used commands such as **Rename document, Document properties, Copy workspace, Workspace units, Print**, and **Close document**.

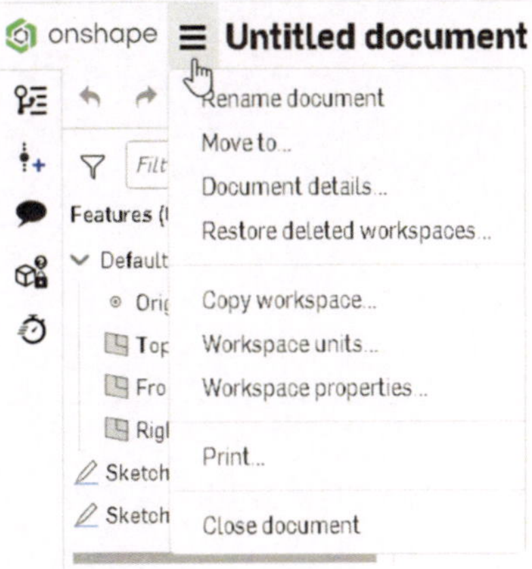

Graphics area

Graphics area is the blank space located below the toolbar. You can draw sketches and create 3D geometry in the Graphics area. The left corner of the graphics area has a **Features** list. It captures the design history of the model. You can edit the sketches and features of the model using the **Features** list. In addition to that, you can Hide/Show the planes, and sketches of the 3D model.

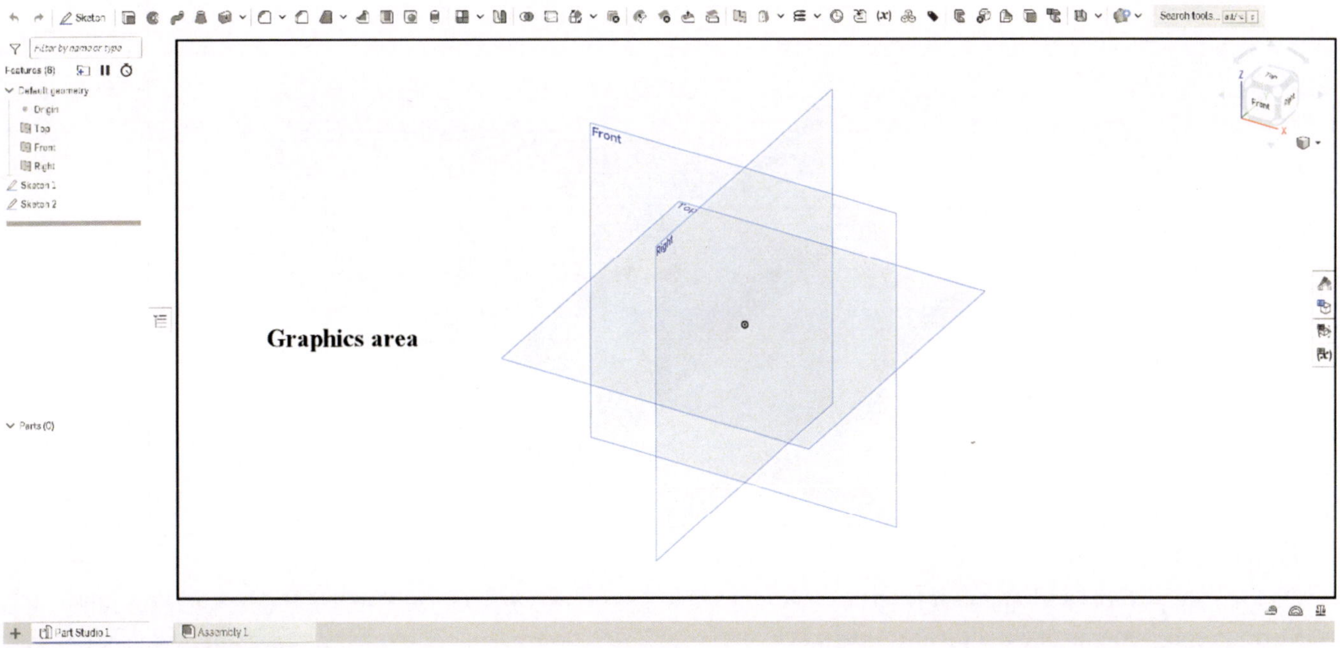

Comments dialog

The **Comments** dialog appears when you click the **Comments** icon located at the left side of the window. You can add comments to the model by clicking the **Tag entity** icon on the **Comments** dialog and selecting an entity from the graphics window. Next, enter the comments in the **Add comment** box and click the **Add** button. You can also attach an image to the comment. To do this, click the **Browse for attachment** icon and select an image.

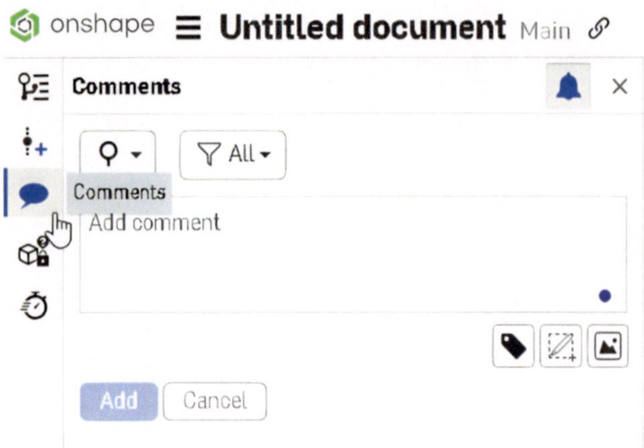

You can also add corrections to the design by clicking the **Markup** icon. Click the green check after adding the corrections.

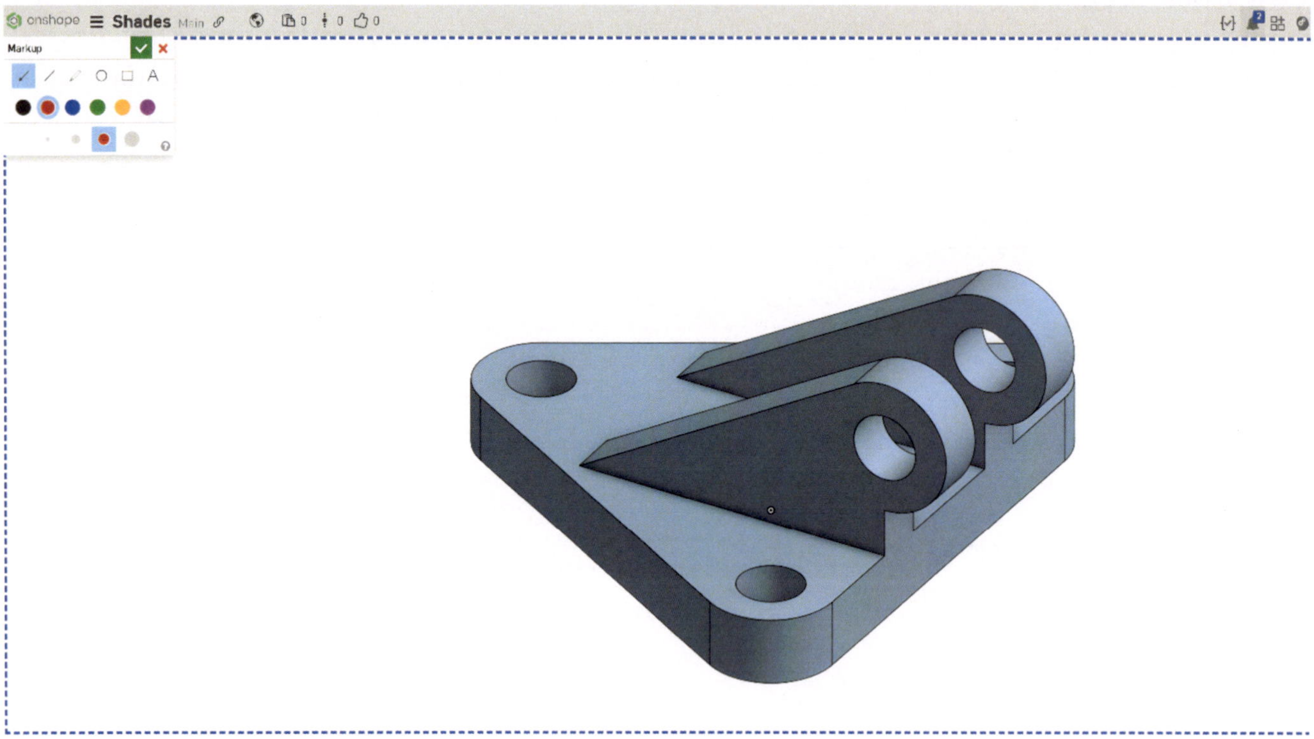

Dialogs

Dialogs are part of Onshape user interface. Using a dialog, you can easily specify many settings and options. Various components of a dialog are shown below.

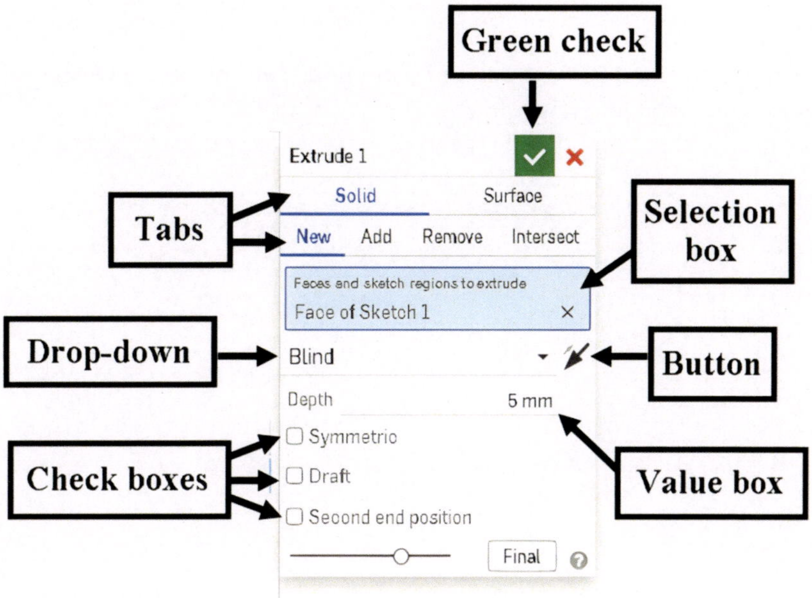

Shortcut menus

Shortcut Menus are displayed when you right-click on the graphics area. Onshape provides various shortcut menus in order to help you access some options very easily and quickly. The options in shortcut menus vary based on the workspace. In addition to that, the options in the shortcut menu depending on the selection.

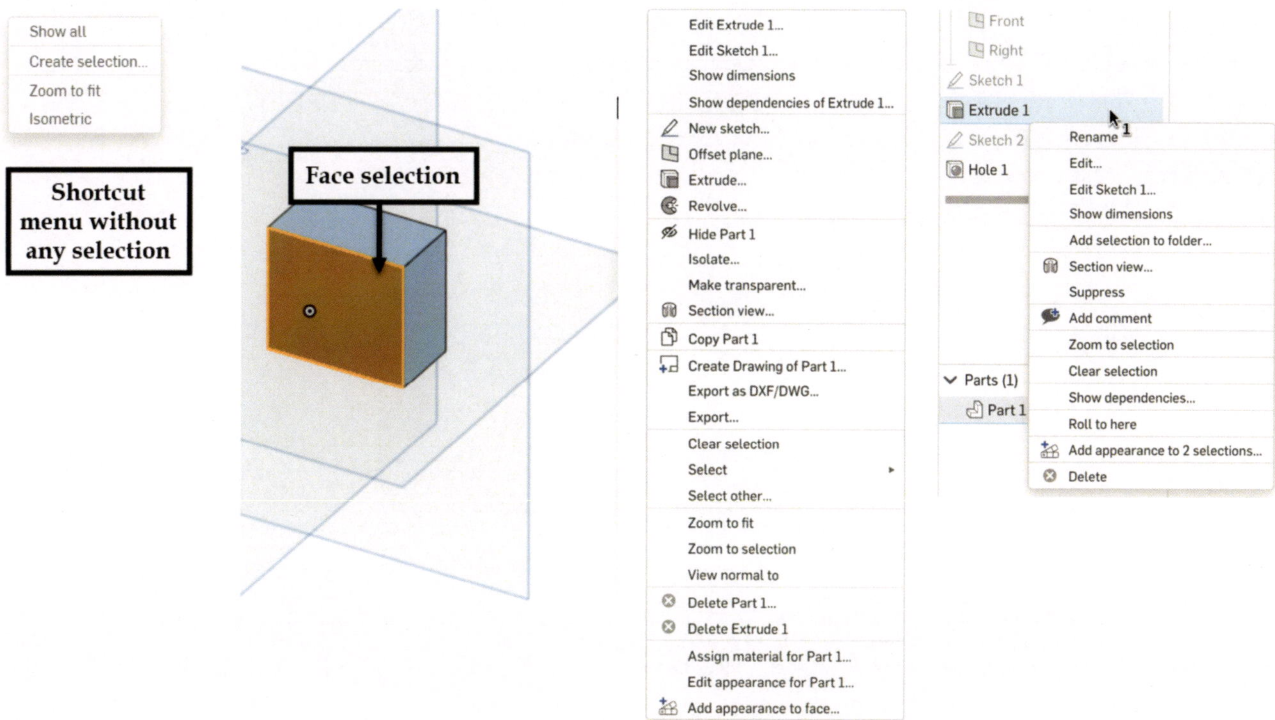

Shortcut menu with selection

Onshape Help

Onshape offers you with the help system that goes beyond basic command definition. You can access Onshape help by clicking on the **Help menu** icon on the right side of the window.

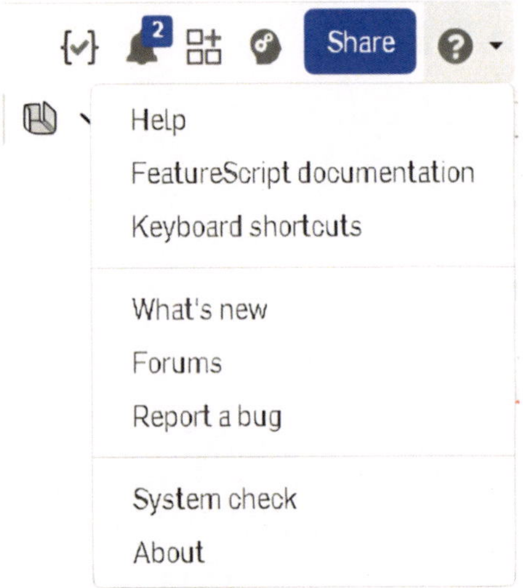

Documents page

The **Documents** page is an essential feature of Onshape. It is used to store, organize, and share the documents. You can display Documents page by clicking the **onshape** icon located at the top left corner of the window. It displays a list of folders and documents created by you.

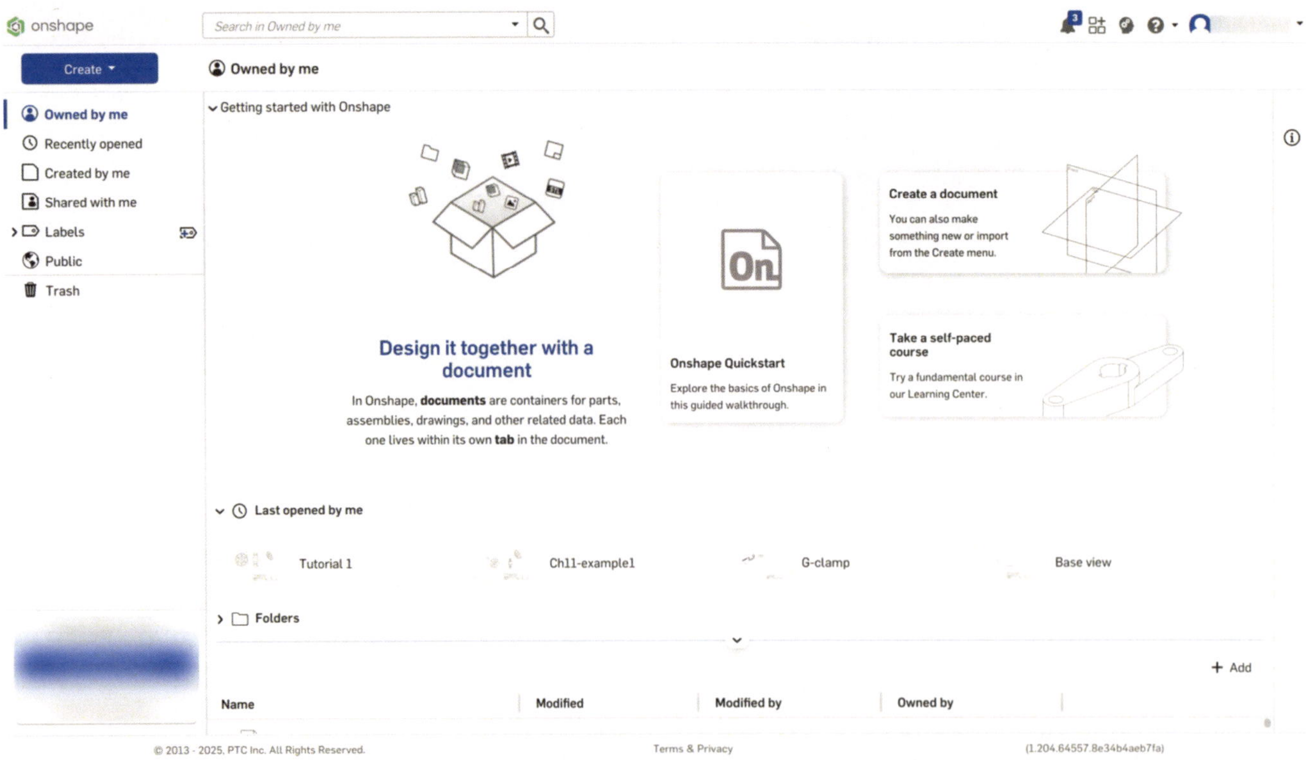

You can create a new folder by clicking the **Create** button and selecting the **Folder** option. Next, enter the folder name and click the **Create** button. After creating the folder, double-click on it. You can upload already existing files by selecting **Create > Import Files**.

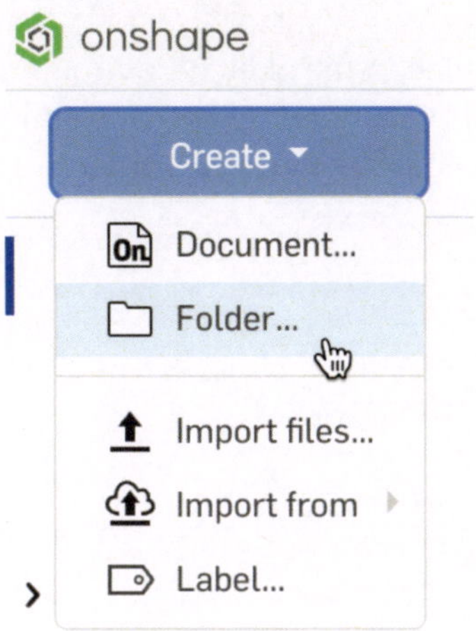

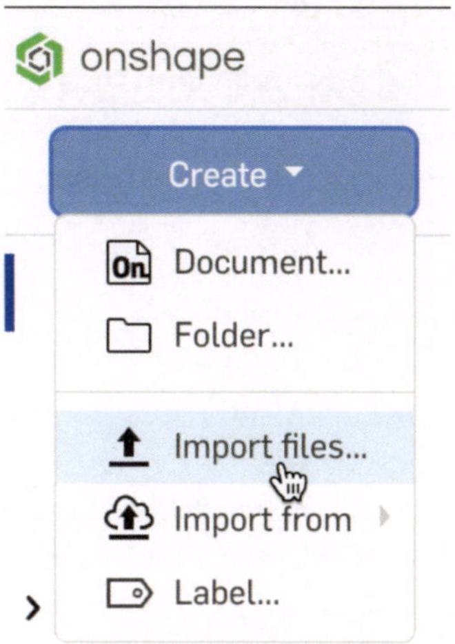

Questions

1. Give one example of where you would establish a relationship between a part's features.
2. How to access ONSHAPE Help.
3. How can you activate the Shortcut menu?
4. How is ONSHAPE a parametric modeling application?
5. How to access the view tools?

Chapter 2: Sketch Techniques

This chapter covers the methods and commands to create a sketch in the Sketch Environment. In Onshape, you create a rough sketch and then apply dimensions and constraints that define its shape and size. The dimensions define the length, size, and angle of a sketch element, whereas constraints define the constraints between the sketch elements.

The topics covered in this chapter are:

- *Sketching in Part Studio*
- *Using constraints and dimensions to control the shape and size of a sketch*
- *Learning sketching commands*
- *Learning commands and options that help you to create a sketch easily*

Starting a New Part Document

To create a new part document, on the dashboard click **Create > Document** and specify the name in the **Document name** field on the **New document** dialog. Click **Create document** to start the part document.

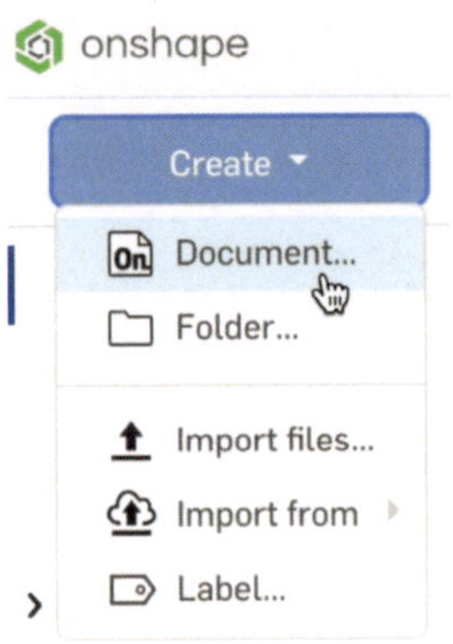

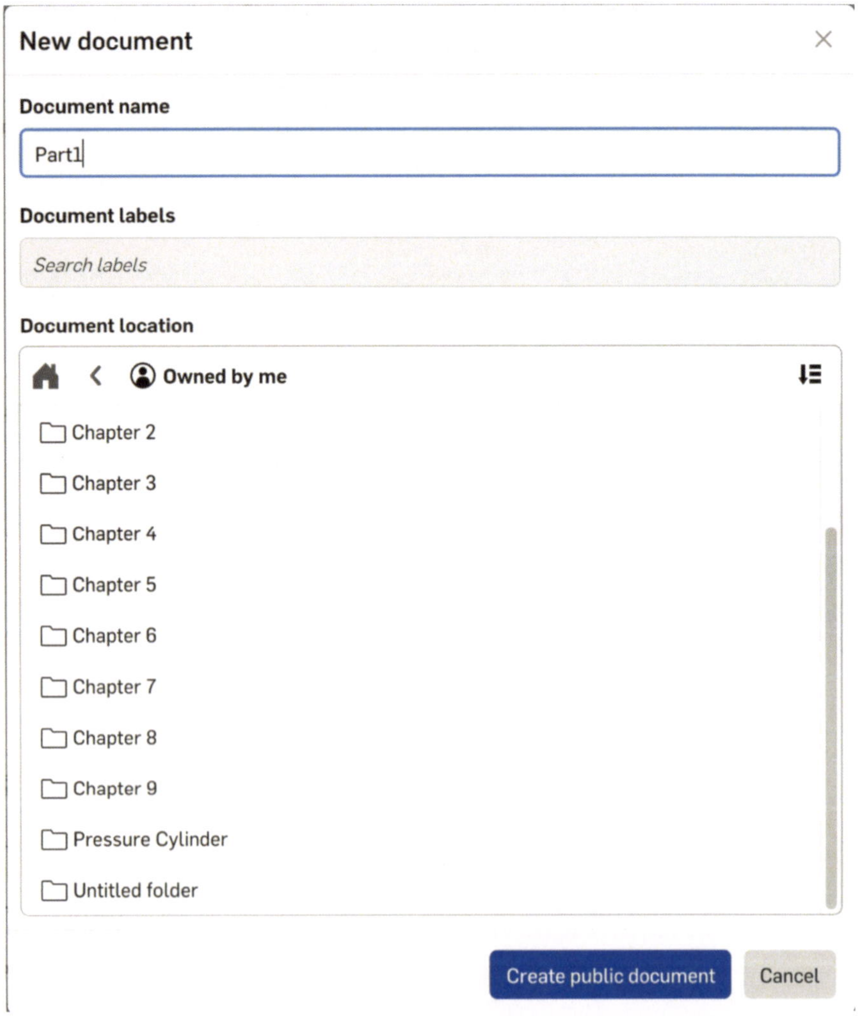

Sketching in the Sketch Environment

Creating sketches in the Sketch environment is very easy. You have to activate the **Sketch** command, and then select a plane on which you want to create the sketch. To do this, click **Sketch** on the toolbar. Next, click on any of the planes located at the center of the graphics window; the Sketch environment is active. You can now start drawing sketches on the selected plane. For example, activate the **Line** command and start sketching lines. After completing the sketch, click the green check on the **Sketch1** dialog. (or) right-click and select **Confirm Sketch1**; the Sketch environment is deactivated.

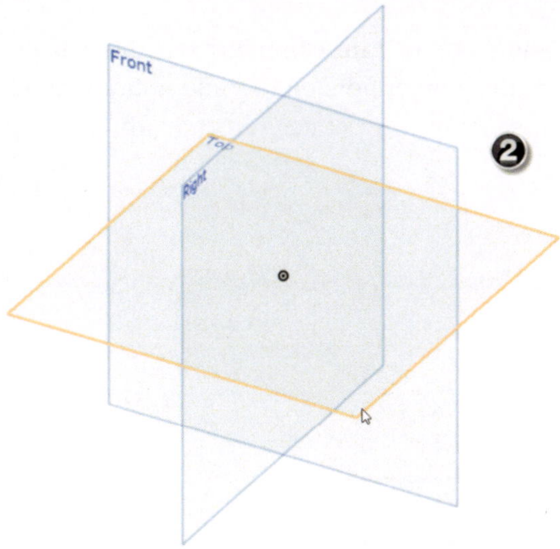

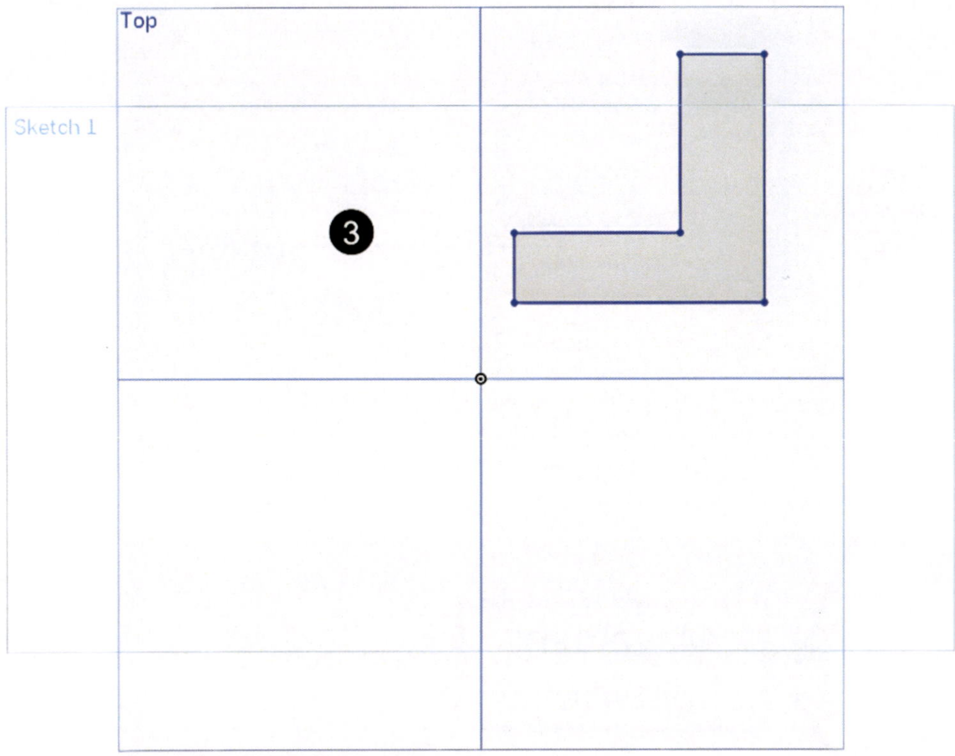

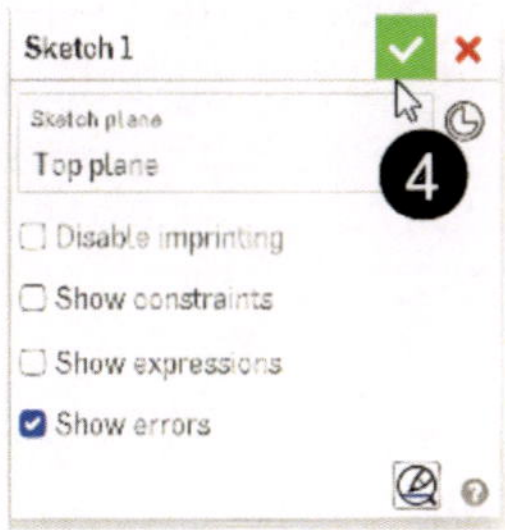

Draw Commands

Onshape provides you with a set of commands to create sketches. These commands are located on the toolbar.

Line Command

The **Line** command is one of the most commonly used commands while creating a sketch. To activate this command, you need to click the **Line** icon on the toolbar. Notice that the mouse pointer changes to a crosshair + indicating that the **Line** command is active. Click in the graphics window to specify the first point of the line. Next, move the pointer horizontally and notice that the horizontal glyph is displayed. Click to create a horizontal line. Likewise, move the pointer vertically upward and click to create the vertical line.

The **Line** command can also be used to draw arcs continuous with lines. Click in the graphics window, move the pointer horizontally toward the right and click. Move the pointer away and place the pointer on the endpoint of the line; the Arc mode is activated.

Move the pointer toward the right and then downwards; the arc appears tangent to the horizontal line.

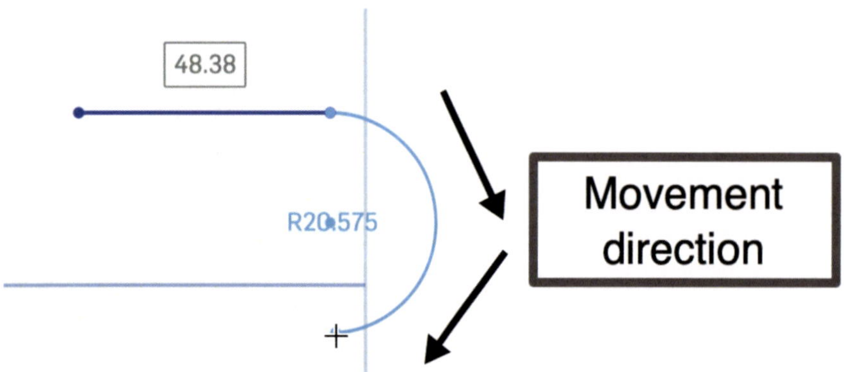

To delete a line, select it and press the **Delete** key. To select more than one line, press and hold the **Ctrl** key and then click on the line segments; the lines will be highlighted. You can also select multiple lines by dragging a box from right to left. Press and hold the left mouse button and drag a box from right to left; the lines inside or crossing the box boundary will be selected. Dragging a box from left to right will only select the lines that are inside the box.

Creating a Midpoint Line

You can create a midpoint line using the **Midpoint Line** command (on the toolbar, click **Line** drop-down > **Midpoint Line**). Next, specify the midpoint of the line, and then move the pointer. Click to specify the endpoint of the line.

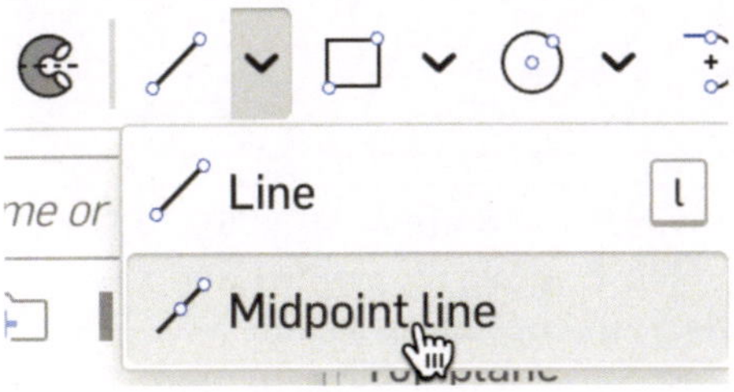

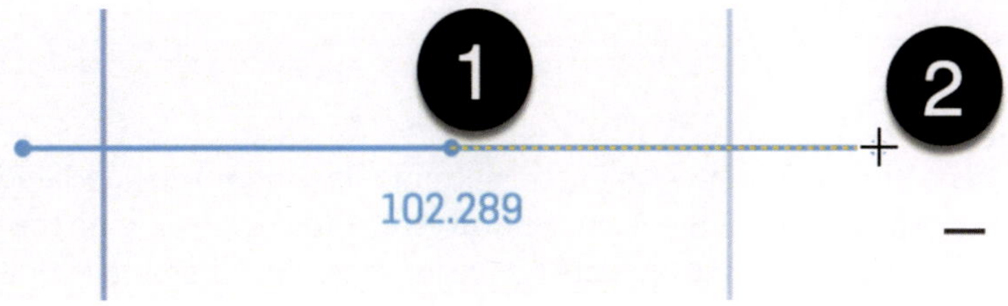

The Tangent Arc Command

This command creates an arc tangent to another entity. On the Toolbar click **Arc** drop-down > **Tangent Arc**. Select the endpoint of a line, move the pointer and then click to create a tangent arc.

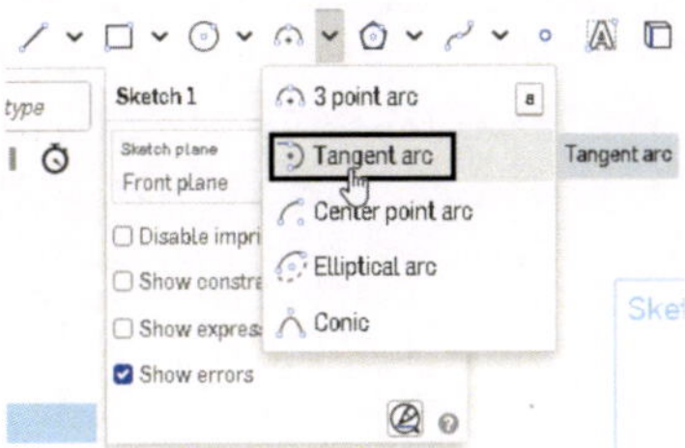

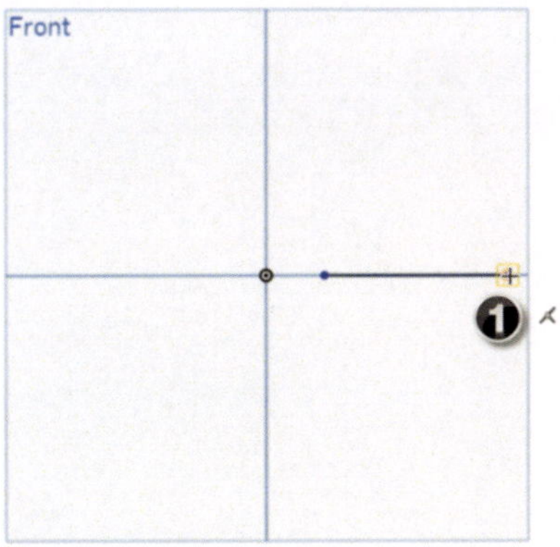

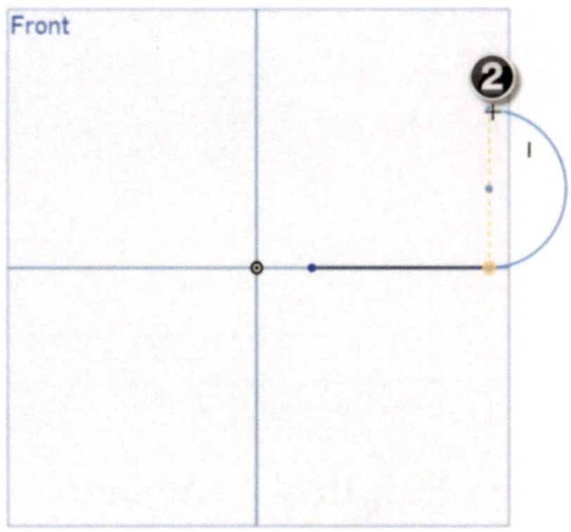

Right-click and select **Esc tangent arc** to deactivate the command.

The Arc by 3 Points command

This command creates an arc by defining its start, end, and radius. Activate this command (On the toolbar, click **Arc** drop-down > **3 point arc**) and click to define the start point of the arc. Next, move the pointer and click again to define the endpoint of the arc. After defining the start and end points, you have to define the size and position of the arc. To do this, move the pointer and click to define the radius and position of the arc. Right-click and select **Esc arc** to deactivate the command.

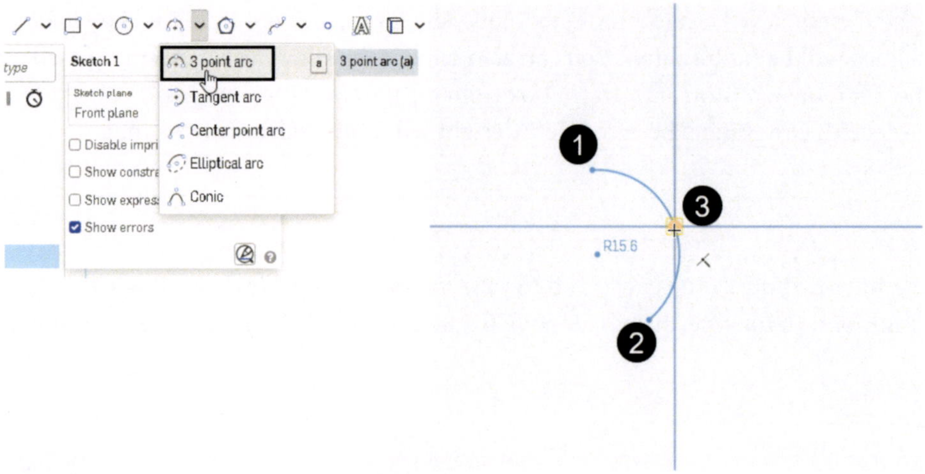

The Arc by Center point command

This command creates an arc by defining its center, start and end points. Activate this command (On the toolbar, click **Arc** drop-down > **Center point Arc**) and click to define the center point. Now, move the pointer and you will notice that a line appears between center and the mouse pointer. This line is the radius of the arc. Now, click to define the start point of the arc and move the pointer. You will notice that an arc is drawn from the start point. Now, click to define the endpoint of the arc.

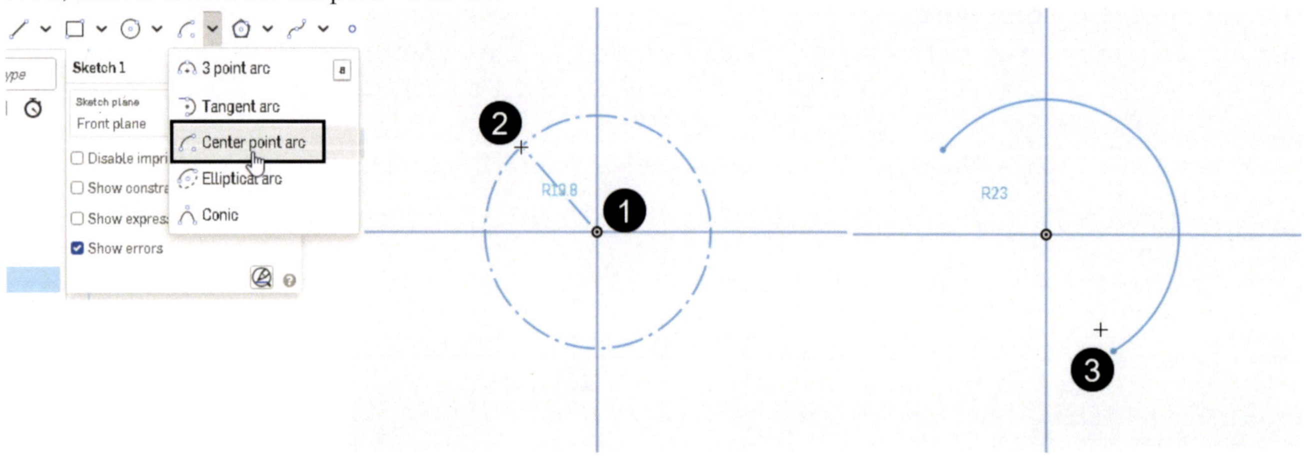

The Arc by Elliptical command

This command creates an elliptical arc by defining its center point, the major axis endpoint, and the arc endpoint. Activate this command (on the toolbar, click Arc drop-down > **Elliptical Arc**) and click to define the center point. Now, move the pointer and you will notice a line appears between the center and the mouse pointer. This line represents the major axis of the ellipse. Click to define the endpoint of the major axis. Now, move the pointer again and you will notice that an arc is drawn along the shape of an ellipse. Click to define the endpoint of the arc.

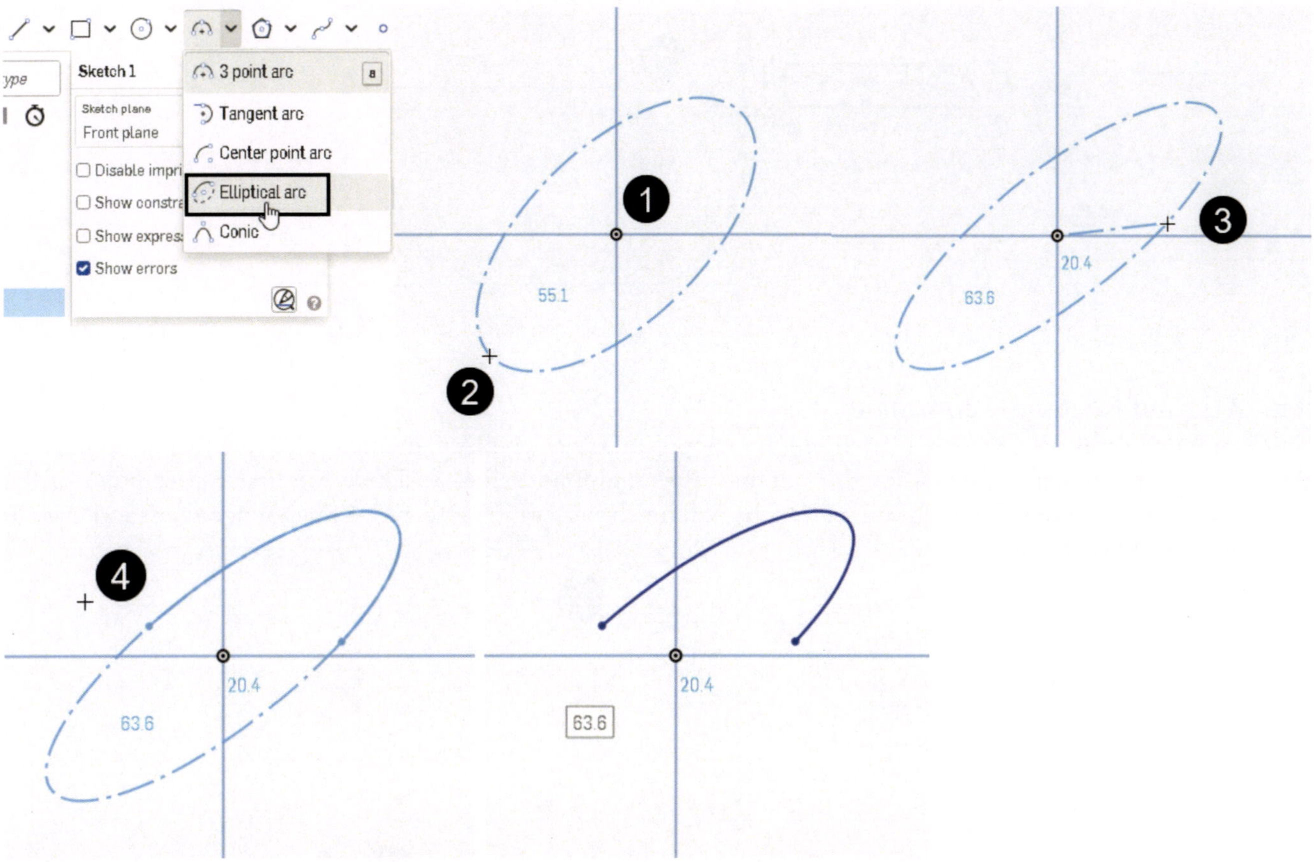

The Center Point Rectangle command

This command creates a rectangle by defining its center and one corner point. Activate this command (on the Toolbar, click **Rectangle** drop-down > **Center Point Rectangle**) and click to define the center point of the rectangle. Move the pointer outward and click to define a corner point of the rectangle.

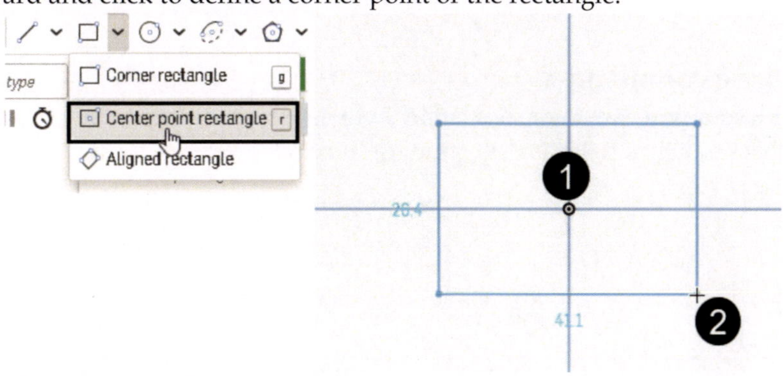

The Corner Rectangle command

This command creates a rectangle by defining its diagonal corners.

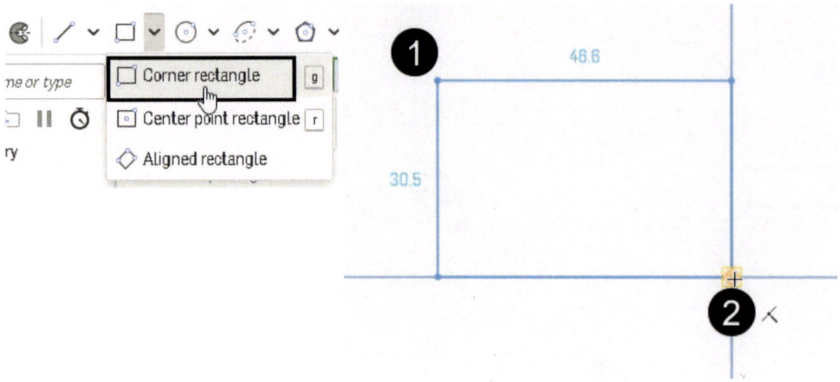

The Aligned Rectangle command

This command creates a rectangle by defining two opposite corner points at an angle. Activate this command (on the toolbar, click **Rectangle** drop-down > **Aligned Rectangle**) and click to define the first corner point of the rectangle. Move the pointer and click to define the second corner point. Now, move the pointer again and click to define the height of the rectangle.

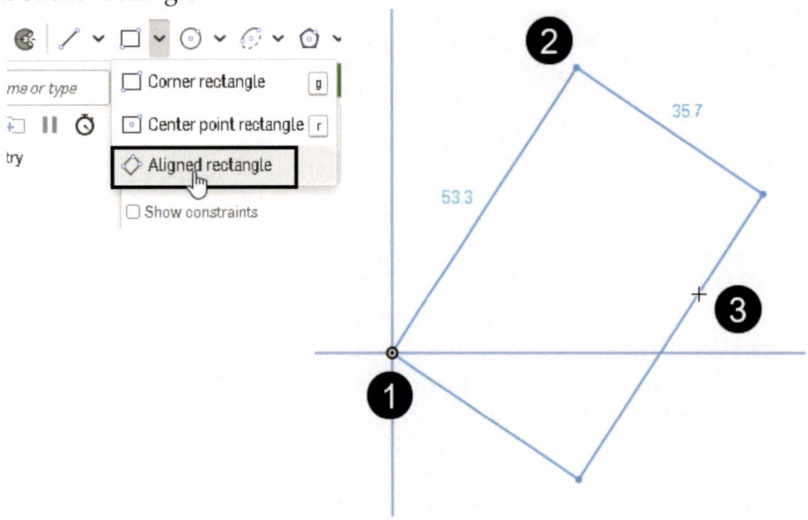

The Center Point Circle command

This command provides a common way to draw a circle. Activate this command (click **Circle** drop-down > **Center point circle** on the Toolbar) and click to locate the center of the circle. Next, move the pointer, and then click again to define the radius of the circle.

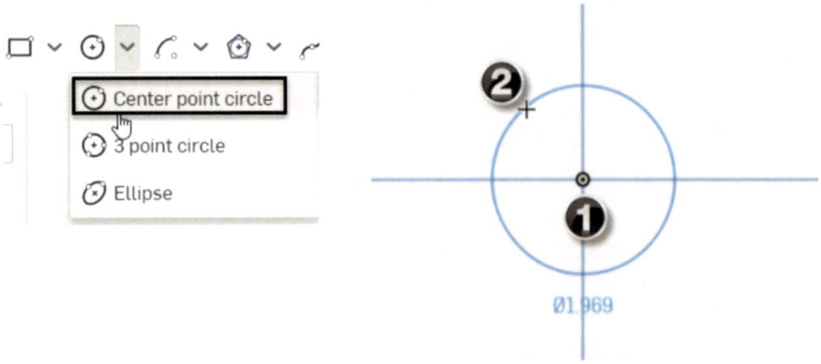

The 3 Point Circle command

This command creates a circle by using three points. Activate this command (On the Toolbar, click tab > **Circle** drop-down > **3 point Circle**) and then select three points from the graphics window. You can also select existing points from the sketch geometry. The first two points define the location of the circle and the third point defines its radius.

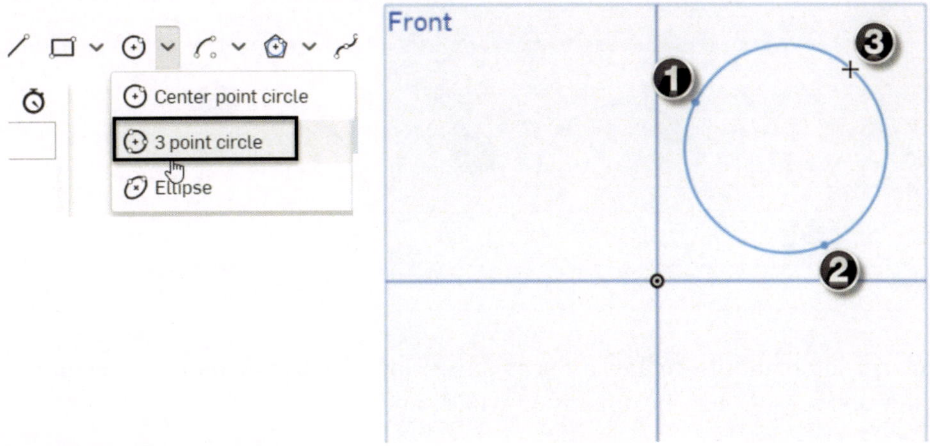

The Slot command

As the name implies, the **Slot** command helps you to create a slot. Activate this command (On the **Sketch** toolbar, click **Offset** drop-down > **Slot**) and select a line or arc. Next, double-click on the diameter dimension attached to the slot. Type-in the slot diameter and press ENTER. Next, click the left mouse button to create the slot.

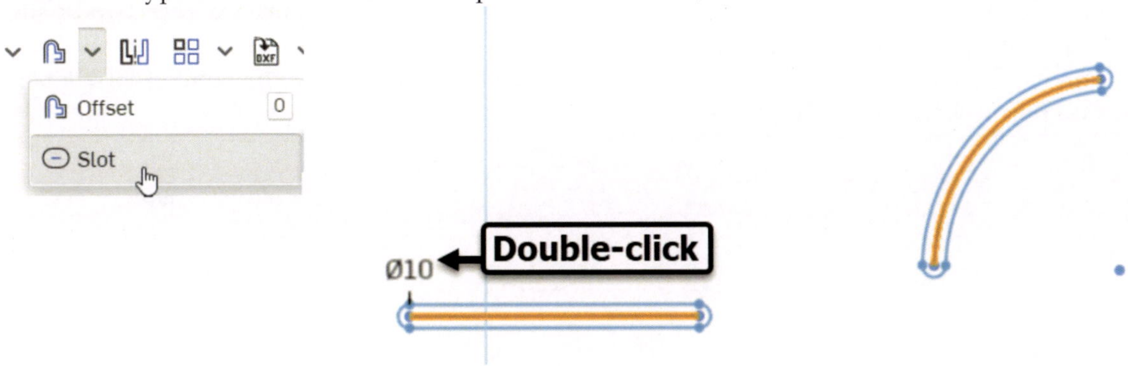

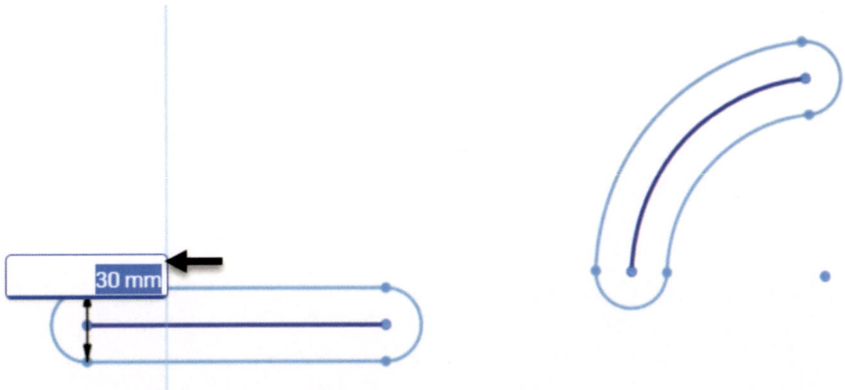

The Dimension command

It is generally considered a good practice to ensure that every sketch you create is fully-constrained before moving on to creating features. The term, 'fully-constrained' means that the sketch has a definite shape and size. You can fully-constrain a sketch by using dimensions and constraints. You can add dimensions to a sketch by using the **Dimension** command. You can use this command to add all types of dimensions such as length, angle, and diameter and so on. This command creates a dimension based on the geometry you select. For instance, to dimension a circle, activate the **Dimension** command, and then click on the circle. Next, move the pointer and click again to position the dimension. Type-in a value in the dimension box, and then press Enter to update the dimension.

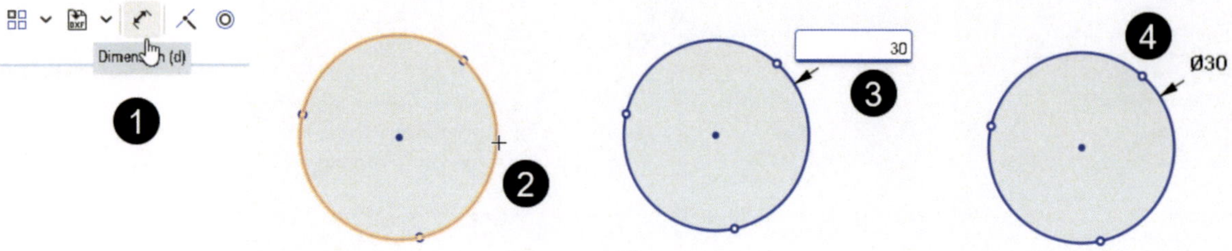

If you click on a line, this command automatically creates a linear dimension. Click once more to position the dimension, and then type-in a value and press Enter; the dimension will be updated.

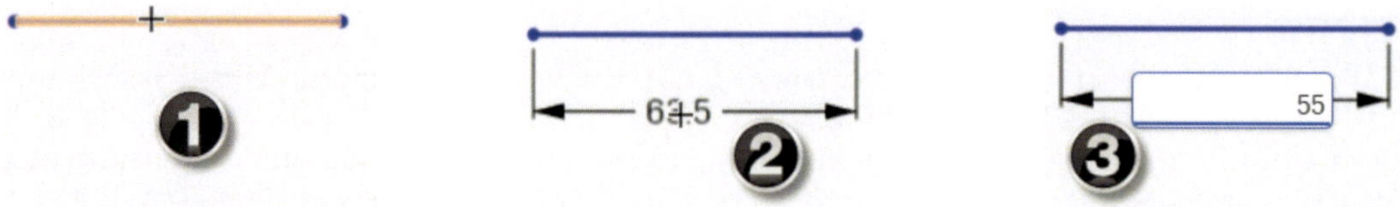

The **Dimension** command can be used to create three different types of linear dimensions between two points. Activate this command and select the centerpoints of the two circles, as shown. Move the pointer vertically downward and notice the horizontal dimension between the two selected points. Move the pointer horizontally and notice the vertical dimension between the points.

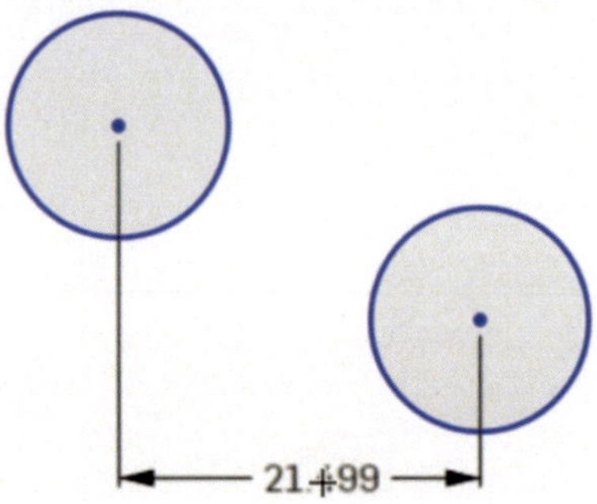

Horizontal Dimension

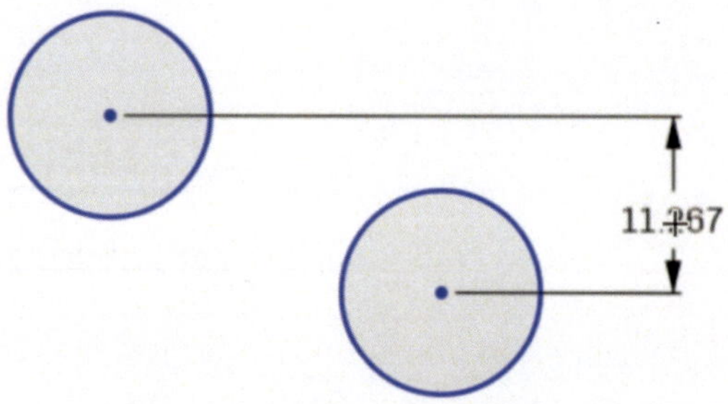

Vertical Dimension

Move the pointer between the two selected points and notice that the dimension is turned into an aligned dimension.

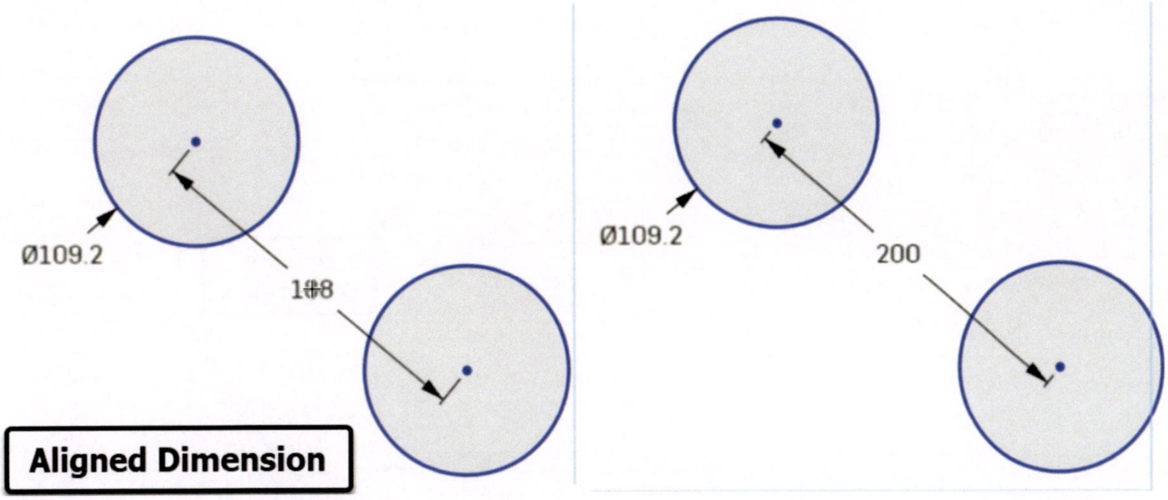

You can also use the **Dimension** command to create an angle dimension. Activate this command and select two lines that are positioned at an angle to each other. Move the pointer between the two lines and click to position the dimension. Type-in a value, and then press Enter.

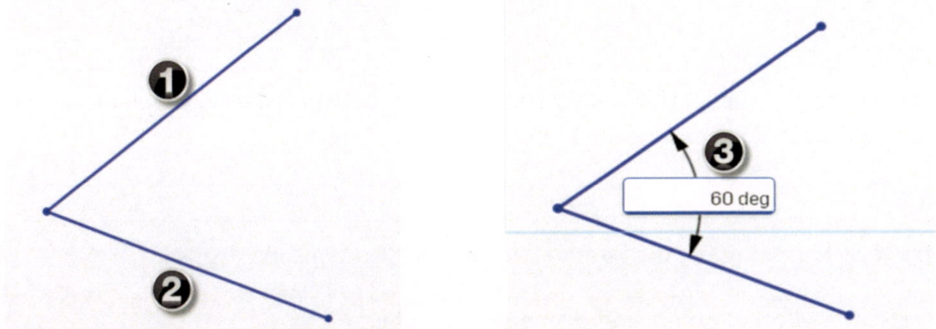

Driving Vs Driven dimensions

When creating sketches for a part, Onshape will not allow you to over-define the geometry. The term 'over-define' means adding more dimensions than required. The following figure shows a fully defined sketch. If you add another dimension to this sketch (e.g. diagonal dimension), then adding this dimension will make the sketch over defined.

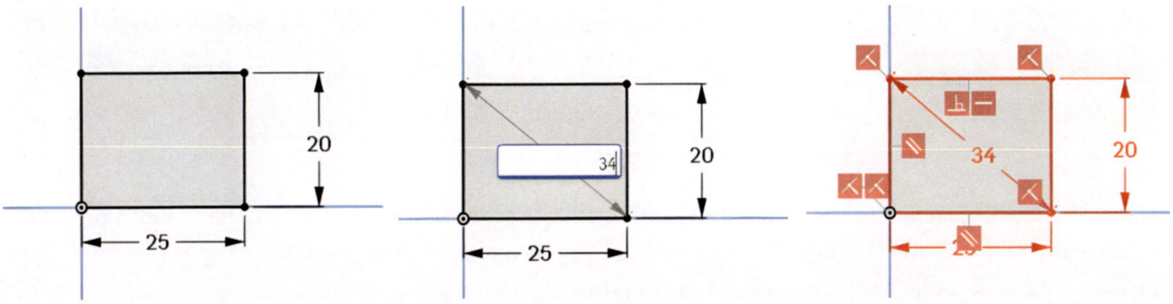

Now, you have to make one of the dimensions as a Driven dimension. Right-click on the diagonal dimension and select **Change to driving dimension**. The driven dimension will be in grey color. Existing driving dimensions (dimensions in black color) already define the sketch geometry. Driving dimensions are so named because they drive the geometry of the sketch. Double-clicking one of the driving dimensions and changing the value will change the geometry of the sketch. For example, if you change the value of the width, the driven dimension along the diagonal updates, automatically. Also, note that the dimensions, which are initially created, will be driving dimensions, whereas the dimensions created after fully defining the sketch are driven dimensions.

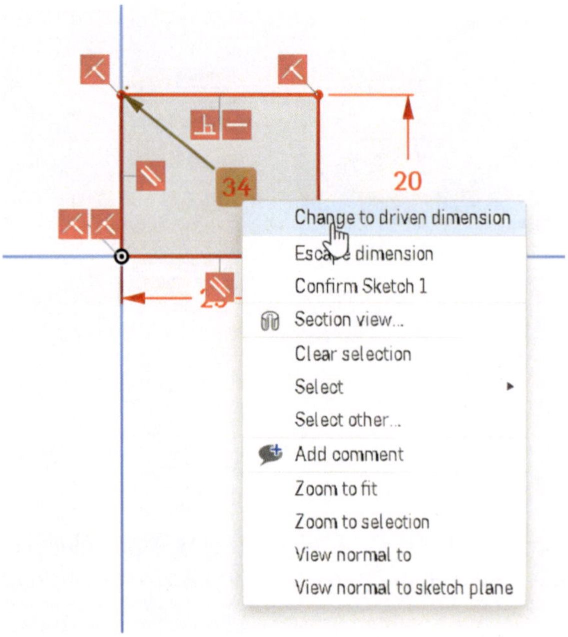

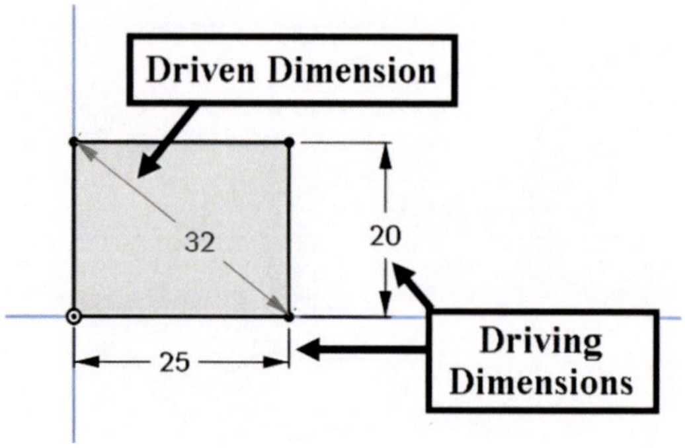

Geometric Constraints

Constraints are used to control the shape of a sketch by establishing constraint between the sketch elements. You can add constraints using the **Constraints** drop-down on the toolbar.

Coincident Constraint

This constraint connects a point to another point. On the **Sketch** toolbar, click **Constraints** drop-down **>** **Coincident** . Select two points. The selected points will be merged together.

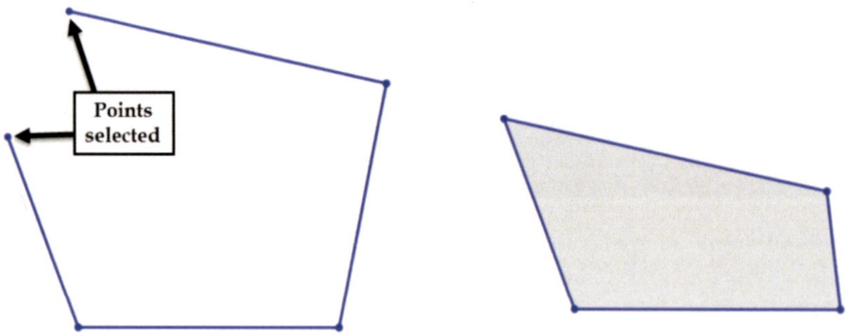

You can also make a point coincident with a line, circle, arc, spline, or ellipse. On the toolbar, click **Constraint** drop-down > **Coincident** and select a point and an entity. The selected point and the entity are made coincident. Click and drag the point and notice that it is movable along the selected line.

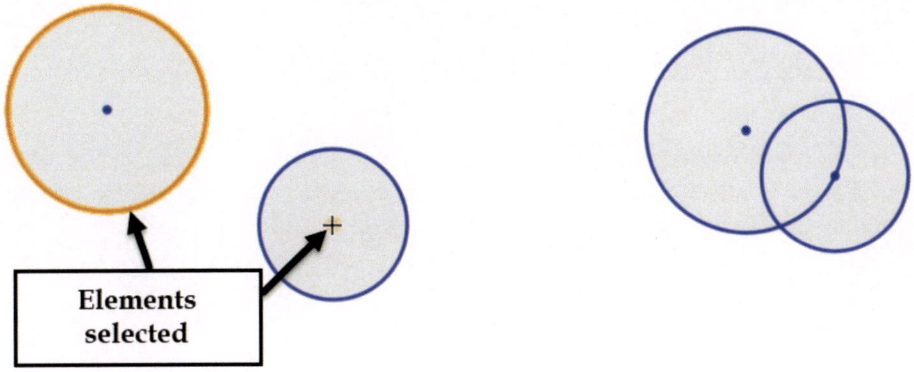

Horizontal

To apply the **Horizontal** constraint, click on a line and click **Horizontal** — on the toolbar.

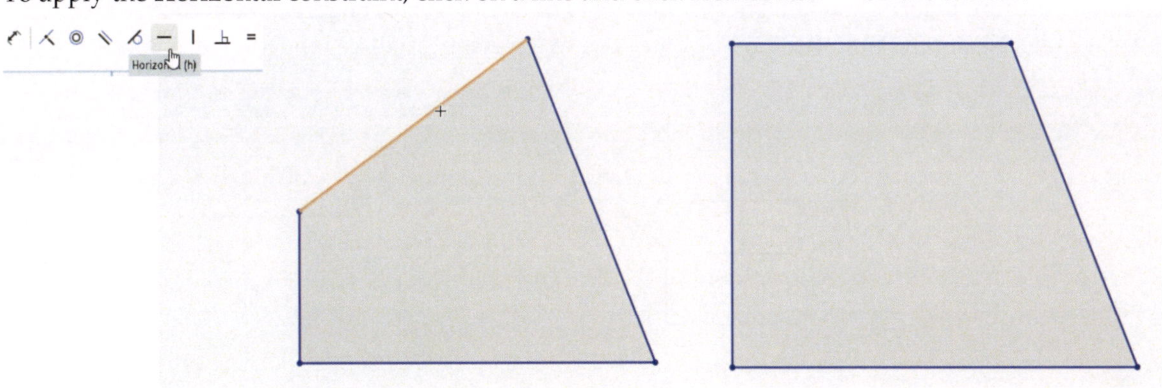

You can also align two points horizontally. Click **Constraint** drop-down > **Horizontal** on the toolbar and select the two points.

Vertical

Use the **Vertical** constraint to make a line vertical. You can also align two endpoints or points vertically by using this constraint.

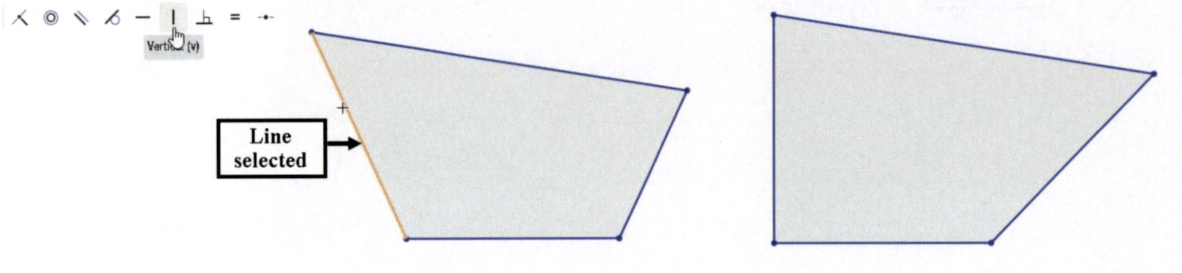

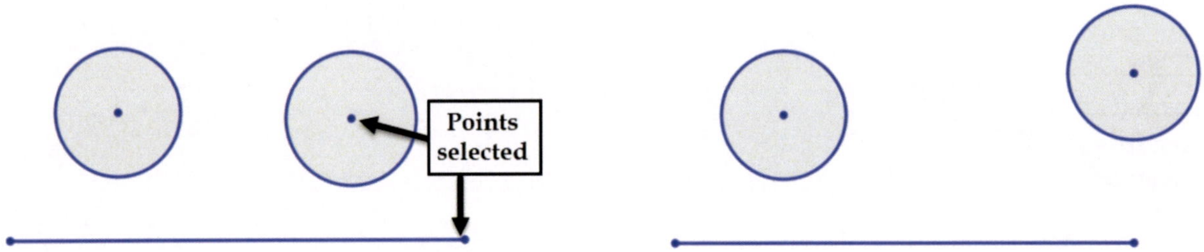

Tangent

This constraint makes an arc, circle, or line tangent to another arc or circle. Click **Tangent** on the toolbar. Select a circle, arc, or line. Next, select another circle, or arc. The two elements will be tangent to each other.

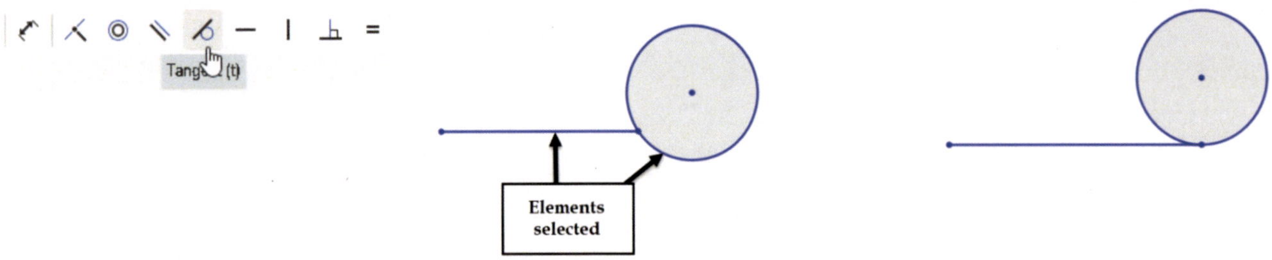

Parallel

Use the **Parallel** constraint to make two lines parallel to each other.

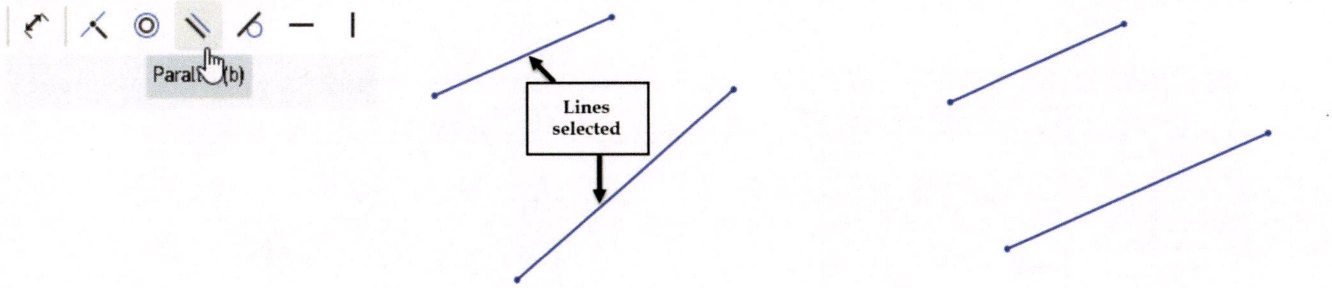

Perpendicular

Use the **Perpendicular** constraint to make two entities perpendicular to each other.

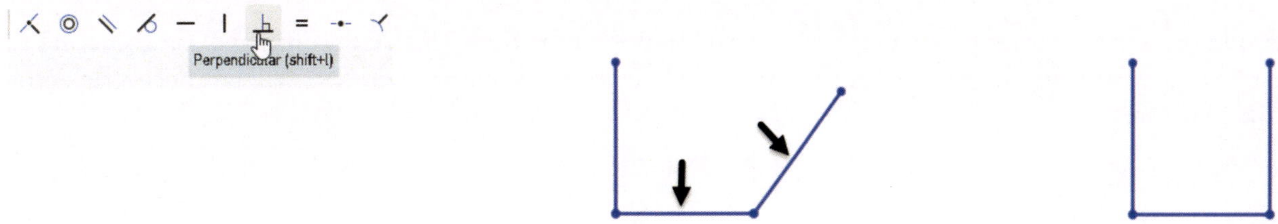

Midpoint

Use the **Midpoint** constraint to make a point coincide with the midpoint of a line or arc. To do this, click **Midpoint** on the toolbar. Next, select and line/arc and a point.

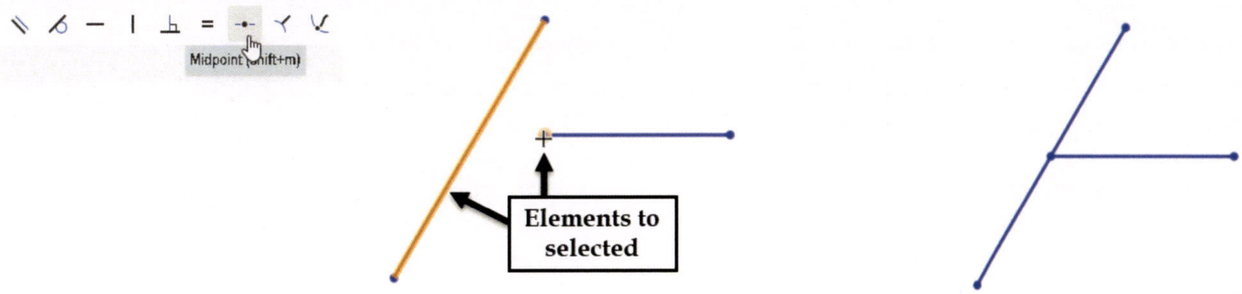

Equal

This constraint makes the selected objects equal in magnitude. For example, if you select two circles, the diameter of the selected circles will become equal. If you select two lines, the length of the two lines will be equal.

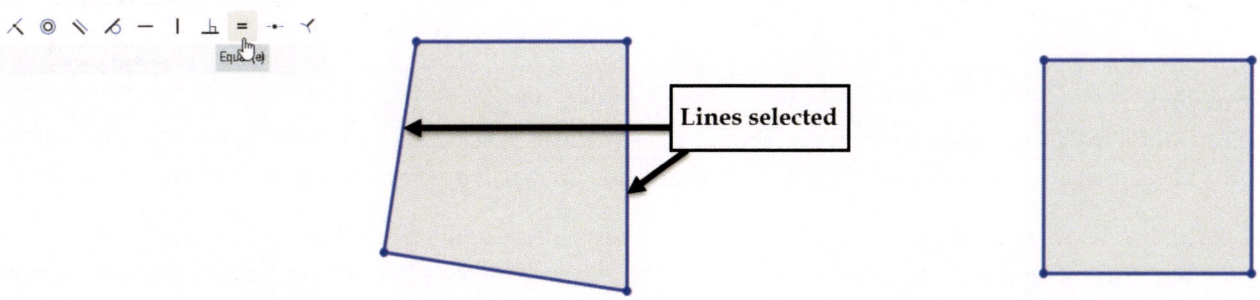

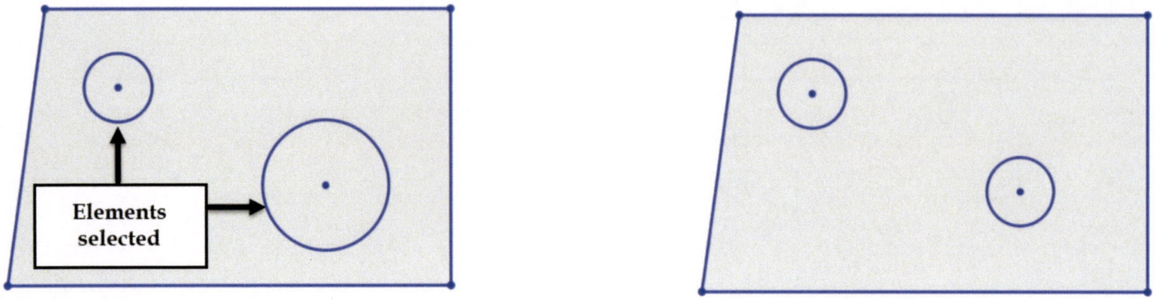

Concentric

This constraint makes the center points of arcs, circles or ellipses coincident. Click **Concentric** on the toolbar. Select a circle or arc from the sketch. Next, select another circle or arc. The first circle/arc will be concentric with the second circle/arc.

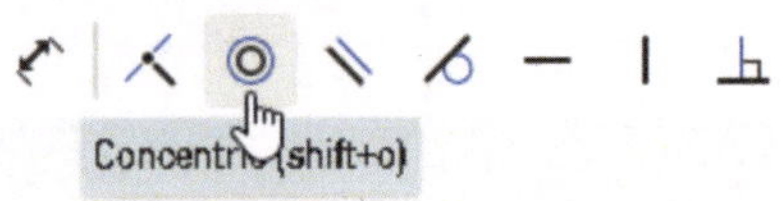

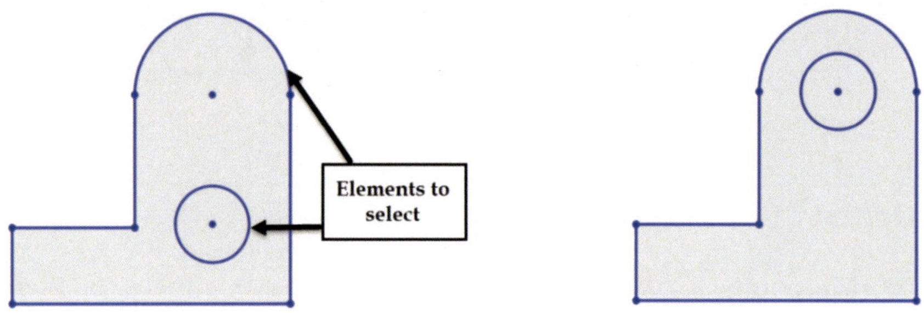

Fix

This constraint fixes a sketch element so that it cannot be moved. Select a sketch element and click **Fix** on the toolbar; it will be fixed at its current position.

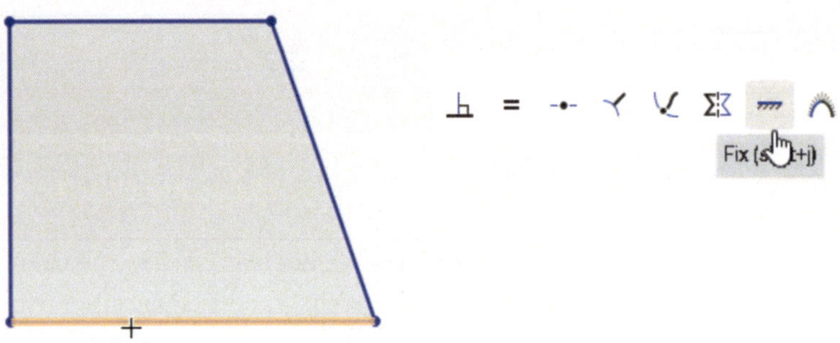

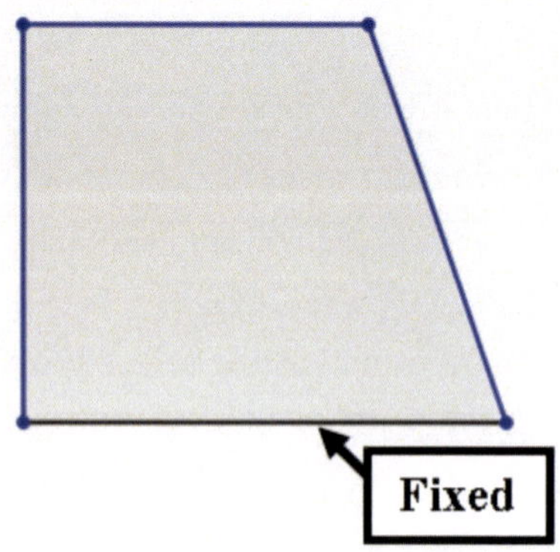

Symmetric

This constraint makes two objects symmetric about a line. The objects will have same size, position and orientation about a line. For example, if you select two circles about a line, they will become equal in size, aligned horizontally, and positioned at an equal distance from the line. To do this, click **Symmetric** on the Toolbar and select the two entities to be made symmetric. Next, select a line to define the symmetry line. The selected objects will be made symmetric about the selected line.

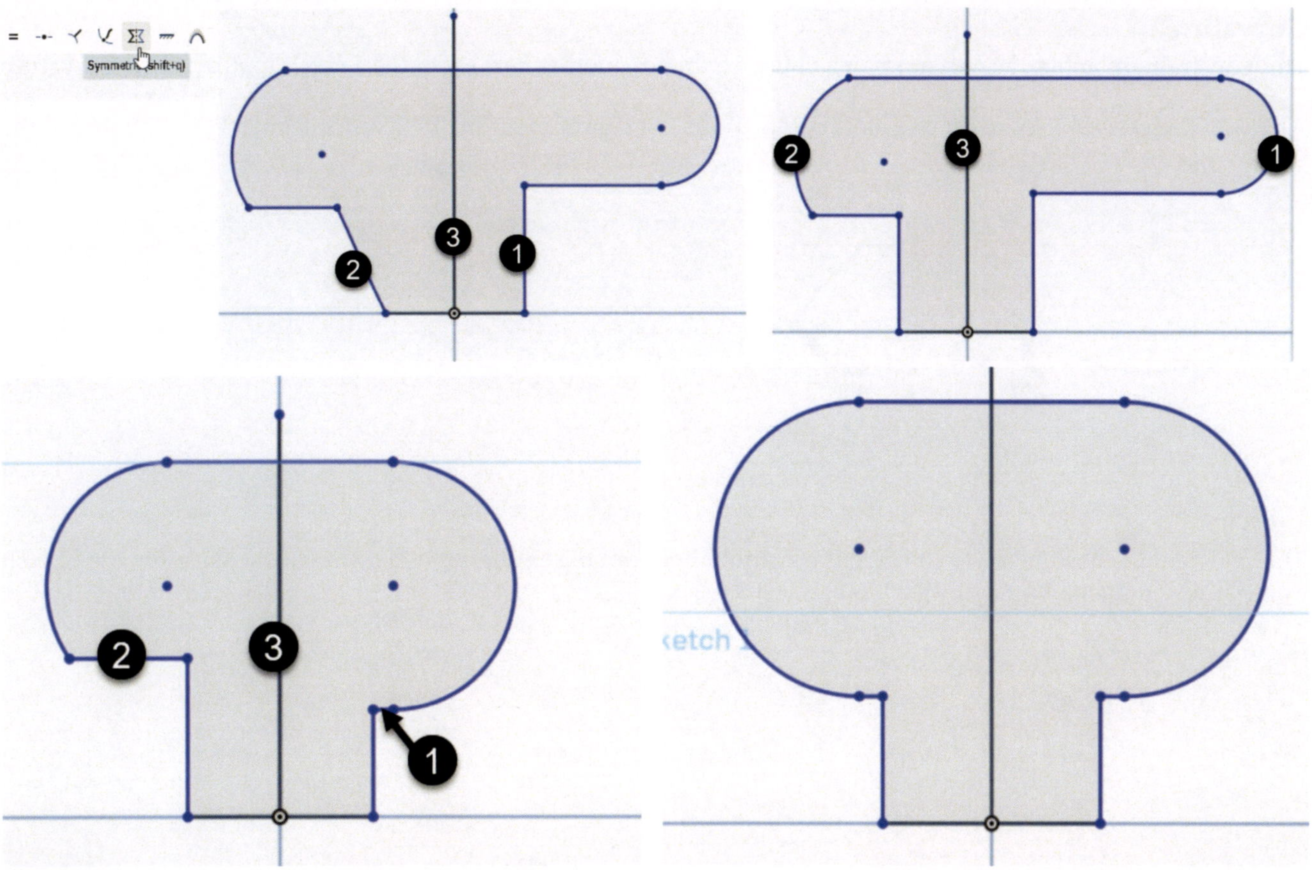

Normal

This constraint makes a line normal to a curve. On the **Sketch** toolbar, click **Constraints** drop-down > **Normal**, and then select a curve and a line; the line is made normal to the curve.

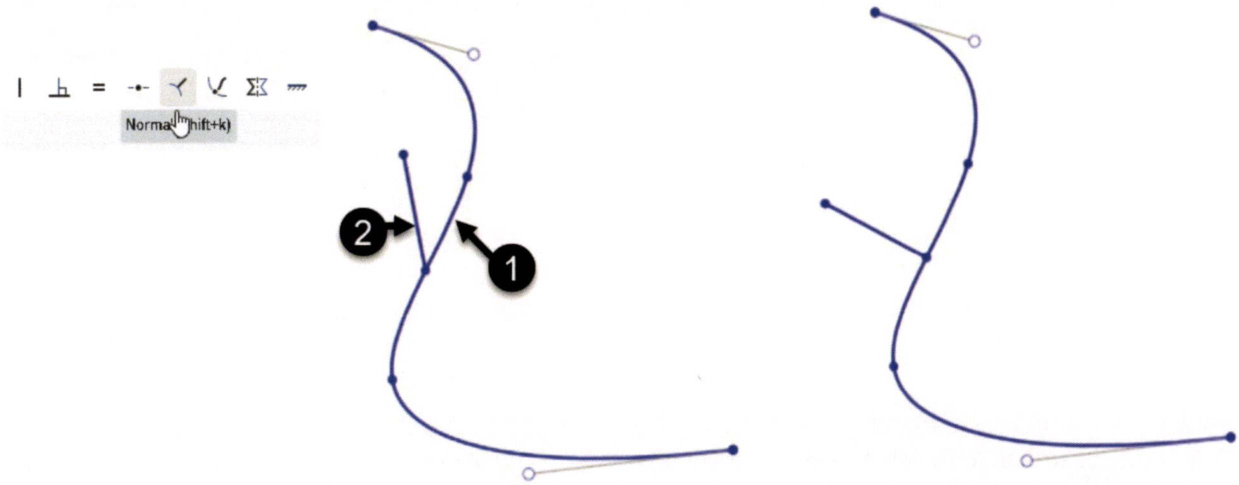

Curvature

This constraint matches the curvature of a spline to that of another curve. On the **Sketch** toolbar, click **Curvature** , and then select a spline. Next, select curve or arc; the curvature of the first spline is matched with that of the second one.

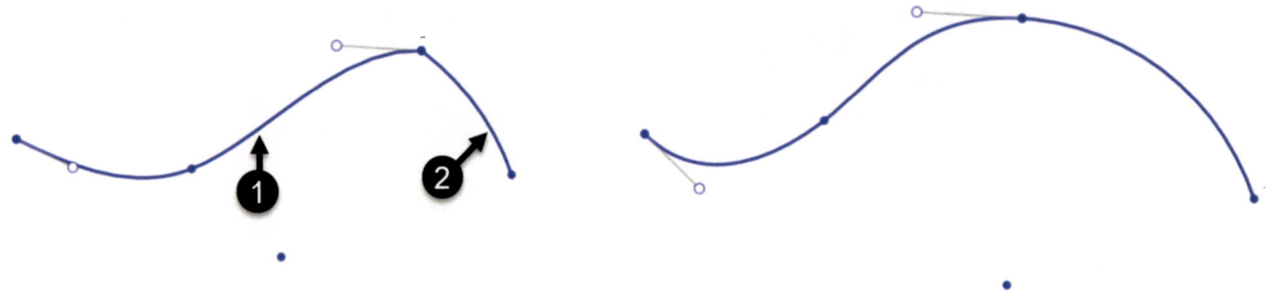

Pierce

This constraint is used to apply coincident constraint between the entities of two different sketches. On the **Sketch** toolbar, click **Pierce**. Next, select the entities of the two sketches.

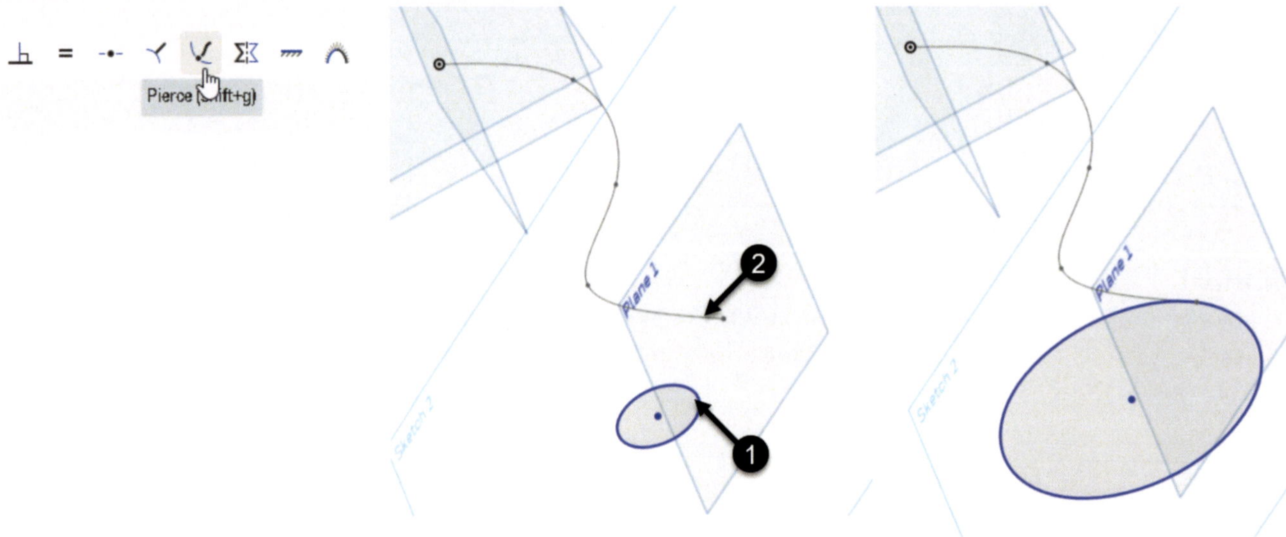

The Construction command

This command converts a sketch element into a construction element. Construction elements are reference elements, which support you to create a sketch of desired shape and size. Click on a sketch element and select the **Construction** 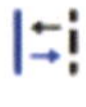 command. The selected element will be converted to a construction element. You can also convert back the construction element to a sketch element by clicking on the element and selecting the **Construction** command.

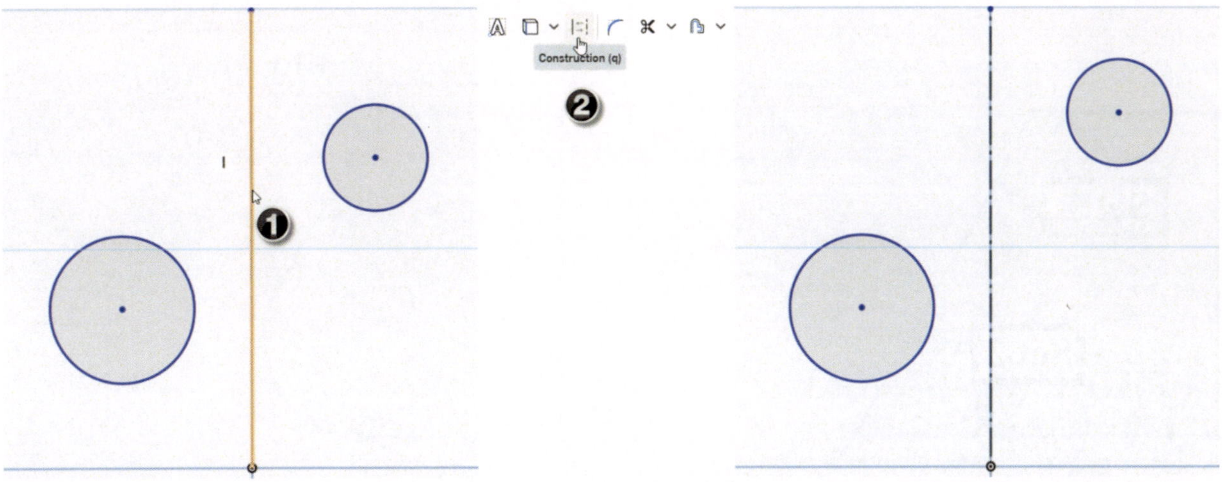

Showing/Hiding Constraints

To show the sketch constraints, check the **Show Constraints** option on the **Sketch** dialog. All the sketch constraints will be displayed. You can hide the sketch constraints, by unchecking the **Show Constraints** option on the **Sketch** dialog.

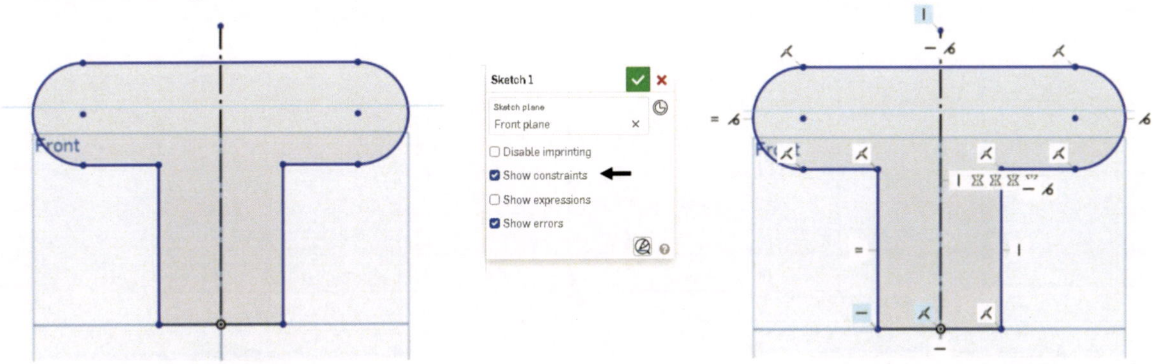

Sketch Constraints OFF

Sketch Constraints ON

Sketch Editing Commands

Sketch editing commands help you to perform various operations such as extending or trimming entities, offsetting, rounding corners, mirroring, and so on. These commands are explained next.

The Sketch Fillet command

This command rounds a sharp corner created by intersection of two lines, arcs, circles, and rectangle or polygon vertices. Activate this command (On the Toolbar, click **Sketch Fillet**) and select the elements' ends to be filleted. Double-click on radius dimension attached to the fillet. Next, type-in a radius value in the **Fillet Radius** box and press Enter. The elements to be filleted are not required to touch each other.

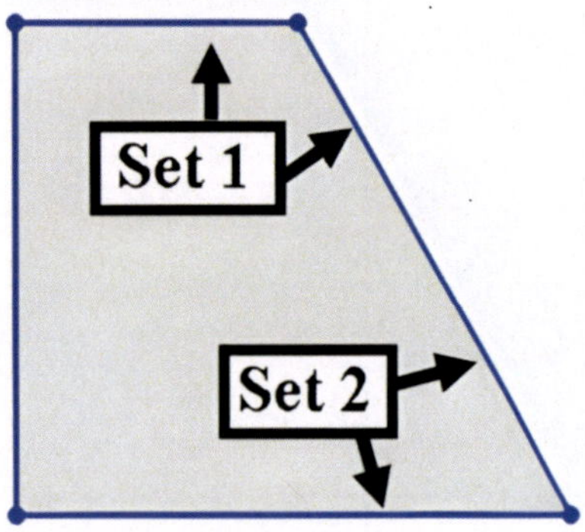

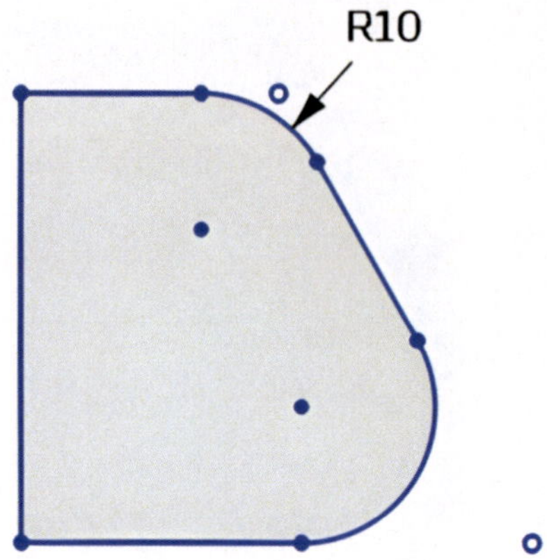

The Trim command

This command trims the end of an element back to the intersection of another element. Activate this command (On the Toolbar, click **Trim**) and select the elements to trim, as shown.

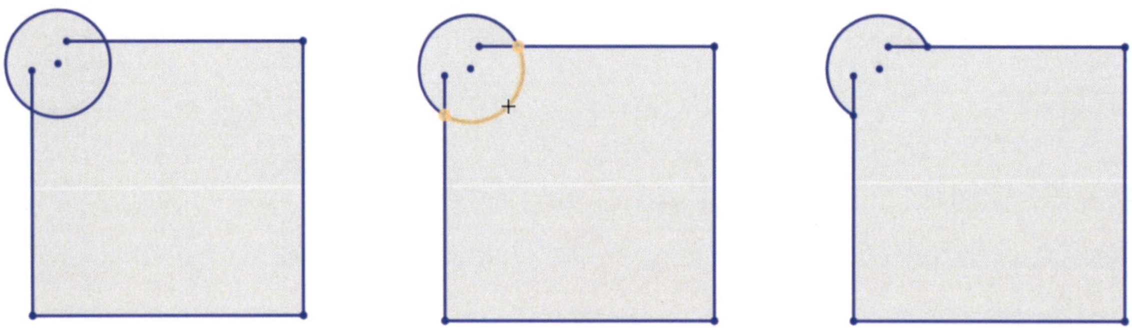

The Extend command

This command extends elements such as lines, arcs, and curves until they intersect another element called the boundary edge. Activate this command (On the Toolbar, click **Trim > Extend**) and click on the element to extend. It will extend up to the next element.

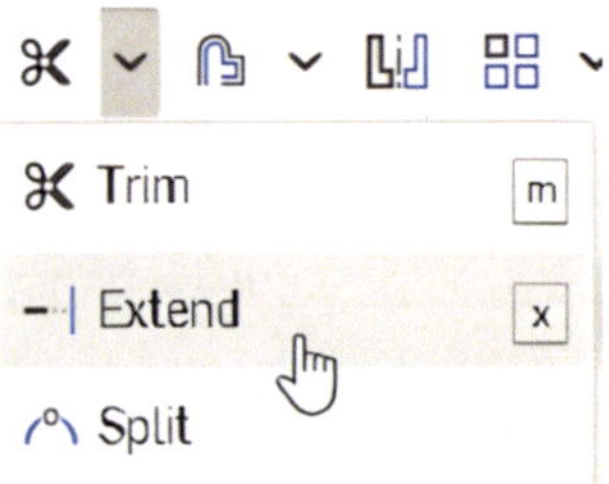

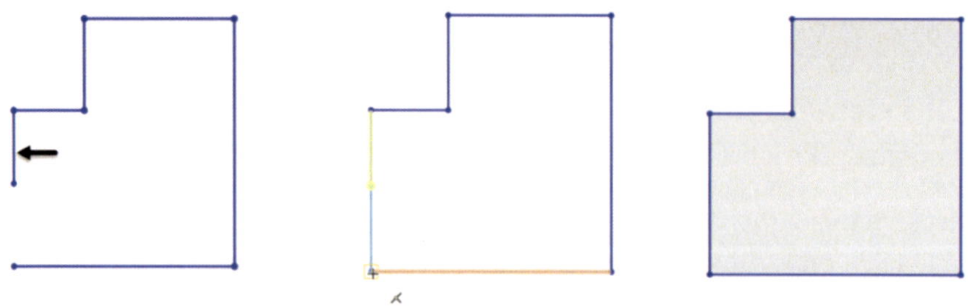

The Split command

This command splits an open or closed entity. Activate this command (On the Toolbar, click **Trim** drop-down > **Split**) and click on an open entity; it will be split at the selected point. If you want to split a closed entity like circle or ellipse, then you need to specify two split points.

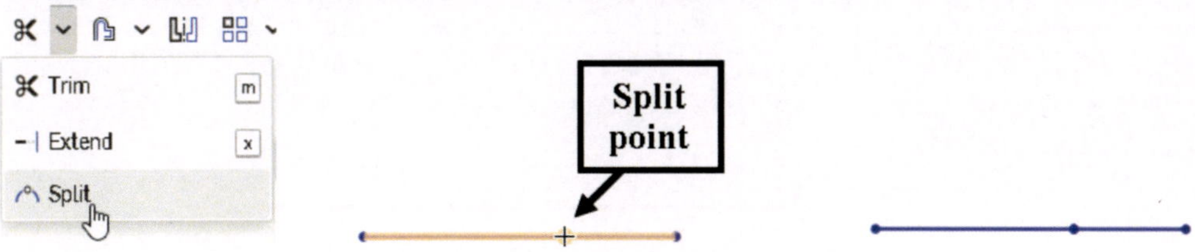

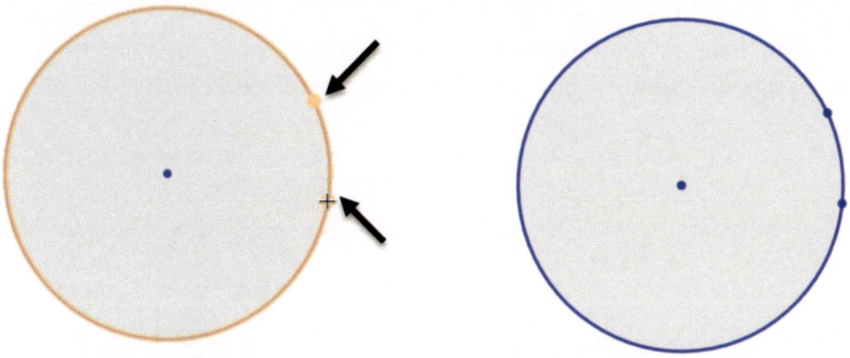

The Offset command

This command creates a parallel copy of a selected element or chain of elements. Click **Offset** on the toolbar and select an element or chain of elements to offset. To select a chain of elements, right-click and select **Select** > **Create selection**. Next, select the **Loop/chain connected** option from the drop-down available on the **Create selection** dialog. Select an entity of a closed chain and click the **Add Selection** button on the **Create selection** dialog; the chain loop is selected. Next, click on the arrow displayed to reverse the offset direction. After selecting the element(s), double-click on the offset distance value to change the value. Type-in a new value in the **Offset Distance** box and press Enter.

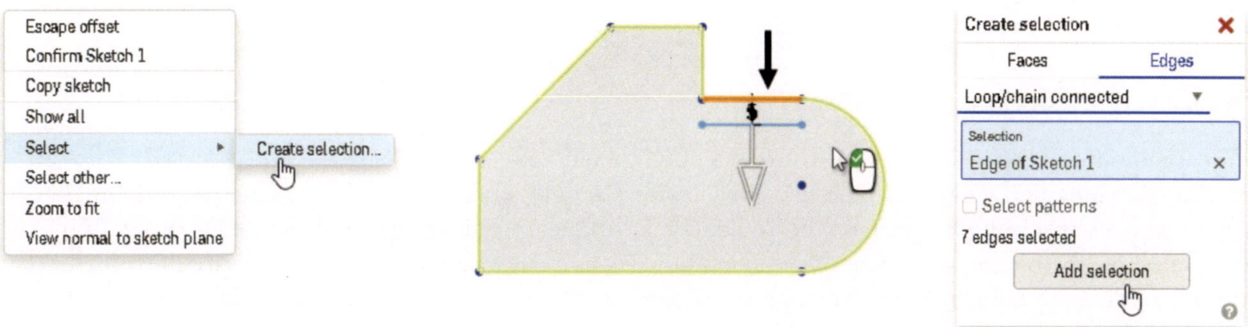

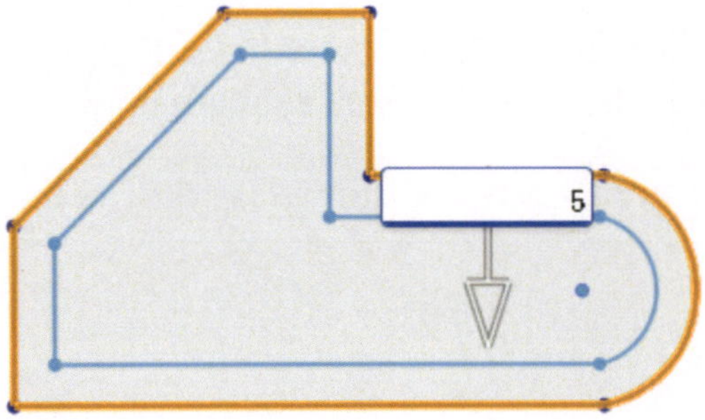

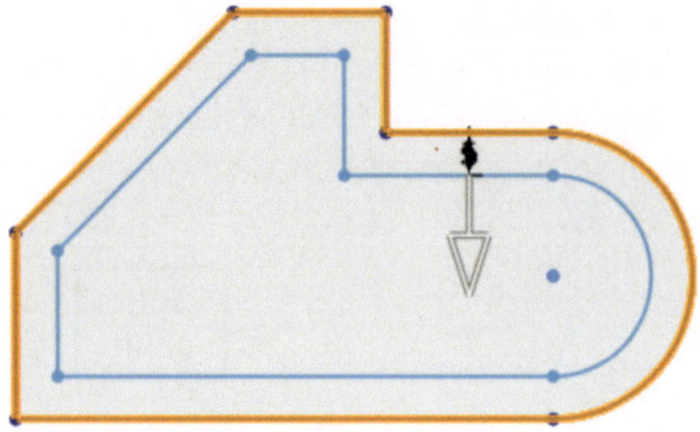

The Mirror command

The **Mirror** command creates a mirrored copy of the selected entities about a line. Create the sketch entities similar to that shown next, and then click the **Mirror** icon on the Toolbar. Select the construction line from the graphics window. Next, select the entities to mirror. Press Enter to complete the mirror operation.

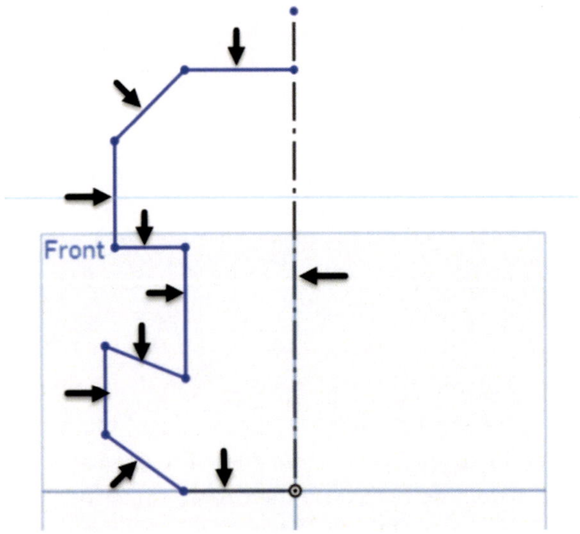

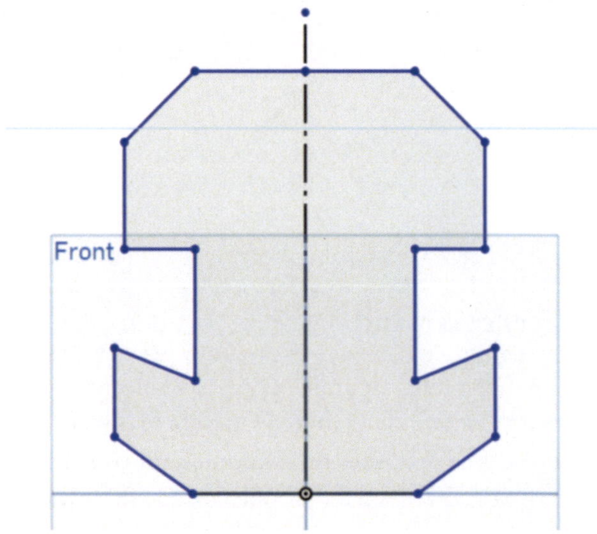

Advanced Draw commands

Onshape provides some advanced drawing commands to create complex sketches. These commands are explained in the following sections.

The Inscribed Polygon command

This command provides a simple way to create a polygon with any number of sides. The **Inscribed Polygon** command, creates a polygon with a dashed circle inside the polygon touching the flat sides. To activate this command, click **Inscribed Polygon** on the Toolbar. Click in the graphics window to define the center of the polygon. Move the pointer away from the center and click to create the polygon. Now, specify the number of sides by moving the pointer. Move the pointer outward to increase the number of sides. Move the pointer inwards to decrease the number of sides. Next, click to create the polygon after specifying the number of sides.

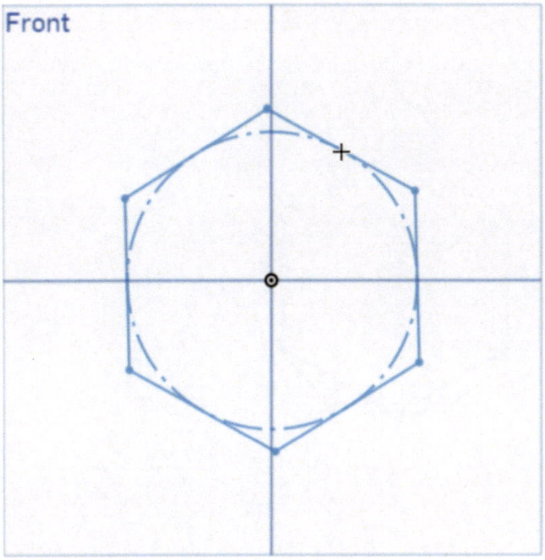

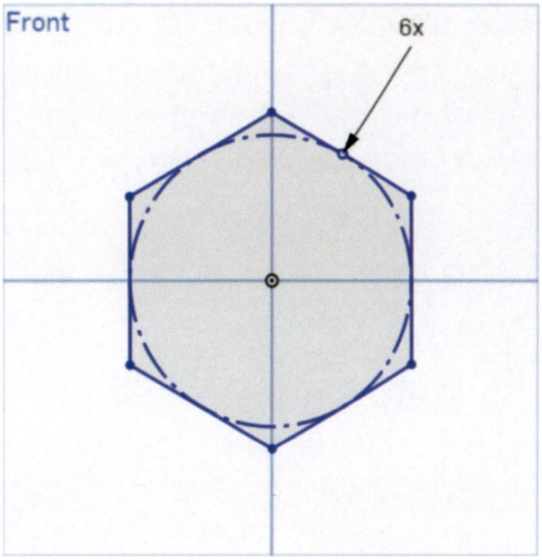

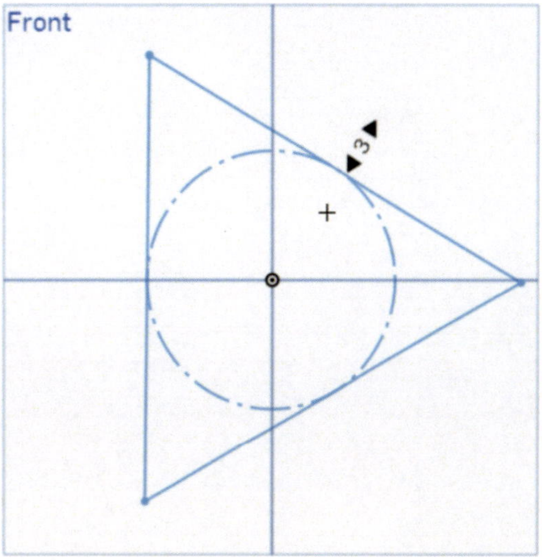

The Circumscribed Polygon command

The **Circumscribed Polygon** command creates a polygon with a dashed circle outside the polygon touching its vertices. To activate this command, click **Inscribed Polygon** drop-down > **Circumscribed Polygon** on the Toolbar. Click in the graphics window to define the center of the polygon. Move the pointer away from the center and click. Now, specify the number of sides by moving the pointer. Move the pointer outward to increase the number of sides. Move the pointer inwards to decrease the number of sides. Next, click to create the polygon after specifying the number of sides.

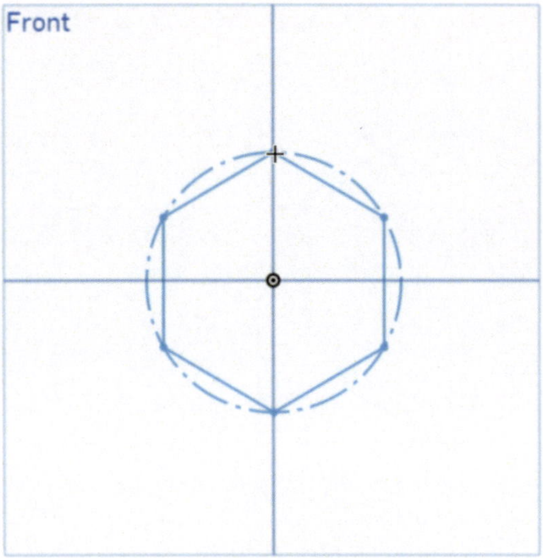

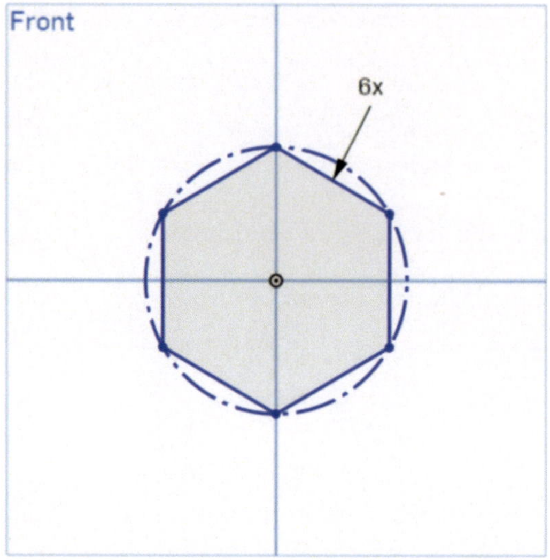

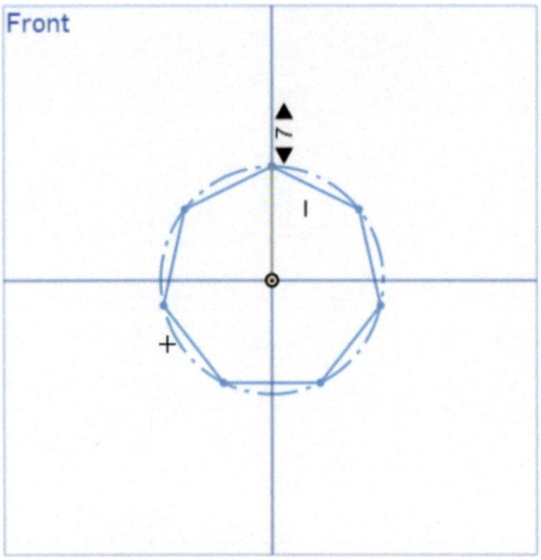

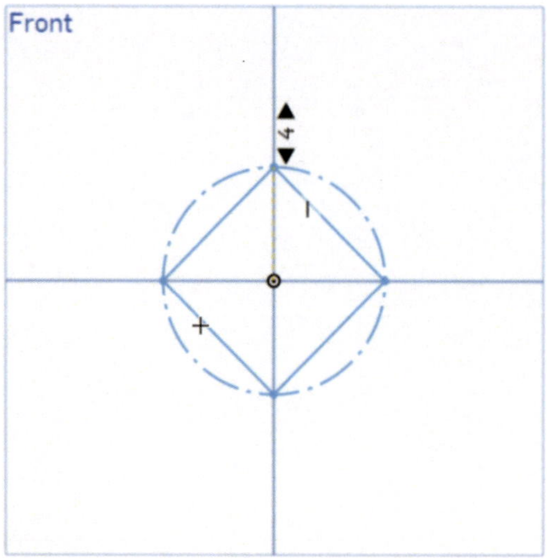

The Ellipse command

This command creates an ellipse using a center point, and major and minor axes. Activate this command (click **Circle** drop-down > **Ellipse** on the **Toolbar**). and click to define the center of the ellipse. Move the pointer and click to define the radius and orientation of the first axis; a preview of the ellipse appears. Next, move the pointer and click to define the radius of the second axis; the ellipse will be drawn.

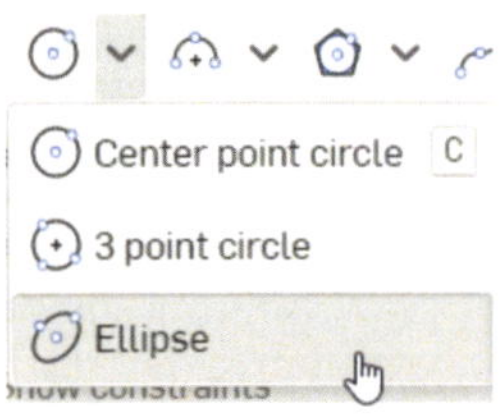

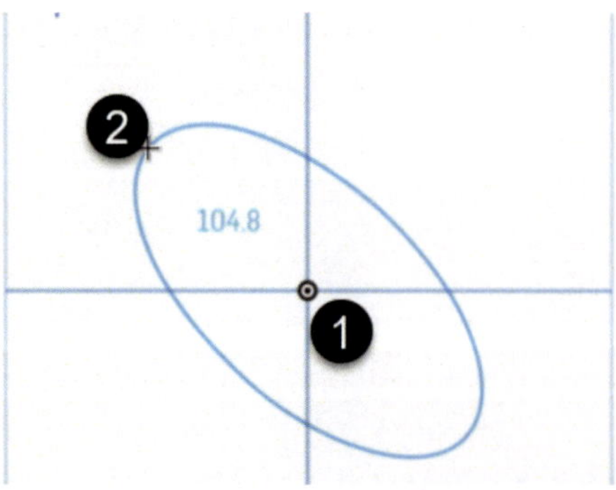

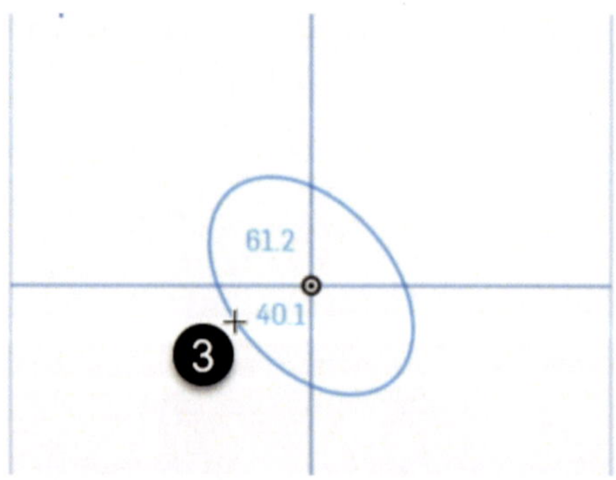

Next, you need to fully-define the ellipse using the constraints and dimensions. First, you need to make the center point of the ellipse coincident with the sketch origin or another sketch entity. You can also make it fixed using the **Fix** constraint. Activate the **Line** and **Construction** command on the toolbar. Next, draw a construction line between the centerpoint of the ellipse and major axis point. Press ESC to end the line chain. Again, activate the **Line** and **Construction** commands. Next, select the centerpoint of the ellipse, move the pointer horizontally toward right and click. Make sure that the Horizontal constraint is applied to the line.

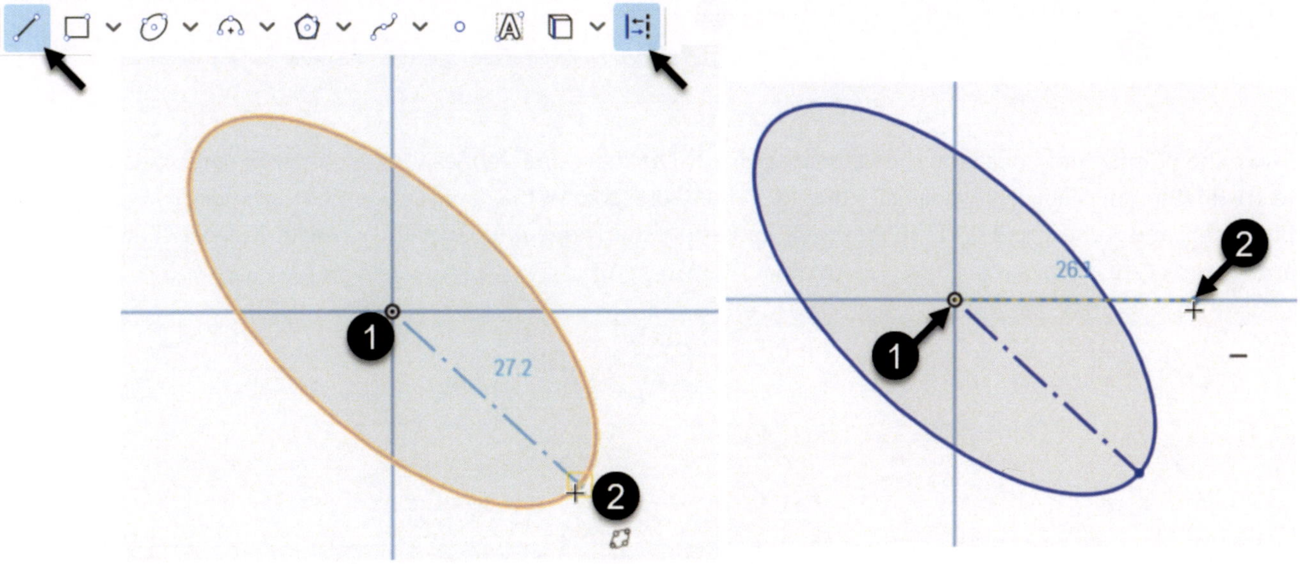

Activate the **Dimension** command and select the two construction lines. Move the pointer between the selected lines and click. Type-in the angle value in the value box and press ENTER.

Select the ellipse on the shorter side and then move the pointer. Click to specify the location of the dimension. Type-in the dimension value and press ENTER.

Select the ellipse on the longer side and move the pointer. Click to specify the location of the dimension. Type-in the dimension value and press ENTER.

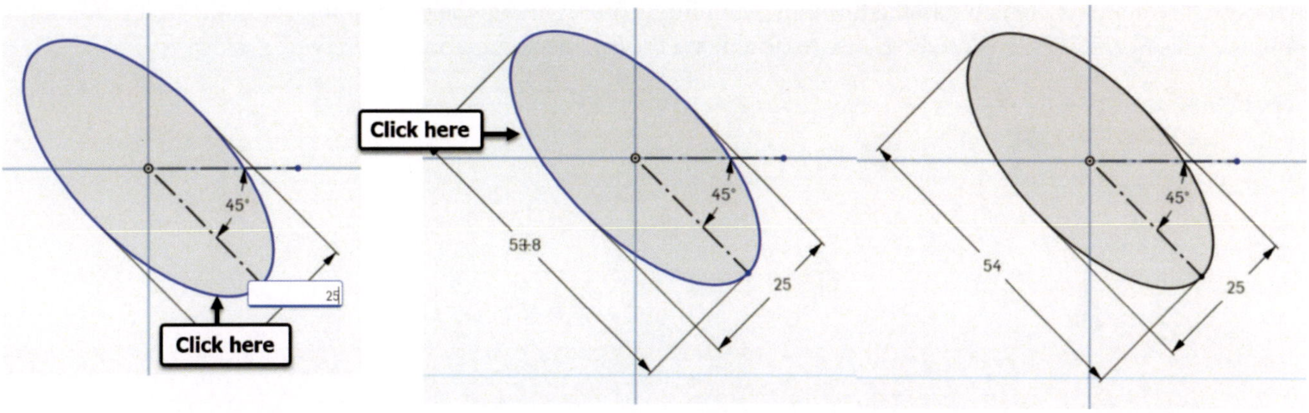

The Conic command

This command creates a conic curve, which is used to connect two open sketch entities. First, you have to create a line and an arc, as shown. Activate the **Conic** command (on the Toolbar, click **Arc** drop down > **Conic)**. Select the endpoints of the line and arc.

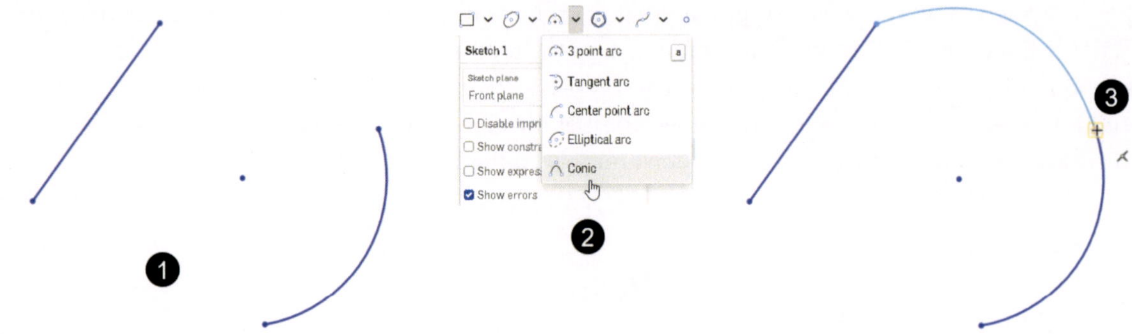

Move the pointer and notice the rho value displayed. The rho value defines the curvature of conic created. Click to create the conic curve. Now, specify the rho value (i.e. ρ box) of the conic curve. You can type-in a value between 0 and 1 and press ENTER. Next, you can apply the Tangent or Curvature constraints between the conic and the adjacent entities.

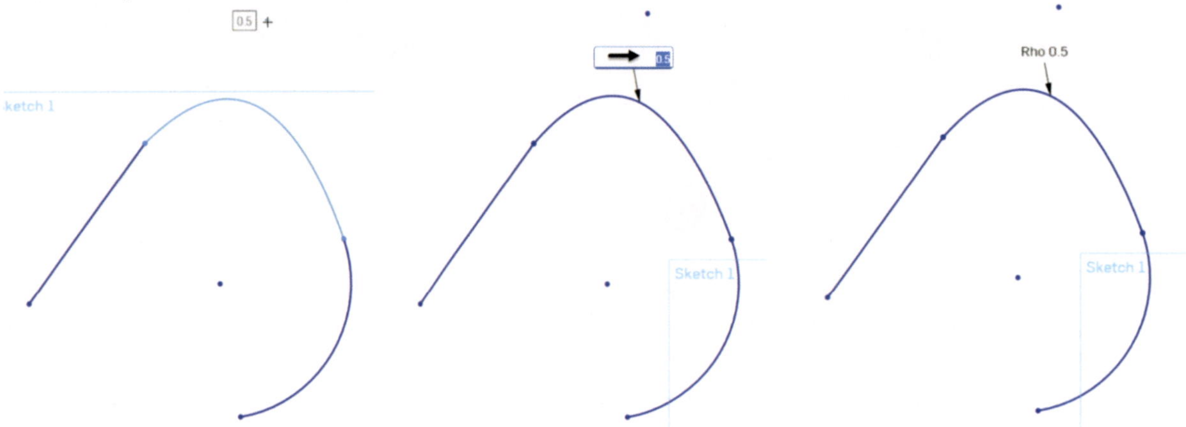

The Spline command

This command creates a smooth B-spline curve along the selected points. B-Splines are non-uniform curves, which are used to create irregular shapes. Click **Spline** on the **Sketch** toolbar and click to specify points in the graphics window. The spline is created passing through the points. You can move the pointer and select the first point of the spline; a closed spline is created. Press Esc to deactivate the **Spline** command.

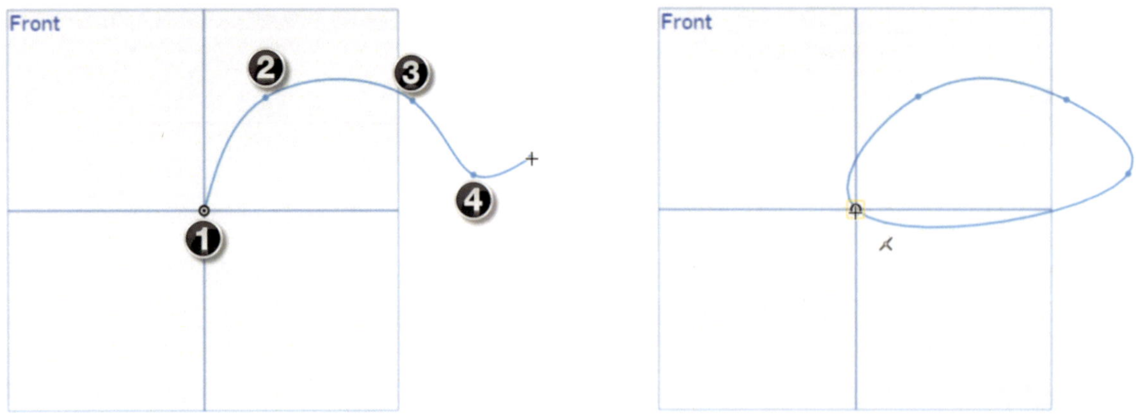

Fully defining a spline is a bit difficult than other sketch entities. For example, create the spline, as shown. Next, activate the **Dimension** command and select the start point of the spline. Select the second point, move the pointer and place the dimension. Type in a value in the box and press Enter. Likewise, create the other two dimensions, as shown.

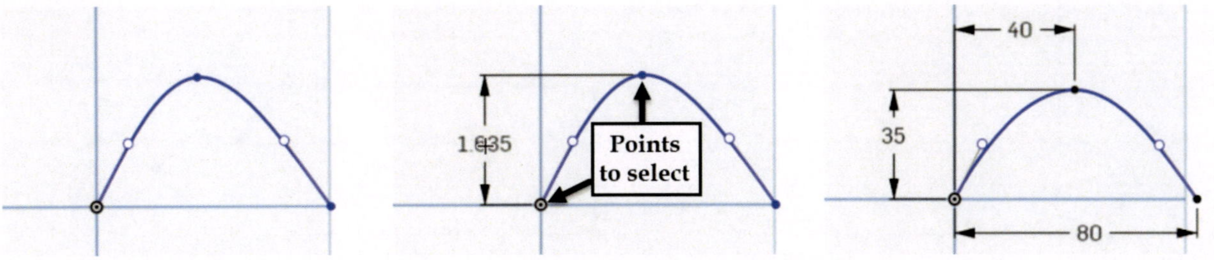

On the Sketch toolbar, click **Constraint** drop-down > **Horizontal** and select the start and end points of the spline. Note the spline handle displayed at the ends of the spline. The spline is modified when you select it and drag the spline handles.

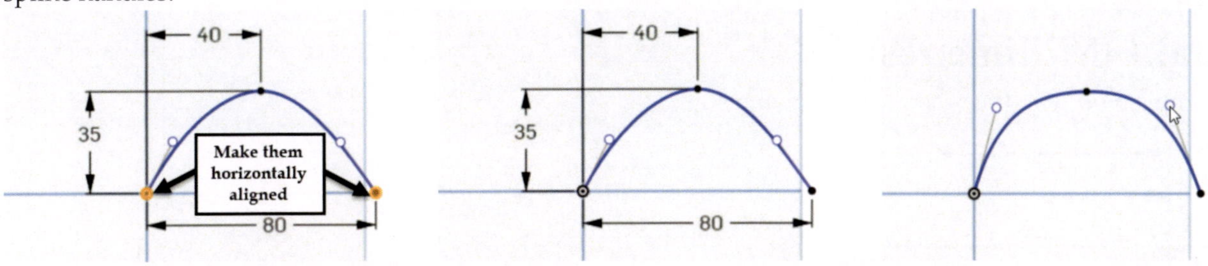

You can control the spline handle by adding dimensions to it. Click the **Dimension** icon on the Sketch toolbar and select the spline handle. Move the pointer and click to specify the dimension location. Type-in the dimension value and press ENTER. Select the spline handle and horizontal axis of the sketch. Next, move the pointer and click to specify the dimension location. Type-in dimension value and press ENTER; the angle dimension is created between the spline handle and the horizontal axis. Likewise, add linear and angular dimensions to the other spline handle.

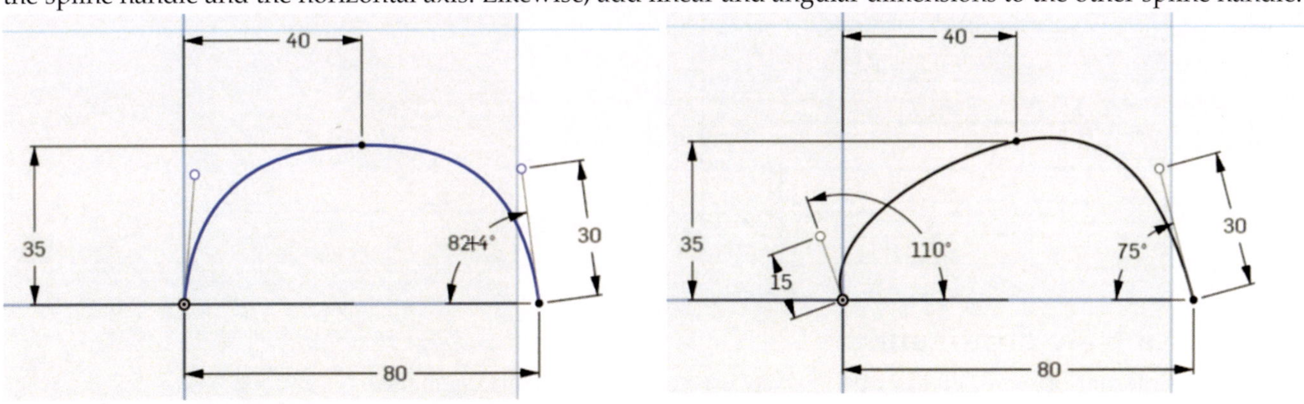

The Spline control point command

This command adds a point to the spline. Click **Spline** drop-down > **Spline control point** on the toolbar. Next, click on the spline at the desired location; the spline point is added. Next, you need to add dimensions and constraints to the newly added spline point to fully define the spline.

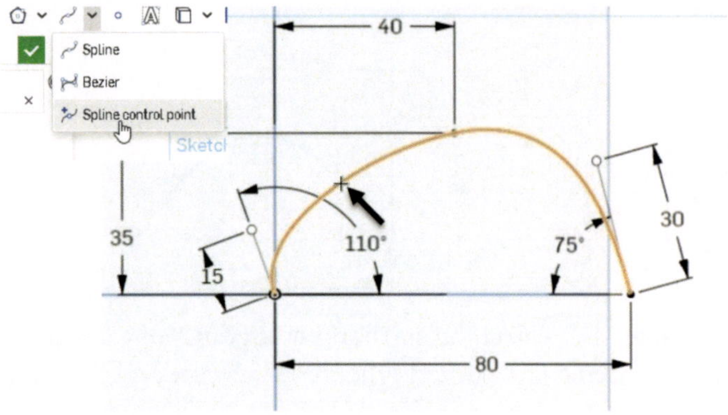

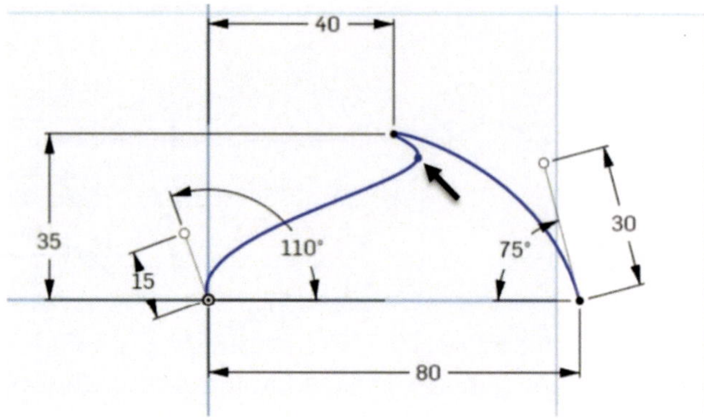

Tutorial 1 (Millimetres)

In this example, you will draw the sketch shown below.

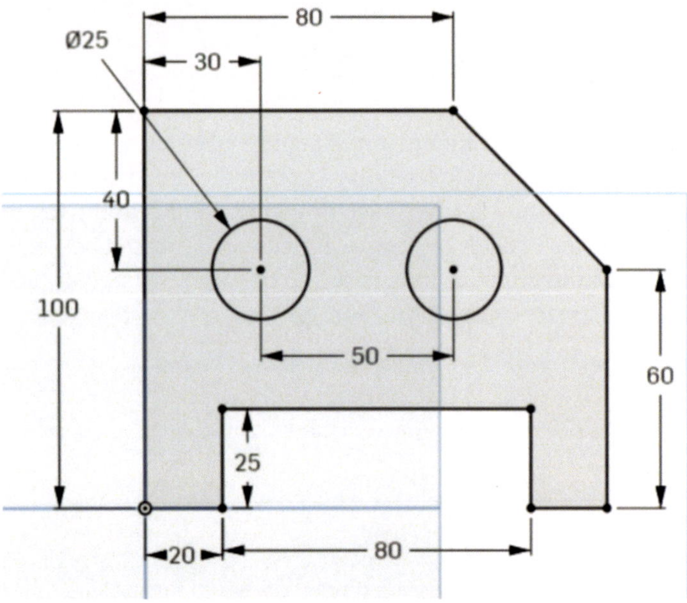

Creating a New document

1. In your Internet Browser, go to https://www.onshape.com to start Onshape.
2. Next, click **SIGN IN** button located on the top right corner side of the web page. Enter the username and password, and then, click **Sign in**.
3. On the Documents page, click **Create > Folder**. Next, type Chapter 2 in the **Folder name** box and then click **Create**.

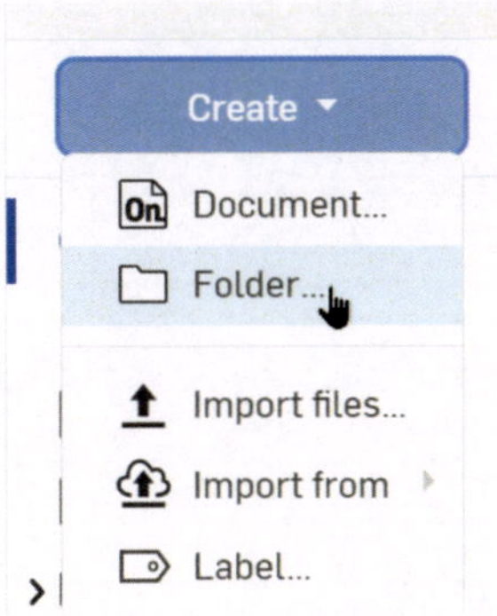

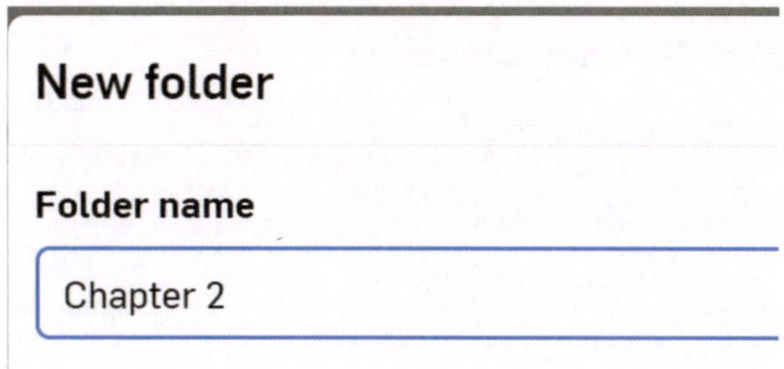

4. Double-click on the **Chapter 2** folder in the **Folders** section; the folder appears.

5. On the Documents page, click **Create > Document**; the **New document** dialog appears on the screen.
6. Enter Tutorial 1 in the **Document name** box and click **OK**; a new document appears.

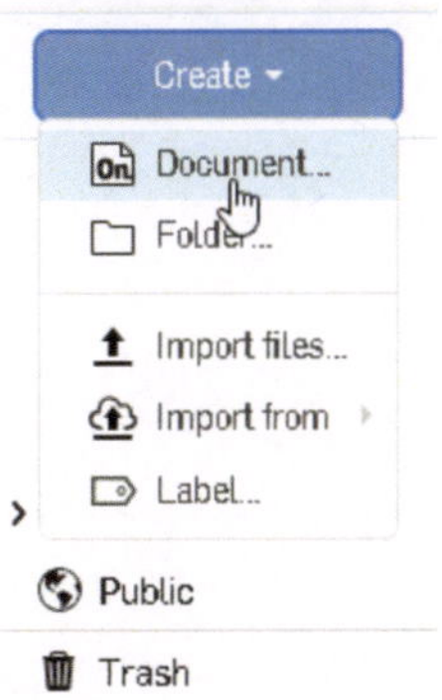

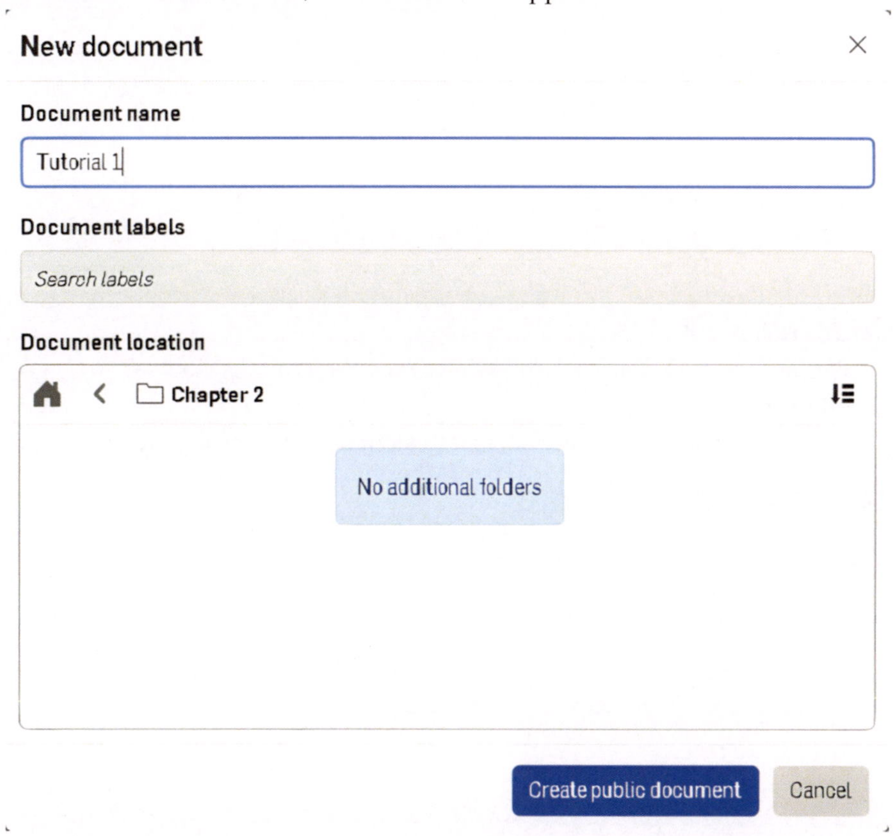

7. Click the **Document menu** located at the top left corner of the window and select **Workspace Units**; the **Workspace Units** dialog appears on the screen.
8. On the **Workspace Units** dialog, select **Length default unit> Millimeter** and **Mass default unit > Gram**.
9. Leave the other default settings and click the green check ✓.

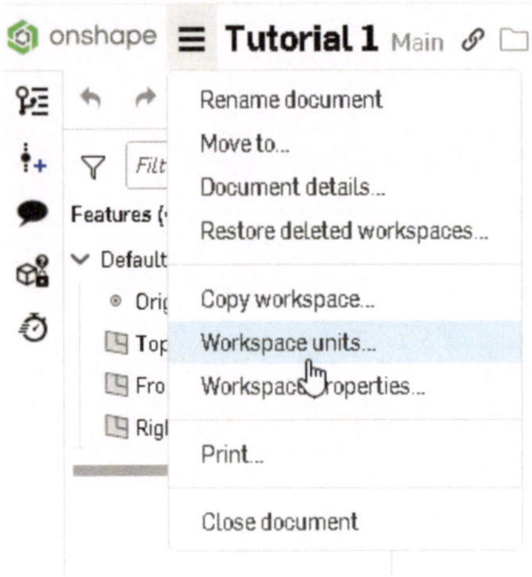

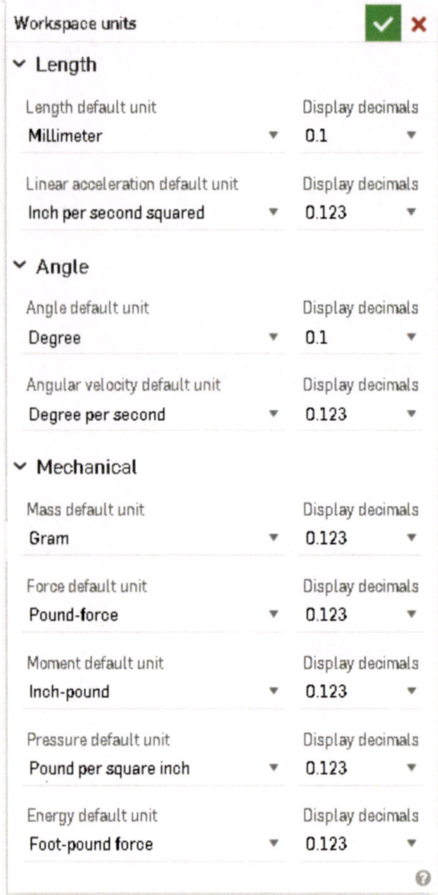

Creating a Sketch

1. To start a new sketch, click the **Sketch** command on the Toolbar.
2. Select the Front plane.
3. Right-click and select **View normal to sketch plane**; the selected plane orients normal to the screen.

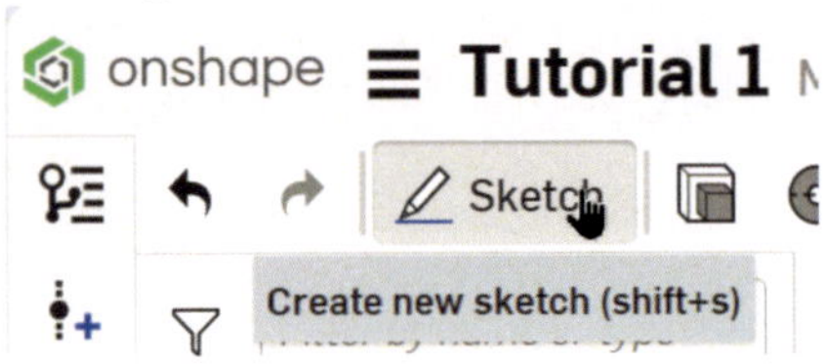

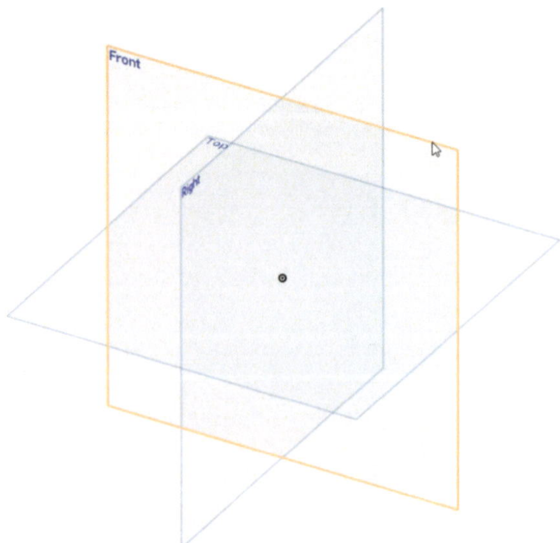

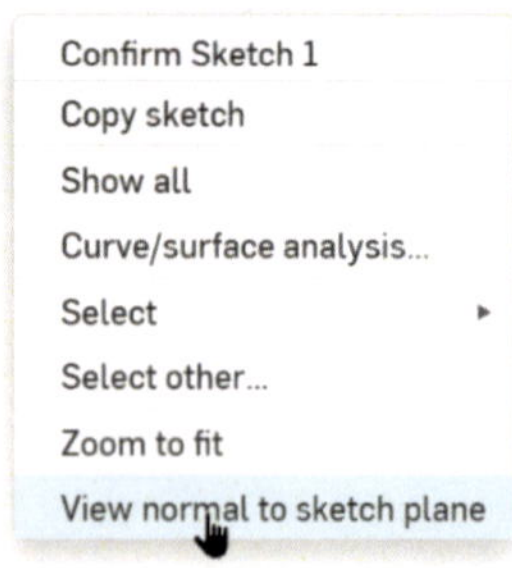

4. Activate the **Line** command (click the **Line** icon  on the Toolbar).

5. Click on the origin point to define the first point of the line.
6. Move the pointer horizontally toward the right.
7. Click to define the endpoint of the line.
8. Move the pointer vertically upward, and then click to draw the second line.

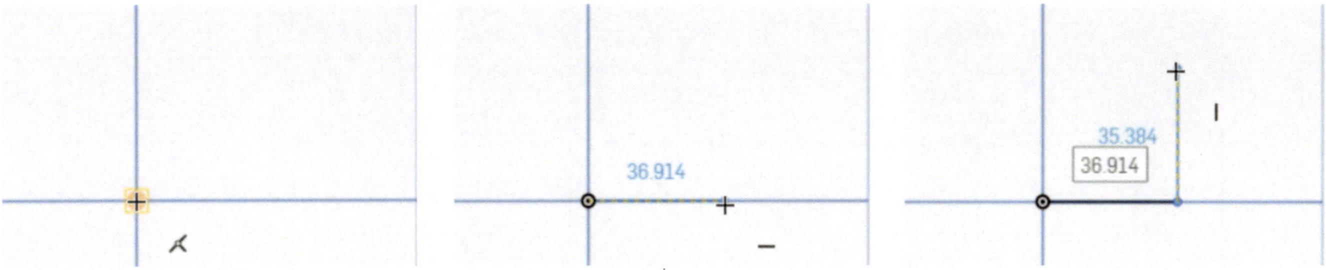

9. Move the pointer horizontally toward the right and click.
10. Move the pointer vertically downward and click when the horizontal trace-lines appear from the sketch origin.
11. Move the pointer horizontally toward right up to a short distance, and then click.

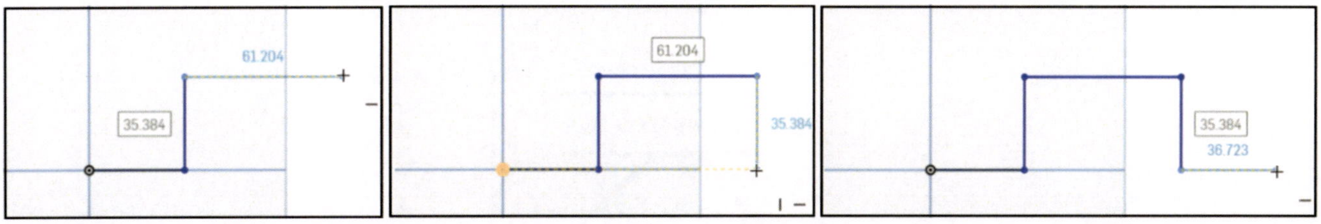

12. Move the pointer vertically upward and click.
13. Move the pointer in the top-left direction and click.
14. Move the pointer horizontally towards left and click when vertical trace-line appears from the origin.

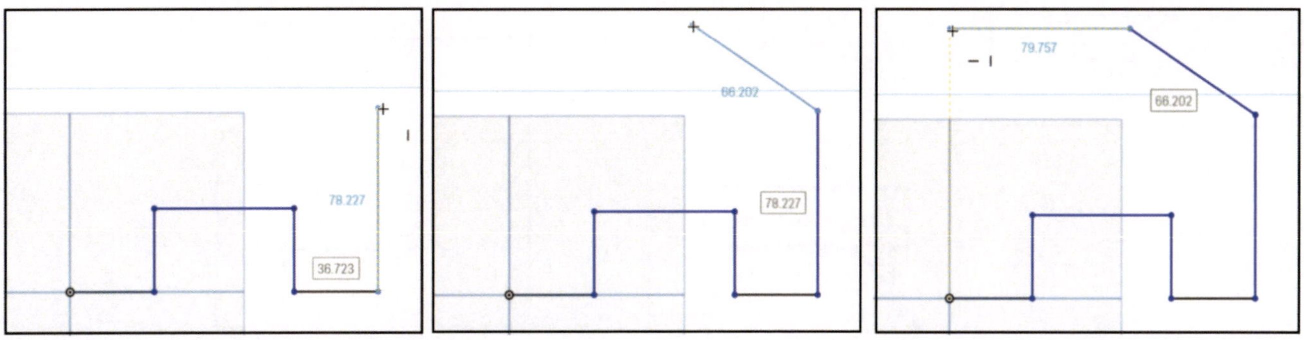

15. Select the start point of the sketch to create a closed sketch. Notice the shade inside the sketch.
16. Right-click and select **Escape Line** (or) press **Esc** to deactivate the **Line** command.

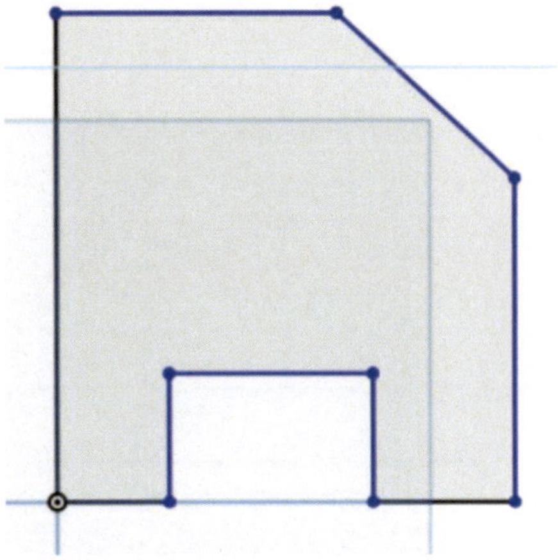

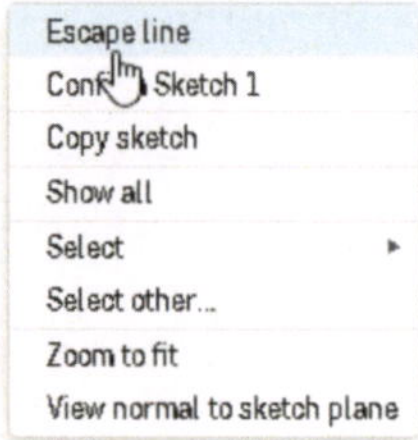

Adding Constraints

1. On the Toolbar, click **Constraint** drop-down > **Horizontal**.
2. Click on the two horizontal lines at the bottom.

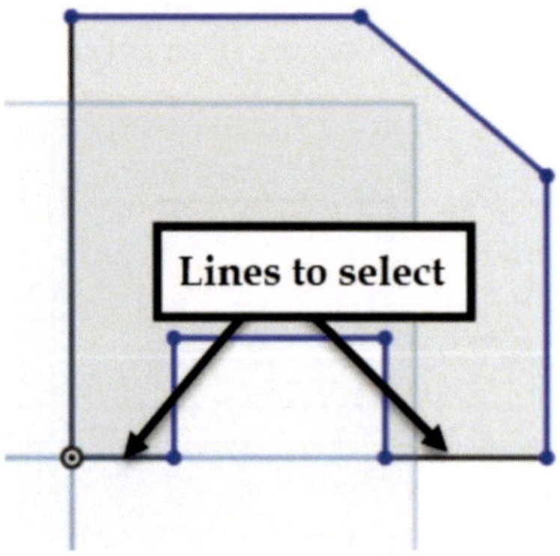

3. On the Toolbar, click **Constraint** drop-down > **Equal** . Next, select the two horizontal lines at the bottom; the selected lines become equal in length.

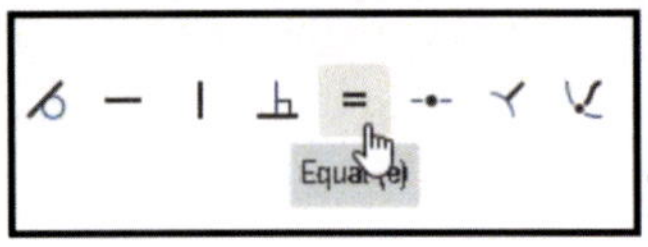

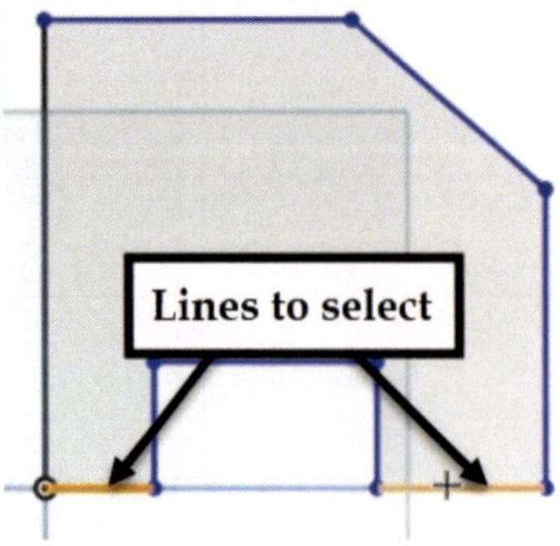

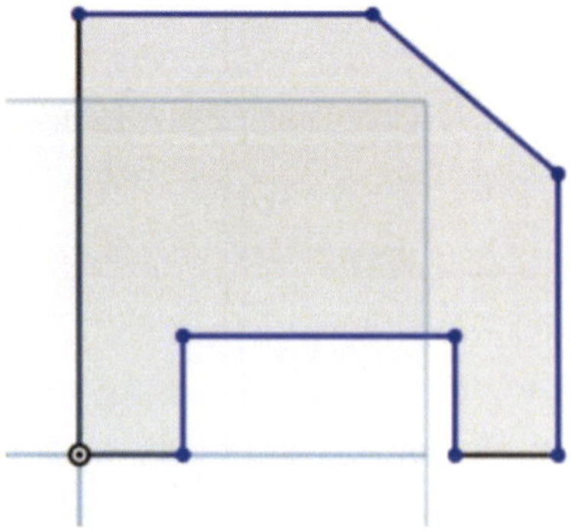

4. Select the small vertical lines; the selected lines are made equal in length.

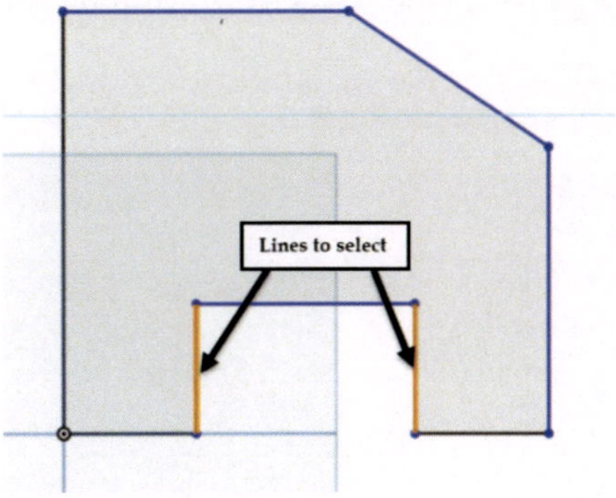

Adding Dimensions

1. Click **Dimension** on the Toolbar and click on the lower left horizontal line. Move the mouse pointer downward and click to locate the dimension.
2. Type-in **20** and press Enter to update the dimension.

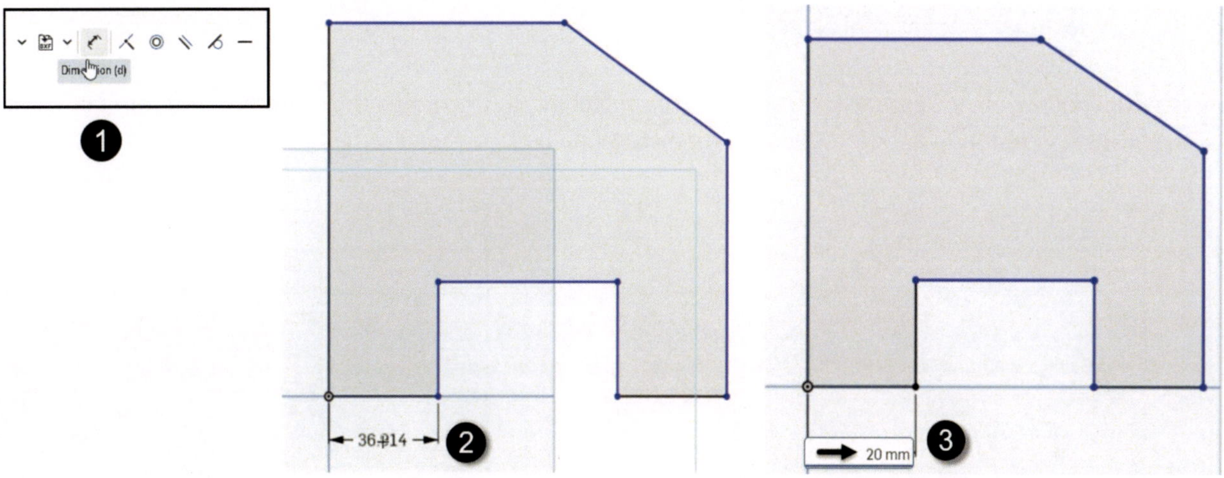

3. Click on the small vertical line located at the left side. Move the mouse pointer towards the right and click to position the dimension.
4. Type-in **25** and press Enter to update the dimension.

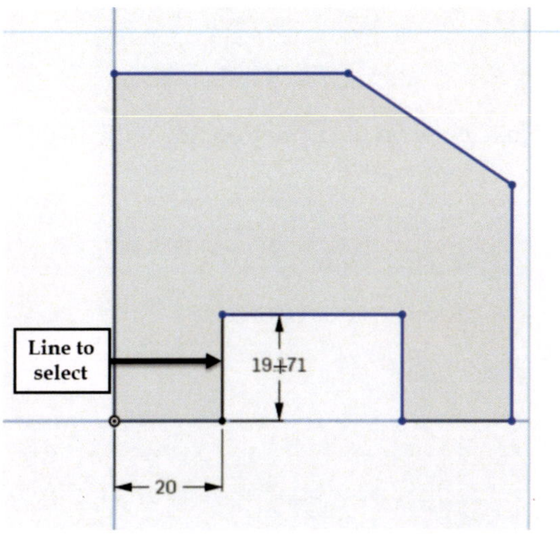

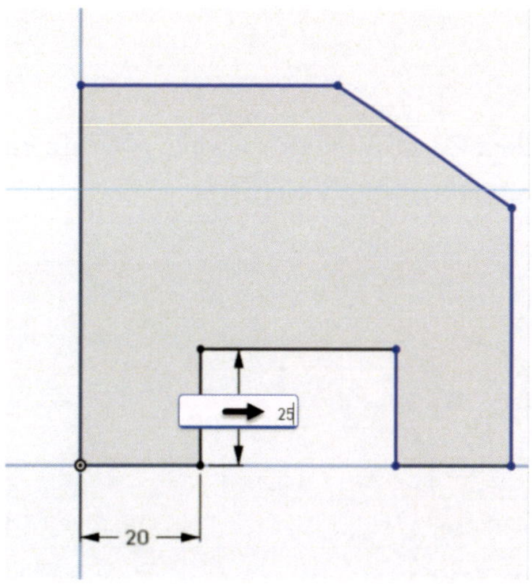

5. Create other dimensions in the sequence, shown below. Press Esc to deactivate the **Dimension** command.

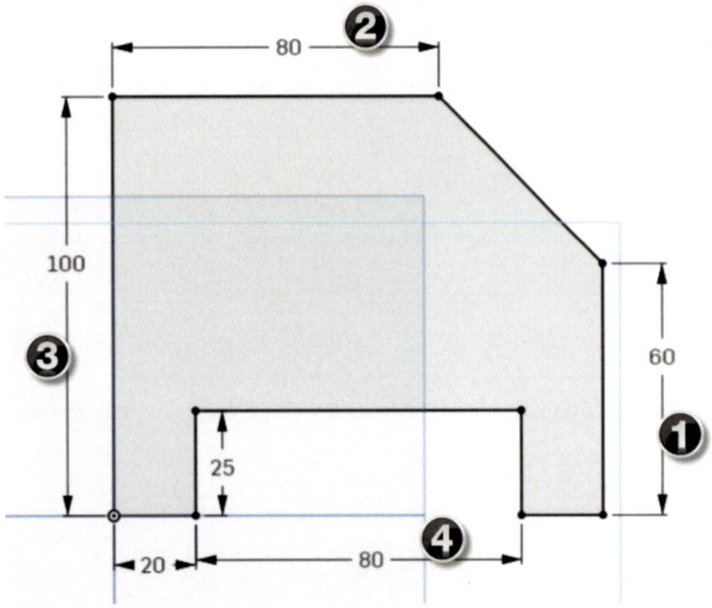

6. On the Toolbar, click **Circle** . Click inside the sketch region to define the center point of the circle. Move the mouse pointer and click to define the diameter. Likewise, create another circle.

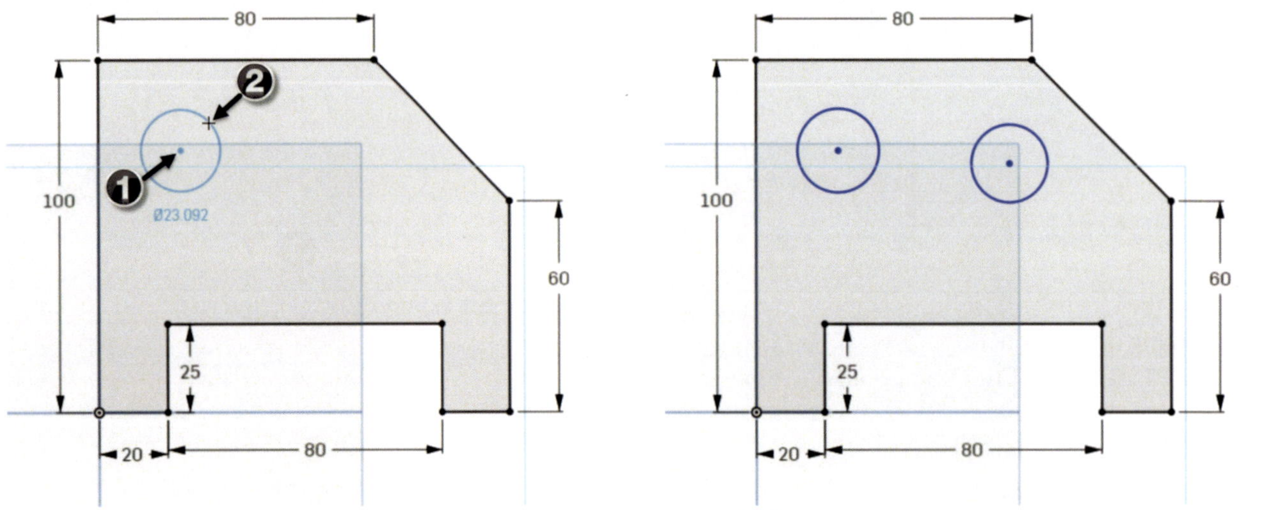

7. On the Toolbar, click **Constraints** drop-down > **Horizontal** . Next, click on the center points of the two circles to make them horizontally aligned.

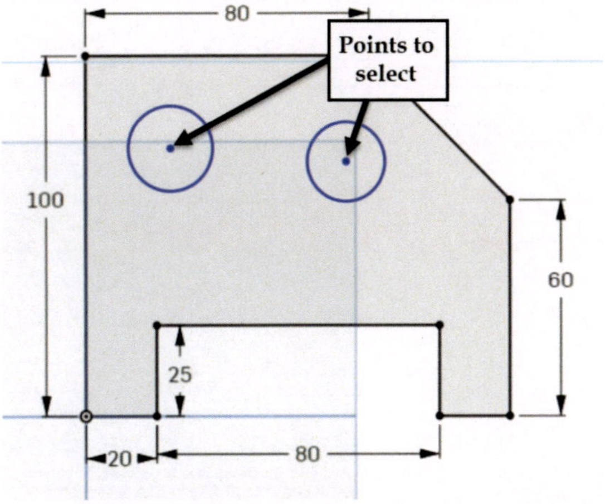

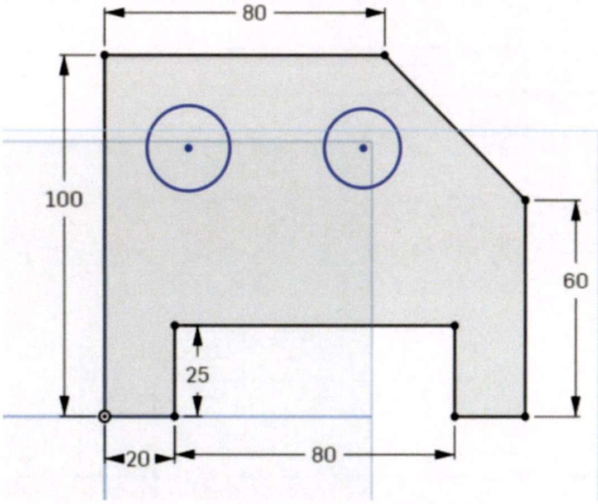

8. On the Toolbar, click **Constraints** drop-down > **Equal**. Next, click on the two circles; the diameters of the circles become equal.

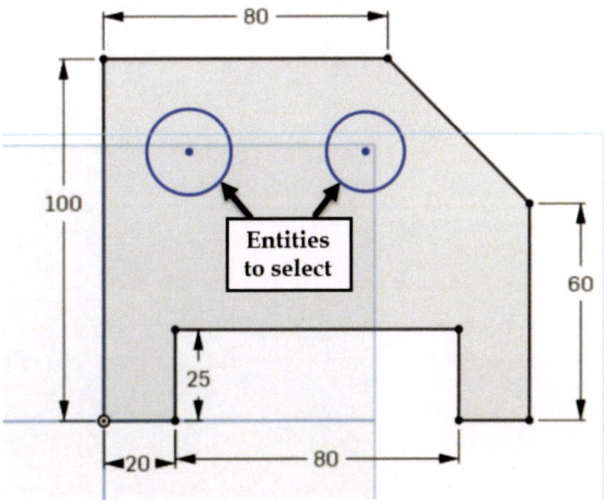

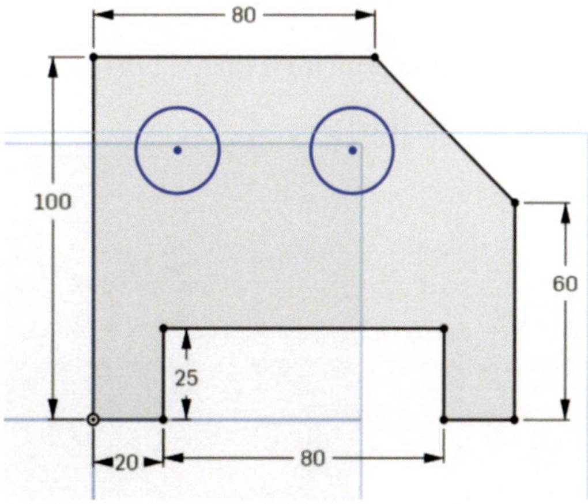

9. Activate the **Dimension** command and click on any one of the circles. Move the mouse pointer and click to position the dimension. Type **25** in the box and press Enter.

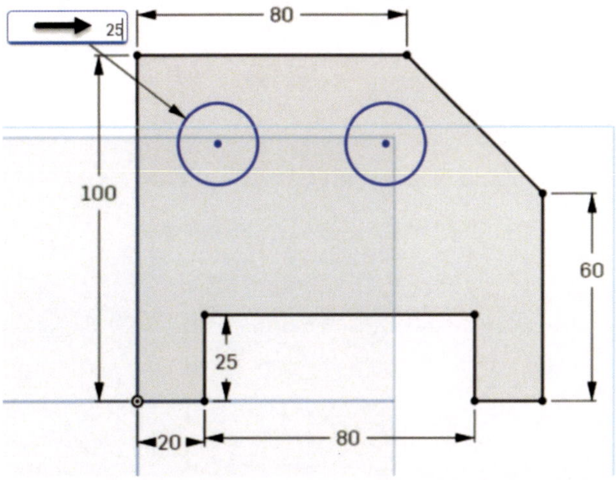

10. Create other dimensions between the circles and the adjacent lines, as shown below.

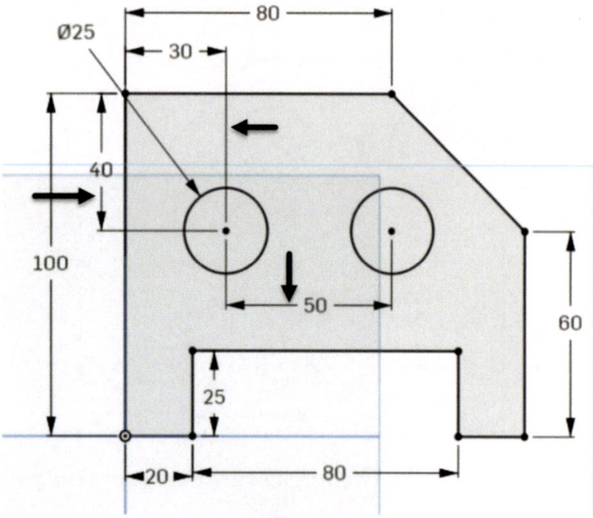

11. Click the green check on the **Sketch 1** dialog or right-click and select **Confirm Sketch 1** to finish the sketch.
12. Click on the **Document menu** located at the top left corner and click **Close document**.

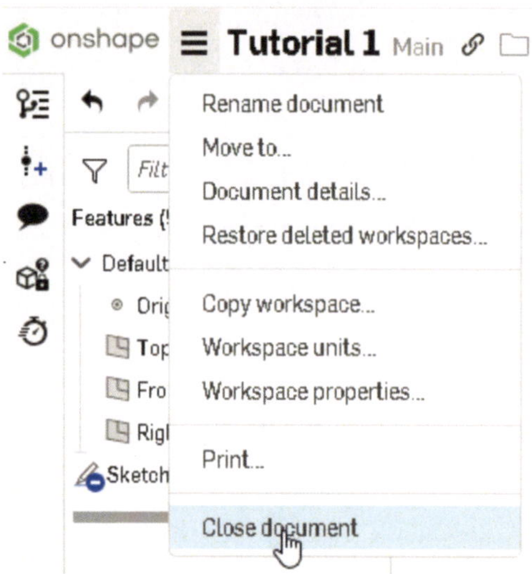

Tutorial 2 (Inches)

In this example, you draw the sketch shown below.

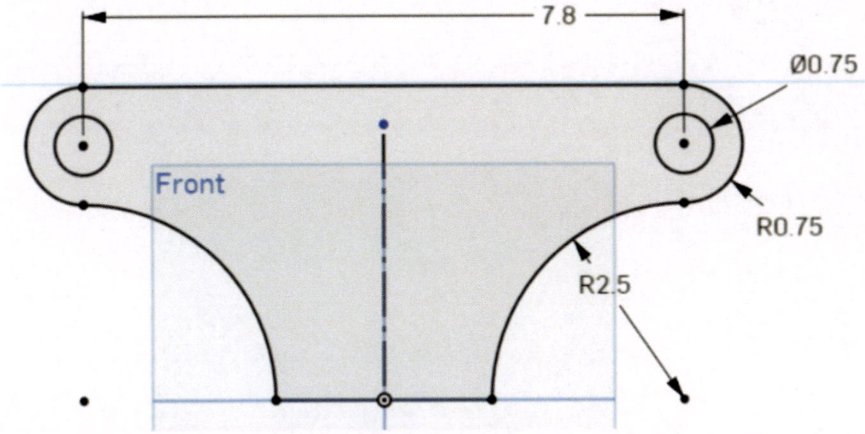

Creating a New document

1. To start **Onshape,** go to https://www.onshape.com.
2. Click the **SIGN IN** button located on the top right corner of the window. Enter the username and password and then click **Sign in**.
3. On the Documents page, click **Create > Document**; the **New document** dialog appears on the screen.

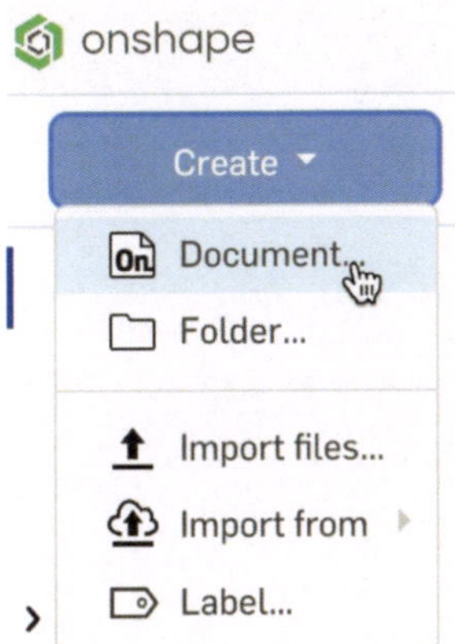

4. On the Documents page, click **Create > Document**; the **New document** dialog appears on the screen.
5. Enter Tutorial 2 in the **Document name** box and click **Create public document**; a new document appears.
6. Click **Document menu** located at the top left corner of the window and select **Workspace Units**; the **Workspace Units** dialog appears on the screen.
7. On the **Workspace Units** dialog, select **Length default unit > Inch** from **Length** section.
8. Select **Mass default unit > Pound** from **Mechanical** section.

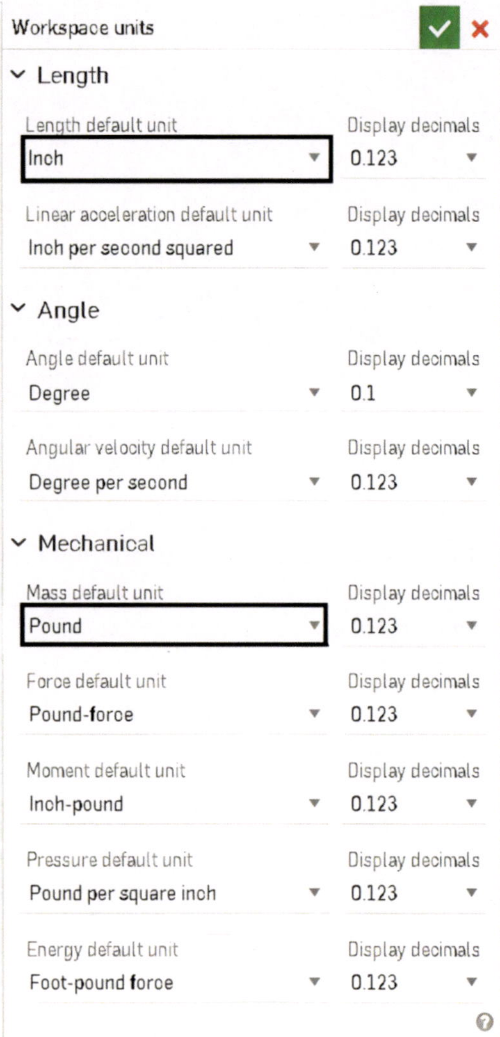

9. Leave the other default settings and click the green check.

Creating a Sketch

1. To start a new sketch, click **Sketch** command on the Toolbar.
2. Click on the Front Plane.
3. Right-click and select **View normal to sketch plane**.
4. Click the **Line** command on the Toolbar.
5. Place the mouse pointer on the origin point and move the pointer horizontally toward the left; the dotted line appears. Click to specify the start point of a line.
6. Move the pointer horizontally towards the right and click to draw a line.

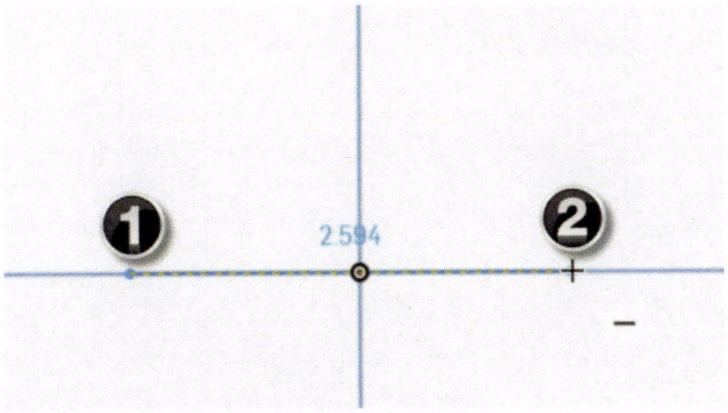

7. Right-click and click **Escape Line**.
8. Click **3 Point arc** on the Toolbar and click on the endpoint of the line.
9. Move the pointer vertically upward, and then move it in the top-right direction.
10. Click to define the endpoint of the arc.
11. Next, move the pointer and click to define the radius of the arc.

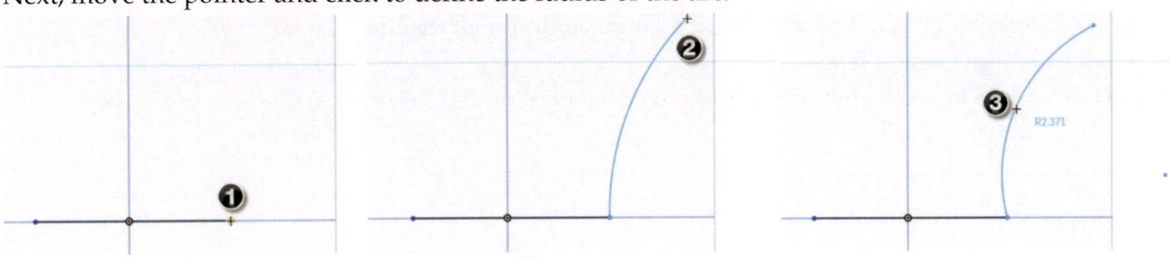

12. Press **Esc** to deactivate the **3 Point arc** command.
13. Click **3 Point arc** drop-down **> Tangent arc** on the Toolbar.
14. Click on the endpoint of the arc.
15. Place the pointer on the endpoint of the arc, and then move it upwards. Click when a vertical dotted line appears, as shown below.

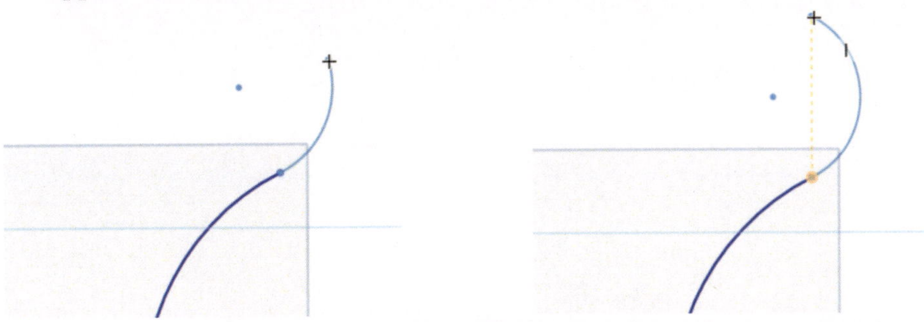

16. Next, right-click and click **Escape tangent arc** to deactivate the **Tangent arc** command.
17. Activate the **Line** command (click the **Line** icon on the Toolbar).
18. Move the mouse pointer towards left and click to create a horizontal line. Note that the length of the new line should be higher than that of the lower horizontal line.

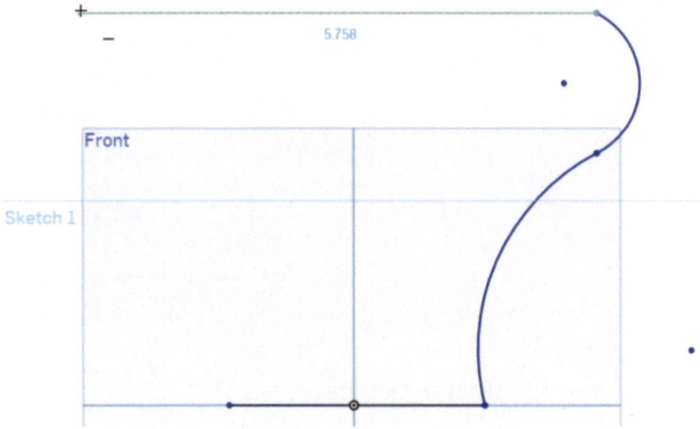

19. Press **Esc** to deactivate the **Line** command.
20. Activate the **Tangent arc** command and click on the endpoint of the line.
21. Move the pointer downwards left.
22. Move the pointer towards the right and click when a vertical dotted line appears, as shown below.

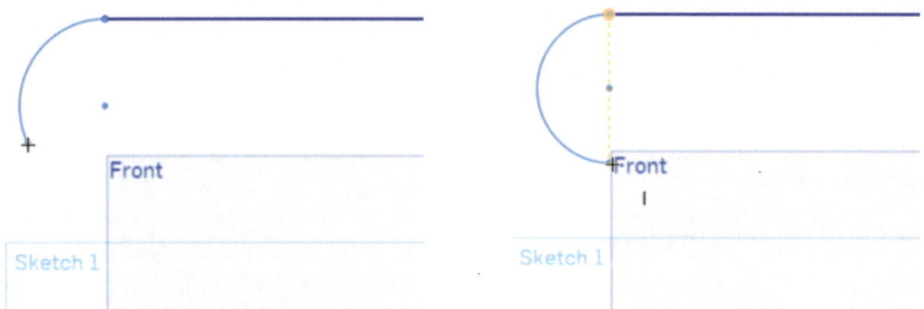

23. Press **Esc** to deactivate the tangent arc.
24. Activate the **3 Point arc** command and click on the endpoint of the tangent arc.
25. Select the start point of the sketch.
26. Move the pointer and click to define the radius of the arc.

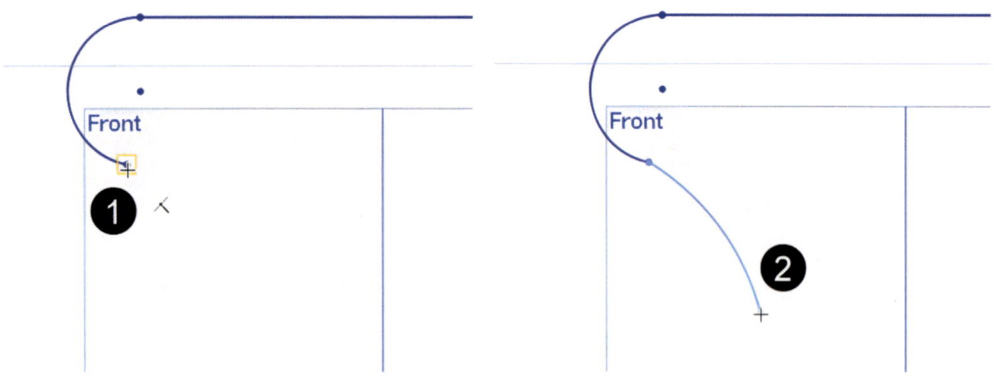

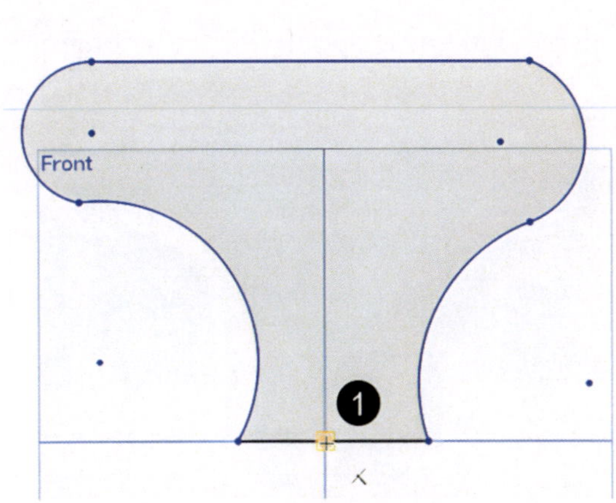

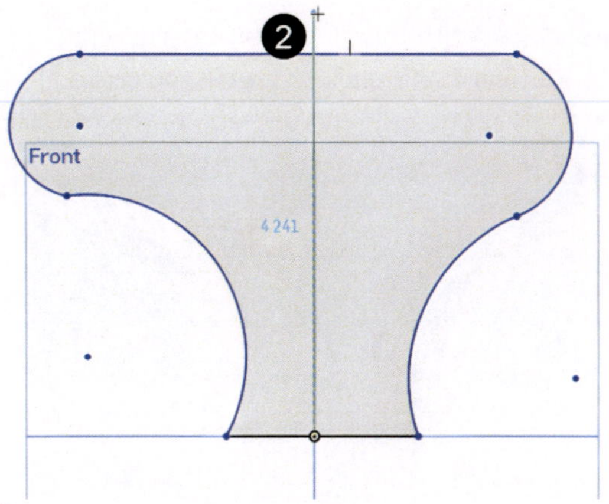

27. Activate the **Line** command (click the **Line** icon on the Toolbar).
28. Click on the origin point of the sketch. Move the mouse pointer vertically up and click to create a vertical line. Next, press Esc to deactivate the **Line** command.

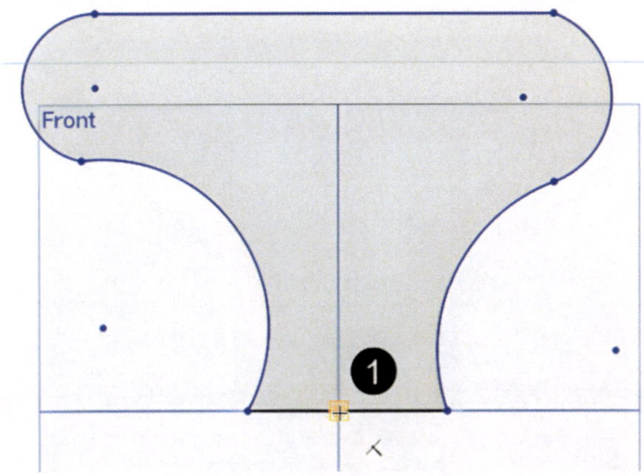

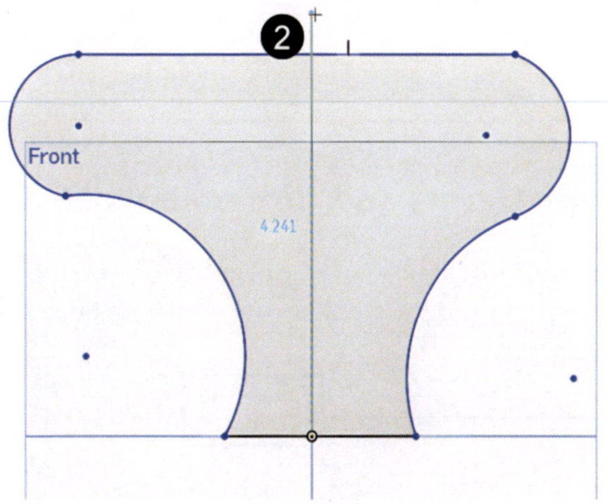

29. Click on the vertical line located at the center, and then click **Construction** command on the Toolbar. The line turns into a construction element.

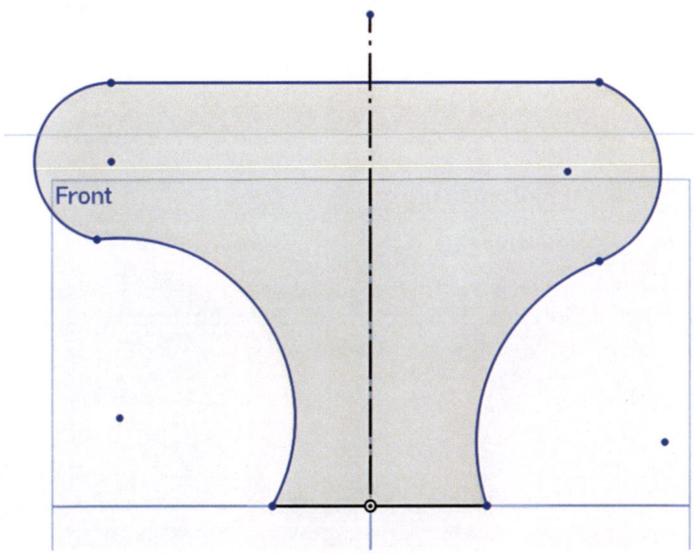

30. Activate the **Circle** command. Click on the right side of the construction line to specify the center point. Move the pointer outward and click to create the circle.
31. Likewise, create another circle on the left side of the construction line.

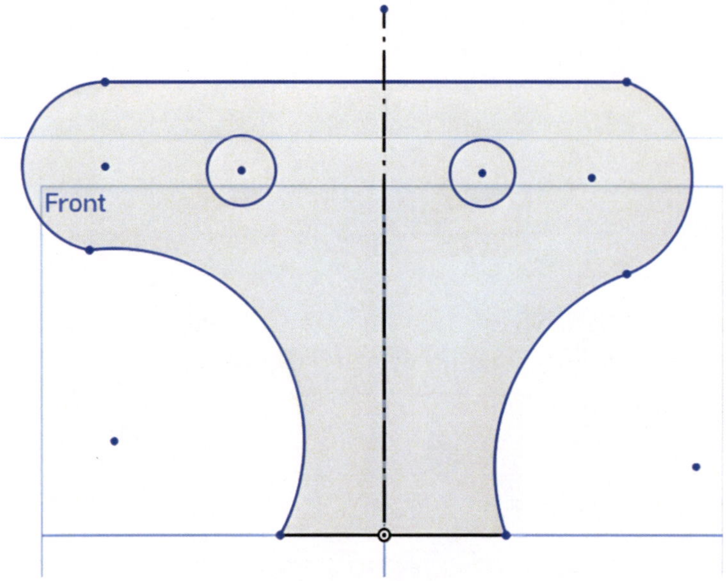

Adding Constraints and dimensions

1. Click **Constraints** drop-down > **Concentric** on the Toolbar.
2. Click on the circle and the small arc on the right side. The circle and arc are made concentric.

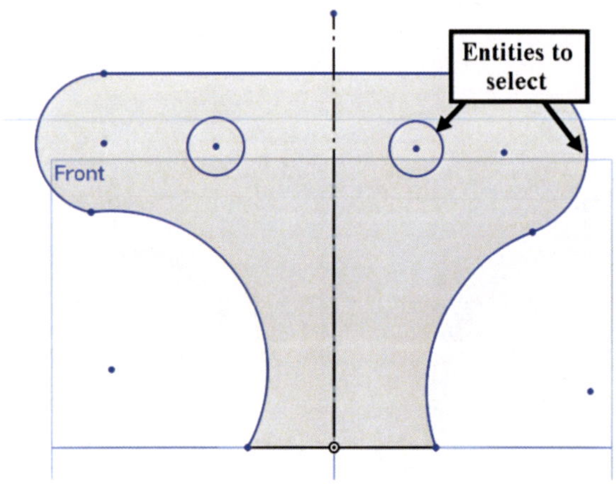

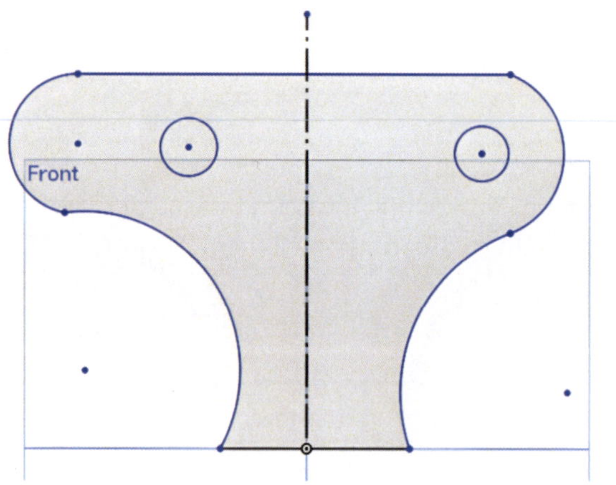

3. Likewise, make the other circle and small arc concentric to each other.
4. On the Toolbar, click **Constraints** drop-down > **Symmetric** .
5. Click on the construction line located at the center.
6. Click on the small arcs on both sides of the construction line. The arcs are made symmetric about the construction line.

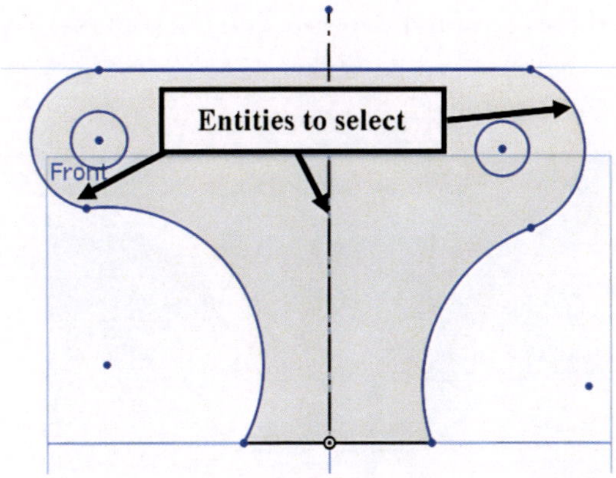

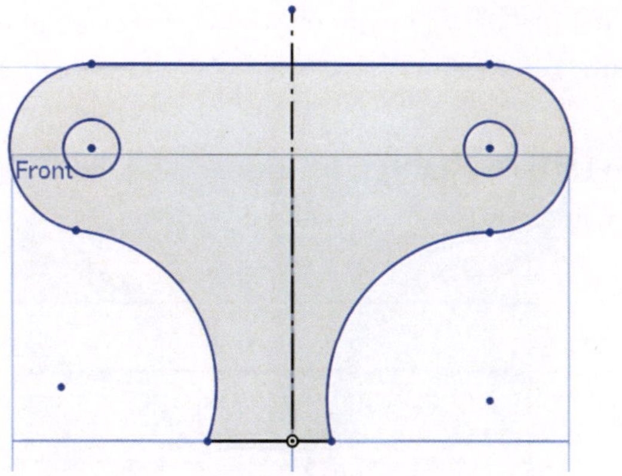

7. Likewise, make the large arcs and circles symmetric about the construction line.

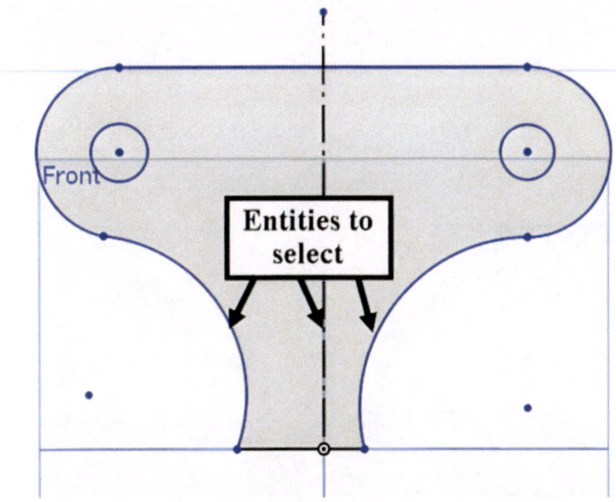

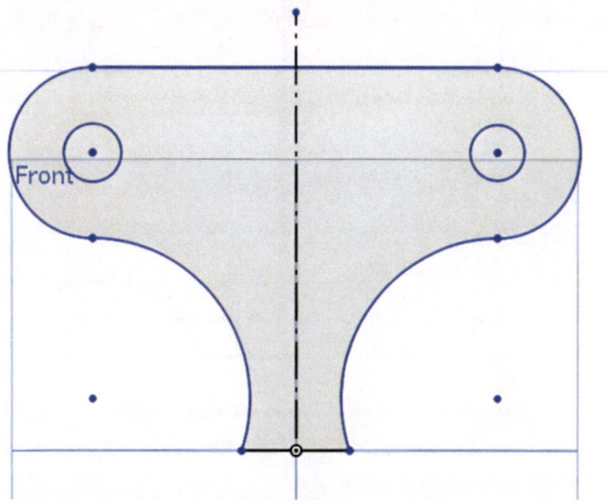

8. On the Toolbar, click **Constraints** drop-down > **Horizontal**. Next, select the center point of any one of the large arcs.
9. Select the origin point of the sketch; the two selected points are aligned horizontally.
10. Activate the **Dimension** command and apply dimensions to the sketch, as shown below.

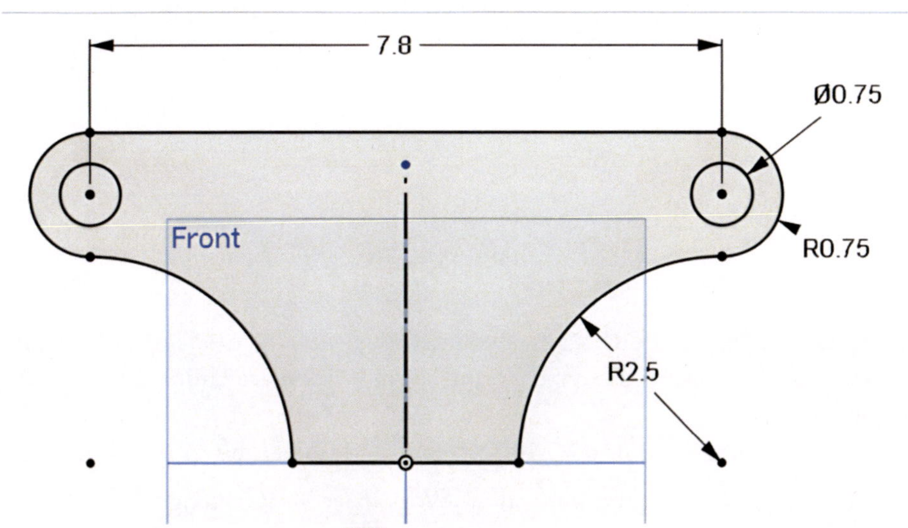

11. Click the green check on the **Sketch 1** dialog to exit the sketch.

12. To close the file, click **Document menu** located at the top left corner of the window and click **Close document**.

Tutorial 3 (Millimetres)

In this example, you draw the sketch shown below.

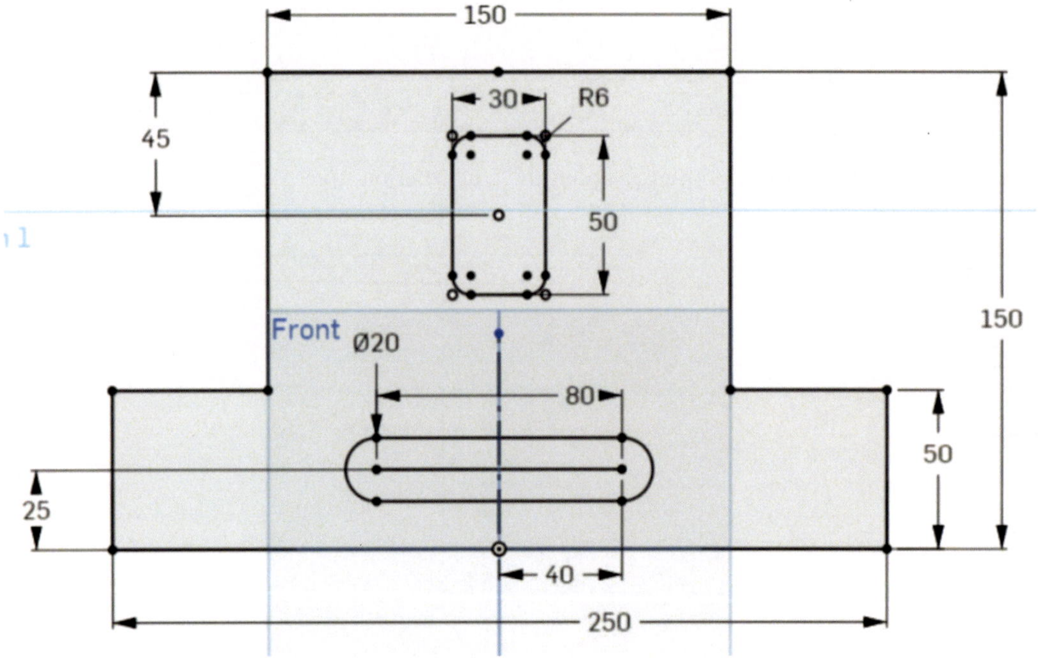

Creating a New Document

1. On the Documents page, click **Create > Document**; the **New document** dialog appears on the screen.

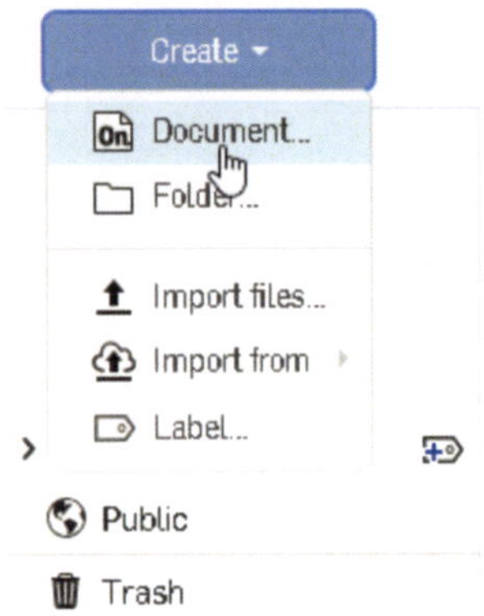

2. Enter Tutorial 3 in the **Document name** box and click **OK**; a new document appears.
3. Click **Document menu** located at the top left corner of the window and select **Workspace Units**; the **Workspace Units** dialog appears on the screen.
4. On the **Workspace Units** dialog, select L**ength default unit > Millimeter** and **Mass default unit > Gram**.
5. Leave the other default settings as it is and click green check on the **Workspace Units** dialog.

Creating a Sketch

1. To start a new sketch, click **Sketch** command on the Toolbar.
2. Click on the Front plane.
3. Right-click and select **View normal to sketch plane**; the selected plane orients normal to the screen.
4. Activate the **Line** command (click the **Line** icon on the Toolbar).
5. Click on the origin point and move the pointer vertically up. Next, click to create a vertical line.

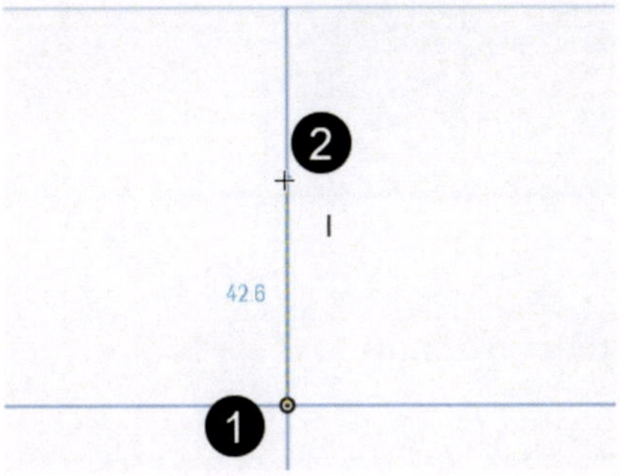

6. Press **Esc** to deactivate the line command.
7. Select the vertical line and click the **Construction** command. It creates a vertical centerline.

8. Activate the **Line** command and click on the origin point.
9. Move the mouse pointer horizontally towards the right and click to define the second point.
10. Draw the lines in the sequence, as shown. Next, right-click in the graphics area and select **Escape line**.

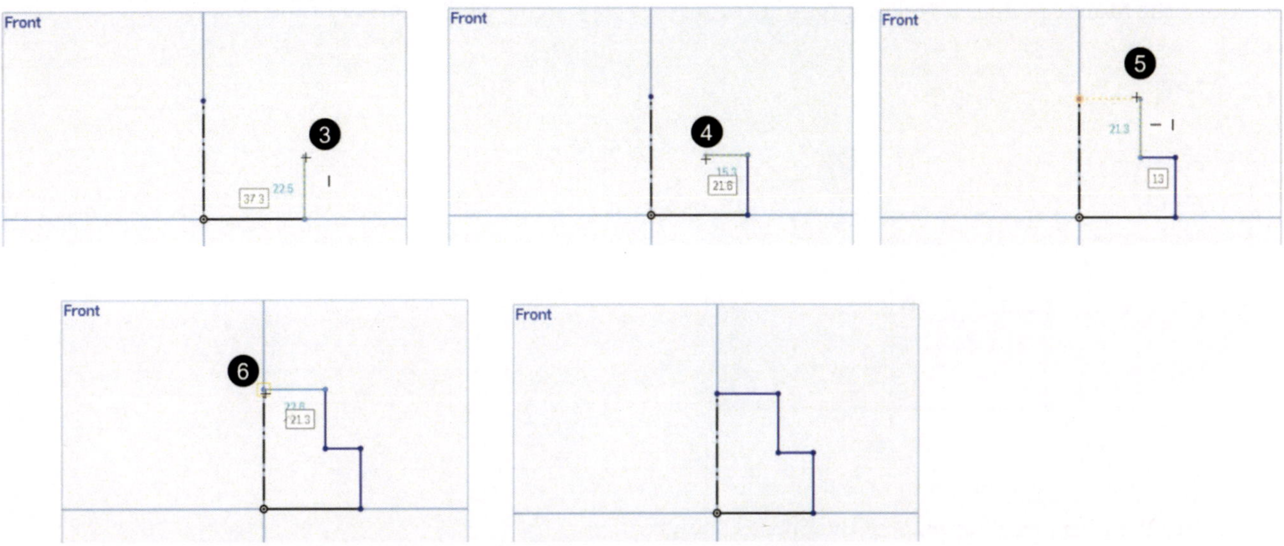

11. Activate the **Mirror** command (On the Toolbar, click the **Mirror**).

12. Select the vertical centreline to define the mirror line.
13. Select the entities to mirror, as shown.

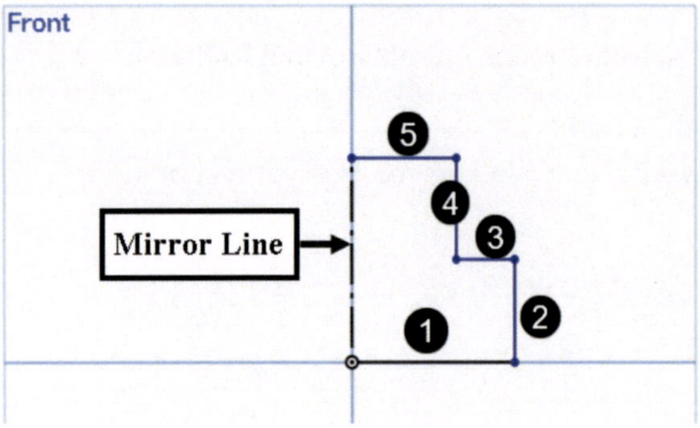

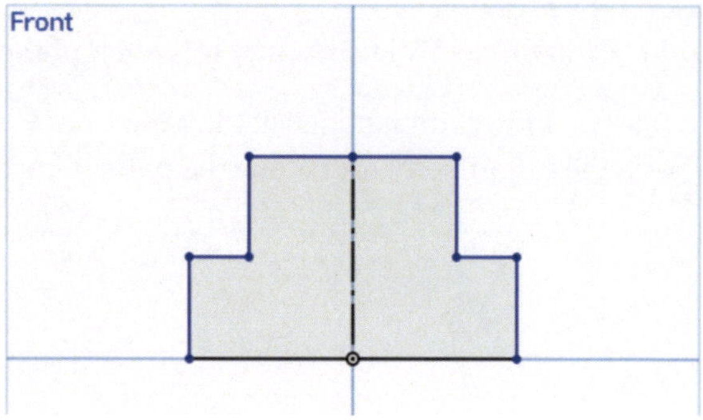

14. Press **Esc** to deactivate the **Mirror** command.
15. On the **Sketch 1** dialog, check the **Show constraints** option to view all the constraints.

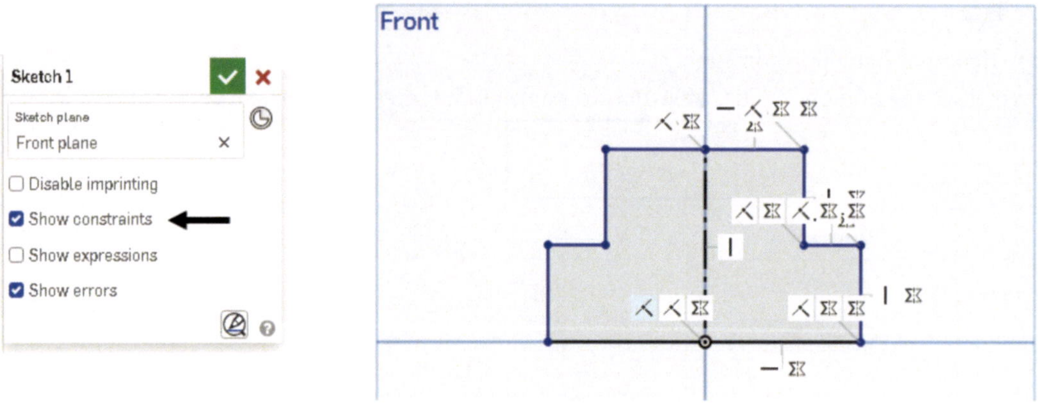

You can notice the symmetric constraints on both sides of the mirror line.

16. On the **Sketch 1** dialog, uncheck the **Show constraints** option to hide the constraints.
17. Click **Rectangle** drop-down > **Center point rectangle** on the Toolbar.
18. Click on the centreline to define the center of the rectangle.
19. Move the mouse pointer towards top right corner and click to define the corner of the rectangle.

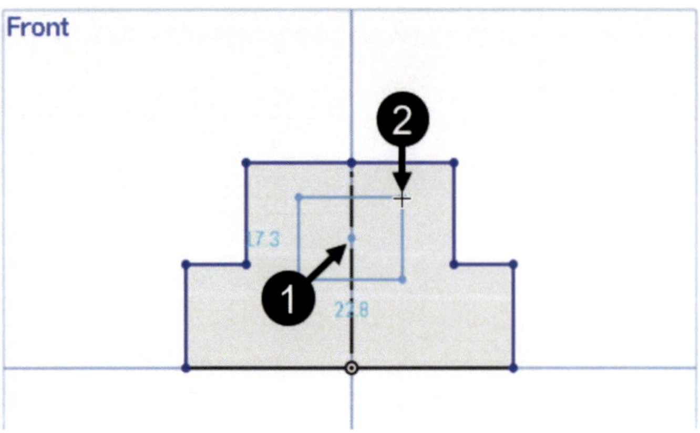

20. Click the **Line** command on the Toolbar.
21. Specify the start and endpoints of the line, as shown.

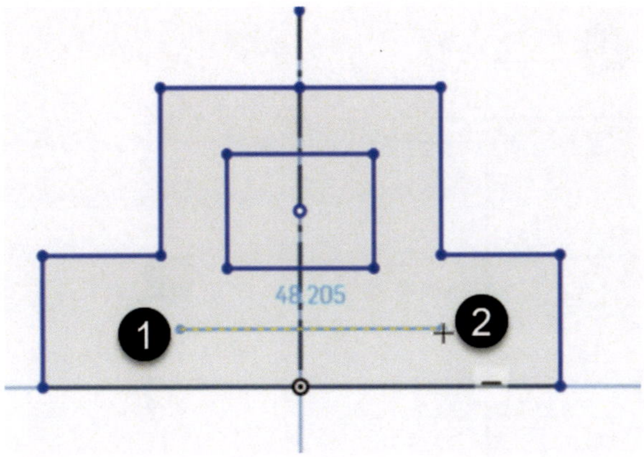

22. On the Toolbar, click **Offset** drop-down > **Slot** and select the horizontal line, as shown.

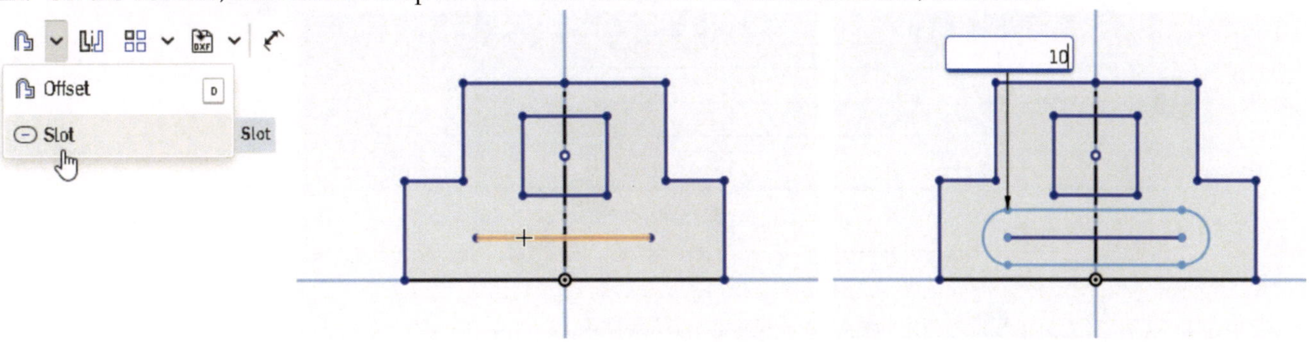

23. Double click on the dimension value attached to the slot, and then enter 10. Next, press Esc to deactivate the **Slot** command.
24. Click the **Sketch Fillet** command on the Toolbar.
25. Select the corners of the rectangle and click to create the fillet, as shown.
26. Double click on the fillet radius value and type-in 6 in the box. Then, press **Enter** to update the radius value.

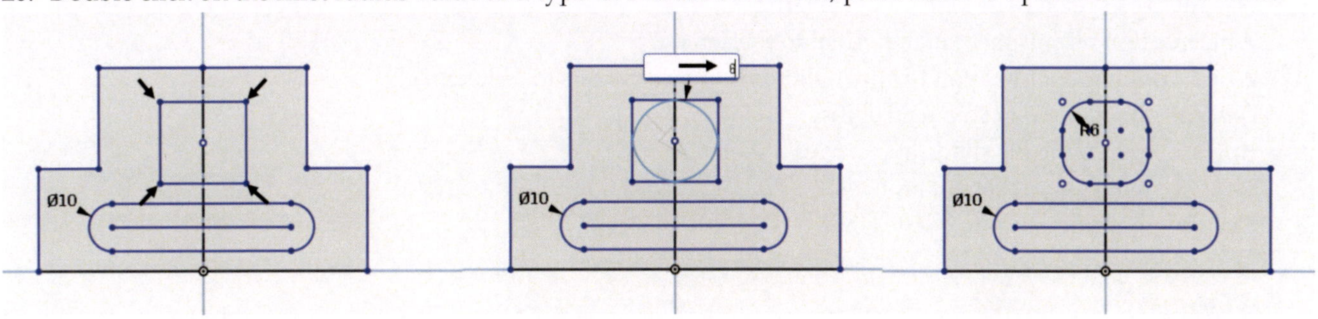

27. Activate the **Dimension** command and apply dimensions in the sequence shown below.

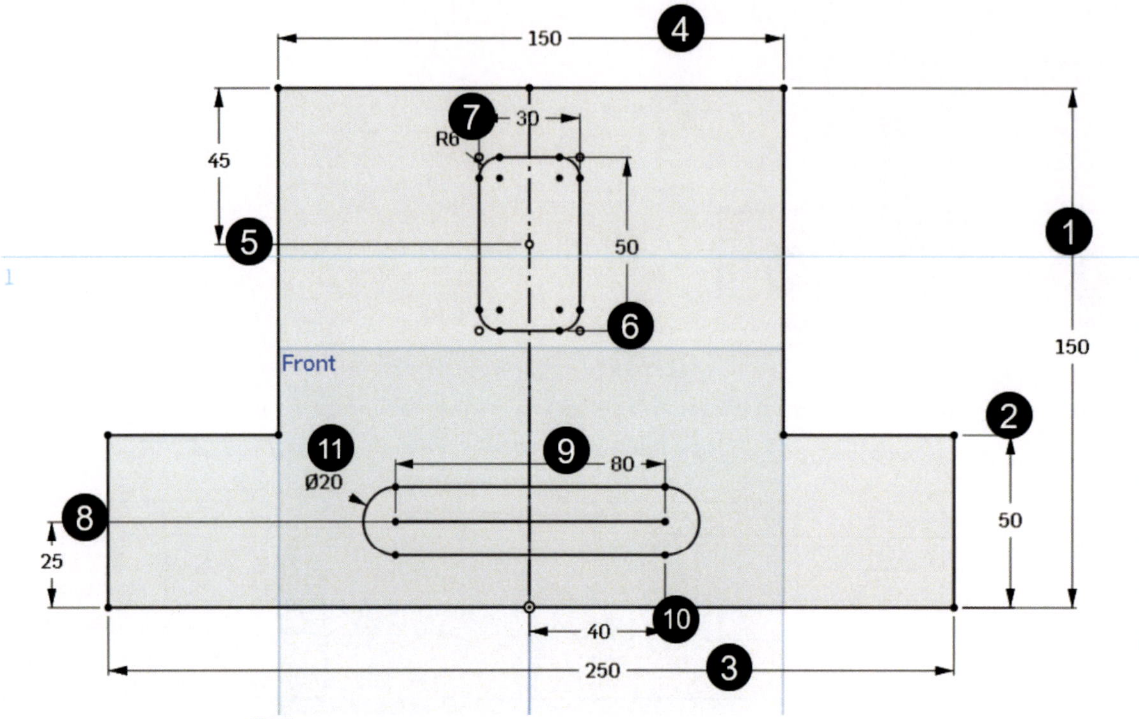

28. Click the green check  on the **Sketch 1** dialog to finish the sketch.
29. Click on the **Document menu** located at the top left corner of the window and click **Close document** to close.

Questions

1. What is the procedure to create sketches in ONSHAPE?
2. List any two sketch *constraints* in ONSHAPE.
3. Which option orients the sketch normal to the screen?
4. Which command allows you to apply all types of dimensions to a sketch?
5. Describe the method to create an ellipse.
6. How do you define the shape and size of a sketch?
7. How do you create a tangent arc?
8. List any two commands to create circles?

Exercises

Exercise 1

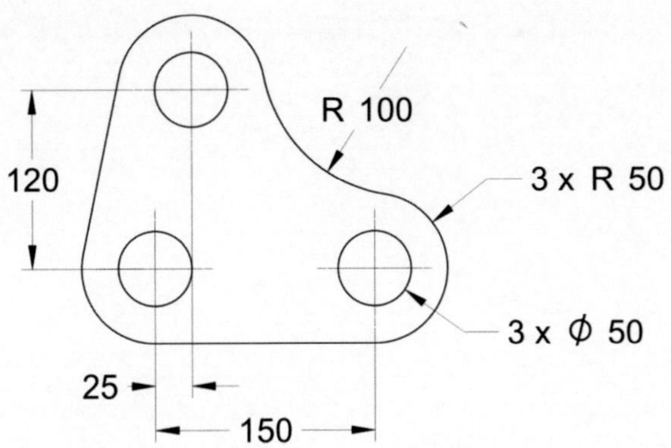

Exercise 2

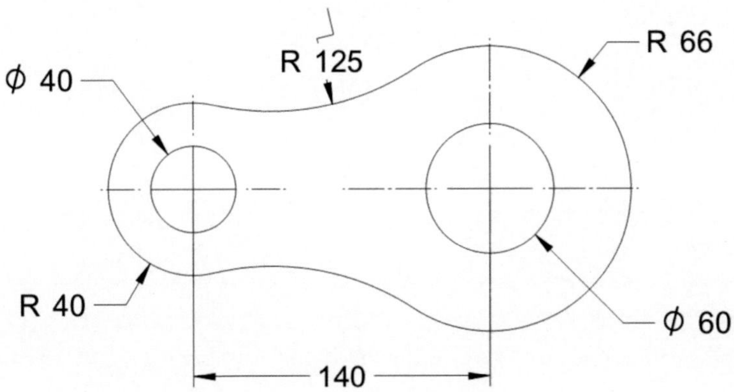

Exercise 3

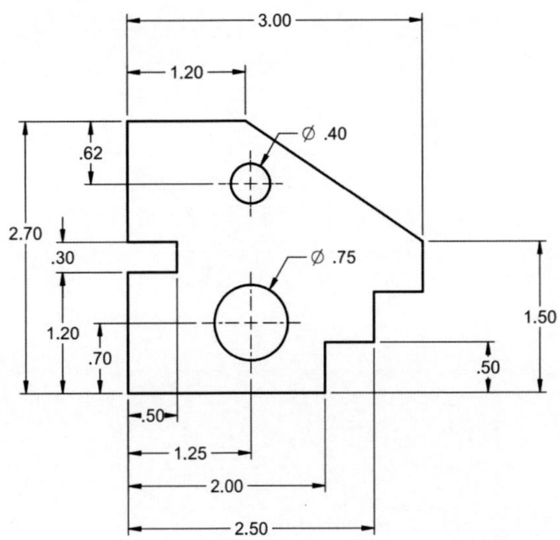

Chapter 3: Extrude and Revolve Features

This chapter covers the methods and commands to create extruded and revolved features.

The topics covered in this chapter are:

- *Constructing Extrude feature*
- *Constructing Revolve feature*
- *Creating Reference Planes*
- *Additional options in the Extrude and Revolve commands*

Extrude Features

Extruding is the process of taking a two-dimensional profile and converting it into 3D by giving it some thickness. A simple example of this would be taking a circle and converting it into a cylinder. To create an Extrude feature, first draw a sketch, and then click the **Extrude** command on the toolbar**.** Click on the sketch profile; notice the preview of the extruded feature with the default depth. Type-in a new value in the **Depth** box on the **Extrude 1** dialog. You can also click and drag the arrow that appears on the extrude preview. If you want to reverse the extrusion direction, click the **Opposite Direction** icon next to the **End type** drop-down of the **Extrude** dialog.

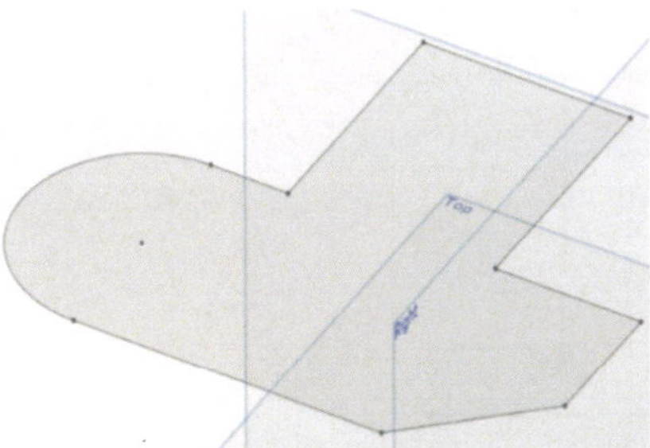

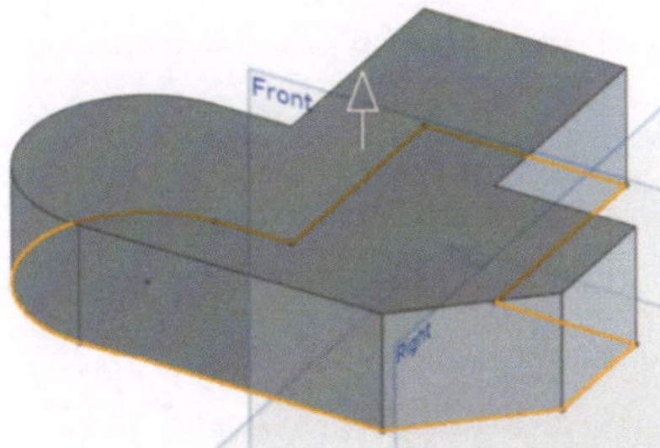

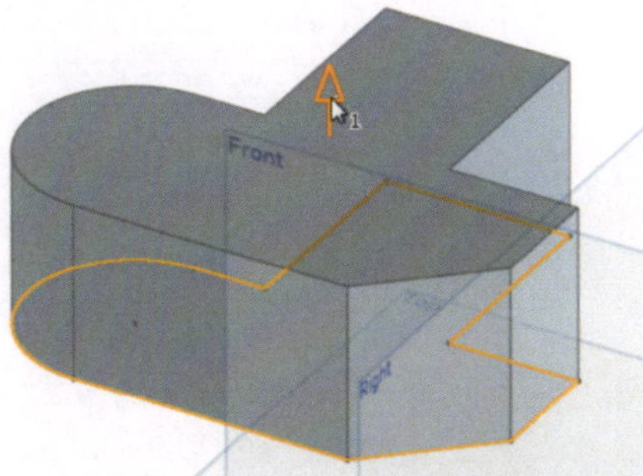

On the **Extrude 1** dialog, check the **Second end position** option to extrude the sketch in two opposite directions. Next, you need to define the depth along the second direction. You can type-in a value in the **Depth** box under the **Second end position** check box.

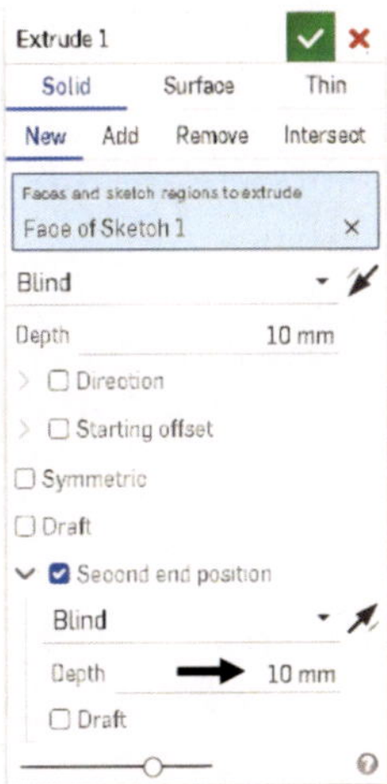

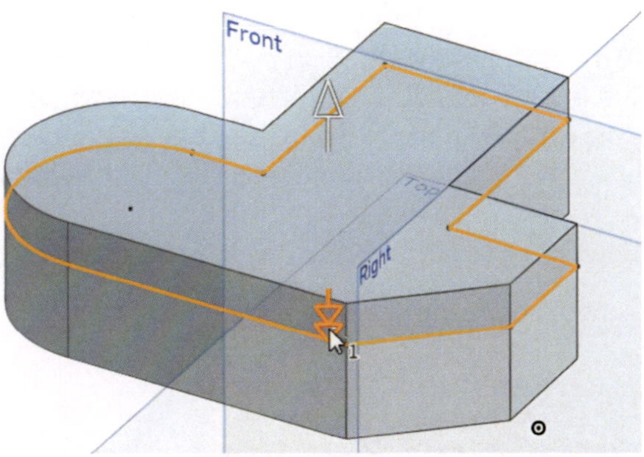

To extrude the sketch equally on both sides, select **Blind** from the **End type** drop-down, enter the desired **Depth**, and then check the **Symmetric** option in the **Extrude 1** dialog to finalize the feature.

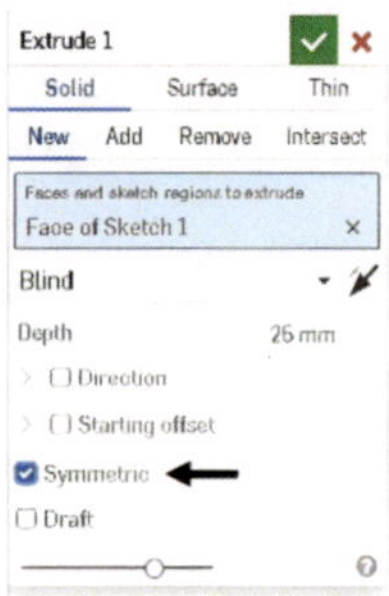

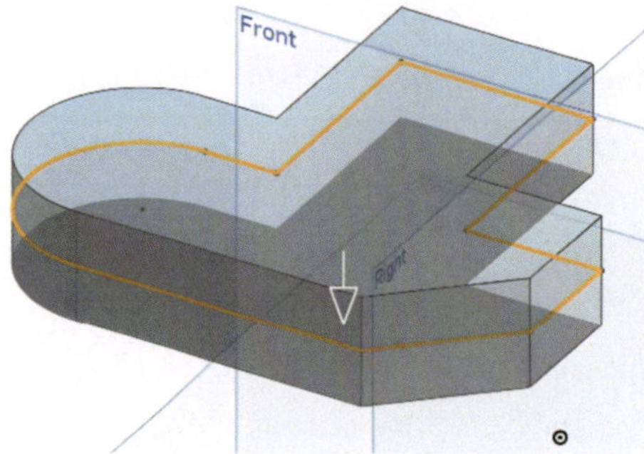

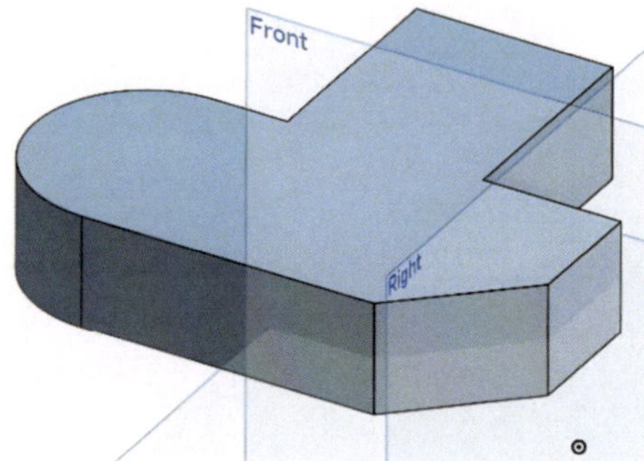

Revolve Feature

Revolving is the process of taking a two-dimensional profile and revolving it about a centerline to create a 3D geometry (shapes that are axially symmetric). While creating a sketch for the *Revolve* feature, it is important to think about the cross-sectional shape that will define the 3D geometry once it is revolved about an axis. For instance, the following geometry has a hole in the center. This could be created with a separate *Hole* feature. But in order to make that hole part of the *Revolve* feature, you need to sketch the axis of revolution so that it leaves a space between the profile and the axis.

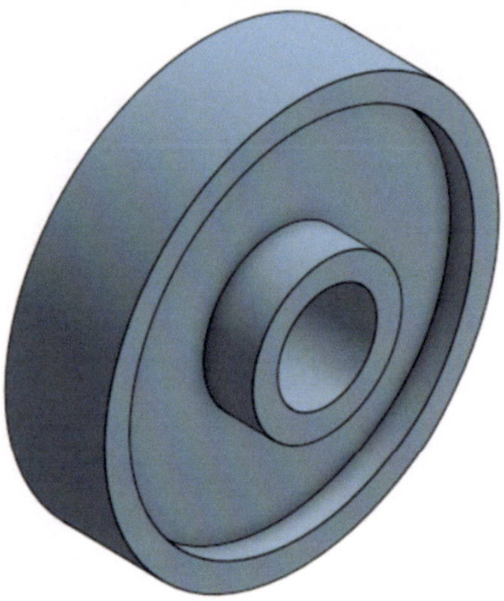

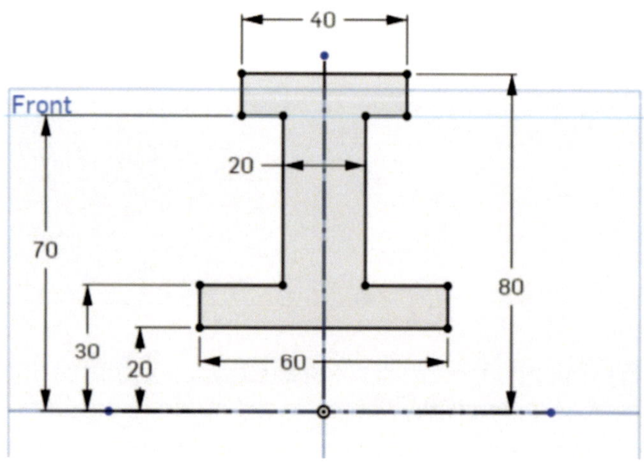

To create a *Revolve* feature, first sketch a revolve profile along with the centreline. Next, confirm the sketch and click **Revolve** on the Toolbar. Next, select the sketch profile to be revolved. Click in the **Revolve axis** selection box on the **Revolve** dialog and select the axis of revolution; the sketch will be revolved by full 360 degrees. If you want to enter a different angle of revolution, then select **One direction** option from the **Revolve type** drop-down on the **Revolve** dialog. Type-in a new value in the **Revolve angle** field. Select the **Symmetric** option from the Revolve type drop-down if you want to revolve the sketch symmetrically on both sides of the sketch. If you want to revolve a sketch asymmetrically, then select the **Two directions** option from the **Revolve type** drop-down.

Type-in values in the **Revolve angle** and **Second revolve angle** fields. Click the green check to complete the *Revolve* feature

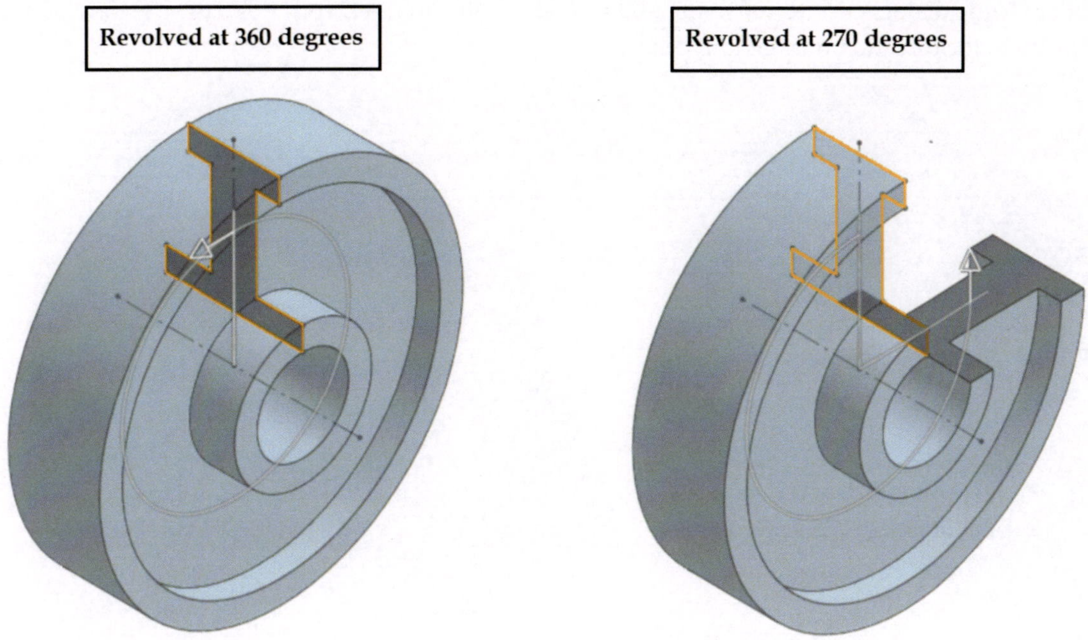

Use (Project/Convert)

This command projects the edges of a 3D geometry onto a sketch plane. To do this, click the Sketch icon on the toolbar and select a plane or model face. Next, click the **Use (Project/Convert)** icon on the Toolbar and click on the edges of the model geometry to project them on to the sketch plane. The projected element will be black in color and fully constrained. Complete the sketch and click the green check.

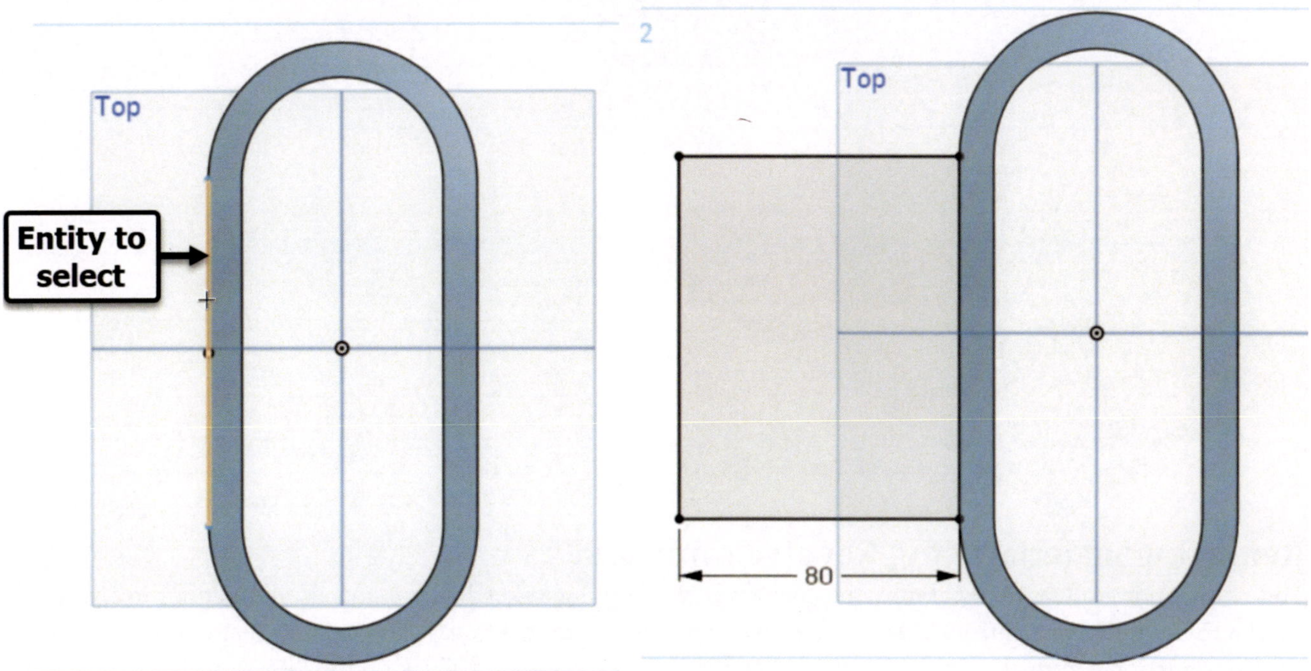

Removing material using the Extrude command

This command removes material from the geometry by extruding a sketch. It functions on the same lines of the **Extrude** command. Draw a sketch on a plane or a model face. On the Toolbar, click the **Extrude** command. Select the sketch. On the **Extrude** dialog, click **Remove** tab and type-in a value in the **Depth** field; the preview of the extruded cut appears in the direction normal to the sketch.

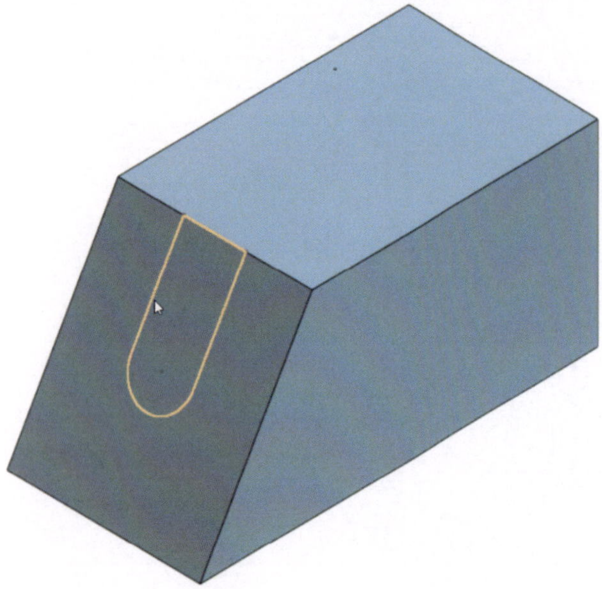

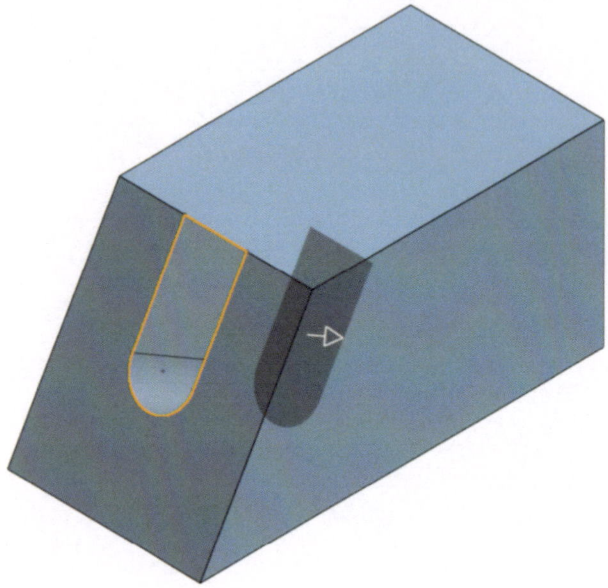

Click green check ✓ to complete the **Extrude** feature.

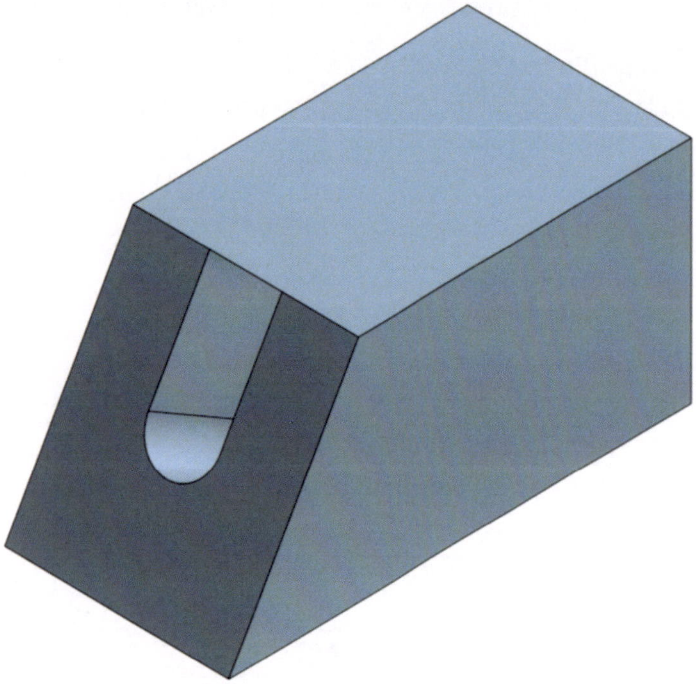

Removing material using Revolve command

This command removes material from the geometry by revolving a sketch about an axis. It functions in a way similar to the **Revolve** command. Draw a sketch on a plane or a model face. Also, draw a construction line using the **Construction** command. On the Toolbar, click the **Revolve** command. Click on the **Remove** tab and select the sketch. Select the construction line. Select the revolve type from the **Revolve** type drop-down. There are four options: *Full, One direction, Symmetric* and *Two direction*. Click green check ✓ to complete the revolved cut feature.

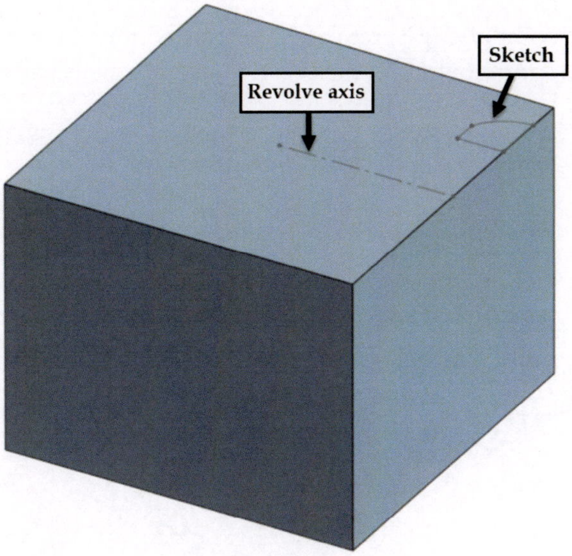

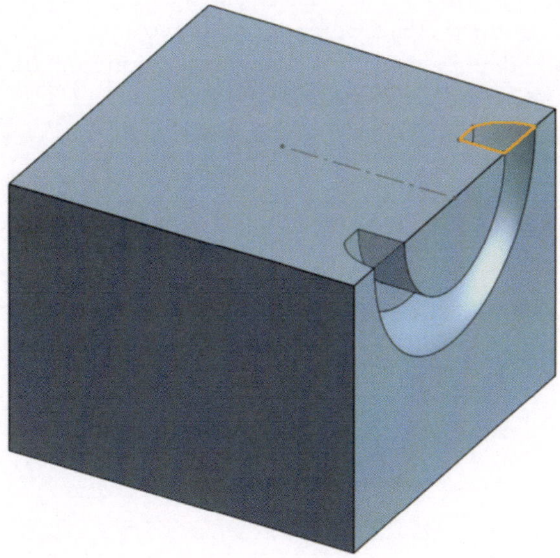

The Plane command

Each time you start a new part file, Onshape automatically creates default Reference planes. Planes are a specific type of elements in Onshape, known as Reference Elements. These features act as supports to your 3D geometry. In addition to the default Reference features, you can create your own additional planes. Until now, you have learned to create sketches on any of the default reference planes (Front, Right, and Top planes). If you want to create sketches and geometry at locations other than default reference planes, you can create new reference planes manually. You can do this by using the **Plane** command.

Offset plane

This method creates a reference plane, which will be parallel to a face or another plane. Click the **Plane** icon on the Toolbar. On the **Plane** dialog, select **Offset** option from the **Plane type** drop-down. Next, select a flat face, and then type-in a value in the **Offset distance** field available on the **Plane** dialog. On the dialog, you can click the **Opposite direction** button to flip the plane to other side of the model face. Check the **Flip normal** option if you want to flip the plane origin. Click green check to create the offset plane.

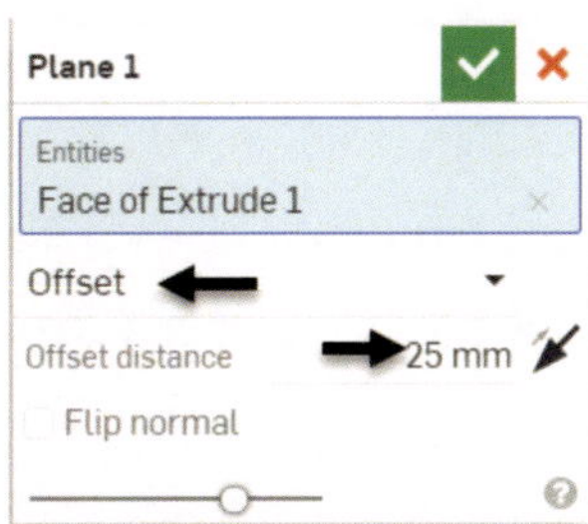

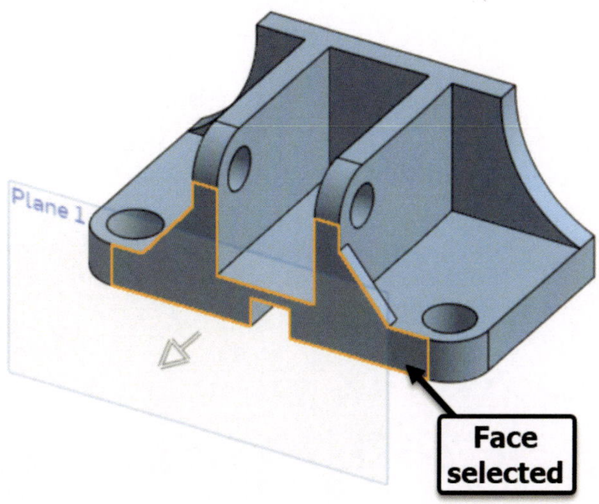

Plane Point

This method creates a plane parallel to a flat face at a selected point or edge. Activate the **Plane** command. On the **Plane** dialog, select the **Plane point** option from the **Plane type** drop-down, and then select a flat face. Select a point to define the parallel plane location.

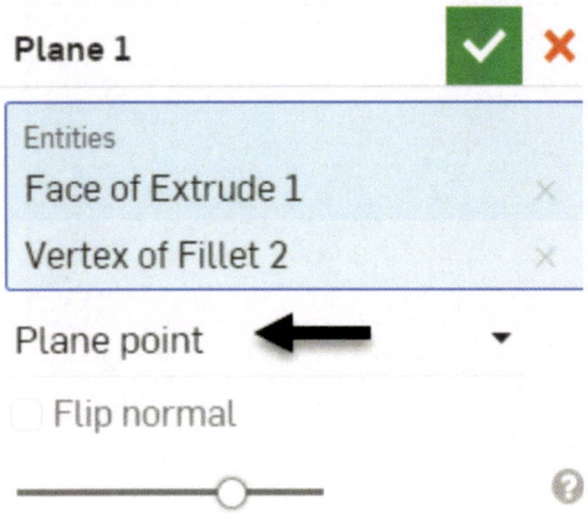

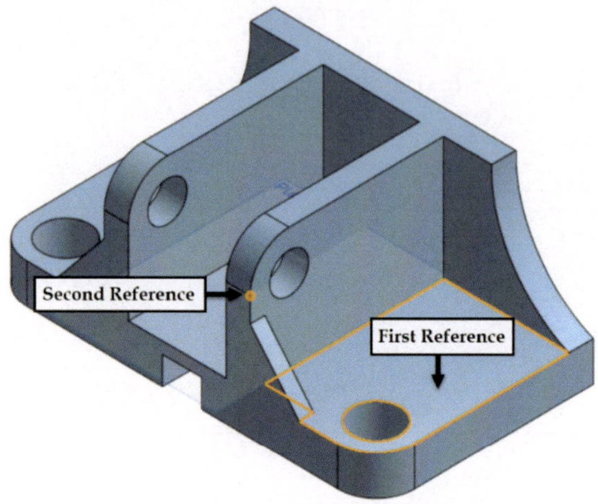

Line angle

This method creates a plane, which will be positioned at an angle to a line. Activate the **Plane** command. Select **Line angle** from the **Plane type** drop-down on the **Plane** dialog. Select a line to define the reference. Click **Opposite direction** button to reverse the direction. Type-in a value in the **Angle** box and click green check .

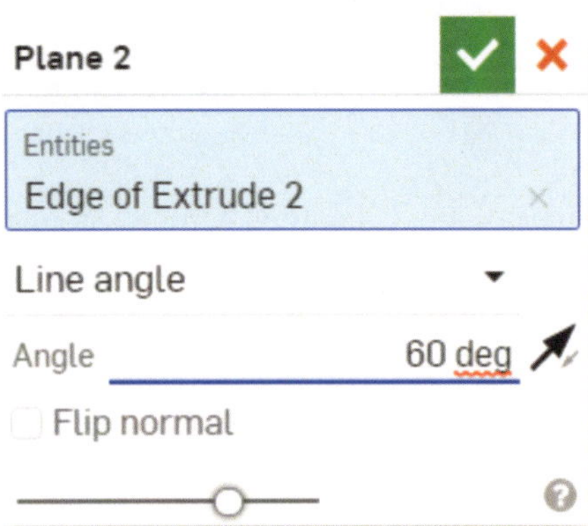

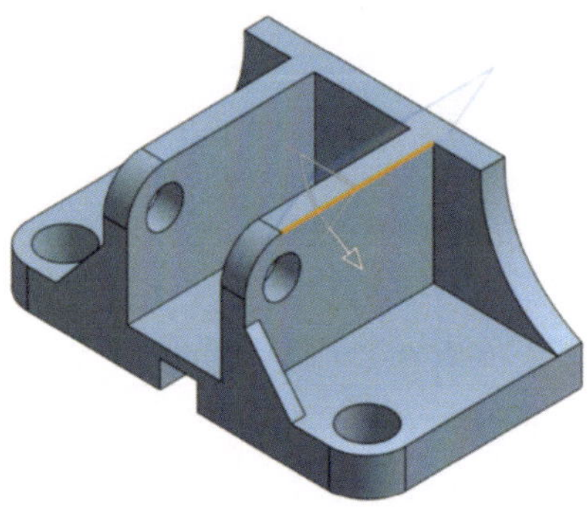

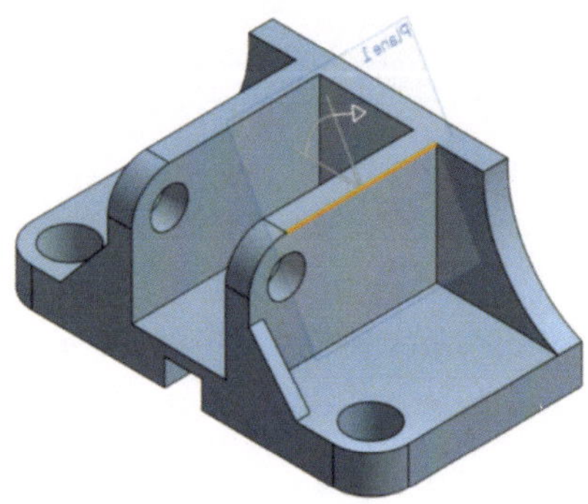

Three points

This method creates a plane by selecting three points. Activate the **Plane** command. Select **Three point** from the **Plane type** drop-down on the **Plane** dialog. Select three points from the model geometry. Click green check to create a plane passing through the points.

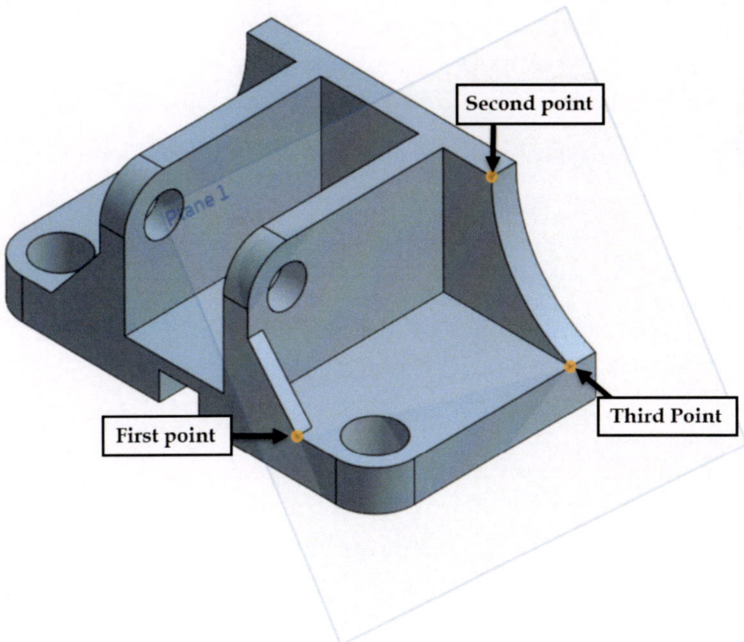

Curve Point

This method creates a reference plane, which will be normal (perpendicular) to a line, curve, or edge. Activate the **Plane** command and select the **Curve point** option from the **Plane type** drop-down on the **Plane** dialog. Select an edge, line, curve, arc, or circle. Click on a point to define the location of the plane. Click the green check ✓ to create the curve point plane.

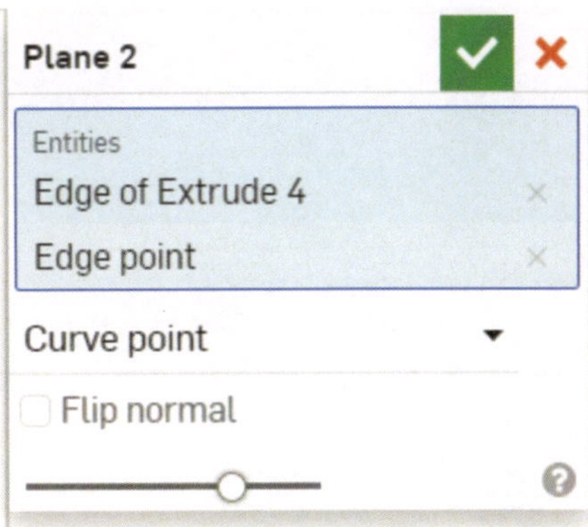

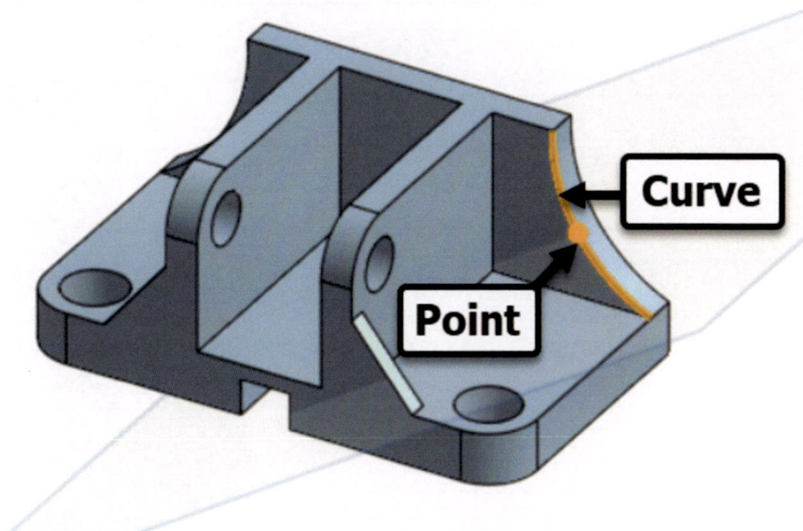

Point normal

This method creates a plane normal to straight line or axis. Activate the **Plane** command and select the **Point normal** option from the **Plane type** drop-down on the **Plane** dialog. Select the cylindrical face from the part geometry; its axis is selected. Next, select a point or vertex from the part geometry; a plane normal to the axis is created at the selected point. Click green check ✓ to create the point normal plane.

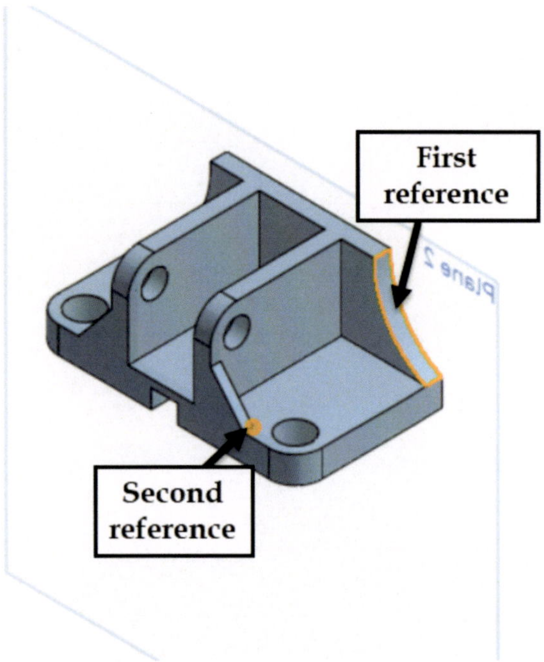

Mid Plane

This method creates a plane, which lies at the midpoint between two selected faces. You can also create a plane passing through the intersection point of the two selected planes or faces. Activate the **Plane** command and select **Mid Plane** option from the **Plane type** drop-down on the **Plane** dialog. Select two faces of the model geometry which are parallel to each other. Click green check to create the mid plane.

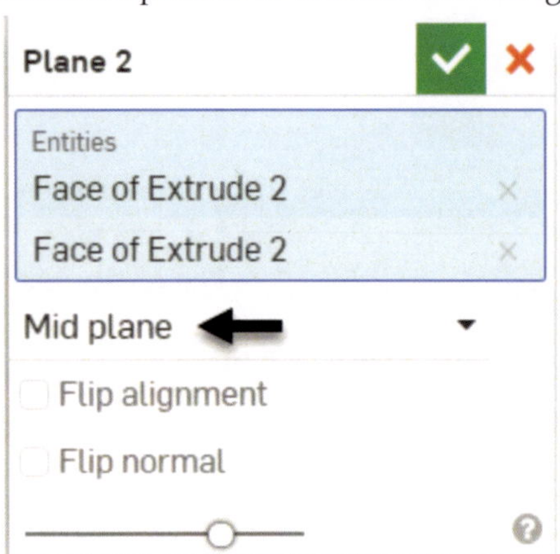

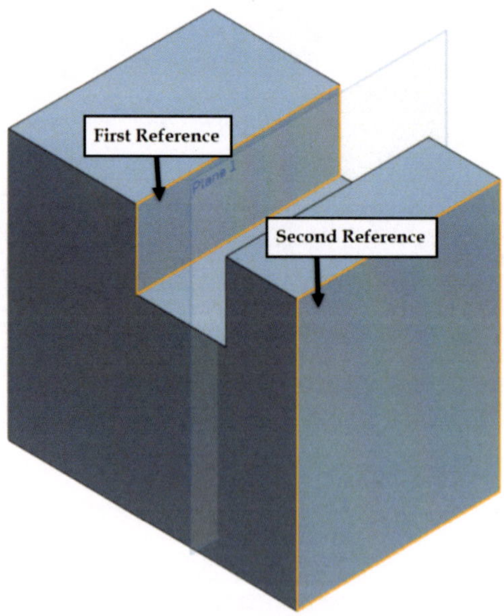

Activate the **Plane** command and select two intersecting faces or planes from the graphics window; the preview of the mid plane appears. On the dialog, check the **Flip Alignment** option; the plane orientation changes. Click green check to create the mid plane.

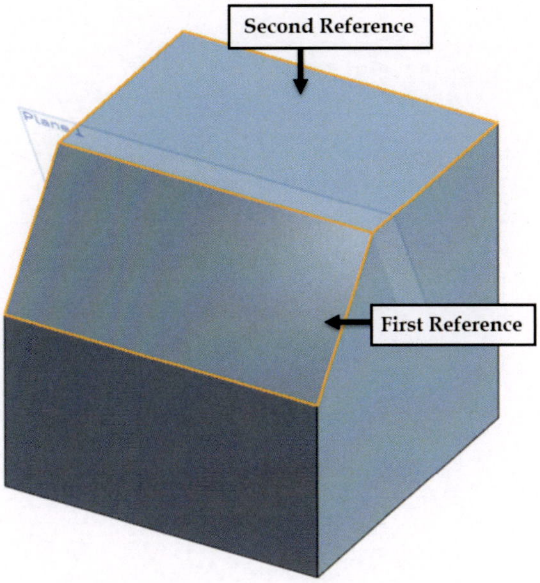

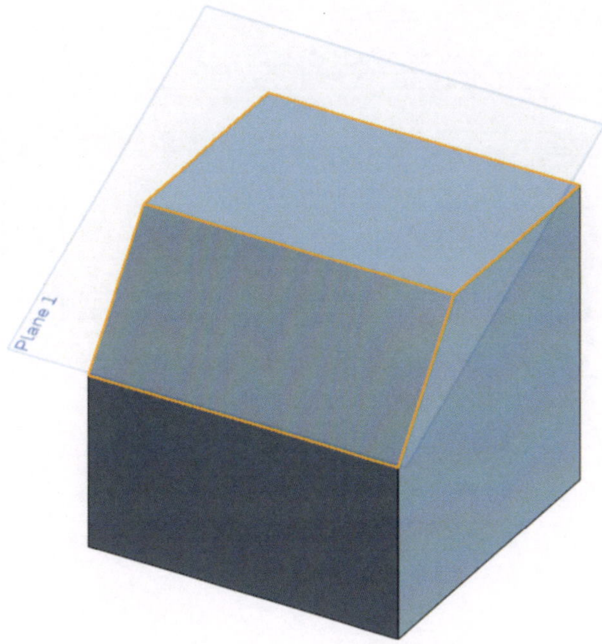

Additional options of the Extrude command

The **Extrude** commands have some additional options to create a 3D geometry, complex features, and so on.

End types

On the **Extrude** dialog, to add or remove material the **End type** drop-down has various options to define the start and end limits of the *Extruded* feature. The options in this drop-down are explained next.

The **Up to next** option extrudes the sketch through the face next to the sketch plane.

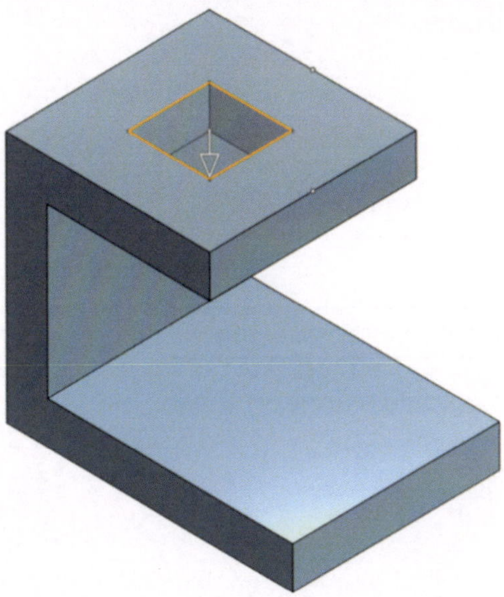

The **Up to face** option extrudes the sketch up to a selected surface.

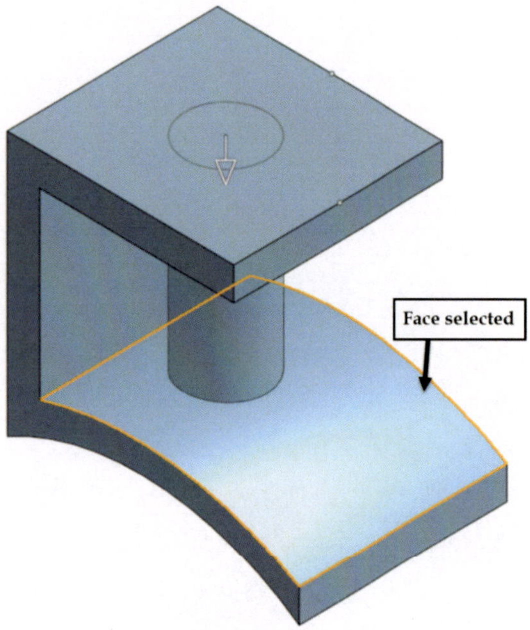

Check the **Offset distance** option to extrude the sketch up to the selected surface but offsets the extrusion by the offset distance that you enter. Click the **Opposite direction** icon, if you want to offset the extrusion beyond the selected surface.

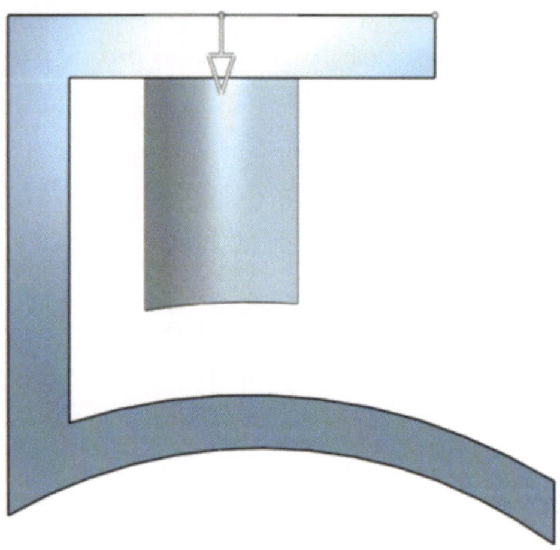

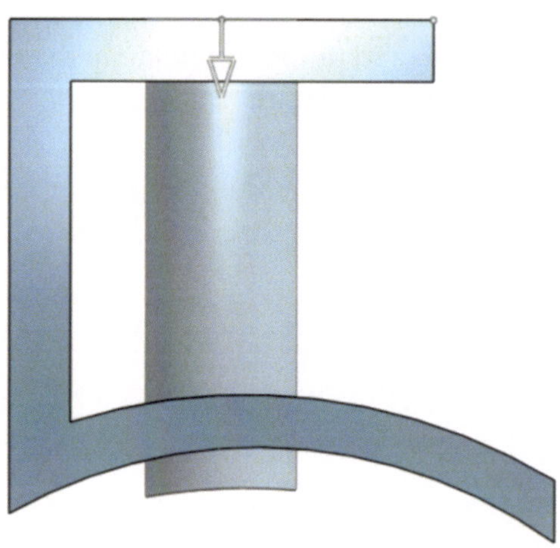

The **Up to vertex** option extrudes the sketch from the sketch plane up to a selected vertex.

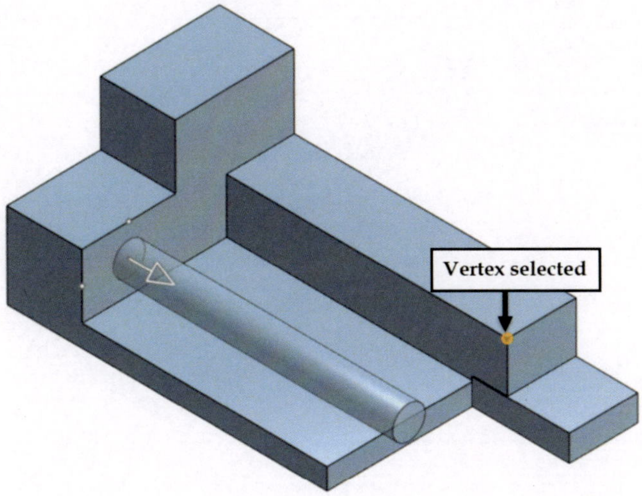

The **Through All** option extrudes the sketch throughout the 3D geometry. The **Blind** option extrudes the sketch up to the specified depth.

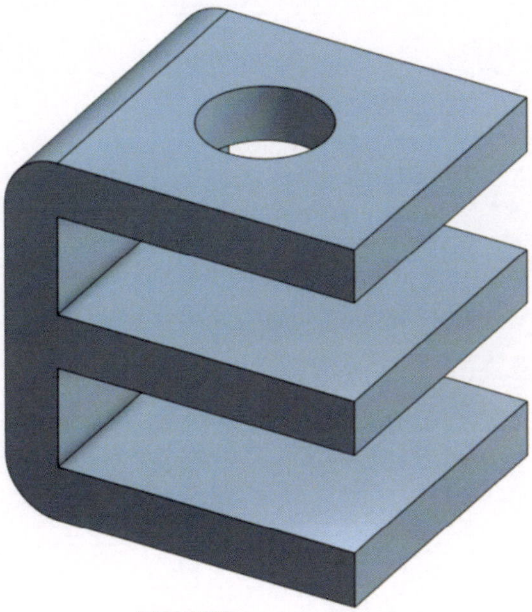

Blind

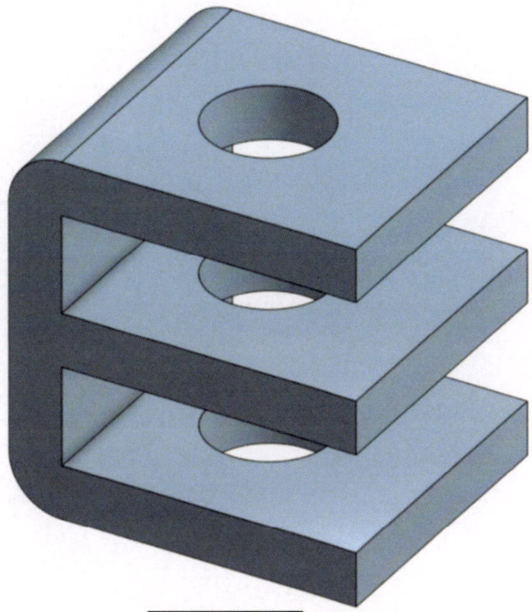

Through All

The **Up to part** option extrudes the sketch up to another part. Select this option from the **End type** drop-down and select an existing part.

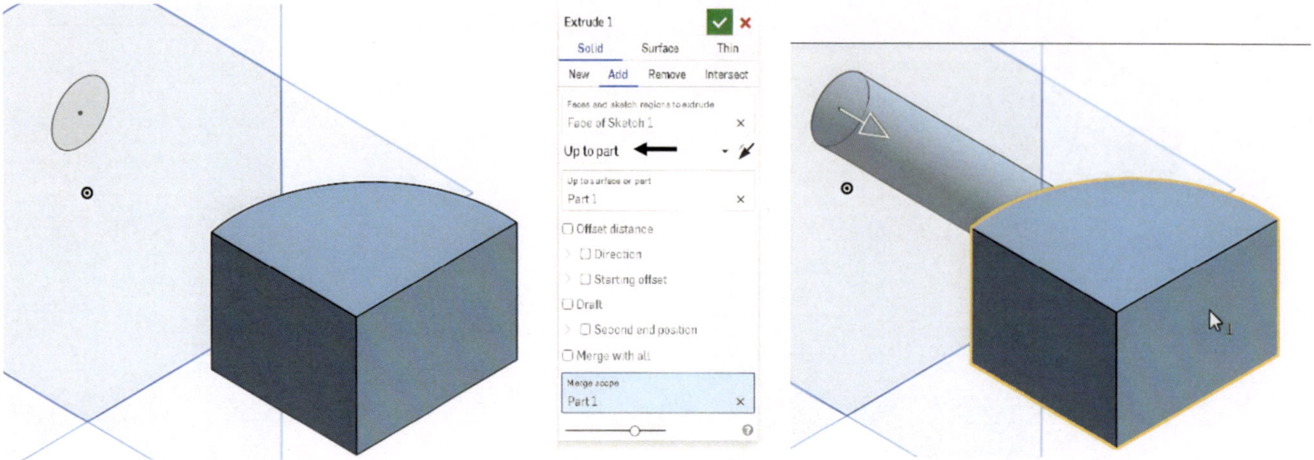

Second end position

Check this option if you want to extrude the sketch on both sides. Additional options appear on checking this option. These options are same as those discussed earlier in this chapter.

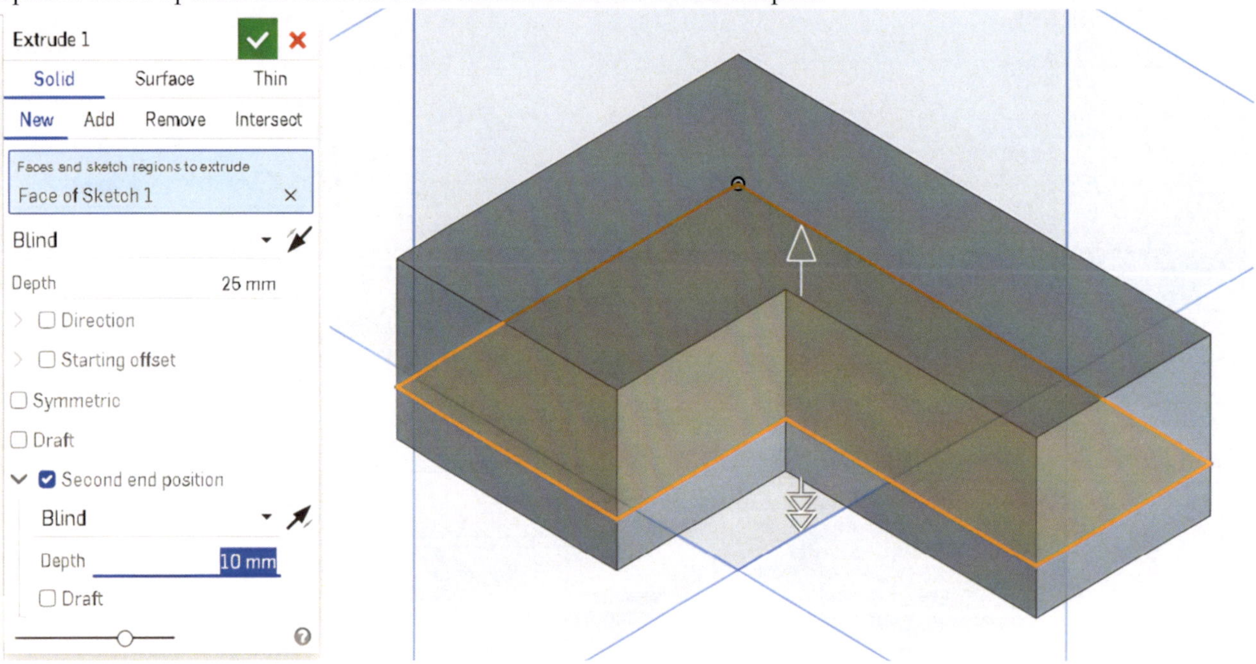

Draft

The **Draft** option will help you to apply draft to the extrusion. Check the **Draft** option on the **Extrude** dialog. Type-in a value in the **Draft angle** field. Click the **Opposite direction** button, if you want to change the draft direction.

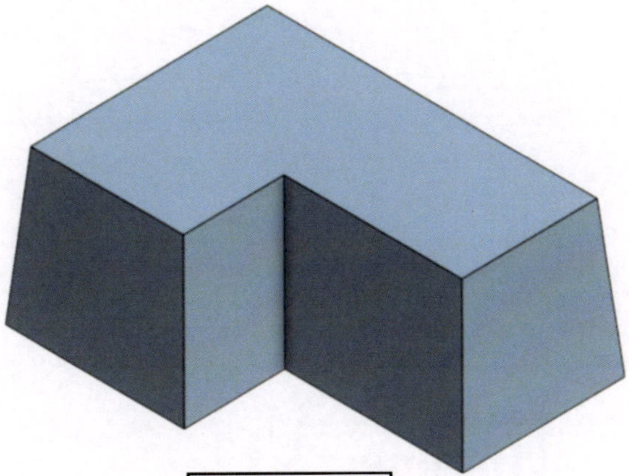

Original direction

Opposite direction

Boolean tabs

When you extrude a sketch, the Boolean options determine whether the material is added, removed or intersected from an existing solid body.

Add

This option adds material to the geometry.

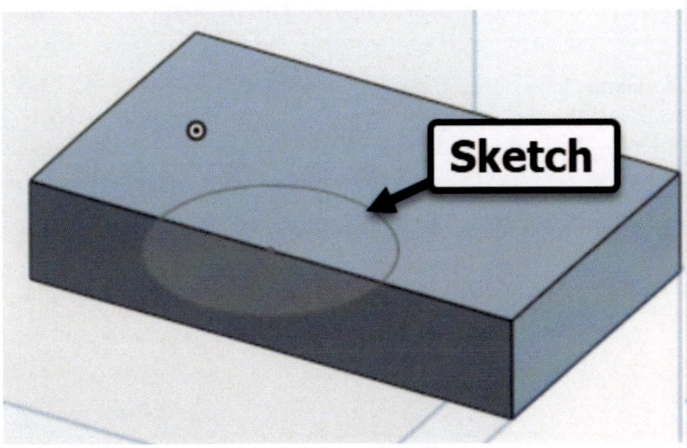

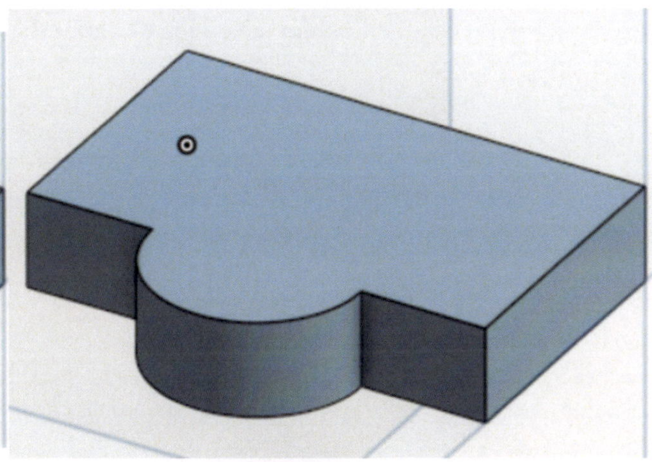

Add

Remove

This option removes material from the geometry.

Intersect

This option creates a solid body containing the volume shared by two separate bodies.

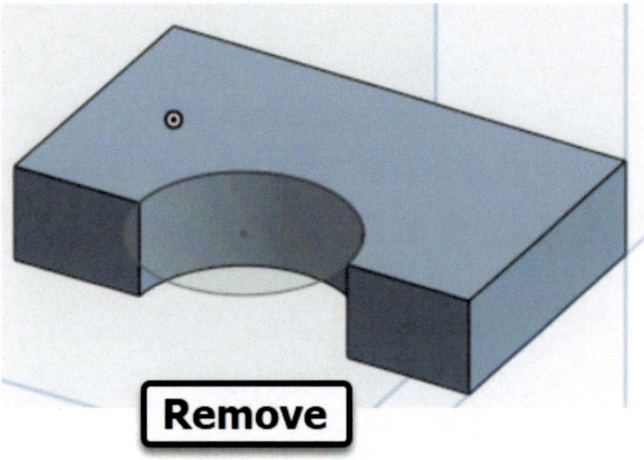

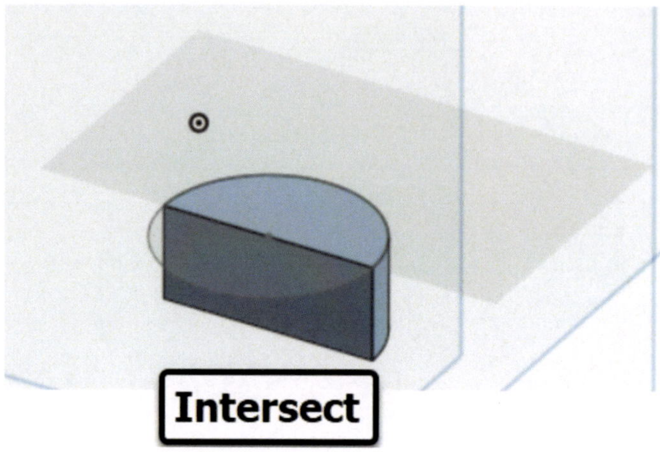

New

This option creates a separate solid body. This will be helpful while creating multi-body parts.

Applying Material to the Geometry

Onshape makes it easy to apply material to the solid geometry. In the Features tree, click the right mouse button on the part and select **Assign material**. The **Material** dialog appears. Select a material from the material list; the selected material is applied to the geometry. Next, click the green check. You can also add a custom material to the part. To do this, click the **Custom** tab on the **Material** dialog. Next, specify the **Name** and **Density** of the material.

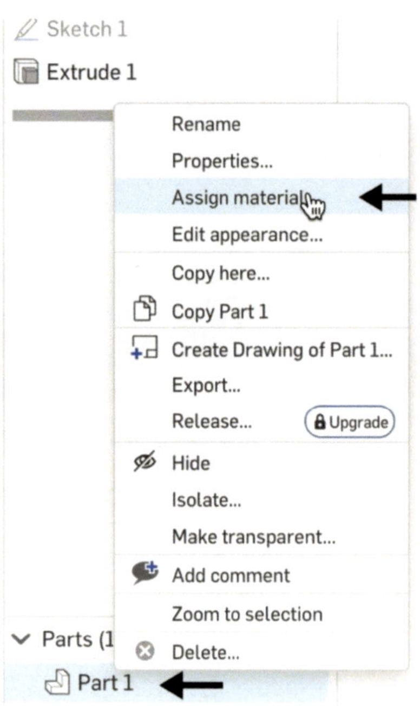

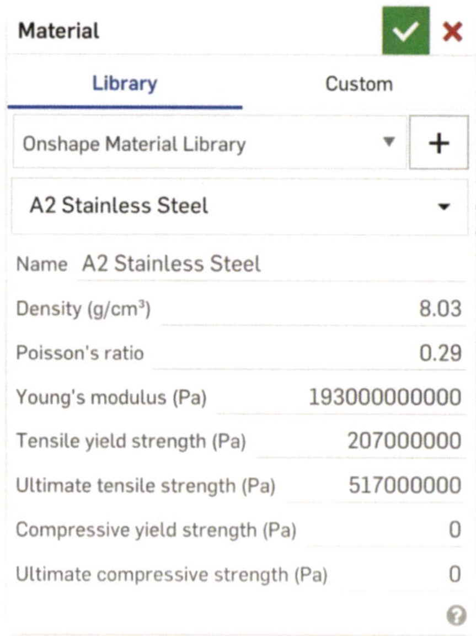

For more detailed engineering simulations, you can also define the material's mechanical properties in the fields provided. These include:

- Poisson's ratio
- Young's modulus
- Tensile yield strength
- Ultimate tensile strength
- Compressive yield strength
- Ultimate compressive strength

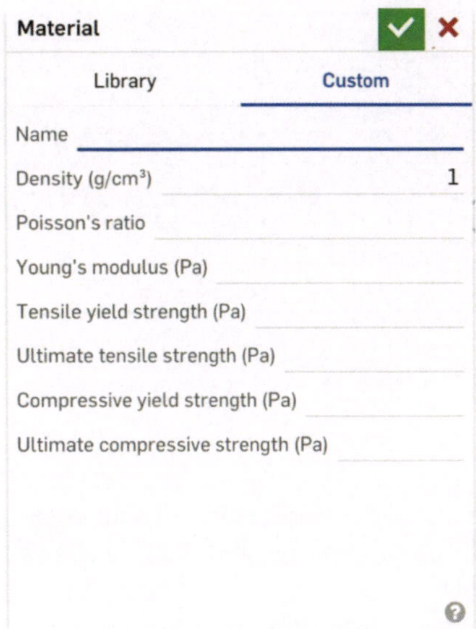

Entering these values allows Onshape to accurately calculate how the part will behave under stress and load during analysis. Once you have finished defining the properties, click the green check to save and apply the new custom material.

View Tools

The model display in the graphics window can be changed using various view options. These options are located at the top-left corner of the graphics window. You can also access these options from the shortcut menu.

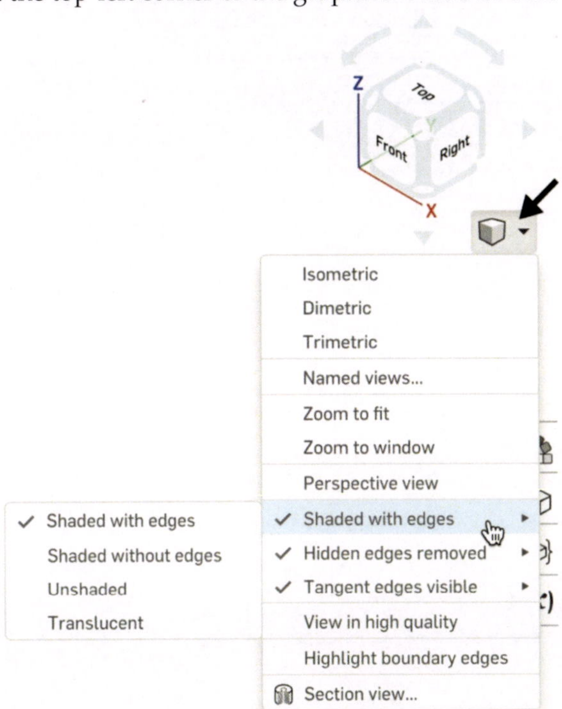

The following are some of the main view options:

Zoom to fit	The model will be fitted in the current size of the graphics window so that it will be visible, completely.	
Zoom to window	Select this option and drag a rectangle. The contents inside the rectangle will be zoomed.	
Shaded with edges	This represents the model with shades along with visible edges.	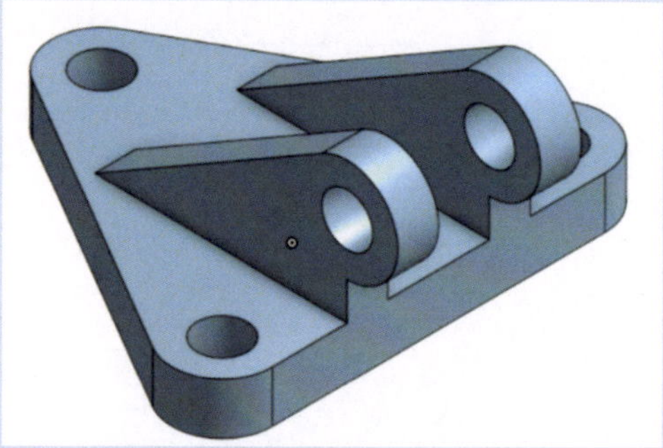
Shaded without edges	This represents the model with shades without visible edges.	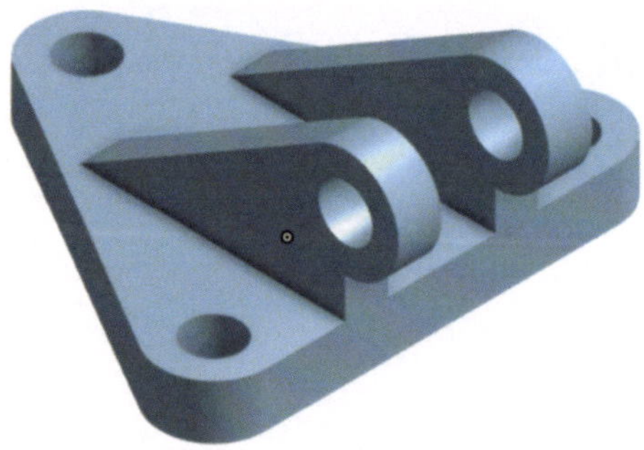
Unshaded	This represents the model using only visible edges, without any surface shading.	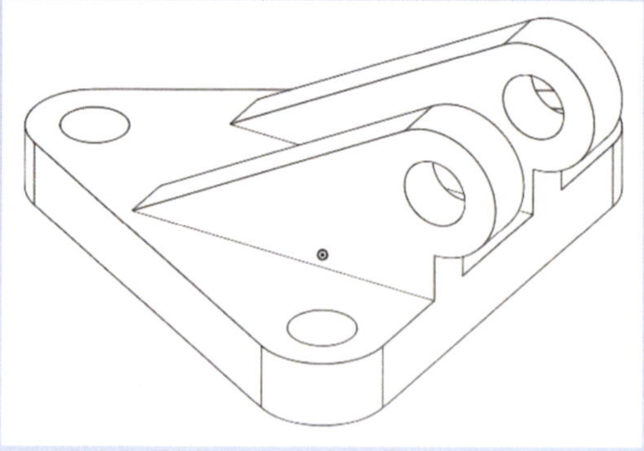

Hidden edge visible	This represents the model with hidden edges.	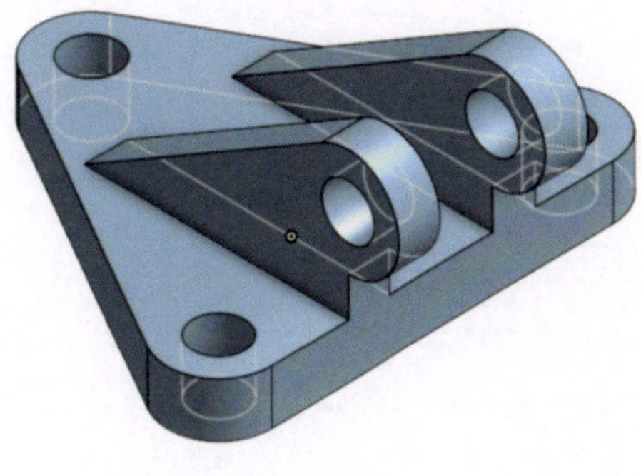
Unshaded	This represents the model in without shades.	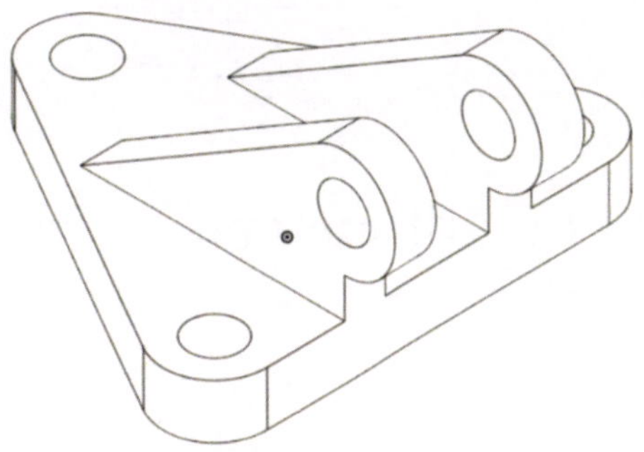
Hidden edges removed	This represents the model without hidden edges	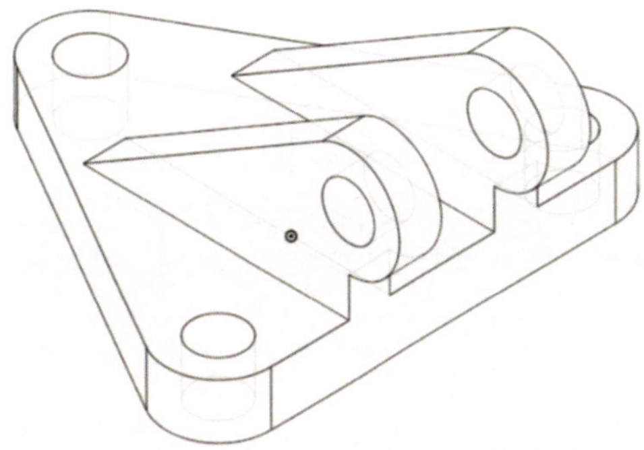
Translucent	This represents the model with translucent shades.	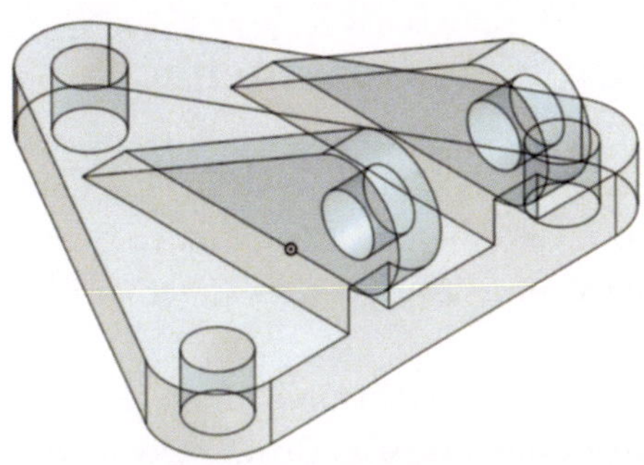

View Cube

It is located at the top right corner of the graphics area and is used to set the view orientation of the model.

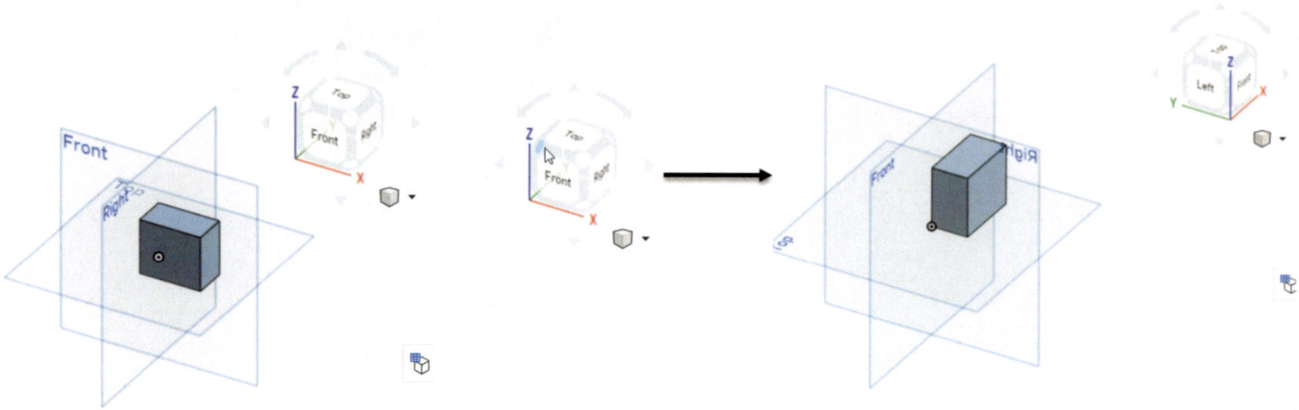

Tutorial 1 (Millimeters)

In this example, you create the part shown below.

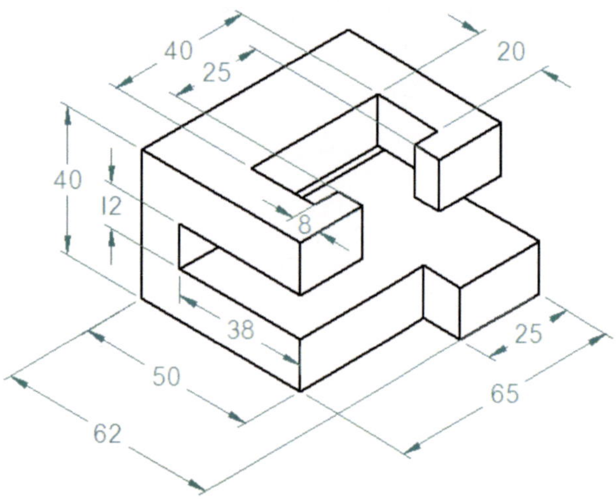

Creating a New Document

1. In your Internet Browser, go to https://www.onshape.com to start Onshape.
2. Next, click **SIGN IN** button located on the top right corner side of the web page. Enter the username and password, and then, click **Sign in**.
3. On the Documents page, click **Create > Folder**. Next, type Chapter 3 in the **Folder name** box and then click **Create**.
4. Double-click on the **Chapter 3** folder in the Folders section; the folder appears.
5. On the Documents page, click **Create > Document**; the **New document** dialog appears on the screen.
6. Enter Tutorial 1 in the **Document name** box and click **Create public document**; a new document appears.
7. Click the **Document menu** located at the top left corner of the window and select **Workspace Units**; the **Workspace Units** dialog appears on the screen.
8. On the **Workspace Units** dialog, select **Length default unit > Millimeter** from the **Length** section.
9. Select **Mass default unit > Gram** from the **Mechanical** section.
10. Leave the other default settings and click the green check .

Creating a Sketch

1. To start a new sketch, click **Sketch** command on the Toolbar.
2. Click on the **Front** plane. Next, right-click and select **View normal to sketch plane**; the selected plane orients normal to the screen.
3. On the Toolbar, click **Rectangle** drop-down > **Corner rectangle**. Next, click the origin point to define the first corner of the rectangle.
4. Move the pointer toward the top right and click to define the second corner.
5. On the Toolbar, click the **Dimension** command.
6. Select the horizontal line, move the pointer upward, and click. Next, type in 50 in the box and press Enter.
7. Likewise, apply a dimension of 40 mm to the vertical line. On the **Sketch 1** dialog, click the green check.

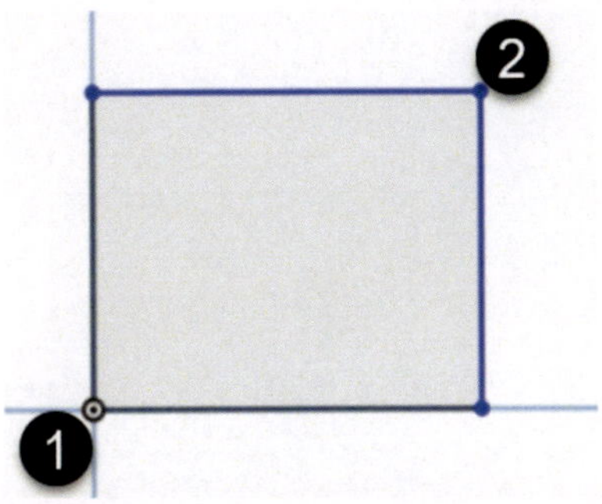

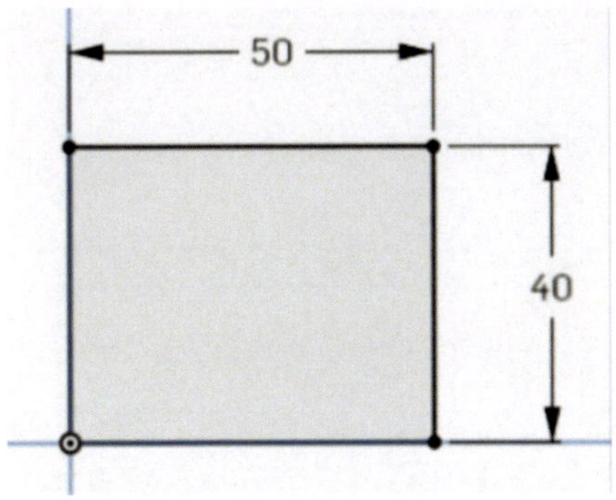

Creating an Extruded Feature

1. On the Toolbar, click the **Extrude** command. Next, click on the region enclosed by the sketch.
2. On the **Extrude** dialog, click **End Type > Blind** and select **Symmetric** option. On the **Extrude** dialog, type-in **65** in the **Depth** box.
3. Click the green check to complete the *Extrude* feature.

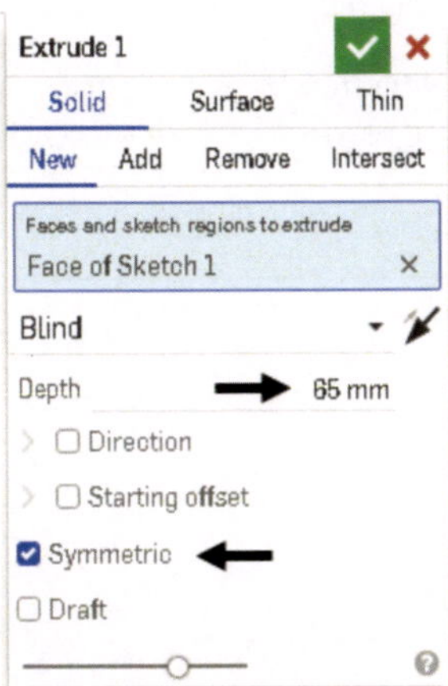

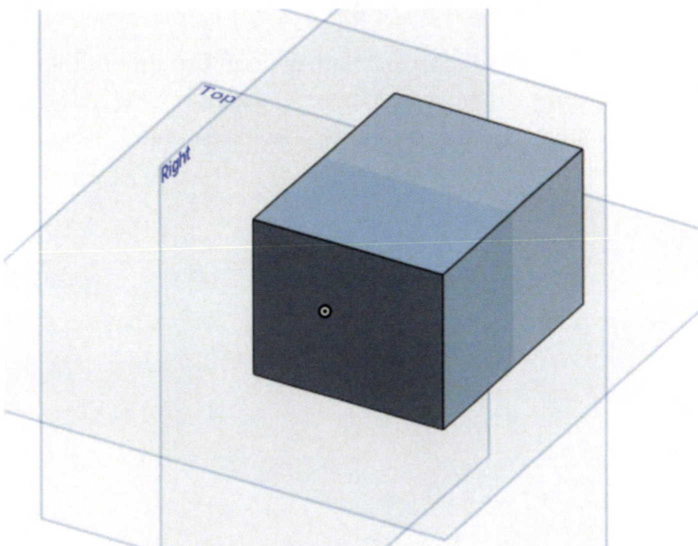

Creating an Extruded Cut Feature

1. Click the **Sketch** command on the Toolbar. Next, click on the front face of the part geometry.
2. To change the view orientation normal to the sketch plane, right-click and select **View normal to sketch plane**.
3. On the Toolbar, click the **Corner rectangle** command.
4. Click on the right edge of the model, move the pointer toward left, and then click.
5. Activate the **Dimension** command and then select the horizontal line of the rectangle. Next, move the pointer upward, and then click to position the dimension. Type **38** in the box, and then press Enter to update the dimension.
6. Select the bottom edge of the model and the lower horizontal line of the rectangle. Move the pointer toward the right and click to position the dimension – type **14** in the box, and then press Enter.
7. Likewise, apply the remaining dimension to the sketch.

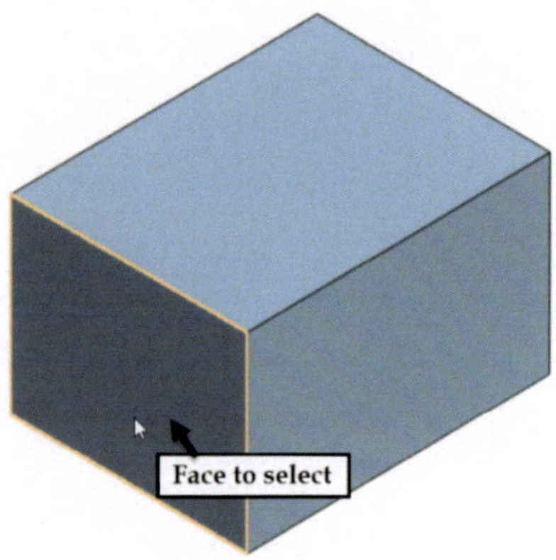

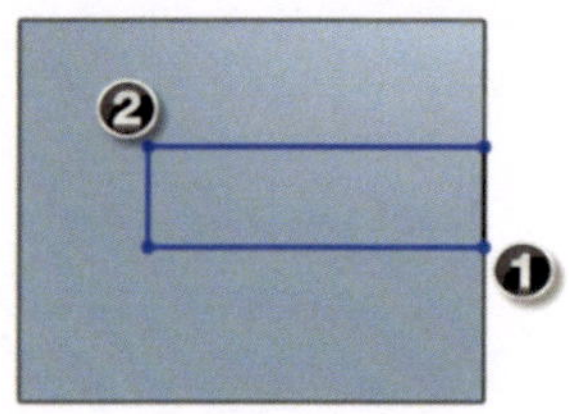

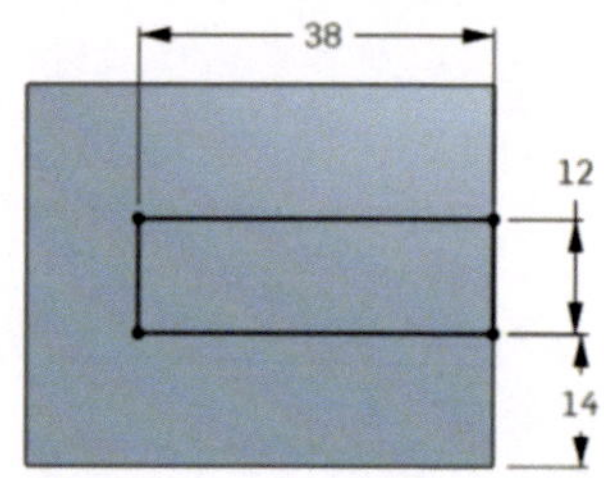

8. On the **Sketch 2** dialog, click green check to confirm the sketch.
9. Click the **Extrude** command on the Toolbar; the **Extrude** dialog pops-up on the screen.
10. Click the **Remove** tab on the **Extrude** dialog. Next, select the sketch from the graphics area.
11. On the **Extrude** dialog, select **End Type > Through All**.
12. Click the green check on the **Extrude** dialog to create the cut throughout the part geometry.
13. Click the **Camera and render options** drop-down located at the right-side in the graphics area.
14. Select the **Isometric** option to change the view orientation to the isometric view.

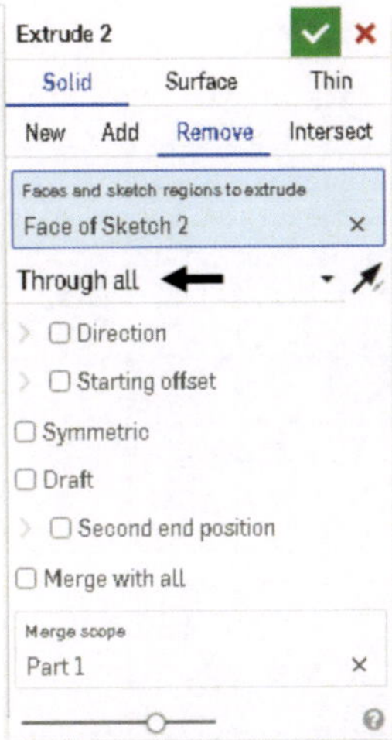

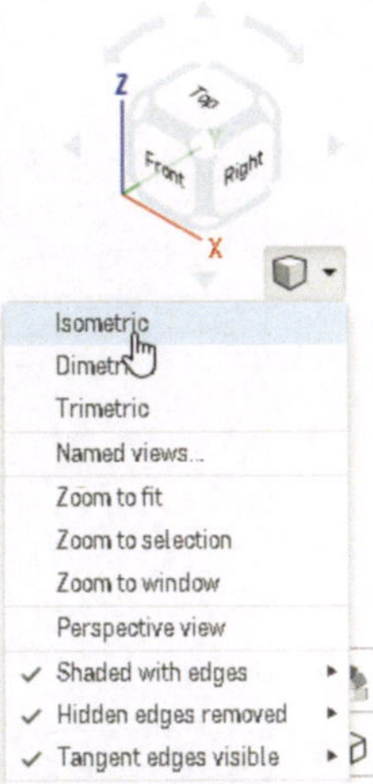

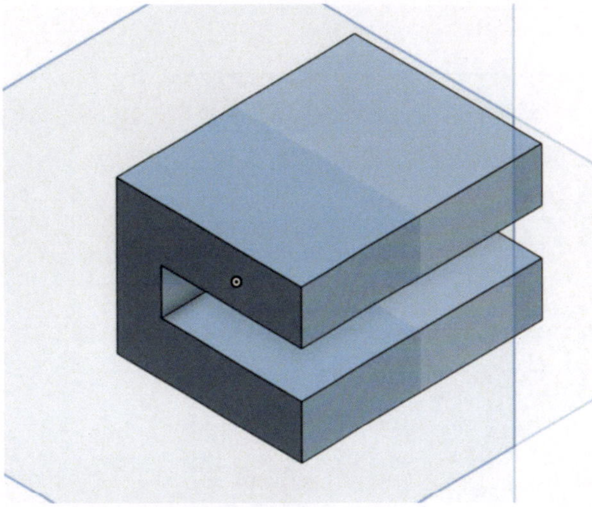

Extruding a sketch Up to the Face next to the sketch plane

1. Click the **Sketch** command on the Toolbar and click on the top face of the part geometry.
2. Click the right mouse button and select **View normal to sketch plane** to change the view orientation normal to the sketch plane.
3. Activate the **Line** command (click the **Line**  icon on the Toolbar).
4. Select the origin point of the sketch, move the pointer towards the right and click.
5. Press **Esc** to deactivate the **Line** command.
6. Select the line from the part geometry and click the **Construction** command on the Toolbar.

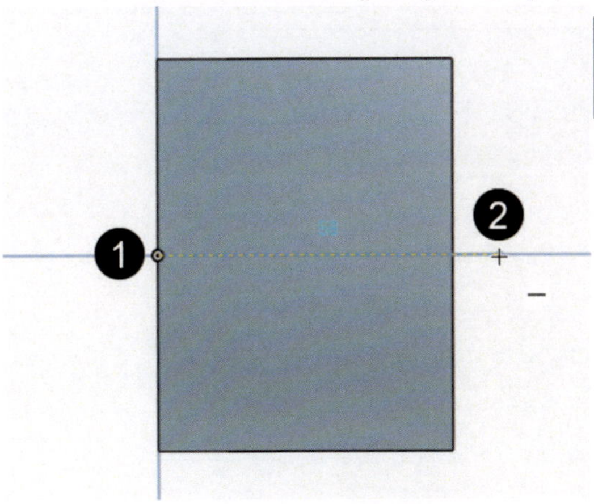

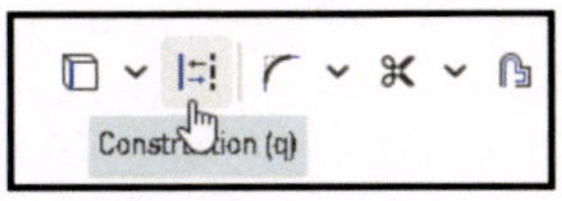

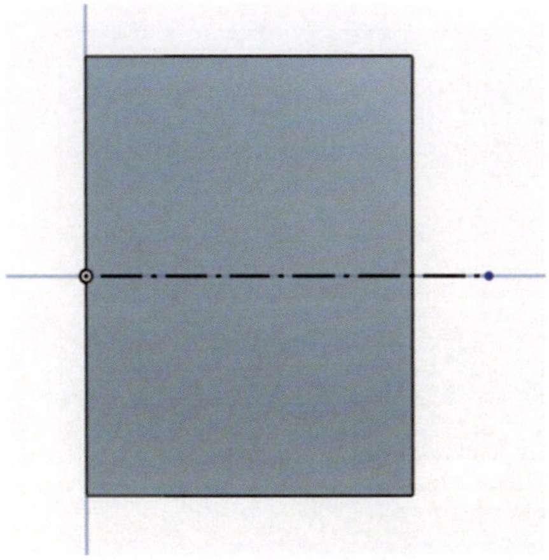

7. Activate the **Line** command and click on the intersection point between the construction line and right model edge.
8. Create the sketch, as shown.

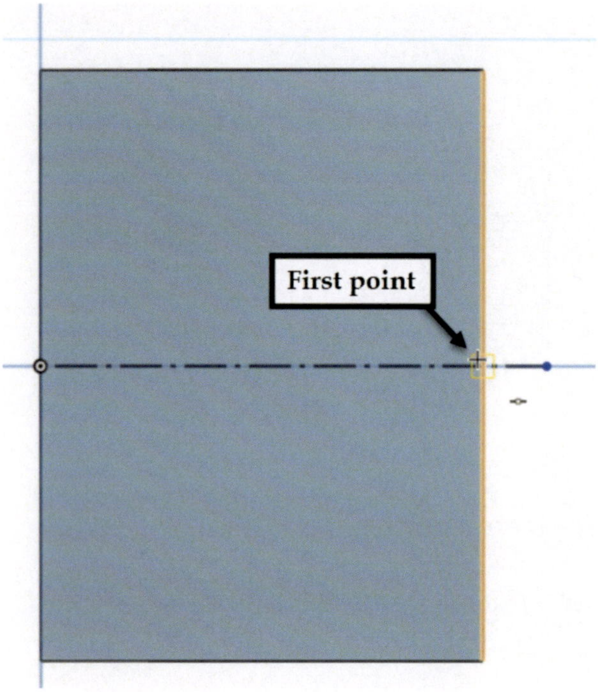

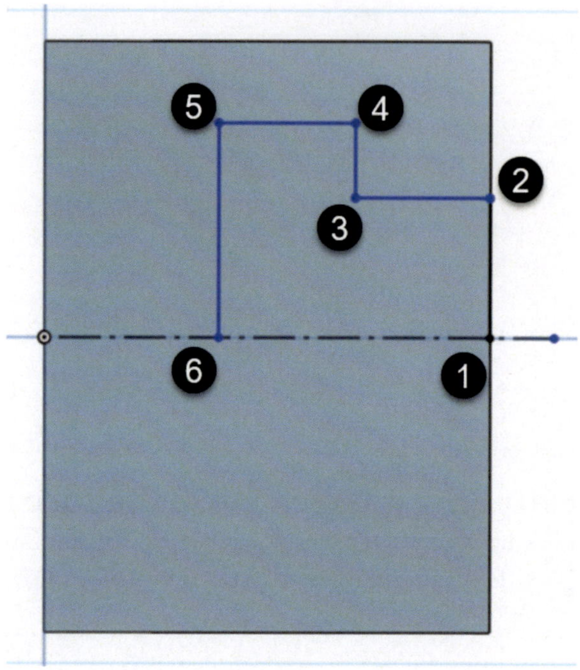

9. On the Toolbar, click the **Mirror** command and select the construction line from the part geometry as the mirror line.
10. Select the other entities to mirror them, as shown. Right click and select Escape mirror.

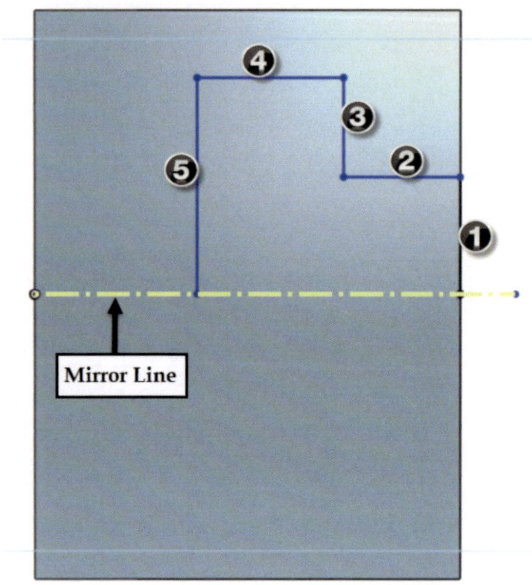

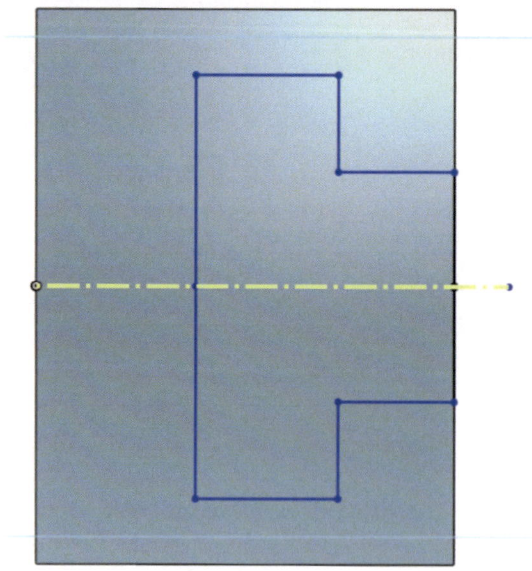

11. Click the **Dimension** command on the Toolbar.
12. Add dimensions to the sketch, as shown.

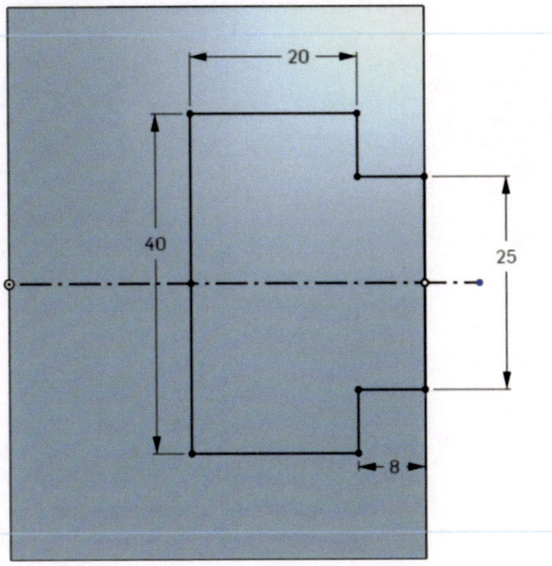

13. Click the green check on the **Sketch 3** dialog to confirm the sketch.
14. Change the view orientation to Isometric by clicking the **Camera and render options** drop-down > **Isometric** located at the right side of the graphics area.
15. Activate the **Extrude** command and select the sketch.
16. Click the **Remove** tab and select **End Type > Up to next** from the **Extrude** dialog.
17. Click the green check to remove the material up to the surface next to the sketch plane.

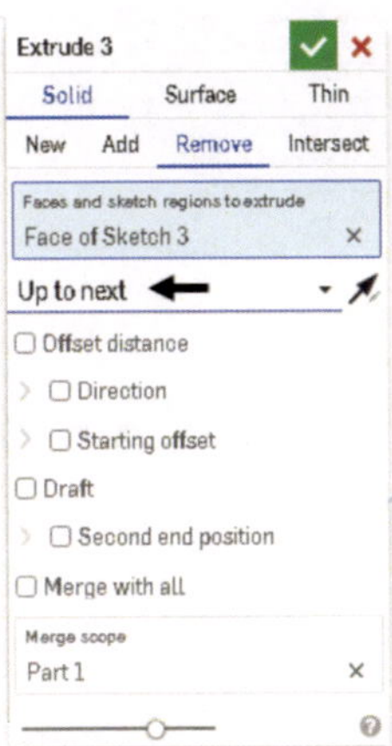

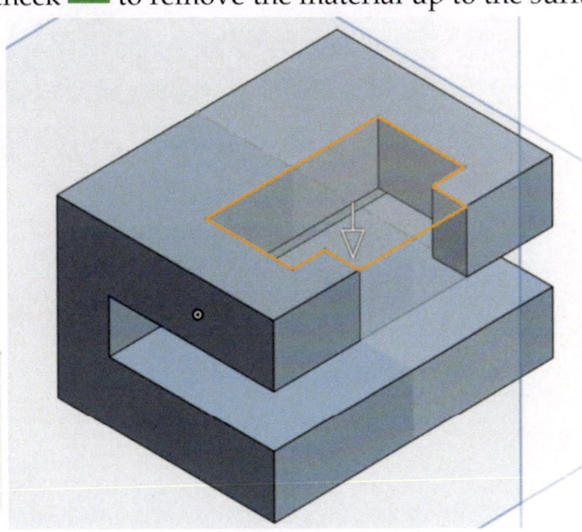

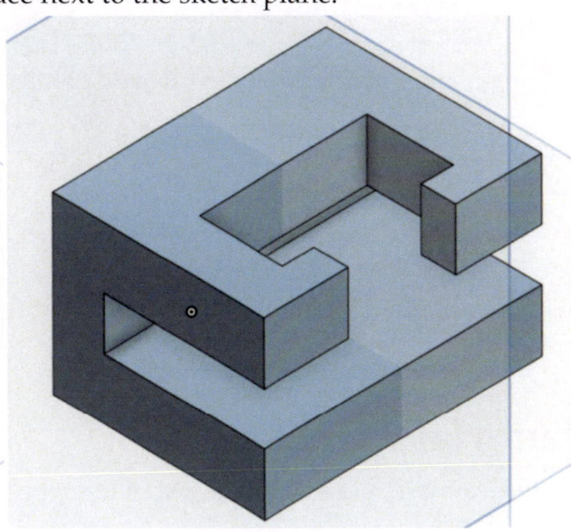

Extruding a sketch up to a selected face

1. Activate the **Sketch** command and select the Top plane.
2. Draw a closed sketch and apply dimensions to it, as shown.
3. On the Toolbar, click **Constraints** drop-down > **Coincident**. Next select the corner point of the rectangle and the model, as shown.
4. Click the green check on the **Sketch 4** dialog to confirm the sketch.

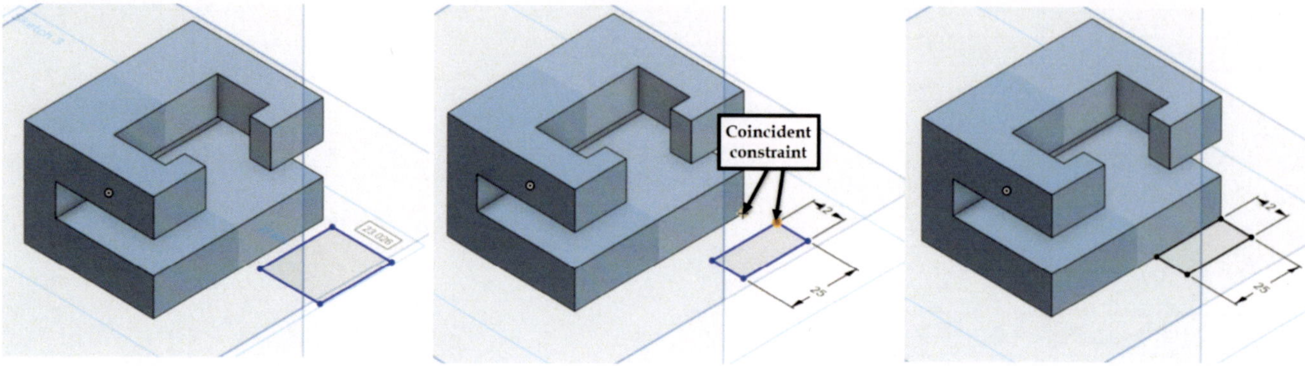

5. Activate the **Extrude** command and select the sketch
6. Select **End type > Up to face** from the **Extrude** dialog. Next, select the horizontal face of the part geometry, as shown.
7. Click the green check on the **Extrude** dialog to complete the part.

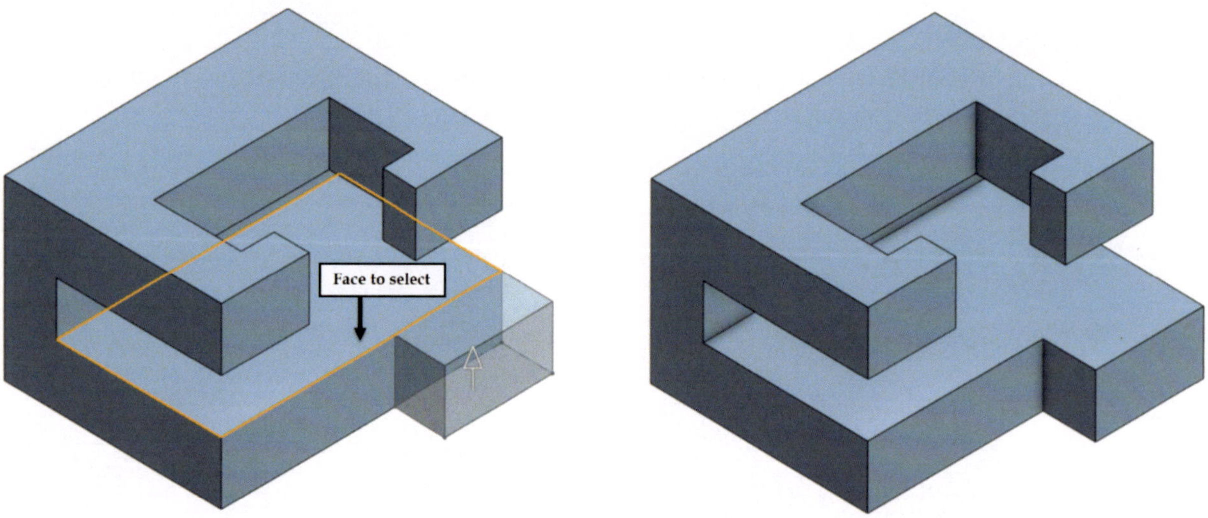

8. Click on the **Document menu** located at the top-left corner of the window, and then select **Close document** to close the document.

Tutorial 2 (Inches)

In this example, you create the part shown below.

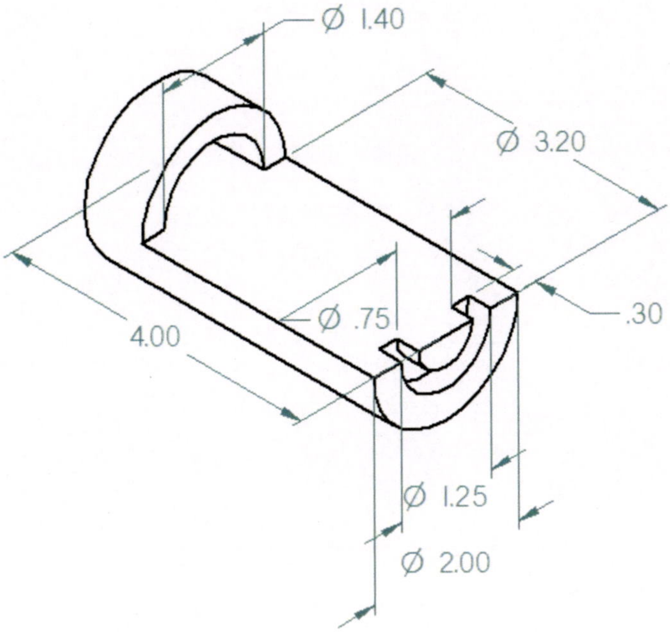

Creating a New document

1. On the Documents page, click **Create > Document**; the **New document** dialog appears on the screen.

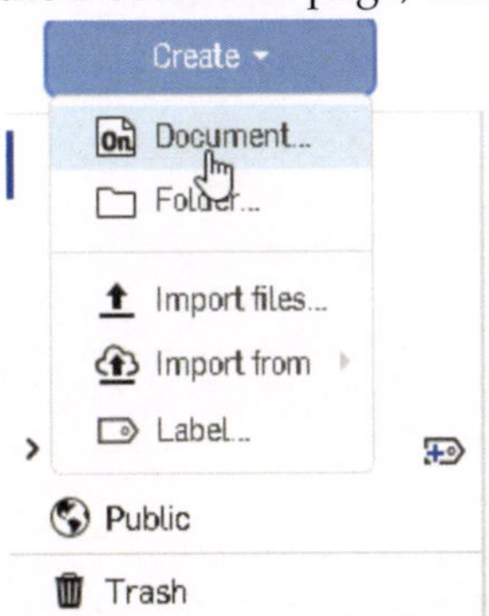

2. Enter Tutorial 2 in the **Document name** box and click **Create public document**; a new document appears.
3. Click **Document menu** located at the top left corner of the window and select **Workspace Units**; the **Workspace Units** dialog appears on the screen.
4. On the **Workspace Units** dialog, select **Length default unit> Inch** from the **Length** section.
5. Select **Mass default unit > Pound** from the **Mechanical** section.
6. Leave the other default settings as it is and click the green check on the **Workspace Units** dialog.

Creating a Revolved Feature

1. Click the **Sketch** command on the Toolbar.
2. Select the Top plane and change the view orientation to normal to the sketch plane.
3. On the Toolbar, click the **Corner rectangle** command.
4. Click the origin point to define the first corner of the rectangle.
5. Move the pointer toward the top right corner and click to define the second corner.
6. Add dimensions to the sketch, as shown. Click the green check on the **Sketch1** dialog to confirm the sketch.

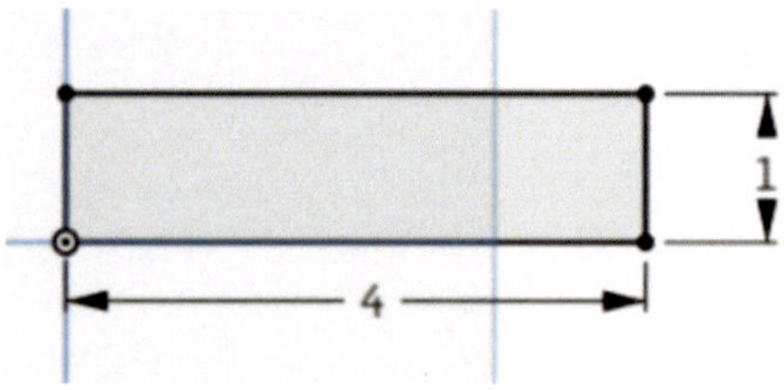

7. On the Toolbar, click the **Revolve** command.
8. Select the sketch and click on the line, as shown.

9. On the **Revolve** dialog, click the **Revolve type** drop-down > **One direction**.
10. Type-in 180 in the **Revolve Angle** field.
11. Click the **Opposite direction** button.
12. Click the green check to create the *Revolved* feature.

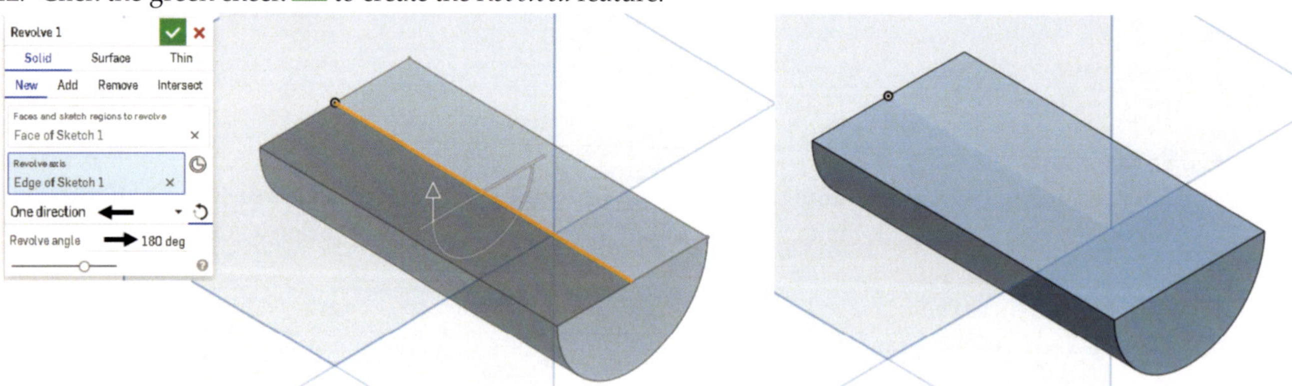

Creating a Revolved Cut feature

1. Click the **Sketch** command on the Toolbar and select the top face of the part geometry.

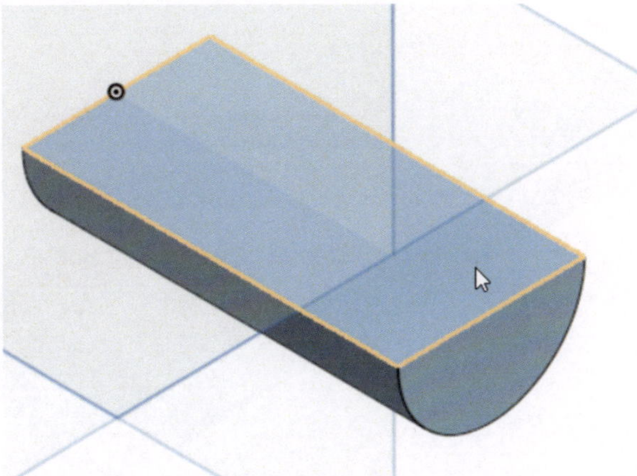

2. Draw a rectangle and apply the dimensions, as shown. In addition to that, draw a horizontal construction line passing through the origin.

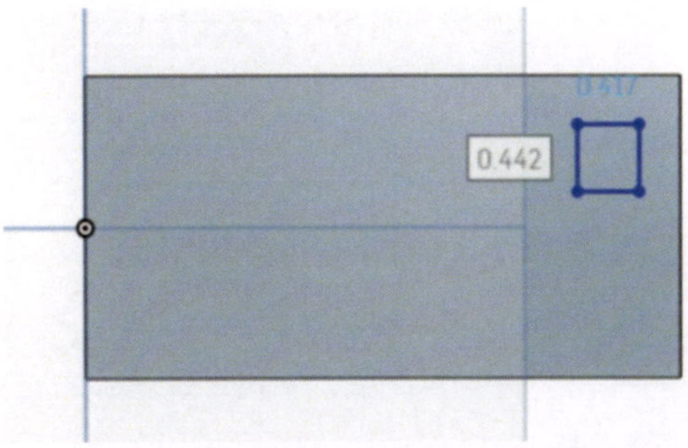

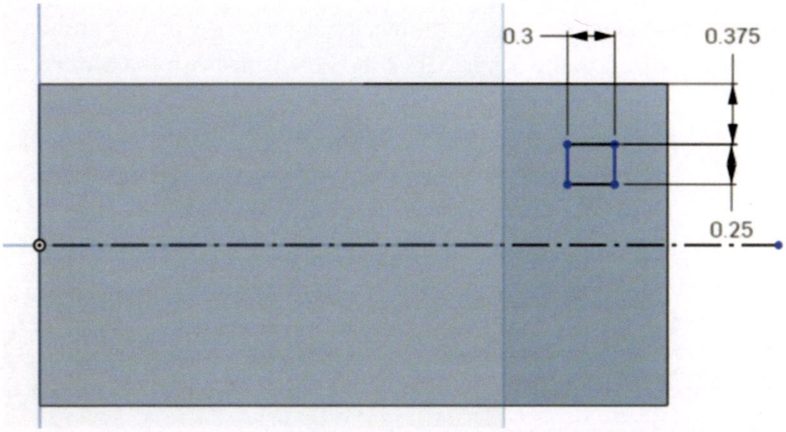

3. Click **Constraints** drop-down > **Coincident** on the toolbar and select the left vertical line of the rectangle. Next, select the left vertical edge of the model. Click the green check on the **Sketch 2** dialog.

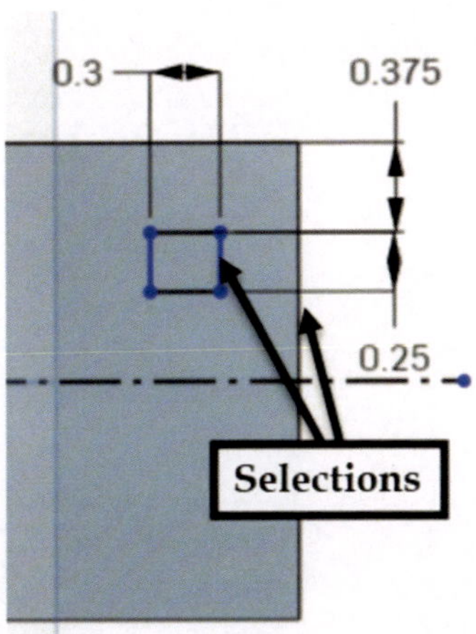

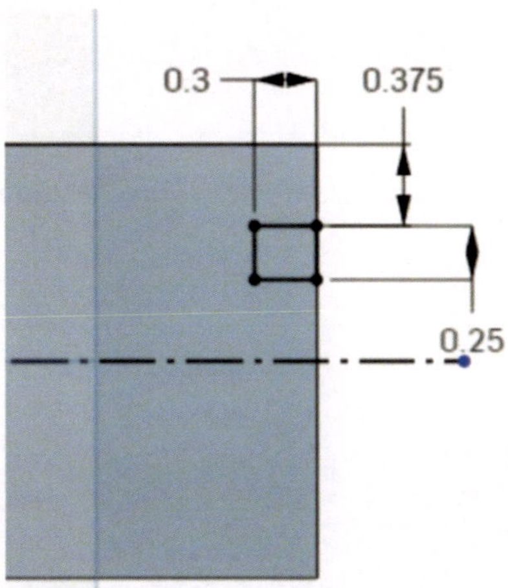

4. On the Toolbar, click the **Revolve** icon and click the **Remove** tab on the **Revolve** dialog.
5. Click on the region enclosed by the rectangle.
6. Click on the **Revolve axis** selection box, and then select the construction line from the part geometry.
7. Click the green check to create the revolved cut.

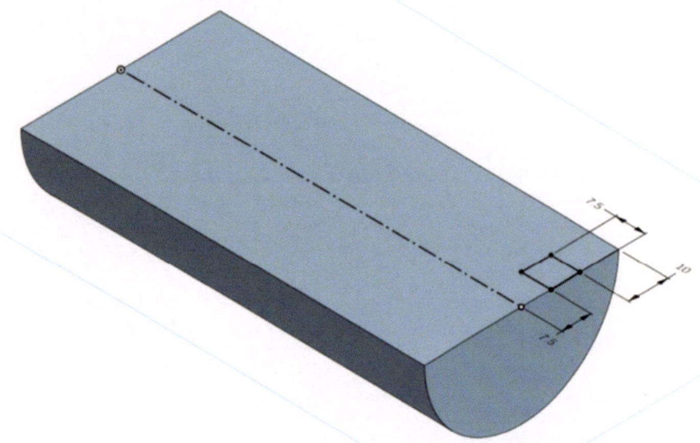

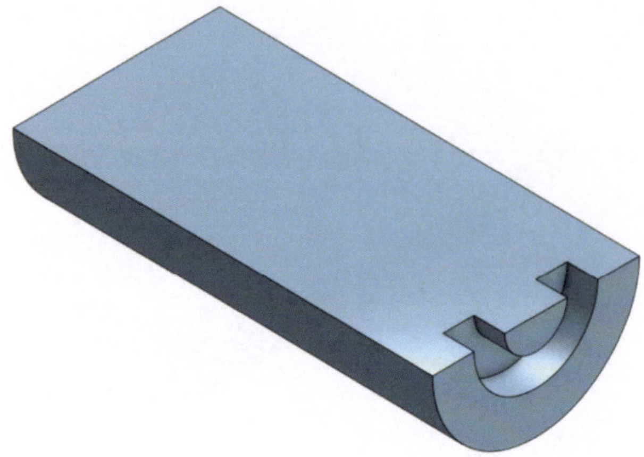

Adding a Revolved Feature to the Model

1. Activate the **Sketch** command and click on the top face of the part geometry.
2. Draw the sketch and apply dimensions and constraint, as shown. Create a horizontal construction line passing through the origin. Click the green check on the **Sketch 3** dialog.

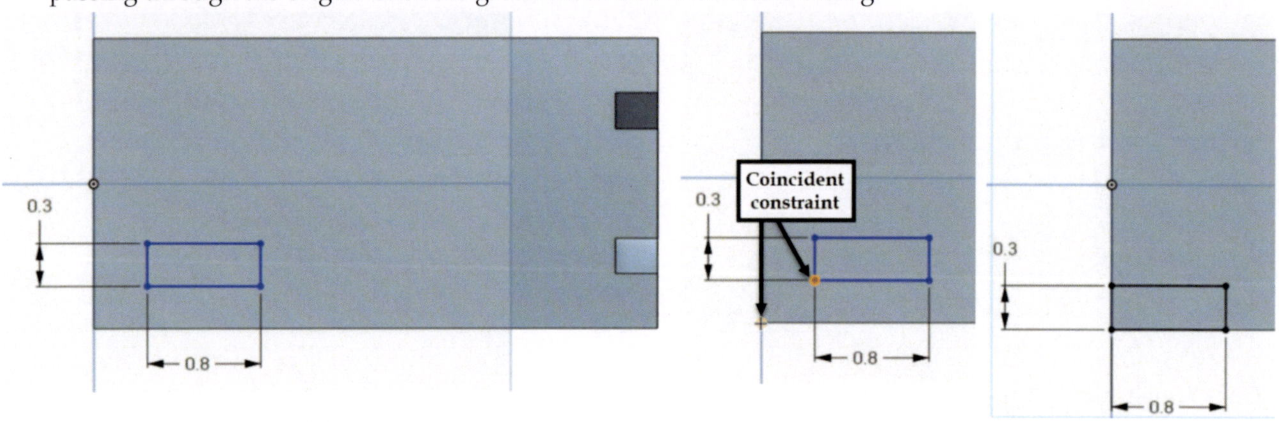

3. Activate the **Revolve** command and select the sketch.
4. On the **Revolve** dialog, click **Revolve axis** and select the construction line from the part geometry.
5. Click the **Revolve type** drop-down > **One direction** and type-in **180** in the **Revolve angle** box.
6. Click the **Opposite direction** button.
7. Click **green check** to add the *Revolved* feature to the geometry.

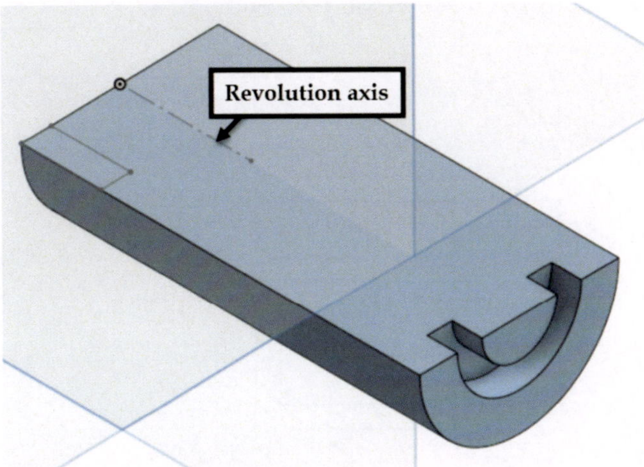

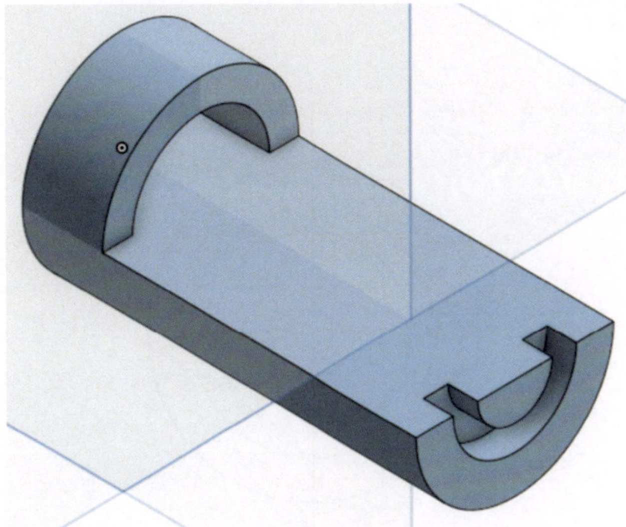

8. Click **Document menu** located at the top-left corner of the window and click the **Close document** option to close the file.

Questions

1. How do you create parallel planes in ONSHAPE?
2. List anyone of the **End types** available on the **Extrude** dialog.
3. How do you create Point normal plane in ONSHAPE?
4. How to add a material to the geometry?
5. How to project edges onto a sketch?

Exercises

Exercise 1

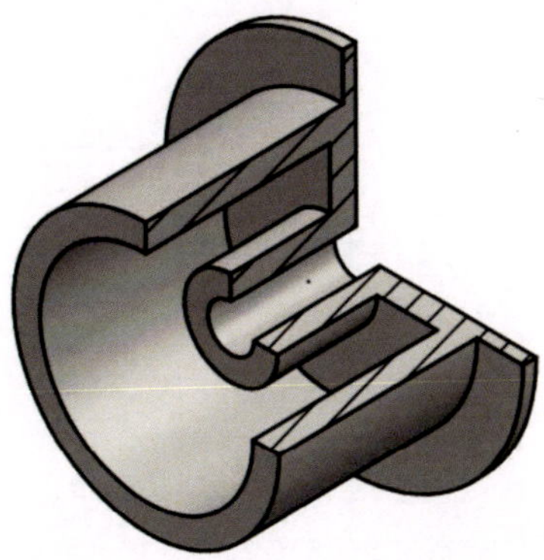

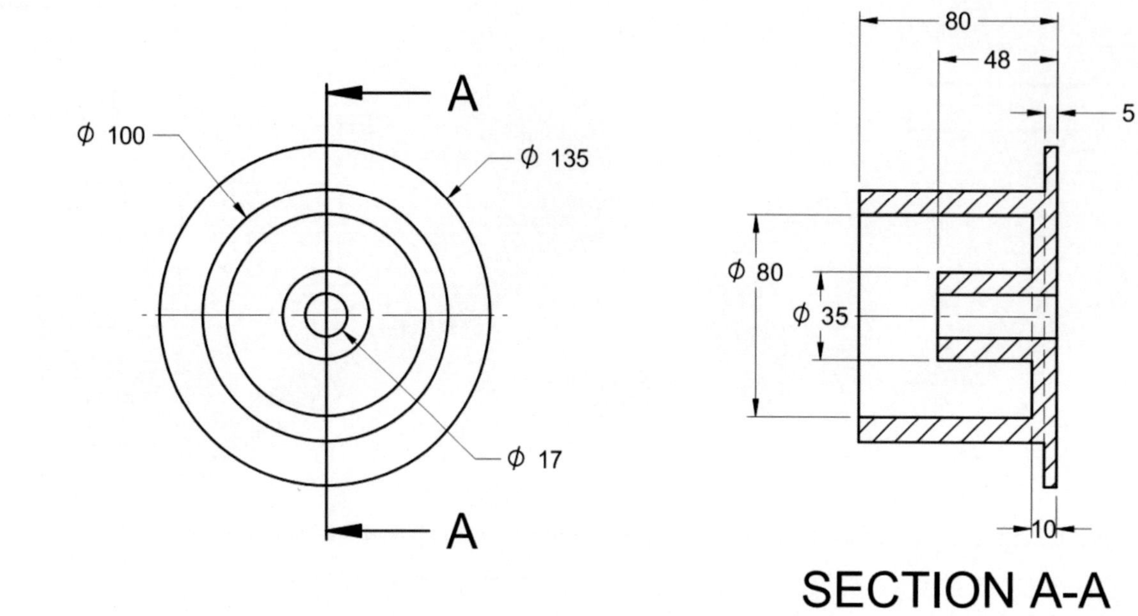
A
A
ϕ 100
ϕ 135
ϕ 17
80
48
5
ϕ 80
ϕ 35
10
SECTION A-A

Exercise 2

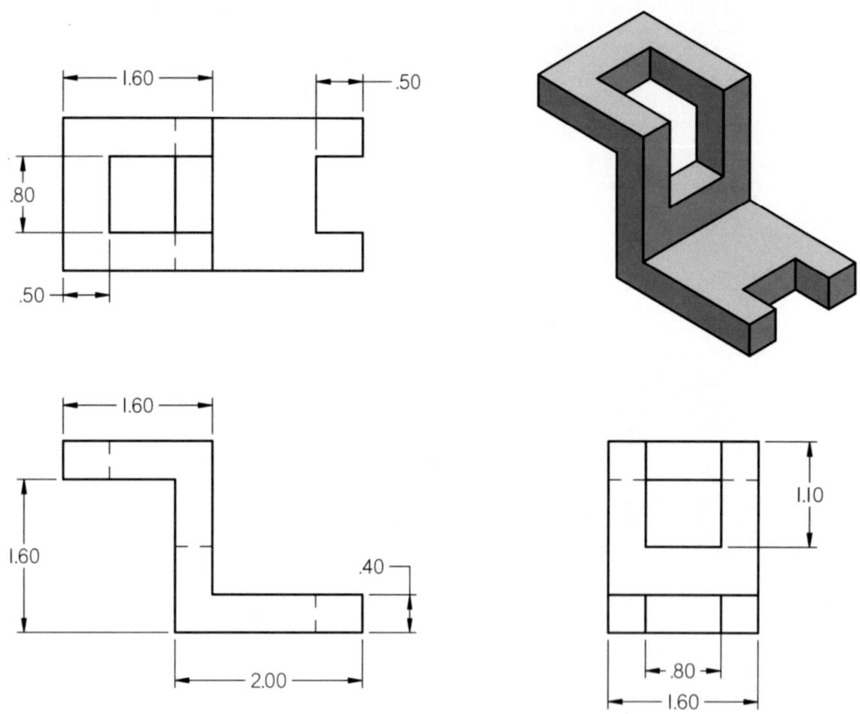
1.60
.50
.80
.50
1.60
1.60
.40
2.00
1.10
.80
1.60

Exercise 3

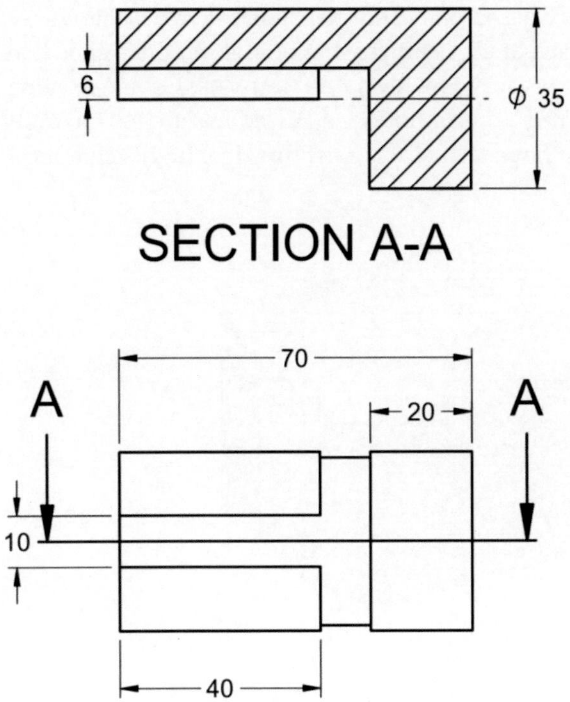

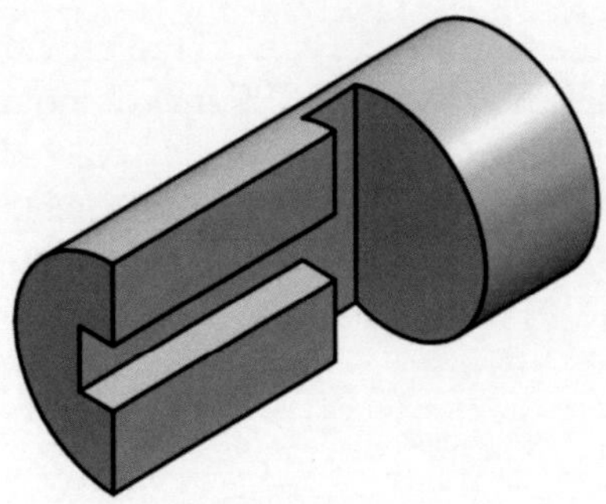

Chapter 4: Placed Features

So far, all of the features covered in the previous chapter are based on two-dimensional sketches. However, there are certain features in ONSHAPE that do not require a sketch at all. Features that do not require a sketch are called Placed features. You can simply place them on your models. However, you must have some existing geometry to add these features. Unlike a sketch-based feature, you cannot use a Placed feature for the first feature of a model. For example, to create a *Fillet* feature, you must have an already existing edge. In this chapter, you learn how to add Holes and Placed features to your design.

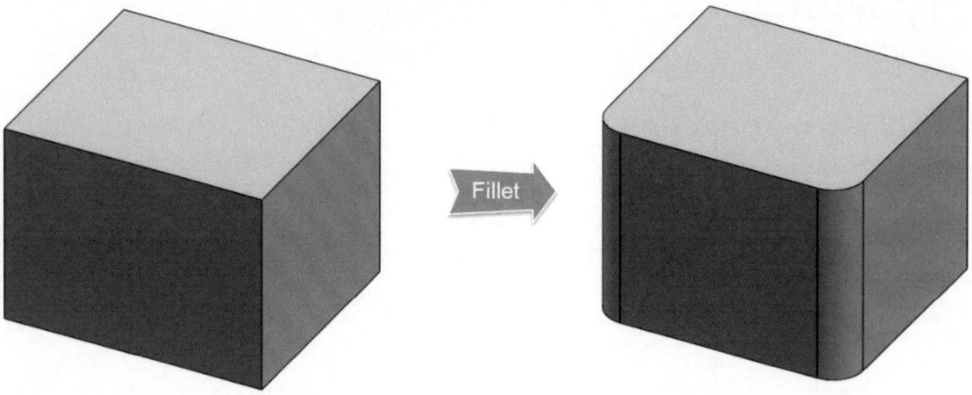

The topics covered in this chapter are:

- *Holes*
- *Fillets*
- *Chamfers*
- *Drafts*
- *Shells*

Hole command

You can create holes simply by creating a circular sketch and remove the material using the **Extrude** command.

But, if you want to create holes that are of standard sizes, the **Hole**  command is a better way to do this. The reason for this is it has many hole types already predefined for you. All you have to do is choose the correct hole type and size. The other benefit is when you are going to create a 2D drawing, Onshape can automatically place the correct hole annotation. To create a hole feature, you need to draw a sketch point on the part geometry. Next, click the **Hole** icon on the Toolbar and then select a hole type from the **Hole** dialog. You can create different types of holes using the options on this dialog.

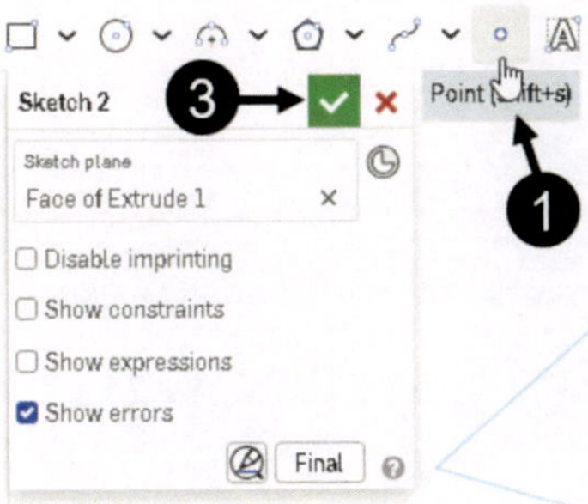

Simple Hole

To create a simple hole feature, click on the **Simple** tab from the **Hole** dialog. The **Simple** hole is the default hole type. Click the **Inch** or **Metric** tab to specify the type of units in which the hole is to be created. Next, specify the hole type, size, and fit from the **Hole type**, **Size**, and **Fastener Fit** drop-down, respectively. Type-in a value in the **Diameter** box. If you want a through hole, click **Termination** > **Through all**. If you want a blind hole, then select **Blind** from the **Termination** drop-down. Next, type-in a value in the **Depth** box.

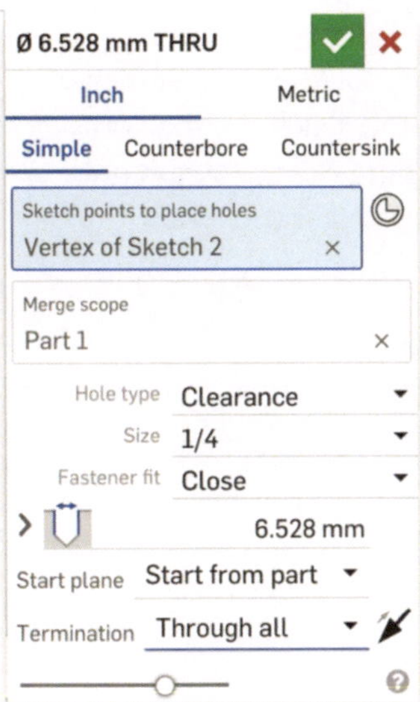

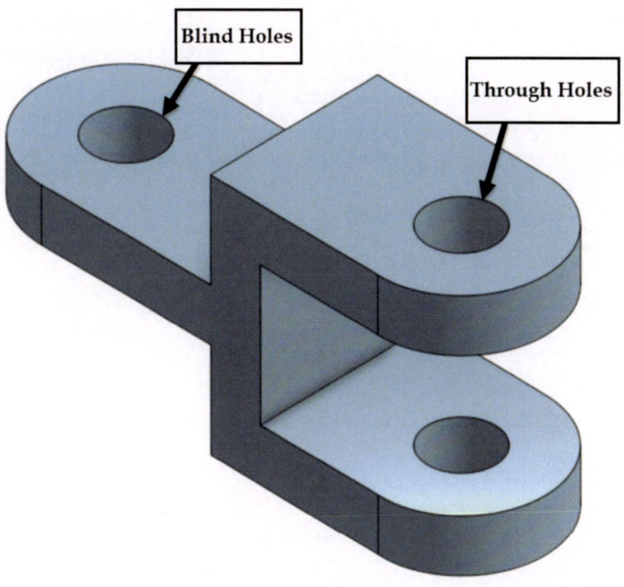

Counterbored Hole

A counterbore hole is a large diameter hole added at the opening of another hole. It is used to accommodate a fastener below the level of the workpiece surface. To create a counterbore hole, click **Hole** on the Toolbar. On the Dialog, click the **Counterbore** tab. Click the **Inch** or **Metric** tab to specify the units. Next, specify the hole type, size, and fit. You can also select the **Custom** option from the **Standard** drop-down and type in the **Diameter**, **Counterbore Diameter**, **Counterbore depth** values. Next, use the **Termination** drop-down to define the hole length.

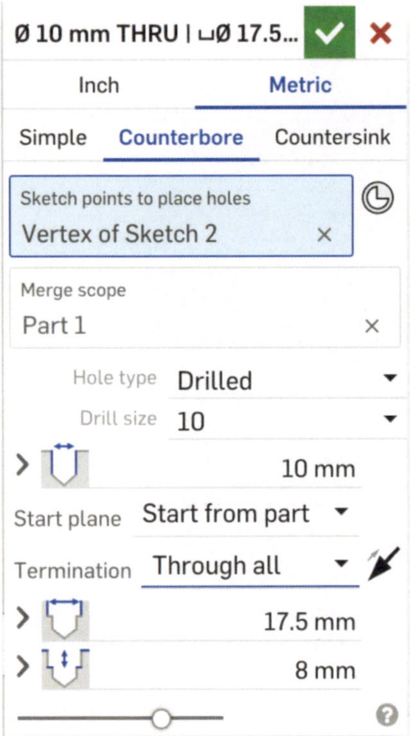

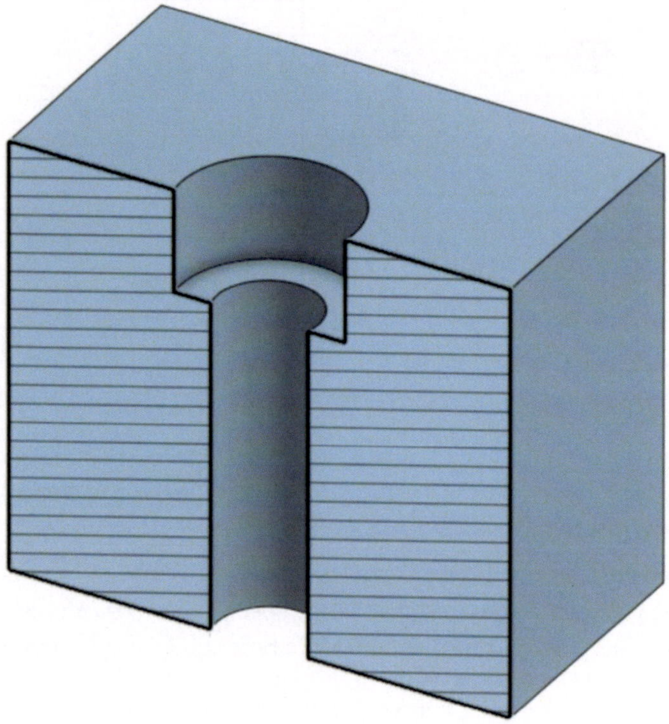

Countersink Hole

A countersink hole has an enlarged V-shaped opening to accommodate the fastener below the level of the work piece surface. To create a countersink hole, click the **Countersink** tab on the **Hole** dialog. Click the Inch or Metric tab, and type-in values in the **Diameter**, **Countersink Diameter**, and **Countersink Angle** boxes. Set the hole depth and end condition.

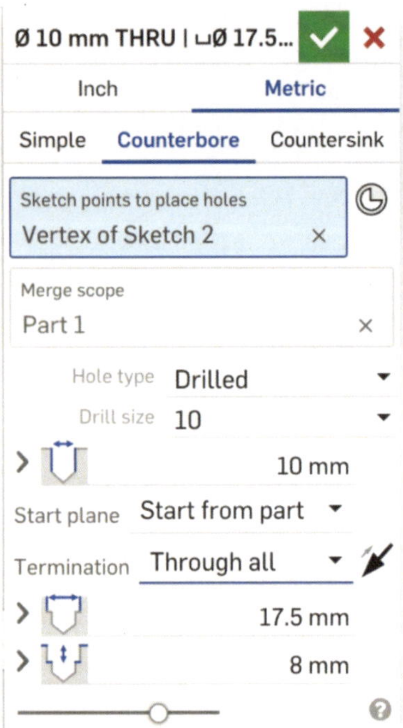

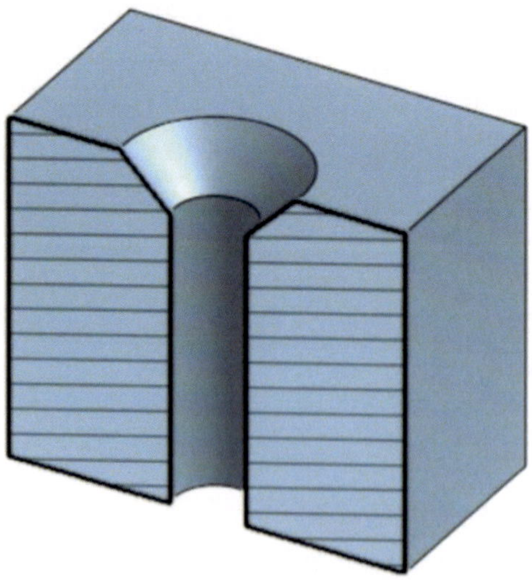

Tapped Hole

To create a tapped hole feature, click the **Inch** or **Metric** tab on the **Hole** dialog. Next, click the select **Simple** tab on the **Hole** dialog. Select **Hole Type** > **Tapped**, which specifies that you are creating internal threads. Following this, you must define the thread's specifications. This involves selecting the **Tap type**, such as a **Straight tap**, **Straight pipe Tap**, or **Tapered pipe tap**, and setting the thread's nominal **Size** and **Pitch**. Based on these parameters, the software determines the correct drill size needed to create the initial hole before the threads are cut. At this stage, you can also refine the thread's precision. The **Thread Class** option allows you to select from various standardized tolerances. These classes, such as 4H, 6G, and the commonly used 6H, define the manufacturing tolerance for the internal threads. The number (e.g., 4, 6, or 7) indicates the tolerance grade. A smaller number means a tighter, more precise fit, while a larger number means a looser fit. The letter (**H** or **G**) specifies the tolerance position or allowance. An **H** position indicates no allowance for a standard fit, while a **G** position provides an allowance that makes the hole slightly larger for a looser fit, which is often used when the threads will be coated. By selecting a class like **6H**, you are specifying a medium tolerance grade with a standard fit.

Similarly, the **Fastener Fit** option (e.g., **Close**, **Normal**, or **Loose**) can adjust the hole's dimensions relative to the fastener, influencing the amount of play or clearance in the final assembly.

Finally, you determine the depth of the hole and threads by setting the **Termination** condition. You can choose the **Through all** option to have the hole go through the entire part or to a specific, blind depth using the **Blind** option. You can also ensure that the threads are cut along the full length of the hole by checking the **Tap through all** option.

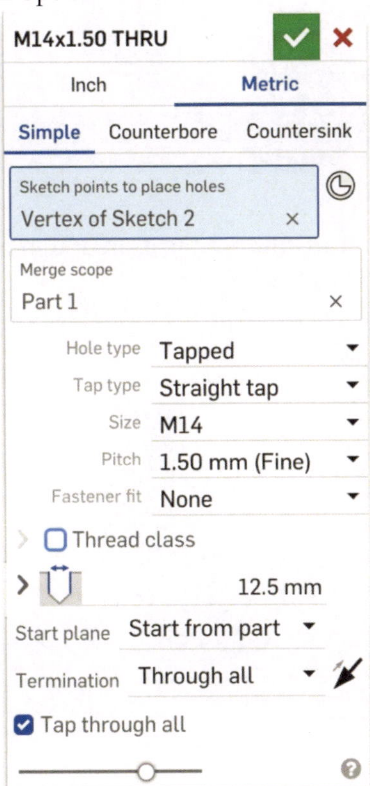

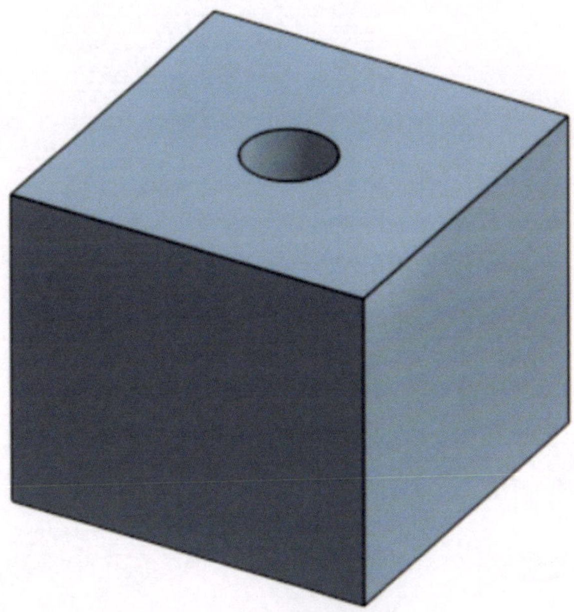

The Fillet command

This command breaks the sharp edges of a model and blends them. You do not need a sketch to create a fillet. All you need to have is model edges. Click the **Fillet** icon on the Toolbar. On the dialog, click the **Edge** tab and select the edges. You can also select all the edges of a face by simply clicking on the face. By mistake, if you have selected a wrong edge, you can deselect it by selecting the edge again. The **Measurement** drop-down allows you to define the fillet's size by either its **Radius** or its **Width**. Next, select the **Distance** option from the **Control** drop-down. It creates a standard circular fillet based on the radius value.

Type a value in the **Radius** or **Width** box available in the **Fillet** dialog. As you change the radius, all the selected edges will be updated. This is because they are all part of one instance. Click the green check to finish this feature. The *Fillet* feature will be listed in the Feature Tree.

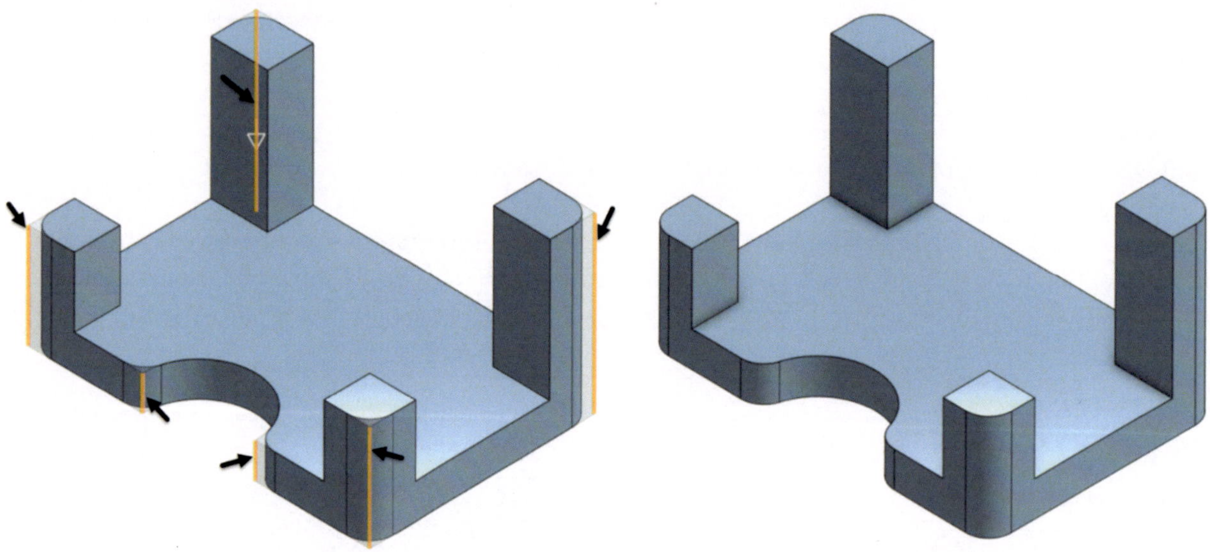

If you want to select all the edges that are tangentially connected, then check the **Tangent propagation** option on the dialog. If you uncheck this option, the selected edge will be filleted ignoring the connected ones.

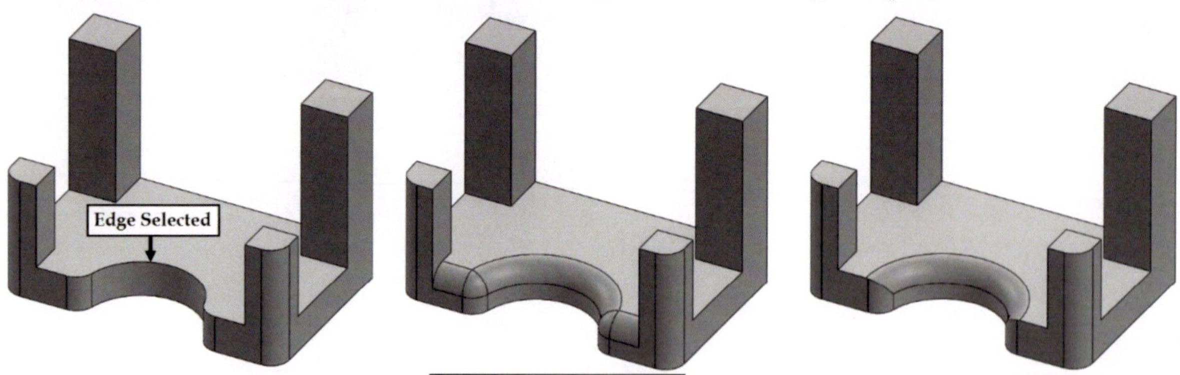

Tangent Propagation ON

Tangent Propagation OFF

Smooth fillet corners

When you fillet two adjacent edges, a sharp juncture appears at the corner. You can avoid this by checking the **Smooth fillet corners** option. It creates a smooth transition between the selected edges.

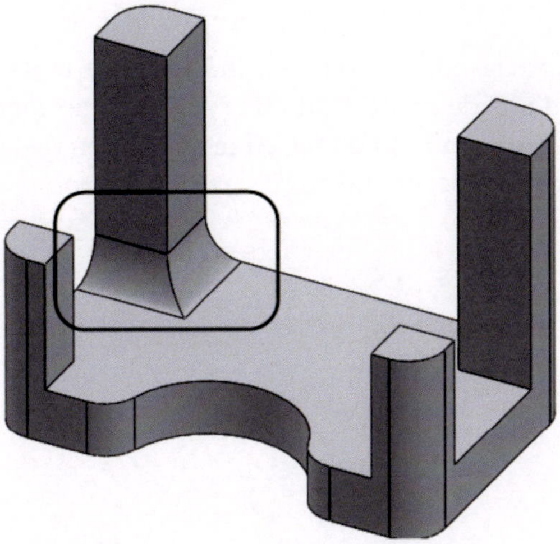

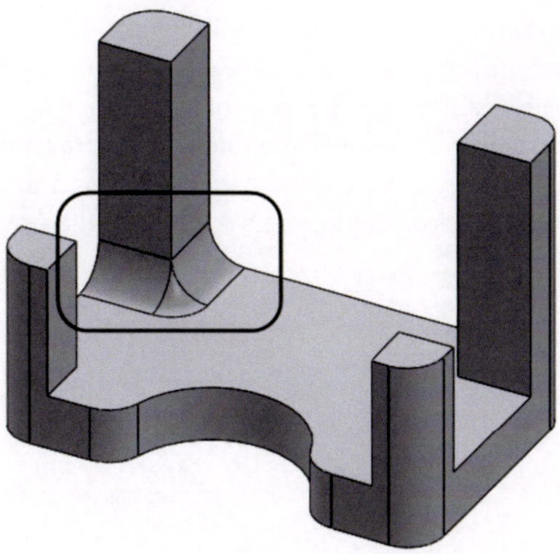

Conic fillets

By default, the fillets have a circular arc profile. However, if you want to create a fillet with conical arc profile, then select **Conic** from the **Cross section** drop-down on the Dialog. Next, type-in a value in the **Rho** box. The fillets with different conic parameters are shown below.

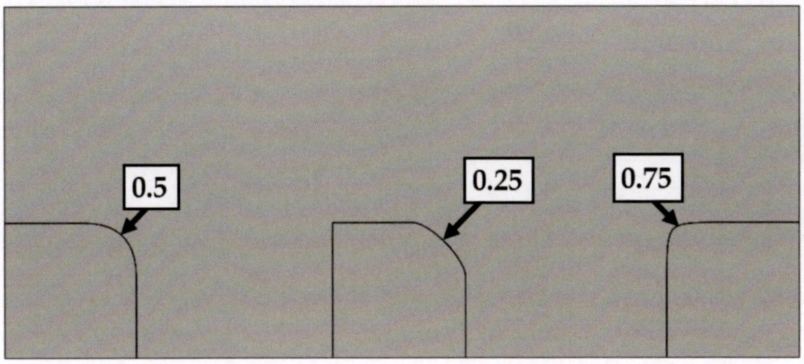

Allow edge overflow

If you create fillets, which intersect with the adjacent edges, the **Allow edge overflow** option will help you to control the geometry. On checking this option, the fillet is preserved by distorting the intersecting edges. On unchecking this option, the adjacent edges are preserved by trimming the overflowing fillets.

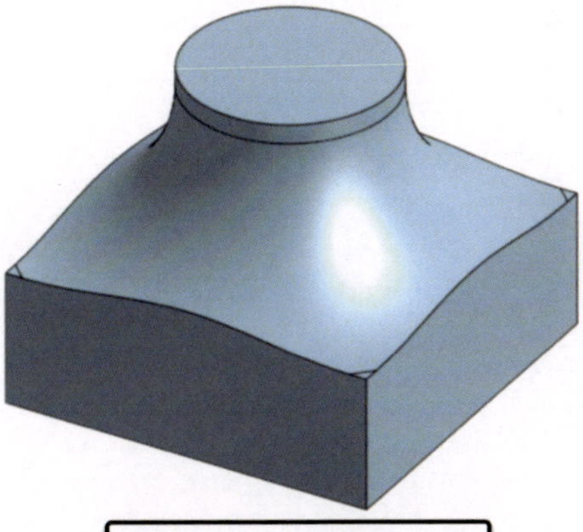

Allow edge overflow ON

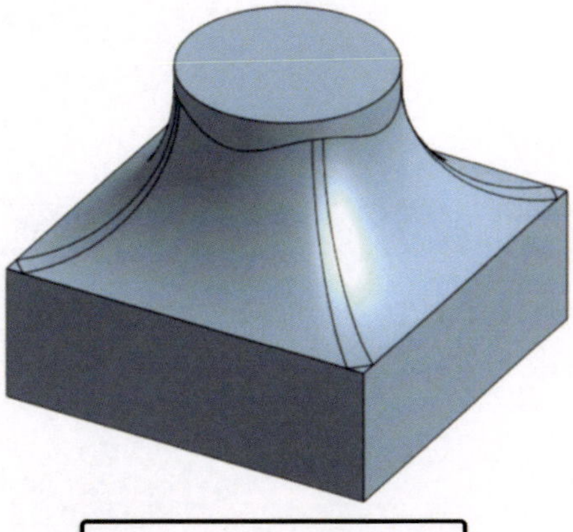

Allow edge overflow OFF

Variable Fillet

Onshape allows you to create a fillet with a varying radius along the selected edge. Click the **Fillet** icon on the Toolbar. On the **Fillet** dialog, select **Measurement > Radius** and click on the edge(s) to fillet. Check the **Variable Fillet** option; the **Points on edges** section appears. Click the **Add point on edge** button and then click on the edge you previously selected to apply the fillet. Next, drag the arrow handle that appears on the edge to position the point, or alternatively, enter a value between **0** and **1** in the **Location** box to specify the point's exact location. After setting the location, define the **Radius** for this first point.

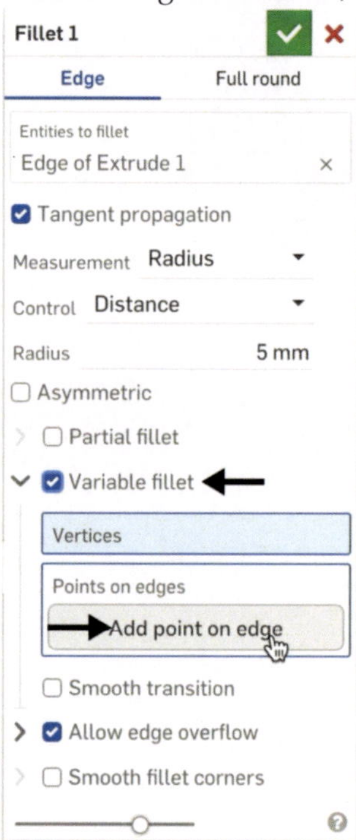

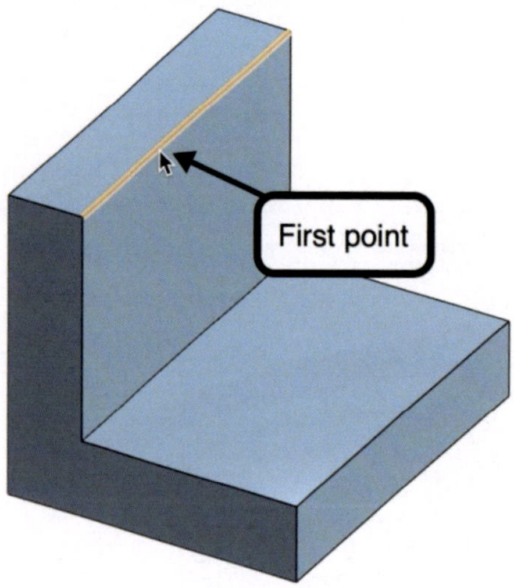

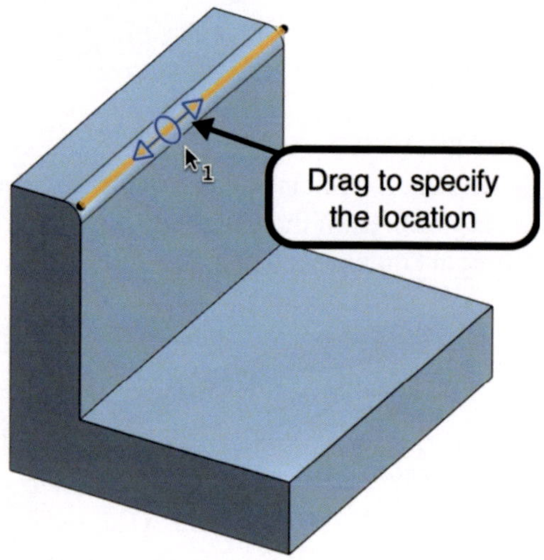

To add more points, click the **Add Point on Edge** button again and select the fillet edge. Specify the location and **Radius** for the second point. Repeat this process to add additional points, each with its own location and radius as required.

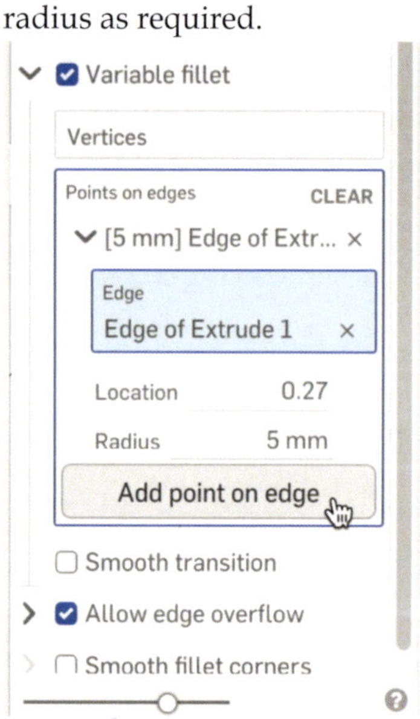

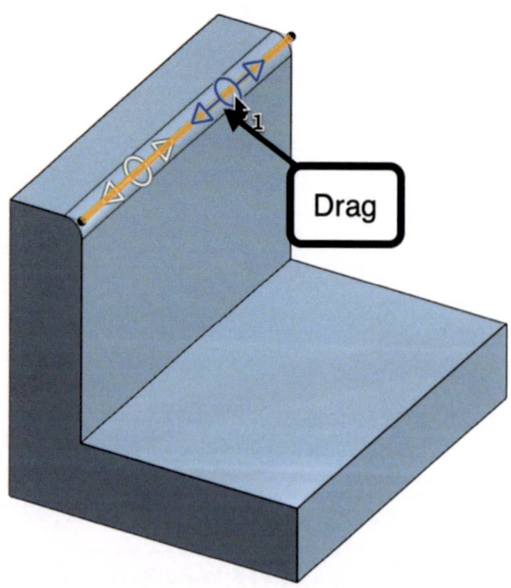

On the Dialog, select **Smooth transition** to get a smooth fillet. Uncheck this option to get a straight transition fillet.

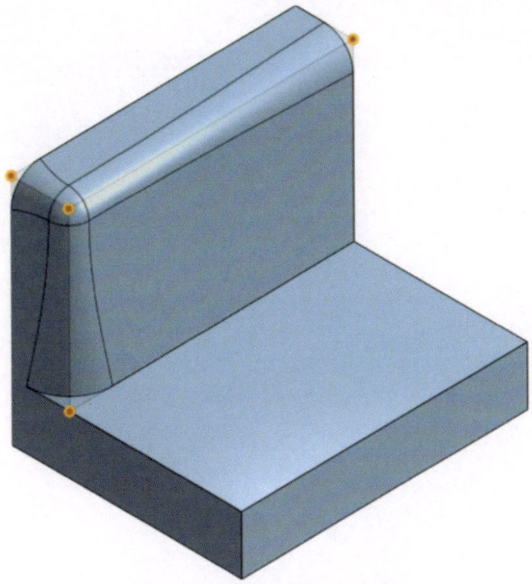

Smooth transition ON

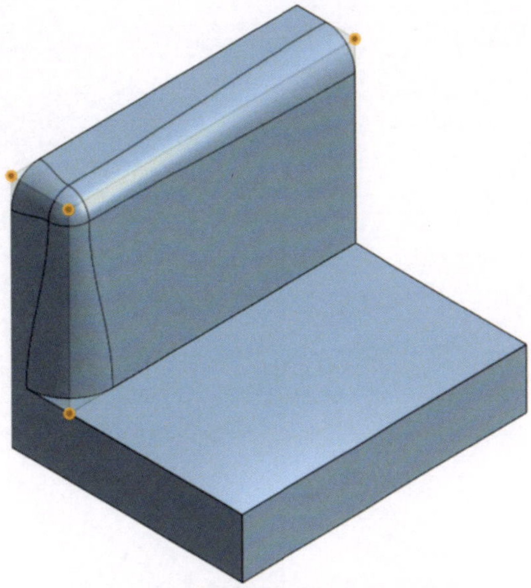

Smooth transition OFF

Click the green check to create the variable radius fillet.

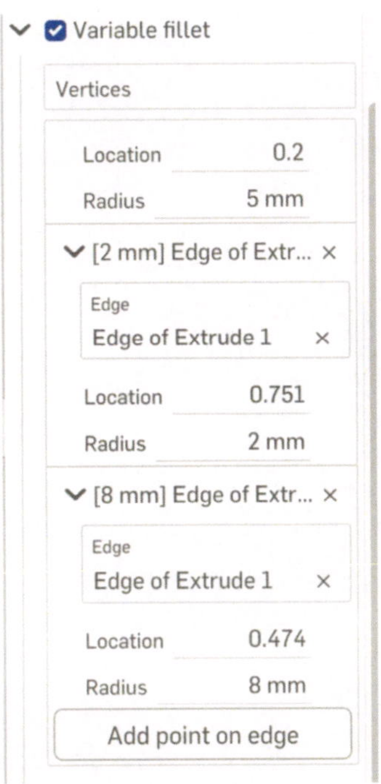

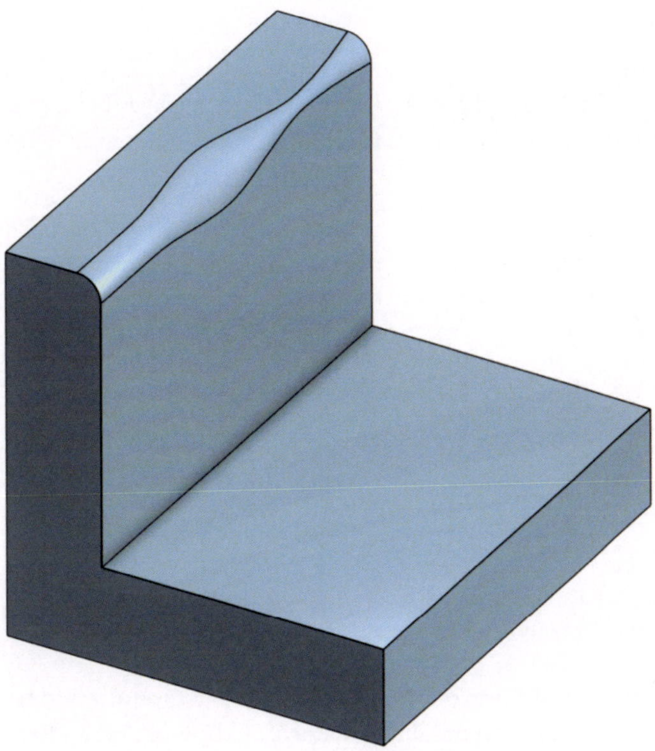

Asymmetric fillets

The **Asymmetric** option allows you specify two different offset distances from the edge instead of a single, uniform radius. You specify the first distance in the **Radius** box and the second, different distance in the **Second**

radius box. This results in a fillet with a non-circular, elliptical-like profile where the curve extends further onto one adjacent face than the other, creating a smooth but uneven transition between the surfaces.

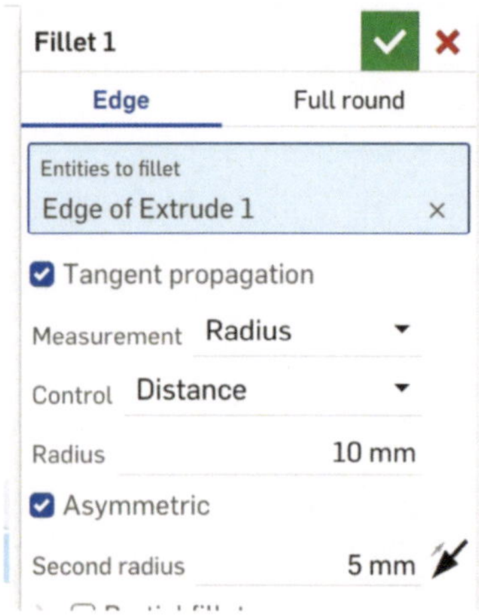

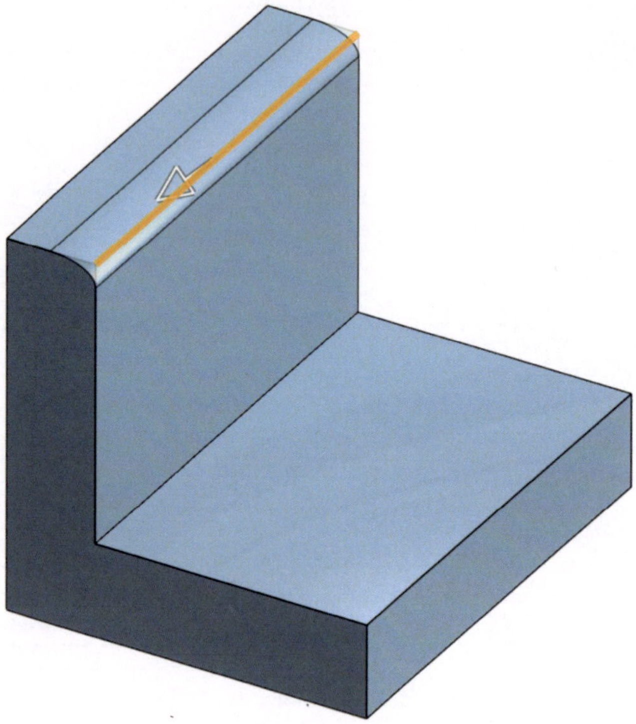

Full Round Fillet

This option creates a fillet between three faces. It replaces the center face with a fillet. Click the **Fillet** icon on the toolbar and click the **Full Round** tab on the **Fillet** dialog. Select the first side face, second side face, and the face to round. Click **OK** to create the full round fillet.

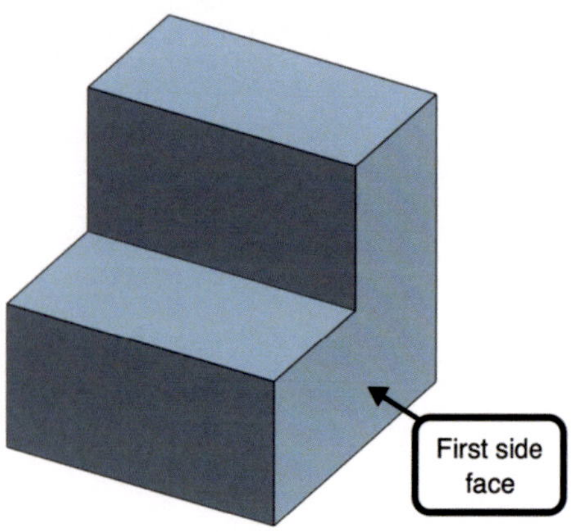

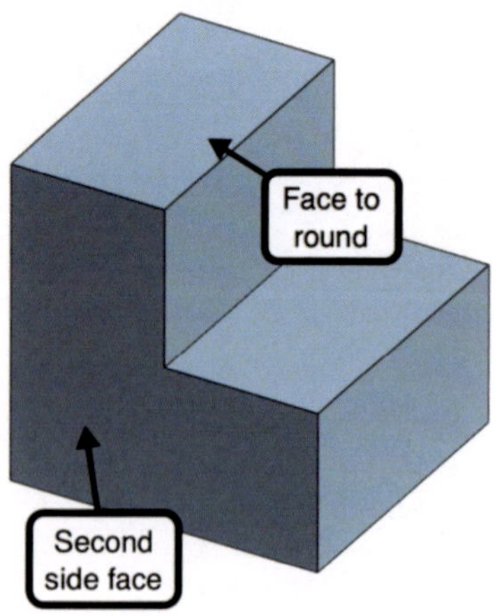

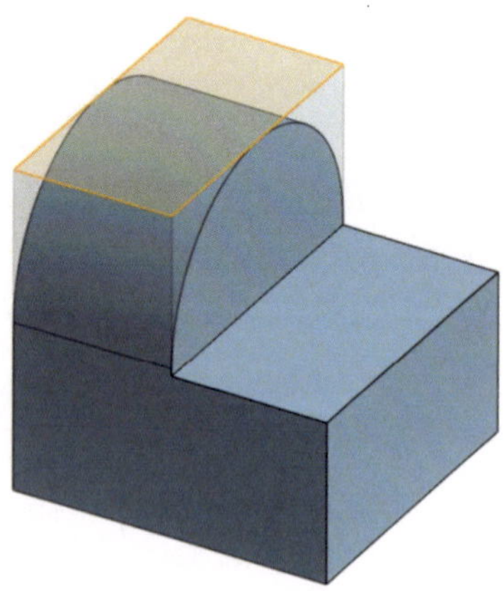

Face Fillet

This option creates a fillet between two faces. The faces are not required to be connected. Click **Fillet** drop-down > **Face Fillet** on the toolbar. Click on the first side face, as shown. On the **Face blend** dialog, click in the **Side 2** selection box and select the second side face, as shown. To apply the face blend to connected faces, check the **Propagation** box and select **Tangent**, **Adjacent**, or **Custom** from the drop-down.

Select the option from the **Cross-section** drop-down. The **Rolling ball** option creates a smooth, constant-radius blend between the faces. Imagine a ball rolling along the intersection to create the shape. The **Swept profile** option creates a variable blend that follows a specified path, such as a curve or an edge (called a spine). The blend's profile stays perpendicular (at a 90-degree angle) to the spine.

Select the option (**Radius** or **Width**) from the **Measurement** drop-down and specify the value in the **Radius** or **Width** box. If the selected faces have a gap between them, ensure the **Radius** or **Width** value is large enough to bridge the distance. Check the **Asymmetric** option if you want to create an asymmetric blend. Click **OK** to create the face fillet.

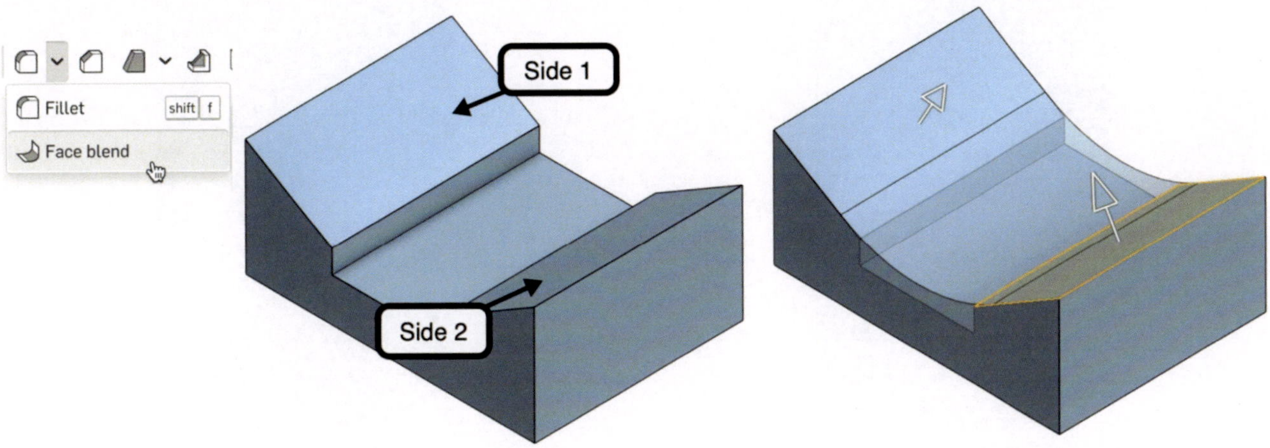

The Chamfer command

The **Chamfer** and **Fillet** commands are commonly used to break sharp edges. The difference is that the **Chamfer** command adds a bevel face to the model. A chamfer is also a placed feature. Click the **Chamfer** button on the Toolbar. On the **Chamfer** dialog, select chamfer **Chamfer type**. You can select **Distance and angle, Equal Distance**, or **Two distances**. If you select **Chamfer Type > Distance and angle**, then type-in the distance and angle values of the chamfer in the **Distance** and **Angle** boxes. Click on the edge(s) to chamfer. Click **OK**.

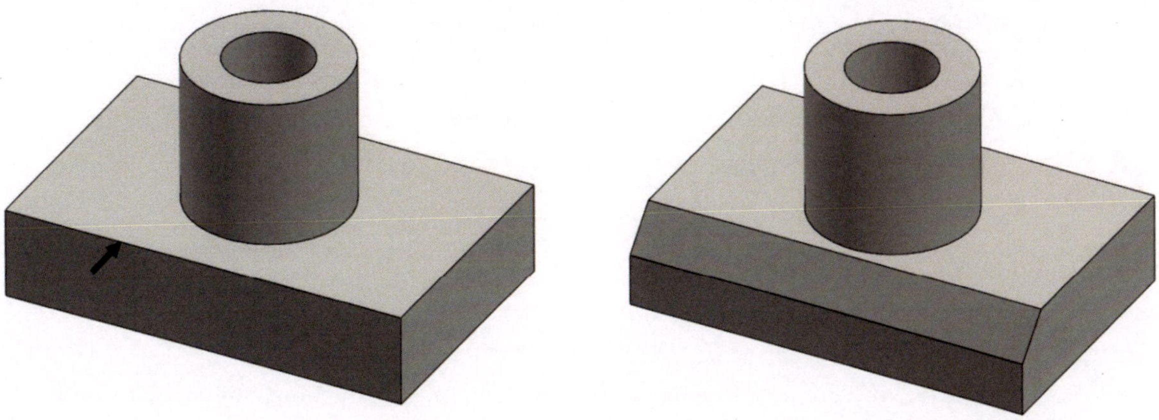

Chamfer Measurement Types for Non-Planar Faces

When creating a chamfer on a curved or angled surface, you must choose how the distance is measured using the **Offset** and **Tangent** options available in the **Measurement** drop-down. For flat surfaces, both options produce the same result.

The **Offset** option measures the chamfer distance from the actual edge that you select. The calculation starts from your first selection and follows the chain of edges.

The **Tangent** option measures the chamfer distance from the theoretical sharp corner where the faces would intersect if they were extended.

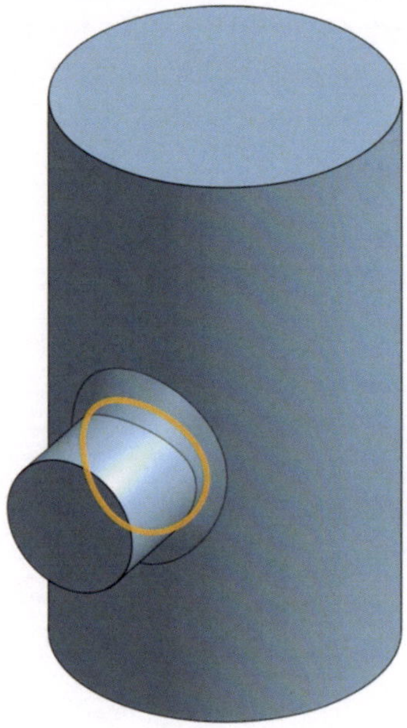

Offset

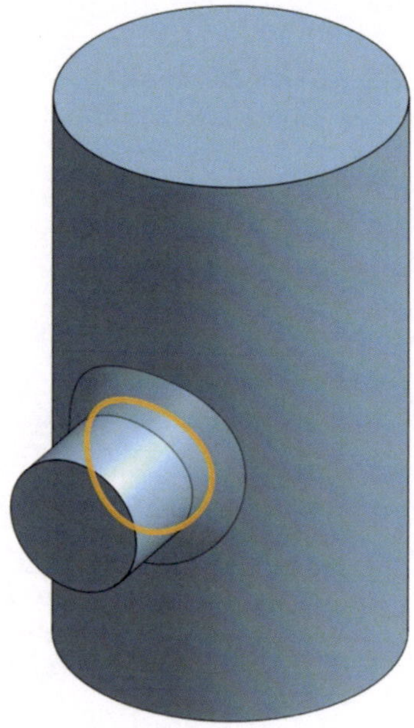

Tangent

Draft

When creating cast or plastic parts, you are often required to add draft on them so that they can be molded easily. A draft is an angle or taper applied to the faces of components so that they can be removed from a mold easily. The following illustration shows a molded part with and without draft.

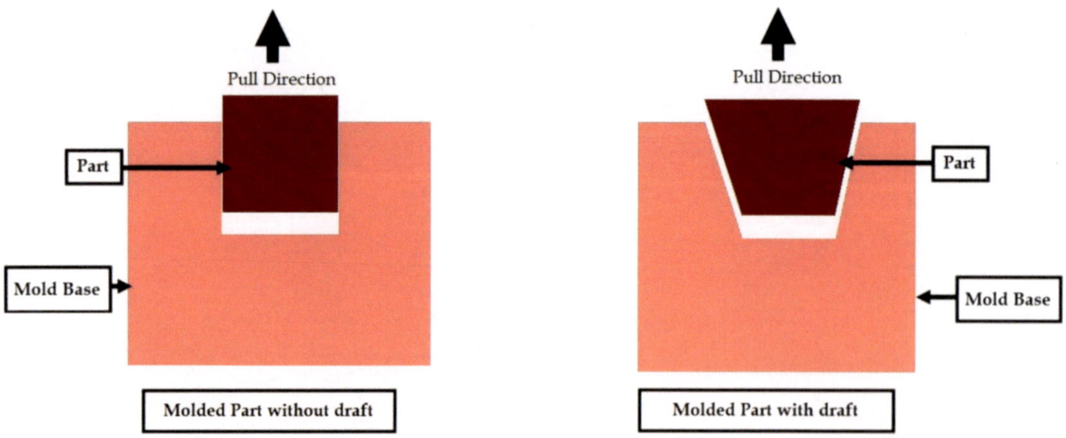

When creating *Extruded* features, you can predefine the draft. However, most of the time, it is easier to apply the draft after the features are created. Click the **Draft** icon on the Toolbar. On the **Draft** Dialog, click the **Neutral plane** tab. Next, select a flat face or plane to define the neutral plane. The draft angle will be measured with reference to this face.

Next, select the faces to draft. The **Tangent propagation** option allows you to select all the tangently connected faces by selecting anyone of them. The **Reapply fillet** option converts the fillet faces to cones and the results are undesirable. Leave this option unchecked; the fillets are treated and reblended resulting in a cylindrical face.

Type-in a value in the **Draft angle** box. This defines the draft angle. If you want to reverse the draft direction, then click the **Opposite direction** icon next to the **Draft angle** box. Click the green check to apply draft.

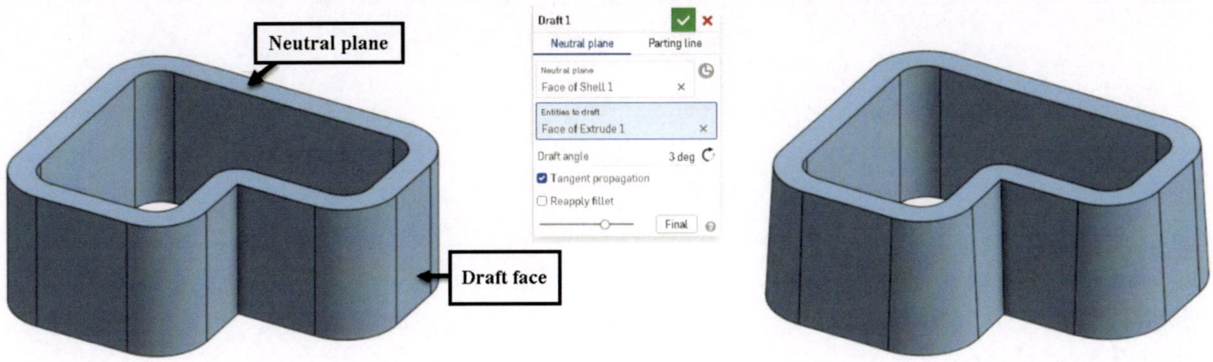

Shell

The **Shell** is another useful feature that can be applied directly to a solid model. It allows you to take a solid geometry and make it hollow. This can be a powerful and timesaving technique, when designing parts that call for thin walls such as bottles, tanks, and containers. This command is easy to use. Create a solid part, and then click the **Shell** icon on the Toolbar. Select the faces to remove. Type-in the wall thickness in the **Shell thickness** box. If you want to add outside thickness, then click the **Opposite direction** icon next to the **Shell thickness** box. Click the green check to finish the feature.

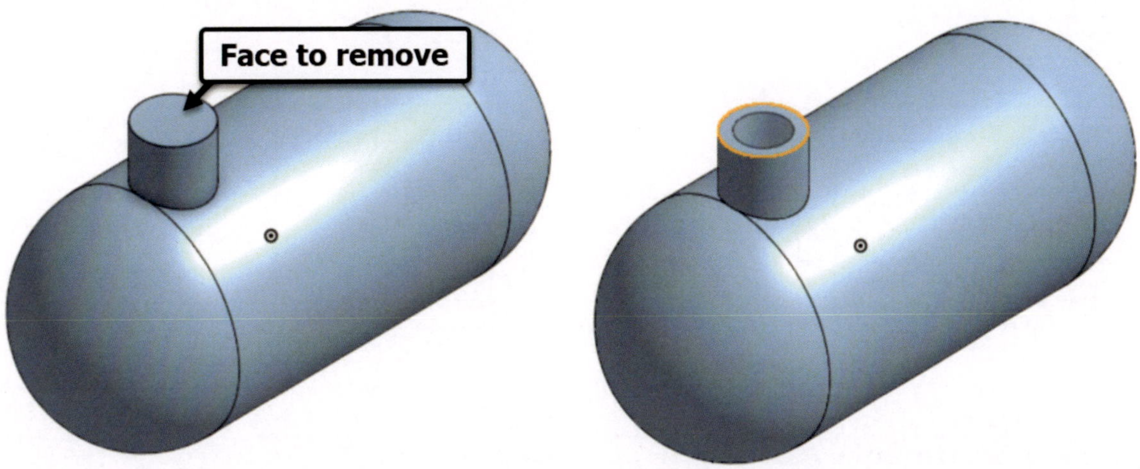

If you want to shell the solid body without removing any faces, then simply check the **Hollow** option and type-in a value in the **Shell thickness** box. Next, select the part to be shelled and click the green check; the part is shelled without removing the faces. Change the **Display Style** to **Hidden edges visible** or **Shade with hidden edges** to view the shell.

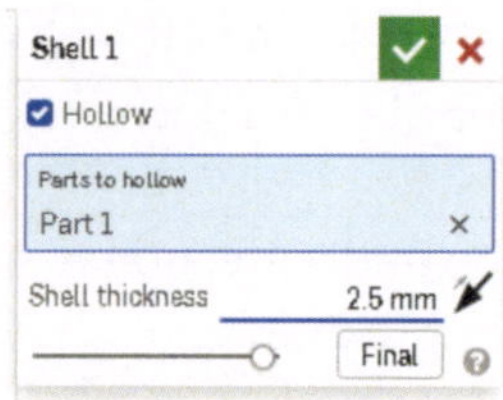

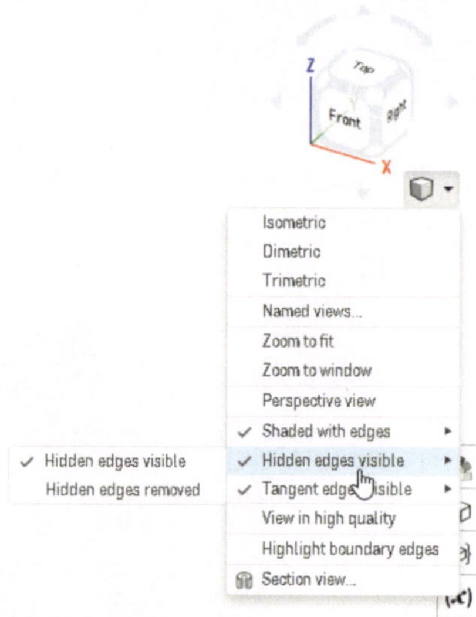

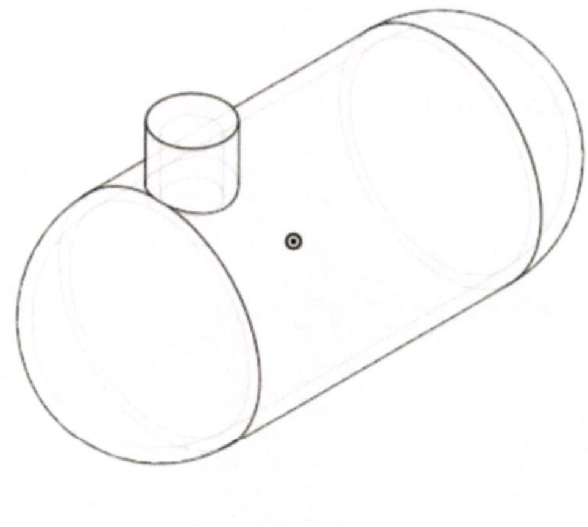

Tutorial 1 (Millimetres)

In this example, you create the part shown below.

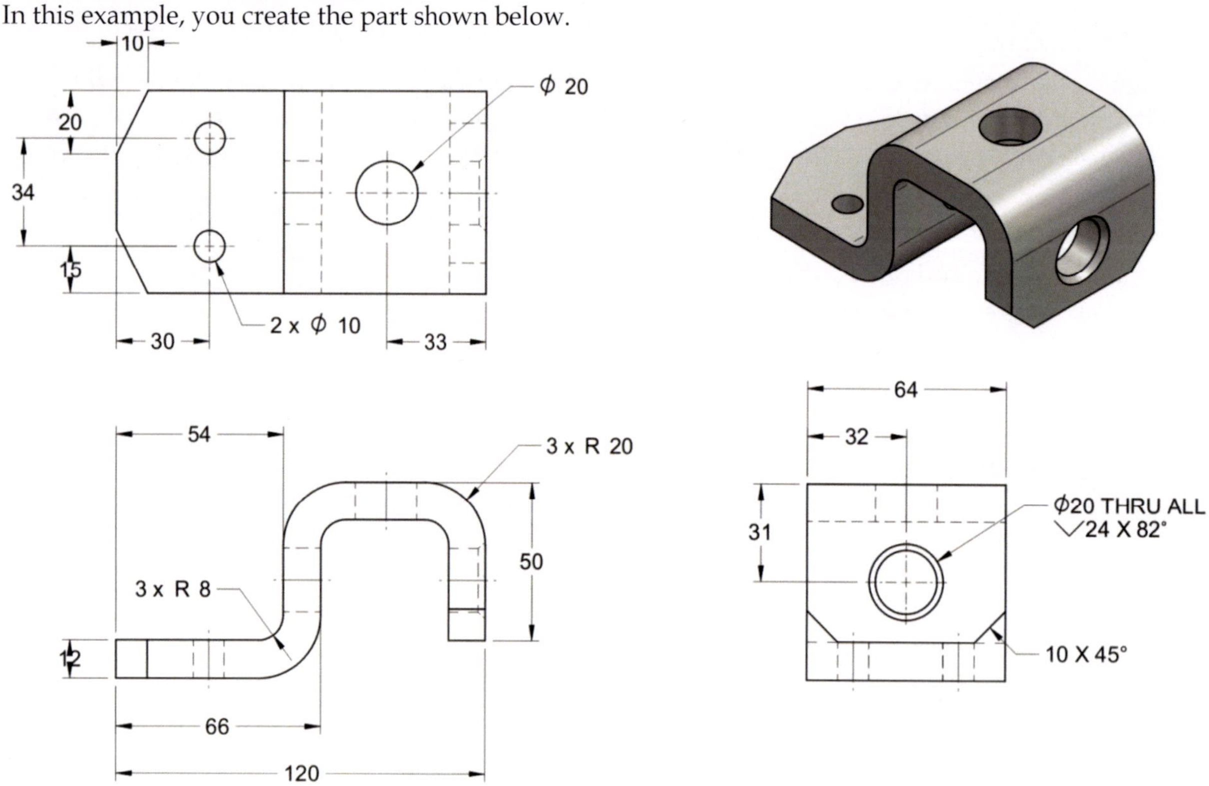

Creating a New document

1. In your Internet Browser, go to https://www.onshape.com to start Onshape.
2. Next, click **SIGN IN** button located on the top right corner side of the web page. Enter the username and password, and then, click **Sign in**.
3. On the Documents page, click **Create > Folder**. Next, type Chapter 4 in the **Folder name** box and then click **Create**.
4. Double-click on the **Chapter 4** folder in the **Folders** section.

5. On the Documents page, click **Create > Document**; the **New document** dialog appears on the screen.
6. Enter Tutorial 1 in the **Document name** box and click **Create public document**; a new document appears.
7. Click the **Document menu** located at the top left corner of the window and select **Workspace Units**; the **Workspace Units** dialog appears on the screen.
8. On the **Workspace Units** dialog, select **Length default unit> Millimeter** from Length section.
9. Select **Mass default unit > Gram** from the **Mechanical** section.
10. Leave the other default settings and click the green check.

Creating the Extruded Feature

1. Click **Sketch** command on the Toolbar. Next, click on the Front plane.
2. Right-click and select **View normal to sketch plane**; the selected plane orients normal to the screen.
3. Activate the **Line** command and create the sketch, as shown.
4. On the Toolbar, click the **Offset** command and select all the lines of the sketch. Next, click the arrow such that it points in the upward direction.

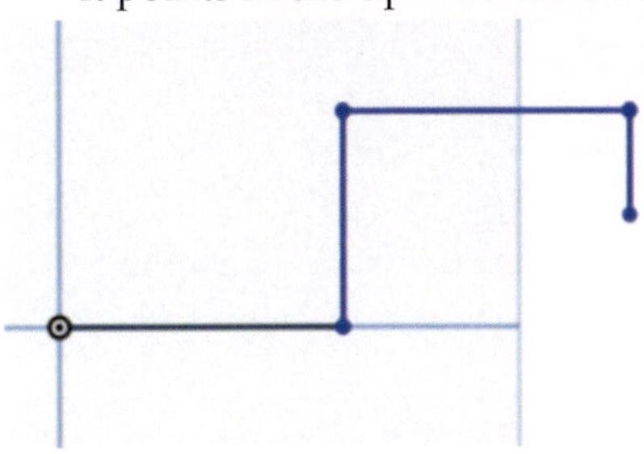
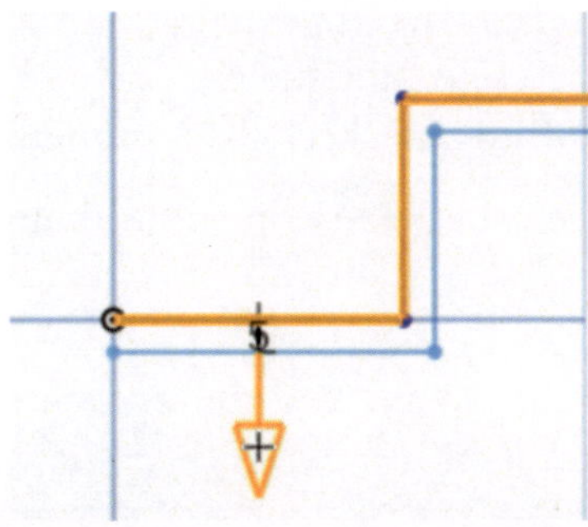
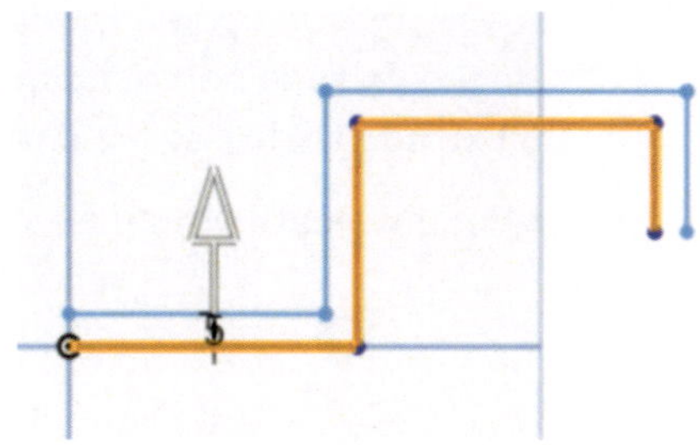

5. Click on the graphics area, and then type 12 in the offset distance box. Next, press Enter.
6. Close the ends of the sketch using the **Line** command.

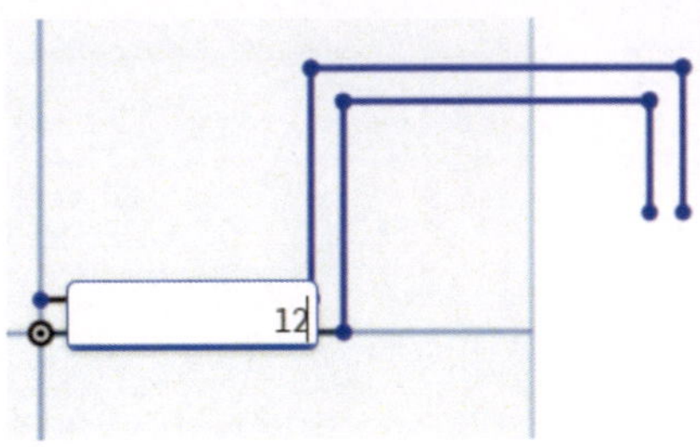

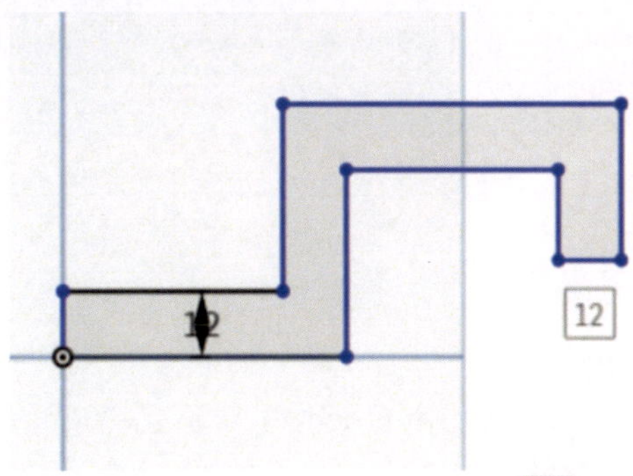

7. Add dimensions to constrain the sketch fully. Click the green check on the **Sketch 1** dialog.

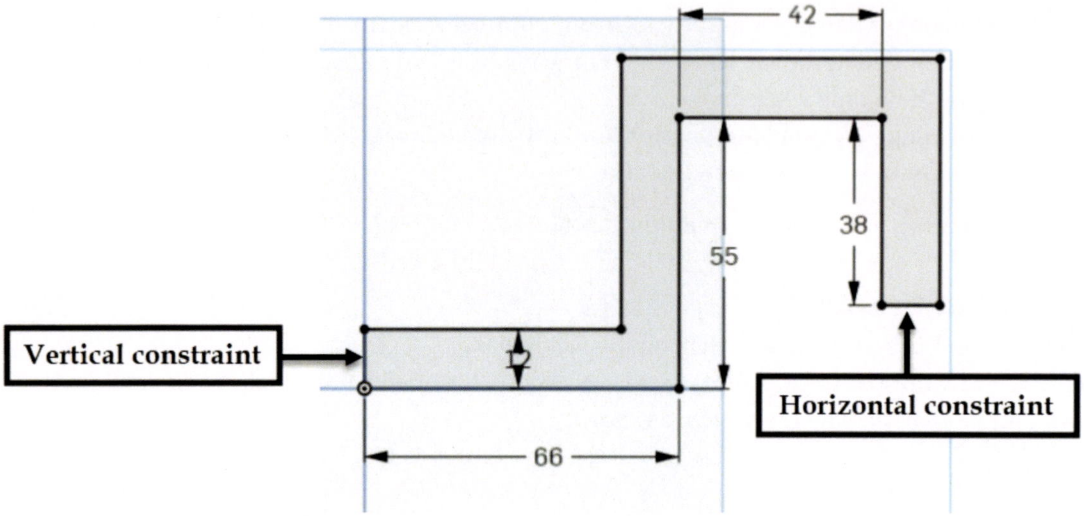

8. Activate the **Extrude** command, and then select the sketch.
9. On the **Extrude** Dialog, select **End type > Blind** and check the **Symmetric** option.
10. Type **64** in the **Depth** box and click the green check icon on the dialog.

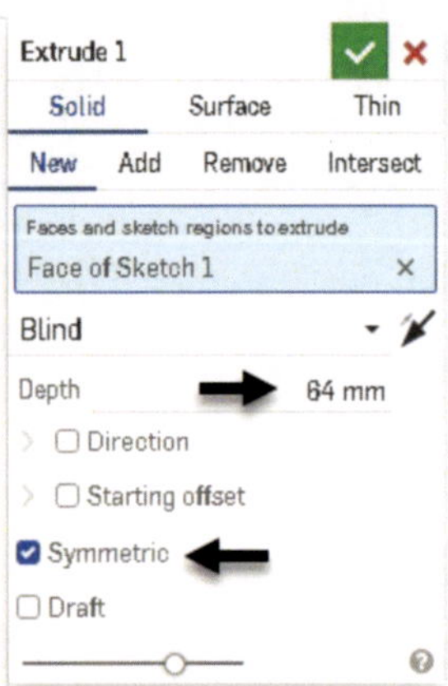

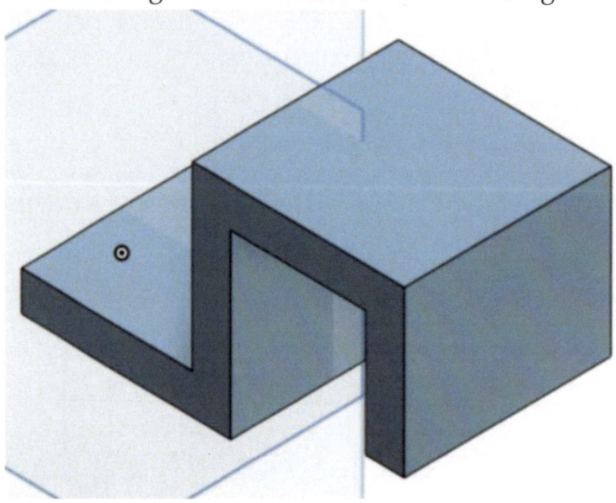

Creating the Hole Features

1. Click the **Sketch** command on the Toolbar, and then click on the right-side face.
2. On the Toolbar, click the **Point** command and then click on the sketch plane.
3. Apply the dimension between the point and the adjacent edges, as shown. Click the green check on the **Sketch 2** dialog.

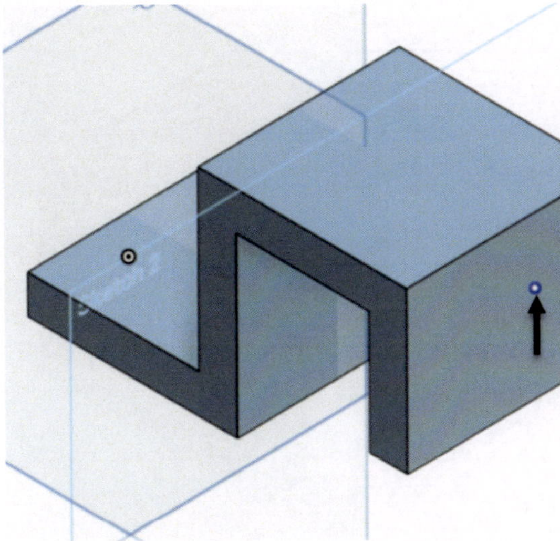

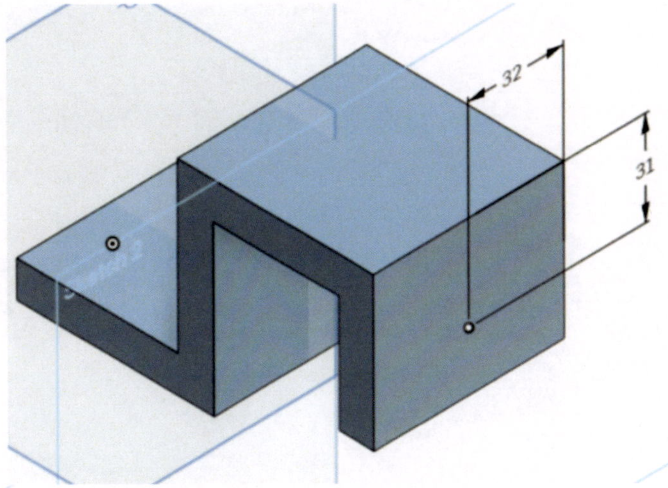

4. On the Toolbar, click the **Hole** command.
5. On the **Hole** dialog, click the Metric tab, and then the **Countersink** tab.
6. Select **Termination > Through** all.
7. Select the **Hole Type > Clearance**.
8. Select **Size > M20** and **Fastener Fit > Close**, respectively.
9. Type-in 24 and 82 in the **Countersink diameter** and **Countersink angle** boxes, respectively.
10. Select the sketch point, and then click the green check on the **Hole** dialog.

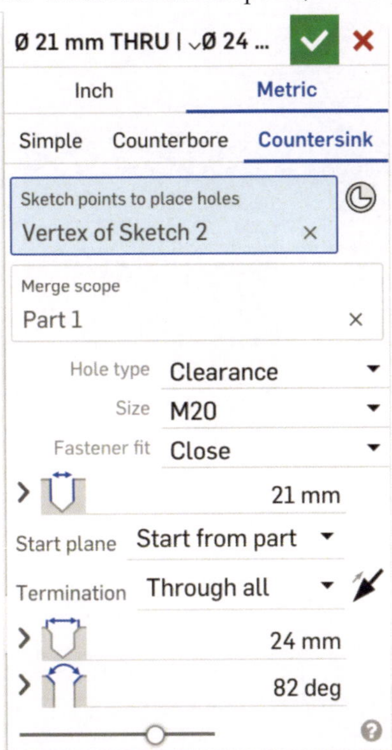

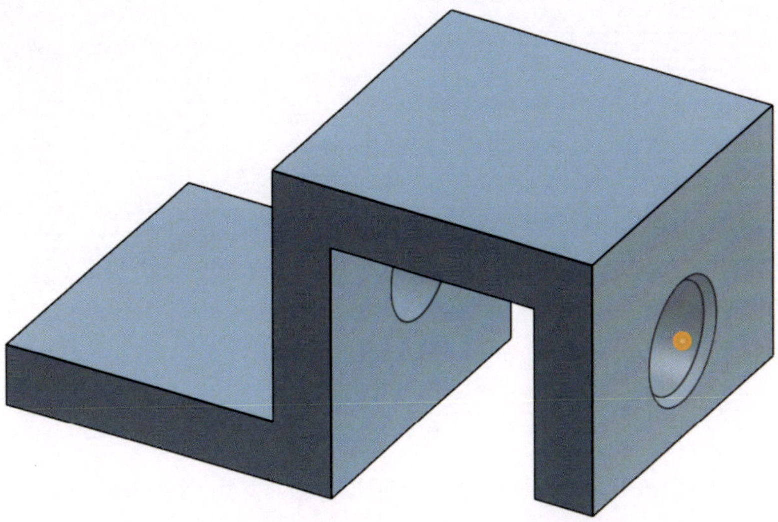

11. Click the **Sketch** command on the toolbar, and then click on the top face.
12. On the Toolbar, click the **Point** command and then click on the sketch plane.
13. Apply the dimension between the point and the adjacent edges, as shown. Click the green check on the **Sketch 3** dialog.

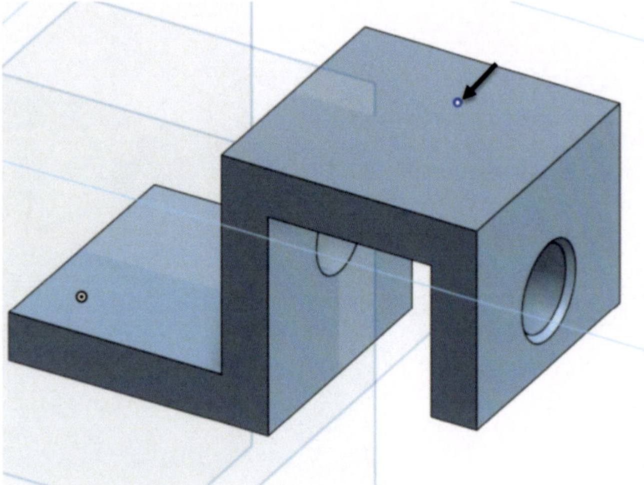

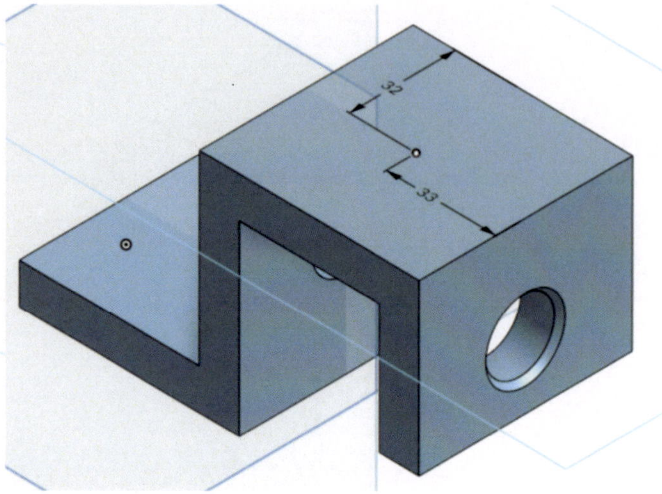

14. On the **Hole** dialog, click the **Metric** tab and then the **Simple** tab.
15. Select **Hole Type > Drill**, and then select **Drill size > 20**.
16. Select **Termination > Through** all.
17. Select the sketch point, and then click the green check on the **Hole** dialog.

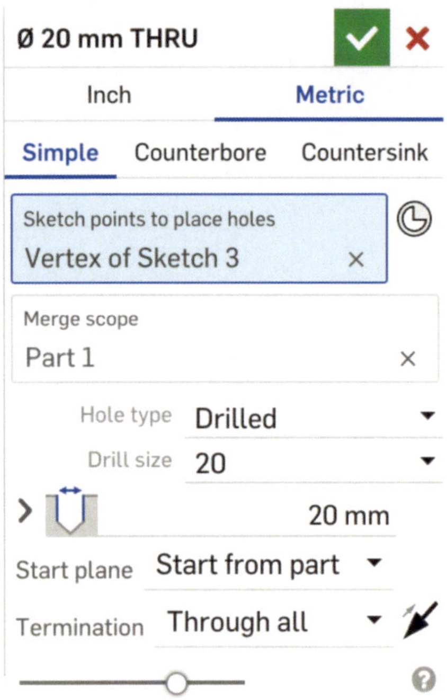

18. On the **View Cube**, click on the top left corner; the view orientation of the model changes.

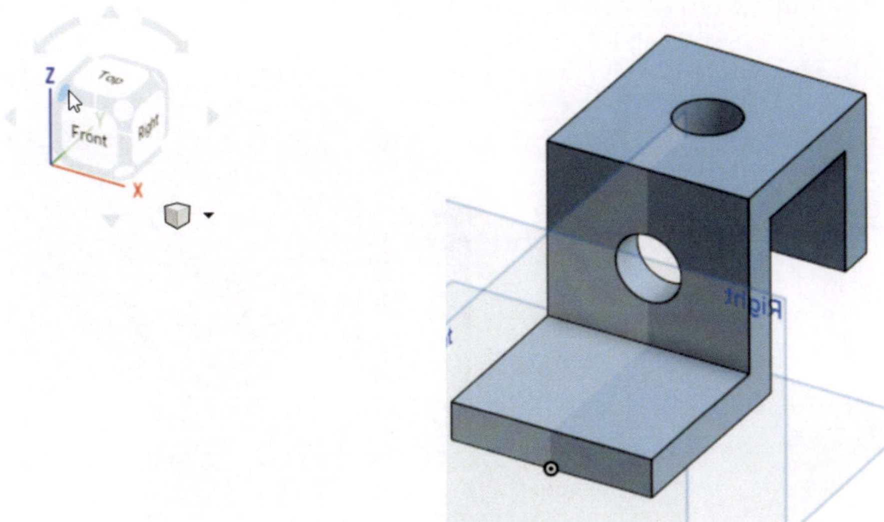

19. Click the **Sketch** command on the Toolbar, and then click on the lower top face of the model.
20. On the Toolbar, click the **Point** command and then click on the sketch plane.
21. Apply the dimension between the point and the adjacent edges, as shown.
22. On the Toolbar, click **Constraint** drop-down > **Vertical**. Next, select the two sketch points to align them vertically.
23. Click the green check on the **Sketch 4** dialog.

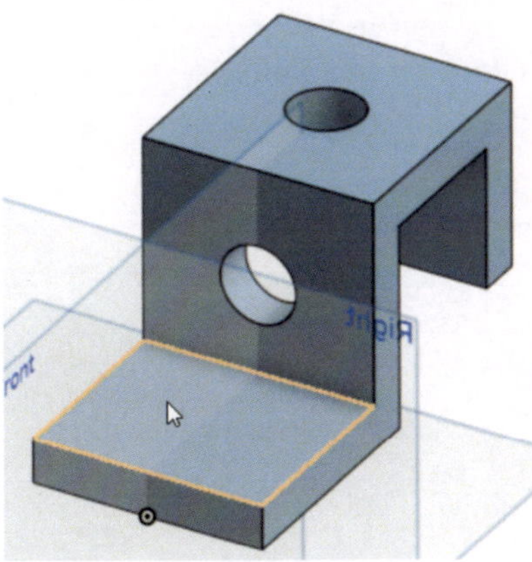
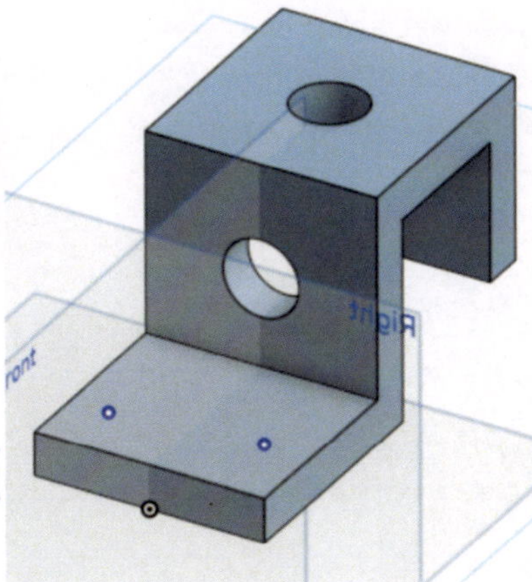
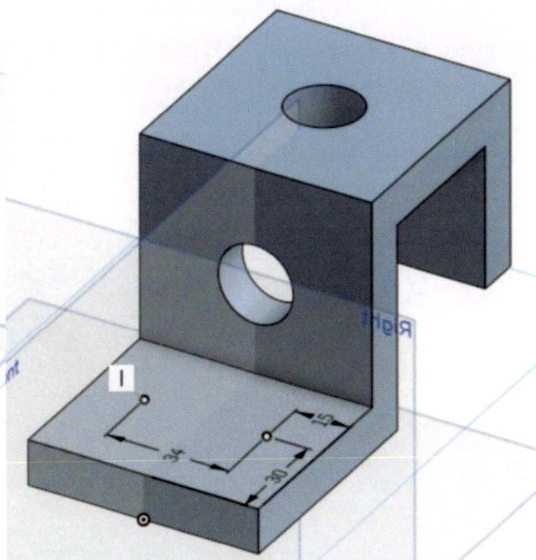

24. On the **Hole** dialog, click the **Metric** tab and then the **Simple** tab.
25. Select **Hole Type > Drill**, and then select **Drill size > 10**.
26. Select **Termination > Through** all.

27. Select the sketch points, and then click the green check on the **Hole** dialog

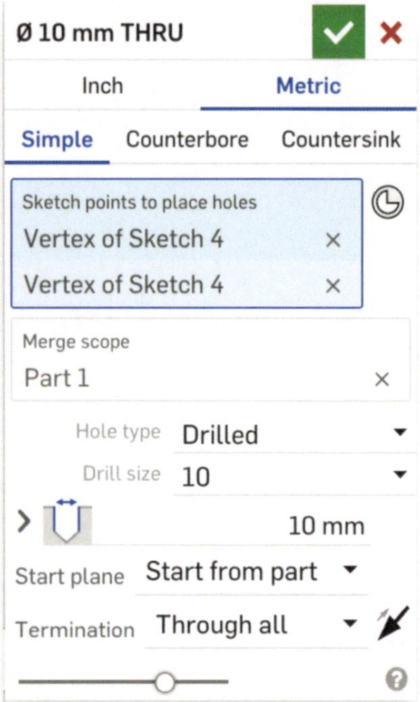

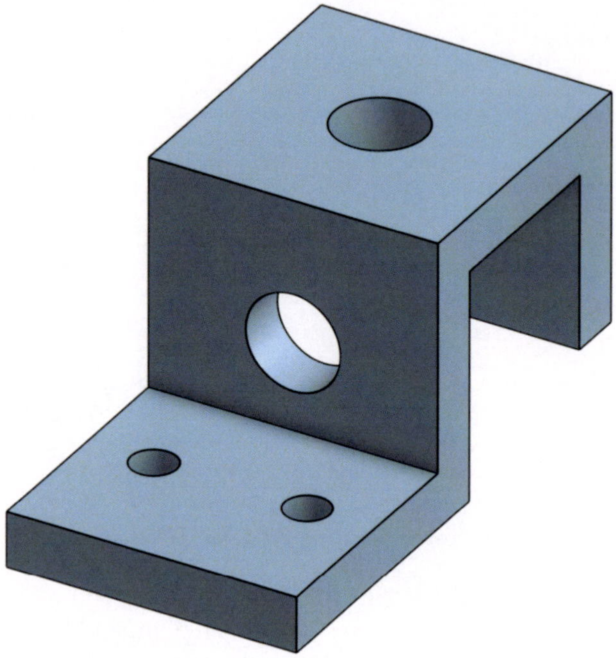

Creating Chamfers and Fillets

1. Click the **Chamfer** command on the Toolbar.
2. On the **Chamfer 1** dialog, select **Chamfer type > Two distances**.
3. Click on the vertical edges of the model, as shown.
4. Set the **Distance 1** and **Distance 2** to **10** and **20**, respectively. Click the green check on the dialog.

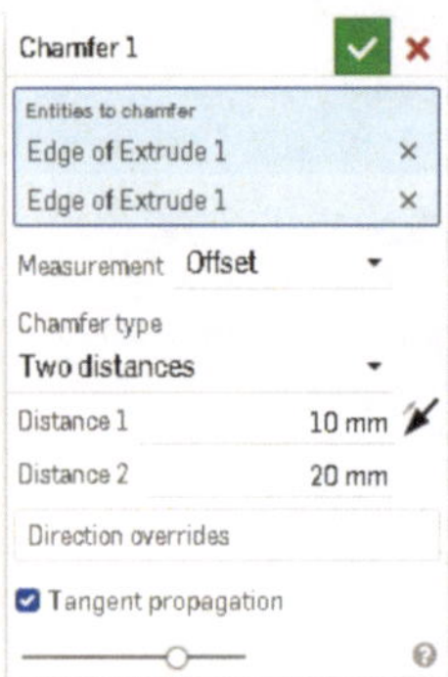

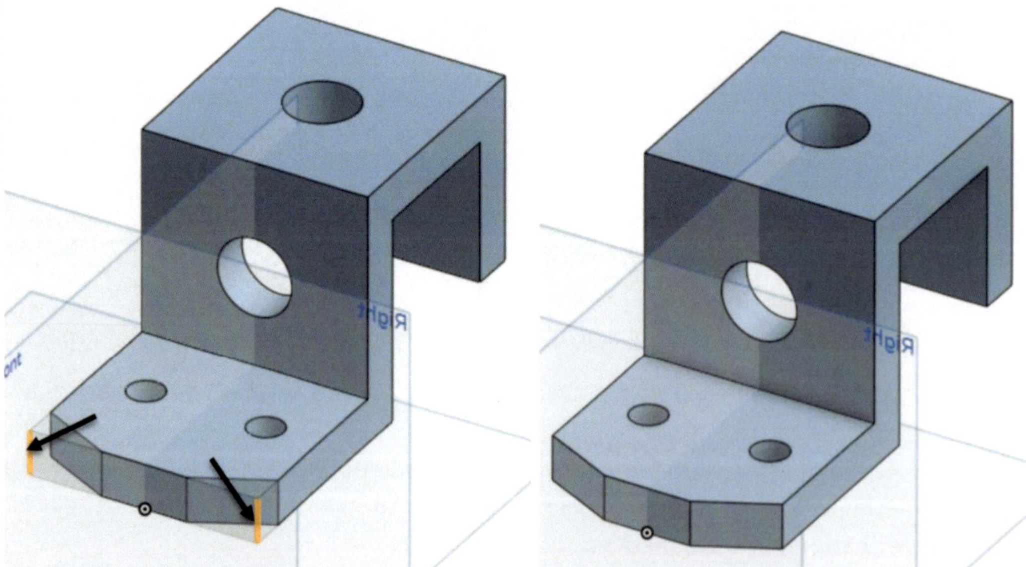

5. Click the **Fillet** command on the Toolbar.
6. On the **Fillet 1** dialog, select **Measurement > Radius**.

7. Click on the horizontal edges of the geometry, as shown below (press and hold the right mouse button and drag to rotate the model).

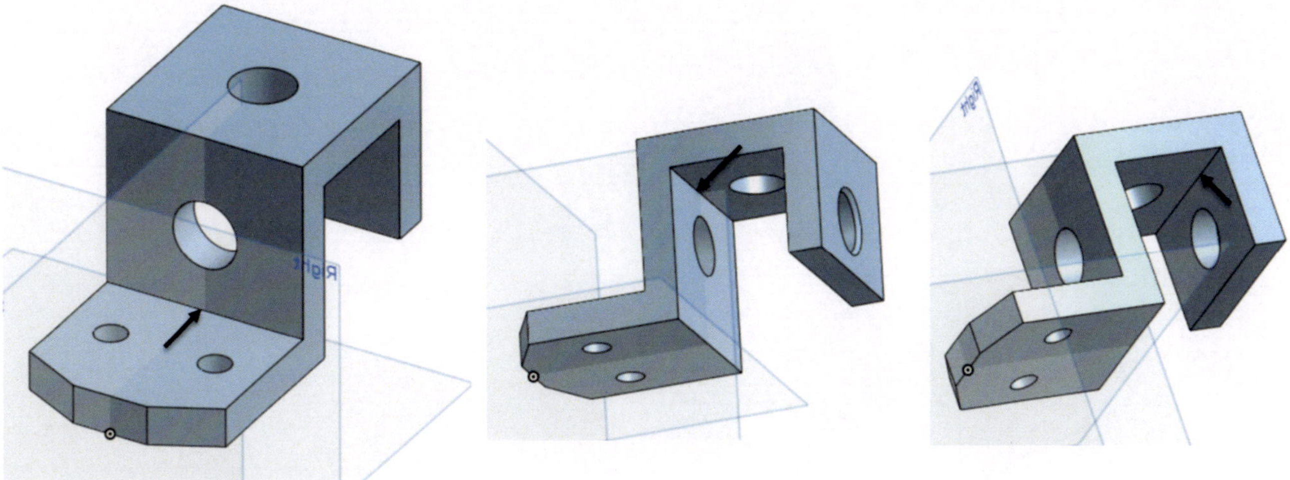

8. Type-in **8** in the **Radius** box, and then click the green check.

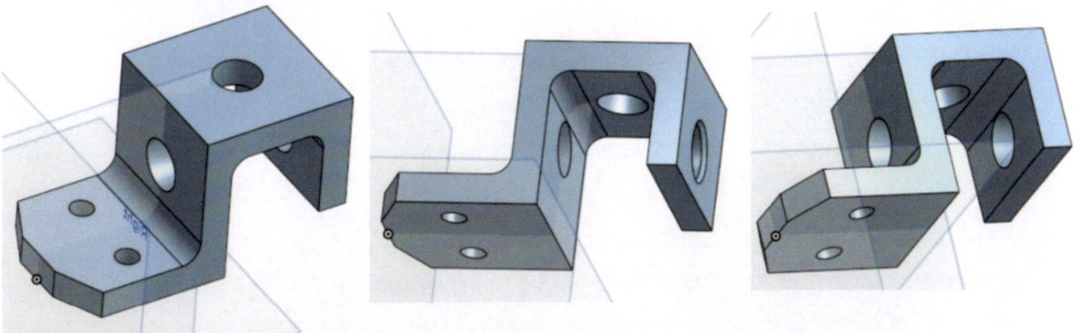

9. Activate the **Fillet** command, and then click on the outer edges of the model, as shown below.

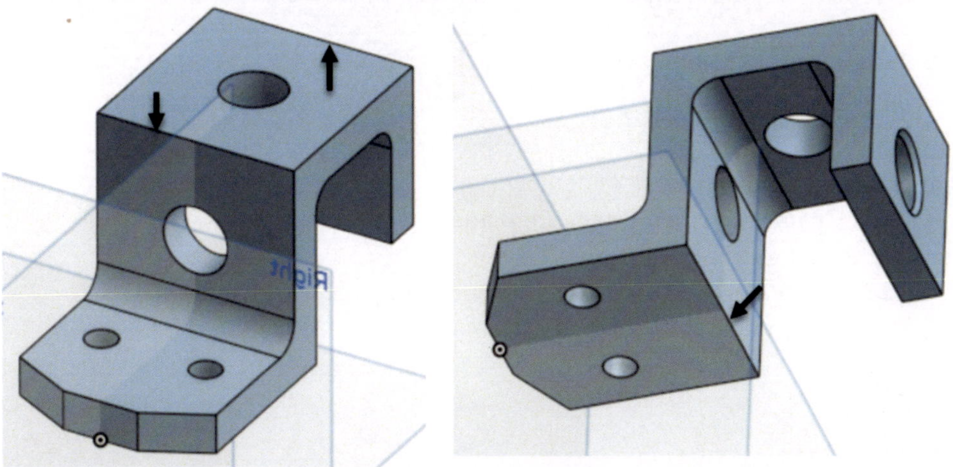

10. Type-in **20** in the **Radius** box. Click the green check to complete the fillet feature.

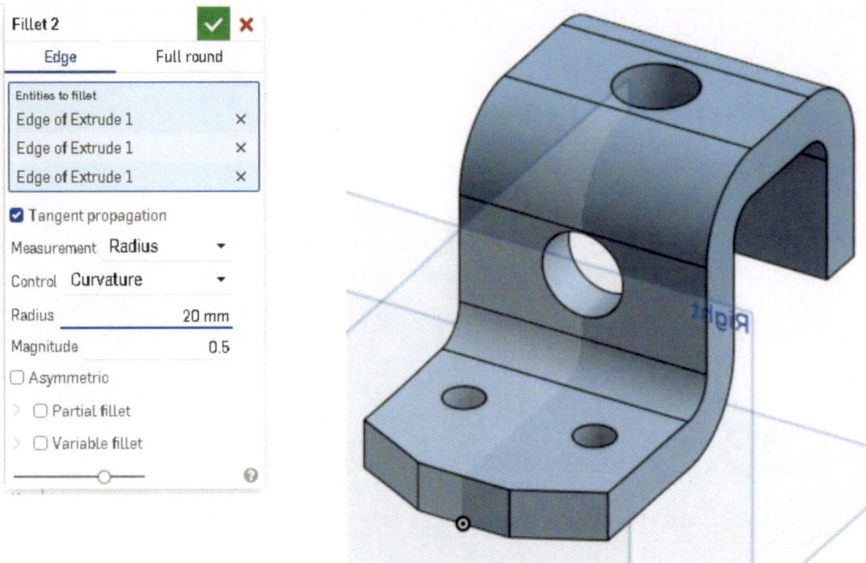

11. Change the orientation of the model view to Isometric by clicking the **Camera and Render options** drop-down, and selecting the **Isometric** option.

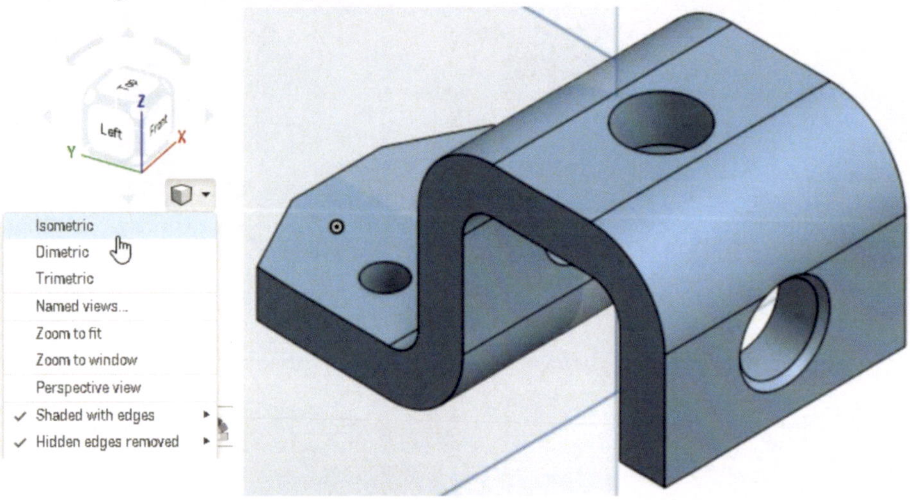

12. Click the **Chamfer** command on the Toolbar.
13. On the **Chamfer 1** dialog, select **Chamfer type > Distance and angle**.
14. Click on the lower corners of the part geometry.
15. Type-in **10** and **45** in the **Distance** and **Angle** boxes. Next, click the green check to chamfer the edges.

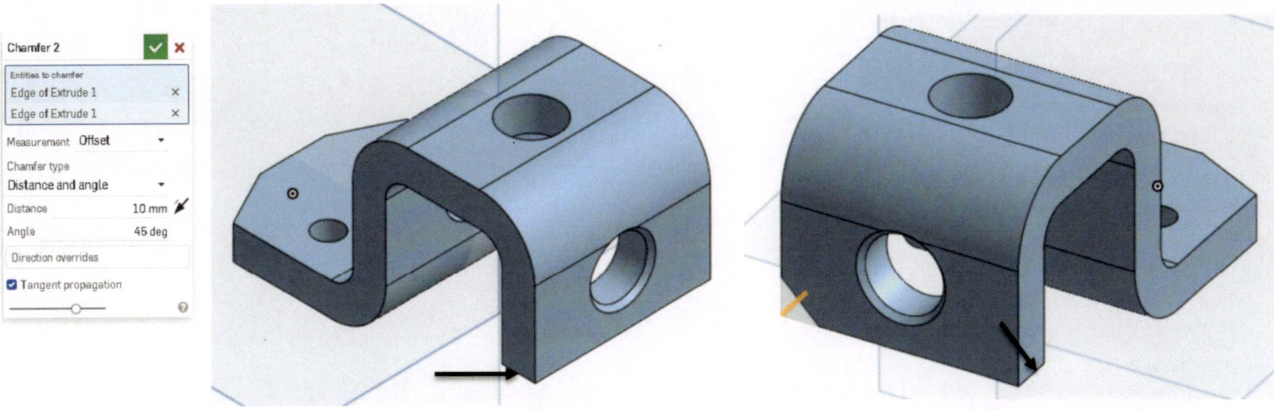

Tutorial 2

In this tutorial, you will create the model given below.

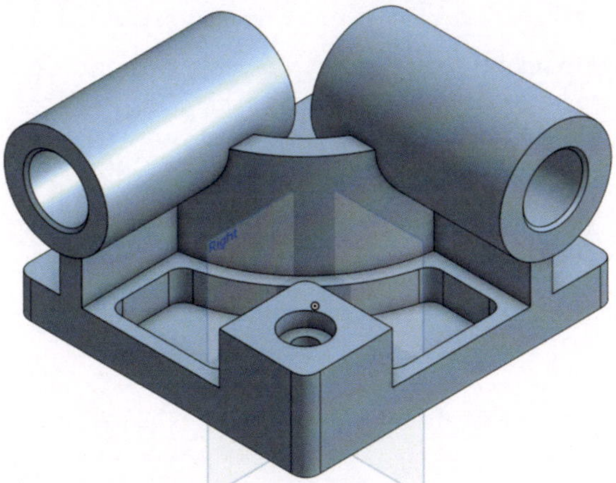

Creating a New document

1. In your Internet Browser, go to https://www.onshape.com to start Onshape.
2. Next, click SIGN IN button located on the top right corner side of the web page. Enter the username and password, and then, click Sign in.
3. On the Documents page, click **Create > Folder**. Next, type Examples in the Folder name box and then click Create.
4. Double-click on the Examples folder in the **Folders** section; the folder appears.
5. On the Documents page, click **Create > Document**; the New document dialog appears on the screen.
6. Enter Tutorial 1 in the **Document name** box and click **Create public document**; a new document appears.
7. Click the **Document** menu located at the top left corner of the window and select **Workspace Units**; the **Workspace Units** dialog appears on the screen.
8. On the **Workspace Units** dialog, select **Length default unit> Millimeter** from the **Length** section.
9. Select **Mass default unit > Gram** from the **Mechanical** section.
10. Leave the other default settings and click the green check.

In Onshape, you define global variables in Variable Studio, and use those variables in Part Studio or Assembly Studio by entering #VariableName directly in dimension or feature fields.

11. To define global variables, click **Insert New tab** and select **Create Variable Studio** on the taskbar.

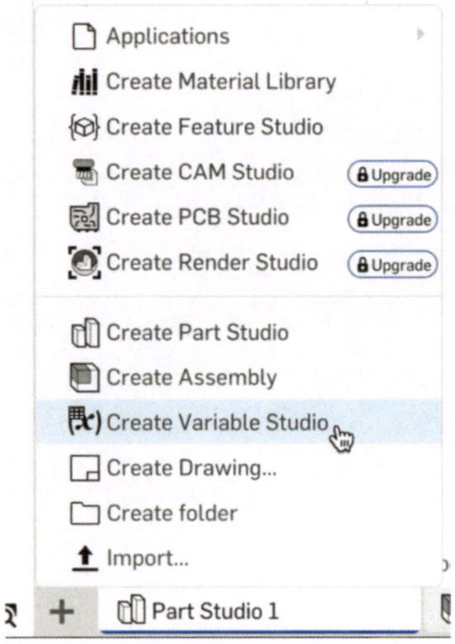

12. In the **Variable Studio** table, click in the field under the **Name** node and then type **A**.
13. Next, select **Variable Type > Length** field next to the A field.
14. Type **213** in the **Value** field next to it.
15. Likewise, create other global variables with the values, as shown.

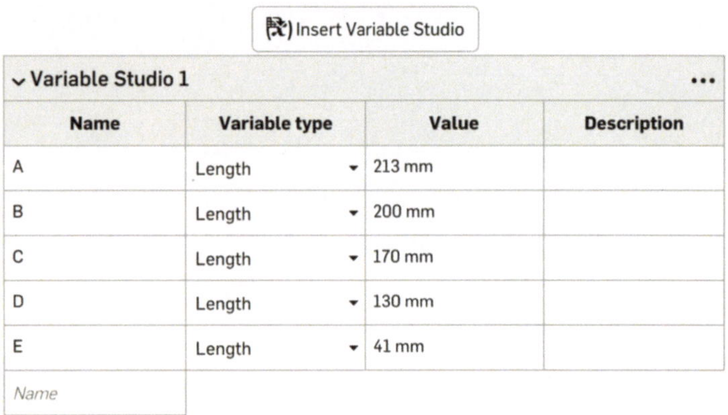

Name	Variable type	Value	Description
A	Length	213 mm	
B	Length	200 mm	
C	Length	170 mm	
D	Length	130 mm	
E	Length	41 mm	
Name			

16. Click in the field below the **E** global variable under the **Name** node, and then type **X**.
17. Next, select **Length** from the **Variable type** next to it.
18. In the **Value** field, type **A** and select the global variable **(x) #A**.
19. Next, type **/3** and press ENTER.

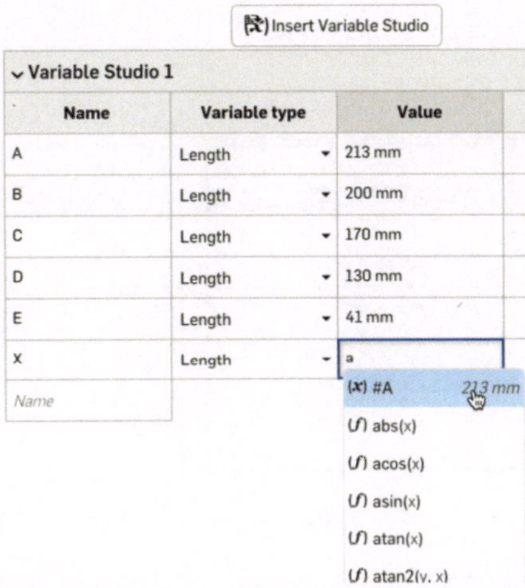

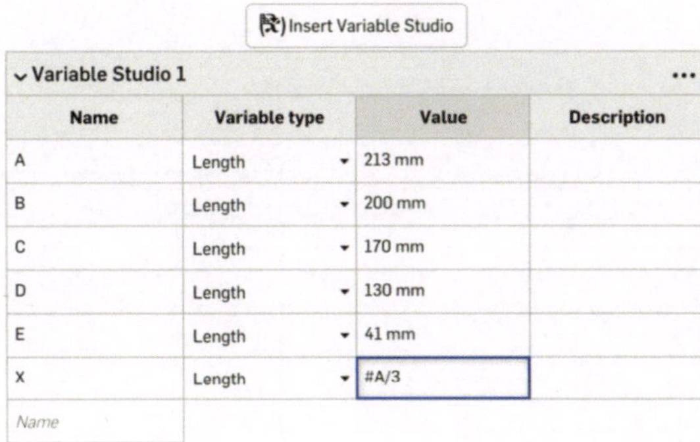

As an alternative, type the full expression **#A/3** directly into the Value field and press ENTER.

20. Click in the field below the **X** global variable under the **Nam**e column, and then type **Y**.
21. Next, select **Length** from the **Variable type** next to it.
22. Click the **Value** field and type **(#B/3)+(10 mm)**. Press Enter. Onshape automatically calculates the value from the expression and populates the result in the **Value** field.

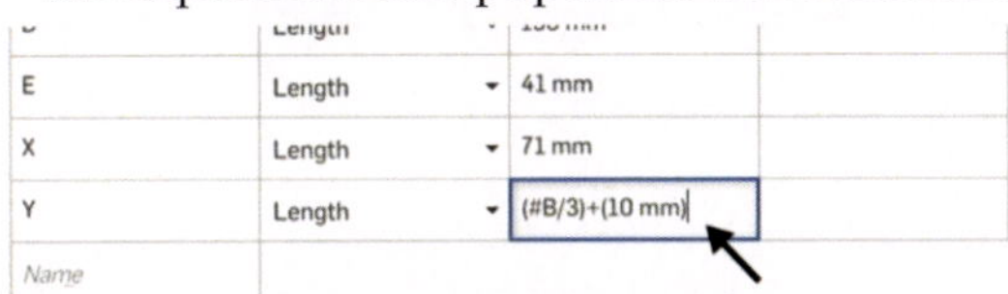

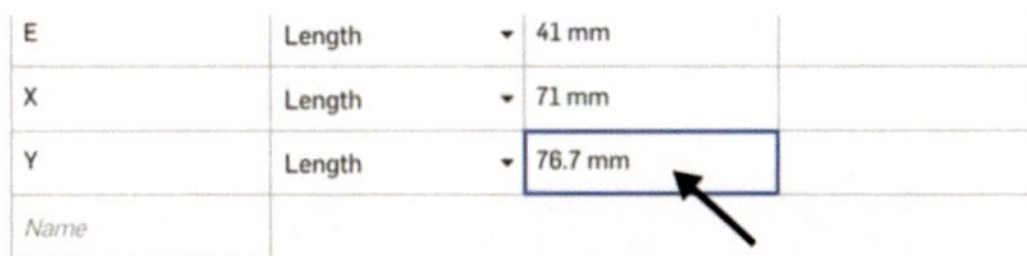

23. Switch to the **Part Studio** from the taskbar at the bottom.
24. Activate the **Sketch** command and click on the **Top** plane from the graphics area.
25. On the Toolbar, click **Rectangle** drop-down > **Center Point Rectangle**. Next, select the sketch origin and move the pointer outward.
26. On the Toolbar, click the **Dimension**  command.
27. Select the vertical line, move the pointer towards left, and click. Next, type in **A** in the dimension box and select **(x) #A**. Next, press Enter.
28. Select the bottom horizontal line, move the pointer downwards, and click.
29. Type **B** in the dimension box and select (x) #B. Next, press Enter.

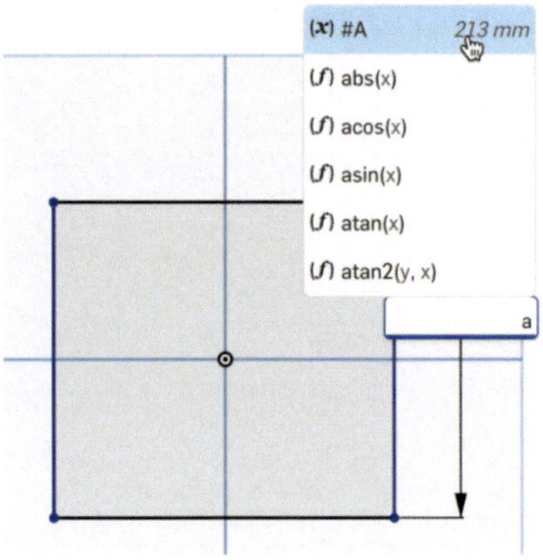

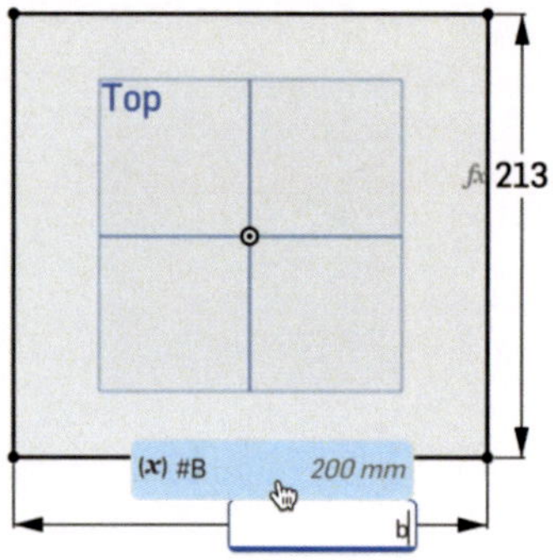

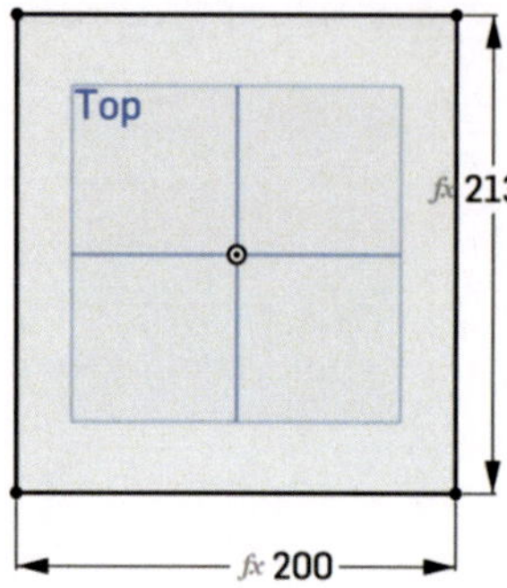

30. On the **Sketch 1** dialog, click the green check.
31. Change the view orientation to Isometric view. (In the graphics area, click the **Camera and render options > Isometric** from the right-side).
32. Click the **Extrude** command on the Toolbar; the **Extrude** dialog pops-up on the screen.
33. Select the sketch from the graphics area.
34. Type **25** in the **Depth** box and click green check on the dialog.

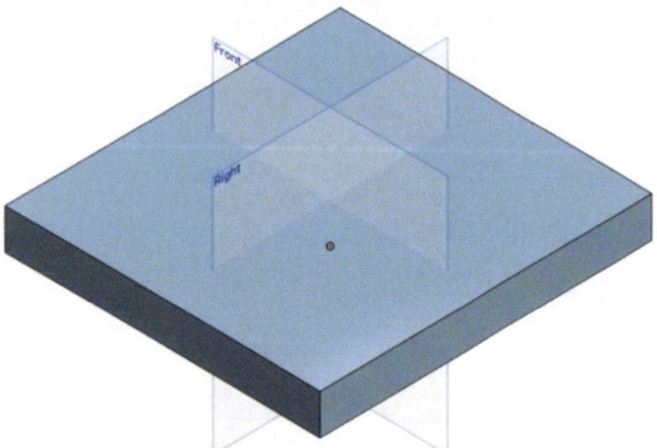

35. Activate the **Sketch** command and click on the top face of the Extruded feature.
36. On the Toolbar, click **Rectangle** drop-down > **Corner Rectangle**.
37. Select the lower right corner of the model. Next, move the pointer toward left and click as shown.
38. Add dimensions to the rectangle, as shown. Next, click green check on the **Sketch2** dialog.

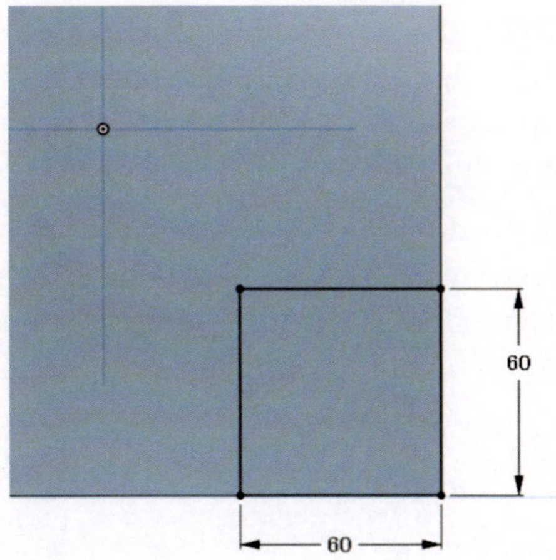

39. On the Toolbar, click **Extrude** command and select the recently created sketch from the graphics area.
40. Type **35** in the **Depth** box and click green check ✓.

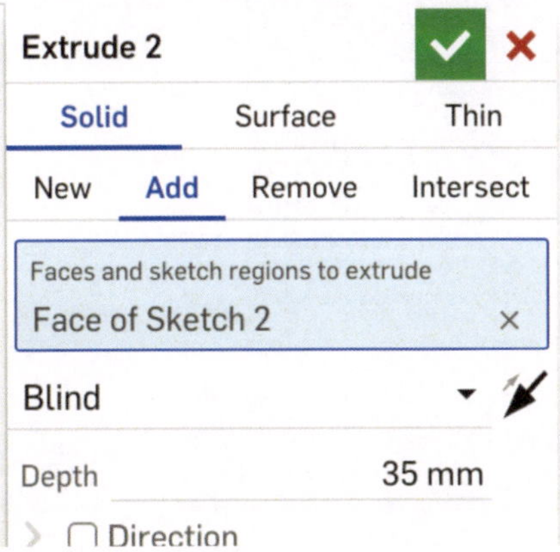

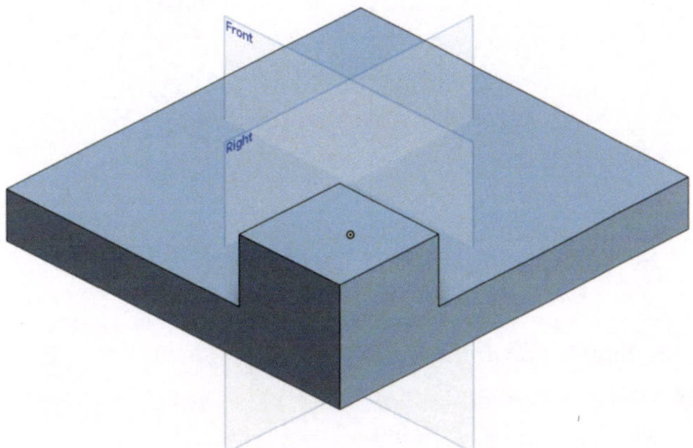

41. Right-click on the **Top** plane in the **Features** window and select **New Sketch**.
42. Click right mouse button anywhere in the graphics area and select **View normal to sketch plane** option.

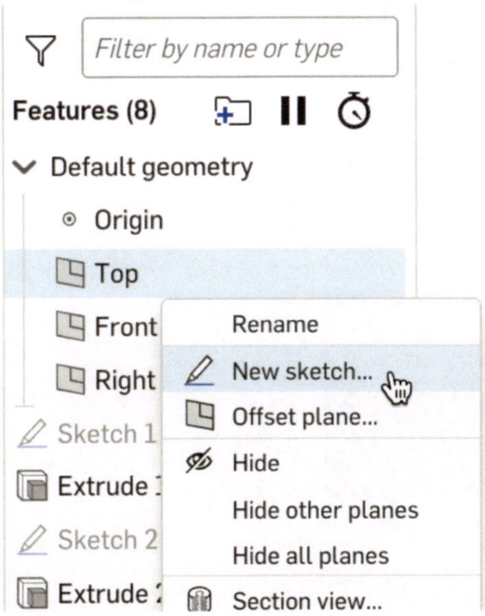

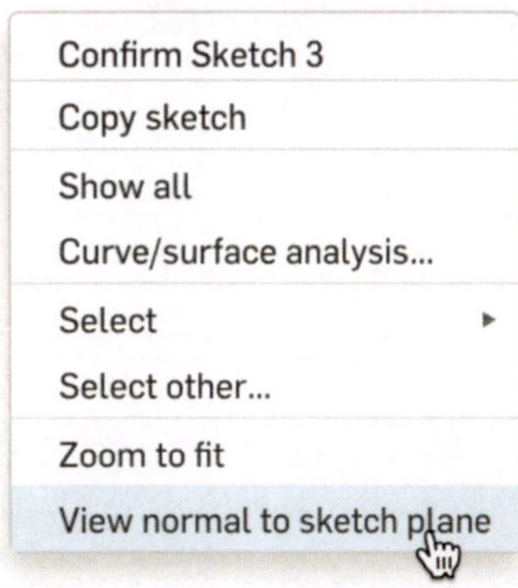

43. On the Toolbar, select the **Line** command.
44. Click on the left vertical edge of the model, as shown.
45. Move the pointer horizontally toward right and click.
46. Move the pointer vertically downward and click on the horizontal edge, as shown.
47. On the Toolbar, click **Arc** drop-down **> Center point arc** .
48. Select the intersection point between the horizontal and vertical line.
49. Click on the vertical line to define the start point of the arc.
50. Move the pointer and click on the horizontal line to define the end point of the arc.

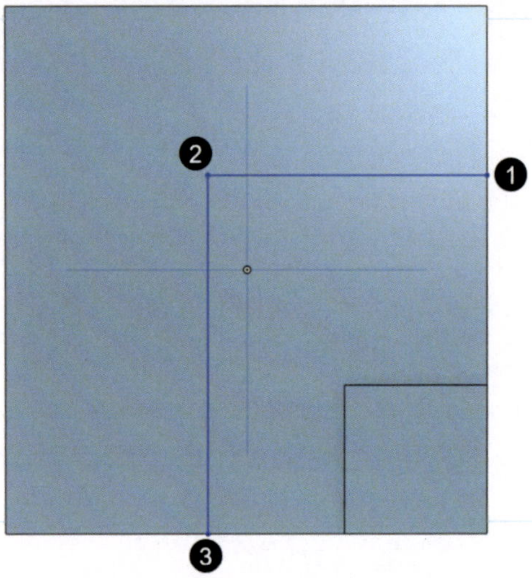

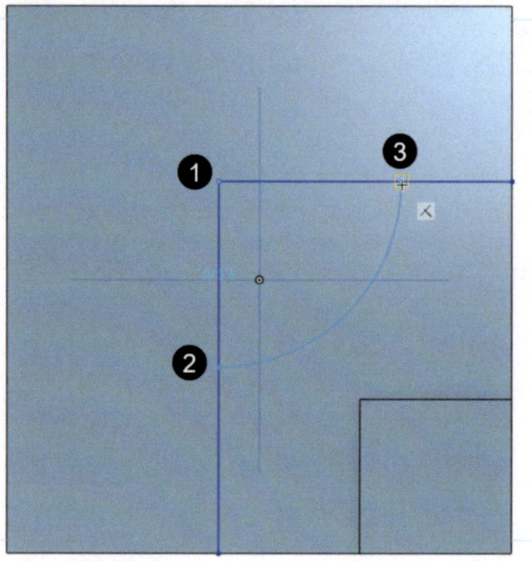

51. Click the **Trim** command on the Toolbar and select the portions of vertical and horizontal lines, as shown.
52. Activate the **Dimension** command and select the horizontal edge. Next, select the horizontal line, as shown.
53. Move the pointer towards right and click.

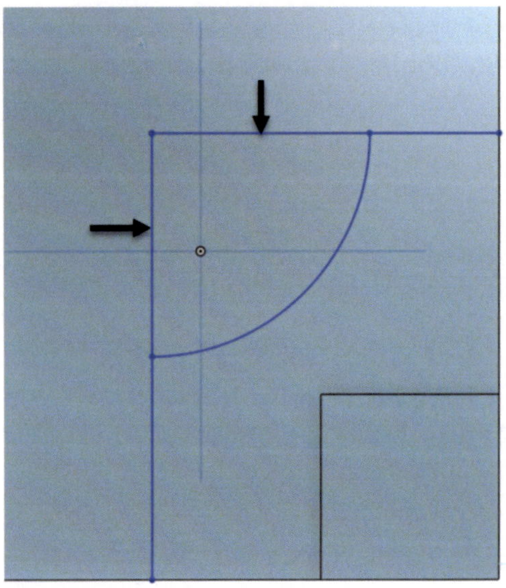

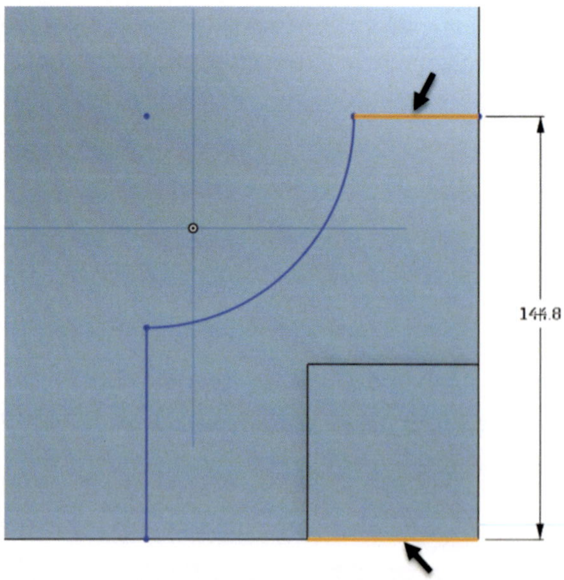

54. Type **#C** in the value box and press Enter.
55. Likewise, create a dimension between the vertical edge and the vertical line using the global variable C.
56. Add dimensions to the vertical and horizontal lines, as shown.

57. On the Toolbar, click the **Horizontal** constraint and select the centerpoint of the arc and end point of the horizontal line.

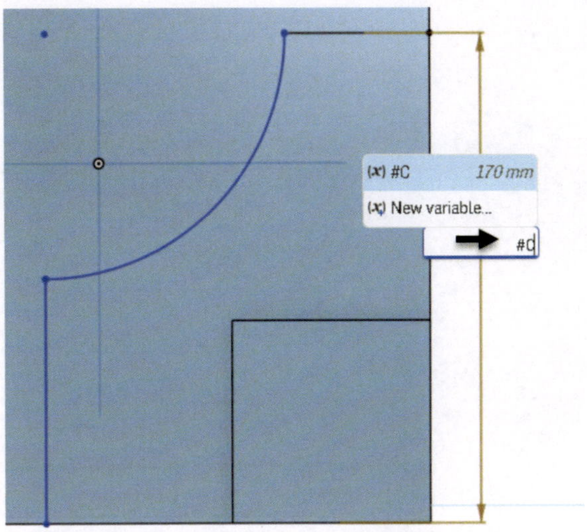

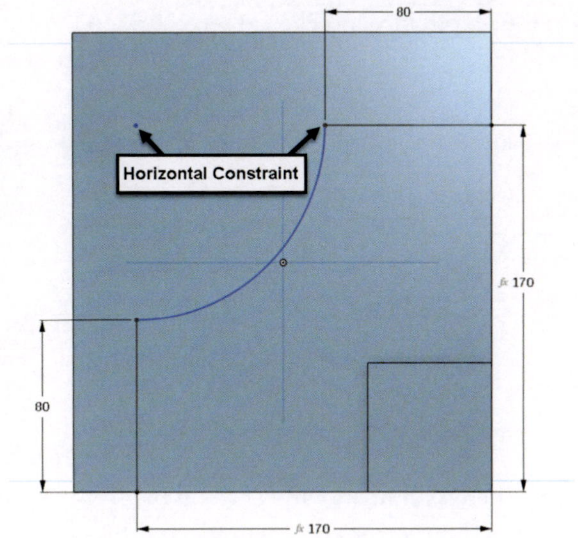

58. Click **Offset** on the Toolbar.
59. Right-click in the graphics window and select **Select > Create Selection**. Select an element from the sketch. Next, click the **Edges** tab and select **Loop/chain connected** option from the drop-down. Click the **Add selection** button.
60. Double-click on the offset value and type **15** in the box. Press Enter.
61. Next, click on the arrow displayed to reverse the offset direction, if the arrow is pointing outwards.
62. Activate the **Line** command and close the cap ends, as shown.

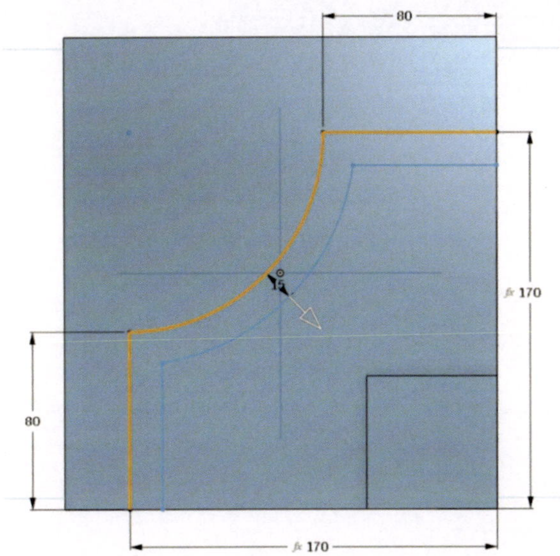

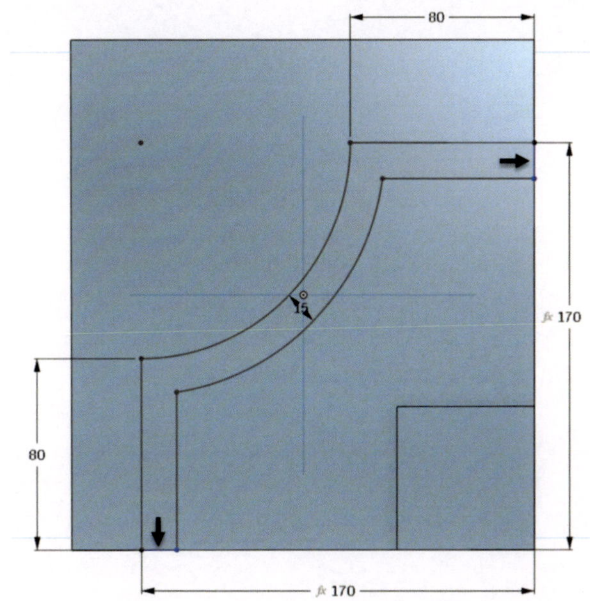

63. Click the green check on the **Sketch3** dialog.

64. Change the view orientation to Isometric view. (In the graphics area, click the **Camera and render options > Isometric** from the right-side).
65. Activate the **Extrude** command and select the sketch from the graphics area.
66. Type **95** in the **Depth** box and click green check on the **Extrude 3** dialog.

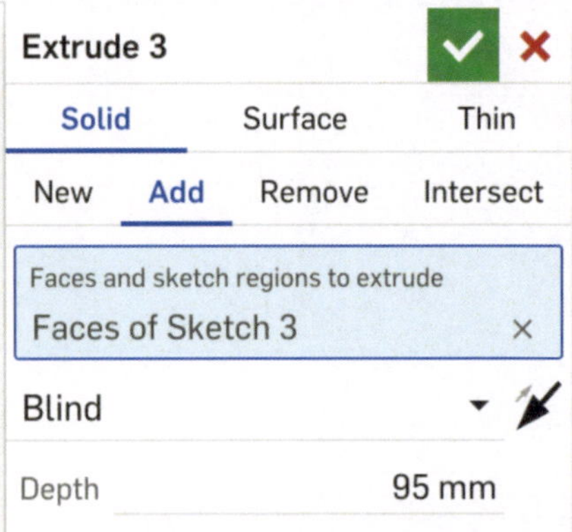

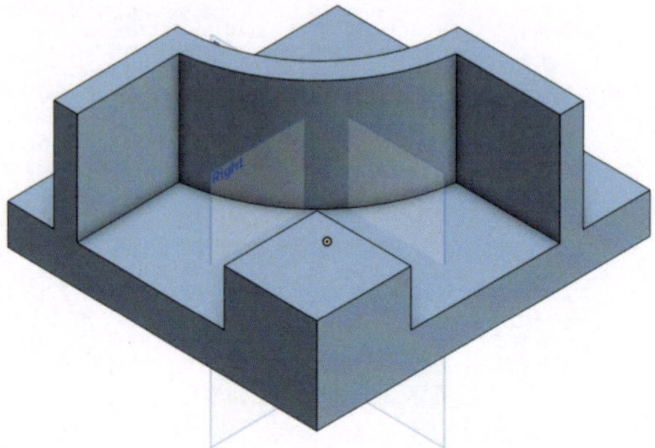

67. Activate the **Sketch** command and click on the front face of the model, as shown.
68. Click right mouse button anywhere in the graphics area and select **View normal to sketch plane** option.
69. On the Toolbar, click **Circle drop-down > Center point circle**.
70. Select the midpoint of the small horizontal edge, as shown.

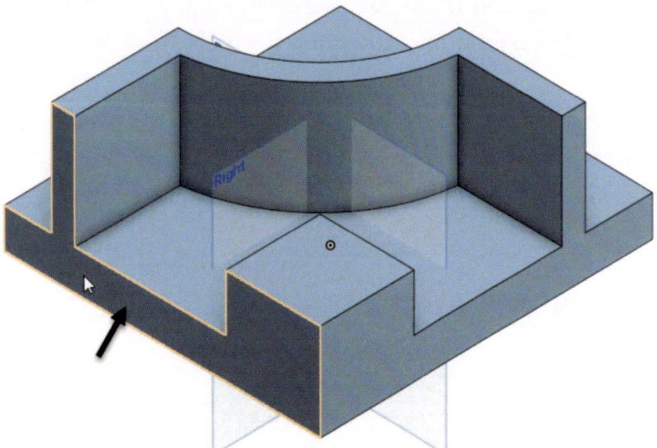

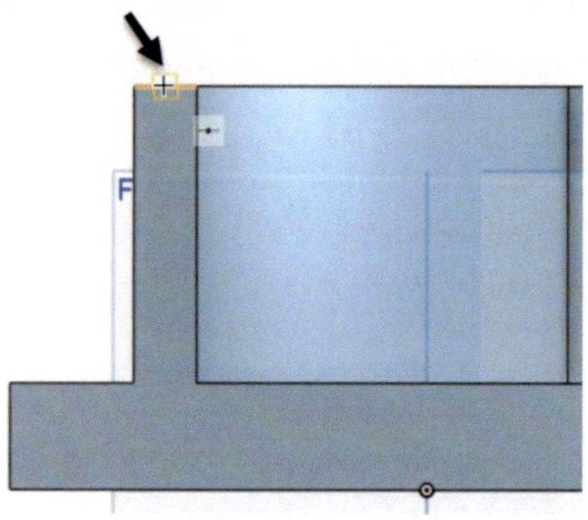

71. Move the pointer outwards and click to create the circle.
72. Activate the **Dimension** command and select the circle.
73. Move the pointer and click to position the dimension.
74. Type **#X** in the box and press Enter twice.

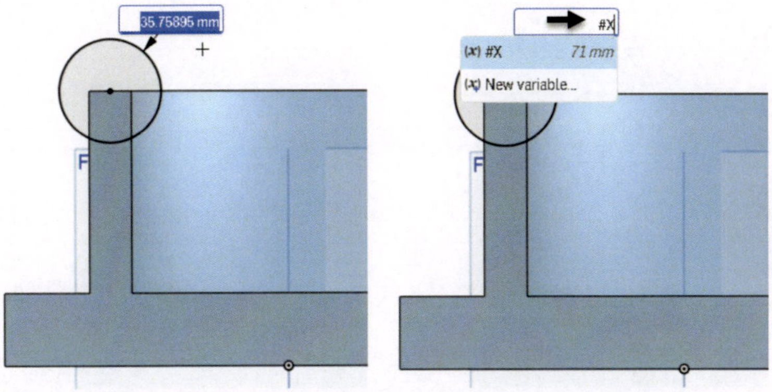

75. Click the **green check** on the **Sketch 4** dialog and change the view orientation to isometric.
76. Activate the **Extrude** command and select the sketch from the Features tree.
77. Select **End type > Blind** and click **Opposite direction** icon next to it.
78. Type **#D** in the **Depth** box.
79. Select the **Starting Offset** option and type **10** in the **Depth** box, as shown.
80. Click green check on the **Extrude 4** dialog.

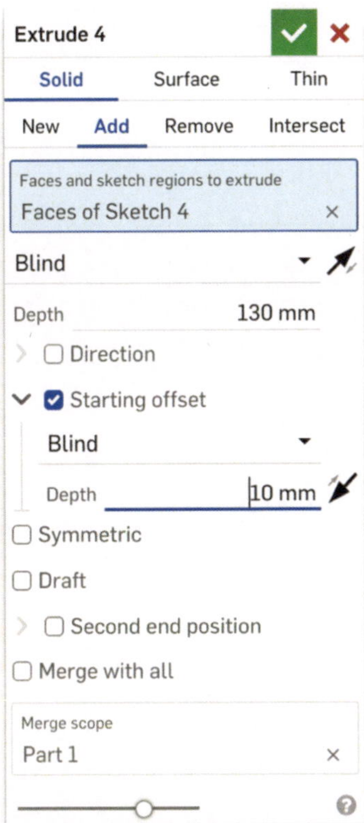

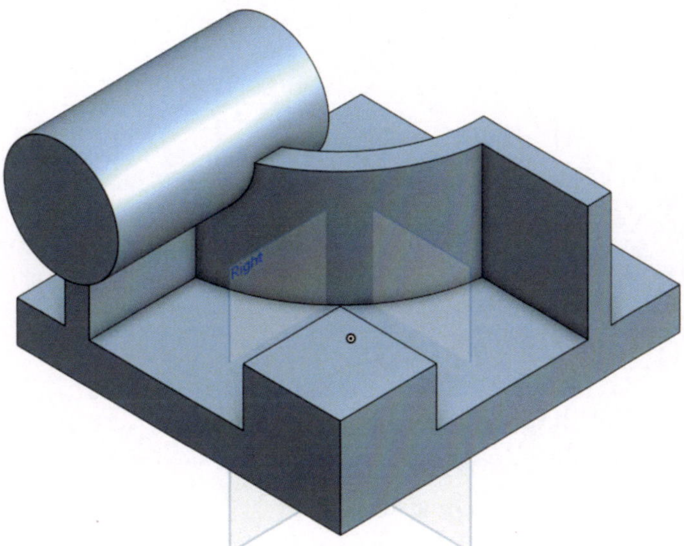

81. Activate the **Sketch** command and right face of the model, as shown.
82. Right-click anywhere in the graphics area and select the **View normal to sketch plane** option.
83. On the Toolbar, click **Circle drop-down > Center point circle**.
84. Select the midpoint of the small horizontal edge, as shown.

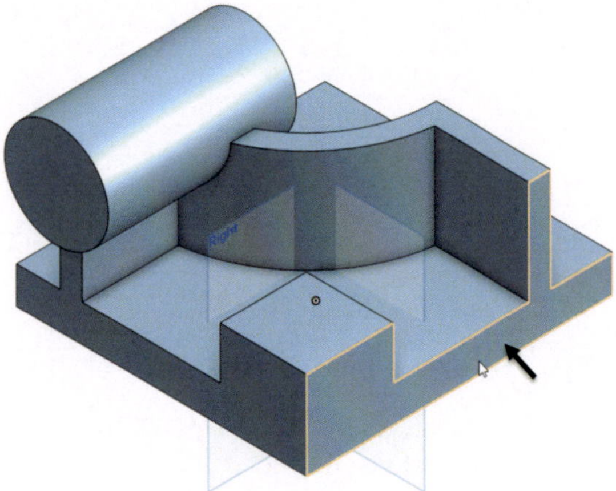

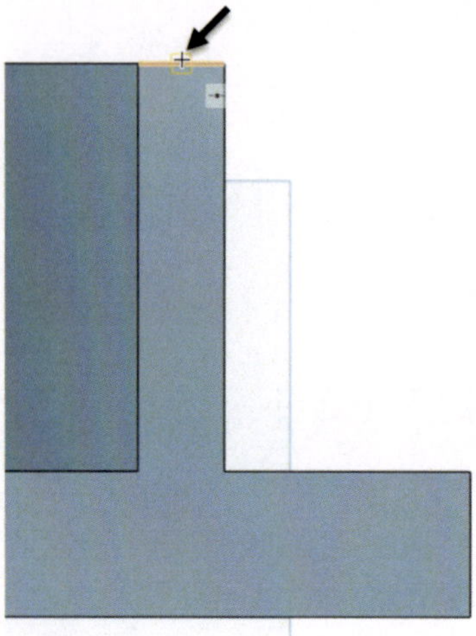

85. Move the pointer outward and click to create the circle.
86. Activate the **Dimension** and select the circle. Move the pointer and click to position the dimension.
87. Type **#Y** in the box and press Enter twice.

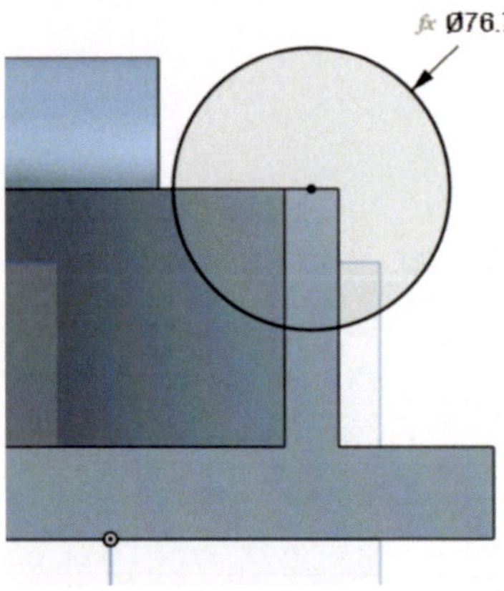

88. Click the green check on the **Sketch 5** dialog.
89. Activate the **Extrude** command and select the recently created sketch from the **Features window.**
90. Select **End type > Blind** and click **Opposite direction** icon next to it.
91. Type **#D** in the **Depth** box.
92. Select the **Starting Offset** option and type **10** in the **Depth** box, as shown.
93. Click the green check on the **Extrude 5** dialog.

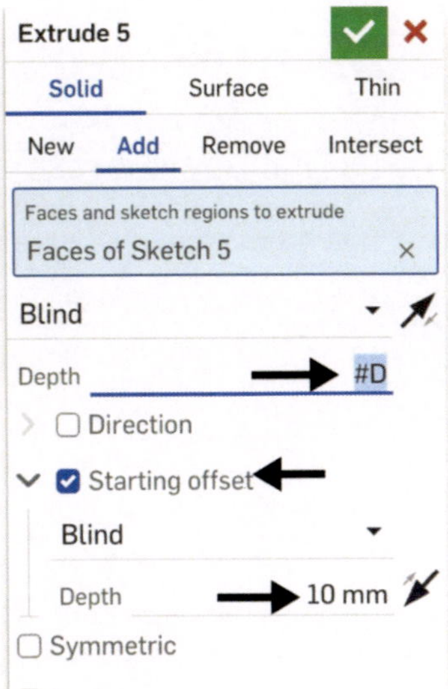

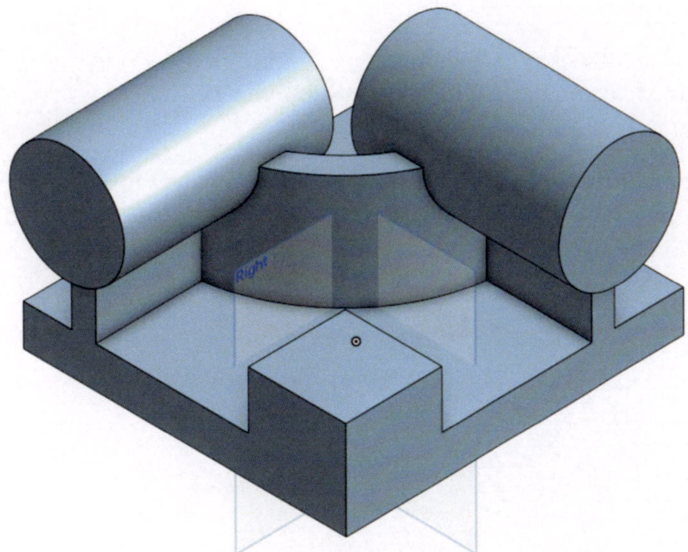

Creating the Fillet

1. Click the **Fillet** command on the Toolbar; a **Fillet** dialog appears on the graphics window.
2. Click on the vertical edge of the geometry, as shown below.
3. Type **9** in the **Radius** box and click green check on the **Fillet 1** dialog.

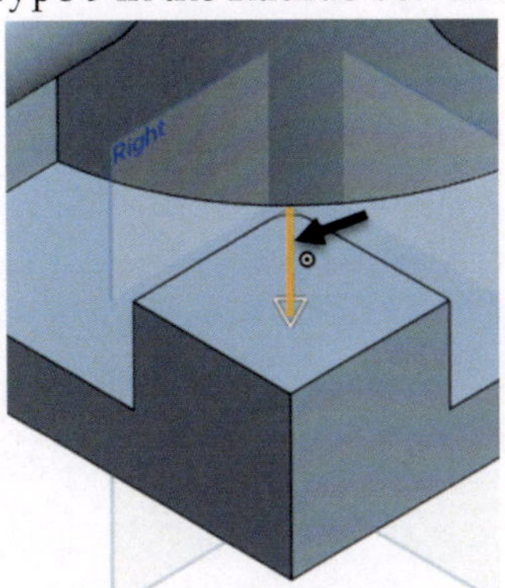

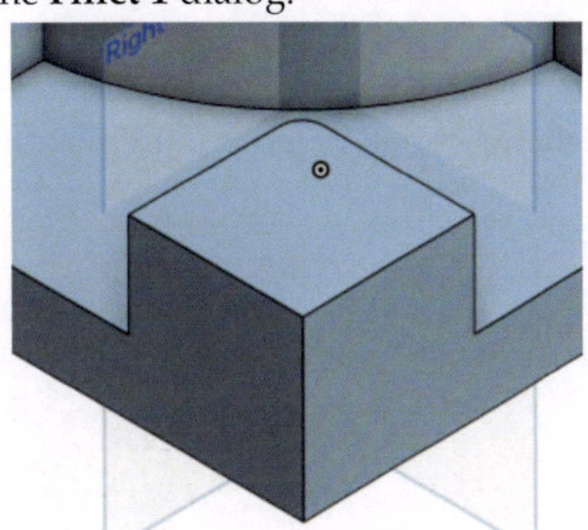

Creating the Extruded Cuts

1. On the Toolbar, click **Sketch** command and select the Top face of the first feature.
2. Click the **Offset** command on the Toolbar, and select the Top face, as shown above.
3. Move the pointer inwards and click.
4. Double-click on the offset value to edit and type **9** in the distance box. Press Enter.

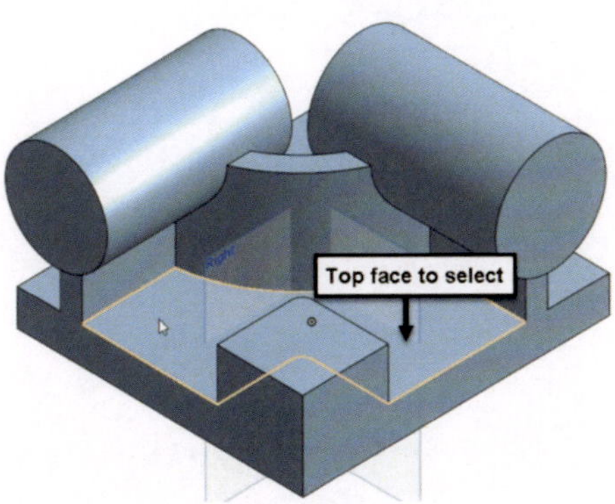

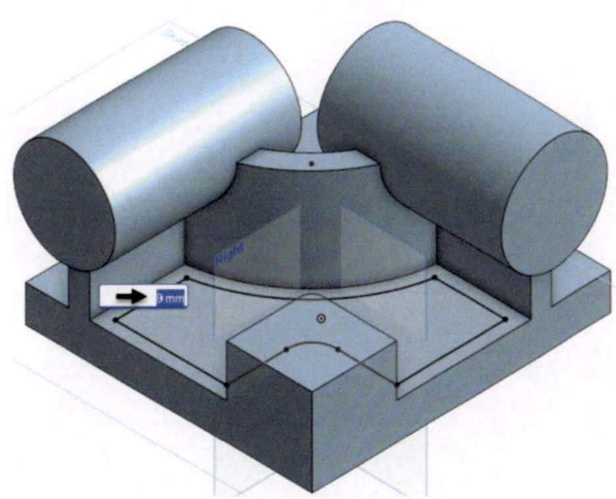

5. Click green check on the **Sketch 6** dialog.
6. Activate the **Extrude** command and click the **Remove** tab.
7. Select the **Offset** sketch from the **Features** window.
8. Select **Up to face** from the **End type** drop-down and click the **Opposite direction** icon next to it.
9. Next, rotate the model and select the bottom face of it, as shown.

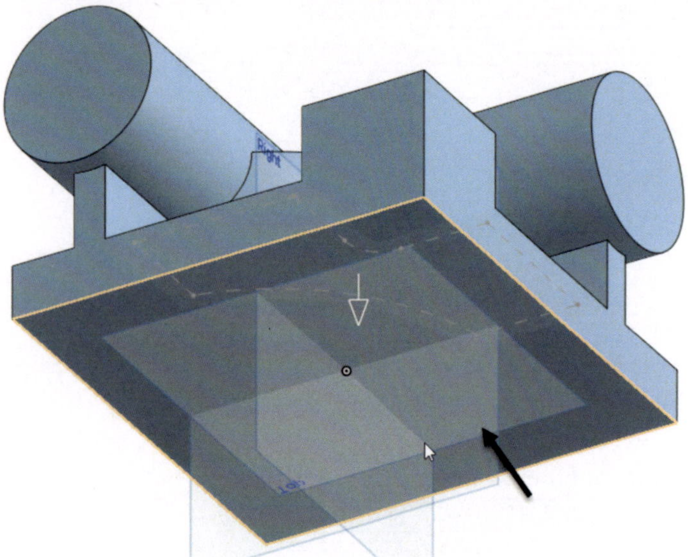

10. Select the **Offset distance** option and type **5** in the offset distance box.

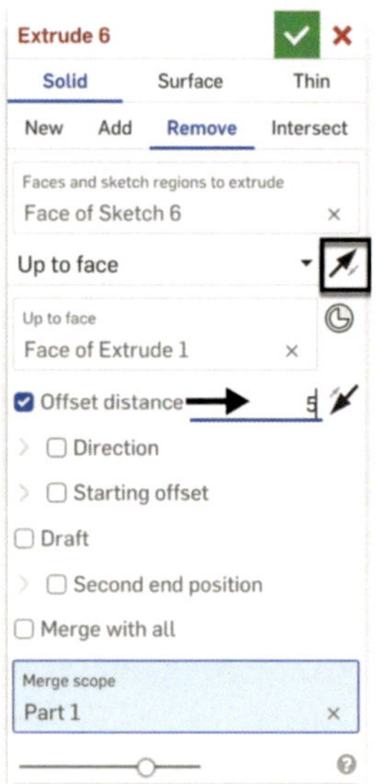

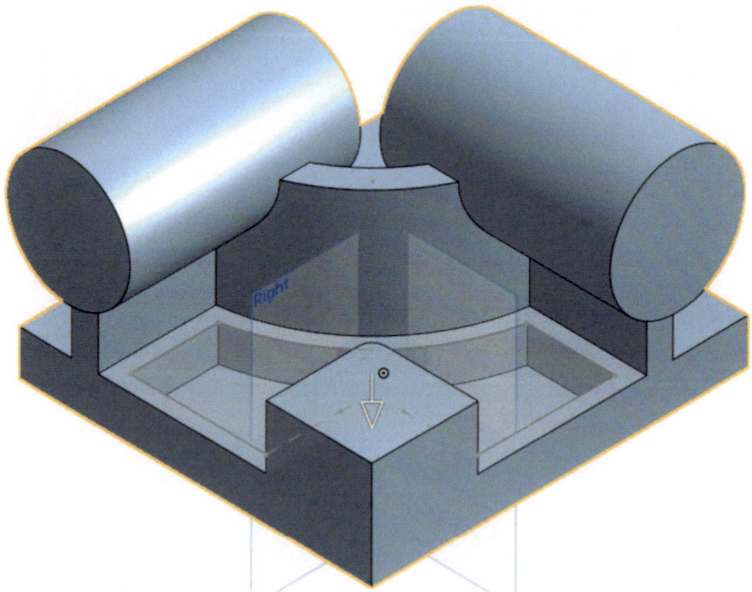

11. Click green check on the **Extrude 6** dialog.
12. Activate the **Sketch** command on the Toolbar and select the front face of the extruded feature, as shown.
13. Right-click anywhere in the graphics area and select the **View normal to sketch plane** option.
14. On the Toolbar, click **Circle** drop-down > **Center point circle**.
15. Click on the centerpoint of the circular edge, as shown.

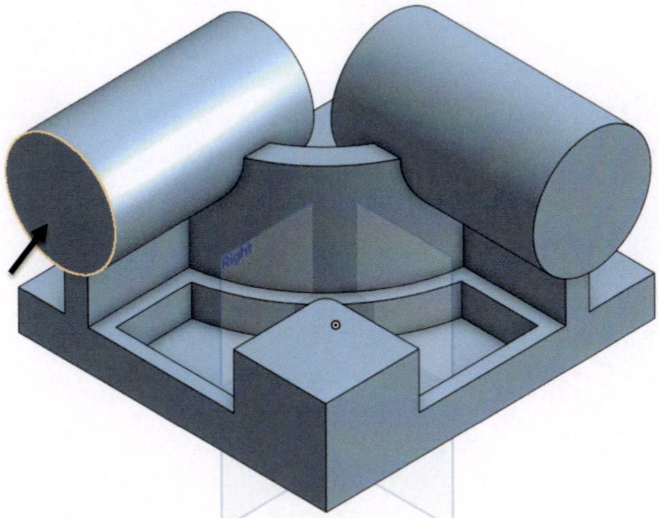

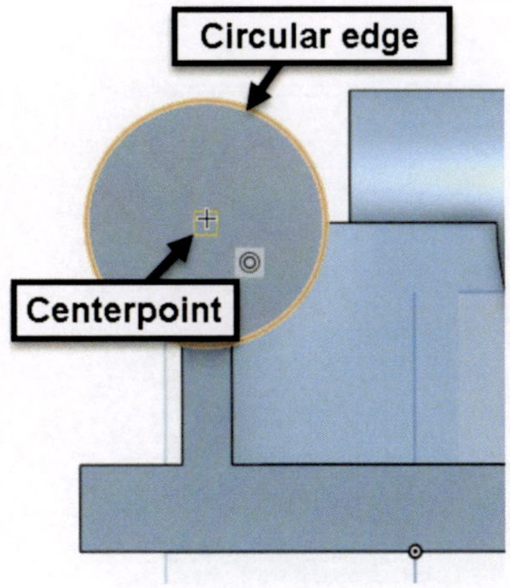

16. Move the pointer outward and click.
17. Activate the **Dimension** command on the Toolbar and select the circle.
18. Move the pointer and click to position the dimension.
19. Type **#E** in the value box and press Enter twice.
20. Click green check ✓ on the **Sketch 7** dialog. Change the view orientation to isometric.
21. On the Toolbar, click **Extrude** command and select the **Remove** tab on the **Extrude** dialog.
22. Select the sketch from the graphics area. Select **End type** drop-down > **Through all** option.
23. Click the green check on the **Extrude 7** dialog.

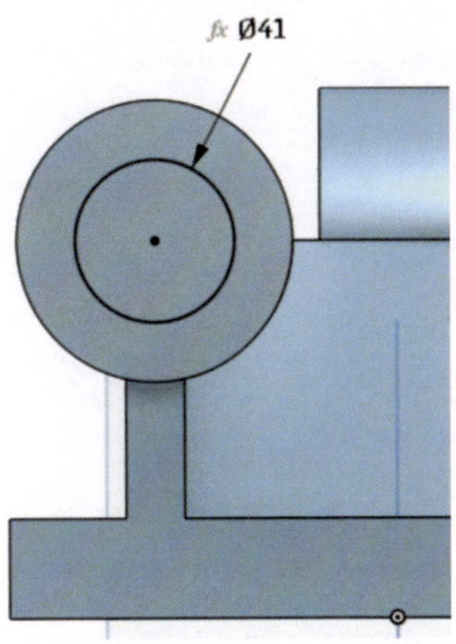

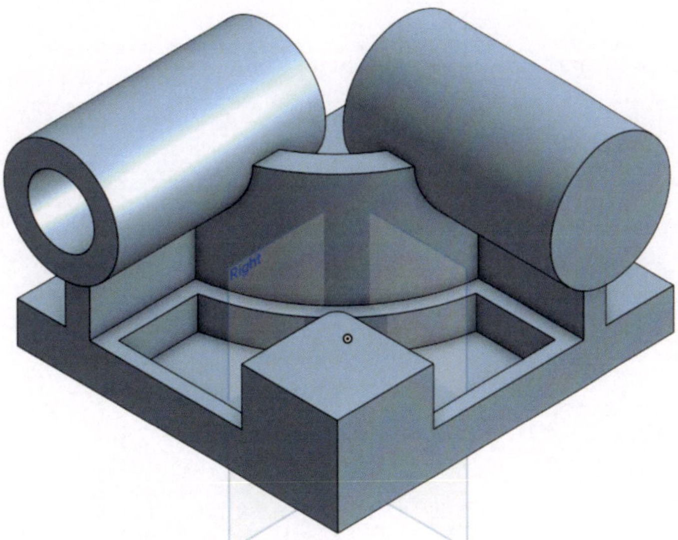

24. Likewise, create the other extruded cut feature, as shown.

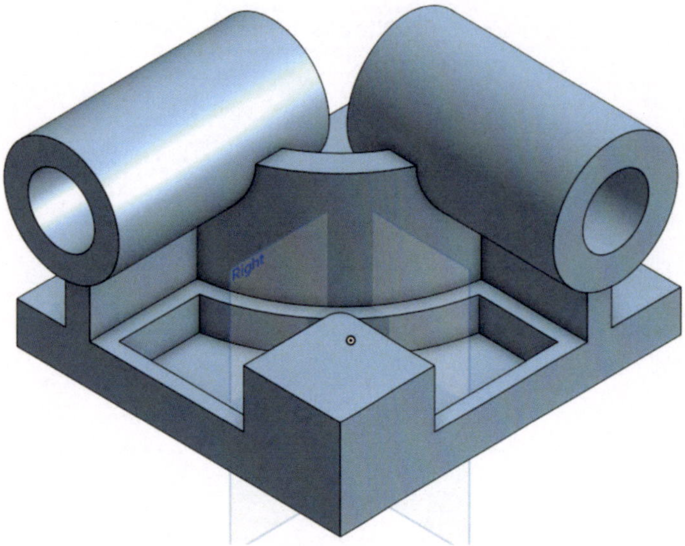

Creating the Hole

1. On the Toolbar, click the **Sketch** command.
2. Click on the top face of the second feature, as shown.
3. Right-click anywhere in the graphics area and select the **View normal to sketch plane** option.
4. On the sketch Toolbar, click the **Point** command. Draw a sketch point on the part geometry.
5. Activate the **Dimension** command and select the sketch point and right vertical edge of the placement face.
6. Move the pointer and click to place the dimension.
7. Next, type **30** in the value box and press Enter.
8. Select the sketch point and bottom edge of the placement face.
9. Move the pointer towards left and click to place the dimension.
10. Type **30** in the value box and press Enter.

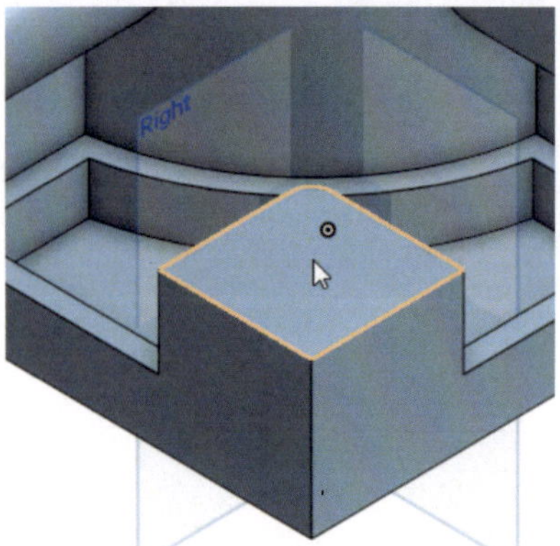

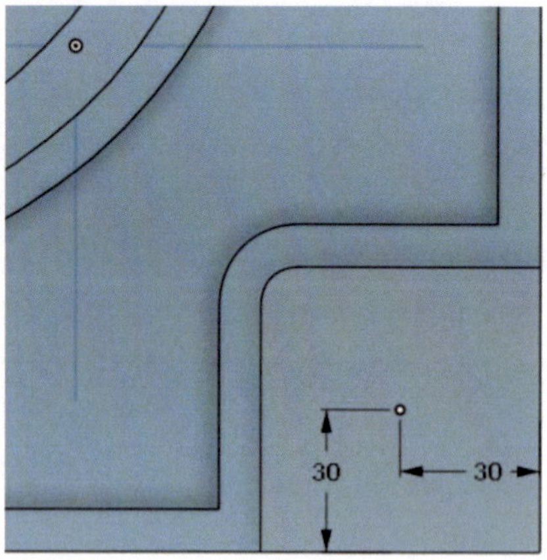

11. Click the green check on the **Sketch 9** dialog.
12. Change the view orientation to isometric.
13. On the Toolbar, click the **Hole** command and select the sketch point.
14. Click the **Metric** tab and the **Counterbore** tab on the **Hole** dialog.
15. Select the **Hole type > Drilled** and **Drill Size > 15**.
16. Select **Through all** from the **Termination** drop-down.
17. Type **30**, and **10** mm in the **Counterbore Diameter** and **Counterbore depth** fields, respectively.
18. Click green check on the **Hole** dialog.

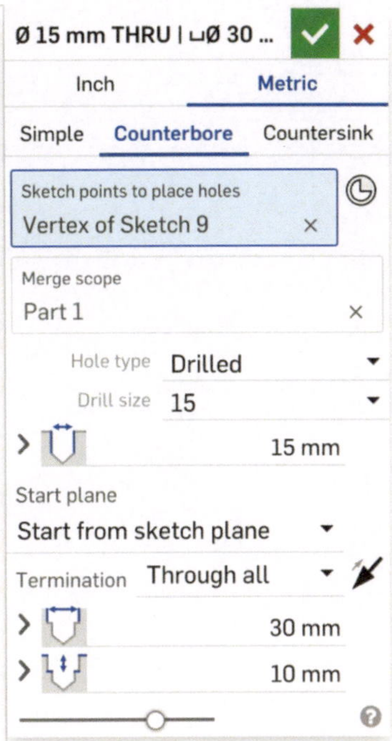

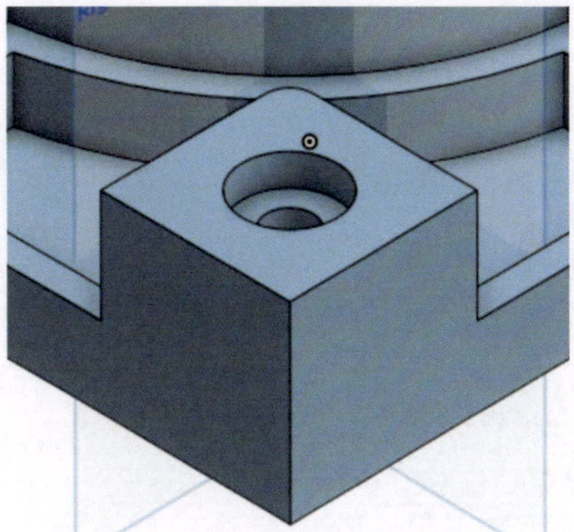

Creating the Fillets and Chamfers

1. On the Toolbar, click the **Fillet** command.
2. Select the vertical edges of the geometry, as shown.

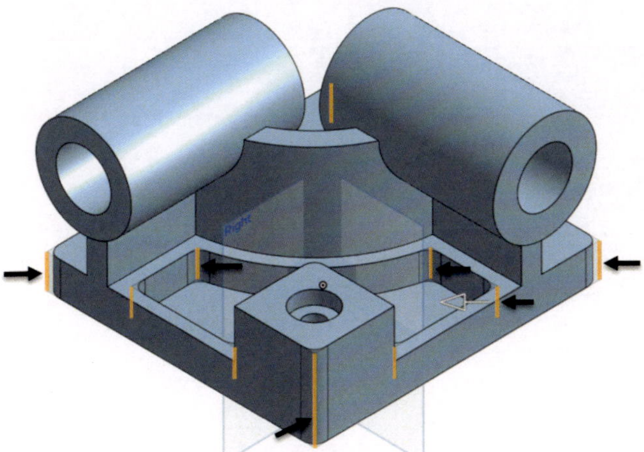

3. Click the **Measurement** drop-down **> Radius** option.
4. Select the **Control > Distance** option.
5. Type-in **10** in the radius box and click green check on the **Fillet** dialog.

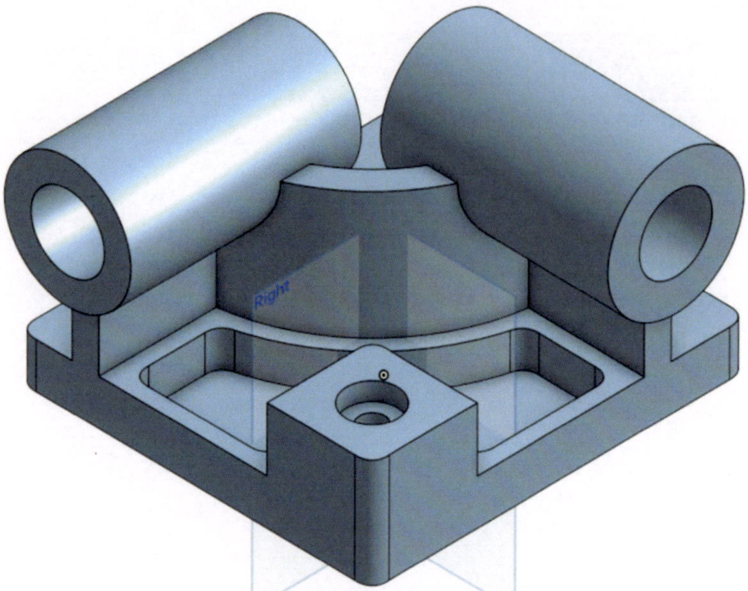

6. Activate the **Chamfer** command on the Toolbar.
7. Select the **Distance and angle** from the **Chamfer type** drop-down.
8. Set the **Distance** and **Angle** to **2** and **45**, respectively.
9. Click on the circular edge of the model, as shown.

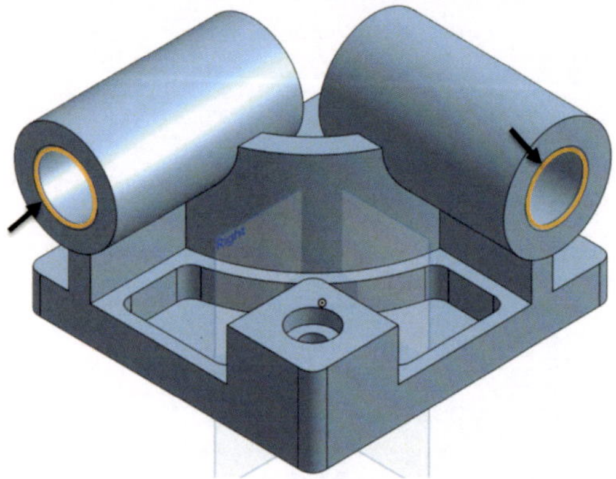

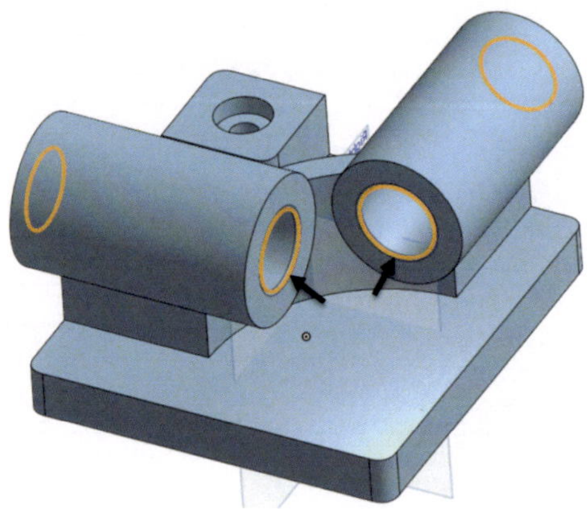

10. Click green check on the **Chamfer** dialog.

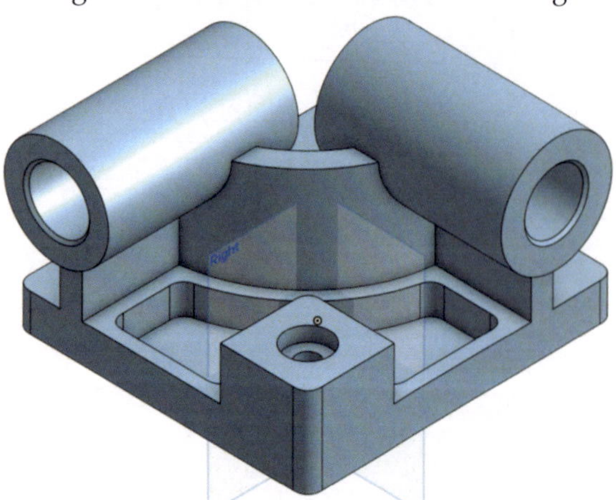

Adding Material to the Model

1. Right click on **Part 1** located at the bottom of the **Instances** window, and then select **Assign material**; the **Material** dialog appears on the screen.
2. Select the **Hardened Alloy Steel** from the **Material** drop-down on the **Material** dialog.
3. Click the green check  on the **Material** dialog to apply.

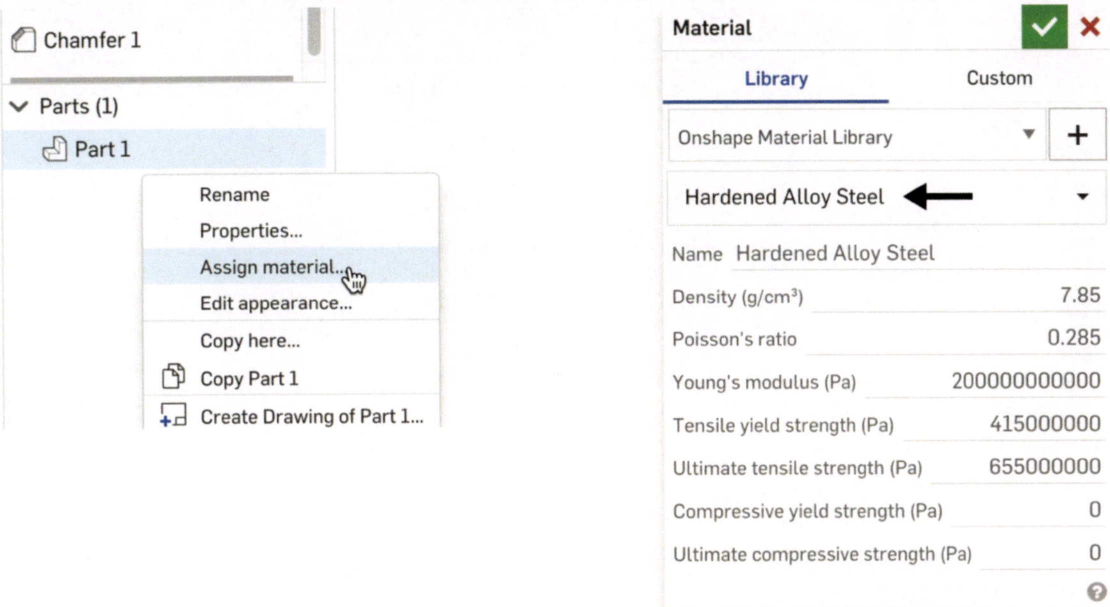

4. Click the **Display mass and section properties** icon located at the bottom right corner of the graphics window and select the **Part 1** from Parts panel.
5. Observe the Mass and section properties and click the **Close** button to close the dialog.

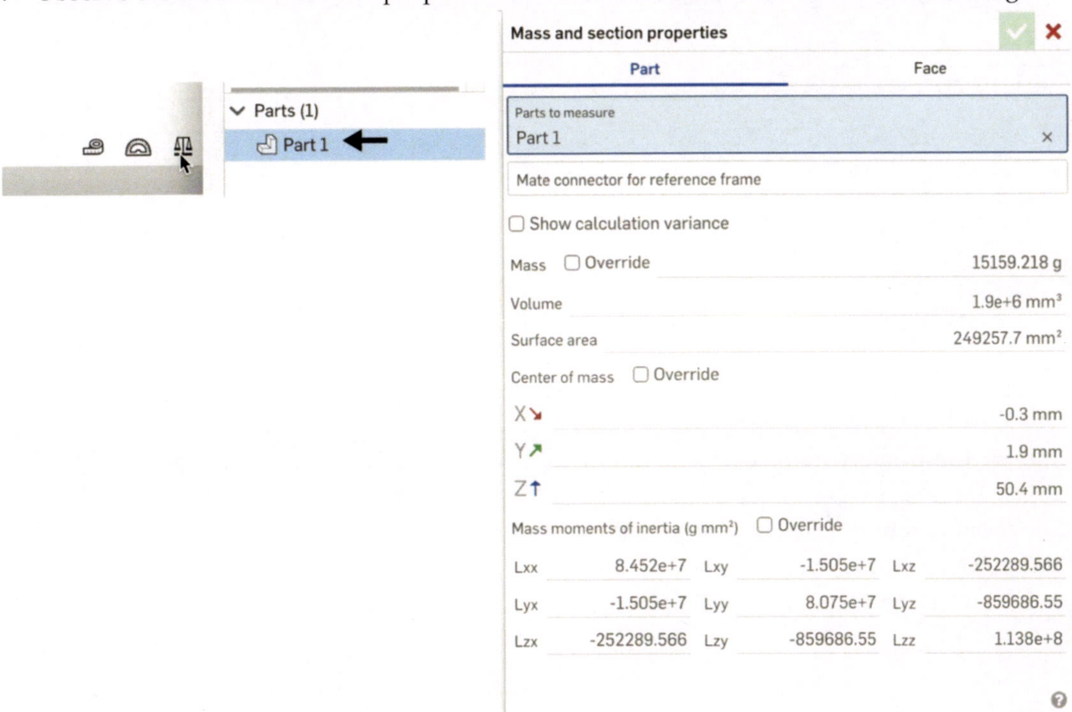

Updating the Model

1. Click the **Variable table** icon on the right pane.
2. On the **Variable table**, select the value in the **Value** box next to the **A** global variable **Name**.
3. Type **225**.
4. Likewise, change the **B, C, D,** and **E** values to **210, 176, 137**, and **39**, respectively.

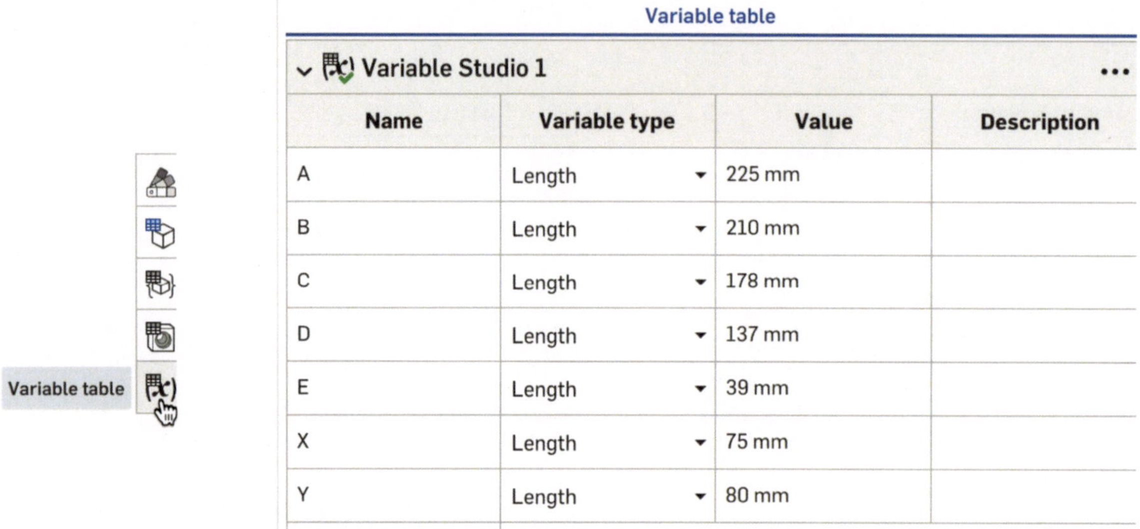

Name	Variable type	Value	Description
A	Length	225 mm	
B	Length	210 mm	
C	Length	178 mm	
D	Length	137 mm	
E	Length	39 mm	
X	Length	75 mm	
Y	Length	80 mm	

5. Click the **Variable table** on the right pane to close.
6. On the Taskbar, click the **Display mass and section properties** icon and select the **Part1** from the **Parts** panel. The mass value is updated.

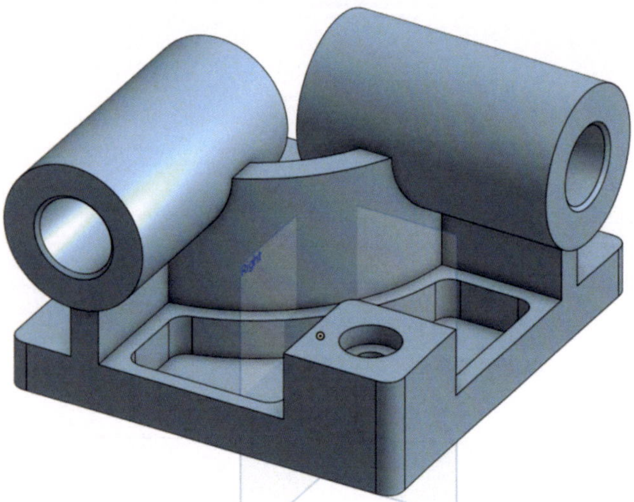

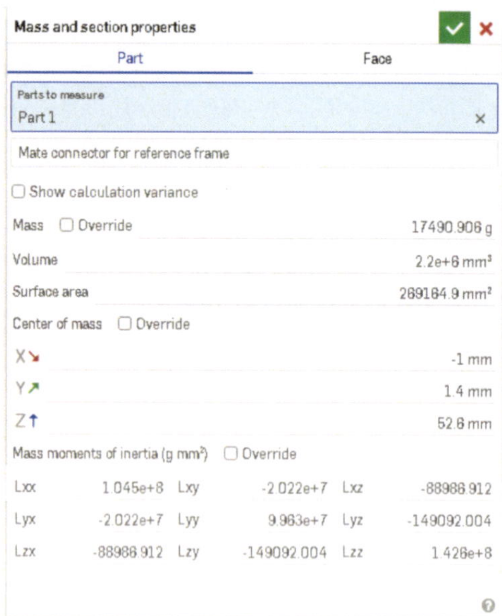

7. Close the **Mass and section properties** dialog.
8. Again, click on the **Variable table** tab on the right pane to change the values.
9. Type **209** in the **Value** box of **Name A**.
10. Likewise, change the **B, C, D,** and **E** values to **218, 169,125** and **41**, respectively.

Variable table

Variable Studio 1

Name	Variable type	Value	Description
A	Length	209 mm	
B	Length	218 mm	
C	Length	169 mm	
D	Length	125 mm	
E	Length	41 mm	
X	Length	69.7 mm	
Y	Length	82.7 mm	
Name			

11. Click the **Variable table** tab on the right plane to close it.

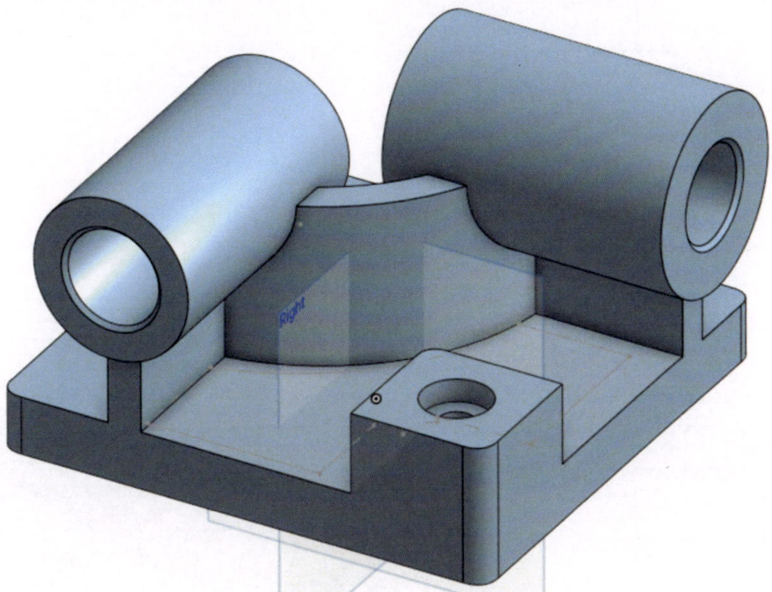

12. On the Taskbar, click the **Display mass and section properties** icon and select the geometry from the graphics window. The mass value is updated.
13. Close the **Mass and section properties**.

Questions

1. What are placed features?
2. How do you create a tapped hole?
3. What are the **Chamfer types** available on the **Chamfer** dialog?
4. Which option allows you to create a variable radius blend?
5. How to create hollow features?

Exercises

Exercise 1 (Millimetres)

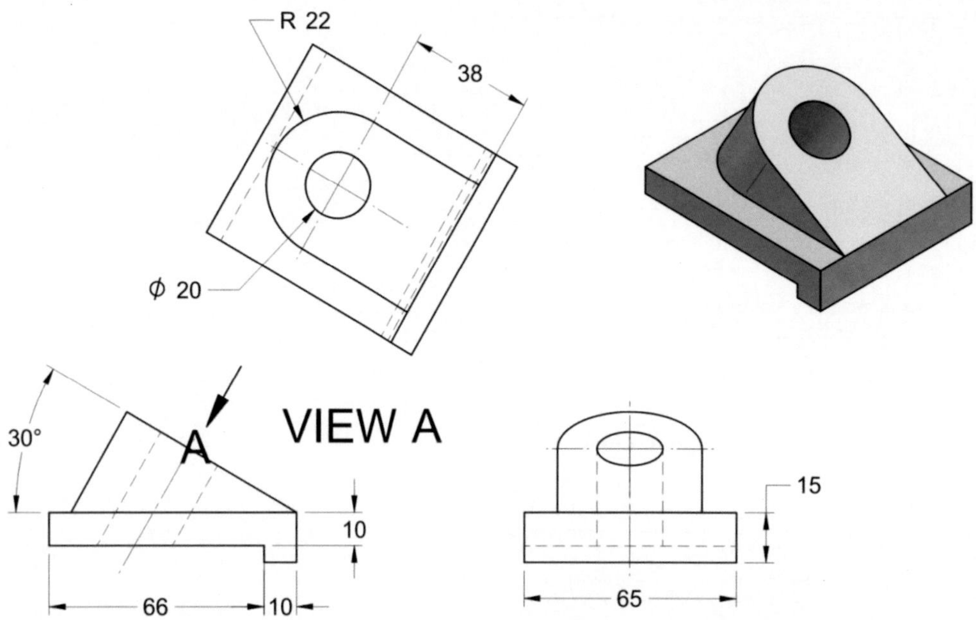

Exercise 2 (Inches)

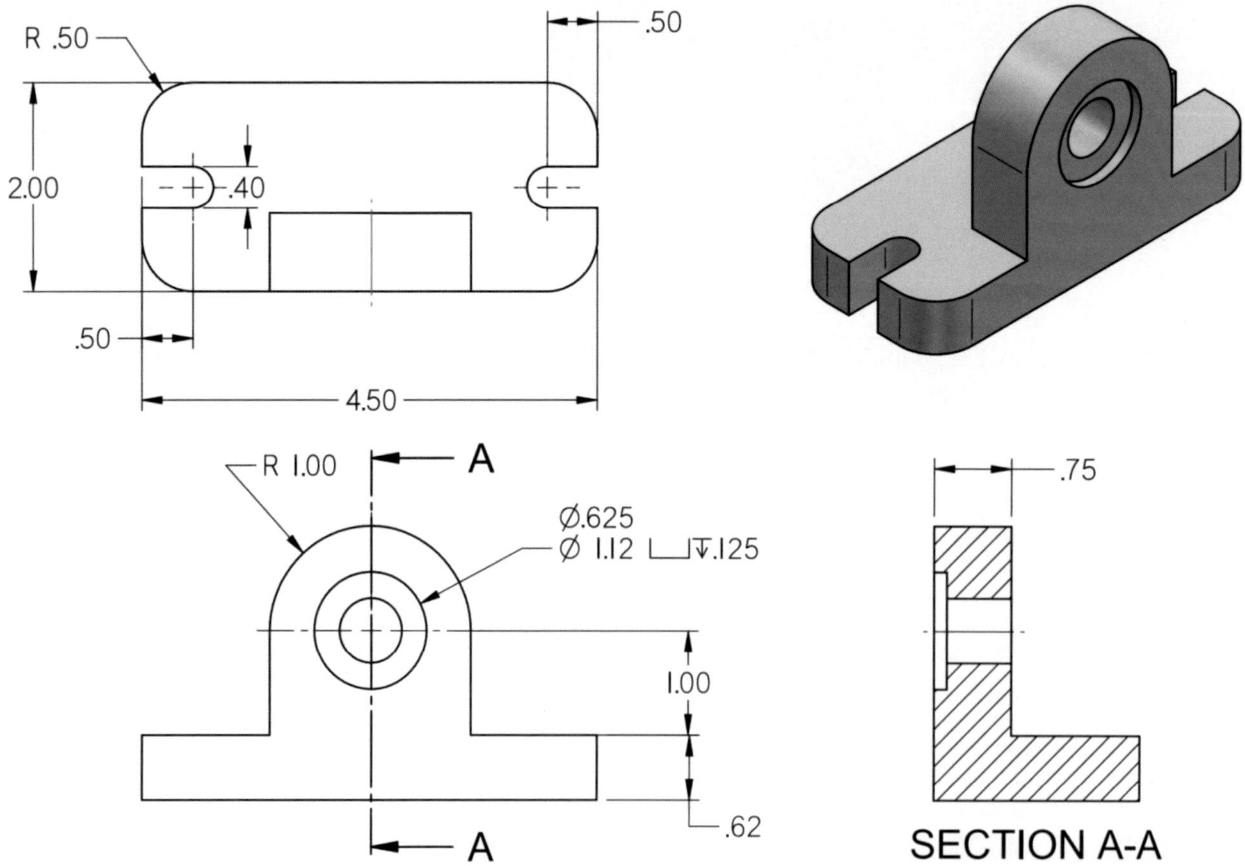

Chapter 5: Patterned Geometry

When designing a part geometry, oftentimes there are elements of symmetry in each part or there are at least a few features that are repeated multiple times. In these situations, Onshape offers you some commands that save you time. For example, you can use mirror features to design symmetric parts, which makes designing the part quicker. This is because you only have to design a portion of the part and use the mirror feature to create the remaining geometry.

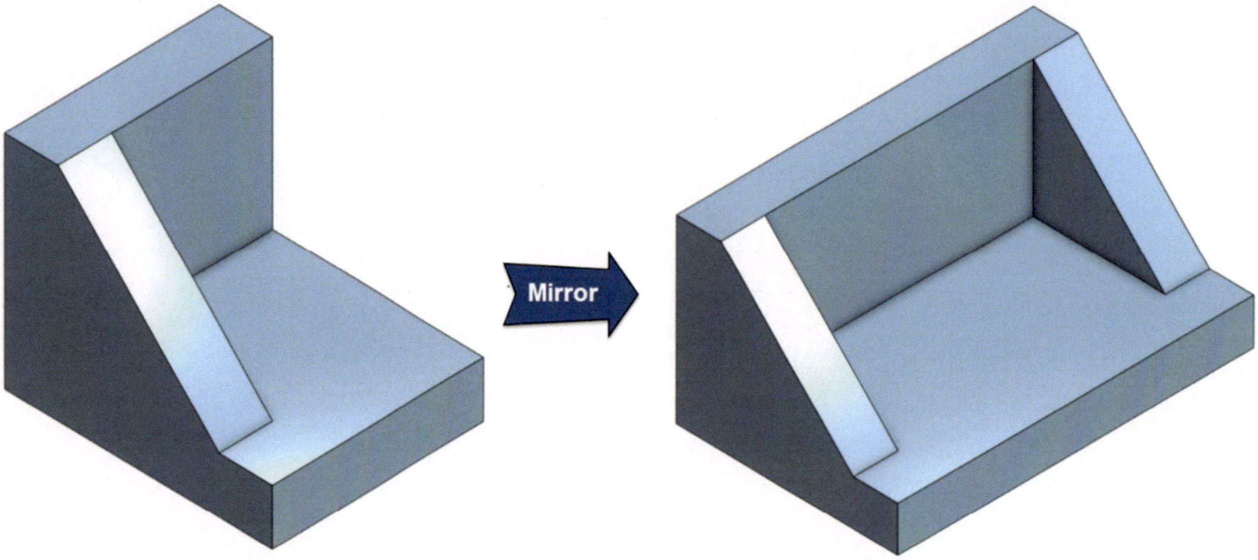

In addition, there are some pattern commands to replicate a feature throughout the part quickly. They save you from creating additional features individually and help you modify the design easily. If the design changes, you only need to change the first feature and the rest of the pattern features will update, automatically. In this chapter, you will learn to create the mirrored and pattern geometries using the commands available in Onshape.

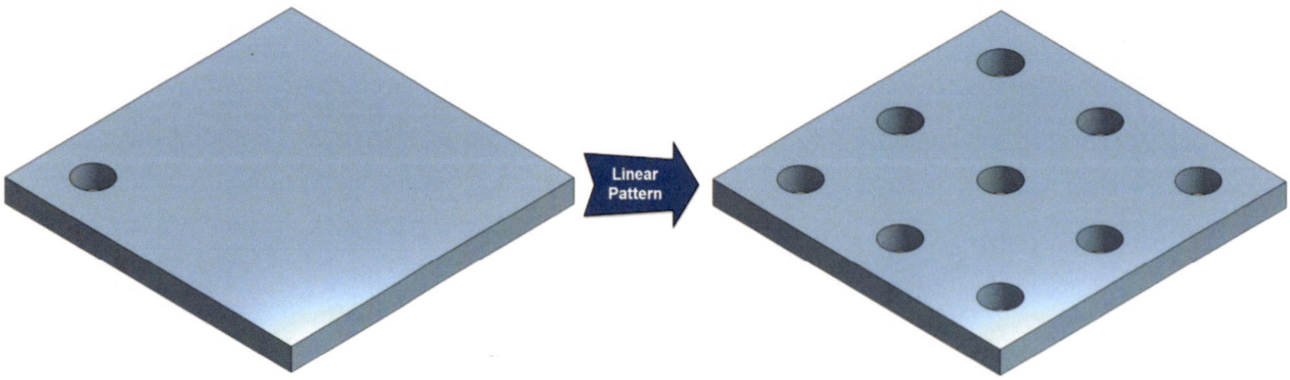

The topics covered in this chapter are:

- *Mirror* features
- *Linear Patterns*
- *Circular Patterns*
- *Curve Patterns*

Mirror

If you are designing a part that is symmetric, you can save time by using the **Mirror** command. Using this command, you can replicate the individual features of the entire body. To mirror features (3D geometry), you need to have a face or plane to use as a reference. You can use a model face, default plane, or create a new plane if it does not exist where it is needed.

Click the **Mirror** icon on the Toolbar. On the **Mirror** dialog, select the **Feature mirror** option from the **Mirror type** drop-down. Next, select the features to mirror. Click on the **Mirror plane** selection box and select the reference plane about which the features are to be mirrored. Check the **Reapply Features** option. This option regenerates the mirrored feature, ensuring its original design parameters are maintained in the new instance. This is crucial for features that adapt to their surrounding geometry. Next, click the green check on the dialog.

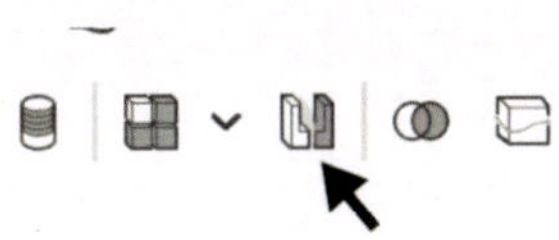

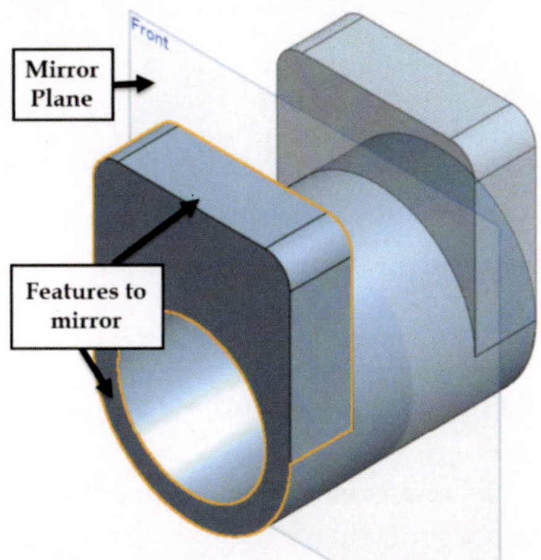

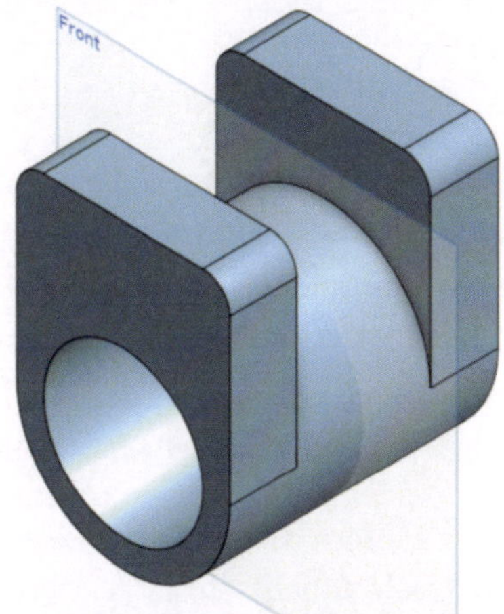

Now, if you make changes to the original feature, the mirrored feature will be updated automatically.

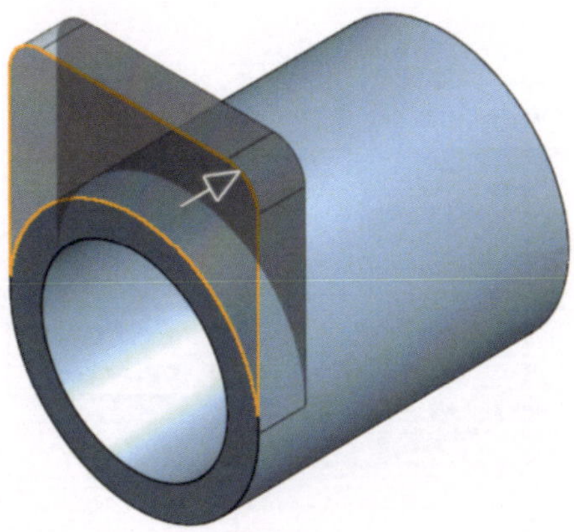

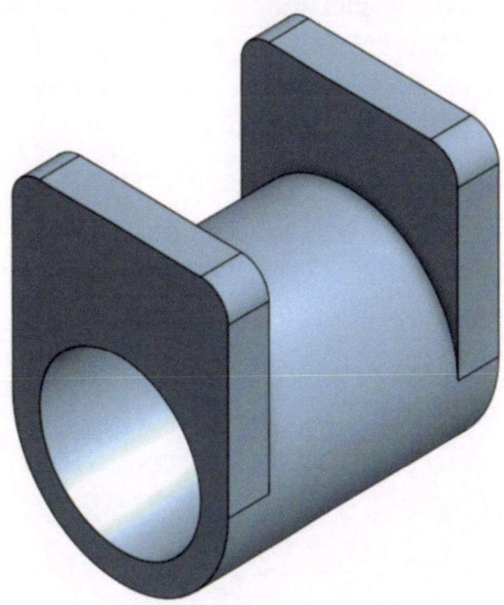

Mirror Bodies

If the part you are creating is completely symmetric, you can save more time by creating half of it and mirroring the entire geometry rather than individual features. Click the **Mirror** icon on the toolbar and select the **Part mirror** option from the **Mirror type** drop-down. Next, click on anyone of the Boolean tabs (**New**, **Add**, **Remove**, or

Intersect). Select the part body to be mirrored. Click the **Mirror plane** selection box and select the face about which the geometry is to be mirrored. Click the green check to complete the mirror geometry.

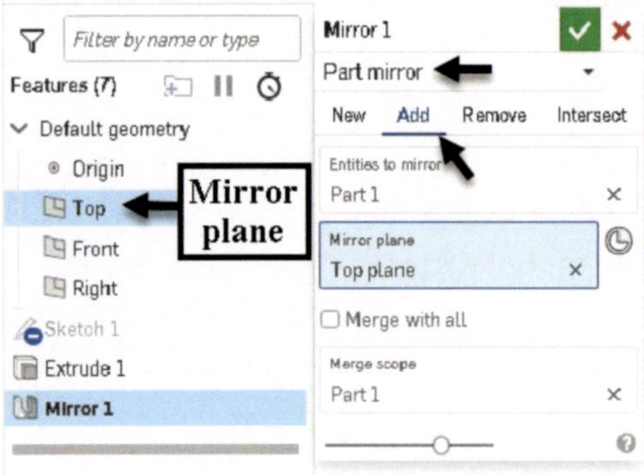

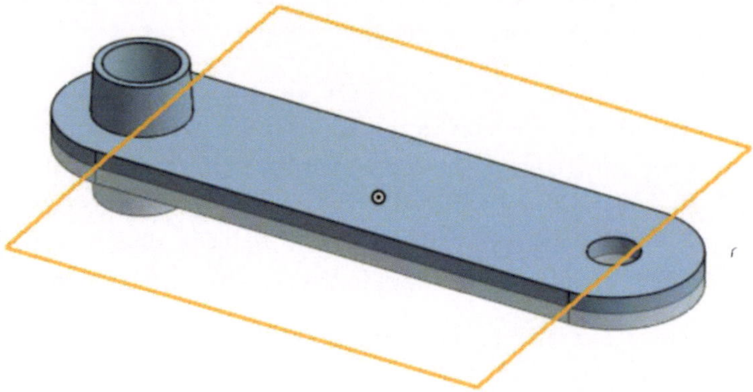

Create Patterns

Onshape allows you to replicate a feature using the pattern commands **Linear Pattern**, **Circular Pattern**, and **Curve Driven Pattern**. The following sections explain the different patterns that can be created using these pattern commands.

Linear Pattern

To create a pattern in a linear fashion, you must first activate the **Linear Pattern** command (On the Toolbar, click **Linear Pattern** drop-down > **Linear Pattern**). Next, select the **Feature pattern** from the **Pattern type** drop-down. Select the feature to pattern from the model geometry.

Click the **Direction** selection box and select an edge, face, or axis to define first direction of the pattern. Type-in values in the **Distance** and **Instance count** boxes. Click the **Opposite direction** icon next to the **Instant count** box to reverse the pattern direction. Check the **Centered** option to pattern the feature on both sides.

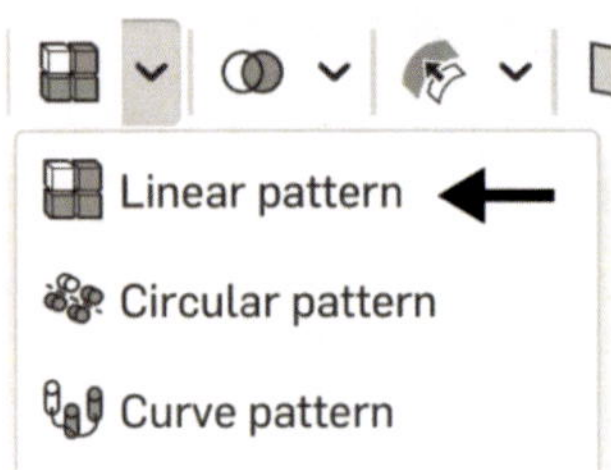

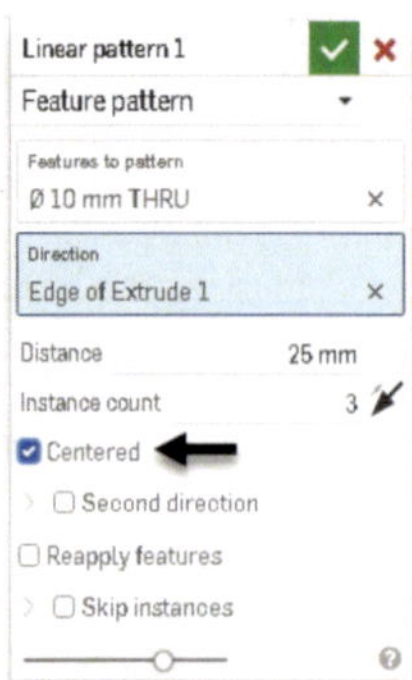

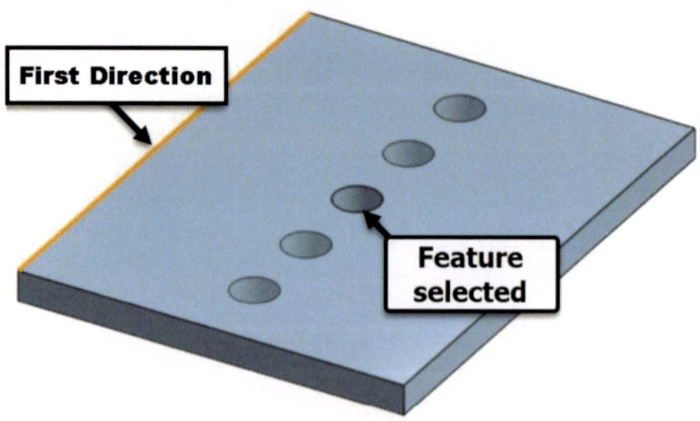

Check the **Second direction** option and select an edge, face or axis to define the second direction of the pattern. Likewise, set the parameters (**Distance** and **Instance count**) of the pattern in second direction.

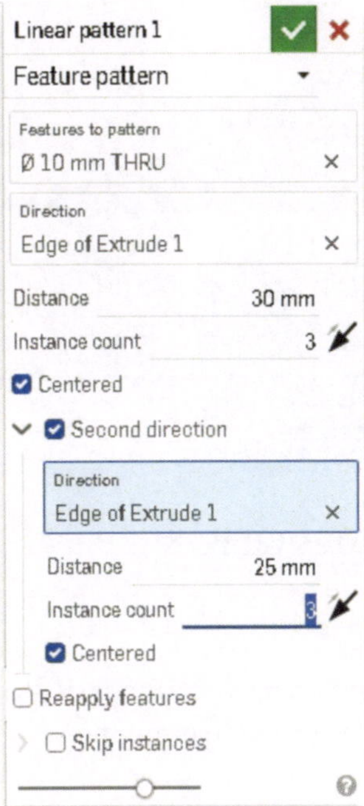

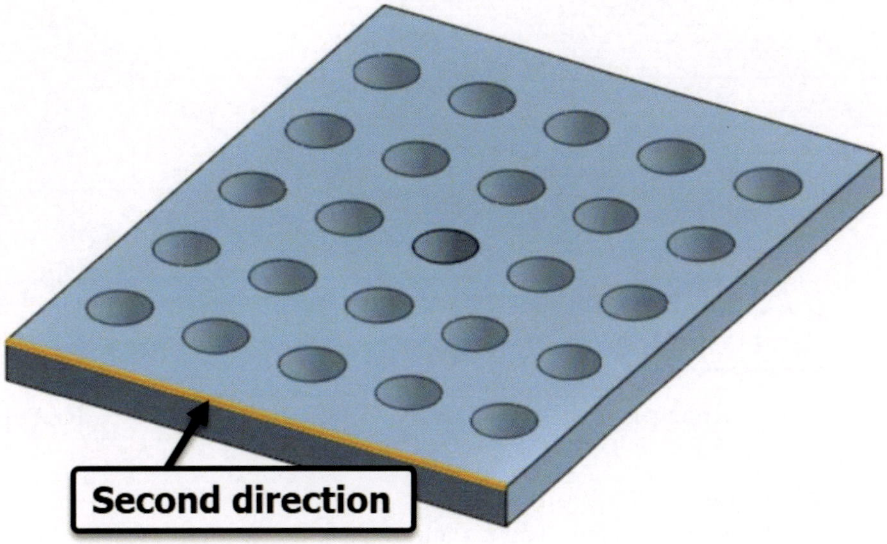

Reapply Features

This option regenerates each instance of the linear pattern such that the feature parameters are maintained. For example, extrude a circle up to a surface, as shown.

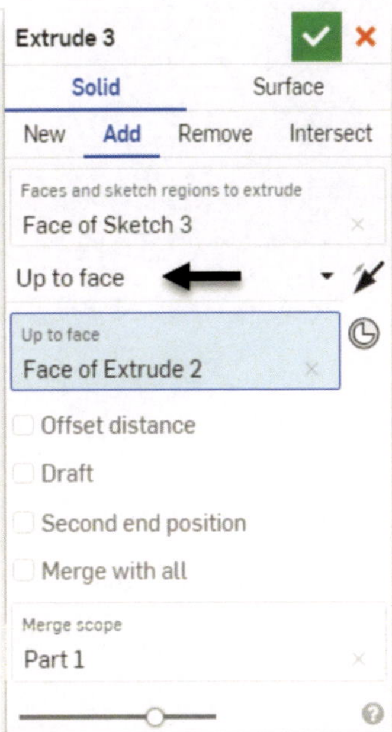

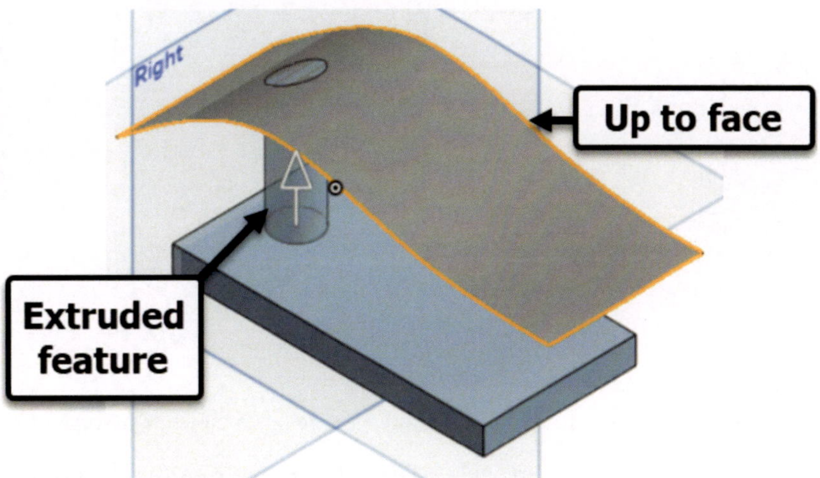

Next, activate the **Linear pattern** command and select the **Feature pattern** option from the **Pattern type** drop-down. Click in the **Features to pattern** selection box and select the cylindrical feature. Click in the **Direction** selection box and select the horizontal edge, as shown. Next, specify the **Distance** and **Instance count** values. Check the **Reapply Features** option and click the green check; the instances of linear pattern are extruded up to the top surface.

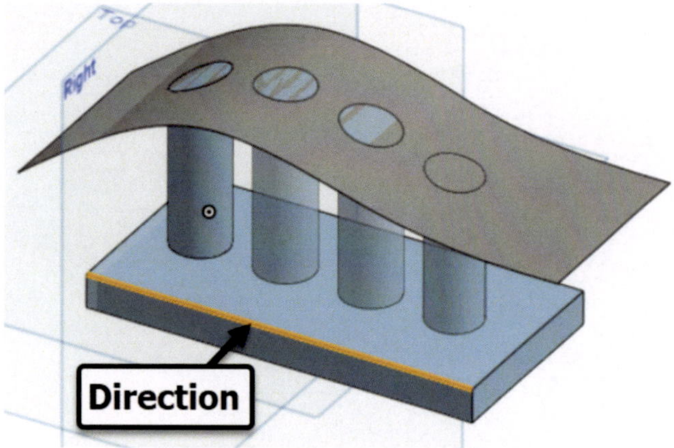

Reapply Features ON

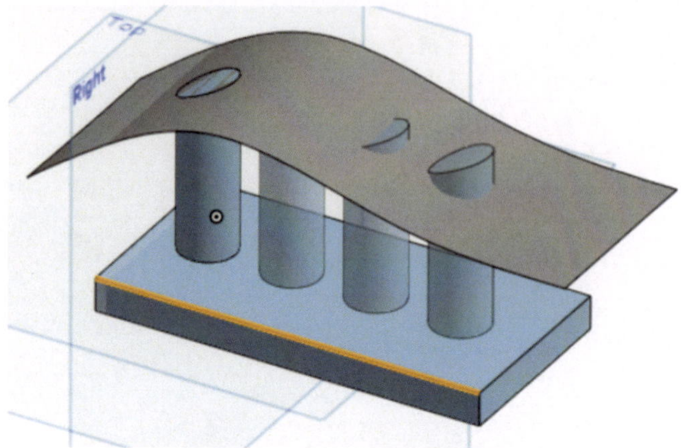

Reapply Features OFF

Patterning the entire geometry

The **Part Pattern** option allows you to pattern the entire part geometry. Activate the **Linear Pattern** command and select the **Part Pattern** option on the **Linear Pattern** dialog. Next, select the bodies to be patterned. Define the direction, instance count, and distance between the instances.

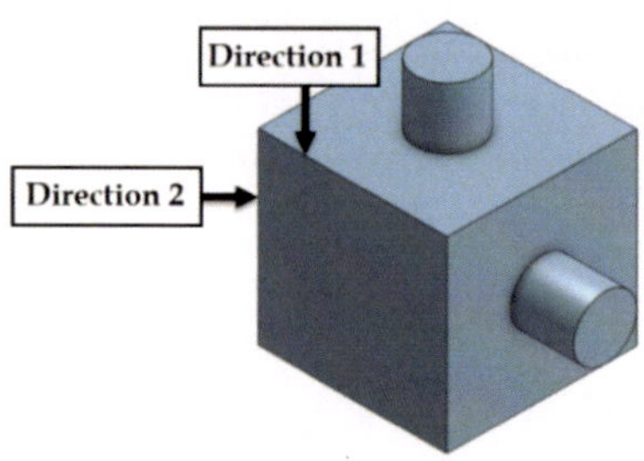

Circular Pattern

The circular pattern is used to pattern the selected features in a circular fashion. Click **Pattern** drop-down **>** **Circular Pattern** on the Toolbar and select **Feature pattern** from the **Pattern type** drop-down. Select the feature to pattern from the model geometry. Click the **Axis of pattern** selection box, and then select the axis from the model geometry or click on a cylindrical face; the axis of the rotation is defined.

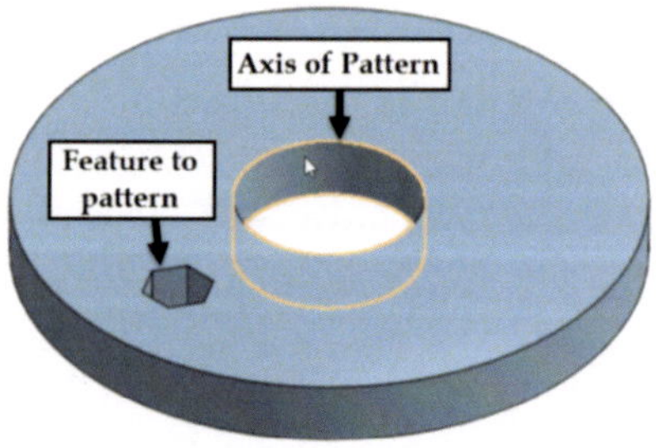

On the **Circular pattern** dialog, select the **Equal Spacing** option. Type-in values in the **Angle** and **Instance count** fields. The total number of instances you specify will be fitted in the occurrence angle.

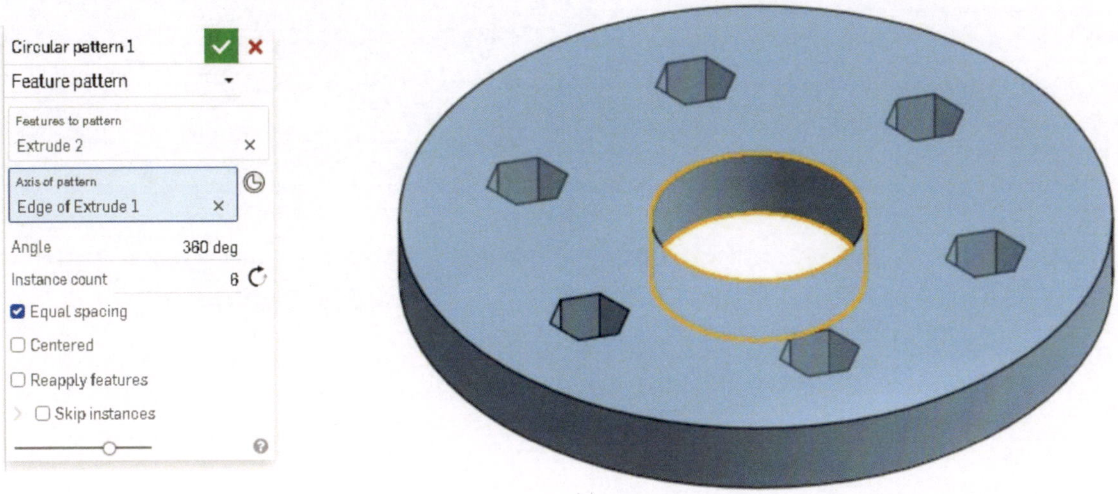

Uncheck the **Equal spacing** option, if you want to type in the instance count and the angle between the individual instances.

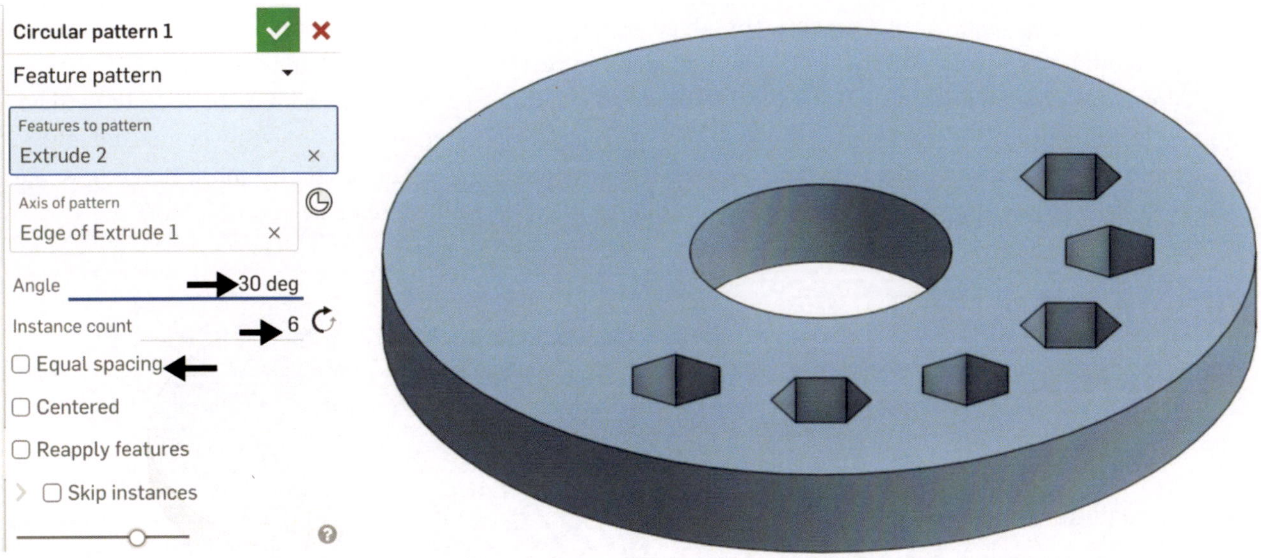

Centered

The **Centered** option is used to create a circular pattern on both sides of the selected feature. Specify the angle between the instances in the **Angle** field and the number of instances in the **Instance count** field. Check the **Centered** option at the bottom of the dialog. Click the green check on the **Circular pattern** dialog to create the centered circular pattern.

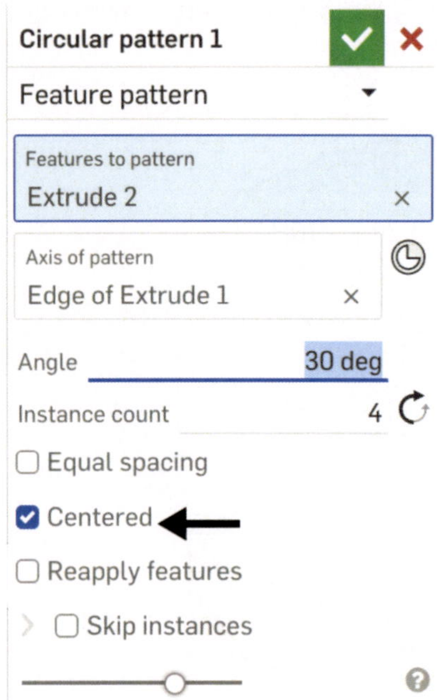

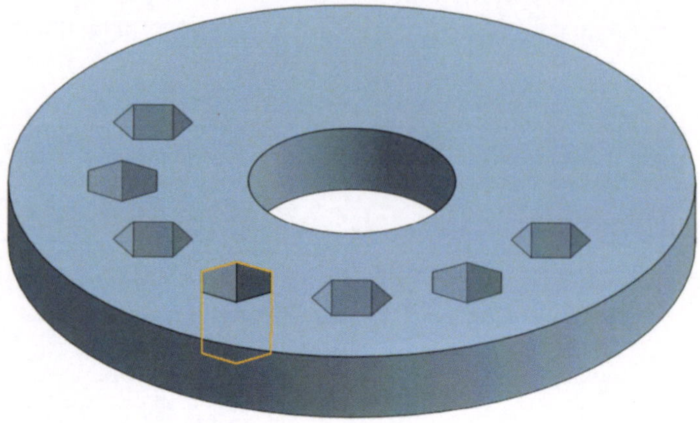

Curve Pattern

You can create a pattern along a selected curve or edge using the **Curve Pattern** command. Activate the **Curve Pattern** command (click **Linear Pattern** drop-down > **Curve Pattern**). On the **Curve Pattern** dialog, click the **Pattern Type** drop-down **> Feature pattern**. Next, click on the feature to pattern. Next, click the **Path to pattern along** the selection button and click on the path, as shown. To select an edge loop or tangently connected edges, right-click and select **Select** > **Create selection**. Next, select any two edges of the tangently connected edges. Next, click the Add Selection button on the **Create selection** dialog. Next, close the **Create selection** dialog.

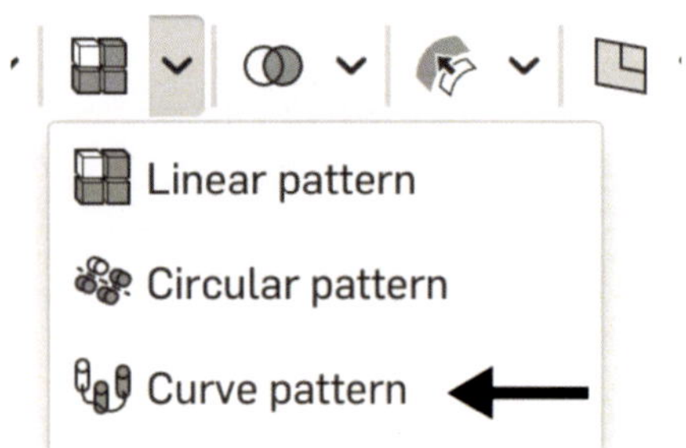

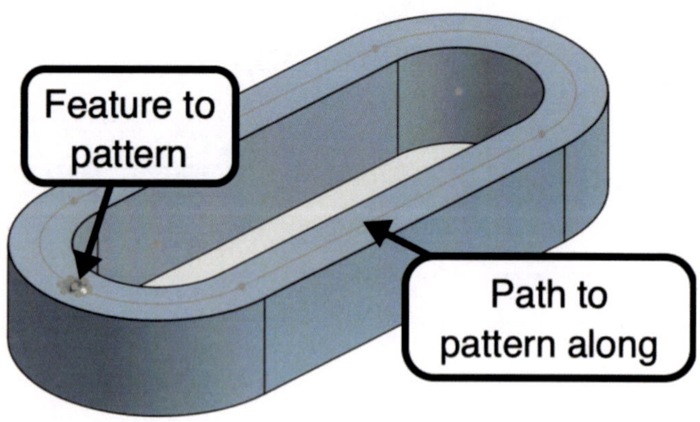

Next, specify the number of instances in the **Instance count** field.

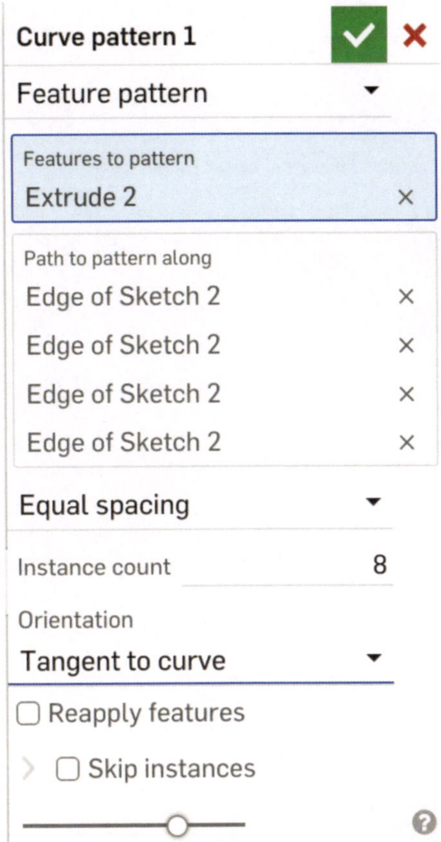

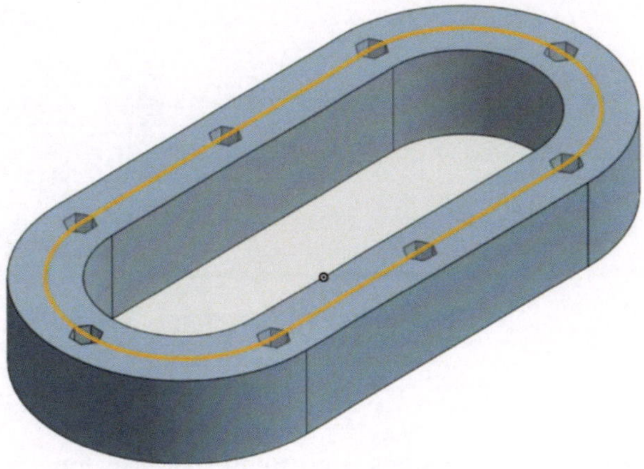

The **Orientation** drop-down allows you to specify the orientation of the pattern instances along the path. The options in this drop-down are explained next.

Tangent to curve: This option makes the pattern instances rotate to follow the bends of the path, like train cars on a curved track. It ensures they stay aligned with the curve's direction at every point.

Normal to face: This option makes the instances to align with the selected face.

Locked: This keeps every pattern instance in the exact same orientation as the original one. No matter how the path curves, the pattern instances will not rotate or tilt at all.

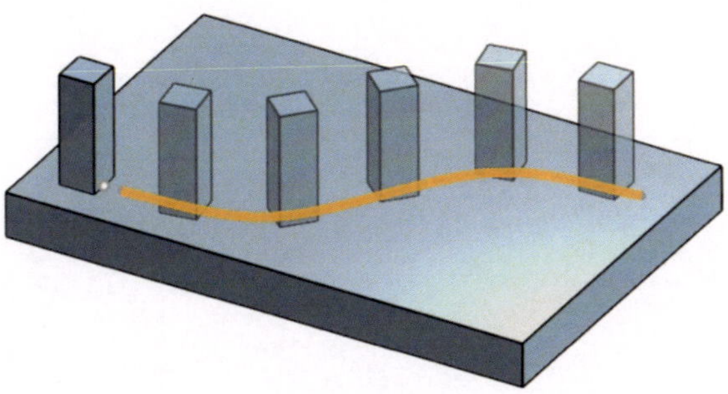

Tangent to curve

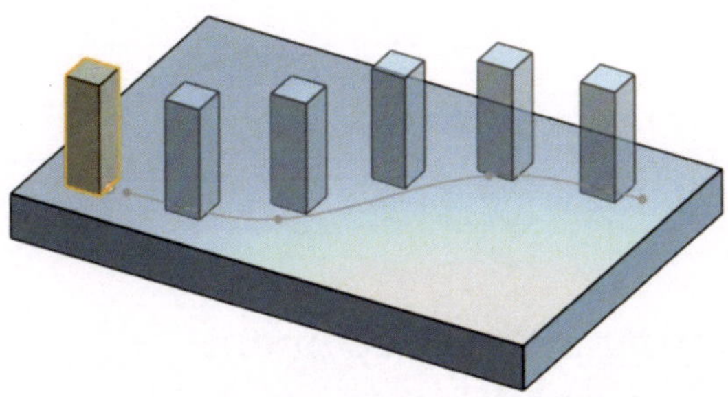

Locked

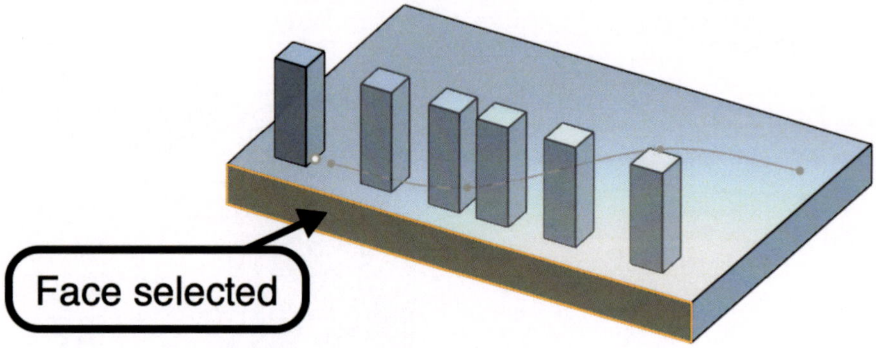

Normal to face

Click the green check ✅ to create the pattern along the curve.

Tutorial 1

In this example, you create the part shown next.

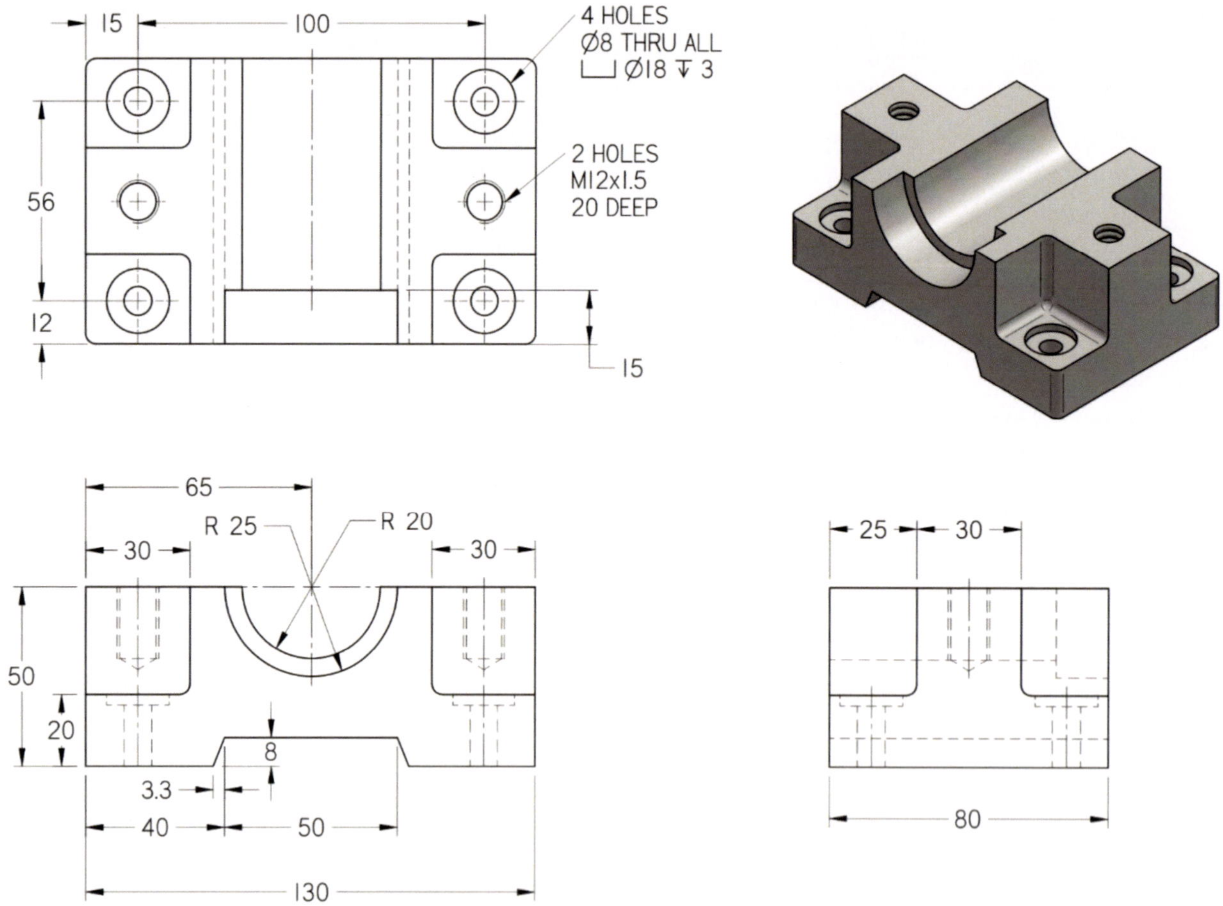

Creating a New document

1. In your Internet Browser, go to https://www.onshape.com to start Onshape.
2. Next, click **SIGN IN** button located on the top right corner side of the web page. Enter the username and password, and then, click **Sign in**.

3. On the **Documents** page, click **Create > Folder**. Next, type Chapter 5 in the **Folder name** box and then click **Create**.
4. Double-click on the **Chapter 5** folder in the Folders section.
5. On the Documents page, click **Create > Document**; the **New document** dialog appears on the screen.
6. Enter Tutorial 1 in the **Document name** box and click **Create public document**; a new document appears.
7. Click the **Document menu** located at the top left corner of the window and select **Workspace Units**; the **Workspace Units** dialog appears on the screen.
8. On the **Workspace Units** dialog, select **Length default unit> Millimeter** from **Length** section.
9. Select **Mass default unit > Gram** from the **Mechanical** section.
10. Leave the other default settings and click the green check.

Creating the Extruded features

1. To start a new sketch, click **Sketch** command on the Toolbar.
2. Click on the Front plane. Next, right-click and select **View normal to sketch plane**; the selected plane orients normal to the screen.
3. On the Toolbar, click **Rectangle** drop-down > **Center Point Rectangle**. Next, select the sketch origin and move the pointer outward.
4. Click to create a rectangle, and then apply dimensions to it. Next, click **green check** on the **Sketch 1** dialog.

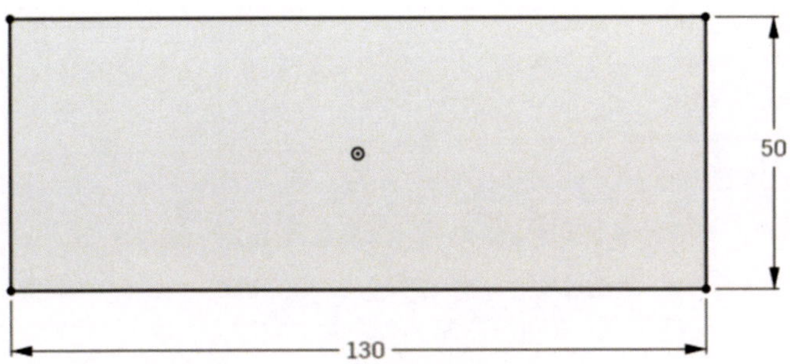

5. Activate the **Extrude** command, and then select the sketch.
6. On the **Extrude** Dialog, click the **End type** drop-down > **Blind**.
7. Select the **Symmetric** option.
8. Type **80** in the **Depth** box and click the green check on the dialog.
9. On the Toolbar, click the **Sketch** command. Next, click on the top face of the part geometry.
10. On the sketch Toolbar, click the **Rectangle** drop-down > **Corner Rectangle**.
11. Click on the corner point of the top face, as shown. Move the pointer in the top-left direction, and then click.
12. Add dimensions to the sketch.

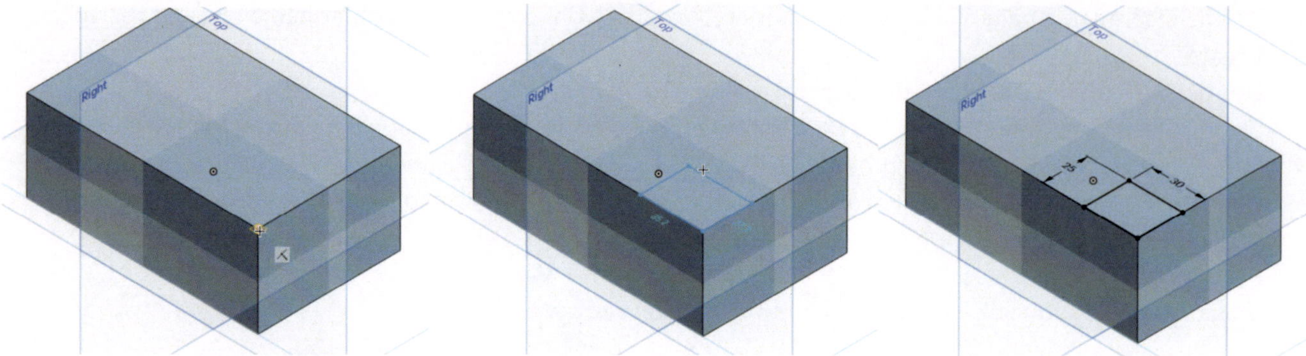

13. Click the green check on the **Sketch 2** dialog.
14. Activate the **Extrude** command and click **Remove** tab on the **Extrude** dialog. Next, select the sketch from the part geometry.
15. Type-in 30 in the **Depth** field.
16. Click the green check on the **Extrude** dialog.

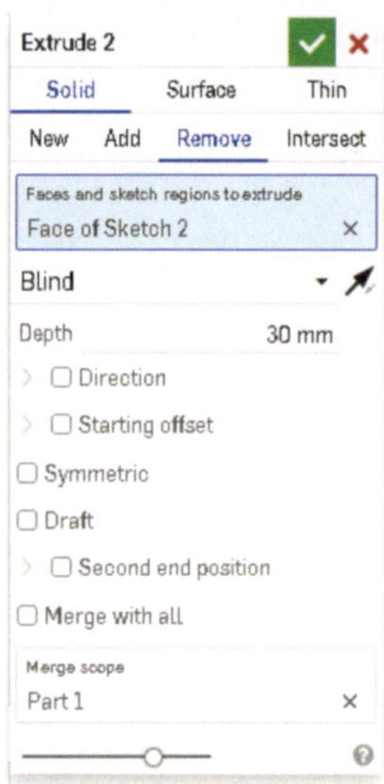

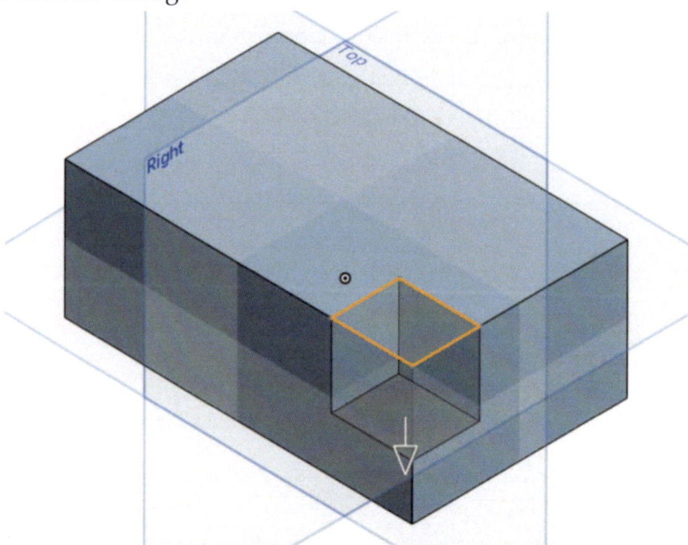

Creating the Hole features

1. On the Toolbar, click the **Sketch** command. Next, click on the bottom face of the **Extrude** cut feature, as shown.
2. Create a sketch point on the bottom face of the Extrude feature. Next, add dimensions to the sketch, as shown.

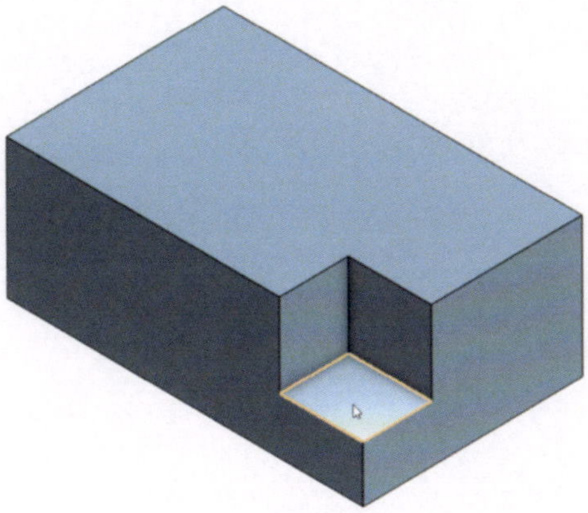

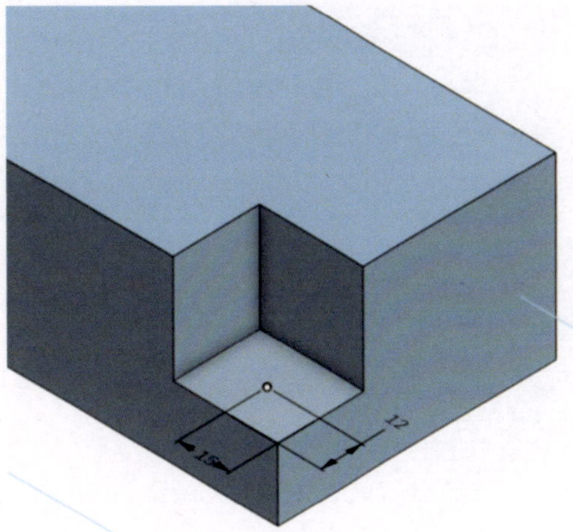

3. Click green check on the **Sketch 3** dialog.
4. Activate the **Hole** command. On the **Hole** dialog, select **Counterbore** tab.
5. Select the sketch point on the part geometry. Next, select the **Termination** drop-down > **Through all.**
6. Set the hole **Diameter** value to **8**.
7. Type-in **18** and **3** in the **Counterbore diameter** and **Counterbore depth** fields, respectively; notice the preview of the counterbore hole on the part geometry.

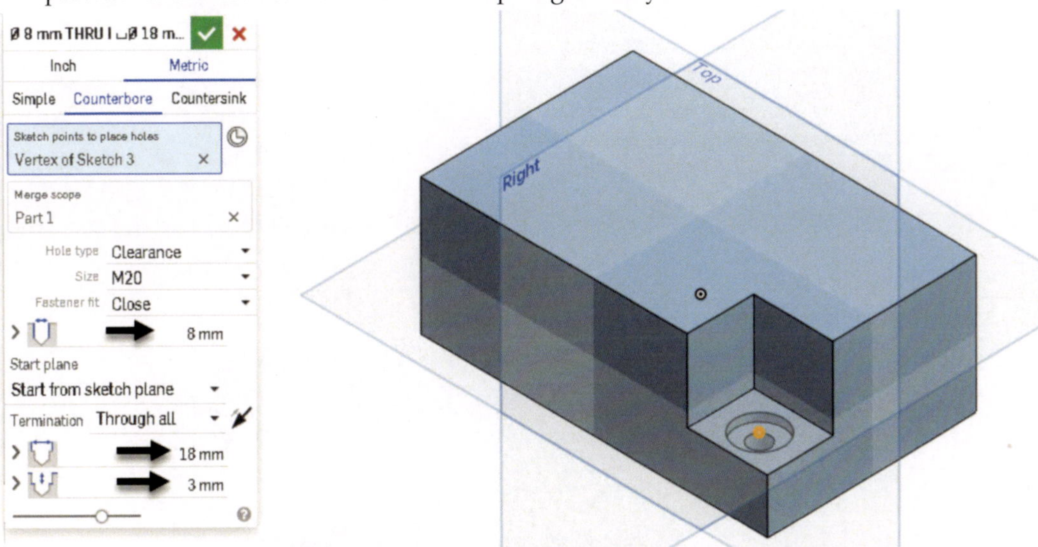

8. Click the green check on the **Hole** dialog to create the counterbore hole.
9. Click the **Sketch** command on the Toolbar. Next, click on the top face of the model.
10. On the sketch Toolbar, click the **Point** command. Next, place the point on the top face of the model.
11. Add dimensions to the sketch point, as shown.

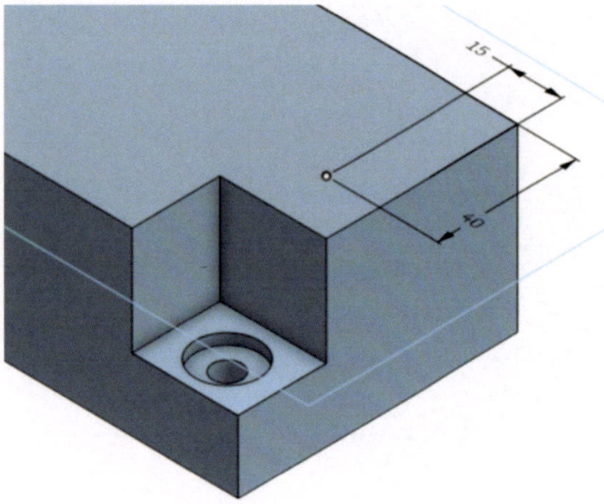

12. On the **Sketch 4** dialog, click the green check to confirm the sketch.
13. Activate the **Hole** command and select the sketch point. On the **Hole** dialog, select the **Simple** tab.
14. Select the **Metric** tab and **Hole type > Tapped**.
15. Select **Size > M12** and select **Pitch > 1.50 mm.**
16. Click the **Termination** drop-down **> Blind**.
17. Type **20** in the hole **Depth** and **Tapped Depth** fields respectively. Next, type **0** in the **Tap Clearance** field.
18. Click the green check on the **Hole** dialog to create the threaded hole.

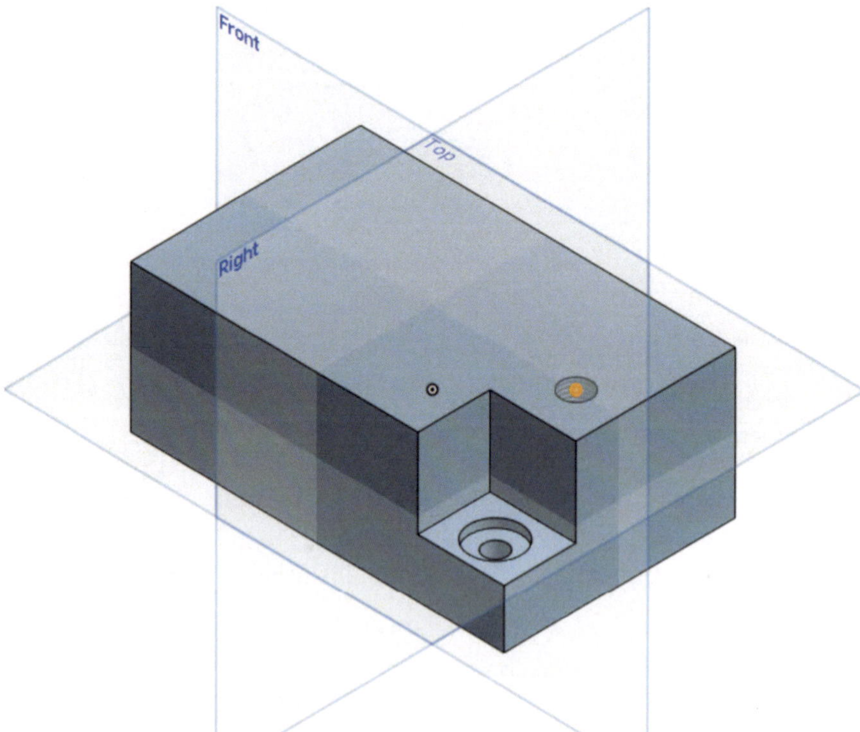

Creating the Linear pattern

1. On the Toolbar, click **Pattern** drop-down > **Linear pattern**.
2. On the **Linear pattern 1** dialog, click the **Pattern type** drop-down **> Feature pattern**.
3. Click the **Features to pattern** selection box.
4. Select the second *Extruded* feature and the *Counterbore Hole* from the part geometry.

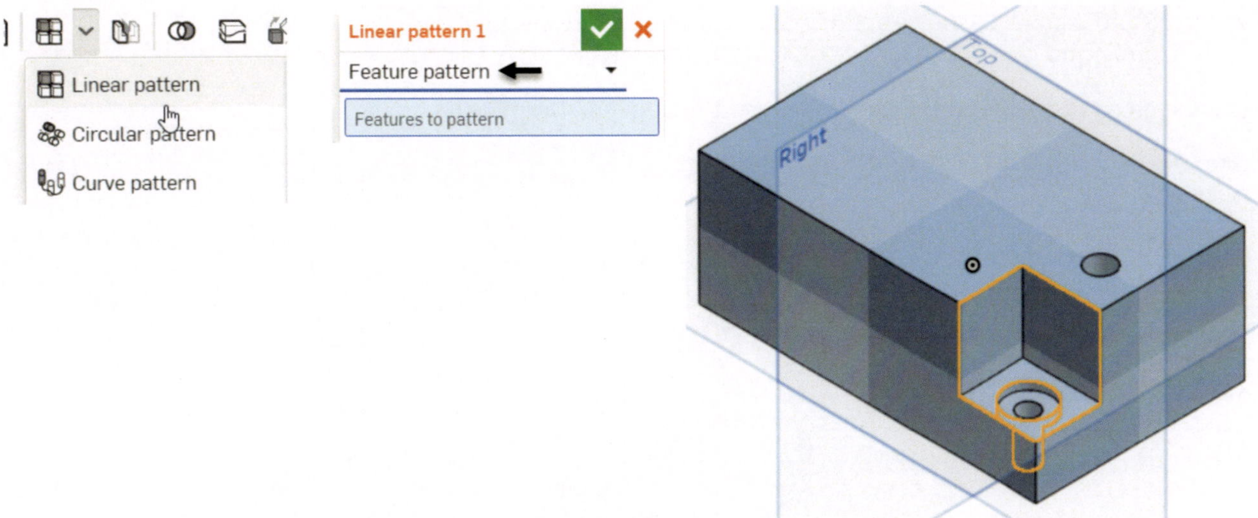

5. Next, click the **Direction** selection box and click on the top front edge of the part geometry.
6. Type-in **100** and **2** in the **Distance** and **Instance count** fields respectively.

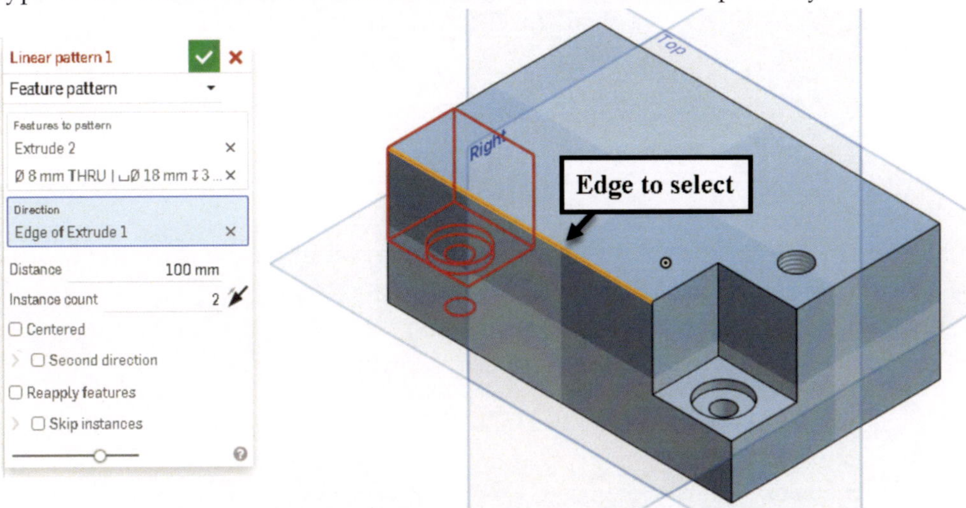

7. Next, check the **Second direction** option at the bottom of the dialog.
8. Click the **Direction** selection box and click on the top-right edge of the part geometry.

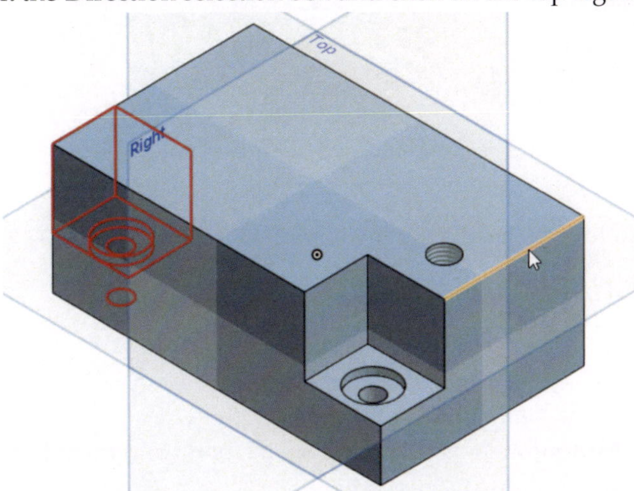

9. Type-in **55** and **2** in the **Distance** and **Instance count** fields, respectively.
10. Check the **Reapply features** option at the bottom of the dialog.
11. Click the green check on the **Linear pattern 1** dialog to pattern the features.

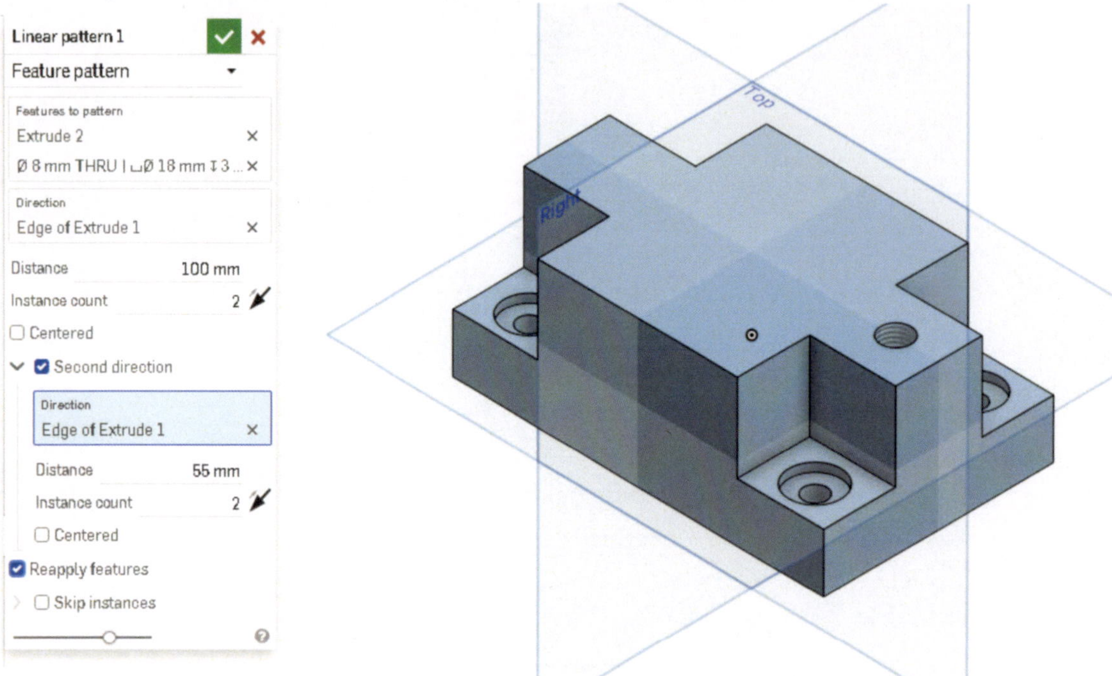

Mirroring the Features

1. On the Toolbar, click the **Mirror** command.
2. Click the **Mirror Type > Feature mirror** on the **Mirror** dialog.
3. Click the **Features to mirror** selection box and select the tapped hole.
4. Click the **Mirror plane** selection box and select the **Right** plane, as shown.

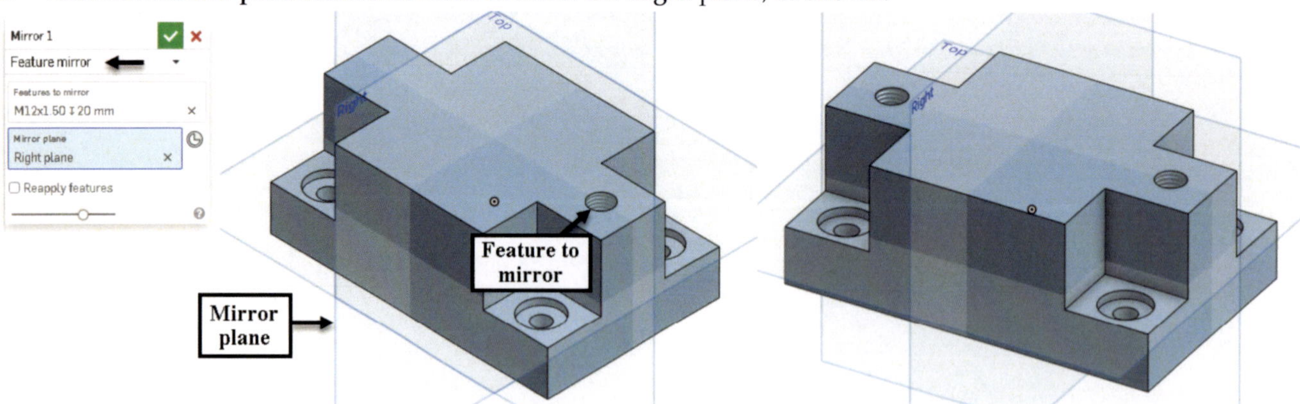

5. Click the green check on the **Mirror** dialog to mirror the selected features.

Creating the Hole and Extruded cut features

1. On the Toolbar, click the **Sketch** command and click on the front face of the part geometry.
2. Click the **Point** command on the toolbar. Next, click anywhere on the sketch plane.
3. On the Toolbar, click **Constraints** drop-down > **Midpoint**. Next, select the sketch point and the top front edge of the model; the point is constrained to the midpoint of the selected edge.

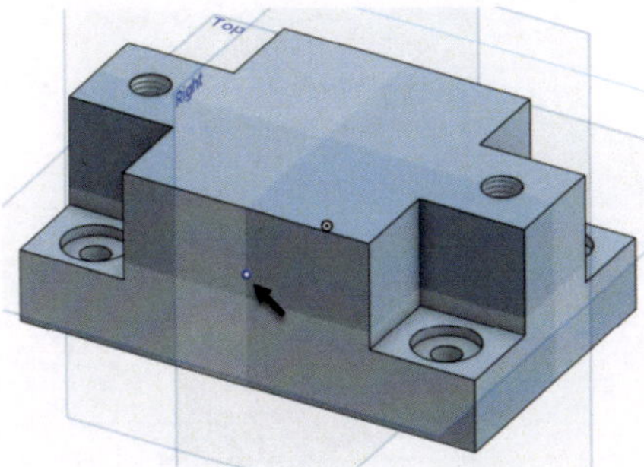

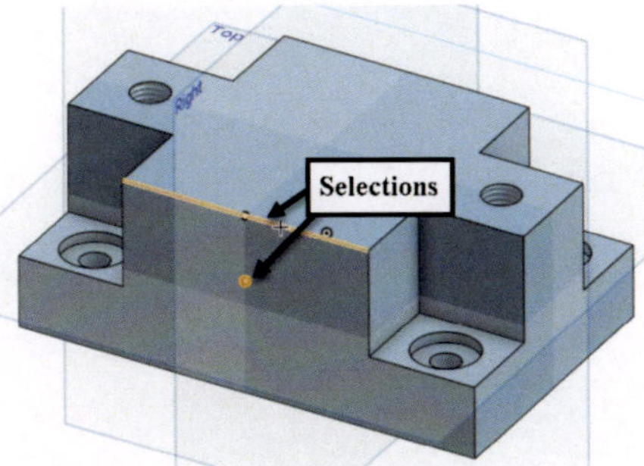

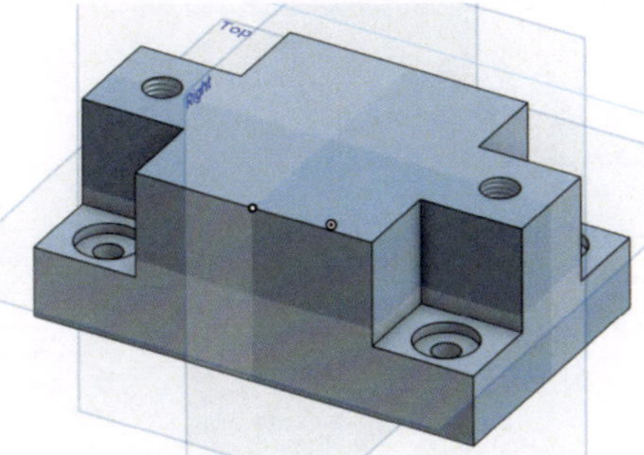

4. Click the green check on the **Sketch 5** dialog to confirm the sketch.
5. Activate the **Hole** command and select the sketch point.
6. On the **Hole** dialog, select the **Counterbore** tab.
7. Select the **Metric** tab on the dialog.
8. Select the **Termination > Through** all.
9. Set the **Hole Diameter** value to **40**.
10. Type-in **50** and **15** in the **Counterbore diameter** and **Counterbore depth** fields, respectively.
11. Click the green check on the **Hole 3** dialog to create the counterbore hole.

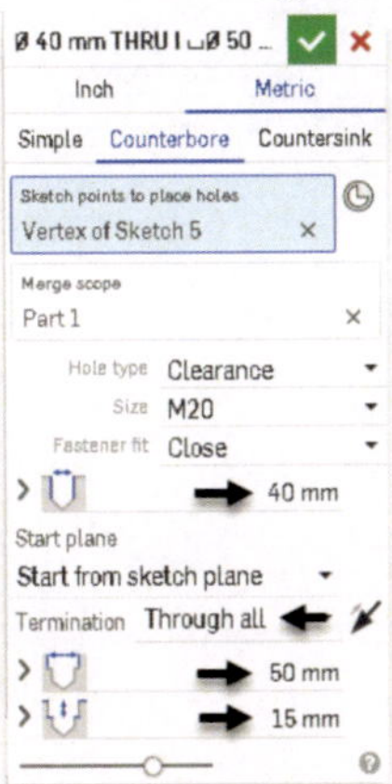

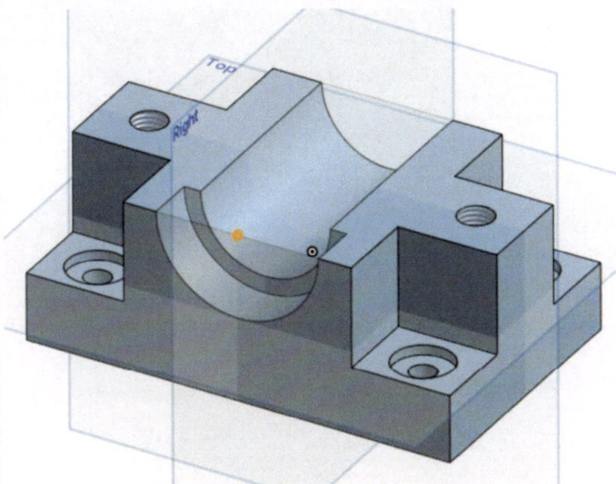

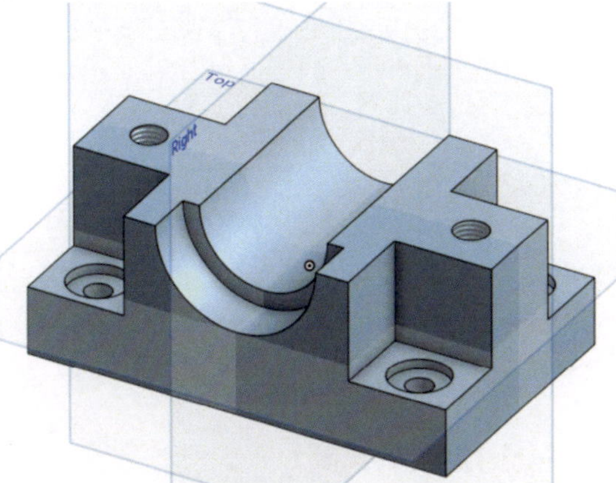

12. Sketch the front face of the part geometry and remove the material throughout the geometry using the **Extrude** command.

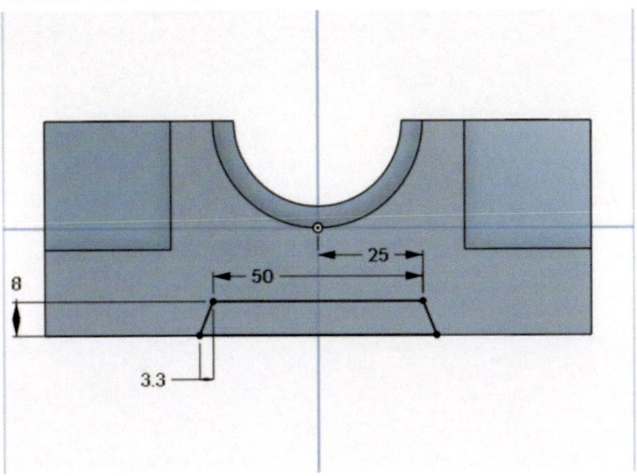

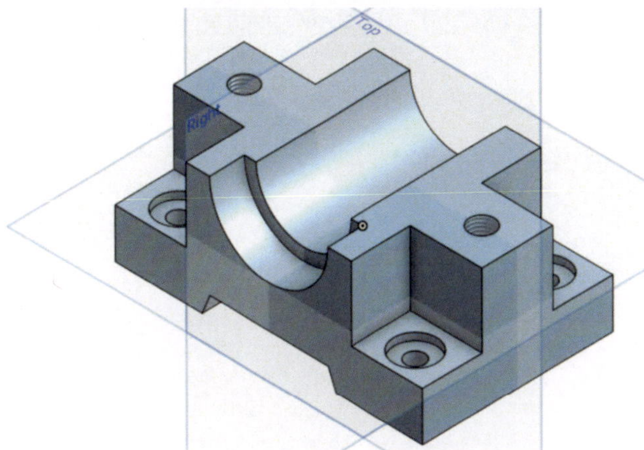

13. Activate the **Fillet** command and select the internal edges of the Extruded cut features, as shown.
14. Type **2** in the **Radius** box and click the green check.

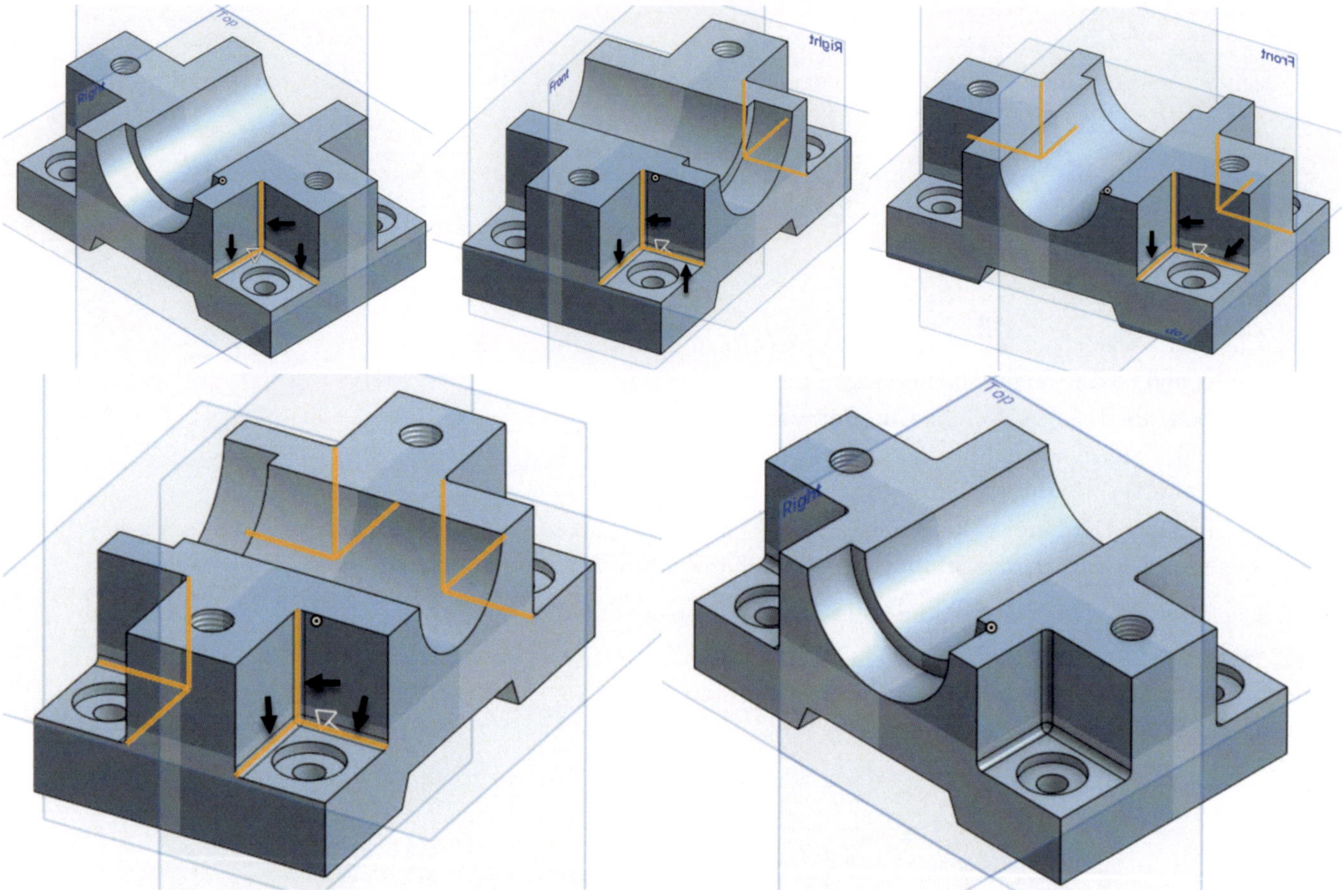

15. Click the **Document menu** located at the top-left corner of the graphics area and click the **Close document** option to close the document.

Questions

1. Describe the procedure to create a mirror feature.
2. List any two types of patterns.
3. List the methods to define spacing in a linear pattern.

Exercises

Exercise 1

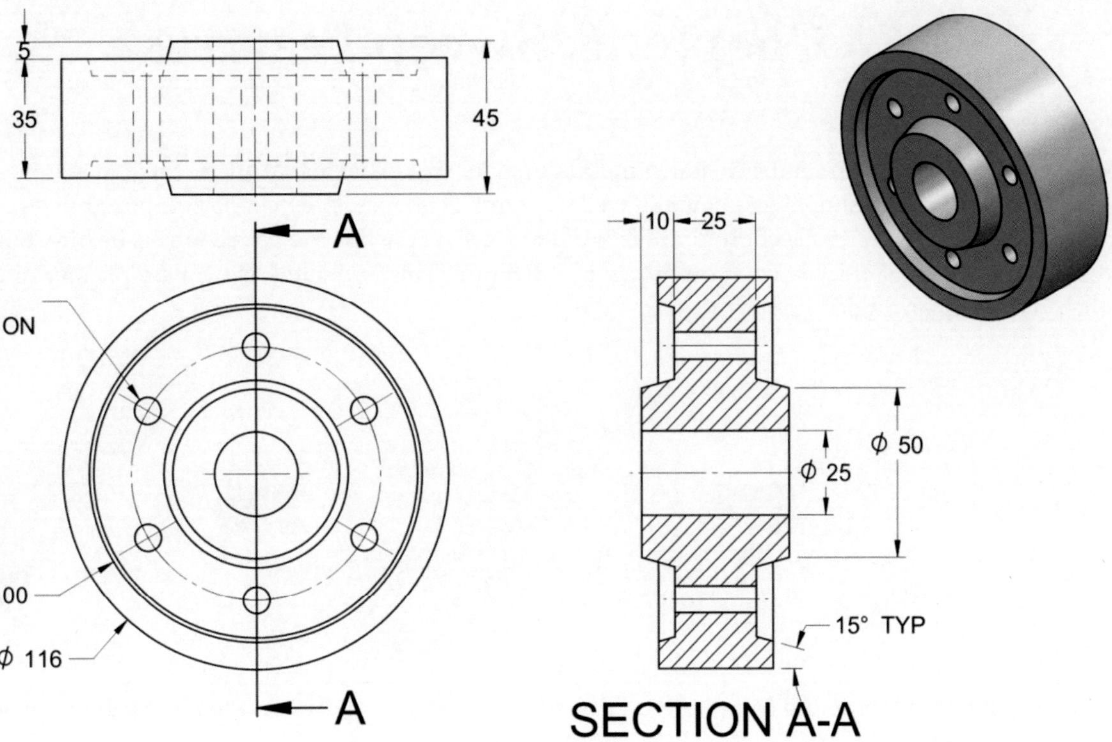
5
35
45
A
6 HOLES Φ 8
EQUI-SPACED ON
75 PCD
Φ 100
Φ 116
A
10
25
Φ 50
Φ 25
15° TYP
SECTION A-A

Chapter 6: Sweep Features

The Sweep feature

The **Sweep** command is one of the basic commands available in Onshape that allow you to generate solid geometry. It can be used to create simple geometry as well as complex shapes. A sweep is composed of two items: a cross-section and a path. The cross-section controls the shape of sweep while the path controls its direction. For example, take a look at the angled sweep feature shown in the figure. This is created using a simple sweep with the ellipse as the profile and an angled line as the path.

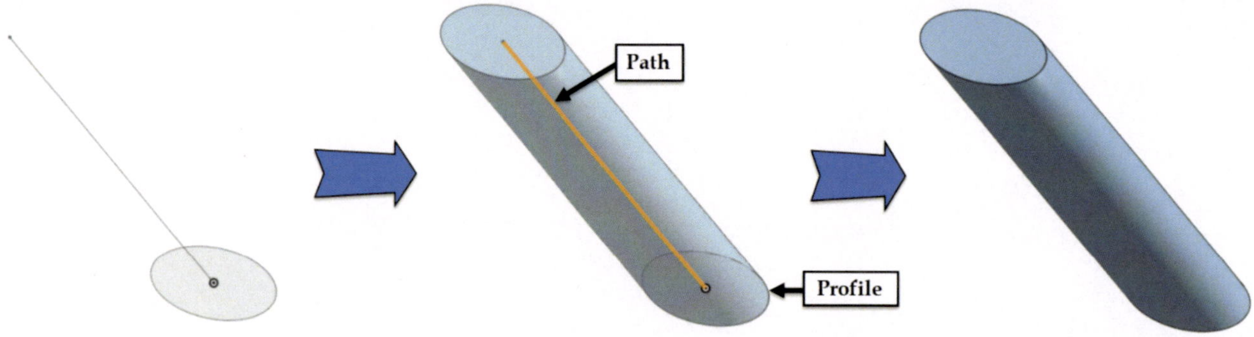

By making the path a bit more complex, you can see that a sweep allows you to create shapes you would not be able to create using commands such as Extrude or Revolve.

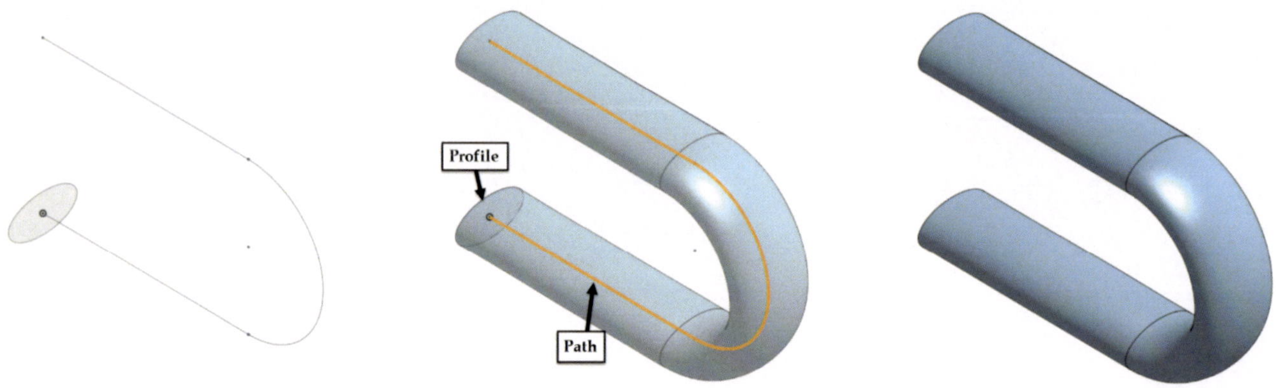

The topics covered in this chapter are:

- *Path sweeps*
- *Profile orientation*
- *Swept Cutouts*

Creating a sweep feature

The sweep feature requires two elements: a path and profile. The profile defines the shape of the sweep along the path. A path is used to control the direction of the profile. A path can be a sketch or an edge. To create a sweep, you must first create a path and a profile. Create a path by drawing a sketch. It can be an open or closed sketch. Next, click **Plane** on the toolbar, and then create a plane normal to the path using the **Curve point** option. Sketch the profile on the plane normal to the path.

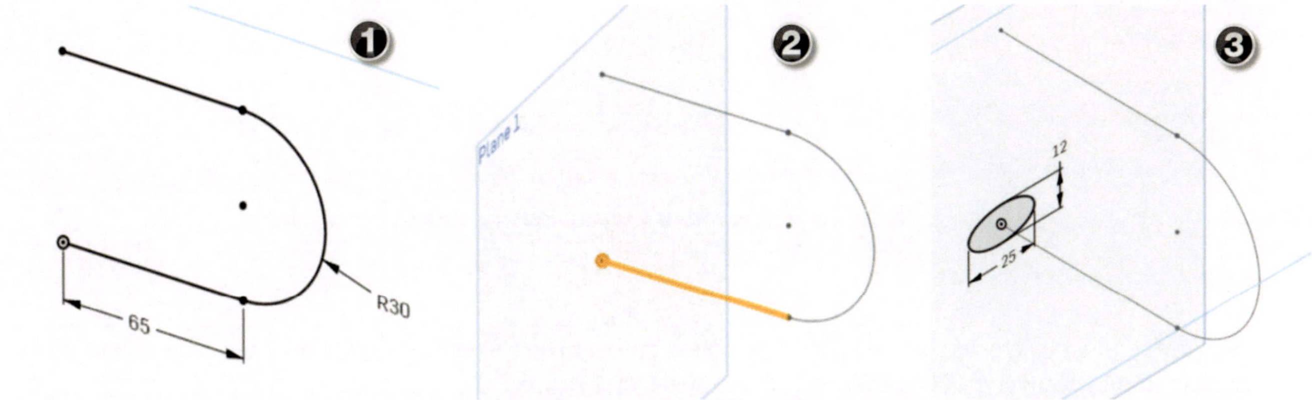

Click **Sweep** on the toolbar, and then select the profile from the graphics window. Next, click the **Sweep path** selection box and select the path. You can select multiple segments of the path in a single click by using the **Create selection** option. To do this, right-click and select Select > **Create selection**. Next, select anyone of the edge of the edge chain, and then click the **Add Selection** button. Next, close the **Create selection** dialog. Alternatively, you can select the path sketch directly from the **Features** list. Click the green check after the desired preview is displayed.

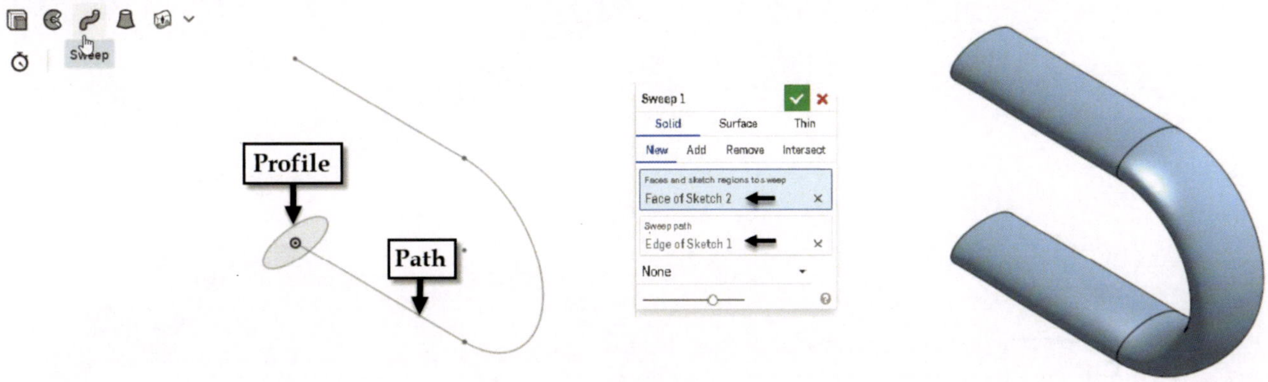

Onshape will not allow the sweep to result in a self-intersecting geometry. As the profile is swept along a path, it cannot come back and cross itself. For example, if the profile of the sweep is larger than the curves on the path, the resulting geometry will intersect and the sweep will fail.

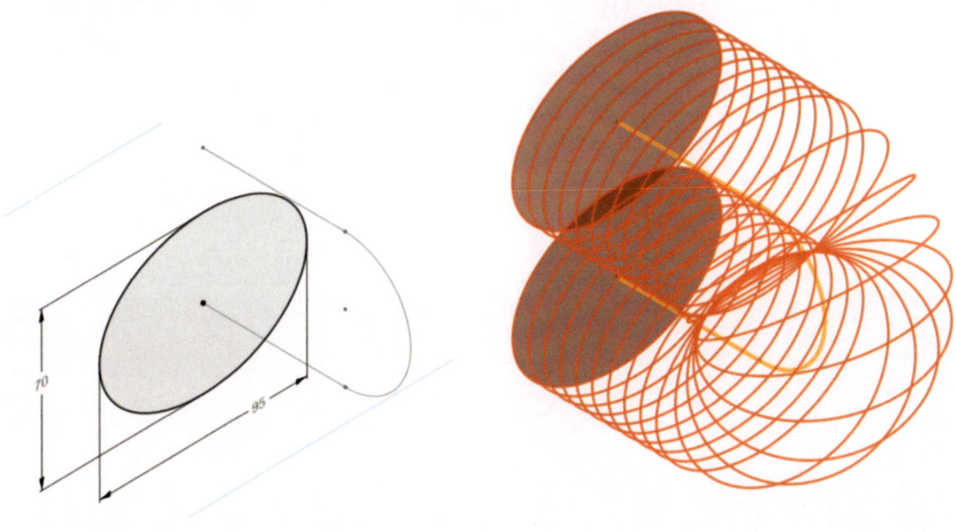

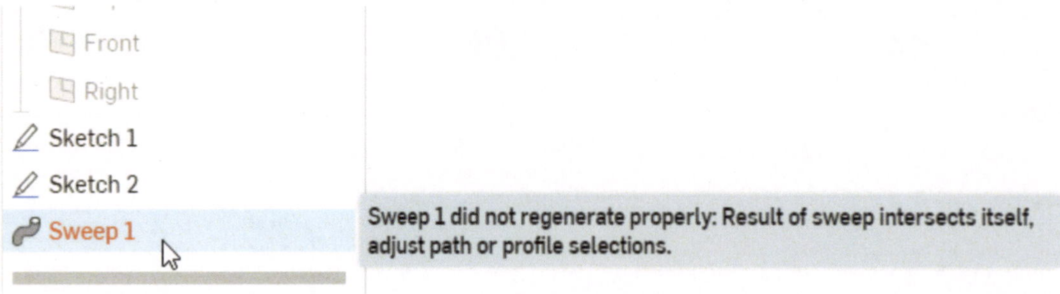

A sweep profile must be created as a sketch. However, a path can be a sketch, curve or an edge. The following illustrations show various types of paths and resultant sweep features.

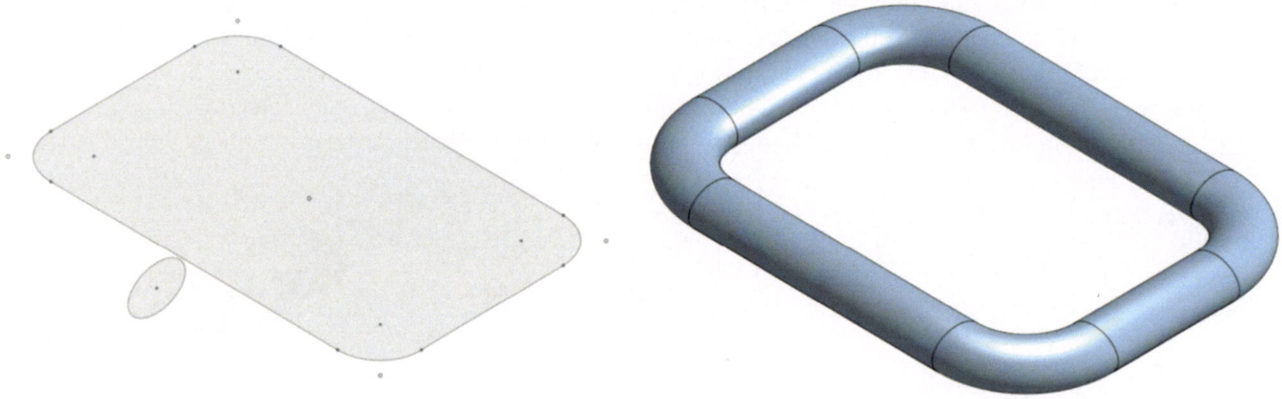

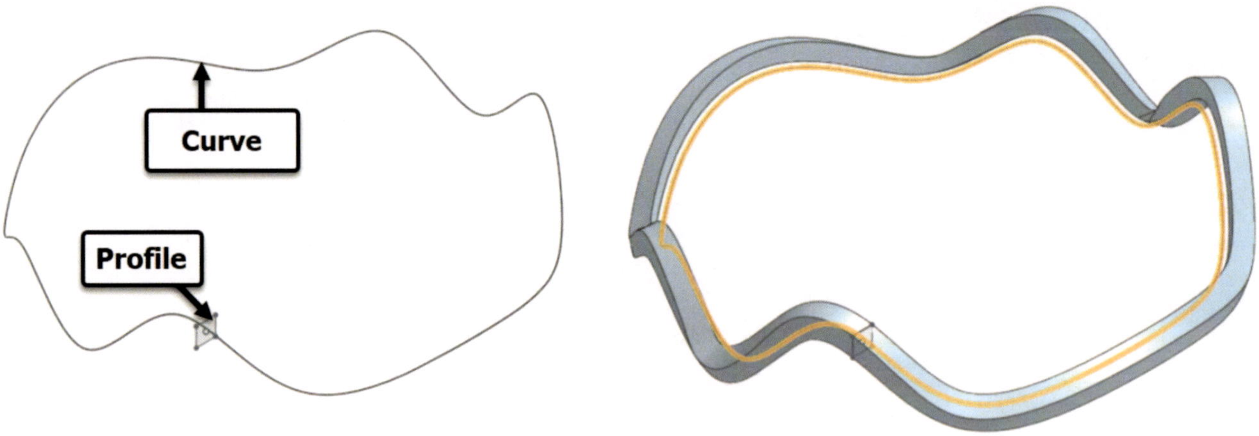

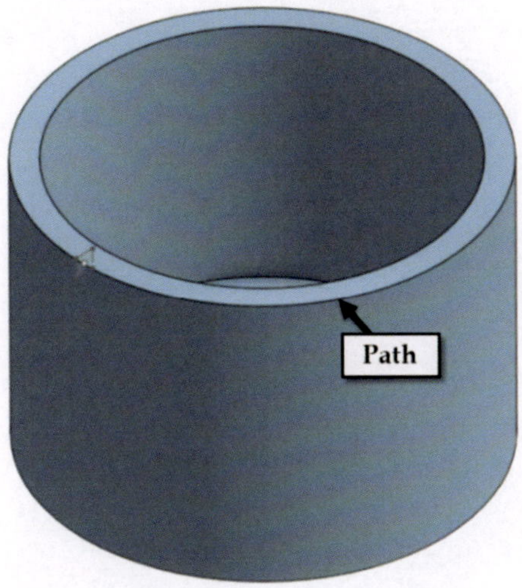

Profile Orientation

The **Profile control** drop-down available in the **Sweep** dialog defines the orientation of the resulting geometry. Select the **Keep profile orientation** option from the **Profile control** drop-down, to maintains the same orientation of the profile along the path. If you select the **None** option, the profile adjusts its orientation to stay perpendicular (at a 90-degree angle) to the path at all times.

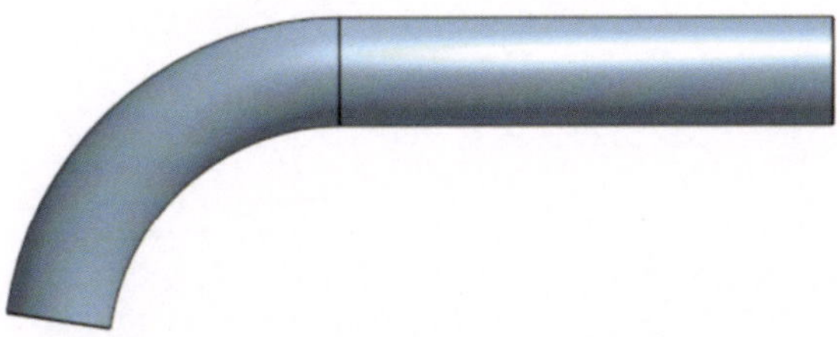

None

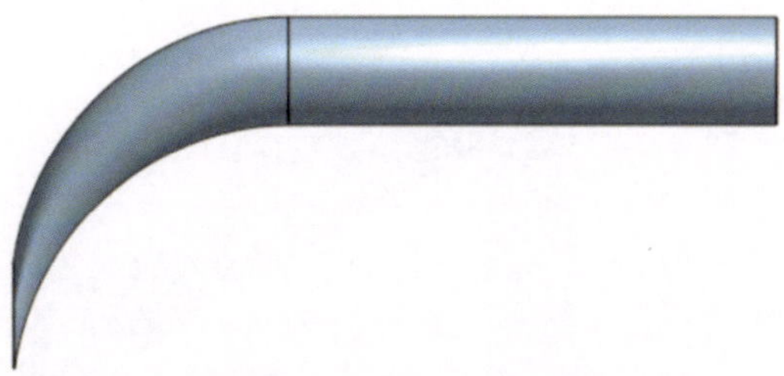

Keep profile orientation

The **Lock profile faces** option locks the selected face or faces of the profile, preventing them from changing shape or deforming as they move along the path. The **Lock profile direction** option locks the profile's orientation relative to a selected direction (such as an axis or plane).

Swept Cut

In addition to adding swept features, Onshape allows you to remove geometry using the swept feature. To do this, activate the **Sweep** command (click **Sweep** on the Toolbar) and click the **Remove** tab on the **Sweep** dialog. Select the profile from the part geometry. Click on the **Sweep path** selection box and select the path. Next, select **Keep profile orientation** option from the **Profile control** drop-down. You can also use the **Merge with all** option to control whether the resulting geometry merges with existing solid bodies or remains separate. Click green check ✓ to create the swept cut.

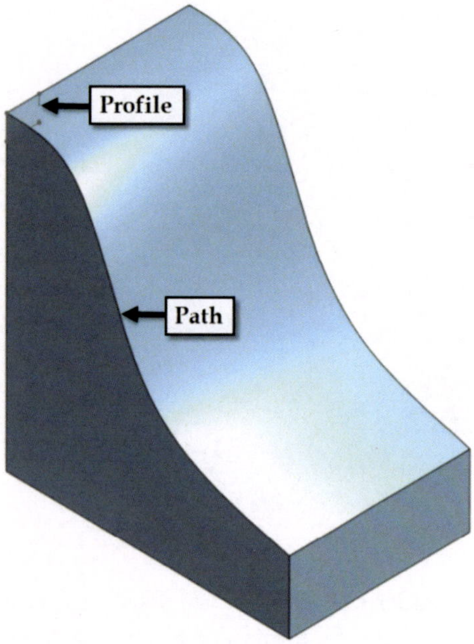

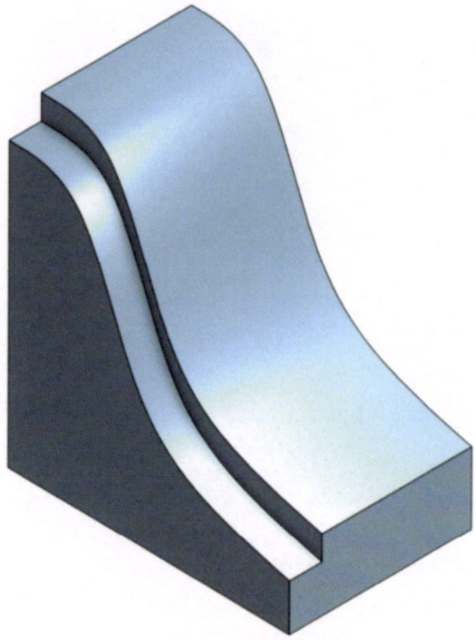

Tutorial 1

In this example, you create the part shown below.

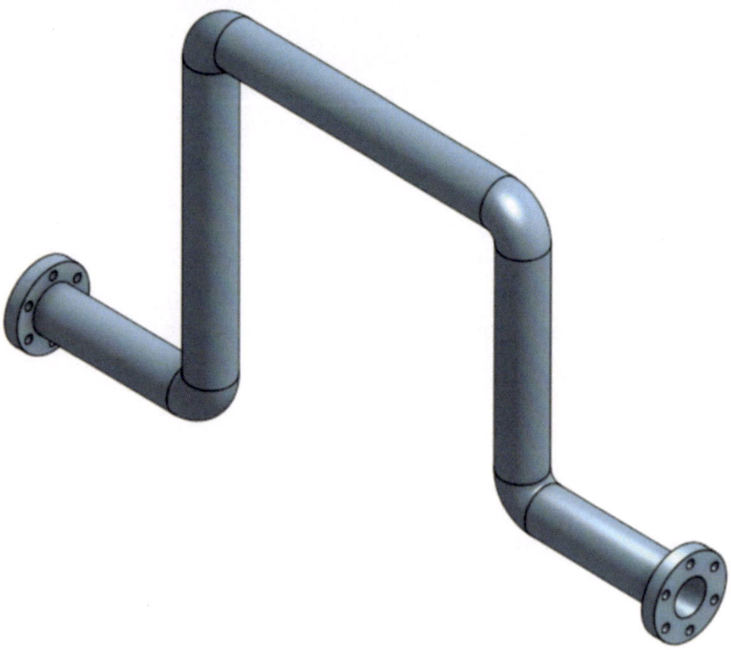

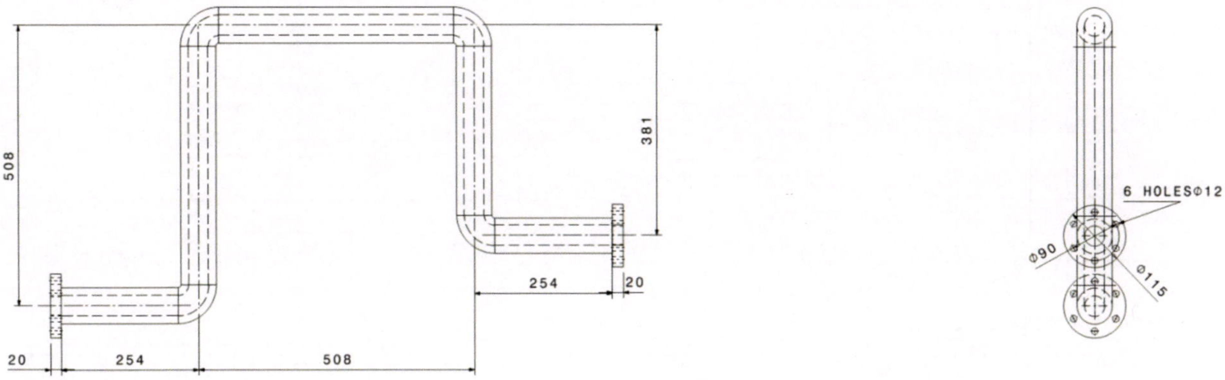

PIPE I.D. 51

PIPE O.D. 65

Creating a New document

1. In your Internet Browser, go to https://www.onshape.com to start Onshape.
2. Next, click **SIGN IN** button located on the top right corner side of the web page. Enter the username and password, and then, click **Sign in**.
3. On the Documents page, click **Create > Folder**. Next, type Chapter 6 in the **Folder name** box and then click **Create**.
4. Double-click on the **Chapter 6** folder in the **Folders** section.
5. On the Documents page, click **Create > Document**; the **New document** dialog appears on the screen.
6. Enter Tutorial 1 in the **Document name** box and click **Create public document**; a new document appears.
7. Click the **Document menu** located at the top left corner of the window and select **Workspace Units**; the **Workspace Units** dialog appears on the screen.
8. On the **Workspace Units** dialog, **select Length default unit> Millimeter** from **Length** section.
9. Select **Mass default unit > Gram** from the **Mechanical** section.
10. Leave the other default settings and click the green check.

Creating the Sweep Feature

1. To start a new sketch, click the **Sketch** command on the Toolbar.
2. Click on the Front plane.
3. Right-click and select **View normal to sketch plane**; the selected plane orients normal to the screen.
4. On the Toolbar, click the **Line** command and select the sketch origin.
5. Create the lines, as shown.
6. Right click and select Escape line.

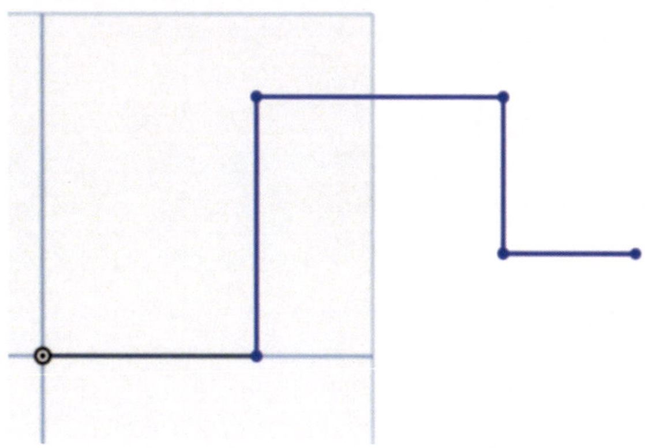

7. On the Toolbar, click the **Sketch fillet** command and select the corner points of the sketch.

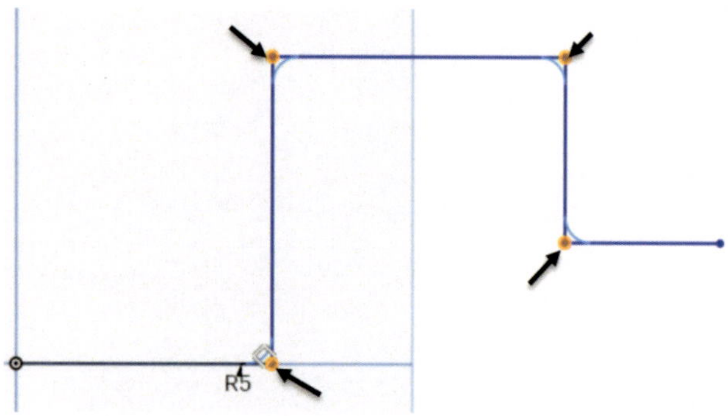

8. Click in the graphics area.
9. Type **38** and press Enter.

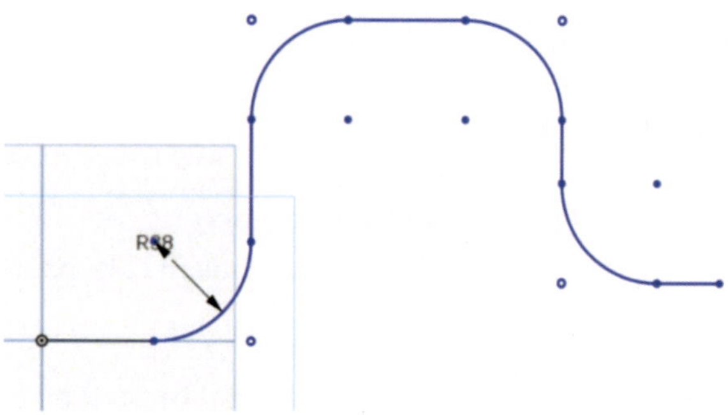

10. On the Toolbar, click the **Dimension** command.
11. Select the origin point and the vertical line.
12. Move the pointer downward and click to position the dimension.

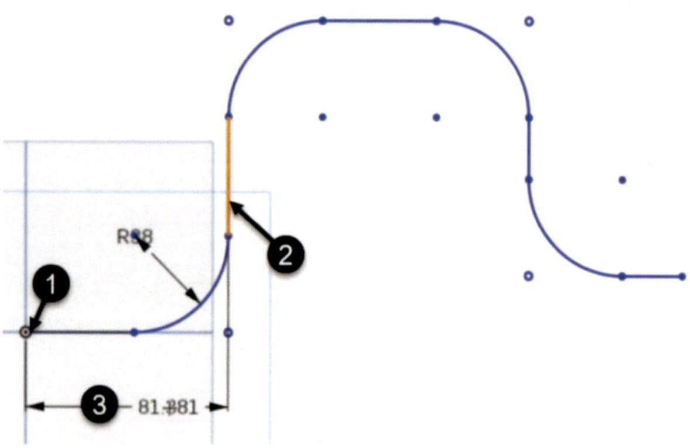

13. Type 254 and press Enter.
14. Select the two horizontal lines of the sketch.
15. Move the pointer toward the left and click to position the dimension.
16. Type 508 and press Enter.

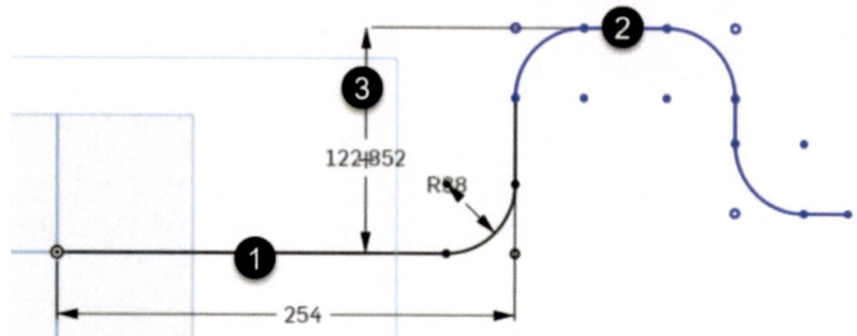

17. Likewise, apply the other dimensions to the sketch.

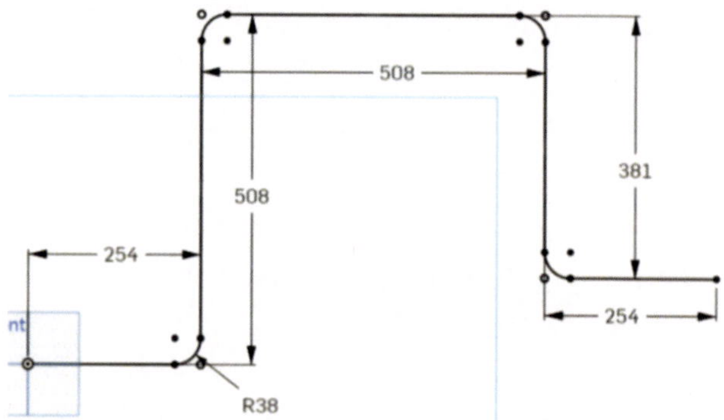

18. Click **green check** on the **Sketch 1** dialog.
19. Change the view orientation to Isometric view. (In the graphics area, click the **Camera and render options > Isometric** from the right-side).
20. On the Toolbar, click the **Plane** command.
21. Click the **Plane type** drop-down **> Point normal**.

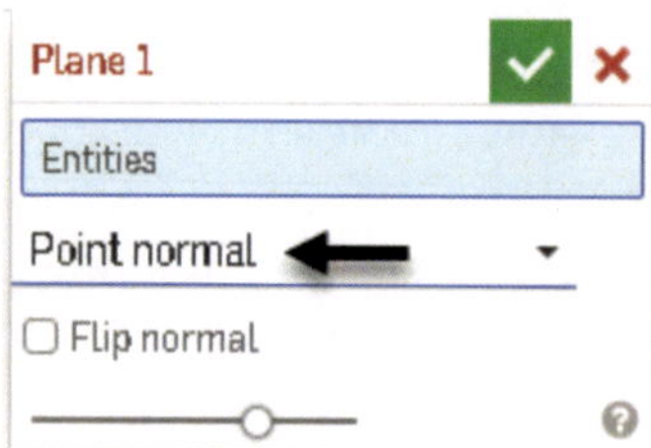

22. Select the lower horizontal line of the sketch to define the first entity.
23. Click on the end-point of the sketch to define the plane location.

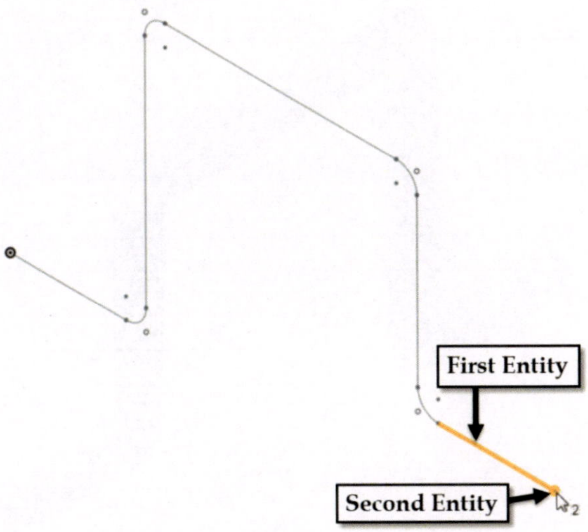

24. Click the green check on the **Plane** dialog to create a new plane.

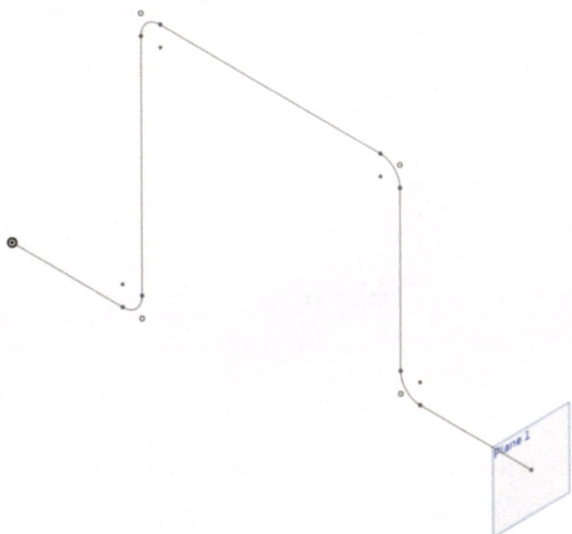

25. On the Toolbar, click the **Sketch** command.
26. Select the newly created plane.
27. On the Toolbar, click **Center point circle** command.
28. Specify the center point of the circle.
29. Move the pointer outward and click to create a circle.
30. Select the center point of the newly created circle.
31. Move the pointer outward and click to create another circle.

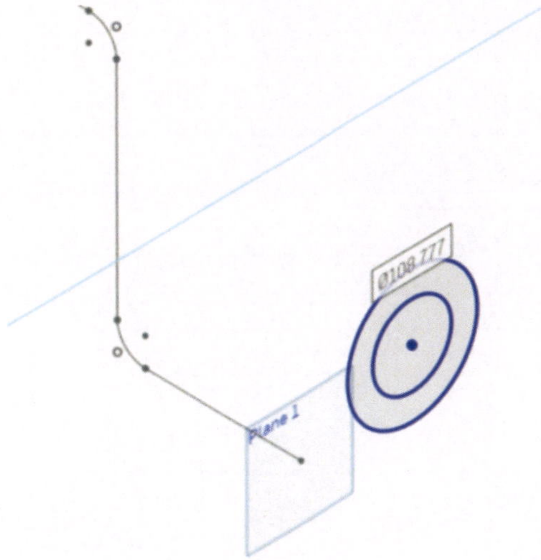

32. On the Toolbar, click Constraints drop-down > Coincident.
33. Select the center point of the circles.
34. Select the endpoint of the line.

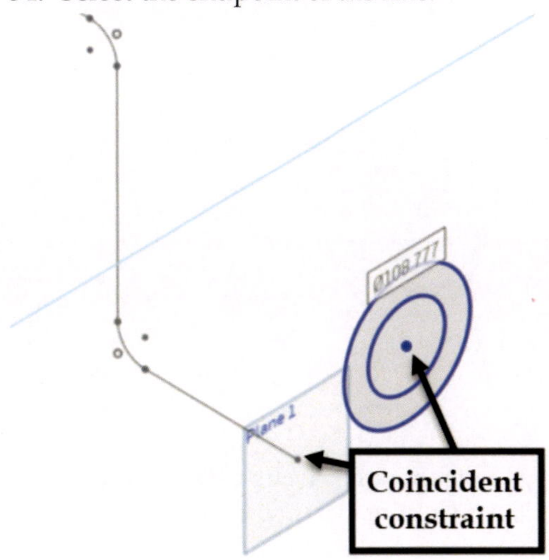

35. On the Toolbar, click the **Dimension** command.
36. Select the outer circle.
37. Type 65 and press Enter.
38. Select the other circle.
39. Type 51 and press Enter.

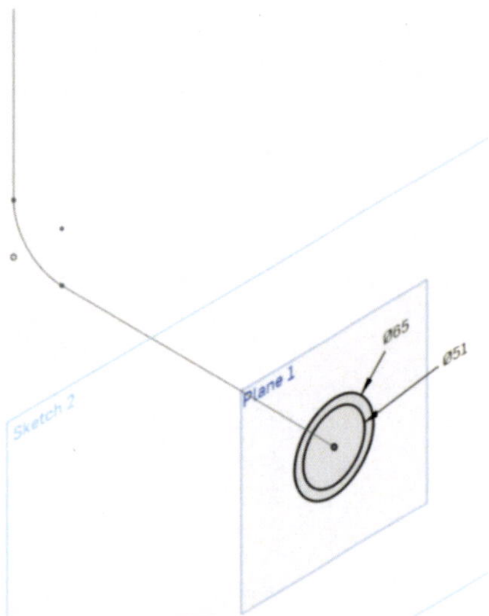

40. Click the green check on the **Sketch 2** dialog.
41. On the Toolbar, click the **Sweep** command.
42. Zoom in to the circles, and then click on the region between the two circles.

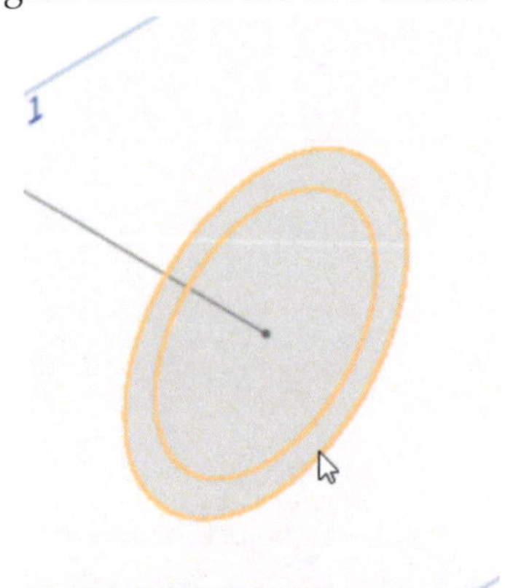

43. Click the **Sweep path** selection box and select the Sketch 1 from the **Features** window.

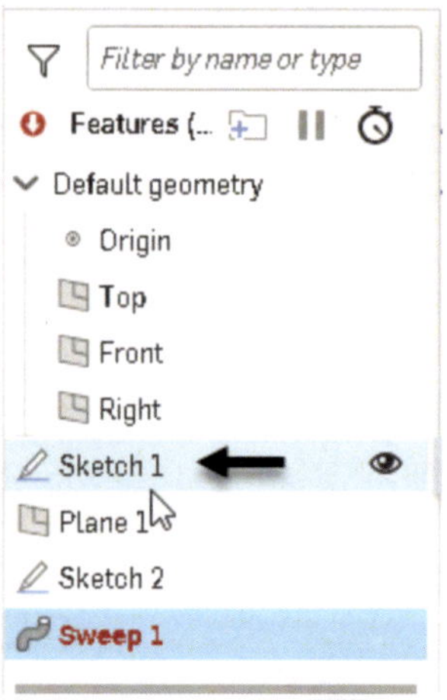

44. Click the green check to create the *Sweep* feature.

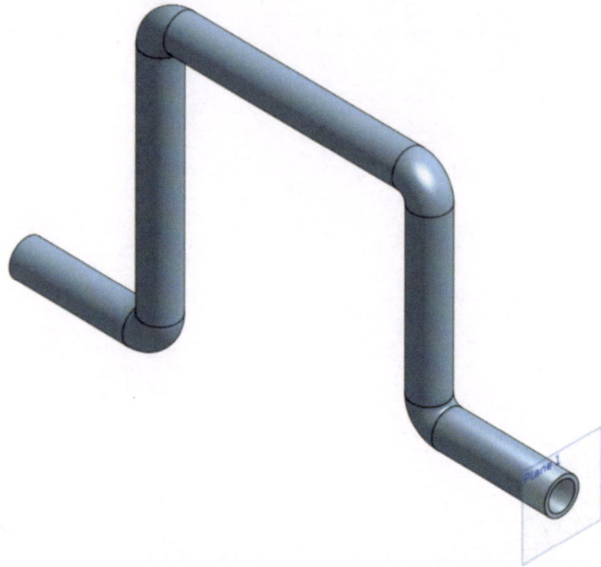

Adding the Extruded Feature

1. Click the **Sketch** command on the Toolbar.
2. Click on the front-end face of the *Sweep* feature.

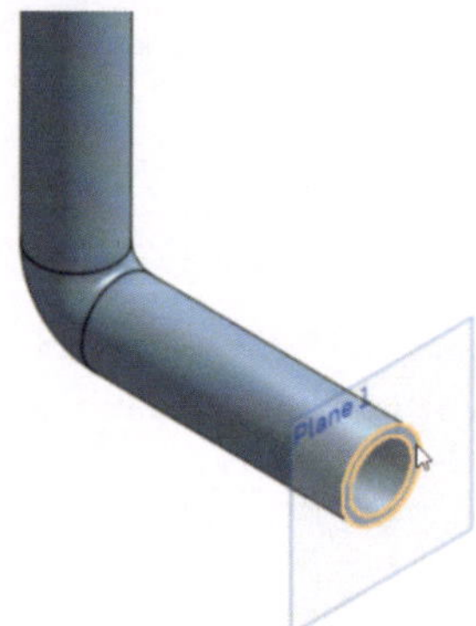

3. On the Toolbar, click the **Use (Project/Convert)** command.
4. Select the inner circular edge, as shown.

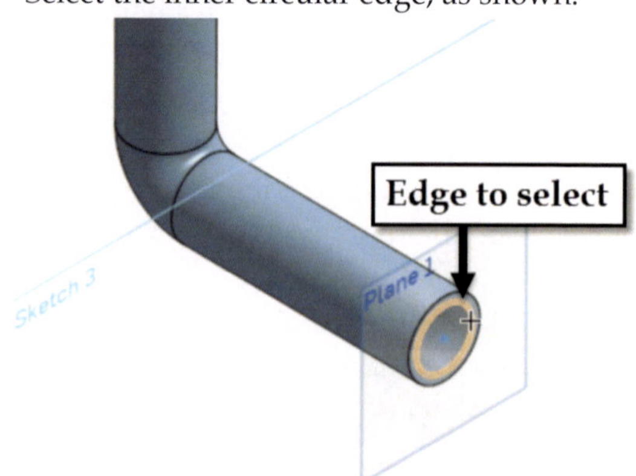

The edge is projected on to the sketch plane.

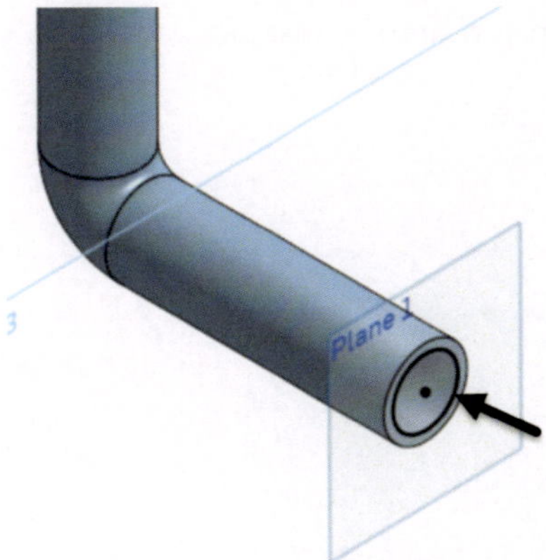

5. Draw a circle of 115 diameters.

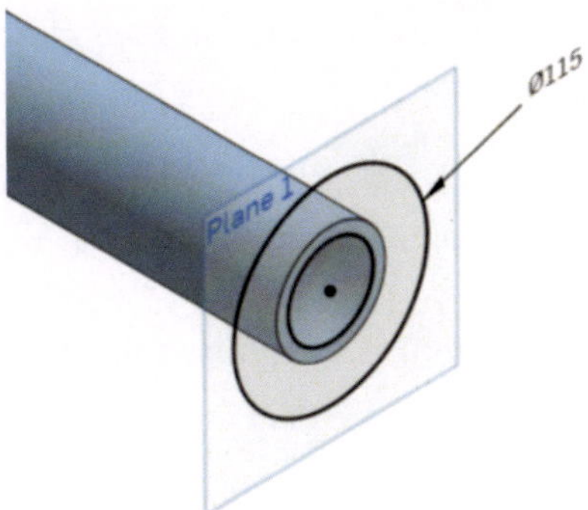

6. Click the green check on the **Sketch 3** dialog to confirm the sketch.
7. Activate the **Extrude** command.
8. Click on the regions enclosed by the sketch, as shown.

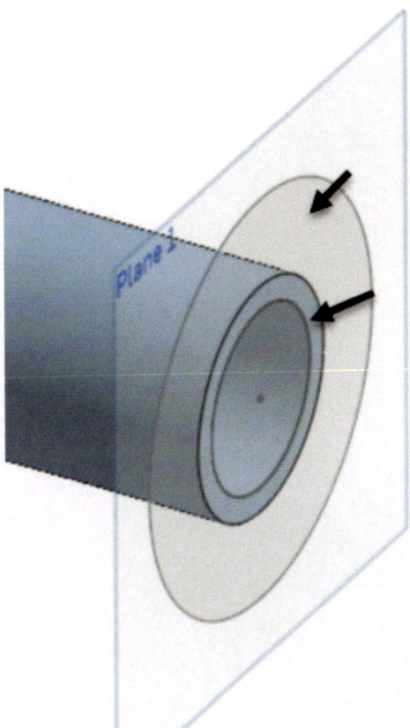

9. Type-in **20** in the **Depth** field. Click the **green** check to complete the *Extrude* feature.

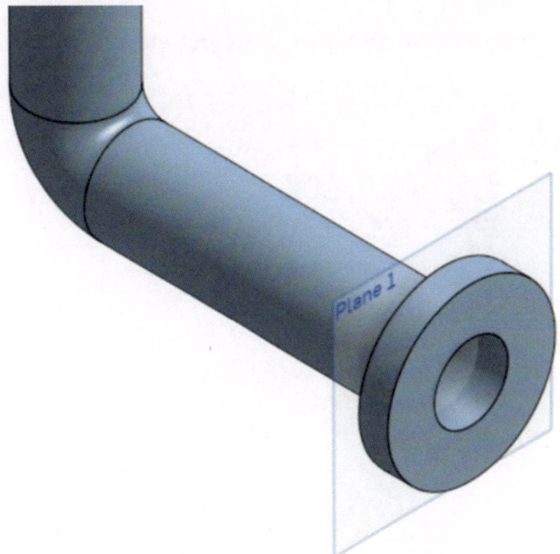

Creating the Circular Pattern

1. Activate the **Sketch** command and select the face of the extruded feature, as shown.

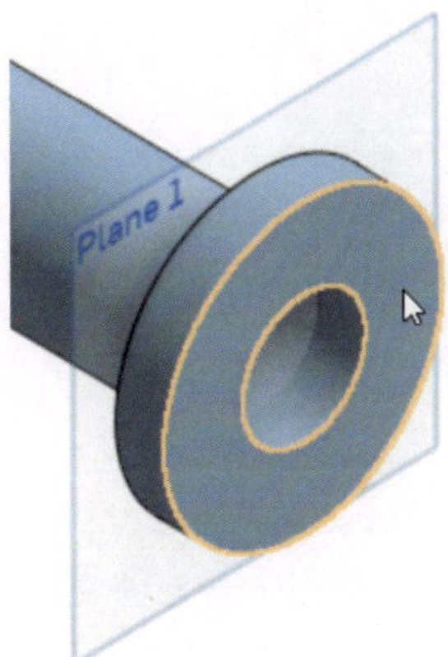

2. On the Toolbar, click the **Point** command and click on the sketch plane.

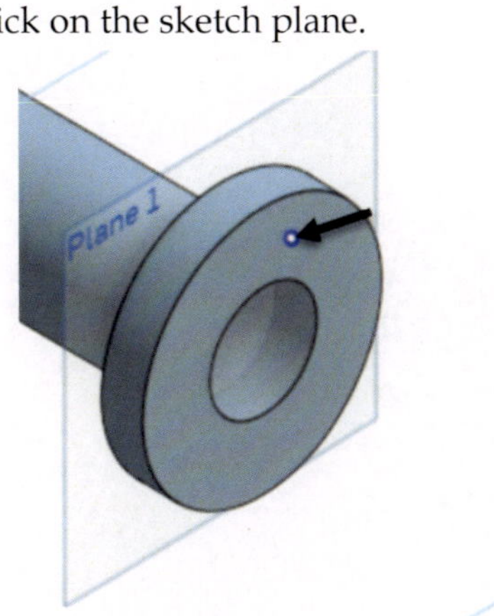

3. Click the **Line** command on the Toolbar.
4. Click the **Construction** command on the Toolbar.
5. Select centerpoint of the inner circular edge.

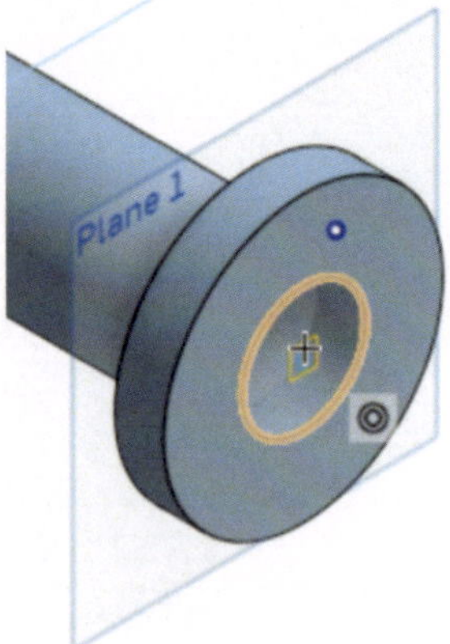

6. Move the pointer vertically upward and click.

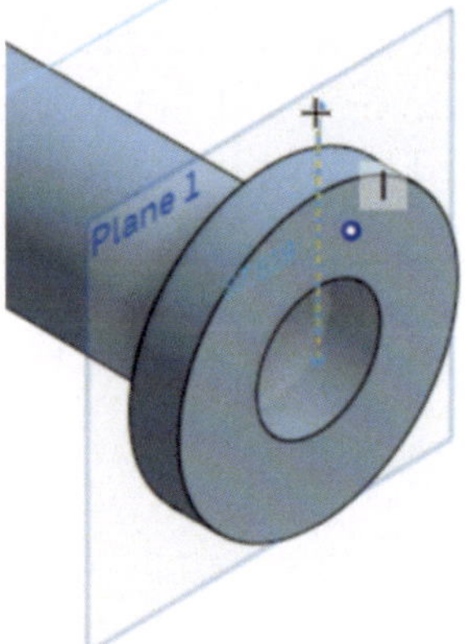

7. Right click and select **Escape line**.
8. On the toolbar, click **Constraints** drop-down > **Coincident**.
9. Select the sketch point and the endpoint construction line.

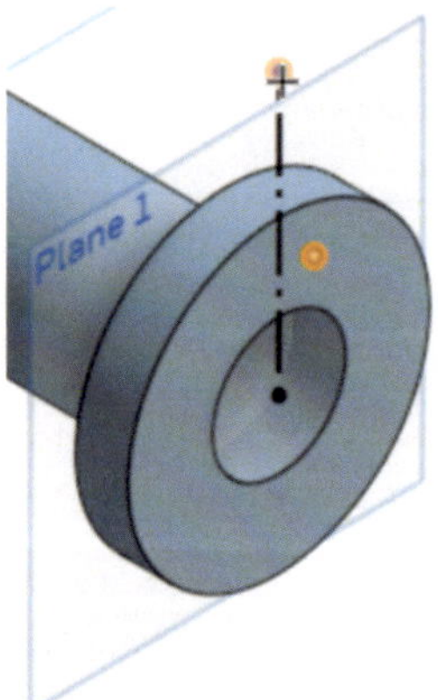

10. Apply dimension to the construction line, as shown.

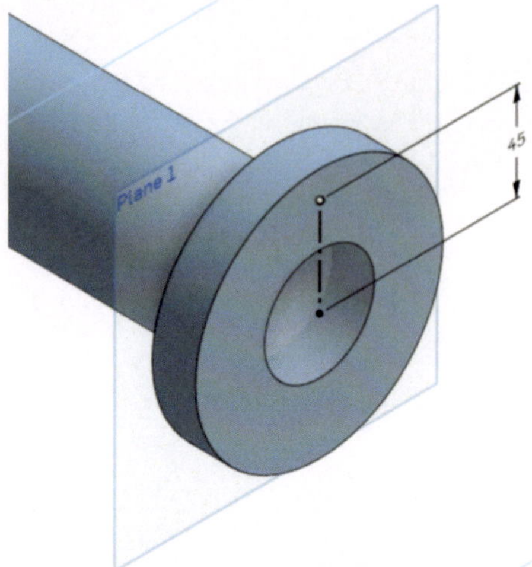

11. Click the green check on the **Sketch 4** dialog.
12. Activate the **Hole** command and select the sketch point.
13. Create a hole of 12 mm diameter on the *Extruded* feature.

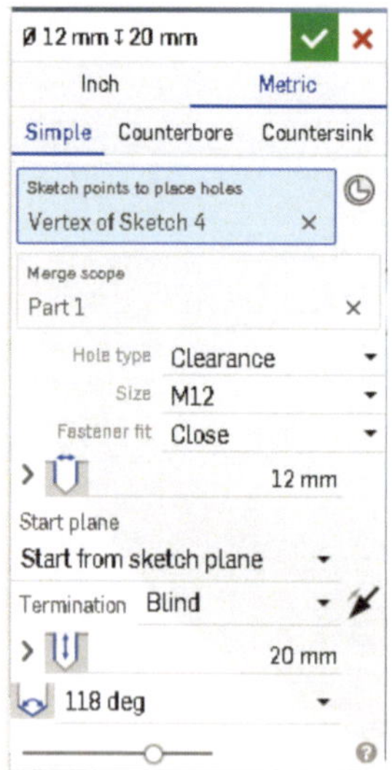

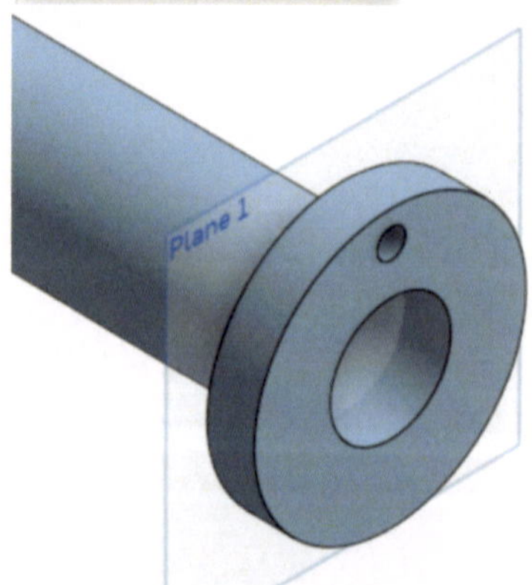

14. On the Toolbar, click the **Linear pattern** drop-down > **Circular pattern** .
15. On the **Circular pattern** dialog, click the **Pattern type > Feature pattern**.
16. Click on the **Features to pattern** selection box and select the 12 mm hole.
17. Click on the **Axis of pattern** selection box and select the outer circular face of the *Extruded* feature.
18. Type-in **360** and **6** in the **Angle** and **Instance count** fields, respectively.
19. Check the **Equal spacing** option and click the green check to pattern the hole.

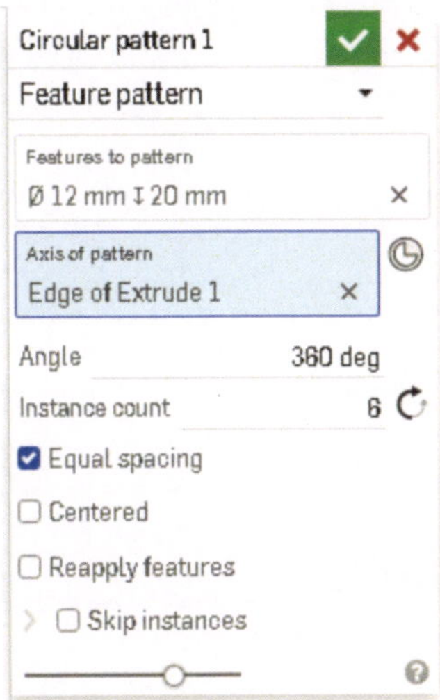

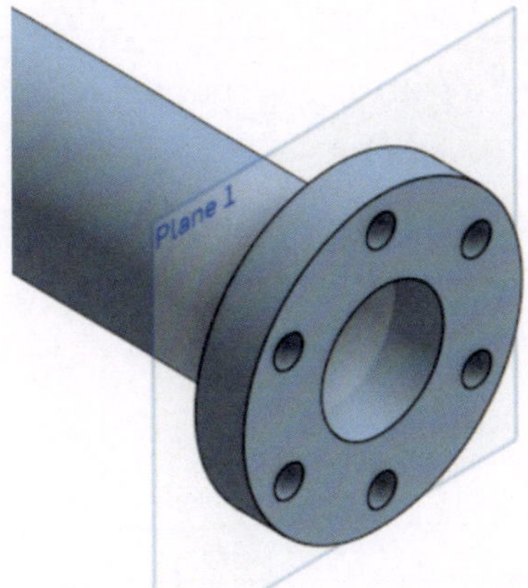

20. Create the *Extruded, Hole,* and *Circular pattern* features on the other end of the model.

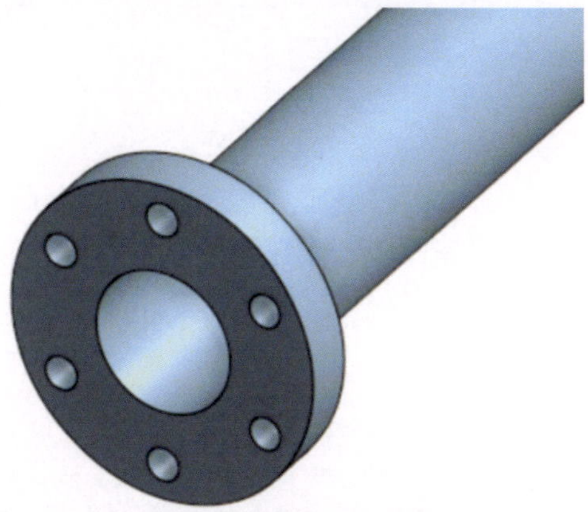

21. Click the **Document menu** located at the top-left corner of the window and click the **Close document** option to close the document.

Questions

1. List the types of a path that can be used to create *Swept* features.
2. How to create a swept cut?
3. What is the use of **Keep Profile orientation** option?

Exercises

Exercise1

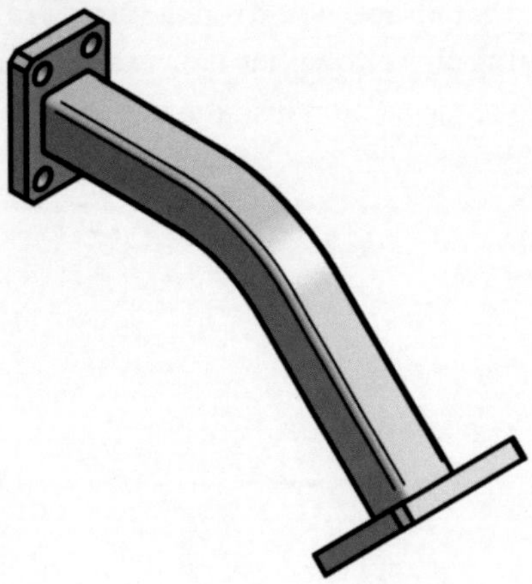

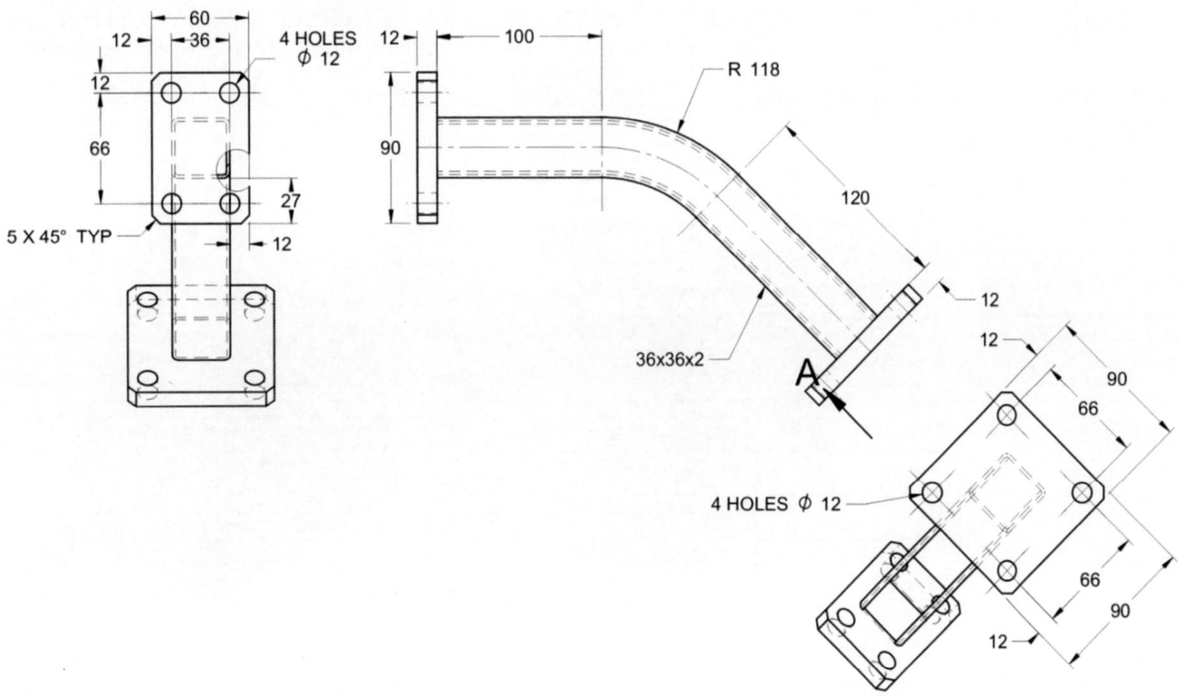

Chapter 7: Loft Features

The **Loft** command is one of the advanced commands available in Onshape that allows you to create simple as well as complex shapes. A basic loft is created by defining two profile and joining them together. For example, if you create a loft feature between a circle and a square, you can easily change the cross-sectional shape of the solid. This ability is what separates the loft feature from the sweep feature.

The topics covered in this chapter are:

- *Basic Lofts*
- *Loft profiles*
- *Start and End Conditions*
- *Loft Cutouts*

Loft

This command creates a loft feature between different profiles. To create a loft first, create two or more profiles on different planes. The planes can be parallel or perpendicular to each other. Activate the **Loft** command (click **Loft** on the Toolbar). Next, click in the **Profile** selection box on the dialog and select two or more profiles. Click green check to create a basic loft feature.

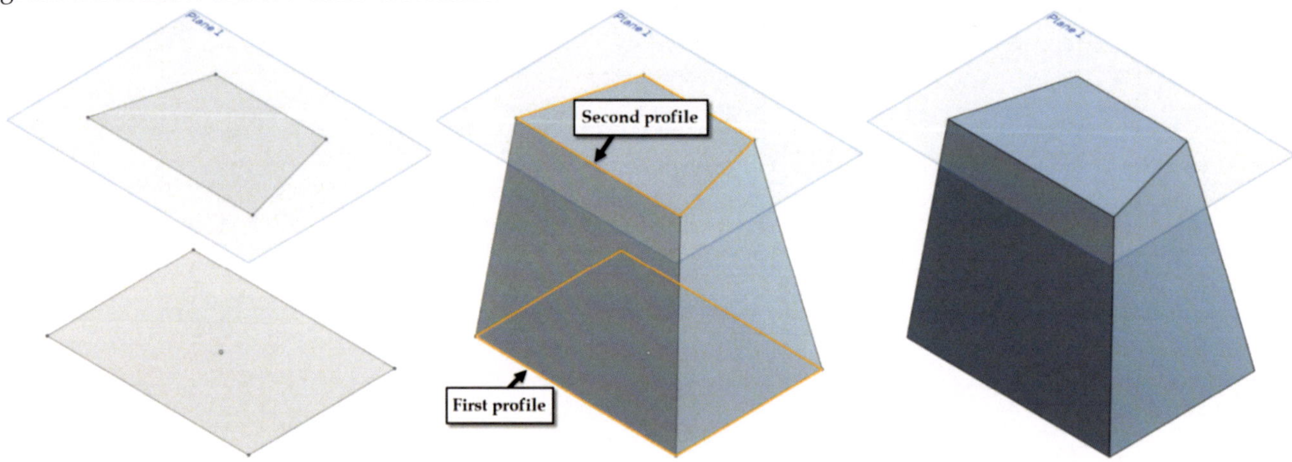

Loft Profiles

In addition to 2D sketches, you can also define loft profiles by using different element types. For instance, you can use existing model faces, surfaces, curves, and points. The only restriction is that the points can be used at the beginning or end of a loft.

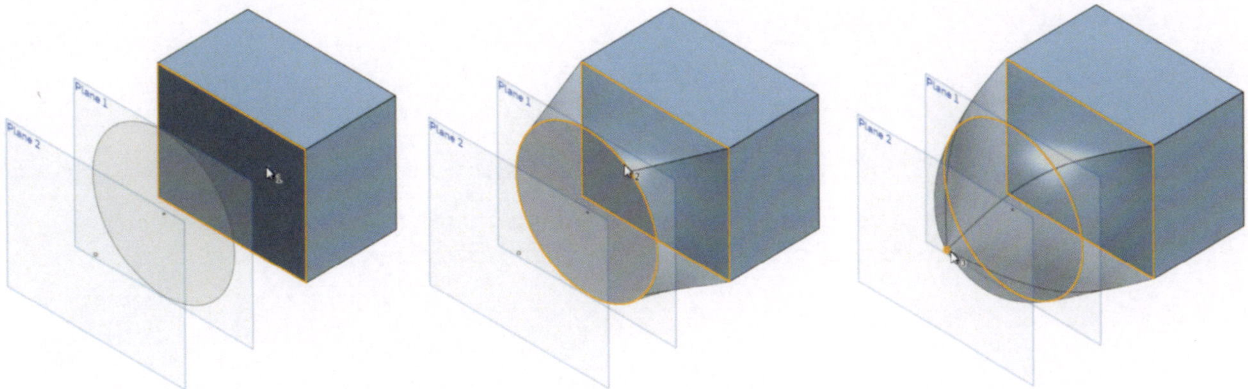

Connections

Profiles used for creating lofts should have a matching number of segments. For example, a four-sided profile will loft nicely to another four-sided profile despite the differences in the shape of the individual segments. The **Loft** command generates smooth faces to join them.

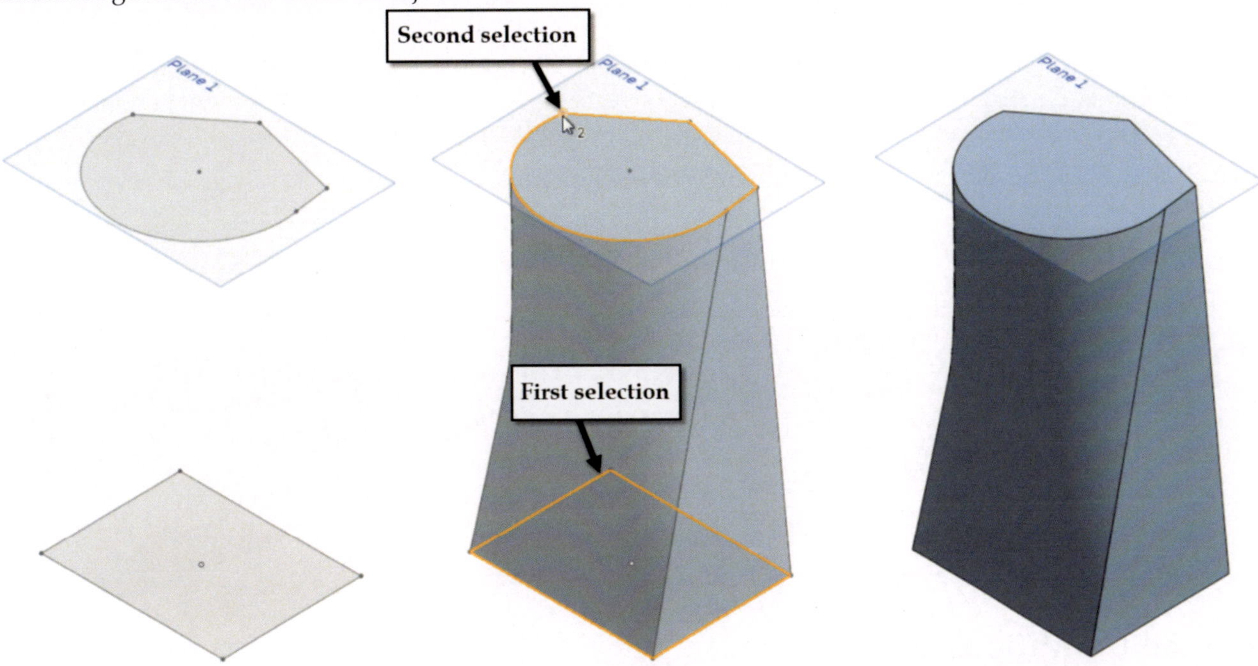

On the other hand, a five-sided profile will not loft nicely to a two-sided profile. Although Onshape succeeds in generating a loft feature, it maps the endpoints incorrectly and you may not get the desired result.

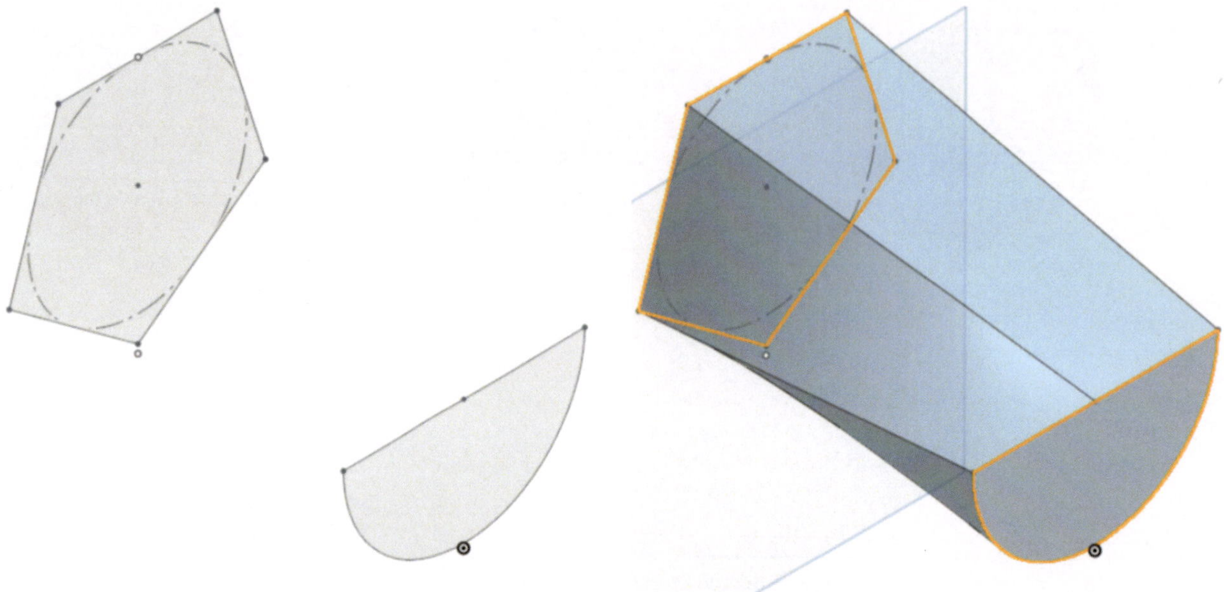

To get the desired result, you have to use the **Connections** option and match the vertices of both the sections. To do this, check the **Connections** option and the first set of vertices of the first and second section, as shown. Next, collapse the selections section in the **Loft** dialog and select the second set of vertices. Likewise, you can specify more sets. Next, click the green check to complete the feature.

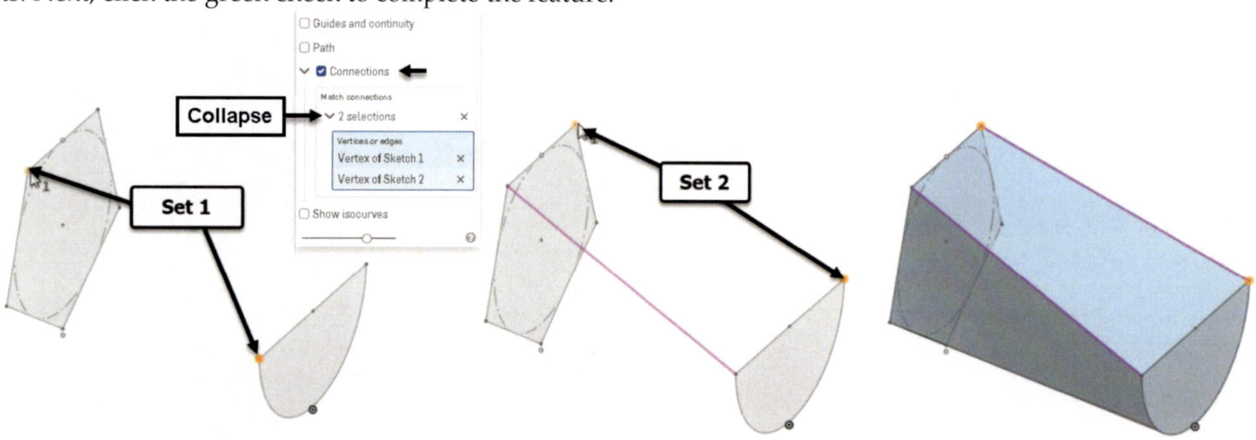

Start-End Conditions

The shape of a simple loft is controlled by the profile sketches and the plane location. However, the **Start profile condition** and **End profile condition** drop-downs can control the behavior of the side faces. You can use these drop-downs if you would like to change the appearance of the side faces.

Normal to Profile

Select the **Start profile condition** drop-down **> Normal to profile** on the **Loft** dialog; the preview of the loft updates. Next, enter the magnitude value in the **Start magnitude** box; the preview of the loft updates. You can notice that the beginning of the loft starts at an angle to the profile. You can control how much influence the angle will have by adjusting the parameter in the **Start magnitude** box. A lower value will have a lesser effect on the feature. As you increase the value, the more noticeable the effect will be, eventually. If you increase the number high enough, the magnitude value will lead to self-intersecting results.

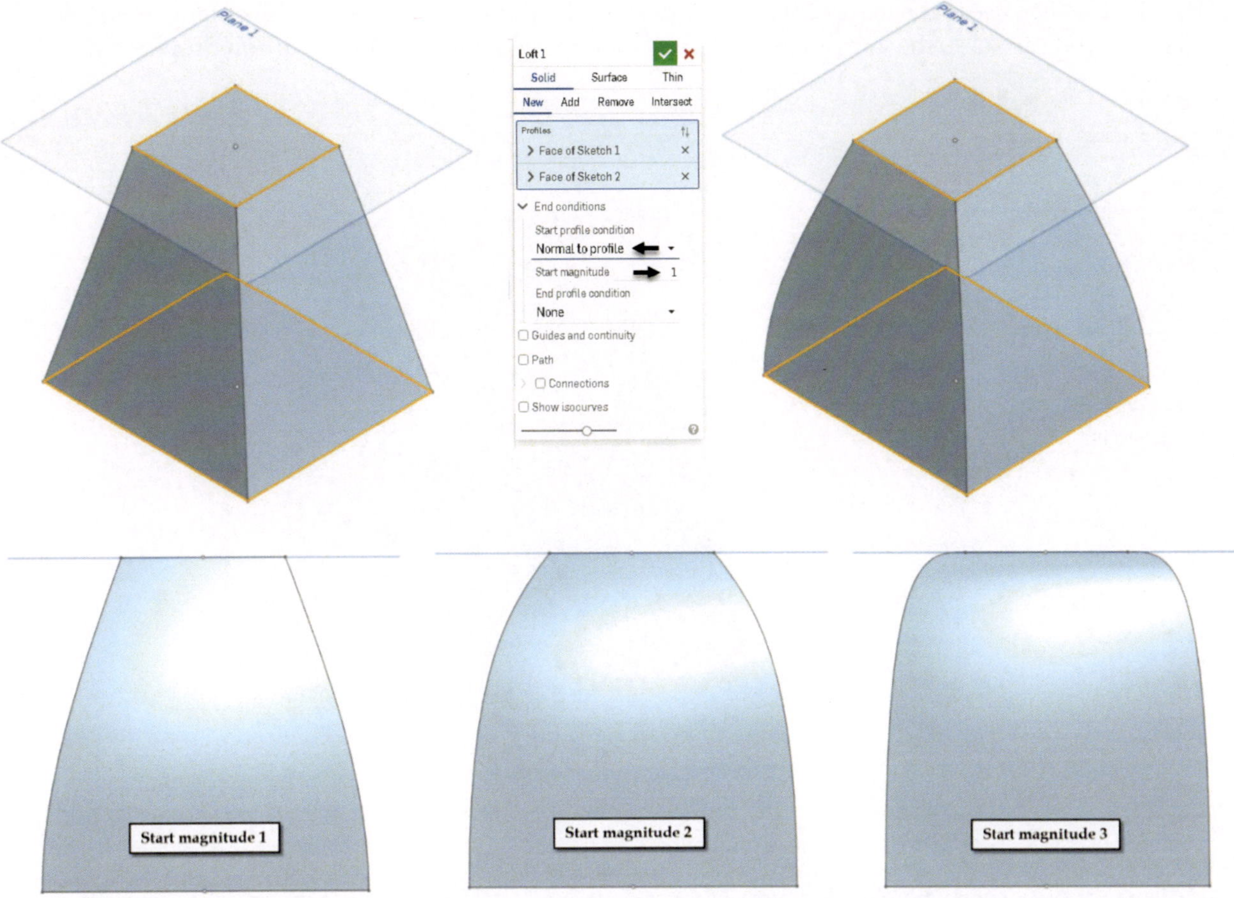

Likewise, you can also apply the **Normal to profile** constraint to the second profile of the loft.

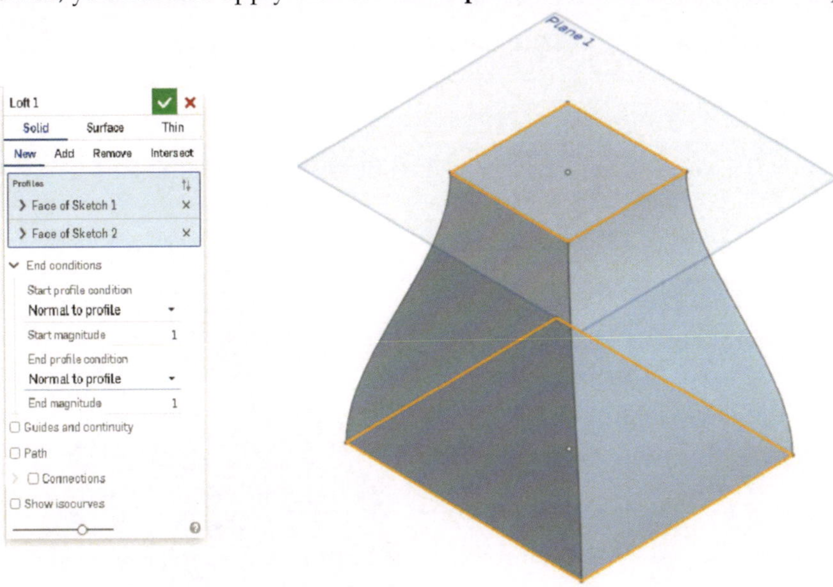

Tangent to Profile

Select the **Start profile condition** drop-down **> Tangent to profile** on the **Loft** dialog; the preview of the loft updates. Next, enter the magnitude value in the **Start magnitude** box; portion of the side faces will be tangent to the start profile. The increase in the magnitude value increases the percentage of the side faces tangent to start profile. Likewise, you can select the **Tangent to profile** option from the **End profile condition** drop-down.

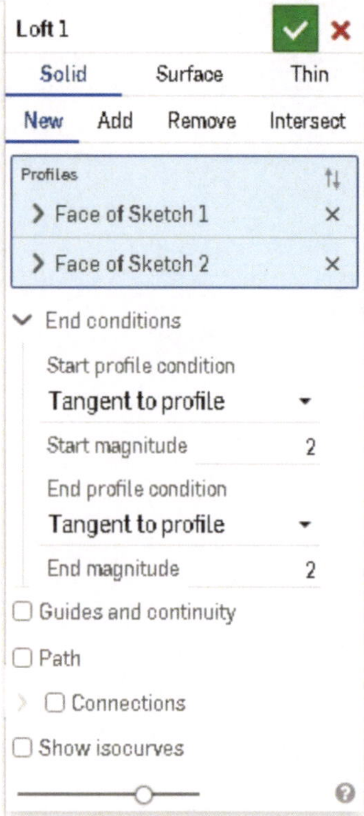

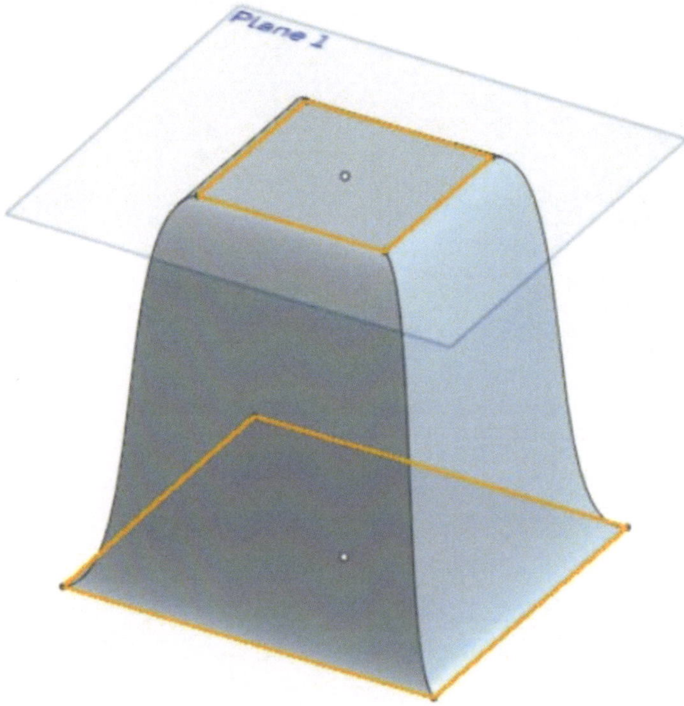

Match Tangent

The **Match Tangent** option is available when you select an existing face loop as one of the profiles. This option makes the side faces of the loft feature tangent to the side faces of the existing geometry. Click an existing face from the part geometry and select the second profile. On the **Loft** dialog, click **Start profile condition** drop-down > **Match tangent** option. Specify the magnitude value in the **Start magnitude** field. Click the green check to create the loft.

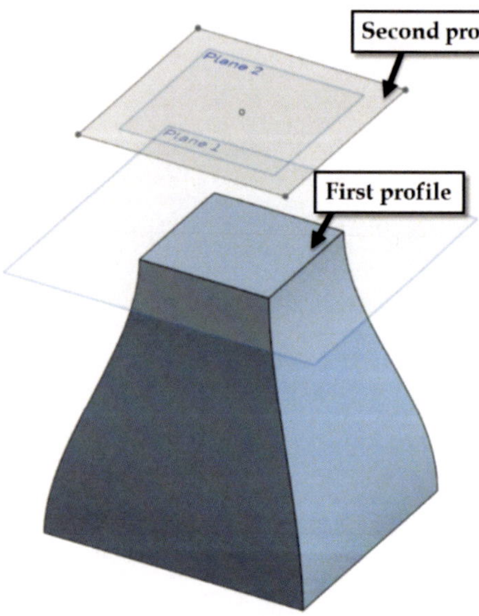

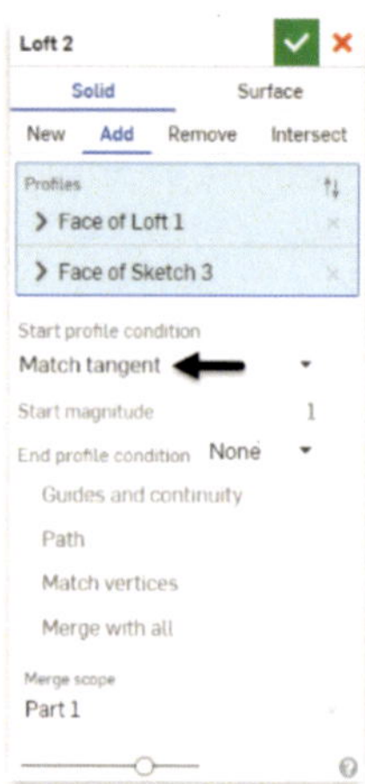

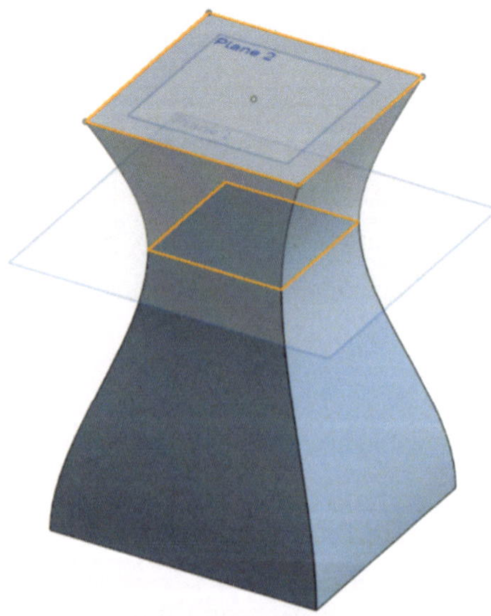

Match curvature

The **Match curvature** option is available when you select an existing face loop as one of the profiles. This option makes the side faces of the loft feature curvature continuous with the side faces of the existing geometry. In the part geometry, click an existing face and select the second profile. Click **Start profile condition** drop-down > **Match curvature** option. Specify the magnitude in the **Start magnitude** field and click the green check to create the loft.

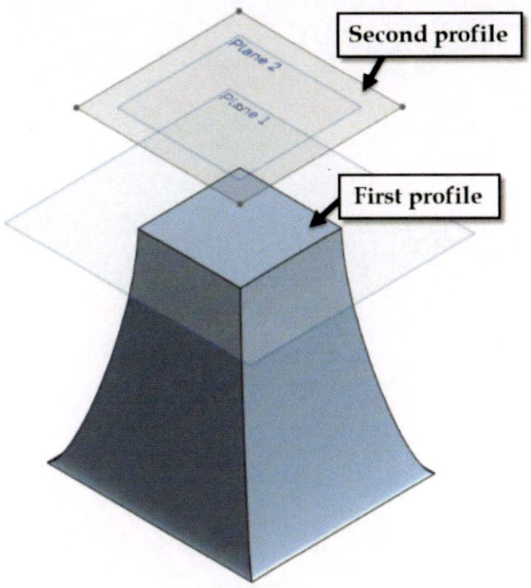

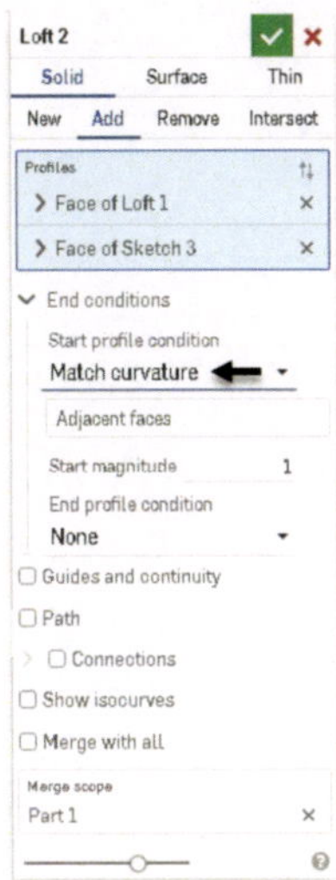

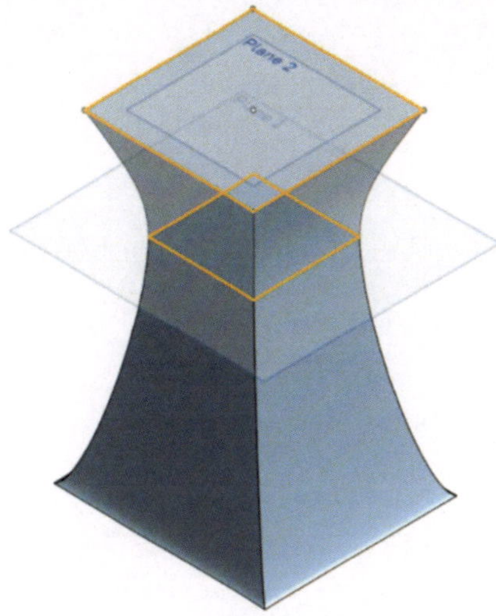

Guide and continuity

Similar to the **Start profile condition** and **End profile condition** options, guide curves allow you to control the behavior of a loft between profile. You can create curves by using 2D or 3D sketches. For example, create sketches on the plane intersecting with the profiles, as shown. Make sure that the sketches are connected to the profiles (use the **Pierce** constraint to connect the profile and guide curves).

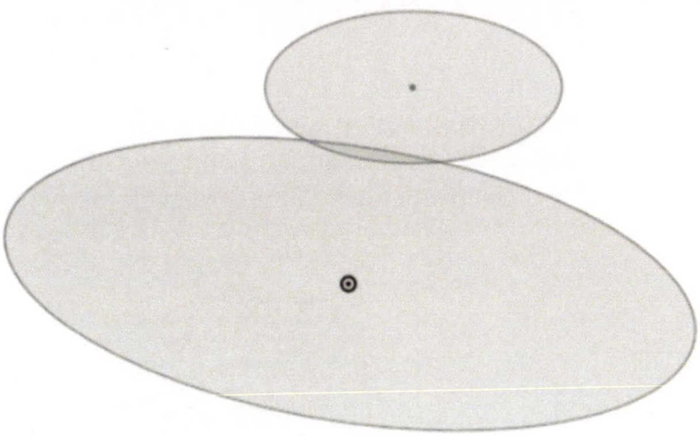

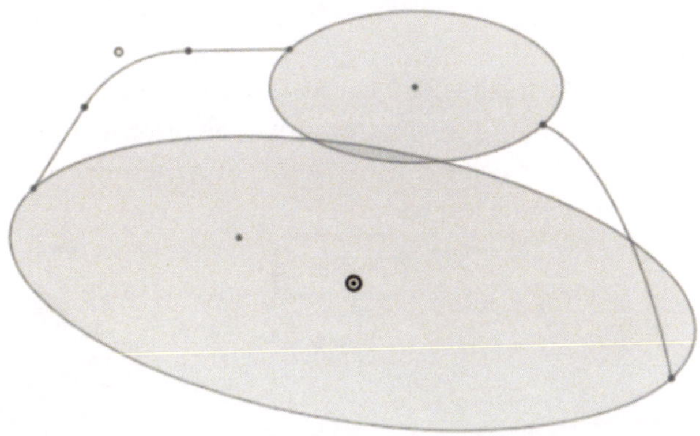

Now, activate the **Loft** command and select the profiles. To select guide curves, check the **Guide and continuity** option and select the guide curves from the **Features** list; you will see that the preview updates. Notice that the edges with guides are affected.

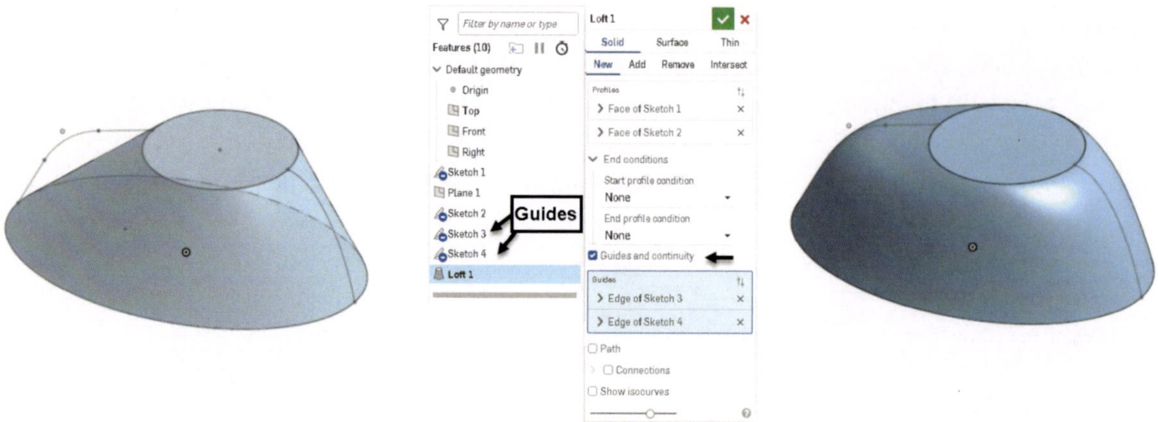

You can expand the guide curve selection on the **Loft** dialog and specify the desired **Continuity** option.

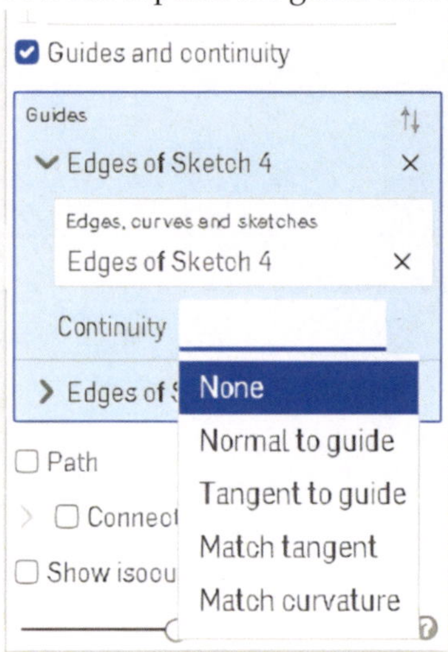

Path

The **Path** option helps you to create a loft feature with the help of a path passing through the selected profiles. First, create a path passing through all the profiles, as shown. Next, activate the **Loft** command and select the profiles. Next, check the **Path** option, and then select the path. Specify the **Section count** value and click green check to create the loft feature.

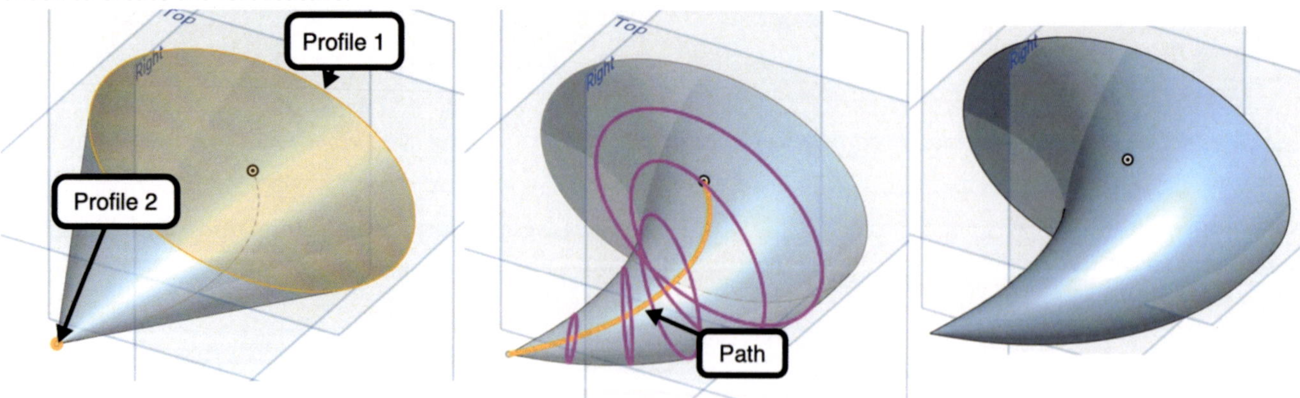

Removing the material using Loft command

Like other standard features such as extrude, revolve and sweep, the loft feature can be used to add material or remove material. You can remove material by using the **Loft** command. Activate this command by clicking **Loft** on the Toolbar and click the **Remove** tab on the **Loft** dialog. Next, select the profiles one-by-one and click the green check to create the lofted cut.

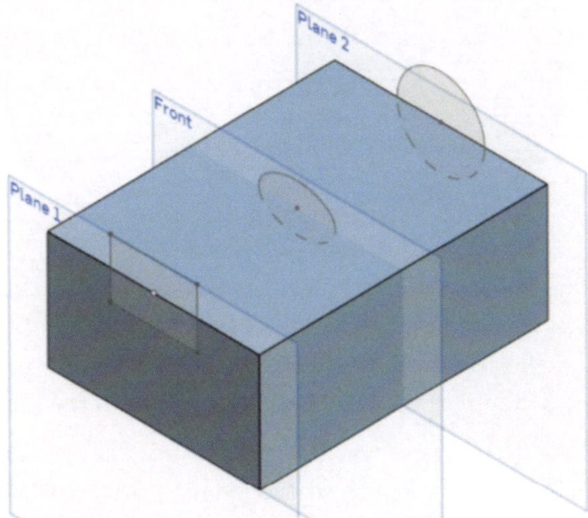

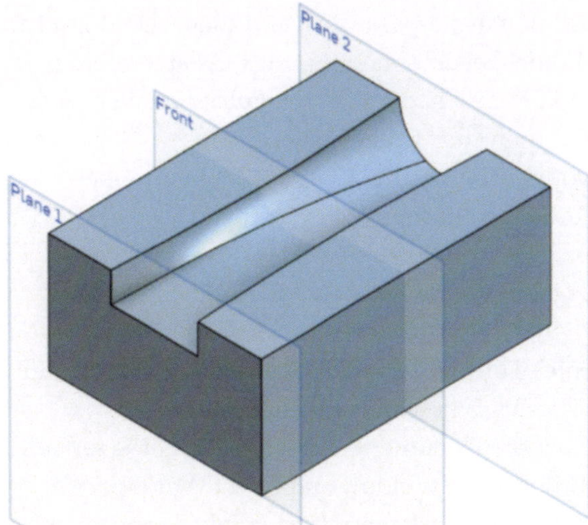

Tutorials

Tutorial 1

In this example, you create the part shown below.

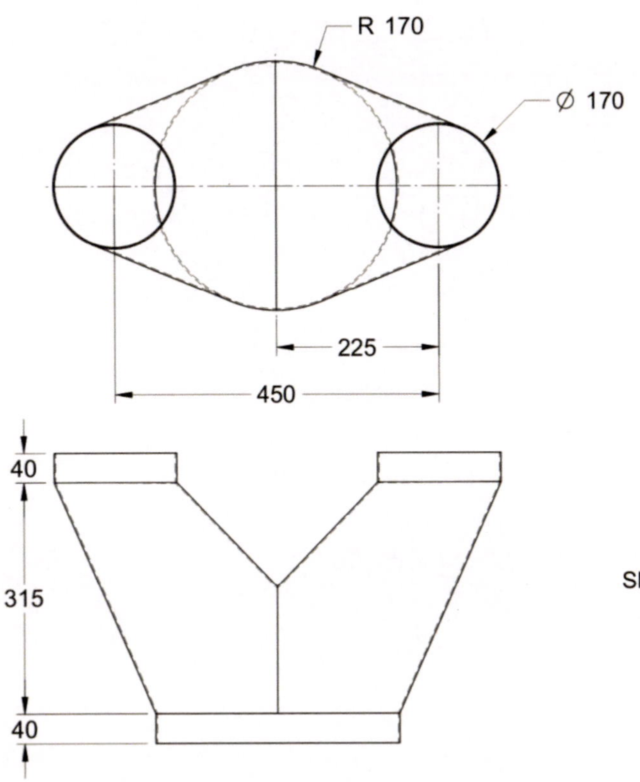

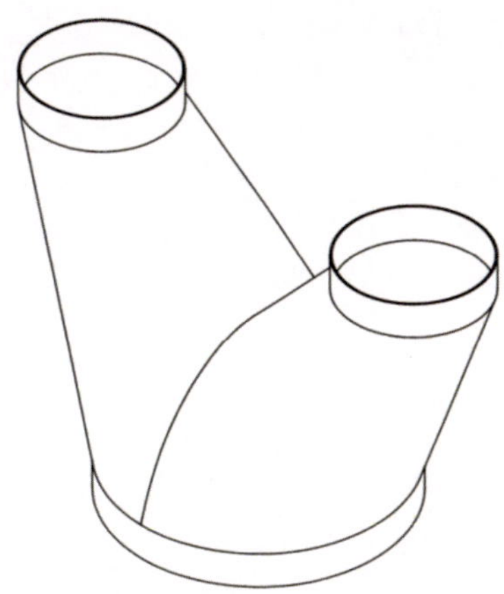

SHELL INSIDE TO 2 mm

Creating a New document

1. In your Internet Browser, go to https://www.onshape.com to start Onshape.
2. Next, click **SIGN IN** button located on the top right corner side of the web page. Enter the username and password, and then, click **Sign in**.
3. On the Documents page, click **Create > Folder**. Next, type Chapter 7 in the **Folder name** box and then click **Create**.
4. Double-click on the **Chapter 7** folder in the **Folders** section.
5. On the Documents page, click **Create > Document**; the **New document** dialog appears on the screen.
6. Enter Tutorial 1 in the **Document name** box and click **OK**; a new document appears.
7. Click the **Document menu** located at the top left corner of the window and select **Workspace Units**; the **Workspace Units** dialog appears on the screen.
8. On the Workspace Units dialog, select **Length default unit> Millimeter** from **Length** section.
9. Select **Mass default unit > Gram** from the **Mechanical** section.
10. Leave the other default settings and click the green check.

Creating a Loft Feature

1. Start a new sketch on the Top plane and draw a circle of **340** mm diameters.

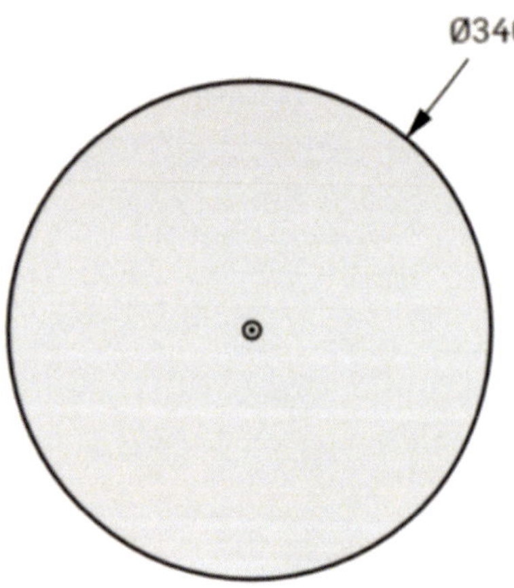

2. Click the green check on the **Sketch 1** dialog.
3. Create an *Extruded* feature of **40** mm depth.

4. On the Toolbar, click the **Plane** command.
5. Click on the top face of the geometry and type in **315** mm in the **Offset distance** field on the **Plane** dialog.
6. Click the green check to create an offset plane.
7. Start a sketch on the offset plane.
8. Draw a circle of **170** mm diameter and add dimensions to it, as shown.
9. Confirm the sketch.

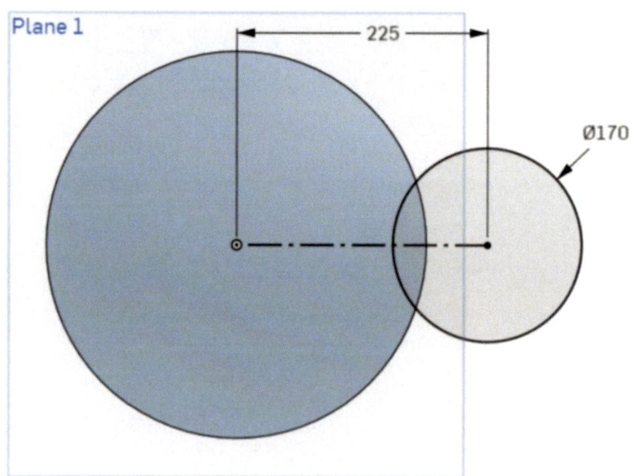

10. Deselect the sketch, if selected.
11. On the Toolbar, click the **Loft** icon.
12. Select the circle.

13. Click on the circular edge of the base to define the second profile, as shown.

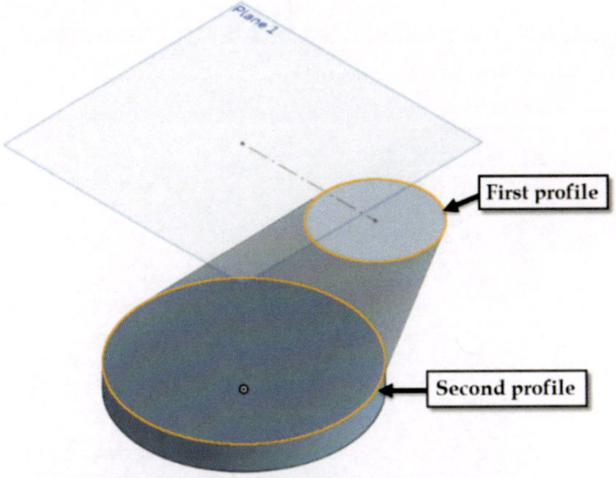

14. Click the green check to create the *Loft* feature.

Extruding a Planar Face of the Model

1. Activate the **Extrude** command and click on the top face of the *Loft* feature.
2. On the **Extrude** dialog, type-in **40** mm in the **Depth** field.
3. Click the green check to create the *Extruded* feature.

Mirroring the Entire Part

1. On the Toolbar, click the **Mirror** command and click the **Mirror type** drop-down **> Part mirror** on the **Mirror** dialog.
2. Select the model from the graphics area.
3. Click on the **Mirror plane** selection box and select the **Right** plane from the **Feature** window to define the mirroring plane.
4. Click the green check to mirror the entire solid body.

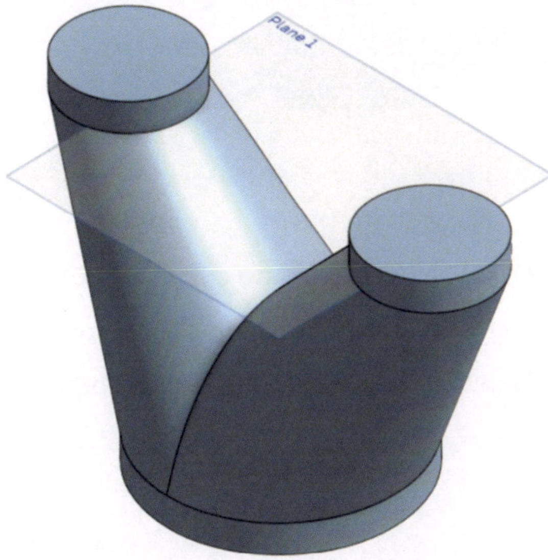

Shelling the Model geometry

1. On the Toolbar, click the **Shell** icon.

2. Click on the flat faces of the model geometry.

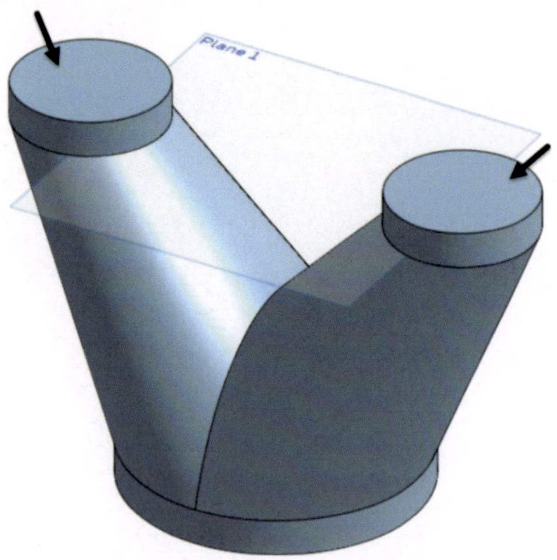

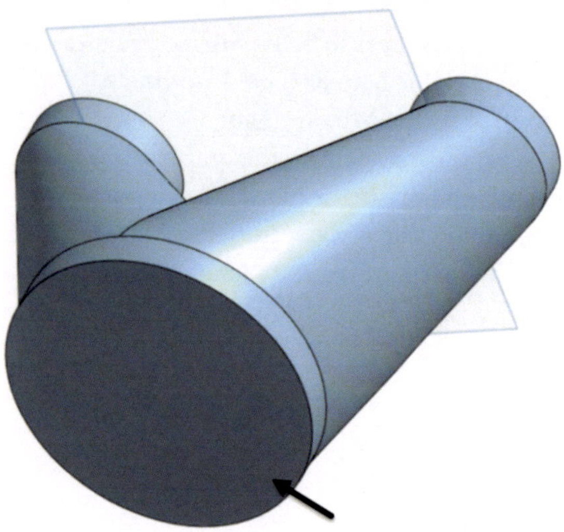

3. On the **Shell** dialog, type-in **2** in the **Shell Thickness** field.
4. Click the green check on the **Shell** dialog to shell the part geometry.

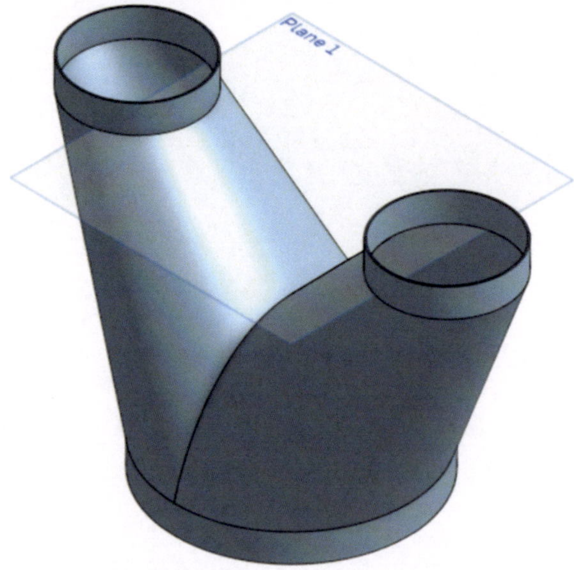

5. Click **Document menu > Close document** to close the document.

Questions

1. Describe the procedure to create a loft feature.
2. List the **Start** and **End condition** options.
3. List the type of elements that can be selected to create a loft feature.

Exercises

Exercise 1

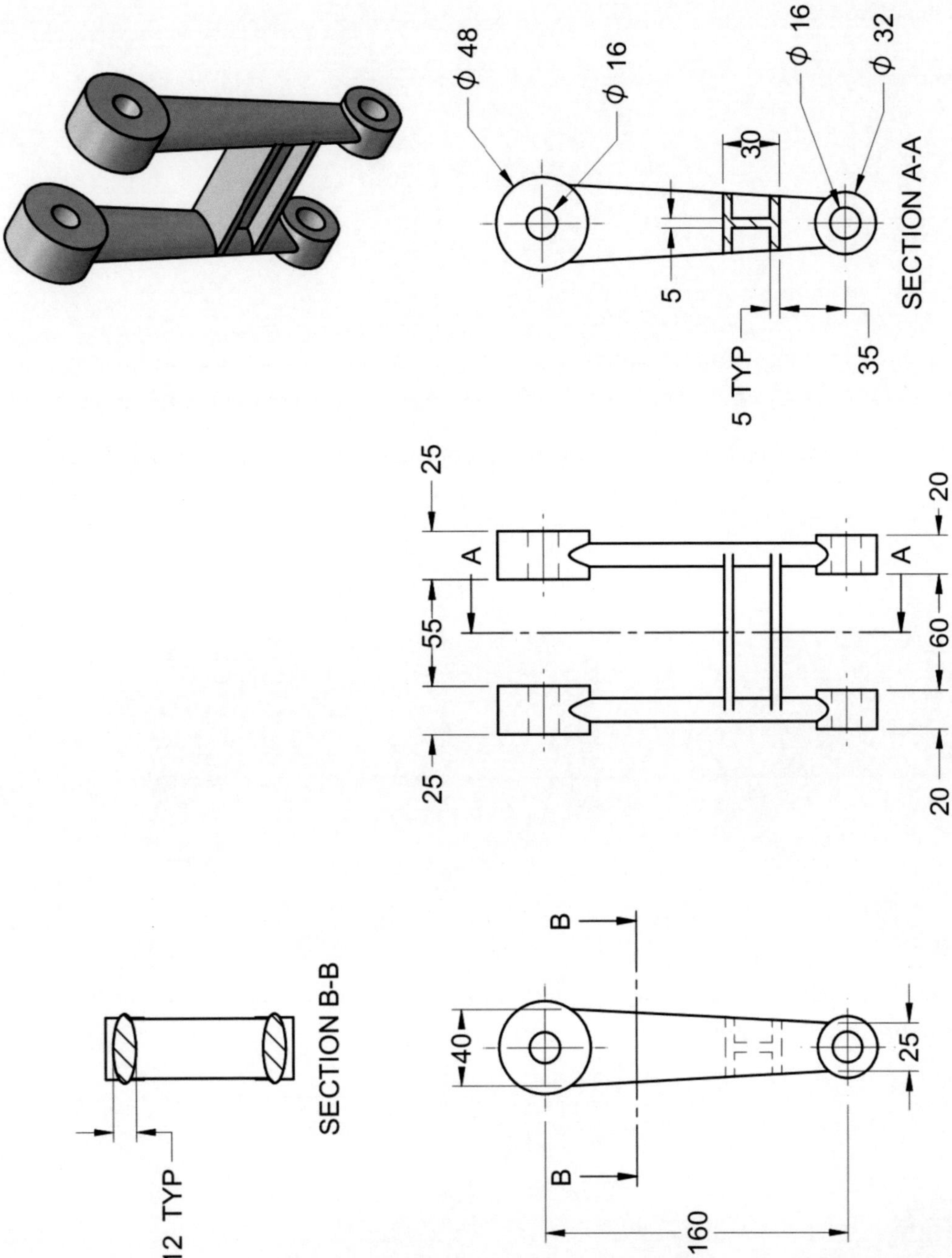

Chapter 8: Additional Features

Onshape offers you some additional commands and features which will help you to create complex models. These commands are explained in this chapter.

The topics covered in this chapter are:

- *Ribs*
- *Multi-body parts*
- *Split bodies*
- *Boolean Operations*

Rib

This command creates a rib feature to add structural stability, strength and support to your designs. Just like any other sketch-based feature, a rib requires a two-dimensional sketch. Create a sketch, as shown in figure and click the **Rib** icon on the Toolbar. Select the sketch and type-in the thickness value of the rib feature in the **Thickness** box displayed on the dialog.

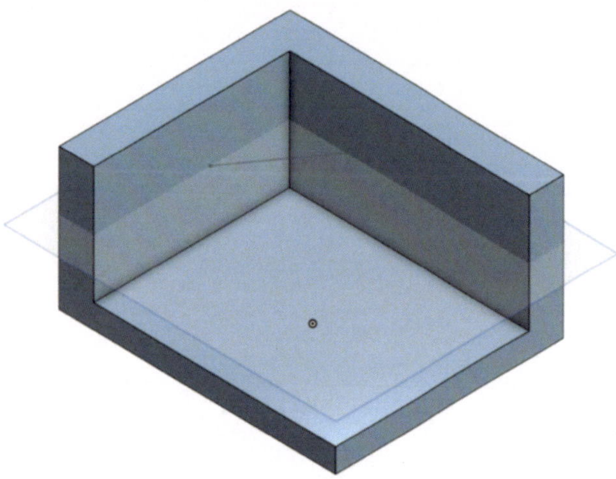

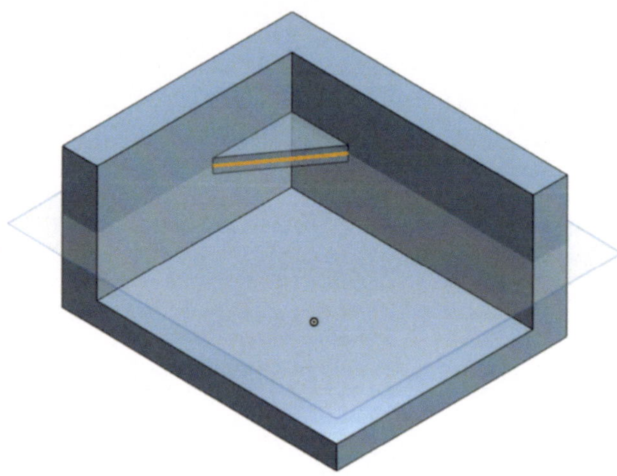

You can define the direction of the rib extrusion by using the **Parallel to sketch plane** or **Normal to sketch plane** option from the **Rib extrusion direction** drop-down.

Parallel to sketch plane

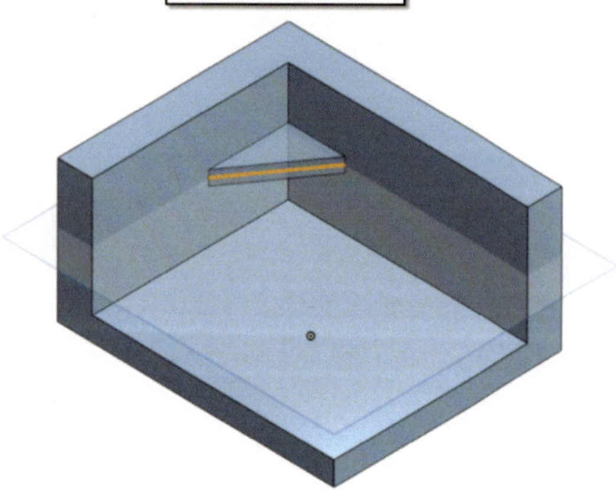

Normal to sketch plane

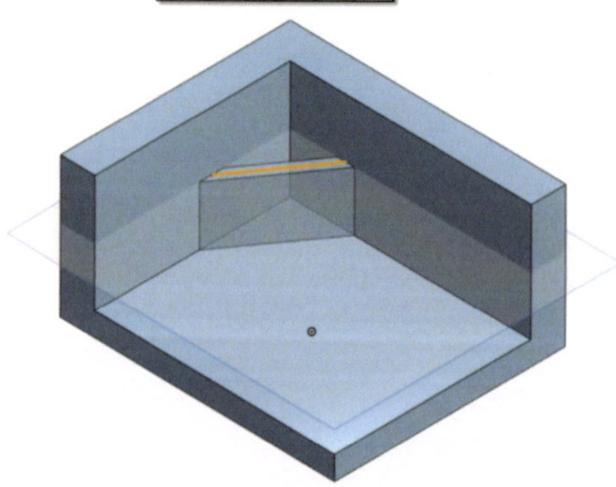

Multi-body Parts

Onshape allows the use of multiple bodies when designing parts. This allow you to use several design techniques that would otherwise not be possible. In this section, you will learn some of these techniques.

Creating Multibodies

The number of bodies in a part can change throughout the design process. Onshape makes it easy to create separate bodies inside a part geometry. Also, you can combine multiple bodies into a single body. In order to create multiple bodies in a part, first create a solid body, and then create any sketch-based feature such as extruded, revolved, swept, or loft feature. While creating the feature, ensure that the **New** tab is selected on the dialog. Click green check on the **Extrude** dialog to create multiple solid bodies. Next, expand the **Parts** folder in the **Features** window and notice the multiple solid parts.

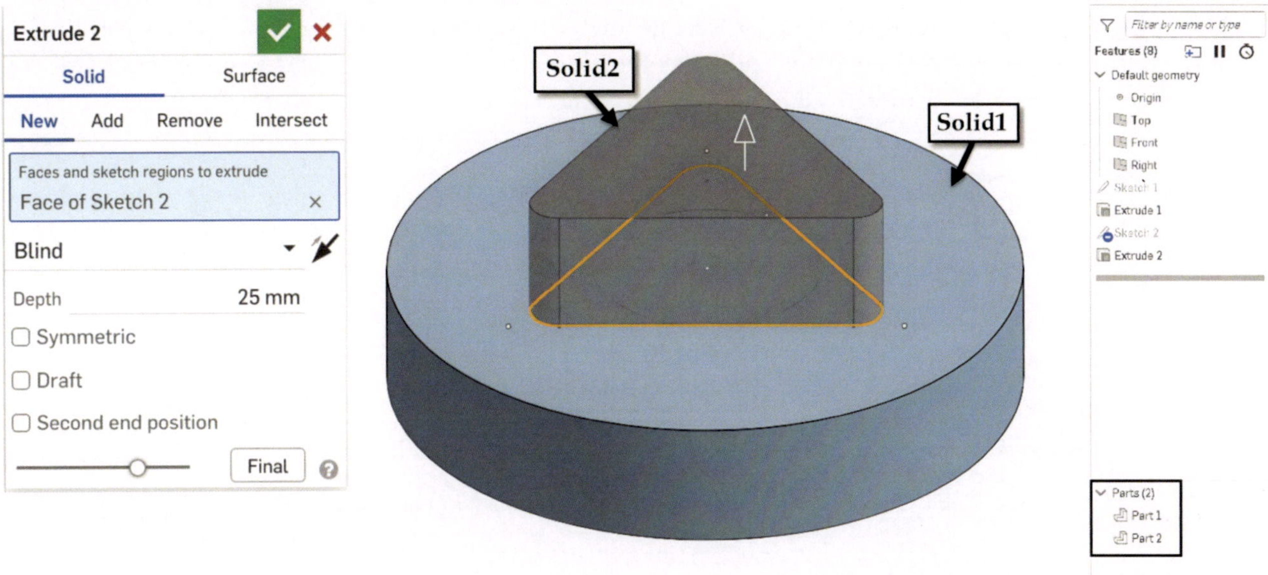

The Split command

The **Split** command can be used to separate single bodies into multiple bodies. This command can be used to perform local operations. For example, if you apply the shell feature to the front portion of the model shown in figure, the whole model will be shelled. To solve this problem, you must split the solid body into multiple bodies (In this case, separate the front portion of the model from the rest).

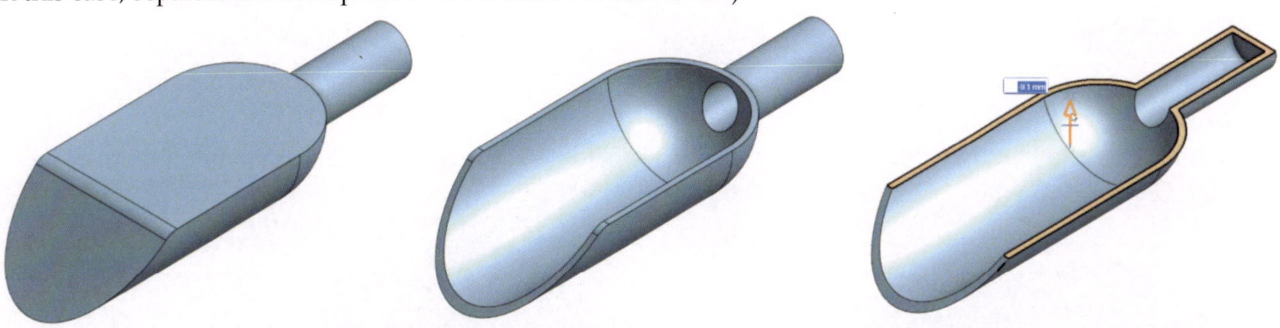

On the toolbar, click **Offset Surface** drop-down > **Fill**. Next, select the edges of the curved face, as shown. Next, click **OK** on the **Fill** dialog; a filled surface is created.

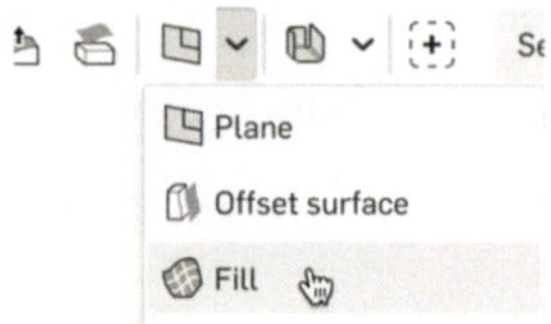

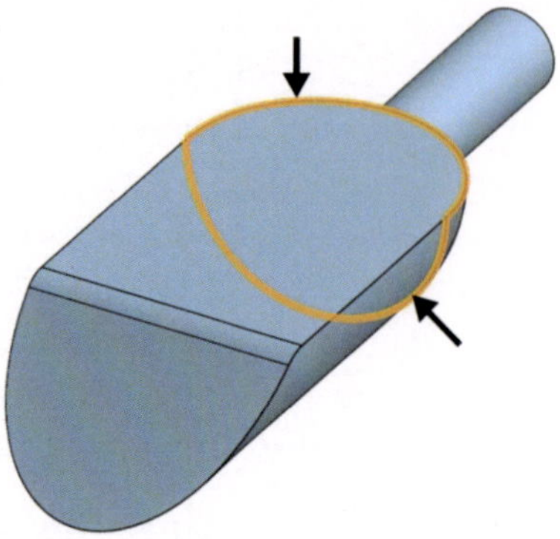

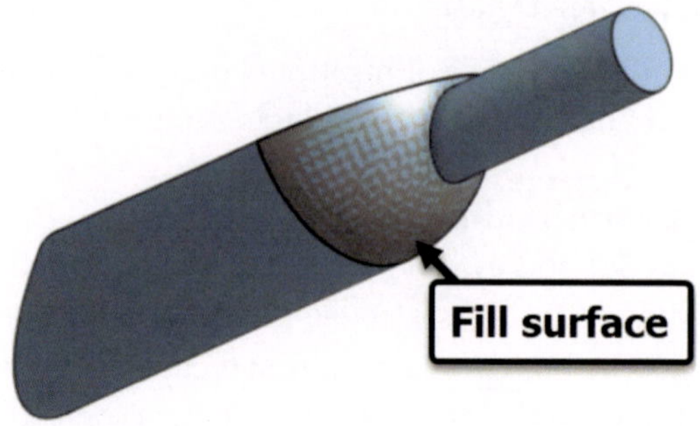

Click the **Split** icon on the toolbar. Select the part geometry from the graphics window. On the **Split** dialog, click in the **Entity to split with** selection box and select the fill surface, as shown. Click the green check; the solid body is split into two separate bodies.

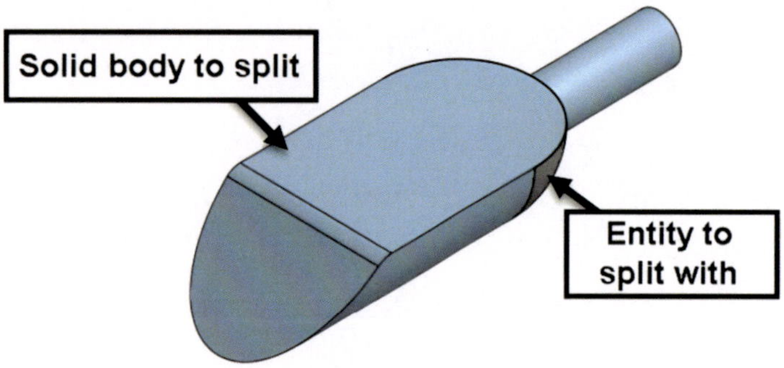

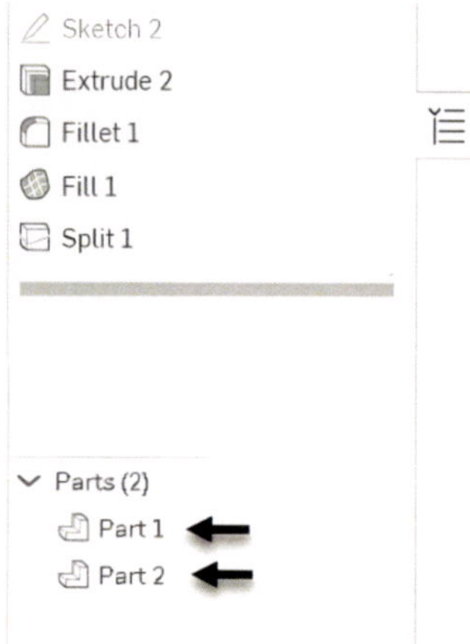

Now, create the shell feature on the split body.

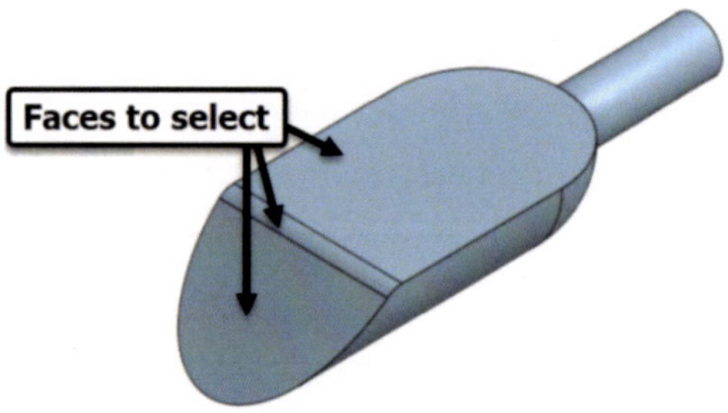

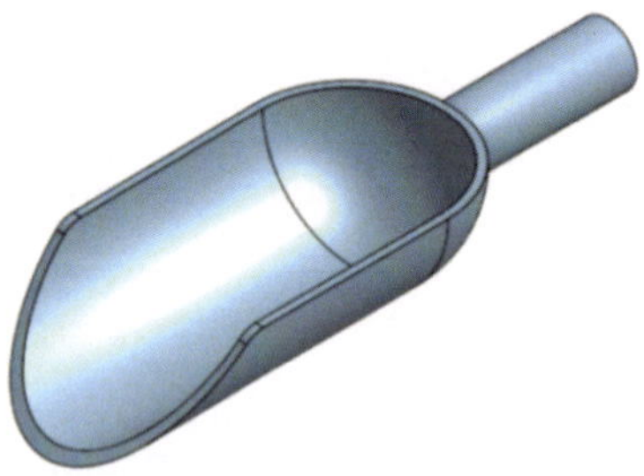

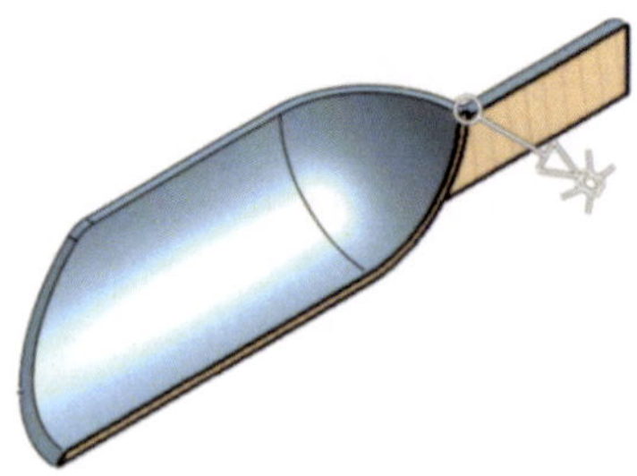

Union

If you apply fillets to the edges between two bodies, it will show a different result as shown in figure. In order to solve this problem, you must combine the two bodies.

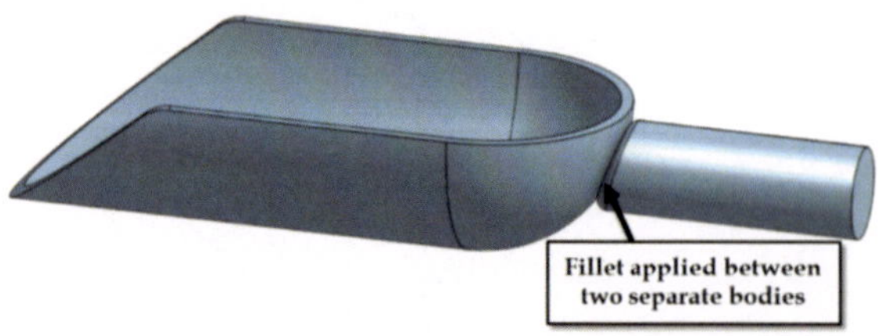

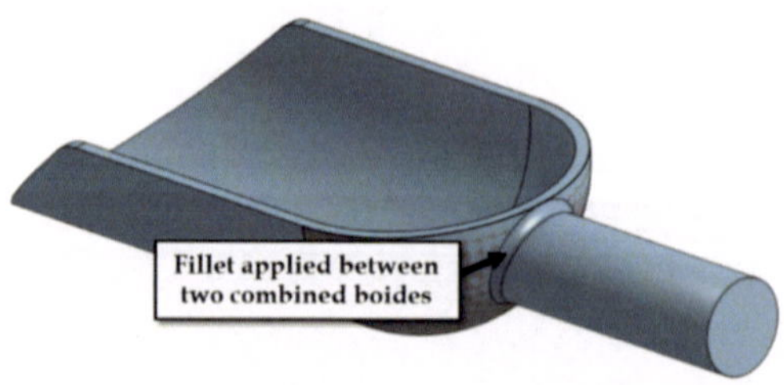

Click the **Boolean** icon on the Toolbar and click the **Union** tab on the **Boolean** dialog. Next, select the two bodies. Enable the **Keep tools** option to preserve the original bodies after the Boolean operation is complete. By default, tool bodies are consumed (deleted) when the final result is created. Click green check to join the bodies. Now, apply fillets to the edges.

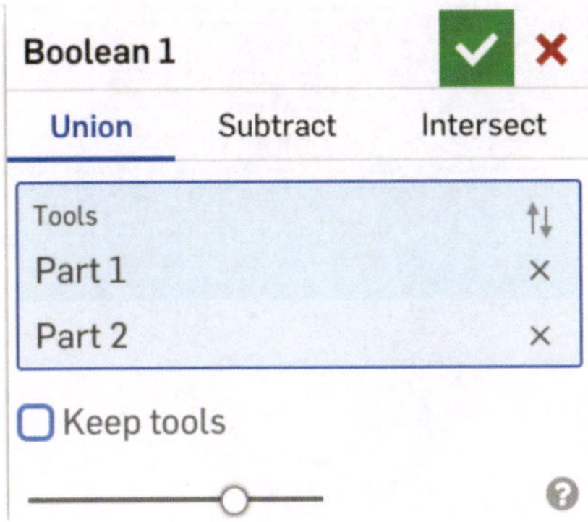

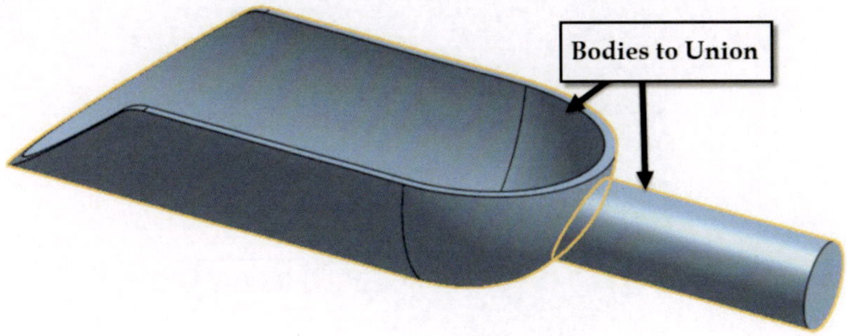

Subtract

This option performs the function of subtracting one solid body from another. Click **Boolean** on the Toolbar and click the **Subtract** tab on the **Boolean** dialog. Next, select the target and tool body. Click green check to subtract the tool body from the main body.

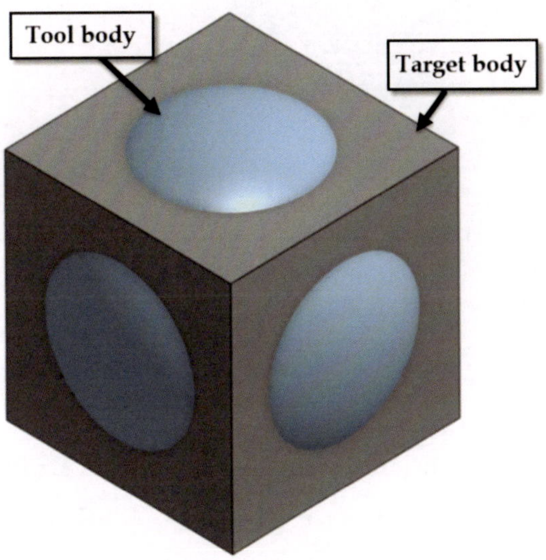

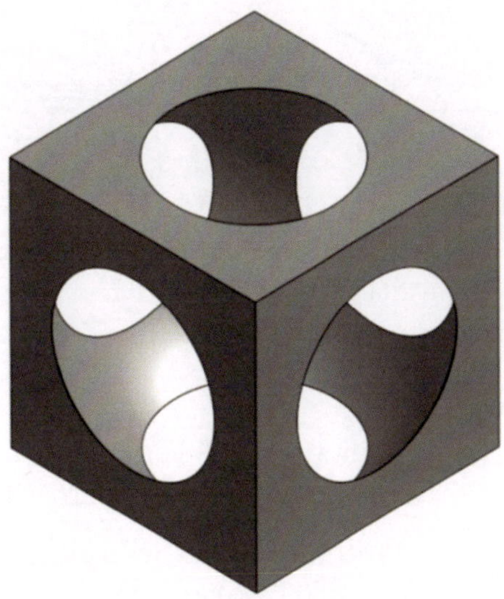

Intersect

By using the **Intersect** option, you can generate bodies defined by the intersecting volume of two bodies. Click **Boolean** on the Toolbar and click the **Intersect** tab on the **Boolean** dialog. Select the two bodies from the part geometry and click green check to see the resultant single solid body.

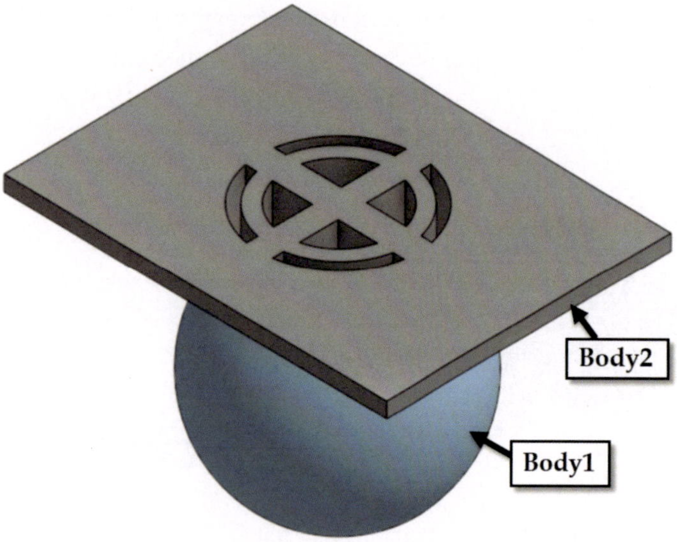

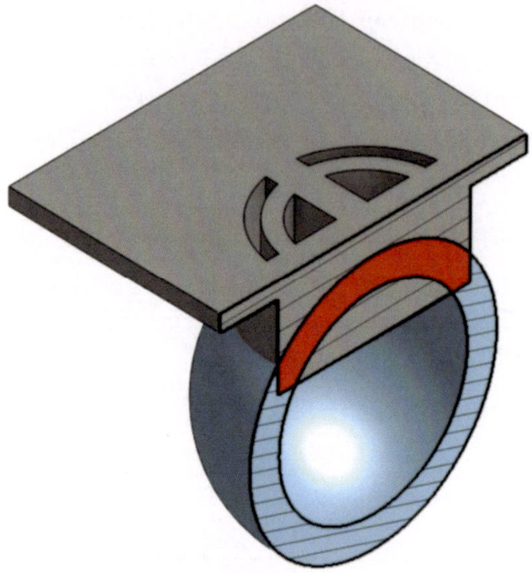

Creating Cut Features in Multi-body Parts

Onshape has some additional options (**Merge with all** and **Merge Scope**) while creating cuts in Multi-body parts. These options are available on all the Extrude or Revolve dialogs. The options in the **Extrude** dialog are explained next.

Merge with all

Create three separate bodies in a part file, and then create a sketch on the active body, as shown. Click the **Extrude** icon on the Toolbar and select the sketch. On the **Extrude** dialog, click the **Remove** tab and select **End type > Through All**. Next, select **Merge with all** option at the bottom of the dialog. Click green check and notice the cut is added to all the bodies of the part.

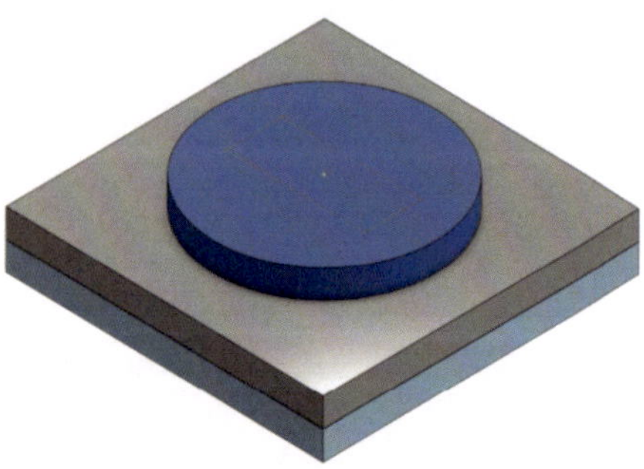

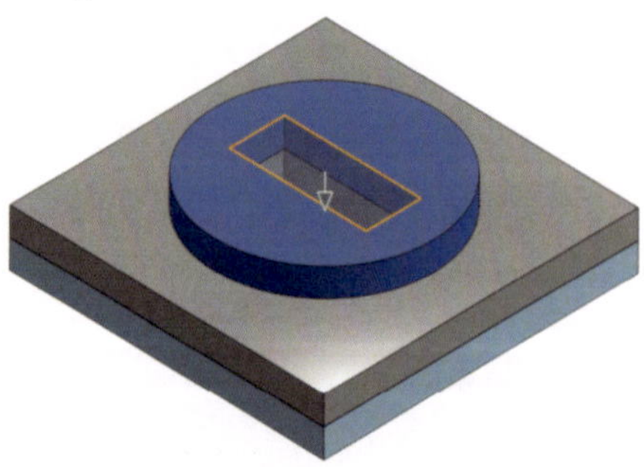

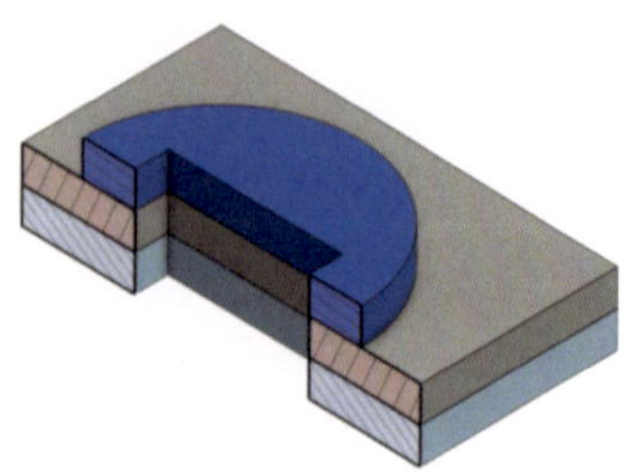

Merge Scope

Click the **Extrude** icon on the Toolbar and select the sketch. On the **Extrude** dialog, click the **Remove** tab and select **End type > Through All**. Next, click in the **Merge scope** selection box and select the bodies from the graphics window. Click green check on the **Extrude** dialog; the cut is added only to the selected bodies.

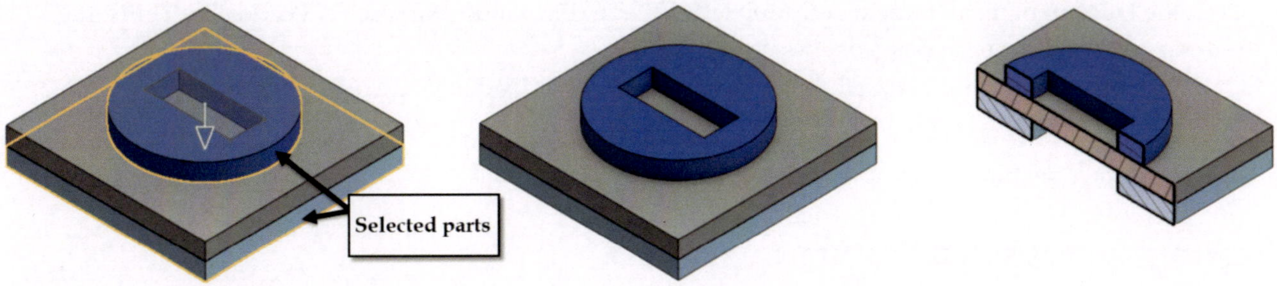

Tutorial 1 (Millimetres)

In this example, you create the part shown next.

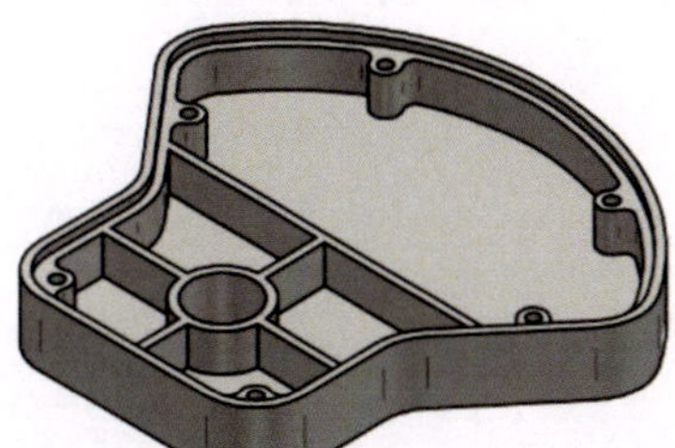

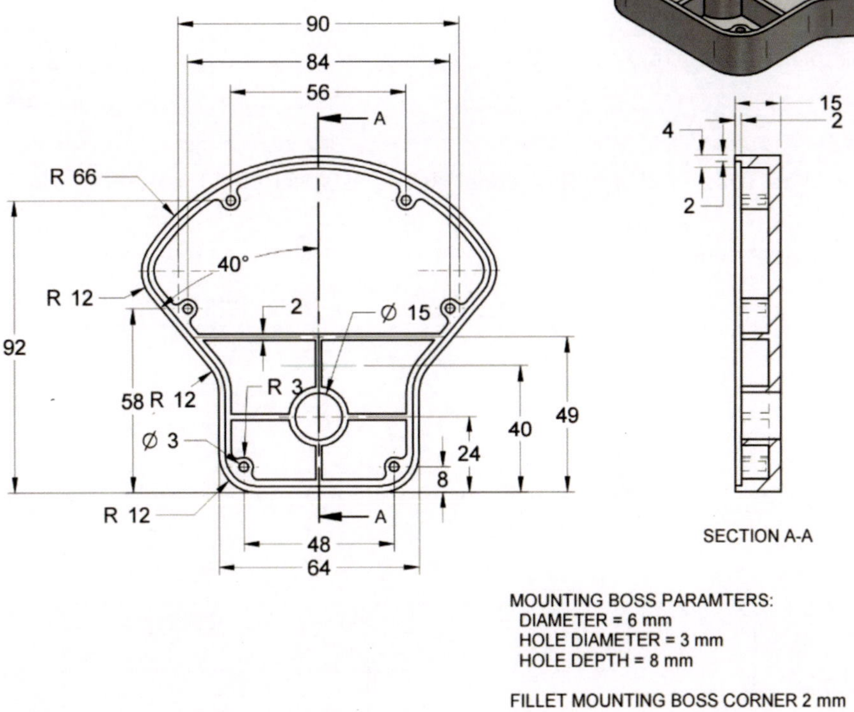

Creating a New document

1. In your Internet Browser, go to https://www.onshape.com to start Onshape.
2. Next, click **SIGN IN** button located on the top right corner side of the web page. Enter the username and password, and then, click **Sign in**.

3. On the Documents page, click **Create > Folder**. Next, type Chapter 8 in the **Folder name** box and then click **Create**.
4. Double-click on the **Chapter 8** folder in the Folders section.
5. On the Documents page, click **Create > Document**; the **New document** dialog appears on the screen.
6. Enter Tutorial 1 in the **Document name** box and click **Create public document**; a new document appears.
7. Click the **Document menu** located at the top left corner of the window and select **Workspace Units**; the **Workspace Units** dialog appears on the screen.
8. On the **Workspace Units** dialog, select **Length default unit> Millimeter** from **Length** section.
9. Select **Mass default unit > Gram** from the **Mechanical** section.
10. Leave the other default settings and click the green check.

Creating the Extruded Feature

1. Click the **Sketch** command on the Toolbar and start a new sketch on the **Top** plane.
2. On the Toolbar, click the **Line** command and draw the sketch, as shown in the figure below.
3. Click the **Mirror** command on the Toolbar, and then mirror the vertical and inclined line about the construction line. Next, apply the **Coincident** constraints between the endpoints, as shown.

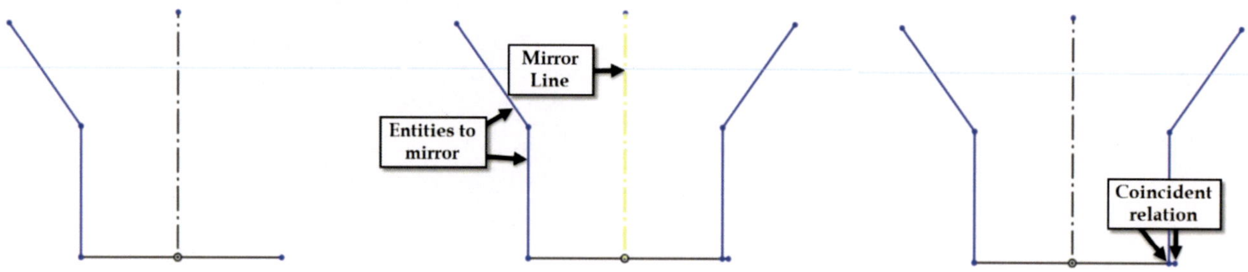

4. On the Toolbar, click the **3-point arc** command, and then create an arc by specifying the points in the sequence, as shown.
5. Apply dimensions to the sketch, as shown.

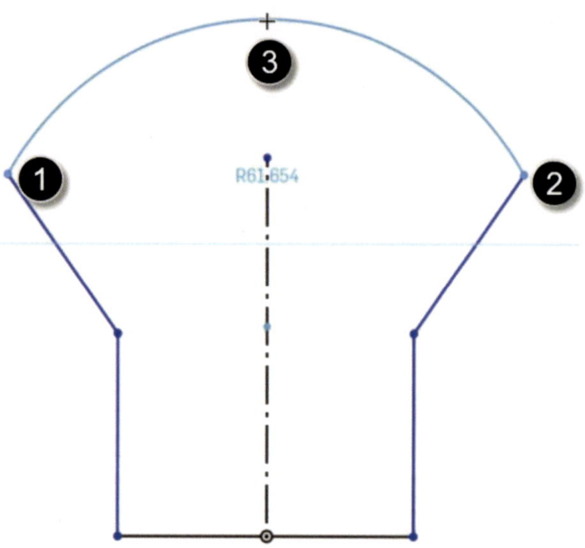

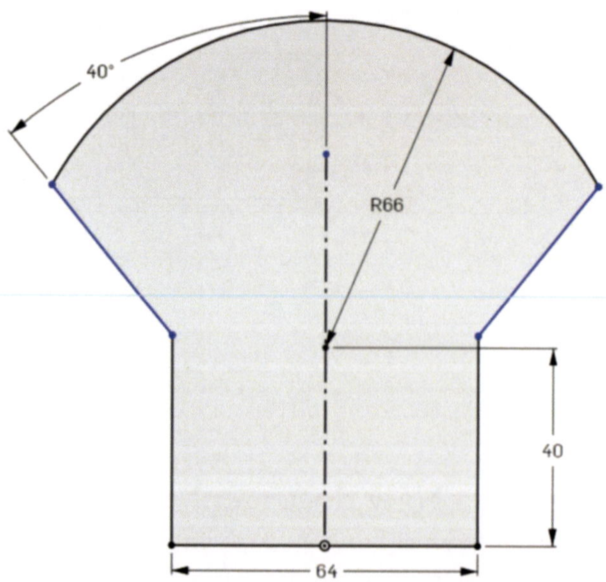

6. Click the **Fillet** command on the Toolbar, and then select the sharp corners to fillet.
7. Press **Enter** and type **12** in the **Radius** box. Again, press **Enter** to update the radius.
8. On the Toolbar, click the **Dimension** command. Add a linear dimension between the centerpoints of the fillets, as shown.

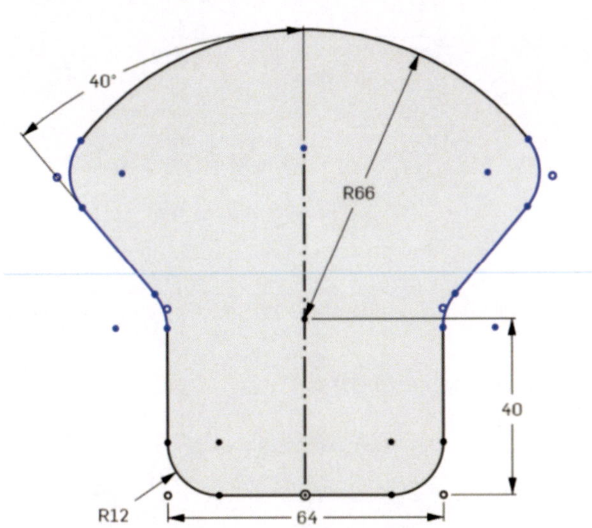

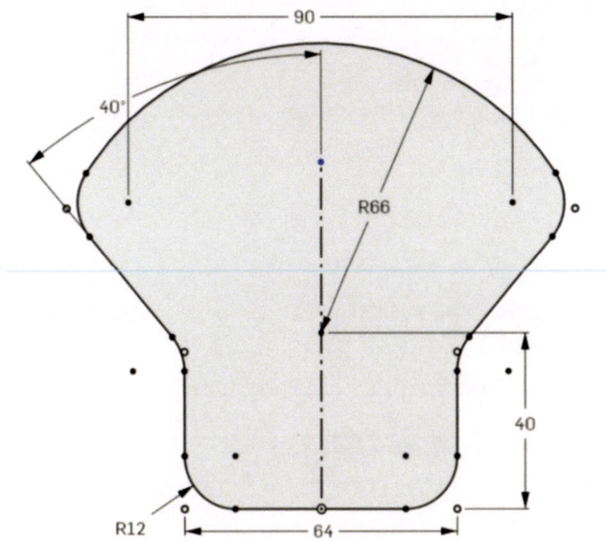

9. Click the green check on the **Sketch1** dialog to confirm the sketch.
10. Activate the **Extrude** command and create the *Extrude* feature of 14 mm depth.
11. Create the *Shell* feature of 4 mm depth.

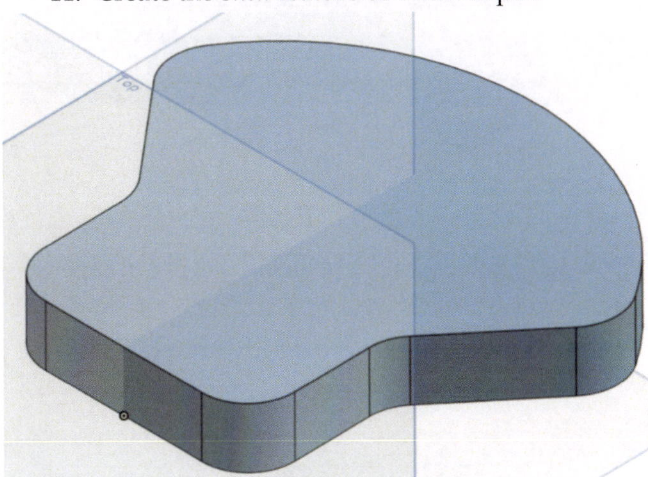

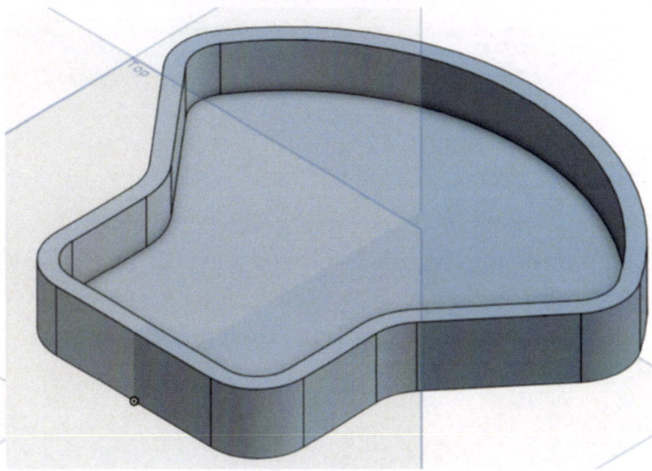

Adding a Lip to the model

1. On the toolbar, click the **Sketch** command and select the top face of the shell feature, as shown.
2. On the toolbar, click the **Offset** command.
3. Right click on the graphics area and select **Create selection**.
4. On the **Create selection** dialog, click the **Edges** tab and select the **Tangent connected** option from the drop-down. Next, select any one of the outer edges of the model.

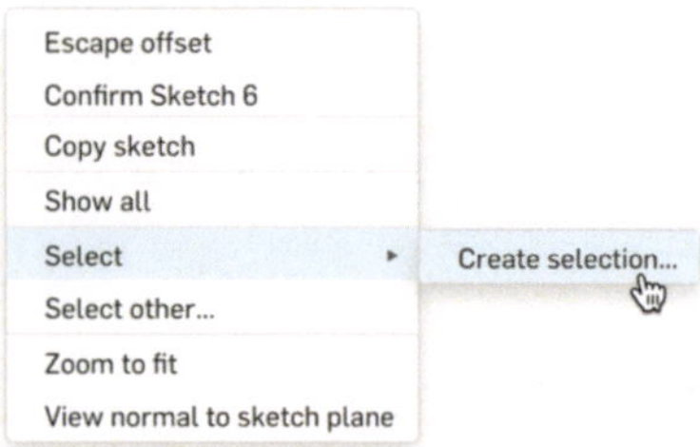

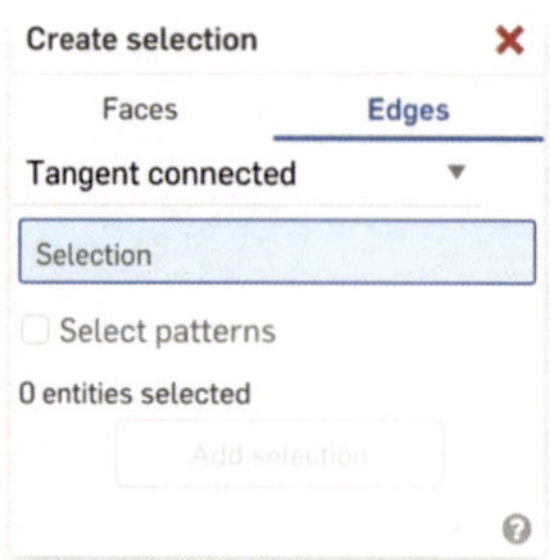

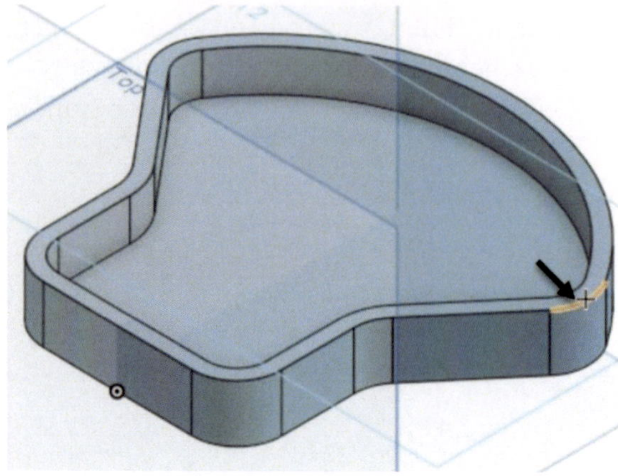

5. Click the **Add selection** button on the **Create selection** dialog; the edges that are tangentially connected to the selected edge are added to the selection.
6. Click on the graphics area and type 2 in the offset distance value box and press Enter.

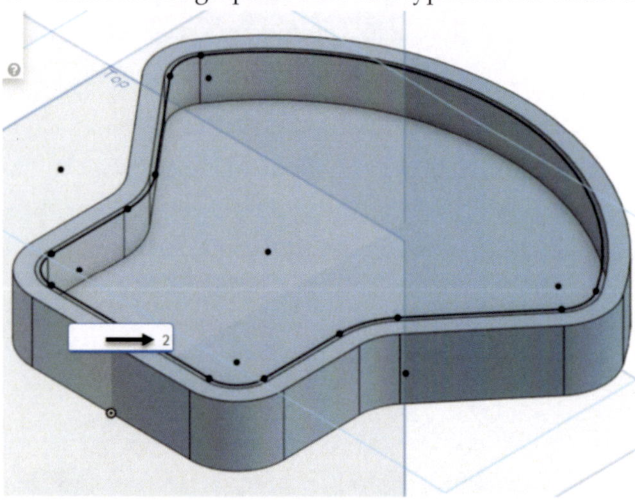

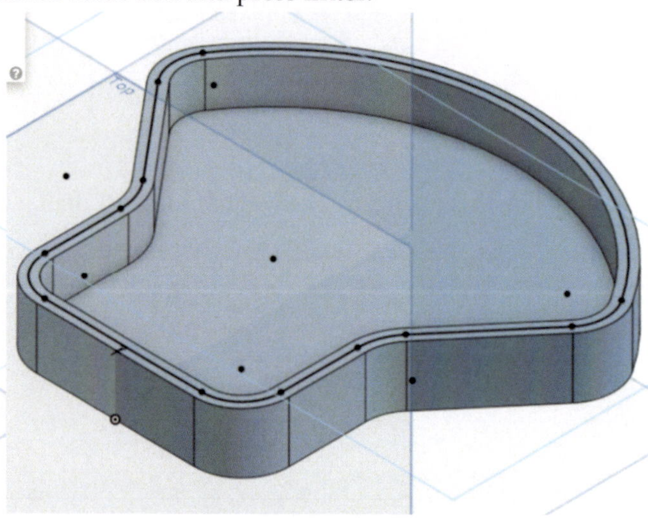

7. Click the green check on the **Sketch 2** dialog.
8. Activate the **Extrude** command and click on the region enclosed by the sketch and inner edge of the shell feature.
9. Click the **Remove** tab on the **Extrude 2** dialog.
10. Select **End type > Blind** and enter **2** in the **Depth** box and click **OK** to create the extruded cut feature.

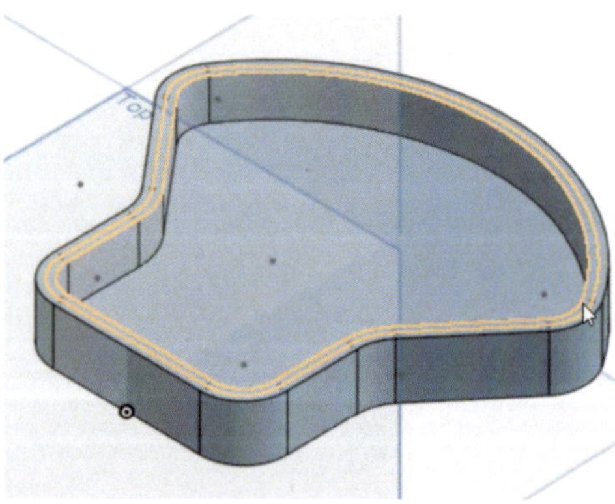

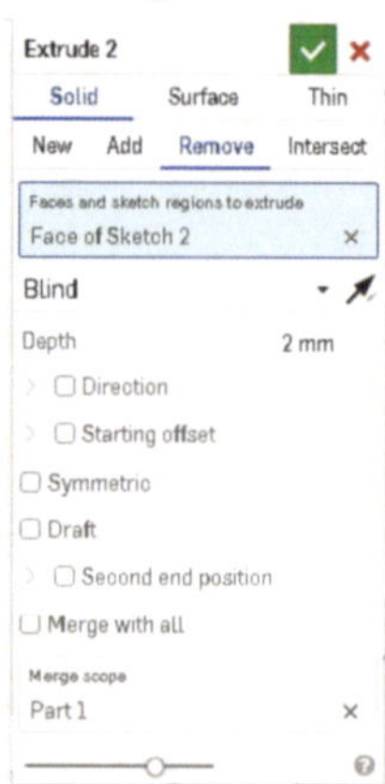

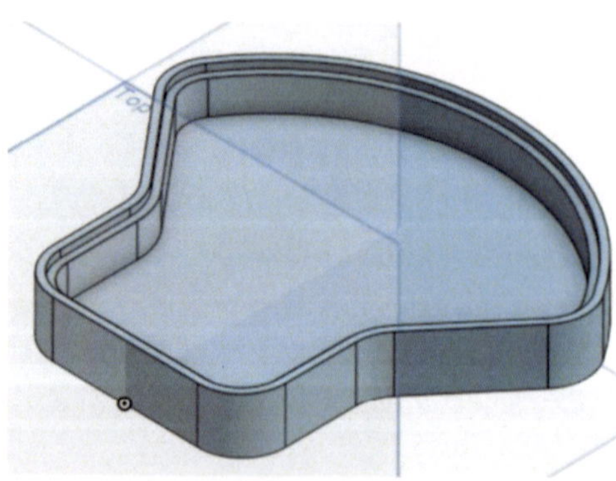

Creating Bosses

1. On the toolbar, click the **Sketch** command, and then click on the bottom face of the extruded cut feature.
2. Draw the three circles on the sketch plane. Next, click **Constraints** drop-down > **Equal** = on the toolbar.
3. Select the first two circles to make them equal in diameter. Next, select the second and third circles to make them equal.
4. Add dimensions to them, as shown. Click the green check on the **Sketch 3** dialog.

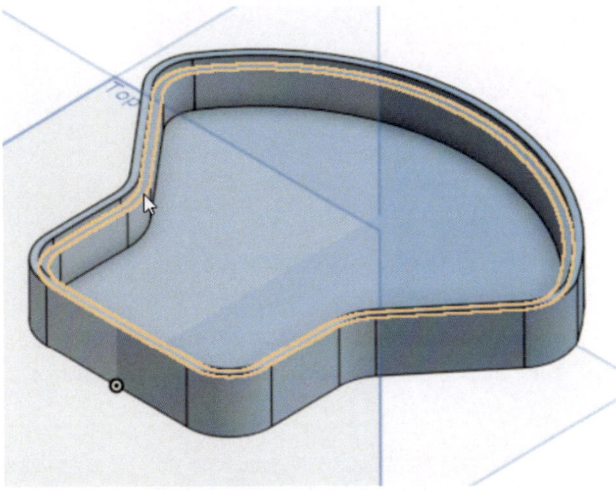

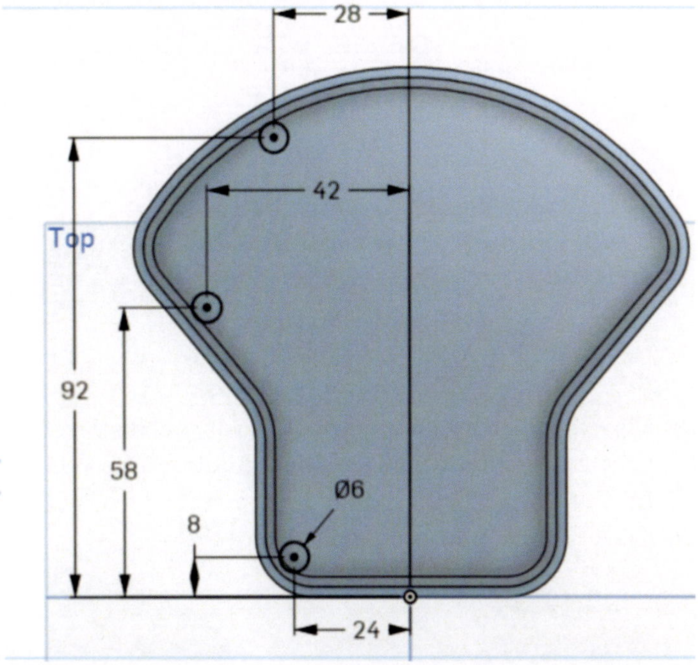

5. On the toolbar, click the **Extrude** command. Click inside the circles.
6. Click the **Add** tab on the **Extrude 3** dialog.
7. On the **Extrude 3** dialog, click **End type > Up to face** and select the bottom surface of the *Shell* feature, as shown.

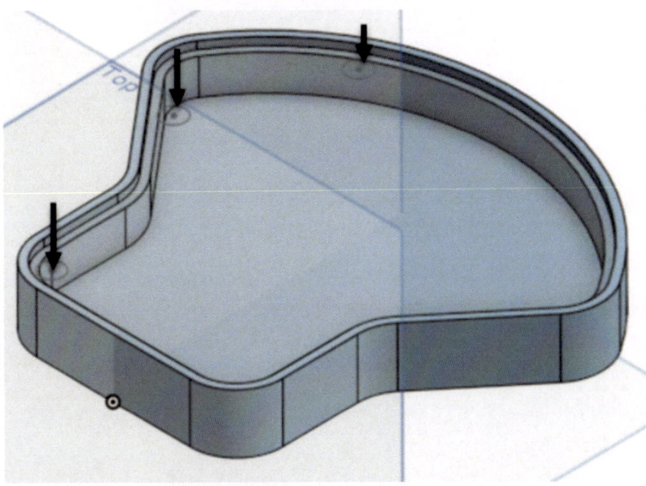

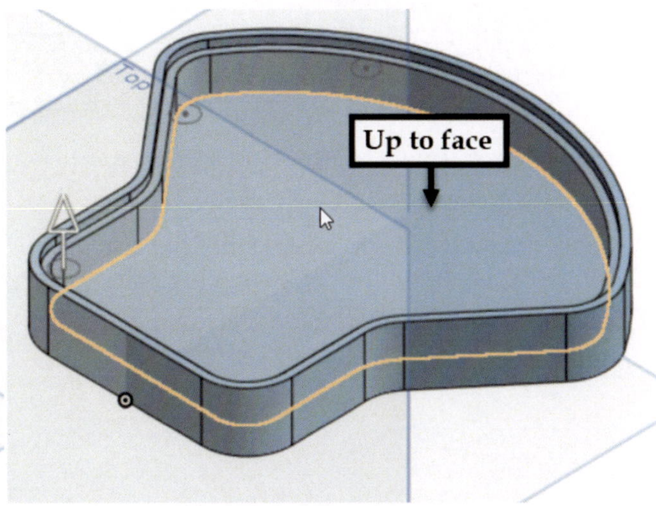

8. Check the **Draft** option and type-in **1** in the **Draft angle** box.
9. Click the green check on the dialog to create the *Extrude* feature.

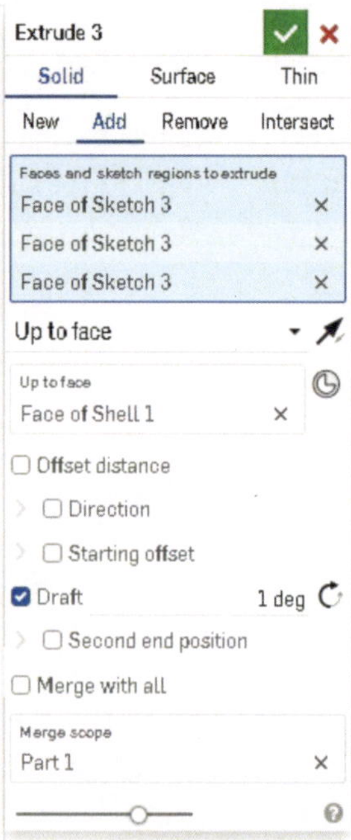

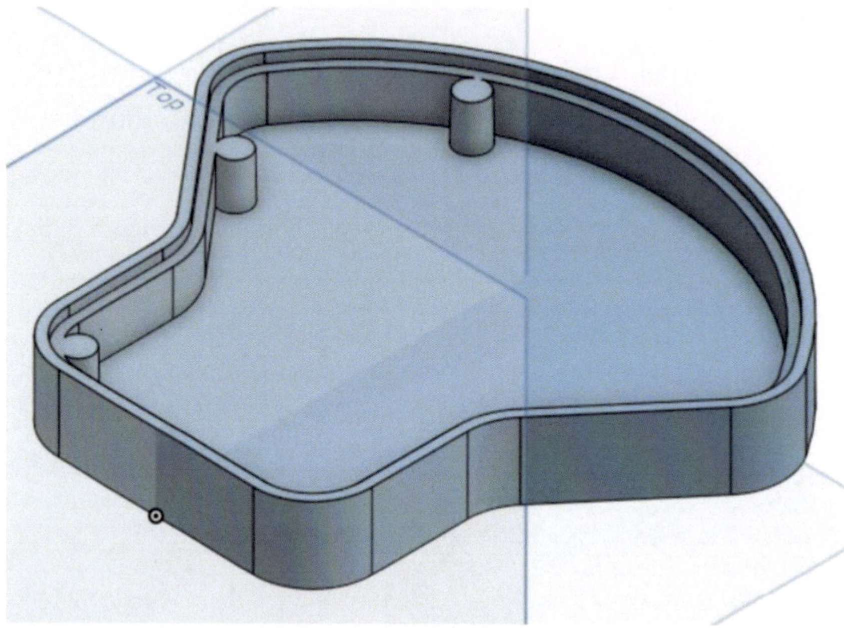

10. Click the **Sketch** command on the toolbar and select the bottom face of the extruded cut feature, as shown.
11. Create circles and apply the **Equal** constraint between them. Also, apply the **Concentric** constraint between the circles and circular edges of the extruded features.
12. Click the green check on the **Sketch 4** dialog.

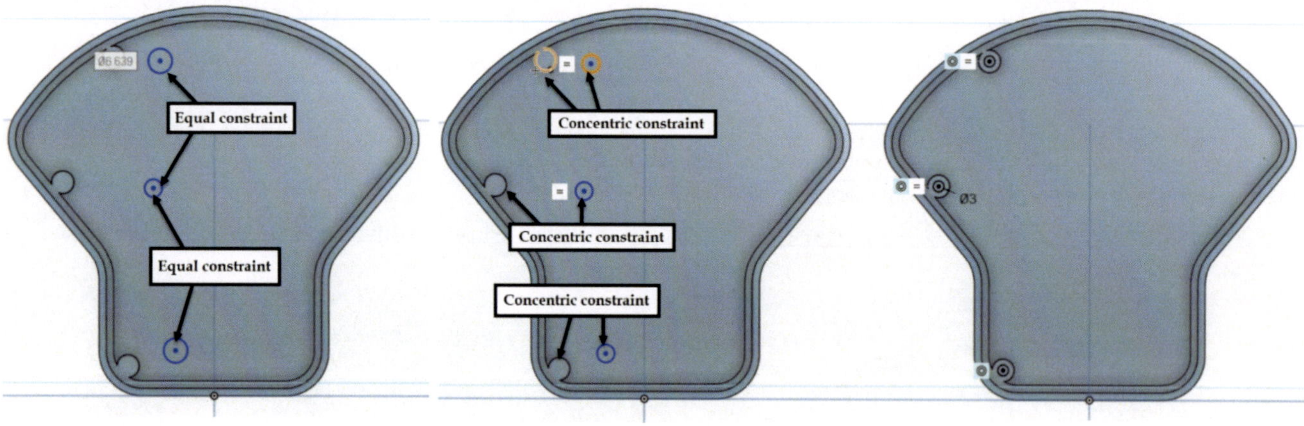

13. Click **Extrude** on the toolbar and select the newly created circles.
14. Click the **Remove** tab on the **Extrude 4** dialog.
15. Click **End type > Blind** and type-in **8** in the **Depth** box.
16. Check the **Draft** option and type-in **1** in the **Draft angle** box.
17. Click the green check on the dialog to create the *Extrude* feature.

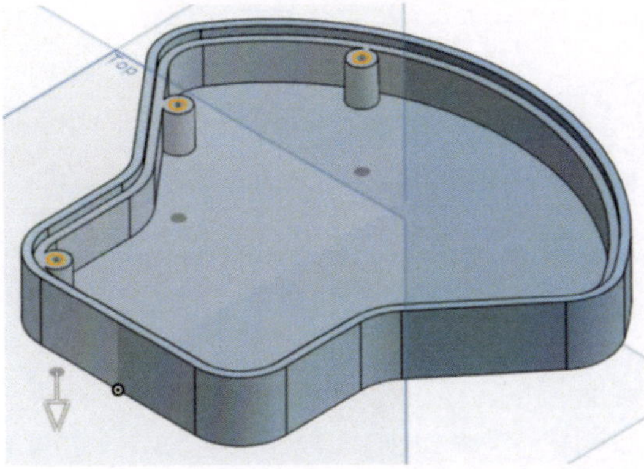

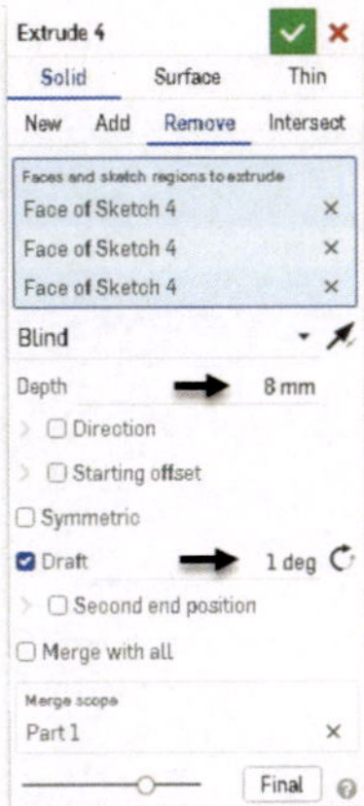

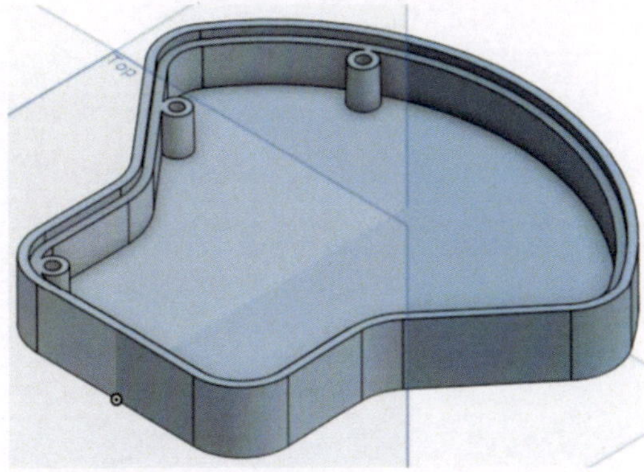

18. On the toolbar, click the **Mirror** command. Next, select **Mirror type > Feature Mirror** on the **Mirror** dialog.
19. Click the **Features to mirror** selection button and select the *Extrude* and *Cut* features from the Features window.
20. Click the **Mirror plane** selection button and select the **Right** plane on the coordinate system.
21. Click the green check to mirror the extrude features.

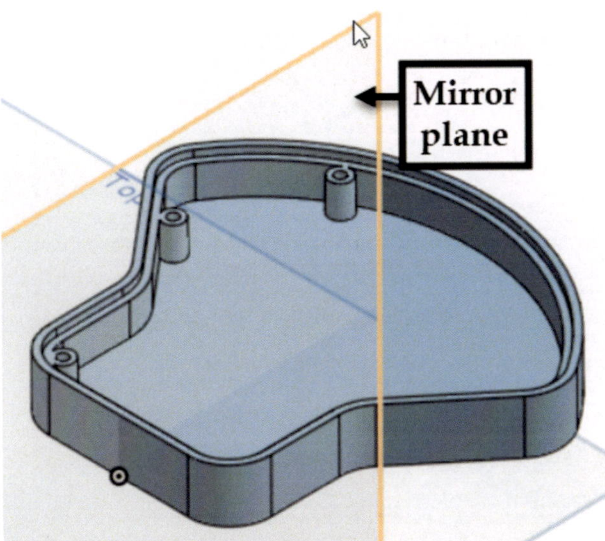

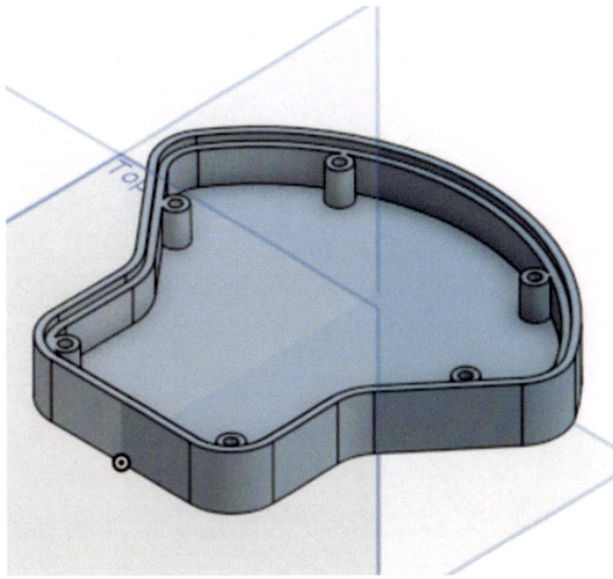

22. Click the **Camera and render options** drop-down located below the ViewCube and select the **Hidden edges visible** option.

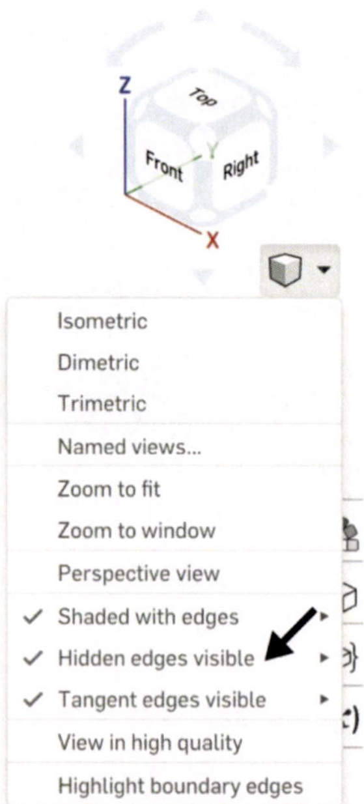

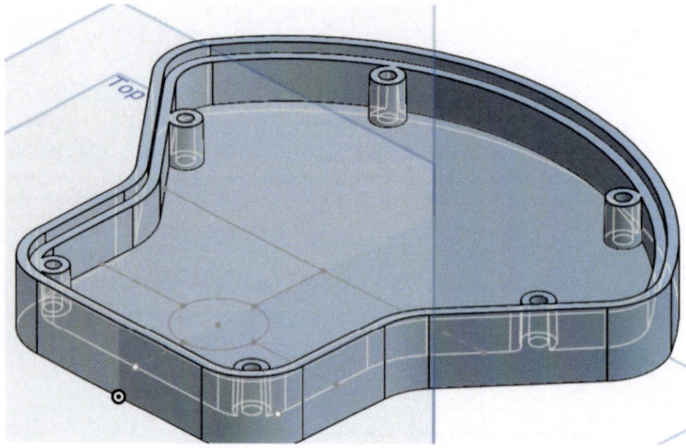

23. On the toolbar, click **Fillet** command and select the edges where the extruded features meet the walls of the geometry.

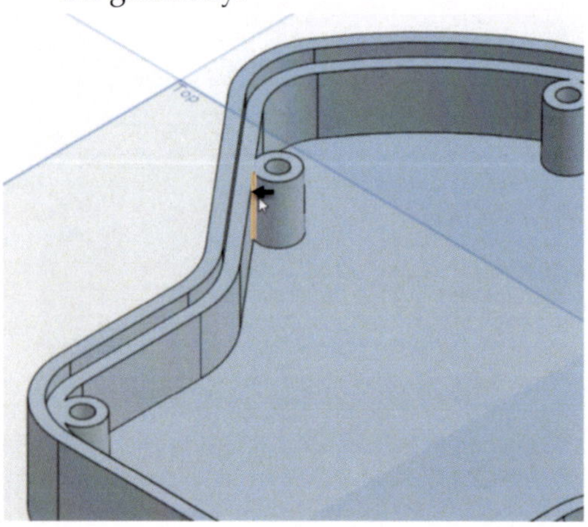

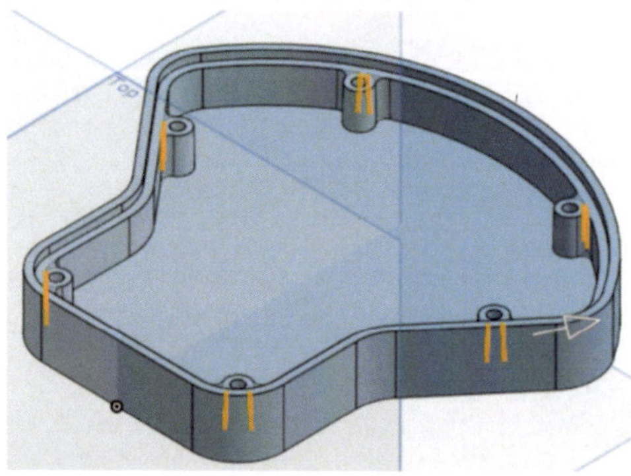

24. Type **2** in the **Radius** box. Click the green check to fillet the selected edges.

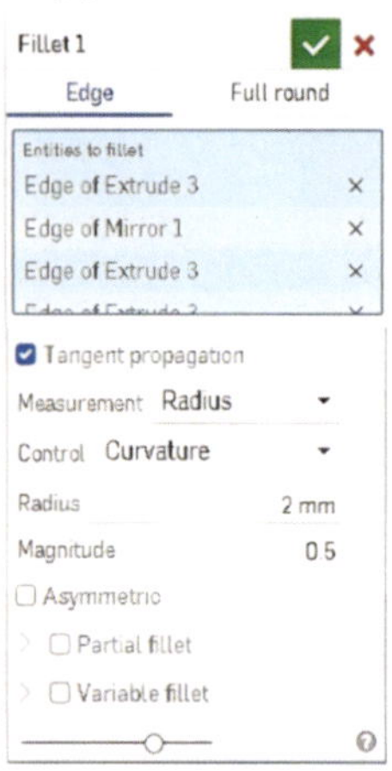

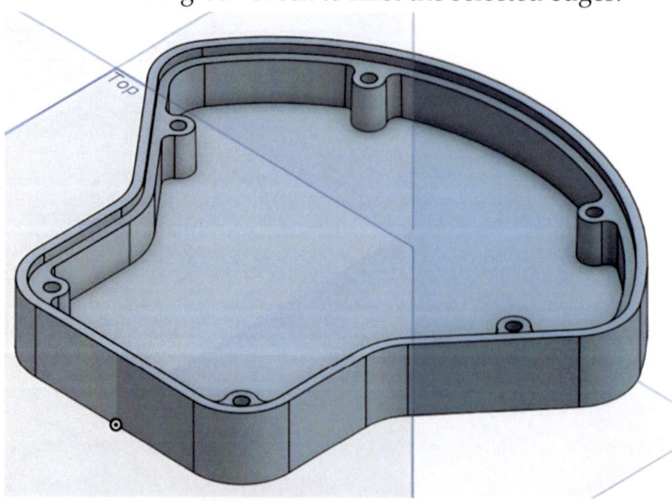

Creating the Rib feature

1. On the toolbar, click the **Sketch** command and select the bottom face of the extruded cut feature.
2. Click the **Center Point Circle** command on the toolbar and create a circle, as shown.
3. Click the Line command on the toolbar and select the midpoint of the lower horizontal edge, as shown. Next, move the pointer vertically upward and click to create a vertical line.
4. On the toolbar, click **Constraints** drop-down > **Midpoint**. Next, select the center point of the circle and the vertical line; the circle is constrained to the midpoint of the line.

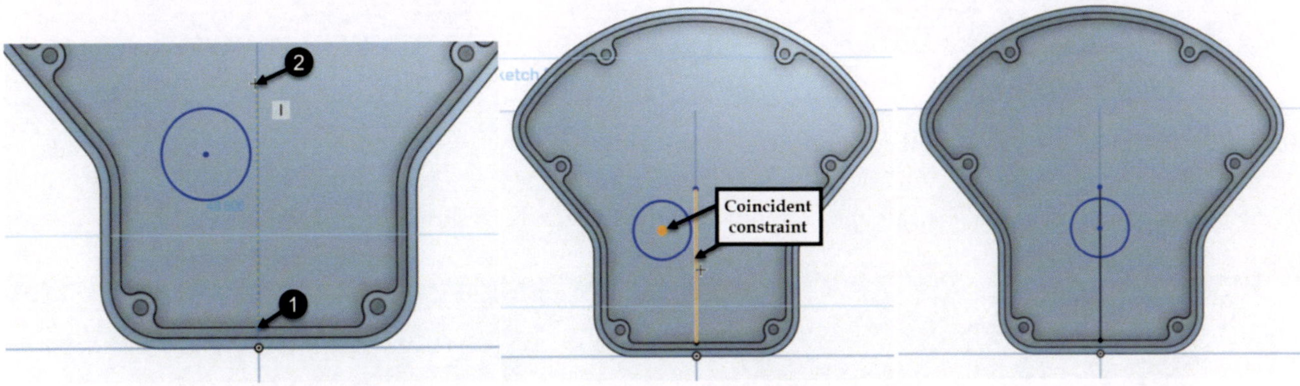

5. Click the **Line** command on the toolbar and create two horizontal lines, as shown.
6. On the toolbar, click **Constraints** drop-down > **Midpoint**. Next, select any one of the horizontal line and the centerpoint of the circle; the centerpoint of the circle is constrained to the midpoint of the horizontal line.
7. Select the other horizontal line and the endpoint of the vertical line; the endpoint of the vertical line is constrained to the midpoint of the horizontal line.
8. Add dimensions to the sketch, as shown.

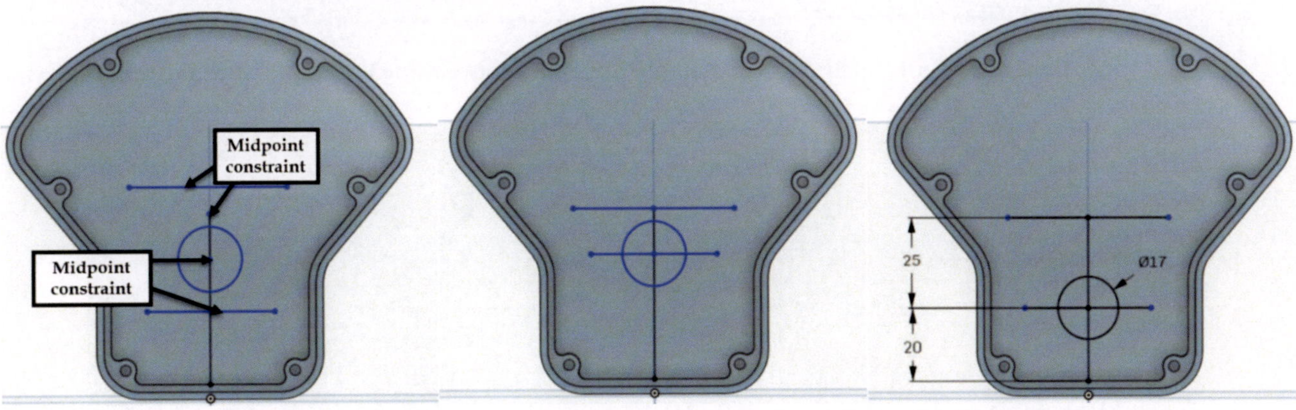

9. Click the **Trim** command on the toolbar and select the lines inside the circle, as shown.

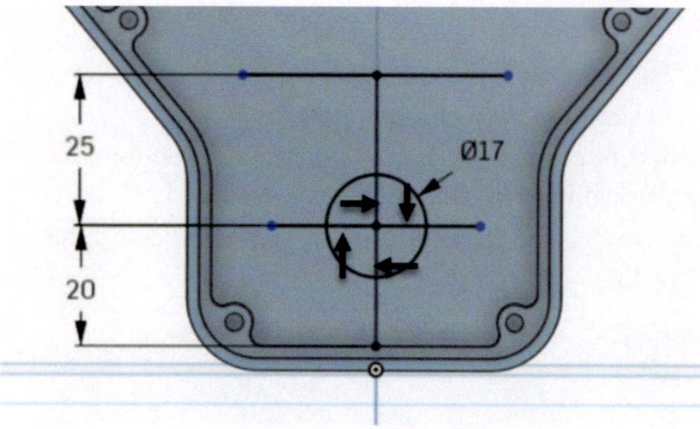

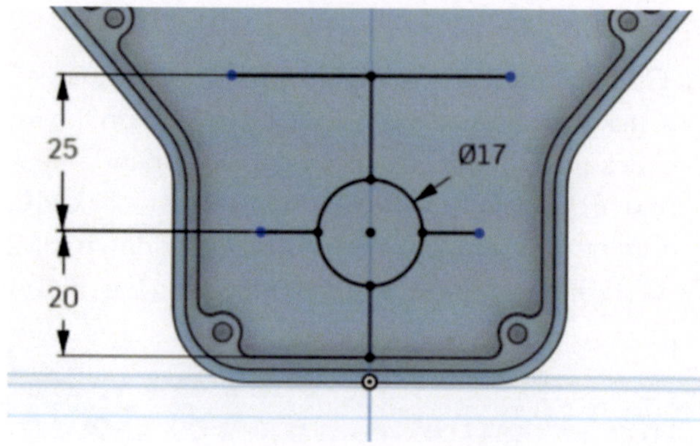

10. On the toolbar, click **Constraints** drop-down > **Coincident** . Next, select the endpoint of the horizontal line.
11. Select the model edge to constrain the endpoint coincident with it, as shown.

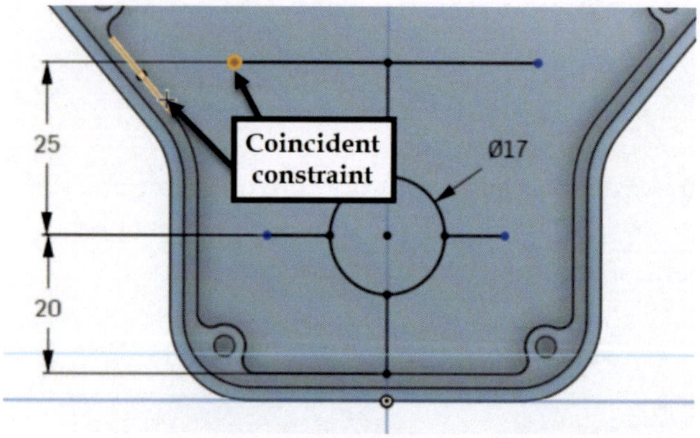

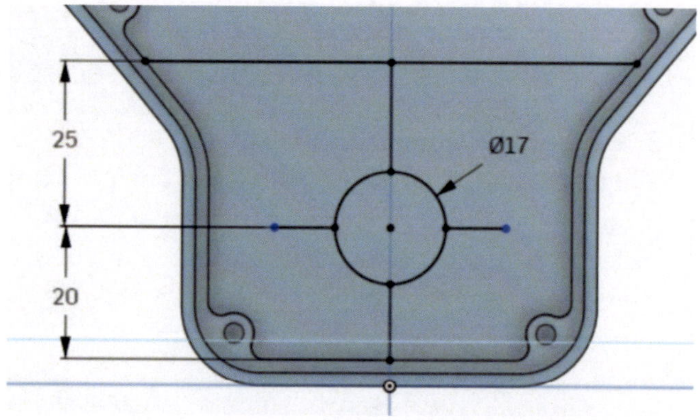

12. Likewise, apply the **Coincident** constraint between the other endpoint of the horizontal line and the model edge, as shown.

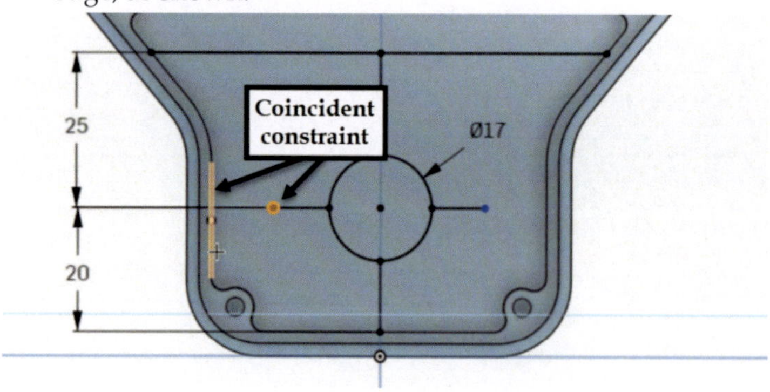

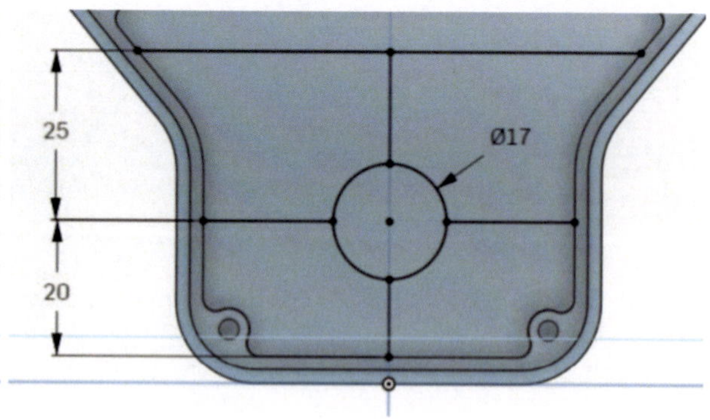

13. Click the green check on the **Sketch 5** dialog.
14. On the toolbar, click the **Rib** command and select the entities of the sketch.
15. On the **Rib** dialog, select **Rib extrusion direction > Normal to sketch plane**.
16. Type **1** in the **Thickness** box to specify the rib thickness.
17. Check the **Merge ribs** option and click **OK** to create the *Rib* feature.

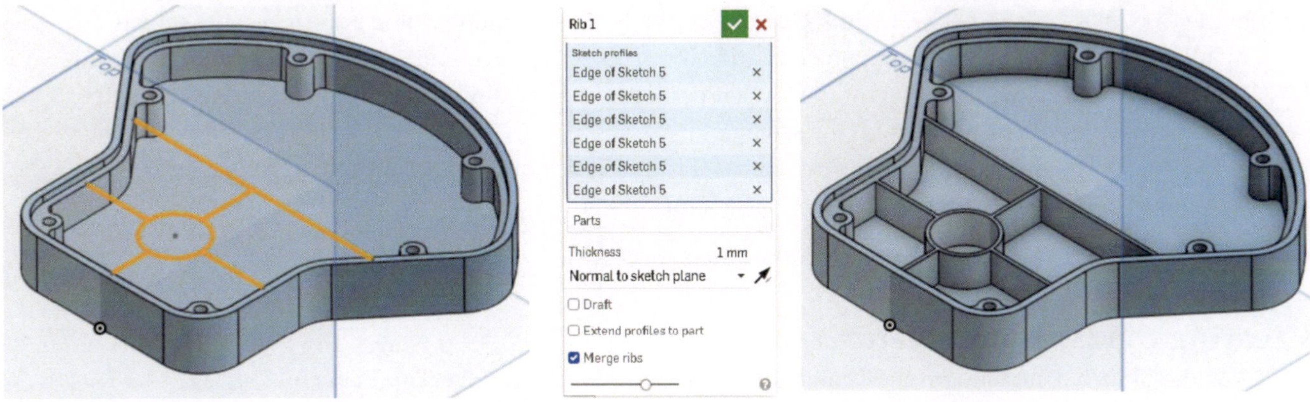

18. Close the file.

Tutorial 2 (Inches)

In this example, you create the part shown next.

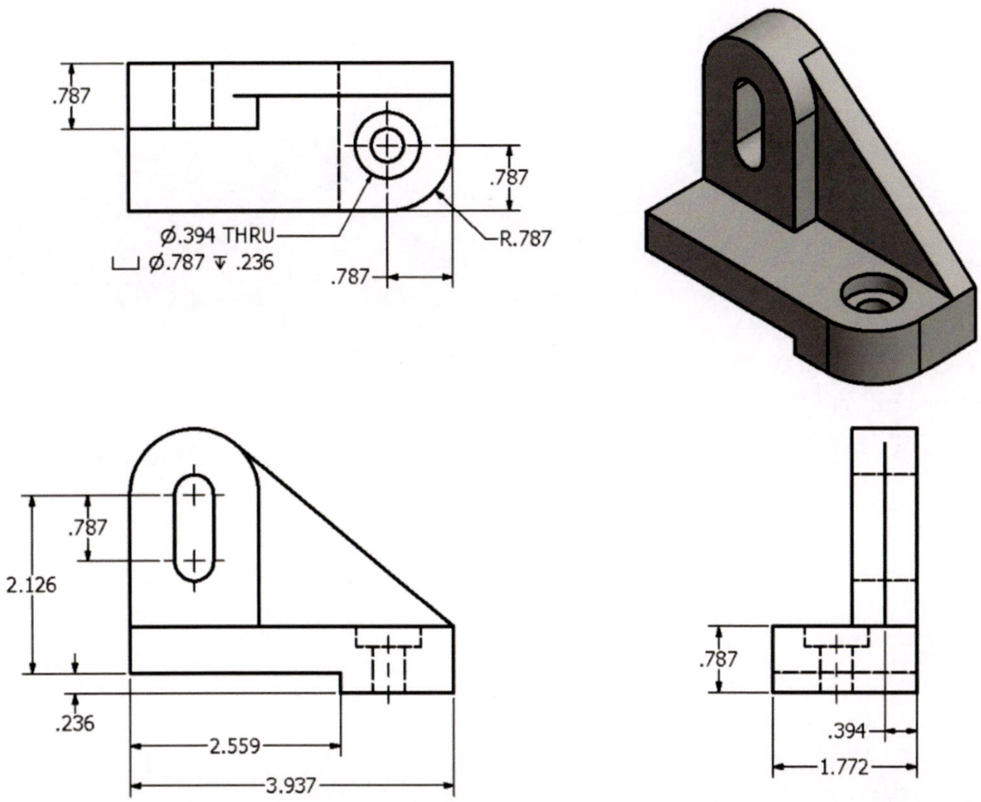

Creating a New document

1. In your Internet Browser, go to https://www.onshape.com to start Onshape.
2. Next, click **SIGN IN** button located on the top right corner side of the web page. Enter the username and password, and then, click **Sign in**.
3. Double-click on the **Chapter 8** folder in the **Folders** section.

4. On the Documents page, click **Create > Document**; the **New document** dialog appears on the screen.
5. Enter Tutorial 2 in the **Document name** box and click **Create public document**; a new document appears.
6. Click the **Document menu** located at the top left corner of the window and select **Workspace Units**; the **Workspace Units** dialog appears on the screen.
7. On the **Workspace Units** dialog, select **Length default unit > Inch** from **Length** section.
8. Select **Mass default unit > Pound** from the **Mechanical** section.
9. Leave the other default settings and click the green check.

Creating the Extruded features

1. Click the **Sketch** command on the Toolbar and start a new sketch on the **Top** plane.
2. Click the **Corner rectangle** command on the toolbar and select the origin point of the sketch. Next, move the pointer toward the right and click.
3. Click the **Dimension** command on the toolbar and apply dimensions to the rectangle, as shown.
4. Click the green check on the **Sketch 1** dialog.
5. On the toolbar, click the **Extrude** command and select the rectangular sketch.
6. On the **Extrude 1** dialog, select **End type > Blind** and enter 0.787 in the **Depth** box. Click the green check to create the *Extrude* feature.

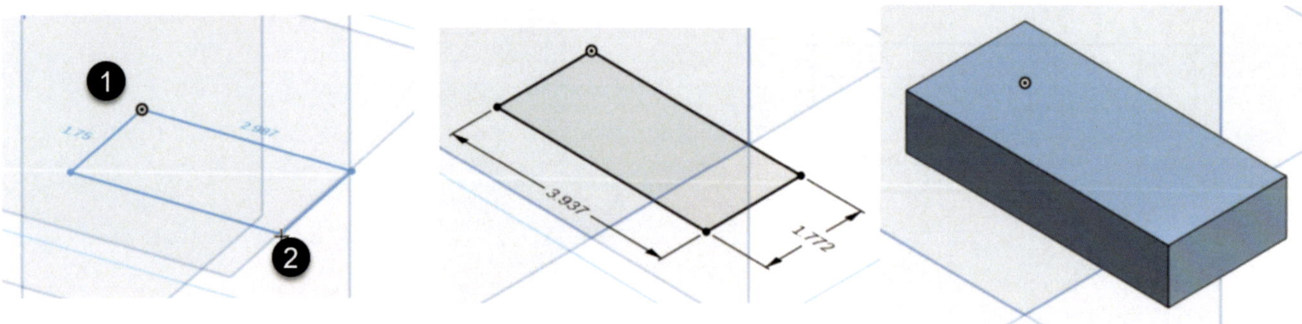

7. Activate the **Sketch** command and select the **Front** plane.
8. Right-click and select **View normal to sketch plane**; the sketch plane orients normal to the screen.
9. Click the **Corner Rectangle** command on the toolbar and specify the first and second corners of the rectangle, as shown.

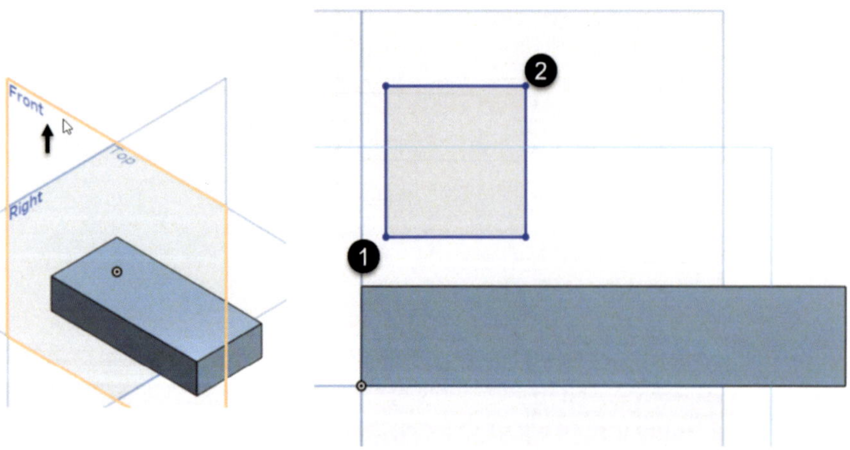

10. On the toolbar, click **Arc** drop-down > **Tangent arc**. Next, select the left vertical line of the rectangle.
11. Move the pointer toward the right and select the top right corner point of the rectangle.

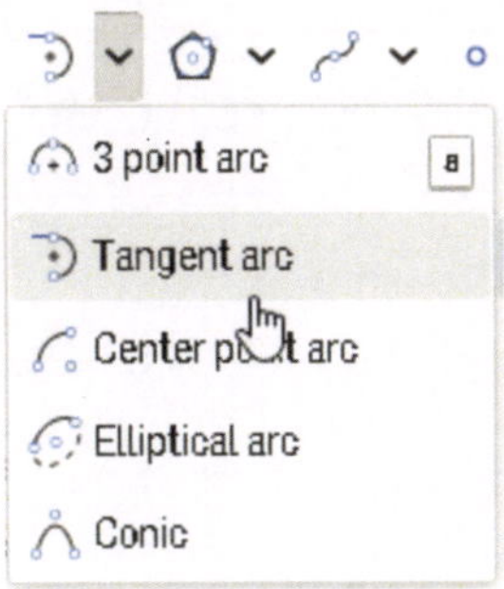

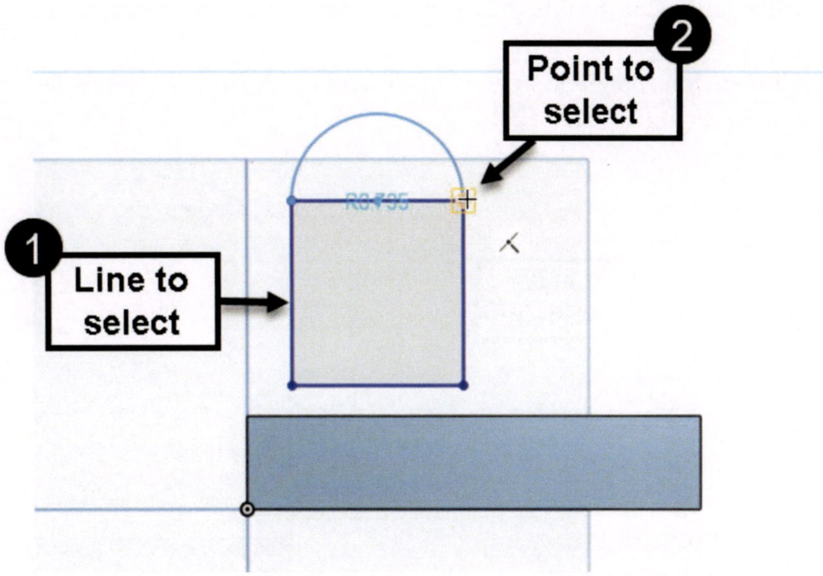

12. Click the **Trim** command on the toolbar and select the horizontal line of the rectangle, as shown.

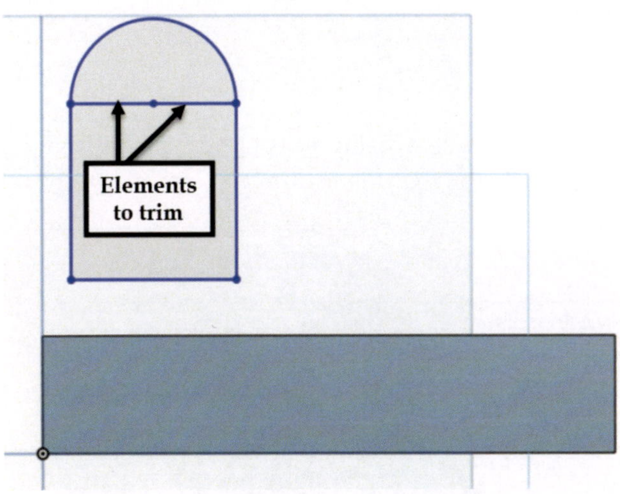

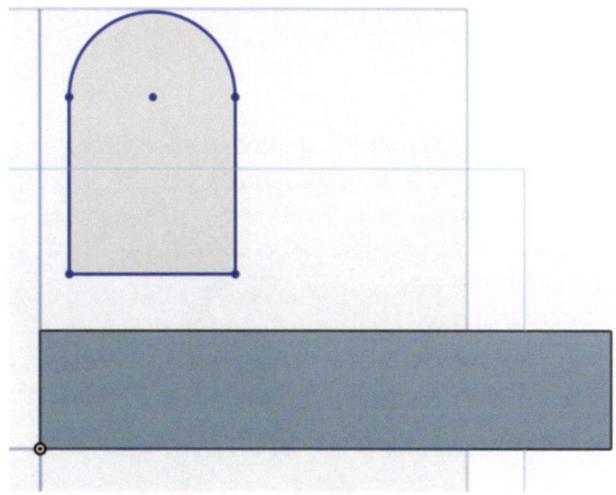

13. Apply the **Coincident** constraint between the horizontal line of the sketch and the top horizontal edge, as shown.
14. Likewise, apply the **Coincident** constraint between the left vertical line of the sketch and the left vertical edge of the model.

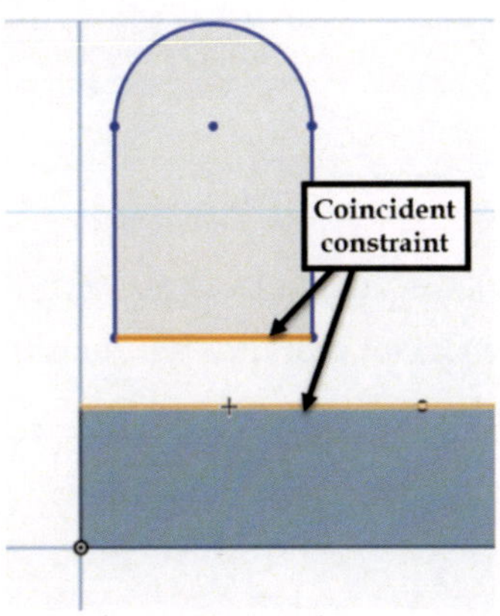

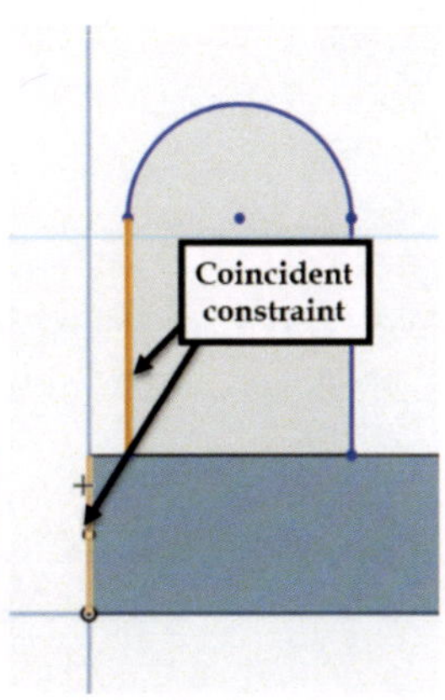

15. On the toolbar, click **Constraints** drop-down > **Tangent** and select the arc and the right vertical line of the sketch.
16. Click the **Dimension** command on the toolbar and create dimensions, as shown. Next, click the green check on the **Sketch 2** dialog.

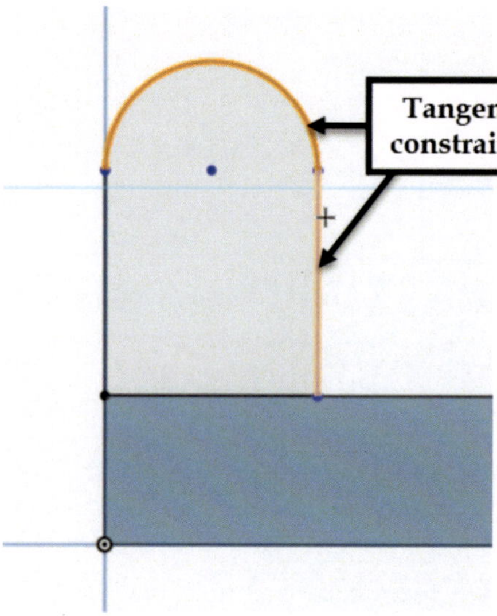

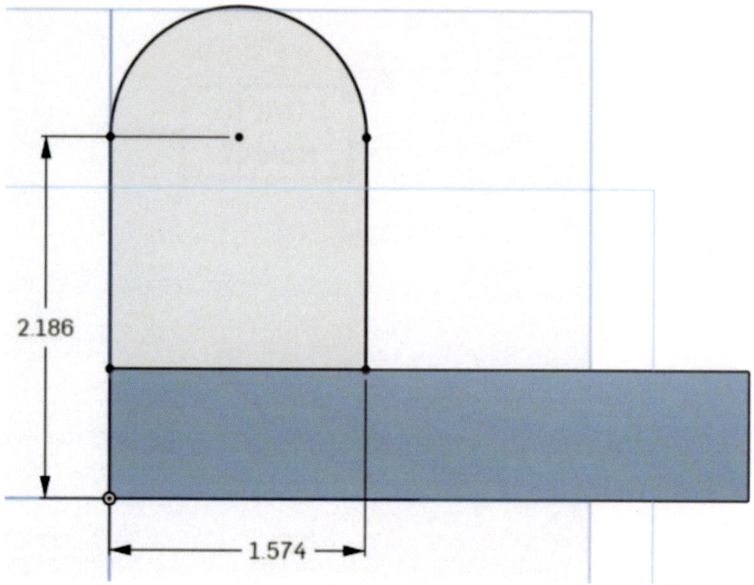

17. Activate the **Extrude** command and select the sketch. On the **Extrude 2** dialog, select **End type > Blind** and enter **0.787** in the **Depth** box. Click the green check to complete the Extrude feature.

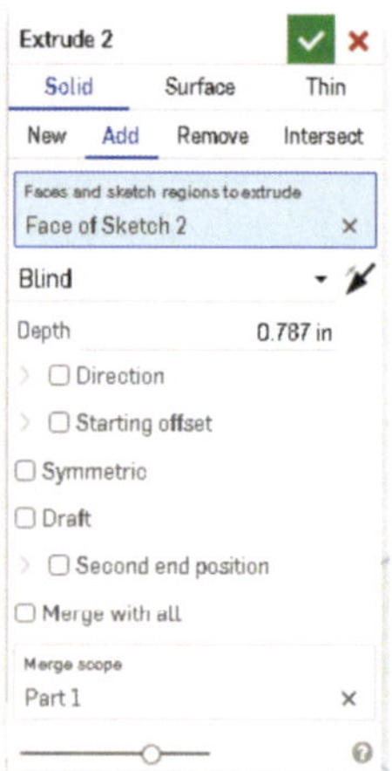

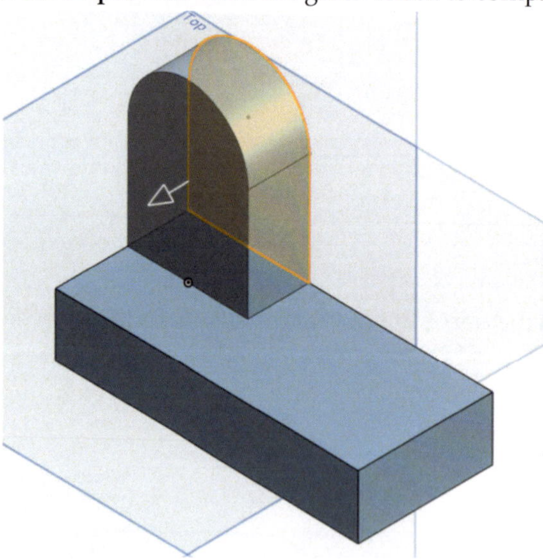

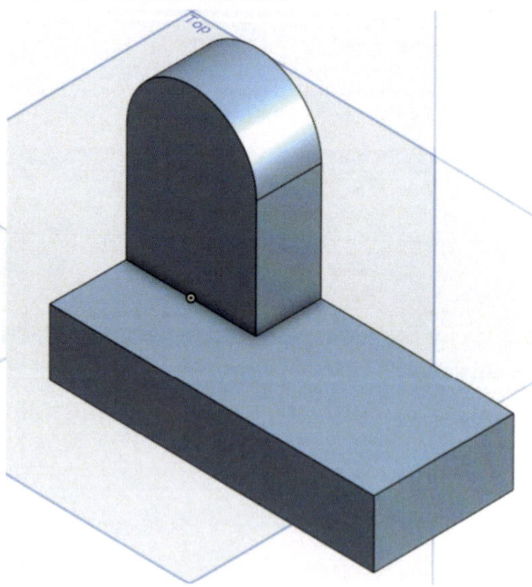

Creating the Rib feature

1. On the toolbar, click the **Plane** command and select the Front plane from the graphics area.
2. Select **Plane type > Offset** from the **Plane 1** dialog. Next, type **0.197** in the **Offset distance** box, and then click the green check.

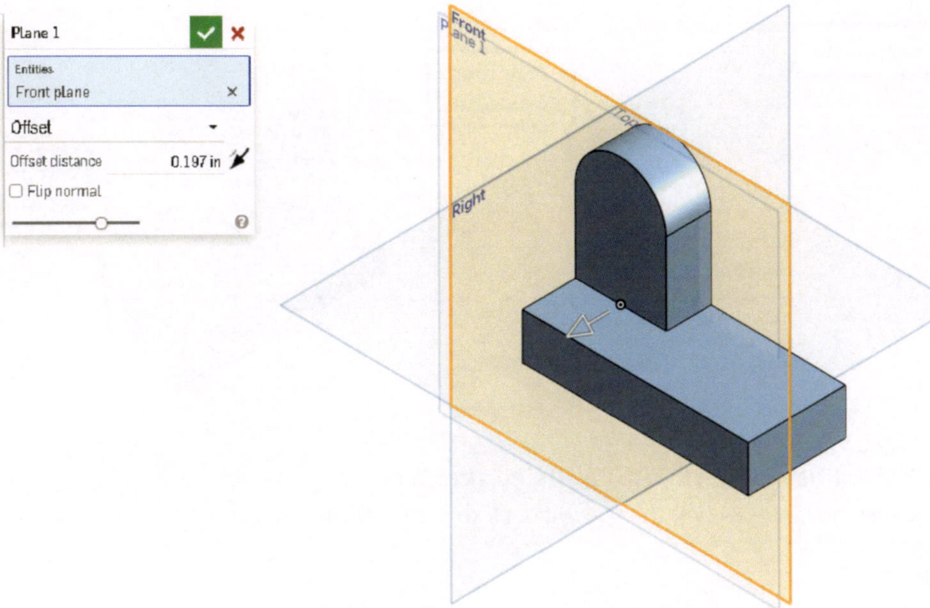

3. Activate the **Sketch** command and select the newly created plane. Draw an inclined line, as shown.

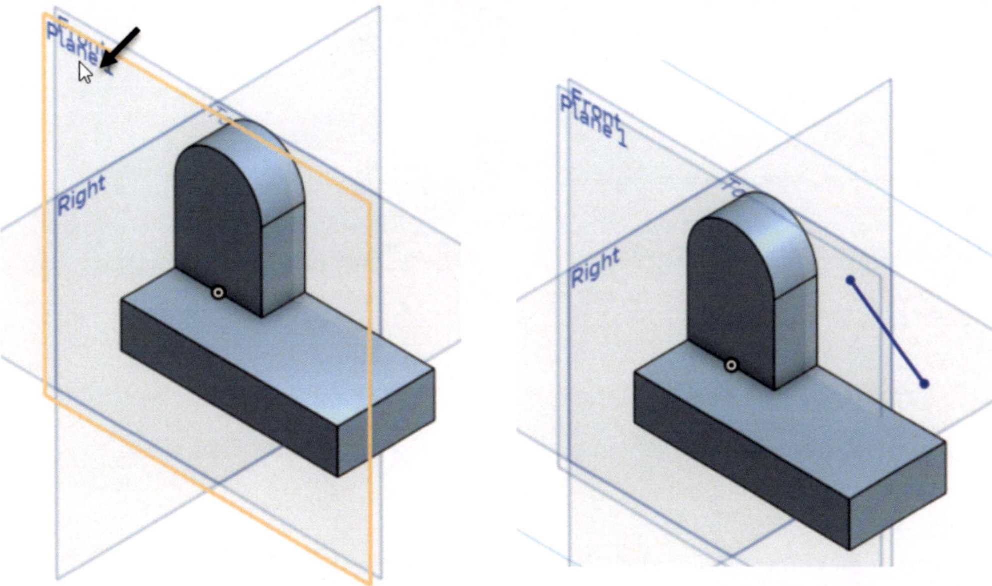

4. On the toolbar, click **Constraints** drop-down **> Tangent**, and then select the inclined line and the curved edge; the line is made tangent to the edge.
5. On the toolbar, click **Constraints** drop-down **> Coincident**, and then select the endpoint of the inclined line and the curved edge; the endpoint of the line is made coincident to the edge.
6. Likewise, make the other endpoint of the line coincident with the vertex point, as shown. Click the green check on the **Sketch 3** dialog.

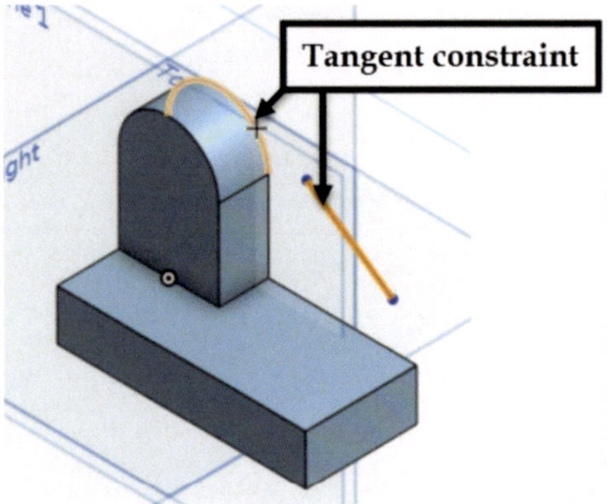

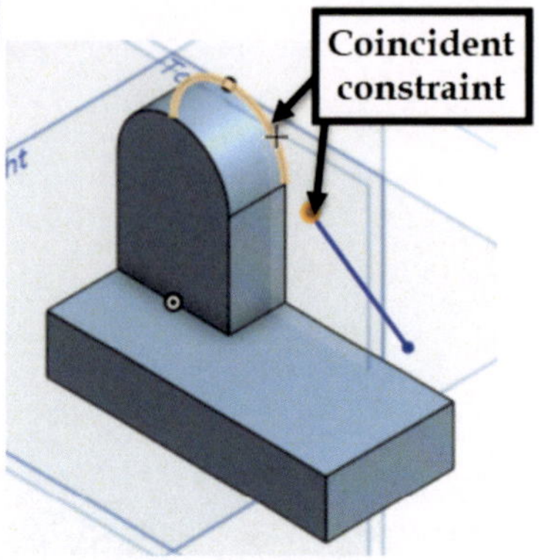

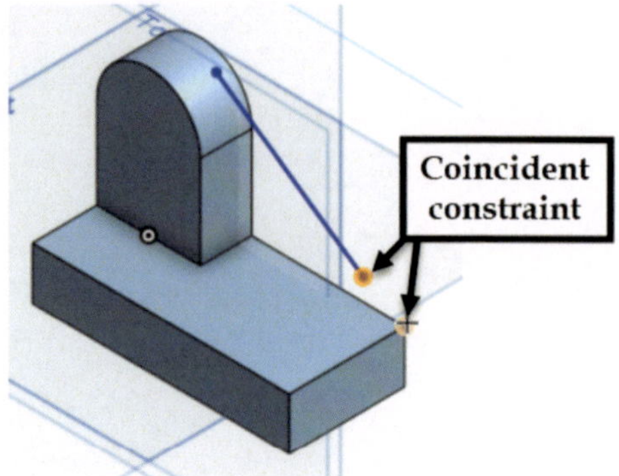

7. Click **Rib** on the toolbar. Next, select the sketch.
8. On the **Rib** dialog, select **Rib extrusion direction > Parallel to sketch plane**.
9. Type-in 0.394 in the **Thickness** box. Next, click the green check to create the *Rib* feature.

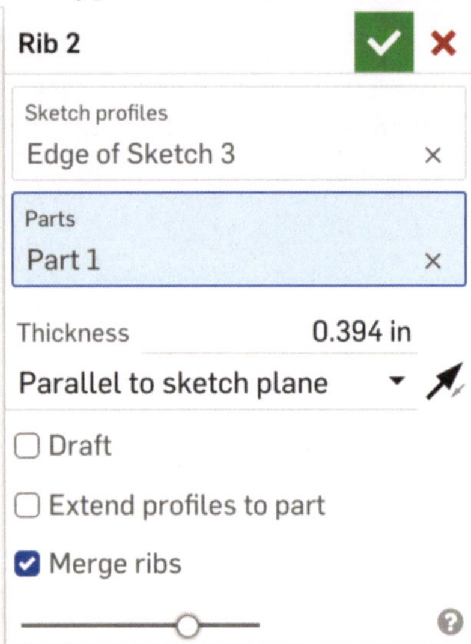

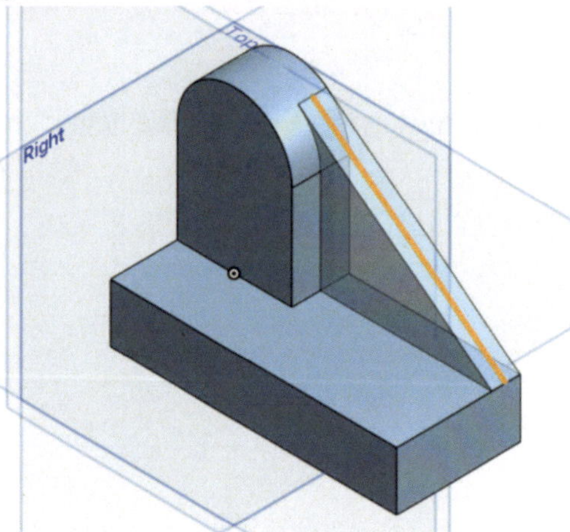

Creating the Extruded Cut features

1. Activate the **Sketch** command and click on the front face of the second feature, as shown.
2. On the toolbar, click the **Line** command.
3. Place the pointer near the centerpoint of the curved edge; the centerpoint is highlighted in orange.
4. Click to select the centerpoint of the curved edge. Next, move the pointer downward and click to specify the second center of the line.
5. Right click and select **Escape line**.

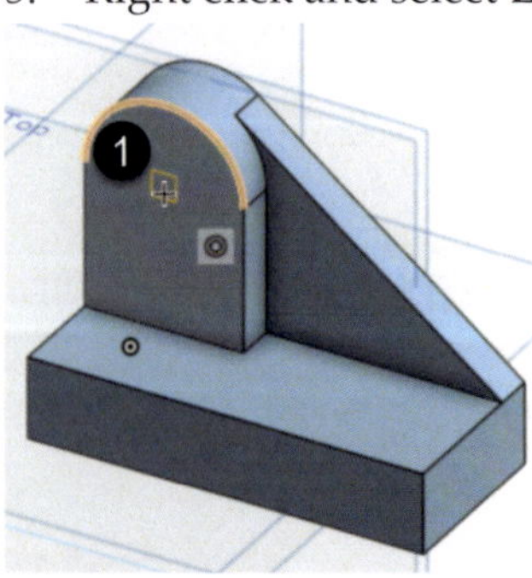

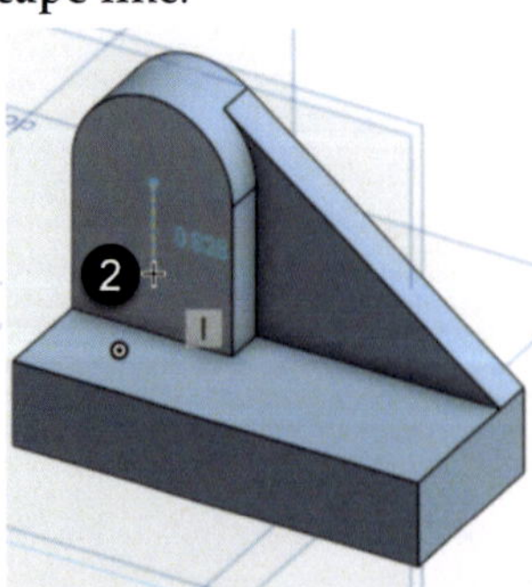

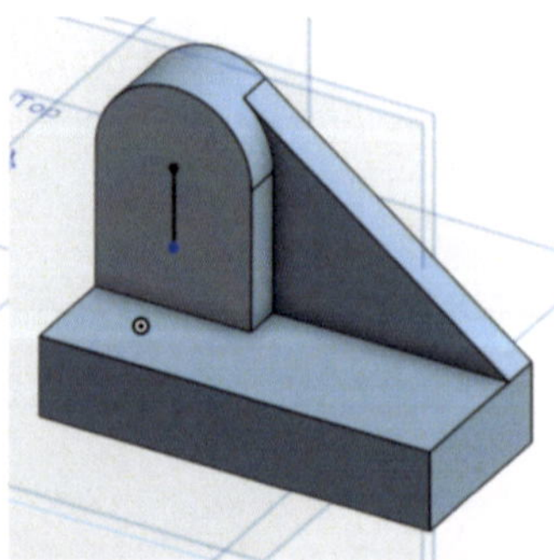

6. On the toolbar, click **Offset** drop-down > **Slot**. Next, select the line created in the previous step.
7. Click on the dimension and enter .474 in the value box.
8. Add dimension to the vertical line, and then convert it into a construction element.

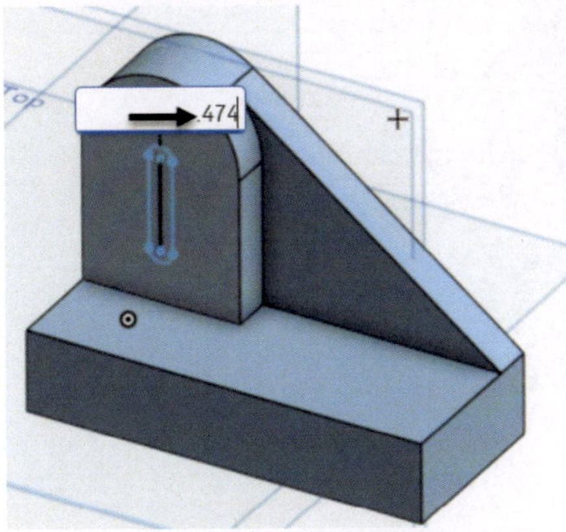

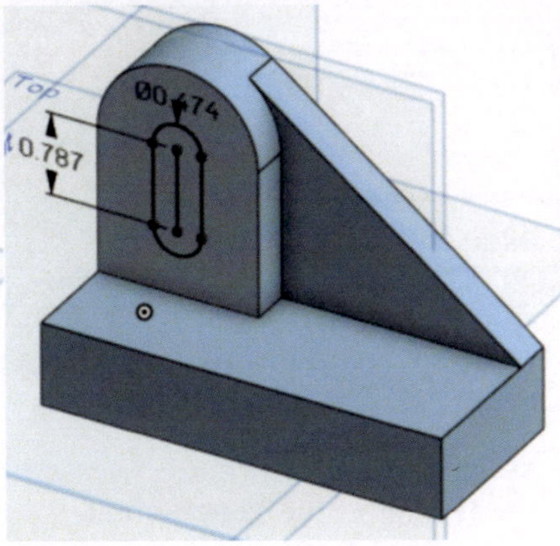

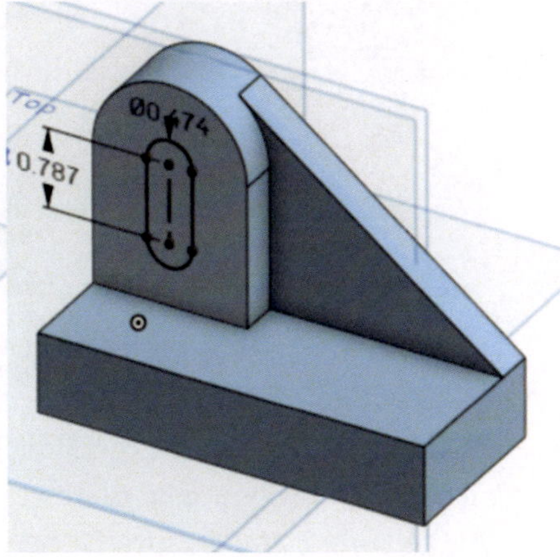

9. Click the green check on the **Sketch 4** dialog.
10. Activate the **Extrude** command and select the sketch.
11. On the **Extrude 3** dialog, click the **Remove** tab and select **End type > Through all**.
12. Click the green check to create the *Extruded cut* feature.
13. Add a fillet of 0.787 in radius to the right vertical edge of the rectangular base.

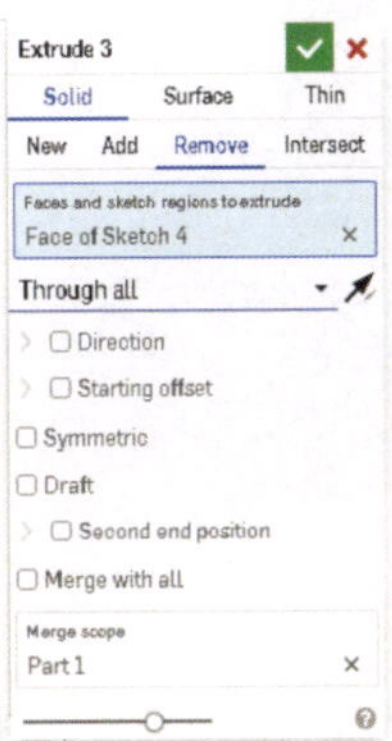

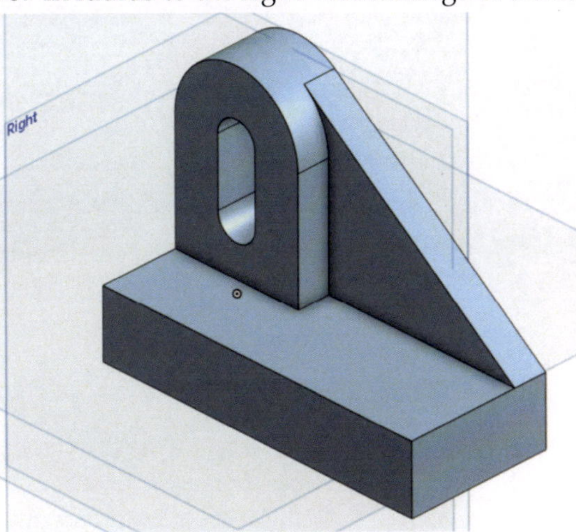

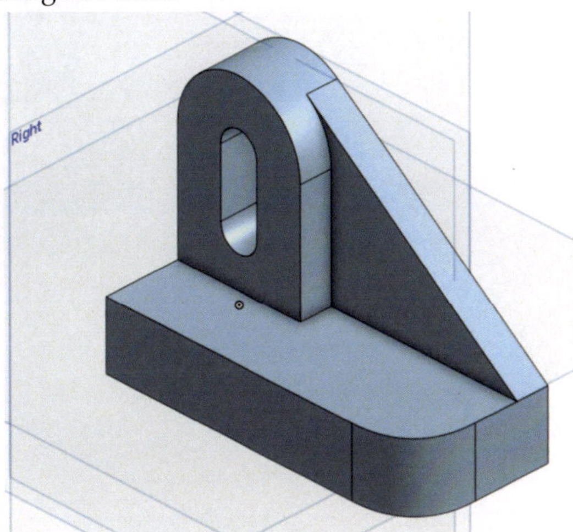

Creating the Fillet and Hole features

1. Activate the **Sketch** command and click on the top face of the first feature.
2. Click the **Point** command on the toolbar and click on the sketch plane.
3. Click **Constraints** drop-down > **Concentric** on the toolbar. Next, select the curved edge of the fillet and sketch point; the point is made concentric to the fillet.

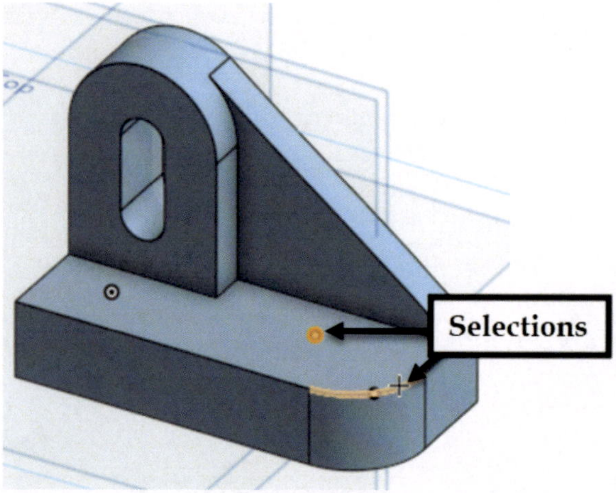

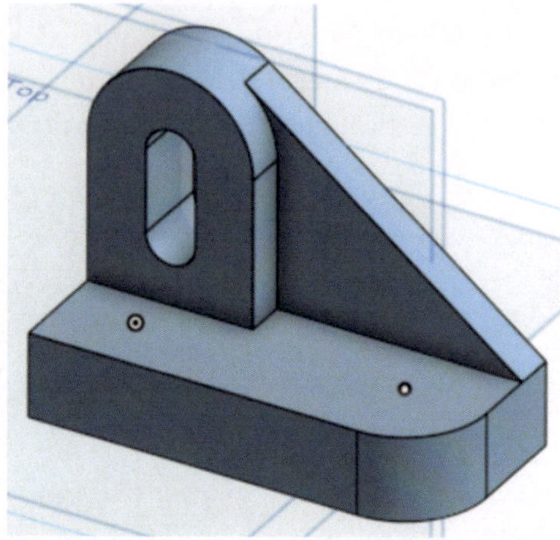

4. Click the green check on the **Sketch 5** dialog.
5. Click the **Hole** command on the toolbar and select the sketch point.
6. On the **Hole 1** dialog, specify the settings, as shown. Next, click **OK** to create the hole.

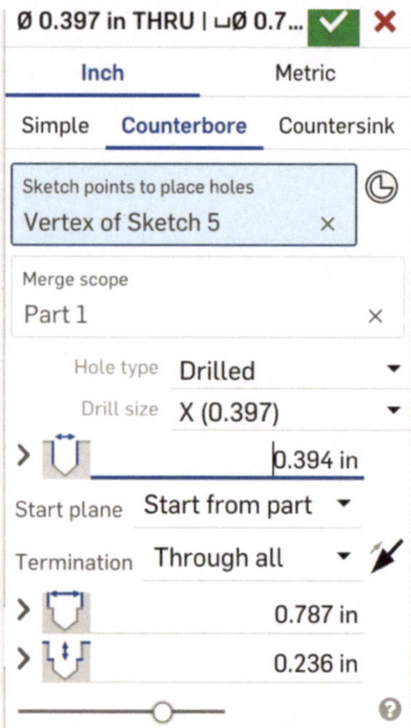

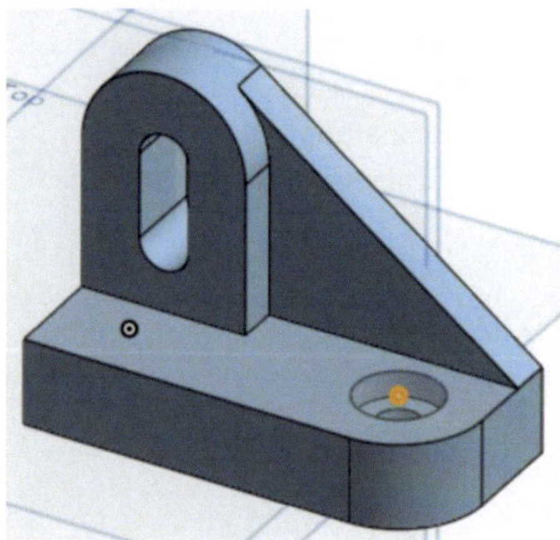

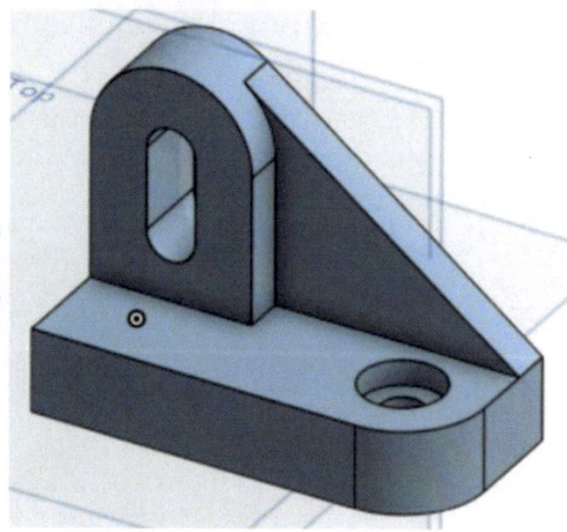

7. Activate the **Sketch** command and select the front face of the rectangular base.
8. Draw a sketch and add dimensions to it. Click the green check on the **Sketch 6** dialog.
9. Create an *Extruded Cut* feature using the sketch.

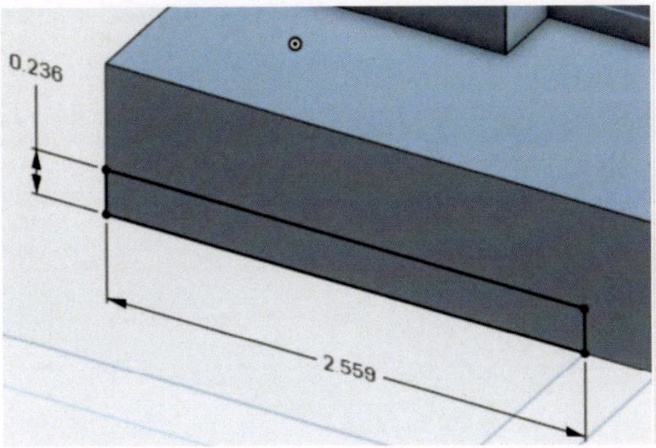

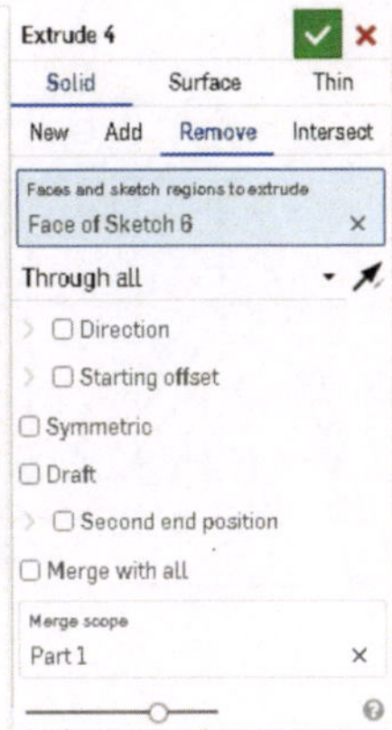

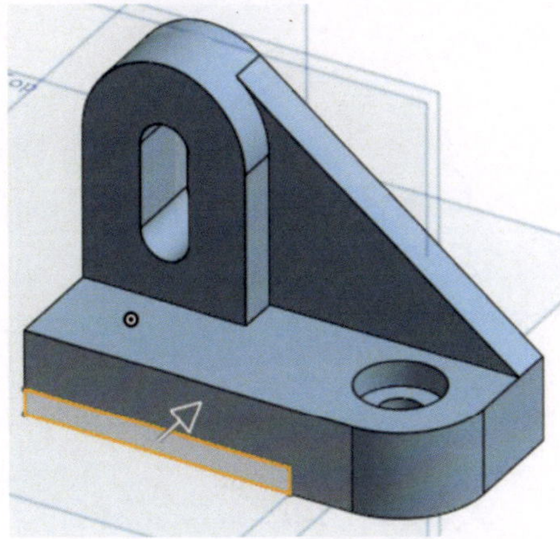

10. Close the part file.

Questions

1. How many types ribs of can be created in ONSHAPE?
2. Why do we create multi body parts?
3. Explain the merge type while creating a cut feature in multi-body part?

Exercises

Exercise 1

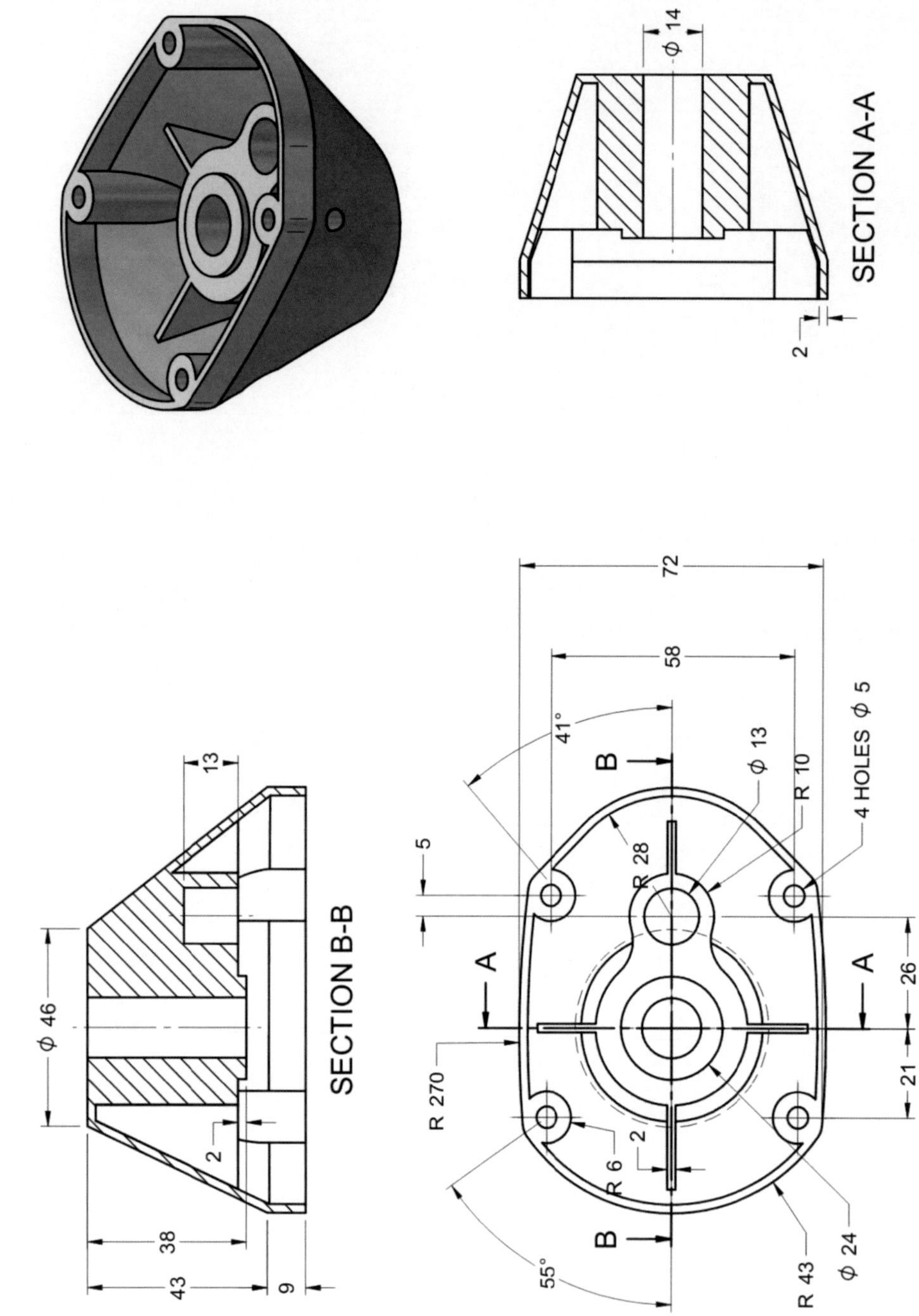

SECTION A-A
ϕ 14
2
SECTION B-B
ϕ 46
13
2
38
43
9
72
58
41°
B
B
ϕ 13
R 10
4 HOLES ϕ 5
5
R 28
A
A
26
21
R 270
R 6
2
55°
R 43
ϕ 24

Exercise 2

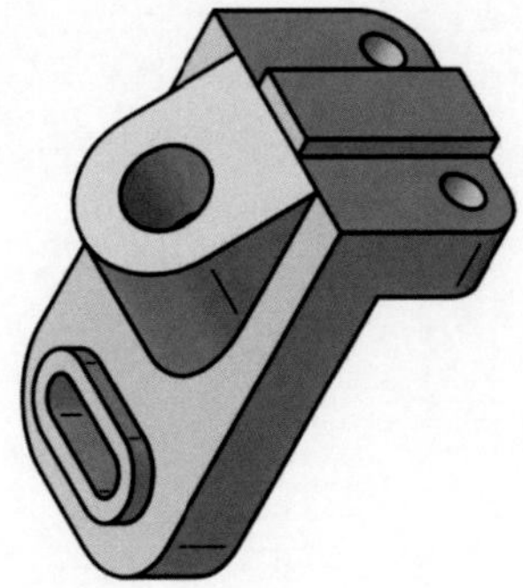

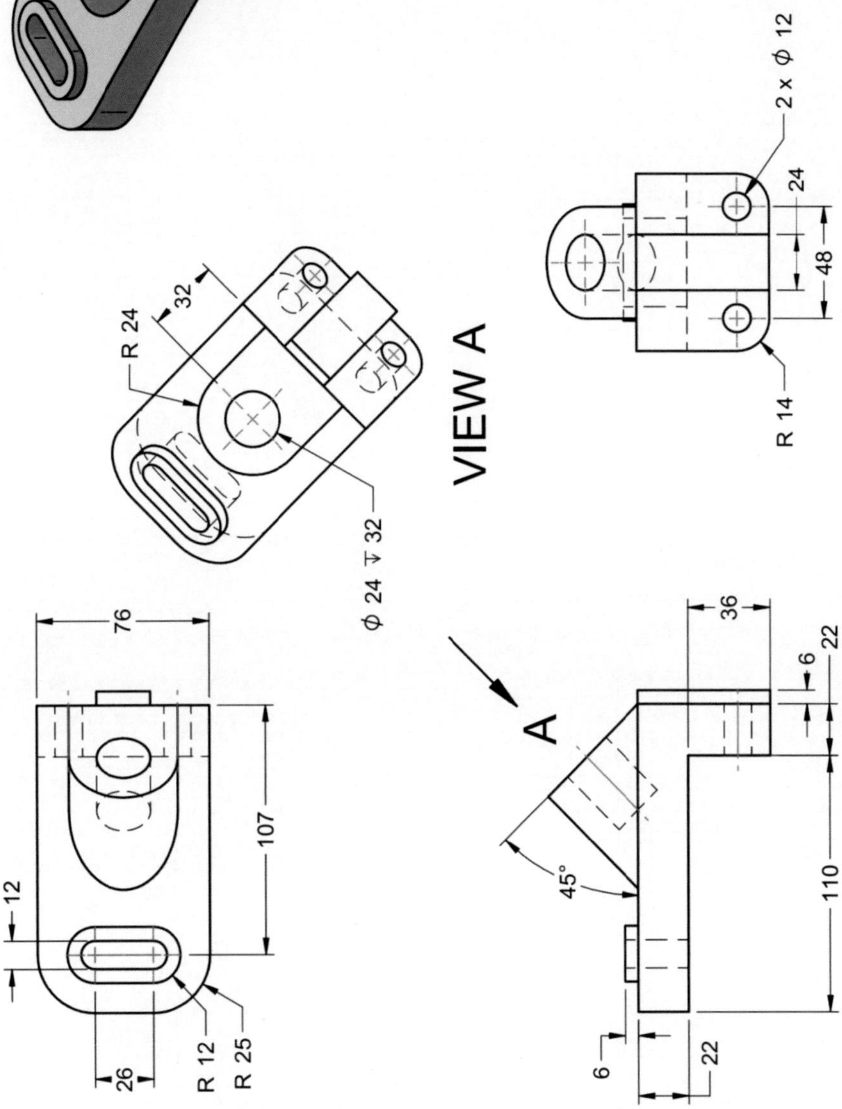
VIEW A
A
R 24
32
Φ 24 ⊽ 32
2 x Φ 12
24
48
R 14
76
107
12
26
R 12
R 25
36
6
22
45°
110
6
22

Exercise 3 (Inches)

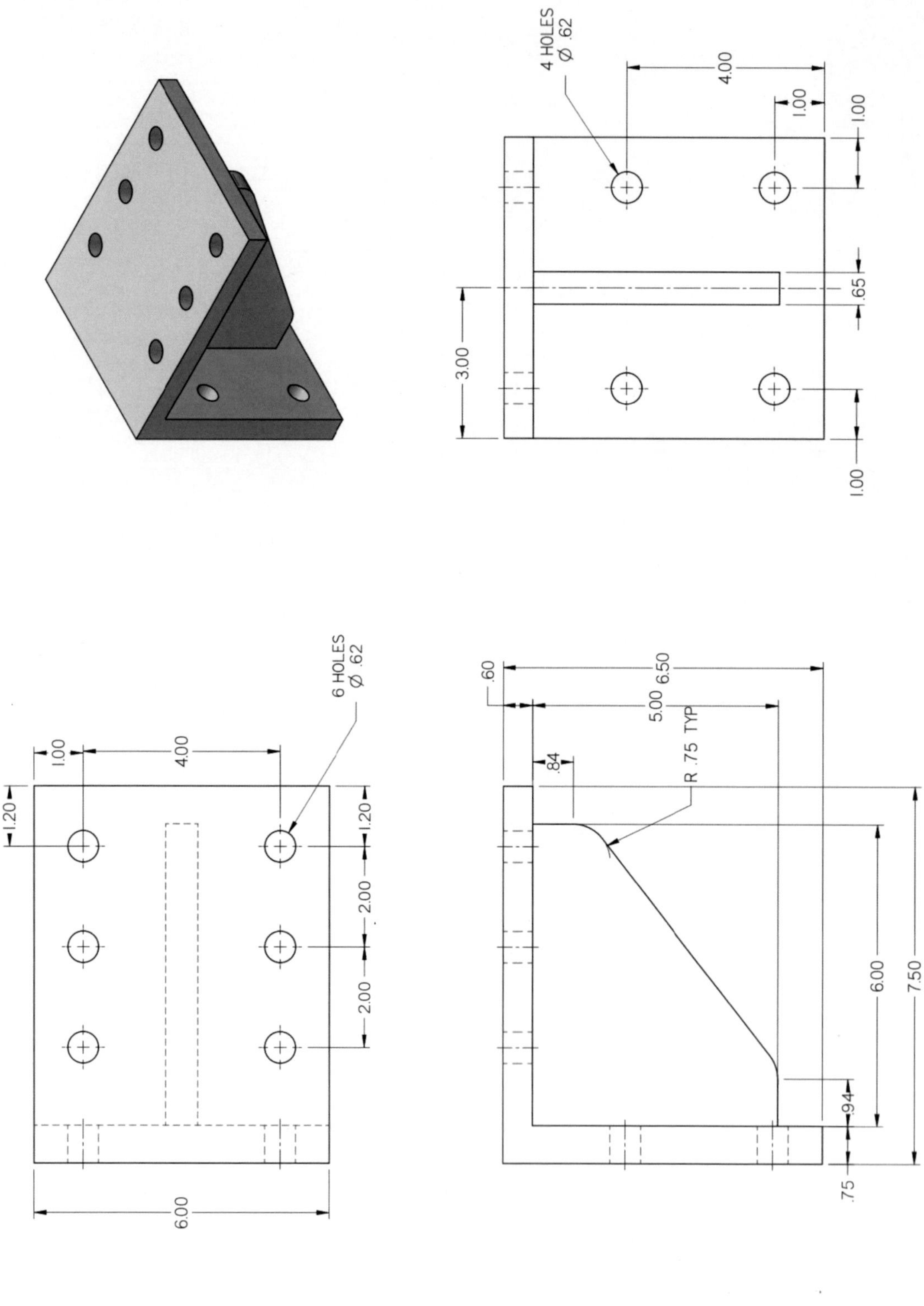

Chapter 9: Modifying Parts

In the design process, it is not required to achieve the final model in the first attempt. There is always a need to modify the existing parts to get the desired part geometry. In this chapter, you learn various commands and techniques to make changes to a part.

The topics covered in this chapter are:

- *Edit Sketches*
- *Edit Features*
- *Suppress Features*

Edit Sketches

Sketches form the base of a 3D geometry. They control the size and shape of the geometry. If you want to modify the 3D geometry, most of the times, you are required to edit sketches. To do this, right-click on the feature and select **Edit Sketch**. Now, modify the sketch and click green check on the dialog. You will notice that the part geometry updates immediately.

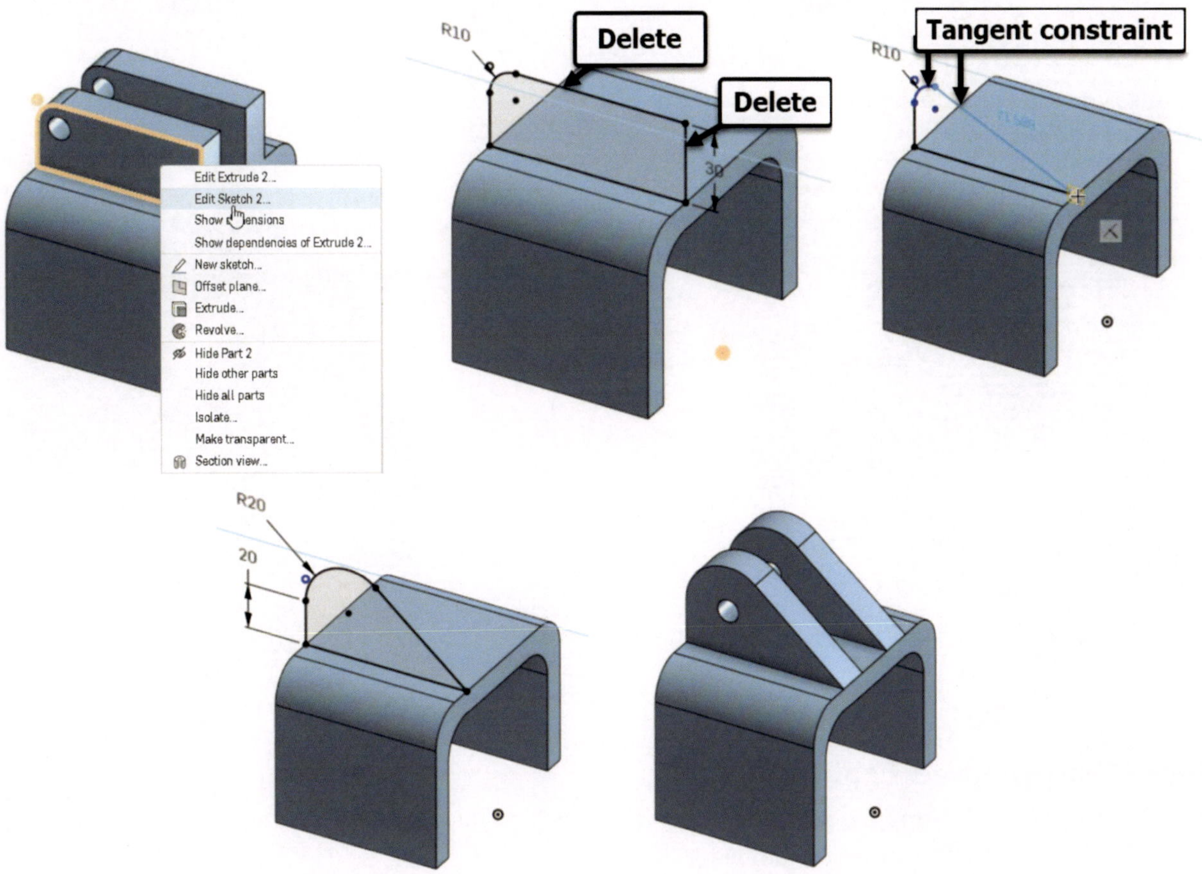

Edit Feature

Features are the building blocks of a model geometry. To modify a feature, click on it and select **Edit** . The dialog related to the feature appears. On the dialog, modify the parameters of the feature and click green check. The changes take place immediately.

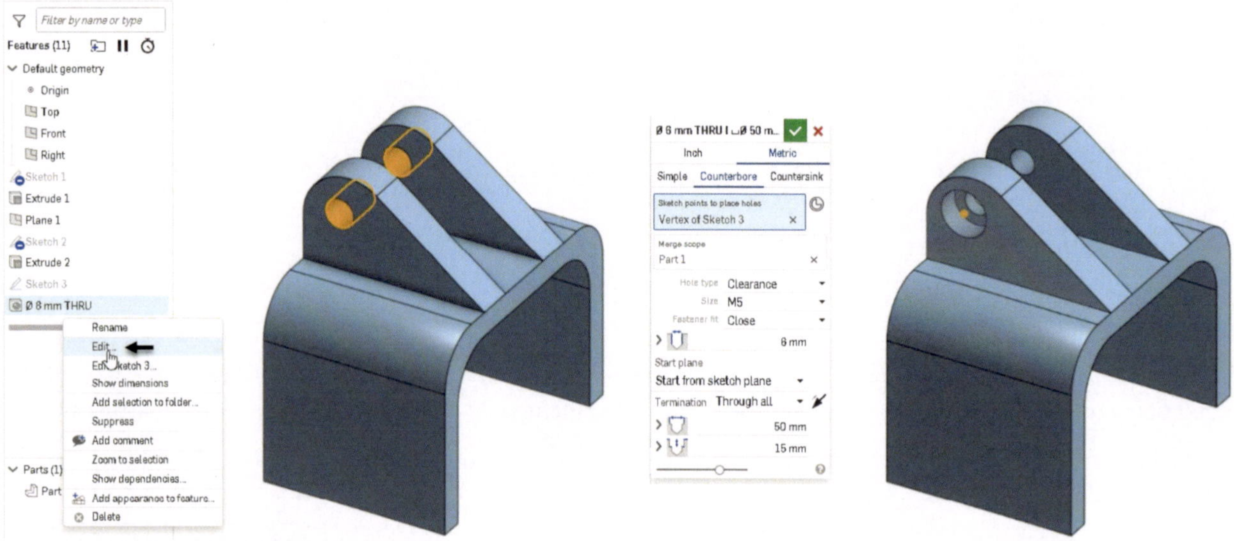

Suppress Features

Sometimes you may need to suppress some features of a model geometry. Right-click on the feature to suppress, and then select **Suppress**.

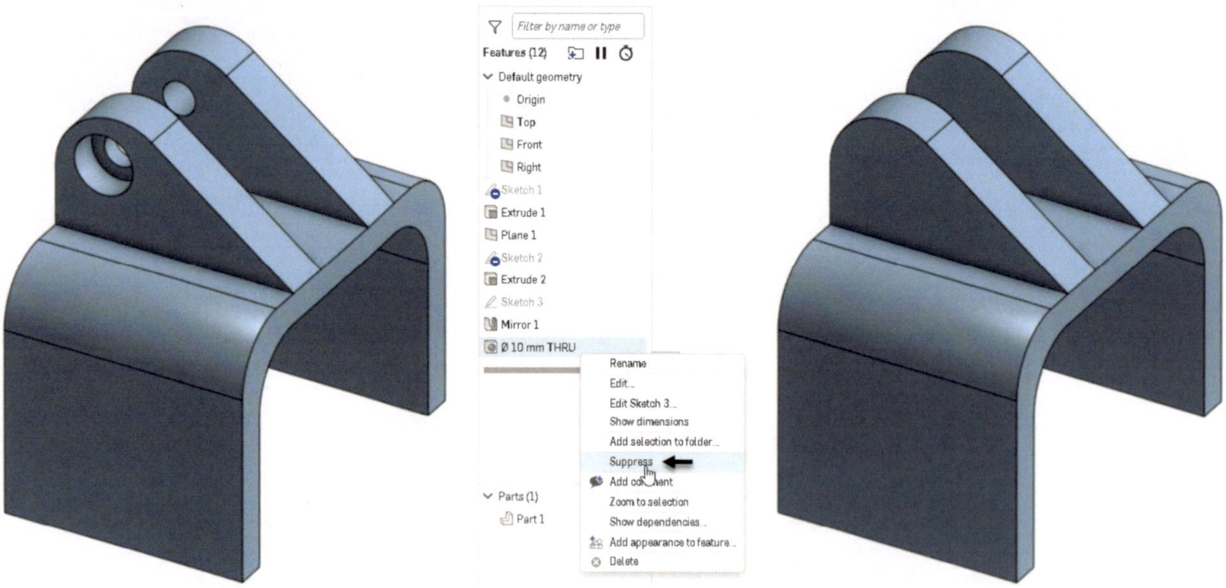

Resume Suppressed Features

If you want to resume the suppressed features, then right click on the suppressed feature in the Features list, and then select **Unsuppress**; the feature is resumed.

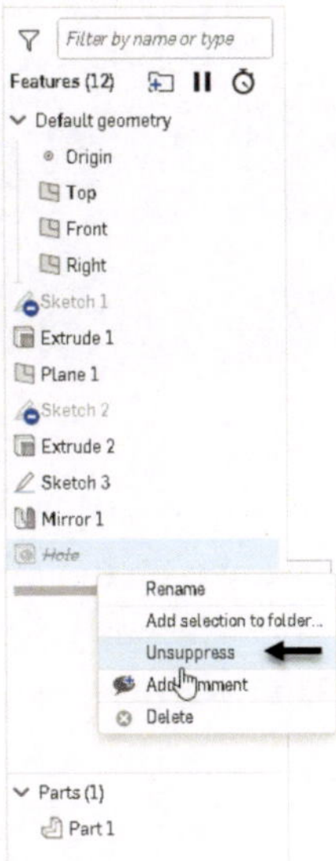

The Move Face command

Onshape provides you with a special tool called **Move Face** to modify faces and planes of part geometry. Click the **Modify face** drop-down > **Move Face** on the Toolbar. You can perform three operations using this tool: **Offset**, **Translate** and **Rotate** faces.

Offset Faces

The **Offset** option moves the selected face in the direction perpendicular to it. To offset a face, select the **Offset** option from the **Move face type** drop-down on the **Move Face** dialog. Next, click on the face to offset, and type-in a value in the **Distance** field available on the **Move Face** dialog. You can change offset direction by clicking the **Opposite direction** button beside the **Direction** field.

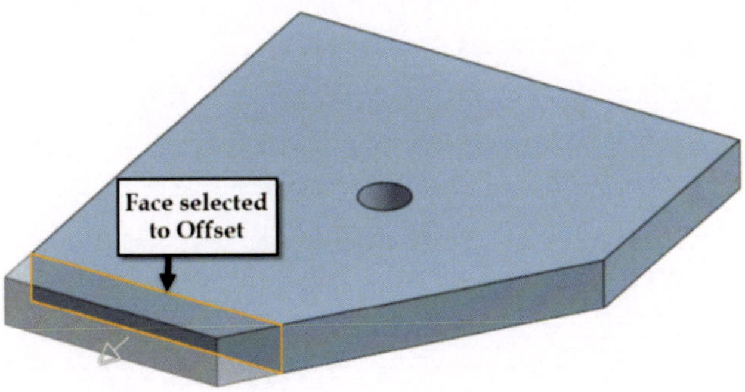

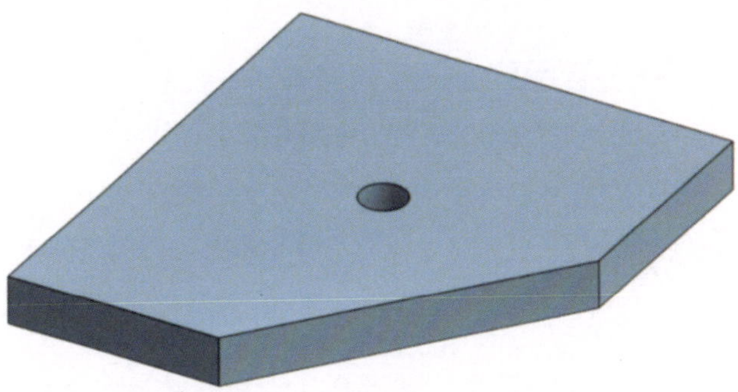

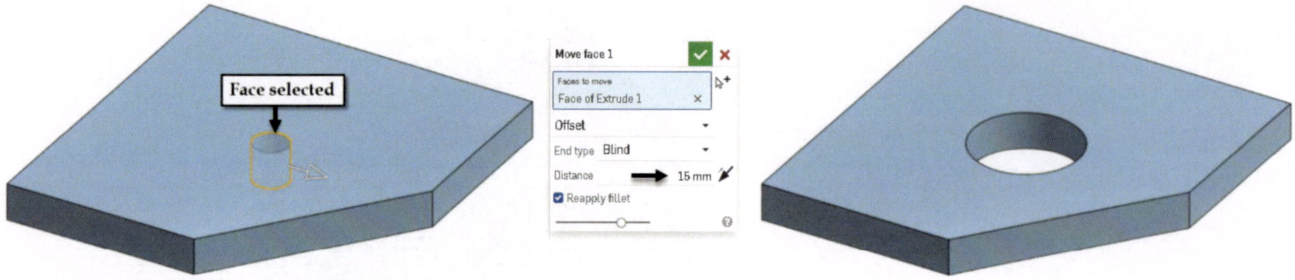

Translate Faces

The **Translate** option allows you to move the selected face(s) along X, Y, or Z directions. To translate faces in a particular direction, select the **Translate** option from the **Move face type** drop-down on the **Move Face** dialog. Next, click on the face to translate. Next, click on the **Direction** selection box and select an edge or face to define the translation direction. Select the **End type** from the drop-down (**Blind** or **Up to entity)**. Next, specify the translation distance in the **Distance** field and click green check to translate.

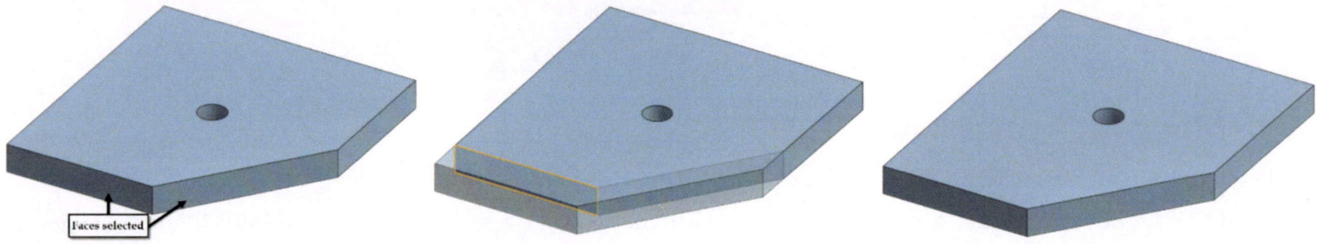

Rotate faces

The **Rotate** option helps you to rotate the selected faces about an axis. To rotate a face, select **Rotation** option from the **Move face type** drop-down on the **Move face** dialog and click on the face to rotate; it displays a manipulator. Click in the **Axis** selection box on the **Move face** dialog, and then select an edge. Now, type-in a value in the **Rotation angle** field and click green check to rotate.

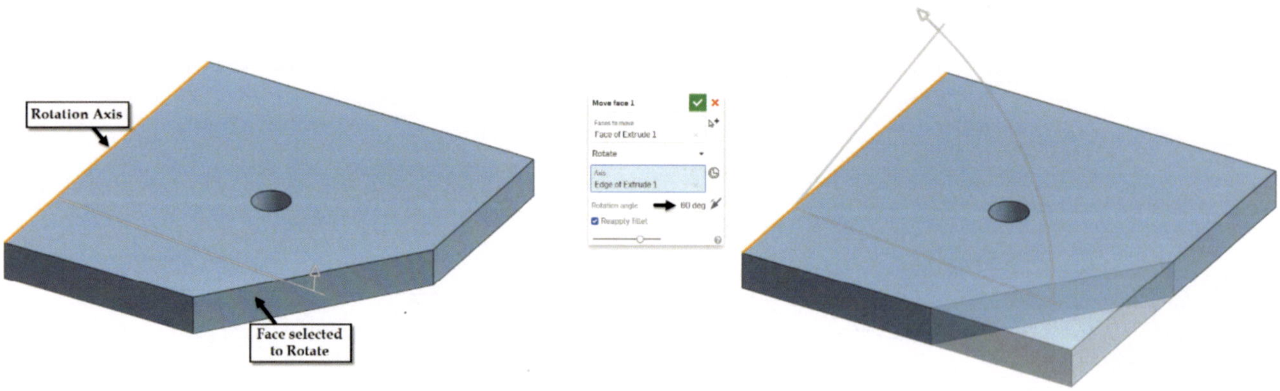

Tutorial 1 (Inches)

In this example, you create the part shown below and then modify it.

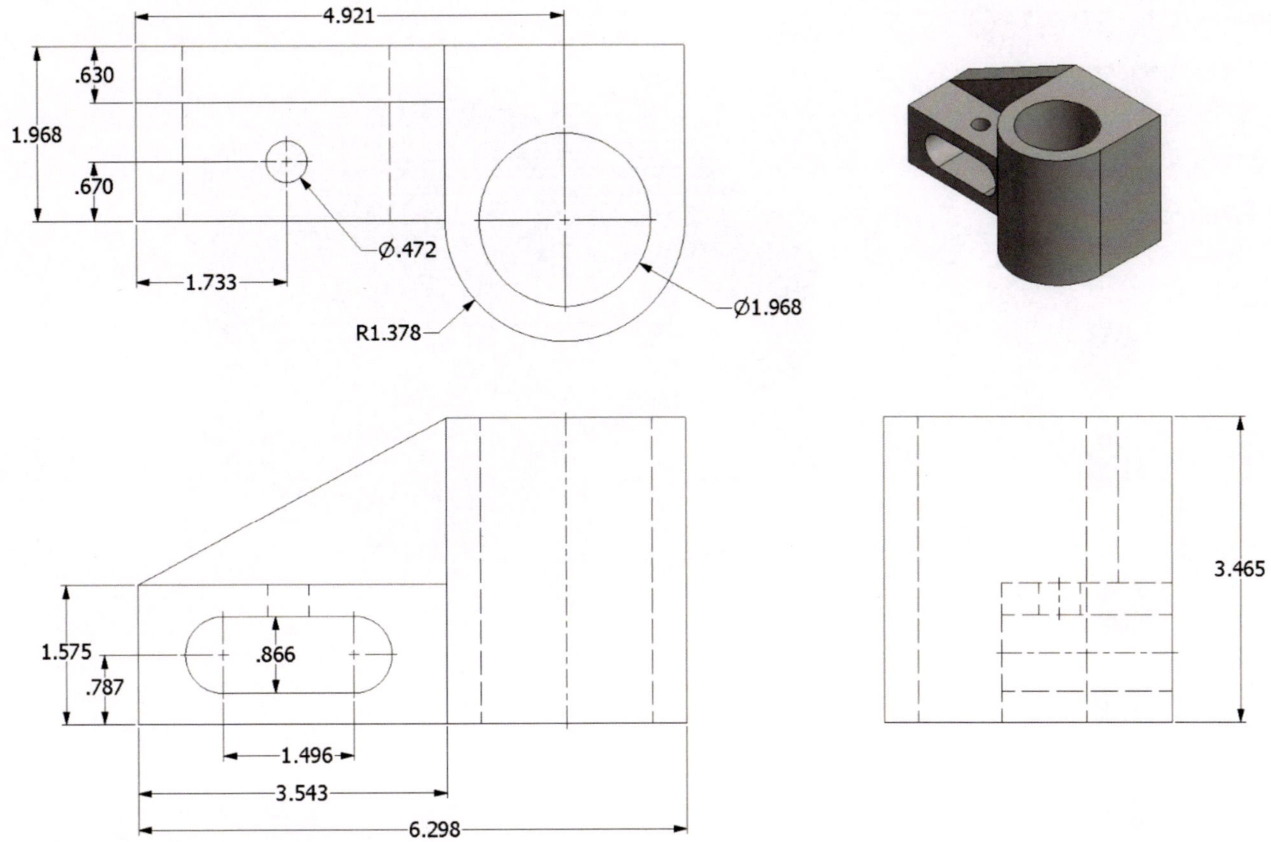

Creating a New document

1. In your Internet Browser, go to https://www.onshape.com to start Onshape.
2. Next, click **SIGN IN** button located on the top right corner side of the web page. Enter the username and password, and then, click **Sign in**.
3. On the Documents page, click **Create > Folder**. Next, type Chapter 9 in the **Folder name** box and then click **Create**.
4. Double-click on the **Chapter 9** folder in the **Folders** section.
5. On the Documents page, click **Create > Document**; the **New document** dialog appears on the screen.
6. Enter Tutorial 1 in the **Document name** box and click **Create public document**; a new document appears.
7. Click the **Document menu** located at the top left corner of the window and select **Workspace Units**; the **Workspace Units** dialog appears on the screen.
8. On the **Workspace Units** dialog, select **Length default unit> Inch** from **Length** section.
9. Select **Mass default unit > Pound** from the **Mechanical** section.
10. Leave the other default settings and click the green check .
11. Create the part using the tools and commands available in Onshape, as shown in the figure. You can also download this file from the companion website.

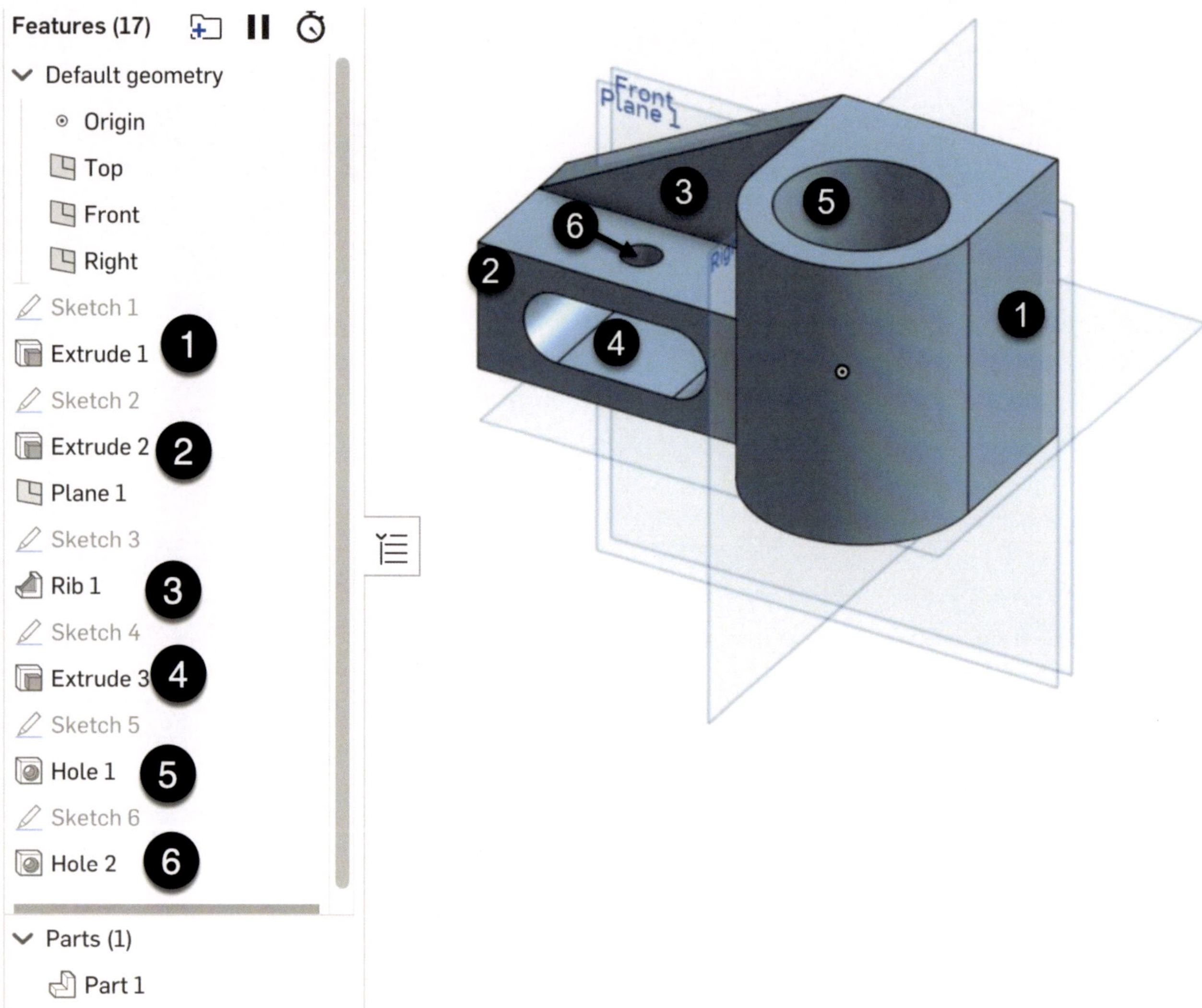

Editing a Feature

1. Click right mouse button on the **Hole 1** in the **Features** window and click **Edit**. On the **Hole 1** dialog, click the **Counterbore** tab.
2. Enter **1.378, 1.968,** and **0.787** in the **Diameter, Counterbore diameter**, and **Counterbore depth** fields, respectively. Click the green check.

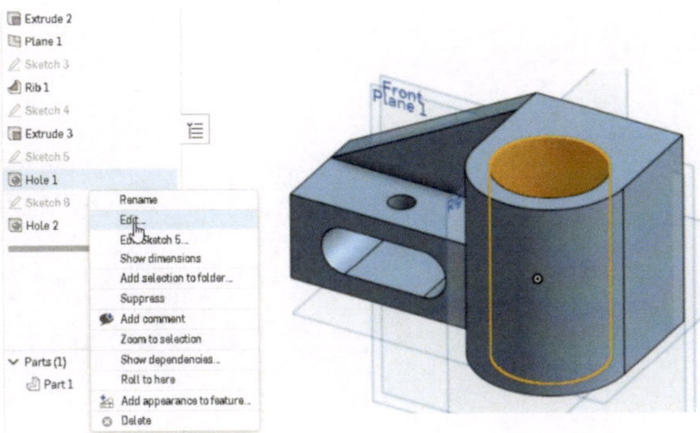

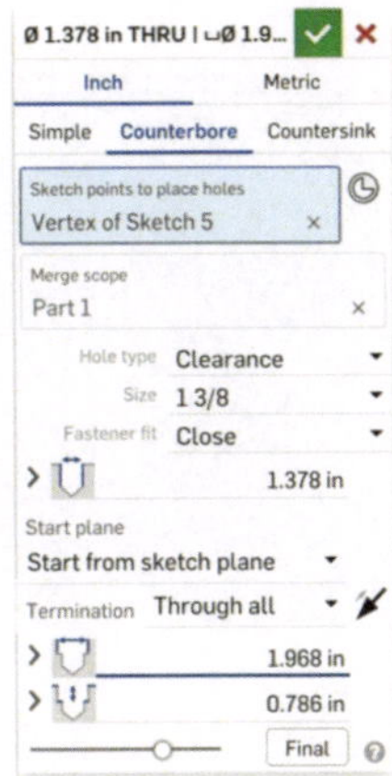

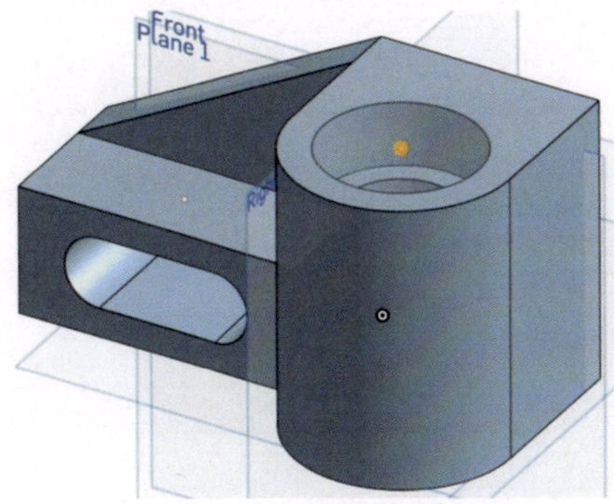

Editing Sketches

1. Right-click on the *Sketch 2* in the **Features** window and select **Edit**. Modify the sketch, as shown. Click **green check**.

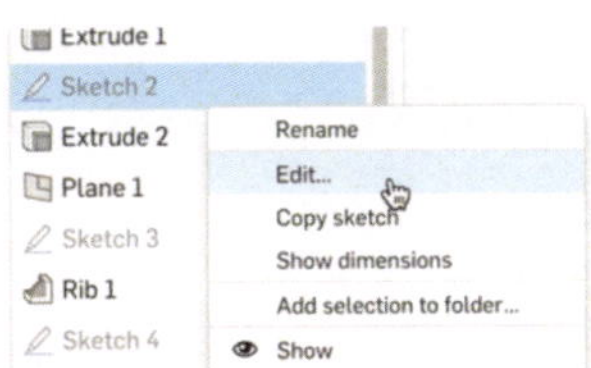

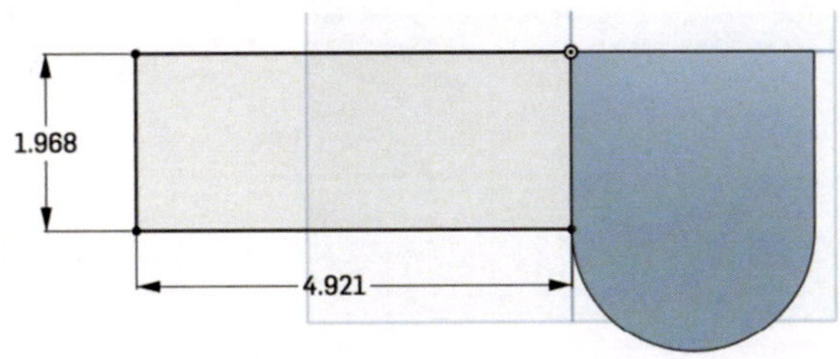

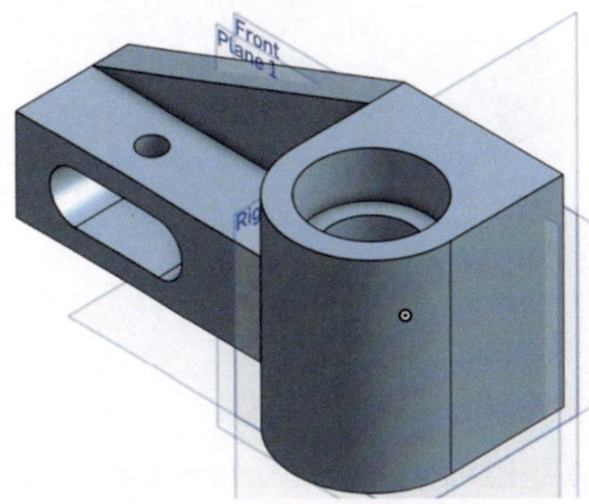

2. Right click on the slot and select **Edit Sketch 4**.
3. Delete the length dimension of the slot, and then add a new dimension between the right-side arc and right vertical edge.

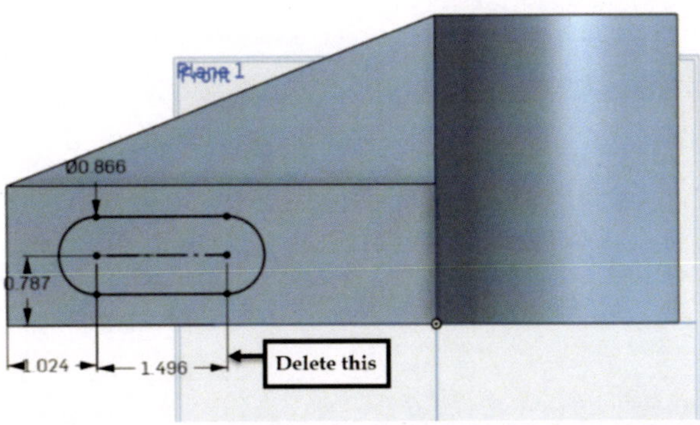

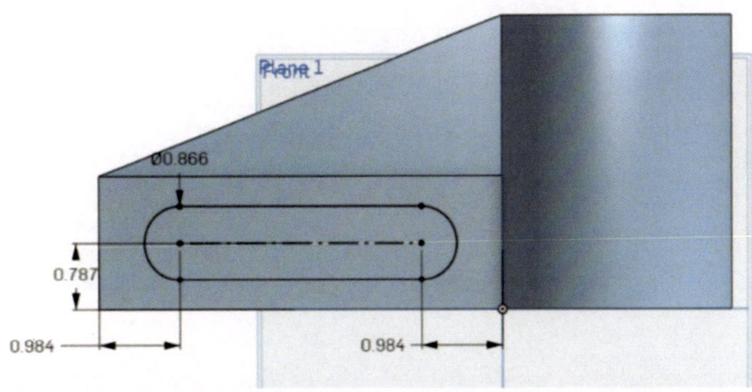

4. Delete the dimension between the centerline of the slot and the horizontal edge.
5. Apply the **Coincident** constraint between the construction line of the slot and the midpoint of the left vertical edge. Click the green check on the **Sketch 4** dialog.

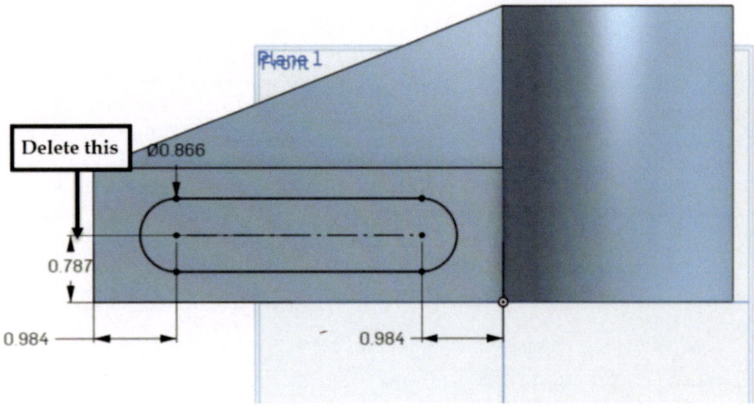

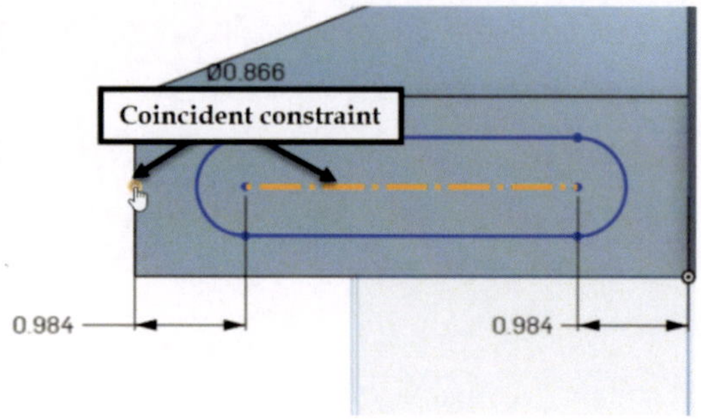

6. Right-click on the small hole, and then select the **Edit Sketch 6** from the menu. Delete the positioning dimensions.

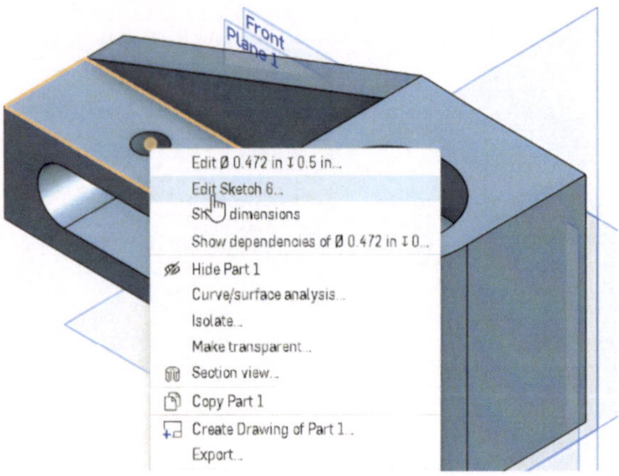

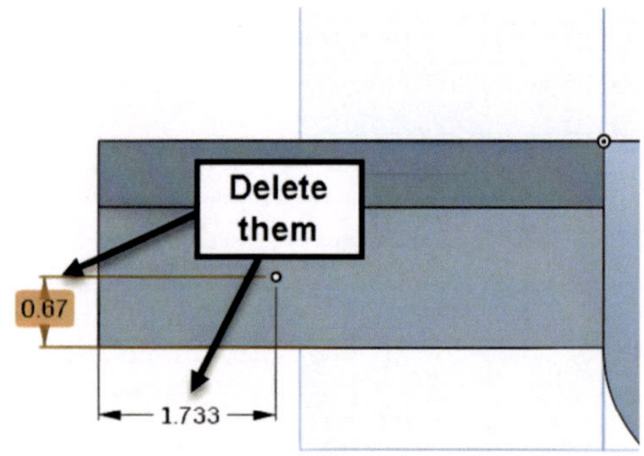

7. Create a construction line and make its ends coincident with the corners, as shown below.
8. On the Toolbar, click the **Midpoint** icon, and select the hole point. Next, select the construction line; the hole point becomes the midpoint of the construction line. Click the green check on the **Sketch 6** dialog.

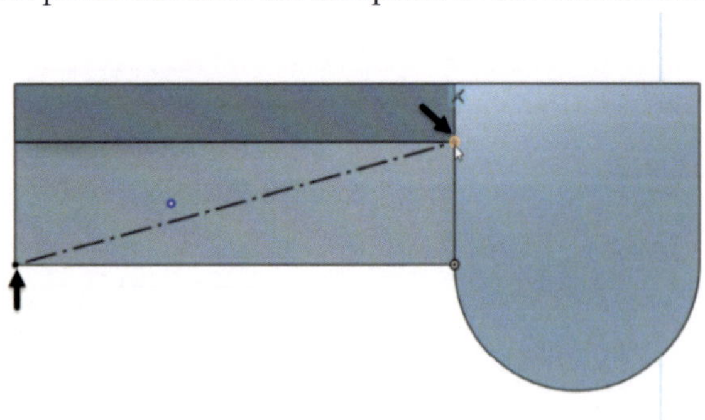

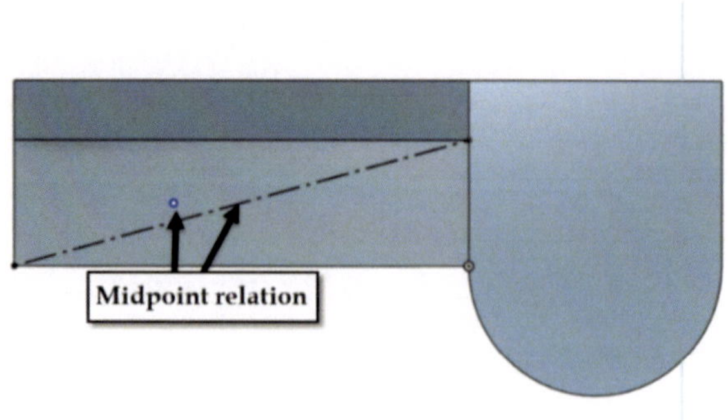

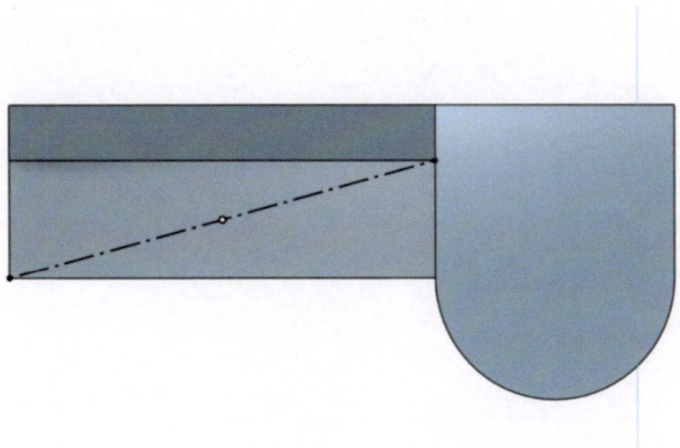

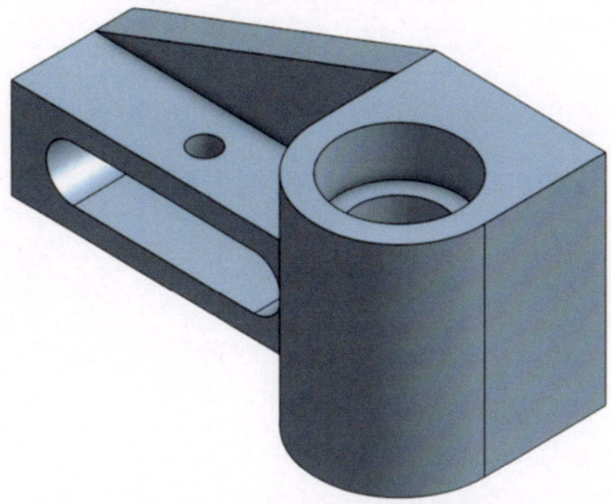

9. Now, change the size of the rectangular extruded feature. Notice that the slot and hole are adjusted automatically.

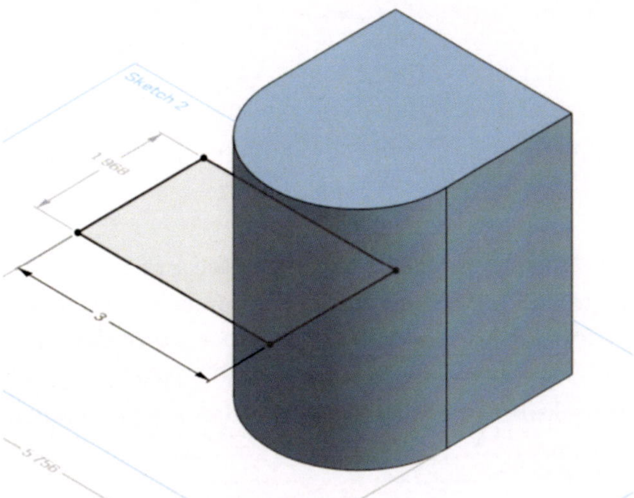

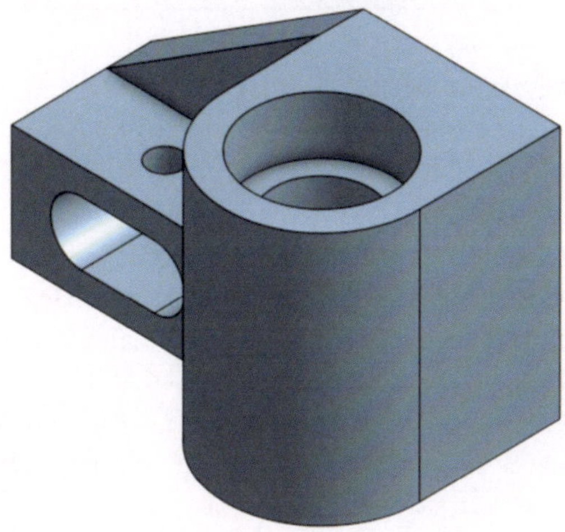

10. Click the **Document menu** located on the top left corner of the window and click the **Close document** option to close the document.

Tutorial 2 (Millimetres)

In this example, you create the part shown below and then modify it using the editing tools.

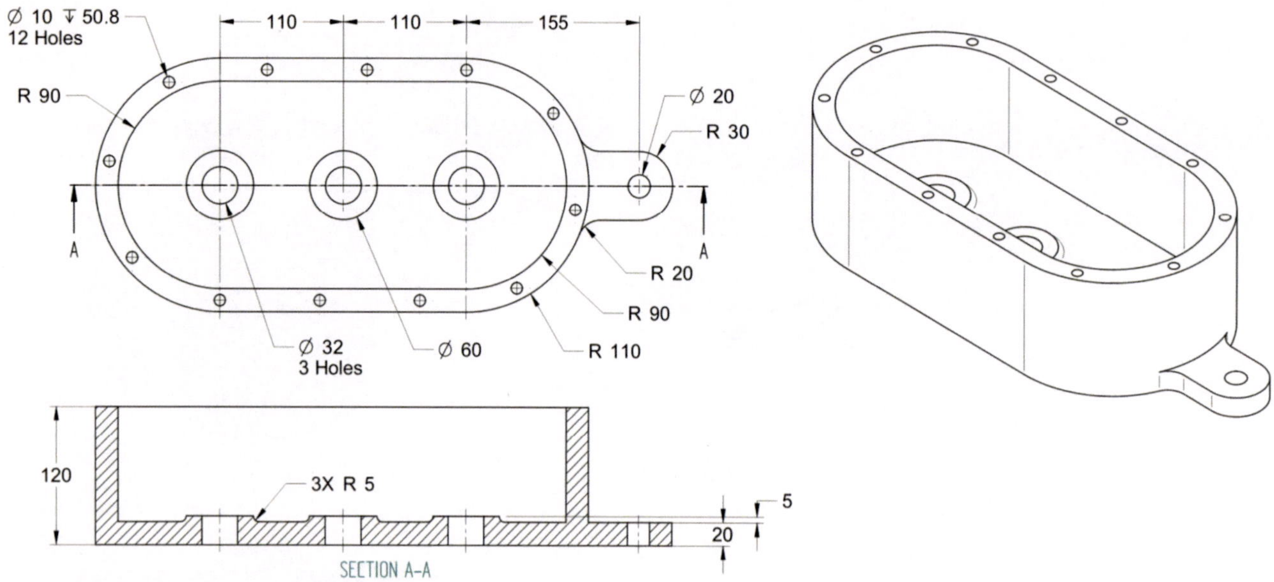

Creating a New document

1. In your Internet Browser, go to https://www.onshape.com to start Onshape.
2. Next, click the **SIGN IN** button located on the top right corner side of the web page. Enter the username and password, and then, click **Sign in**.
3. Double-click on the **Chapter** 9 folder in the **Folders** section.
4. On the Documents page, click **Create > Document**; the **New document** dialog appears on the screen.
5. Enter Tutorial 2 in the **Document name** box and click **Create public document**; a new document appears.
6. Click the **Document menu** located at the top left corner of the window and select **Workspace Units**; the **Workspace Units** dialog appears on the screen.
7. On the **Workspace Units** dialog, select **Length default unit> Millimeter** from **Length** section.
8. Select **Mass default unit > Gram** from the **Mechanical** section.
9. Leave the other default settings and click the green check.

Creating the Extruded and Shell Features

1. Activate the **Sketch** command and select the **Top** plane from the graphics area.
2. Click a horizontal line and apply the **Midpoint** constraint between the line and origin.
3. Click the **Offset** drop-down > **Slot** on the toolbar and select the line. Next, click in the graphics area to create a slot.
4. Select the line used to create the slot, and then click the **Construction** command on the toolbar.
5. Click the **Dimension** command on the toolbar and apply dimensions to the slot. Next, click the green check on the **Sketch 1** dialog.

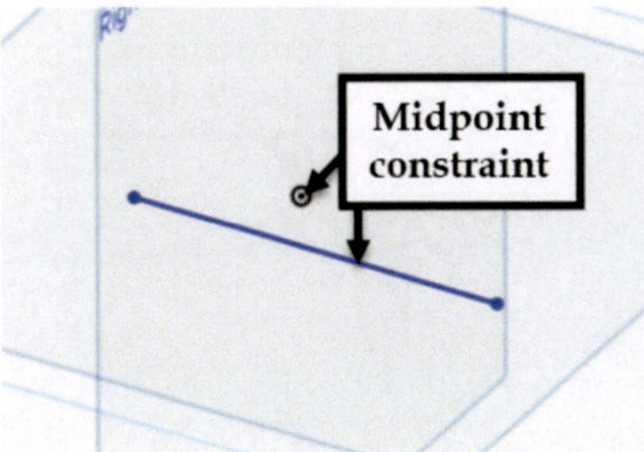

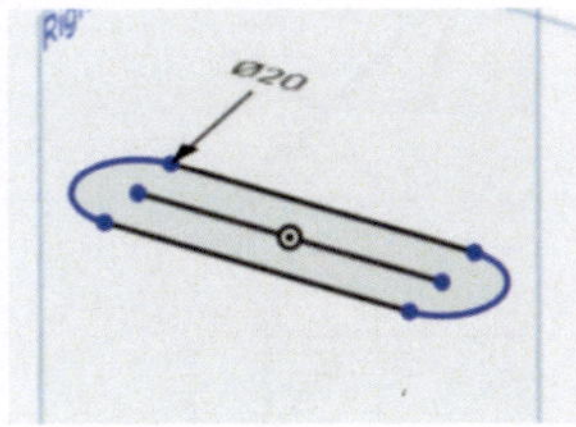

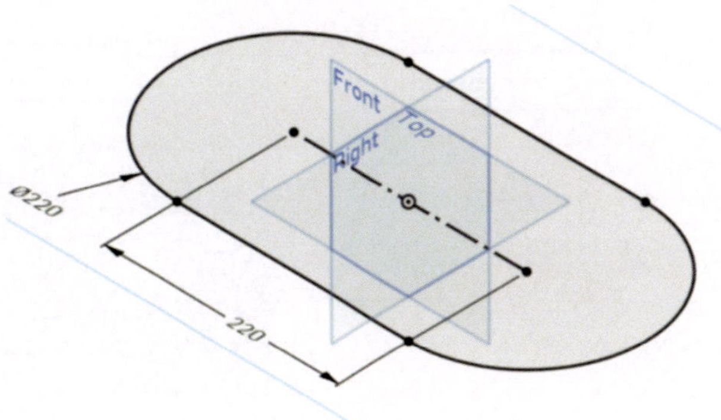

6. Click the **Extrude** command on the toolbar and select the slot. Next, type **120** in the **Depth** box and click the green check on the **Extrude 1** dialog.
7. Click the **Shell** command on the toolbar and select the top face of the model. Type **20** in the **Shell thickness** box and click the green check.

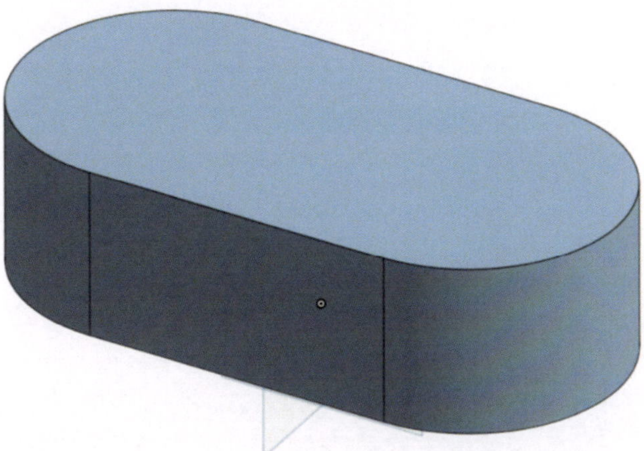

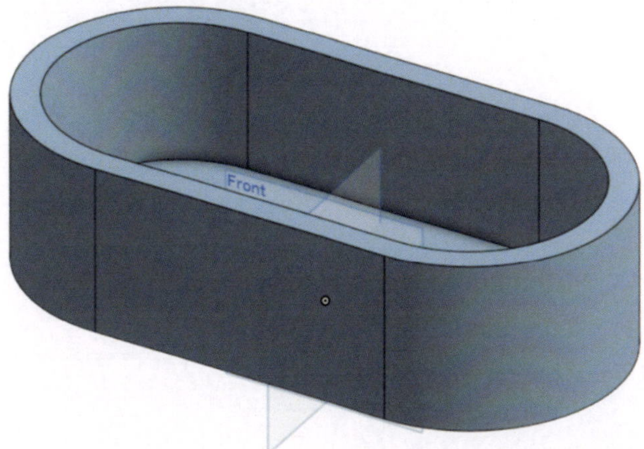

Adding the Extruded and Hole features

1. Click the **Sketch** command and select the Top plane from the **Features** window.
2. Click the **Use (Project/Convert)** command on the toolbar. Next, select the circular edge of the model, as shown.
3. Create two lines and arc using the **Line** and **3 point arc** commands, respectively.

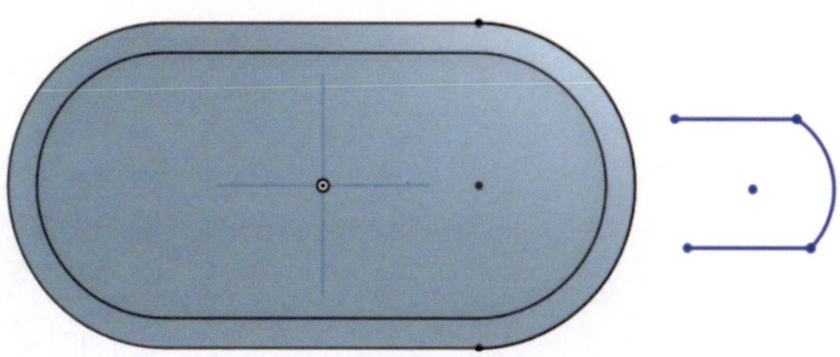

4. Apply the **Equal** constraint between the two lines.
5. Apply the **Tangent** constraint between the arc and the two lines.
6. Apply the **Coincident** constraint between the endpoints of the lines and the projected edge.

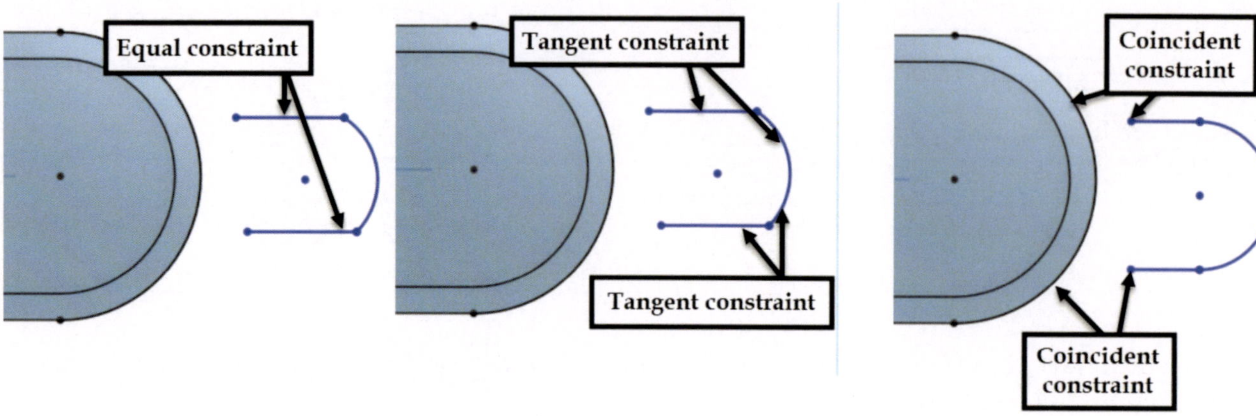

7. Add dimensions to the sketch, as shown.
8. Click the **Trim** command on the toolbar and select the portions of the projected entity, as shown. Next, click the green check on the **Sketch 2** dialog.

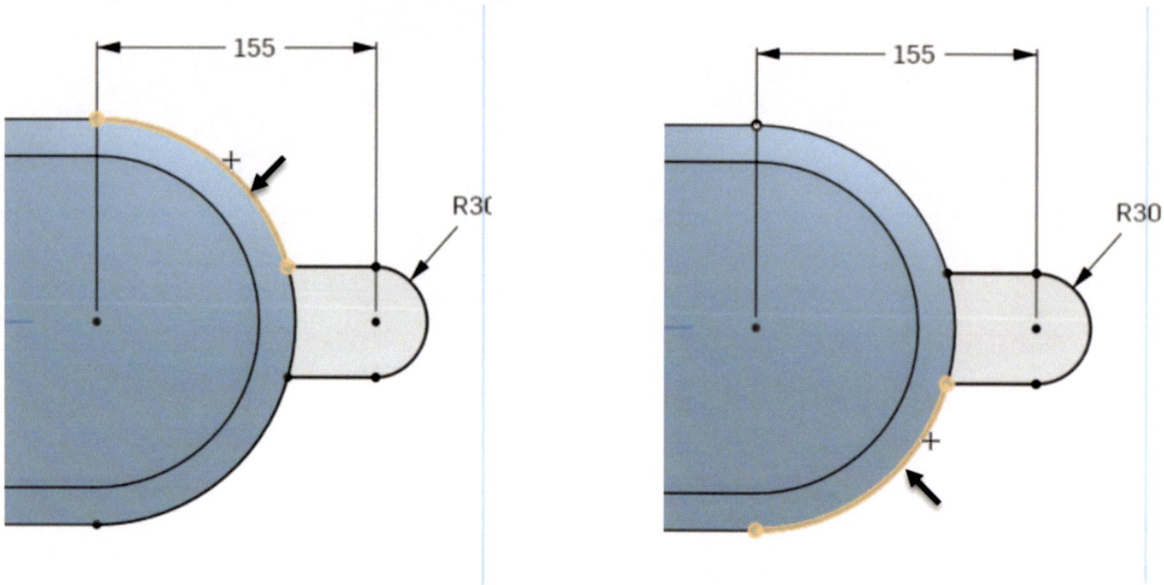

9. Click the **Extrude** command on the toolbar and select the newly created sketch.
10. Type **20** in the **Depth** box and click the green check on the **Extrude 2** dialog.

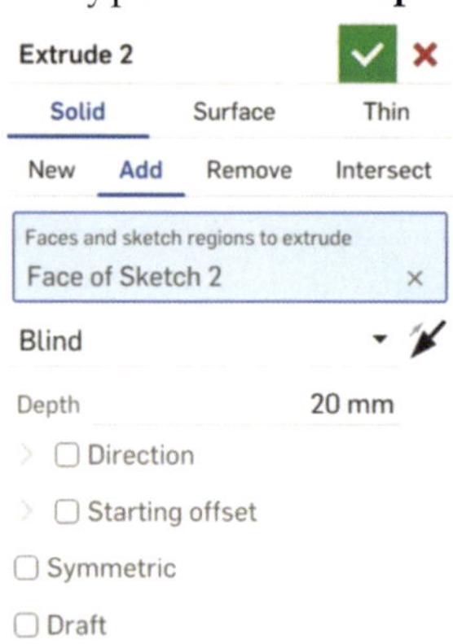

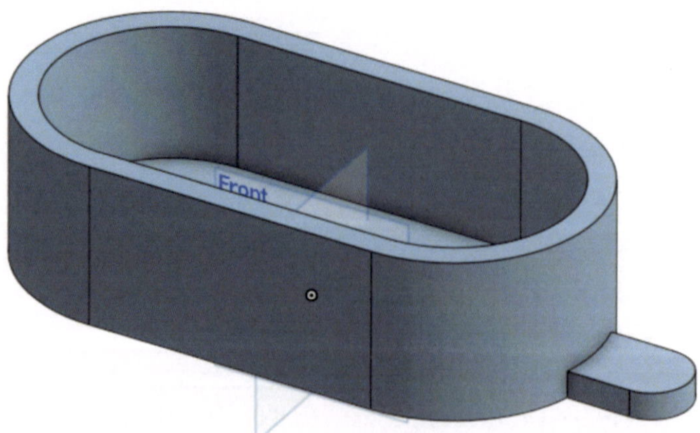

11. Create a hole of 20 mm diameter on the newly created extruded feature.

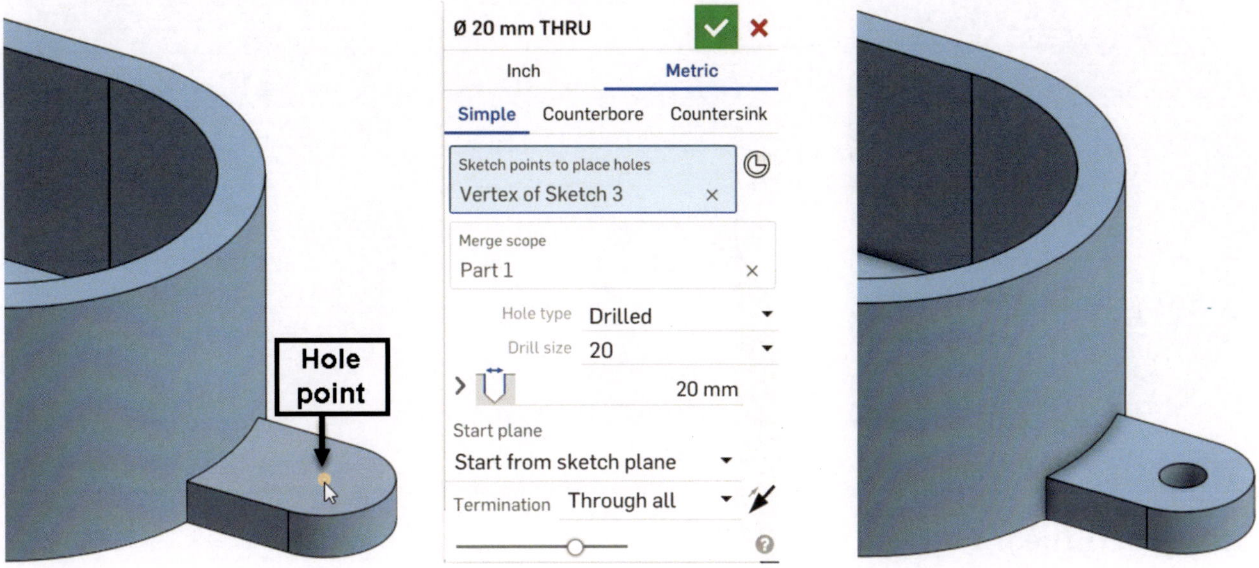

12. Create an extruded feature of **5 mm** depth on the inner bottom face of the shell feature.

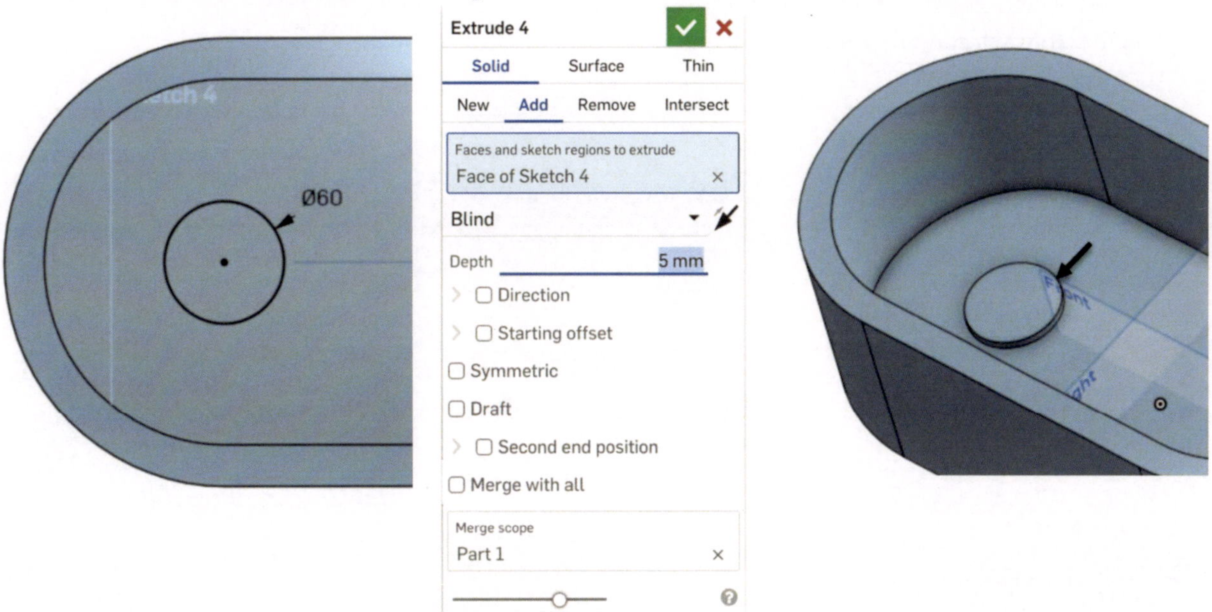

13. Create a hole of 32 mm diameter on the newly created extruded feature.

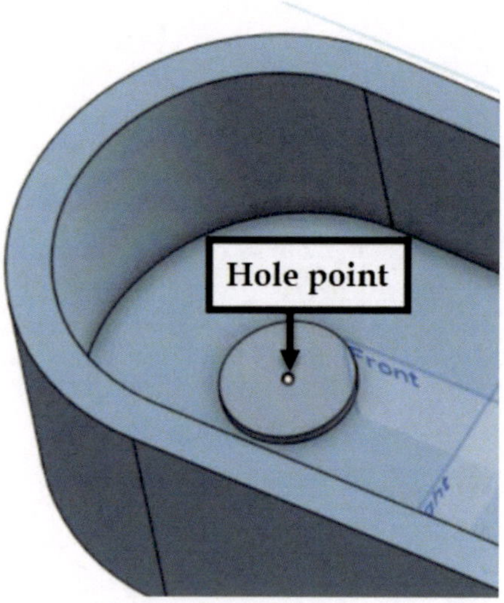

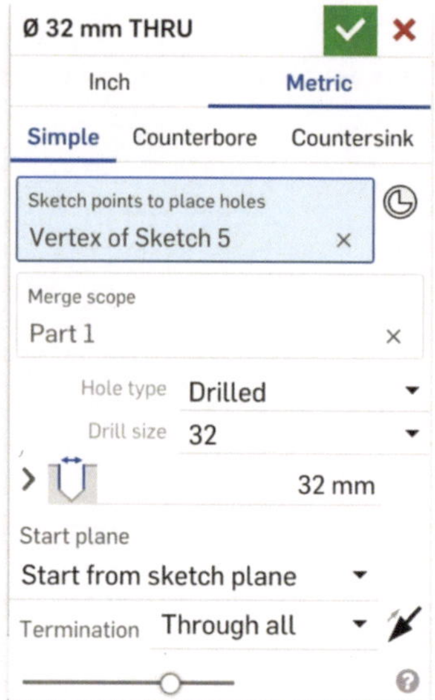

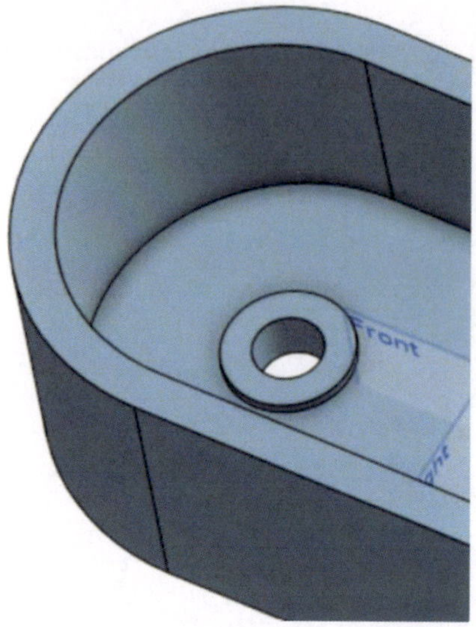

Creating the Linear Pattern

1. Click the **Linear Pattern** command on the toolbar and select the **Feature pattern** option from the **Pattern type** drop-down available on the **Linear pattern 1** dialog.
2. Select the newly created extruded feature and the hole, as shown.
3. Click the **Direction** selection box and select the edge of the model, as shown.

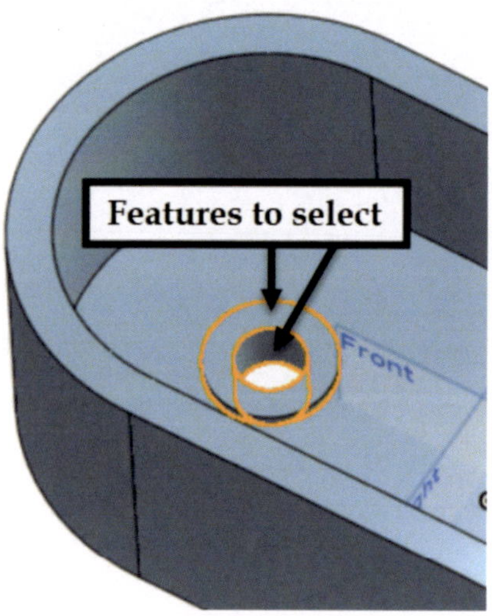

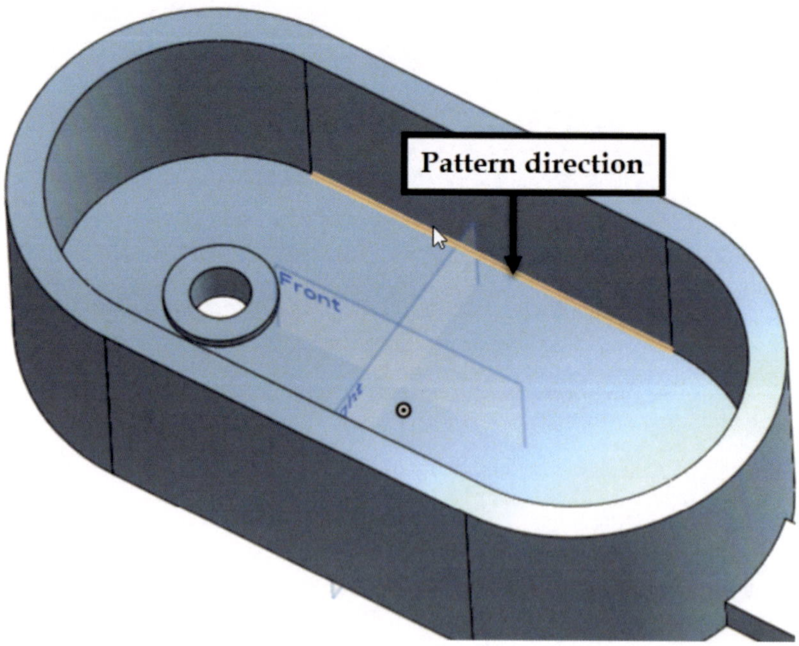

4. Type 110 and 3 in the **Distance** and **Instant count** boxes, respectively. Next, click the green check on the **Linear pattern 1** dialog.

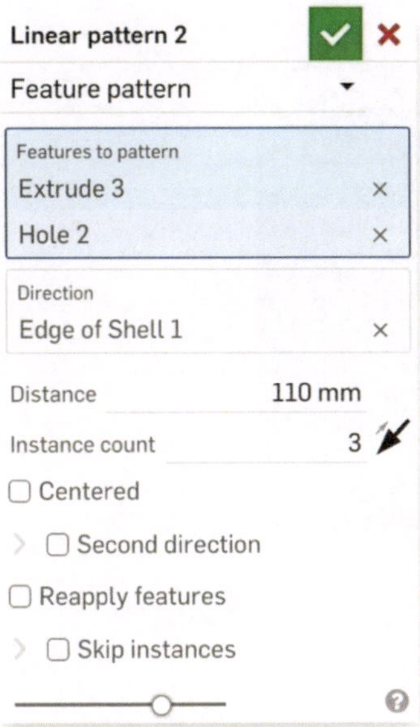

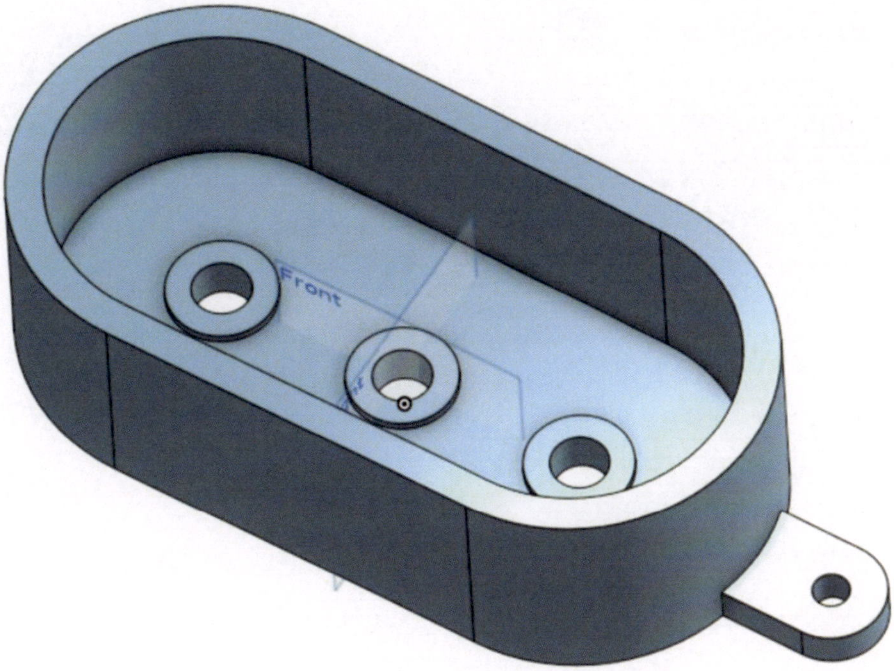

Creating the Curve pattern

1. Click the **Sketch** command on the toolbar and select the top face of the model, as shown.
2. Place a point and add dimensions to it, as shown. Next, click the green check on the **Sketch 6** dialog.

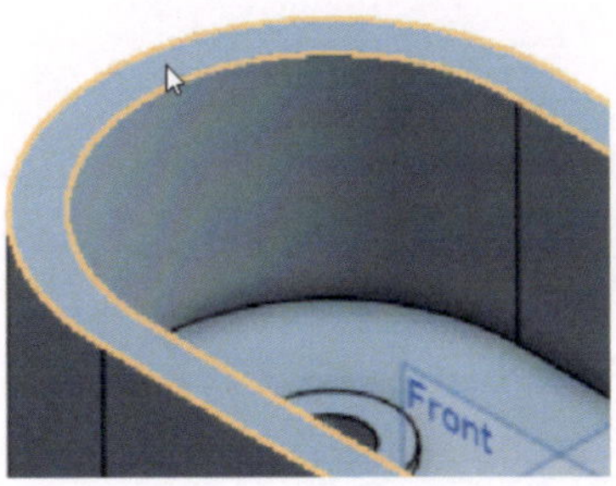

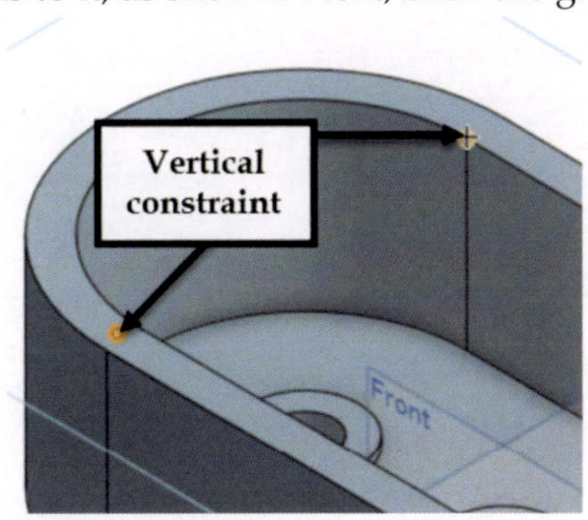

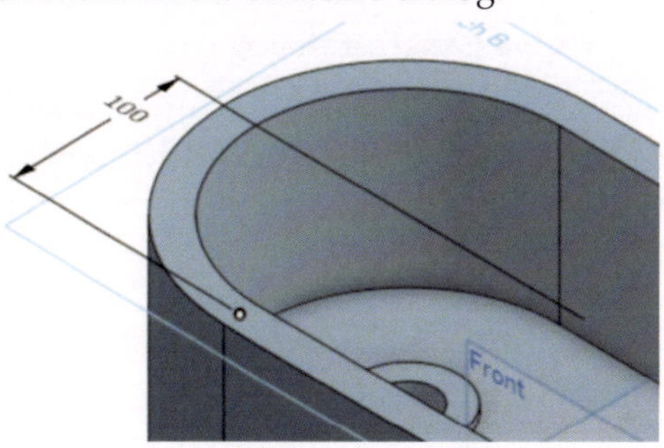

3. Click the **Hole** command on the toolbar and select the newly created sketch point.
4. Specify the parameters on the **Hole 1** dialog, as shown. Next, click the green check to complete the **Hole** feature.

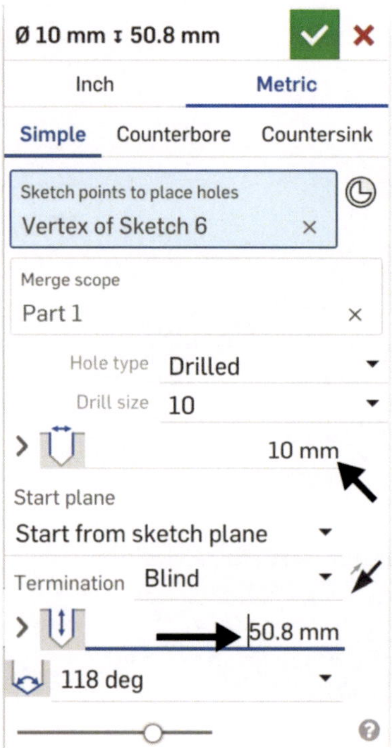

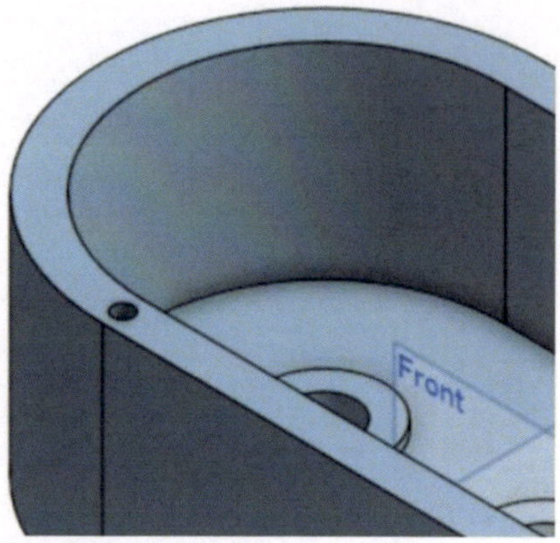

5. On the toolbar, click the **Pattern** drop-down > **Curve pattern**. Next, select the **Feature pattern** option from the **Pattern type** drop-down.
6. Select the newly created hole from the model. Next, click the **Path to pattern along** selection box from the **Curve pattern 1** dialog.

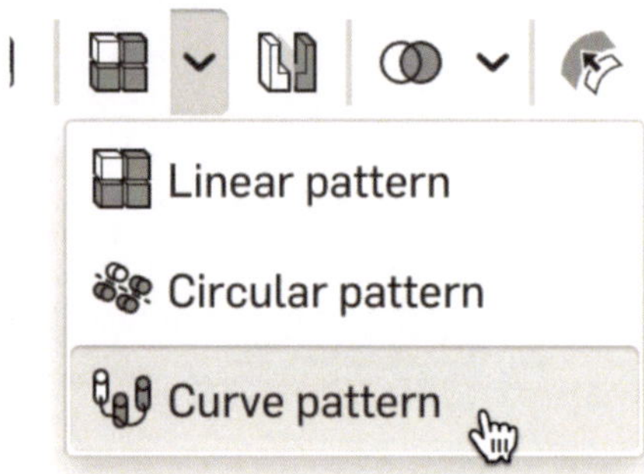

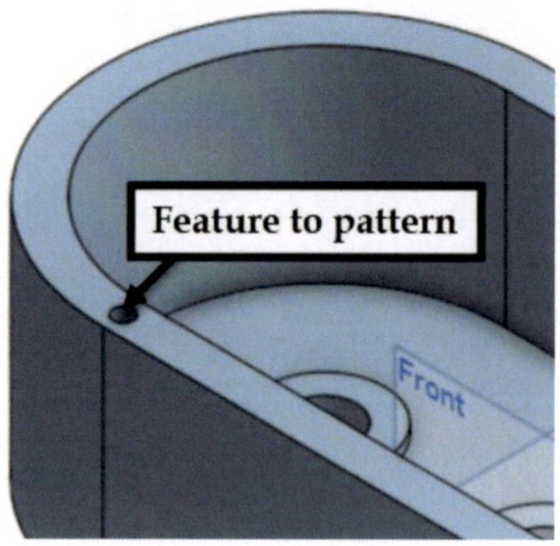

7. Right click and select Select > **Create selection** from the shortcut menu. Next, select **Tangent connected** from the drop-down available on the **Create selection** dialog.
8. Click the inner circular edge of the shell feature, as shown; the edges that are connected tangently to the selected edge are highlighted.
9. Click the **Add selection** button on the **Create selection** dialog. Next, close the **Create selection** dialog.

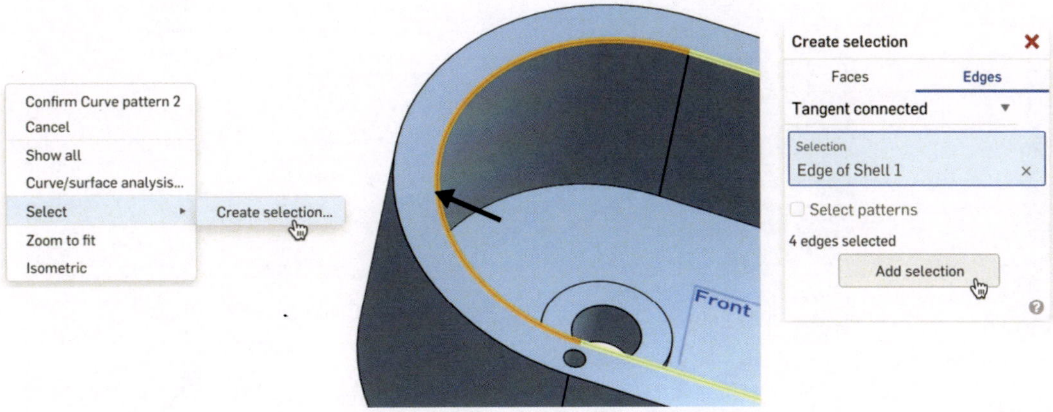

10. Type 12 in the **Instant count** box and click the green check on the **Curve pattern 1** dialog.

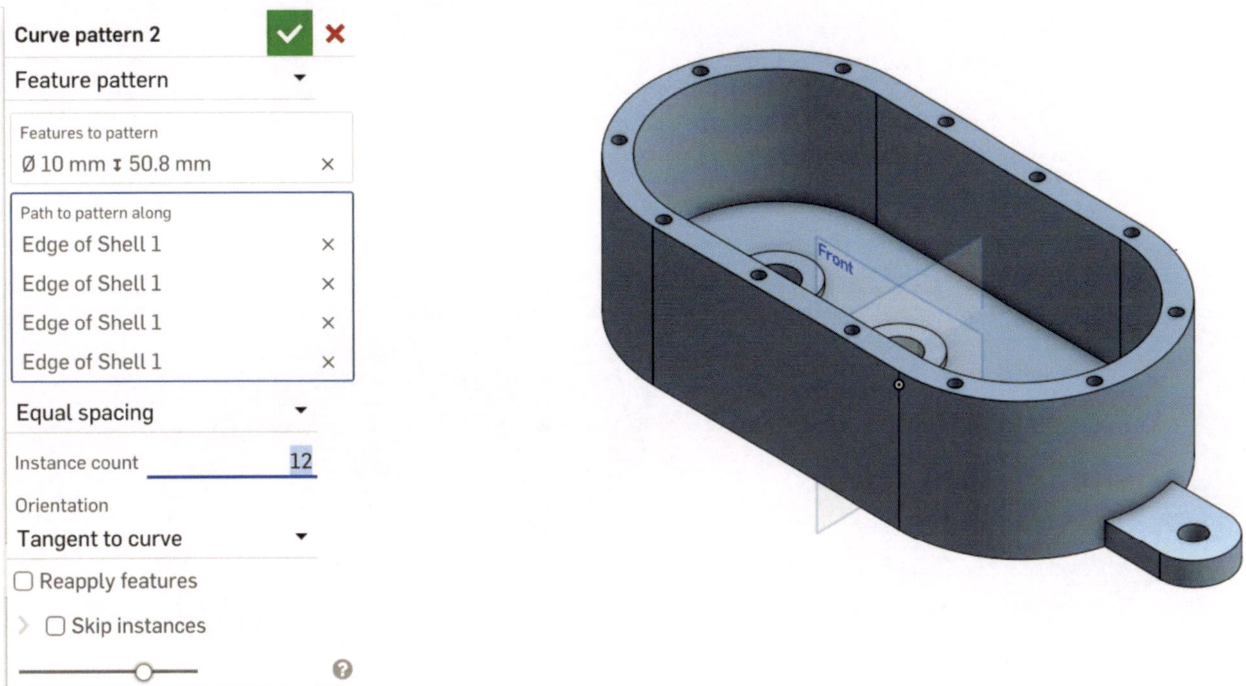

Creating the Fillet features

1. Click the **Fillet** command on the toolbar and select the edges of the model, as shown.
2. Type 20 in the **Radius** box and click the green check.

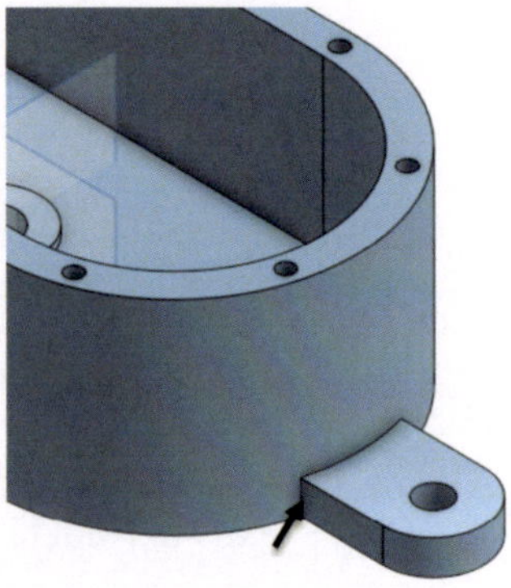

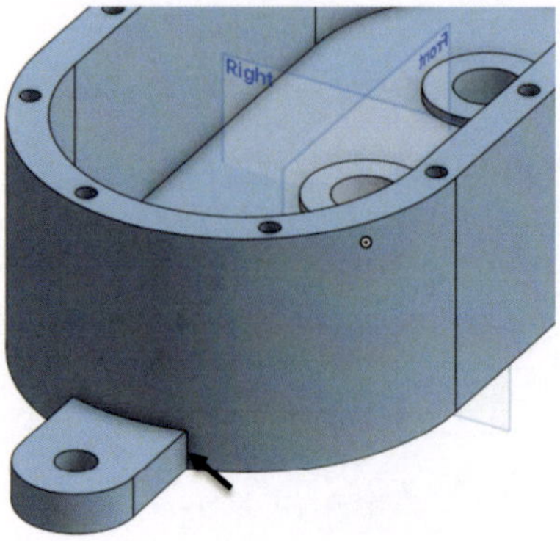

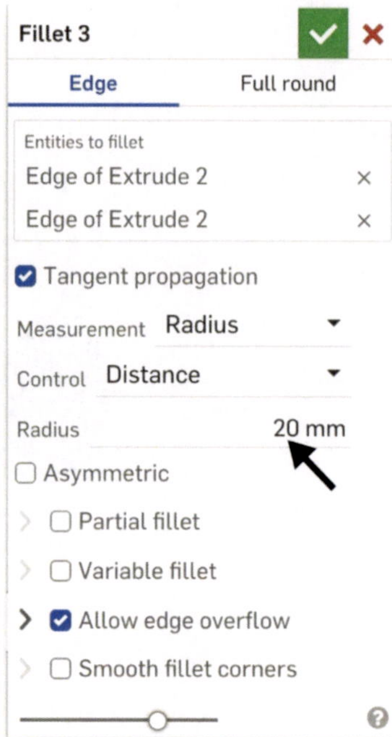

3. Apply fillets of 5mm radius to the edges of the extruded features, as shown.

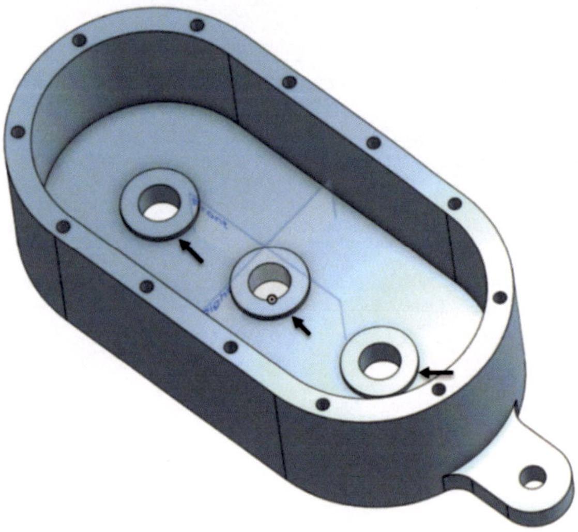

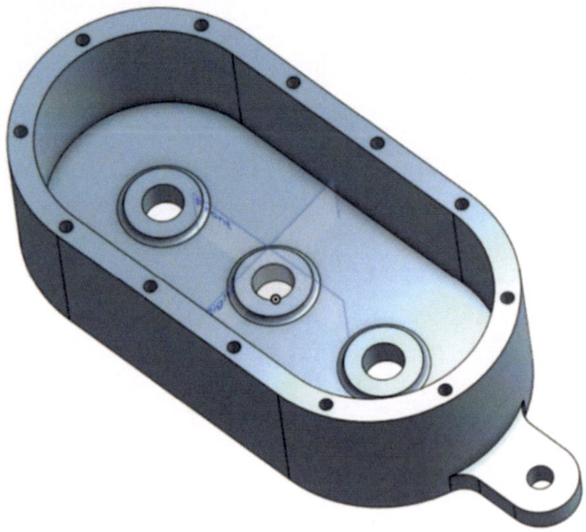

Editing the Hole feature

1. Click on the 20 mm diameter hole, and then select **Edit ∅20 mm THRU**; the dialog appears.
2. On the **Hole** dialog, click the **Counterbore** tab.
3. On the **Hole** dialog, enter **20**, **30**, and **10** in the **Diameter**, **Counterbore diameter**, and **Counterbore depth** boxes, respectively. Click the green check to close the dialog.

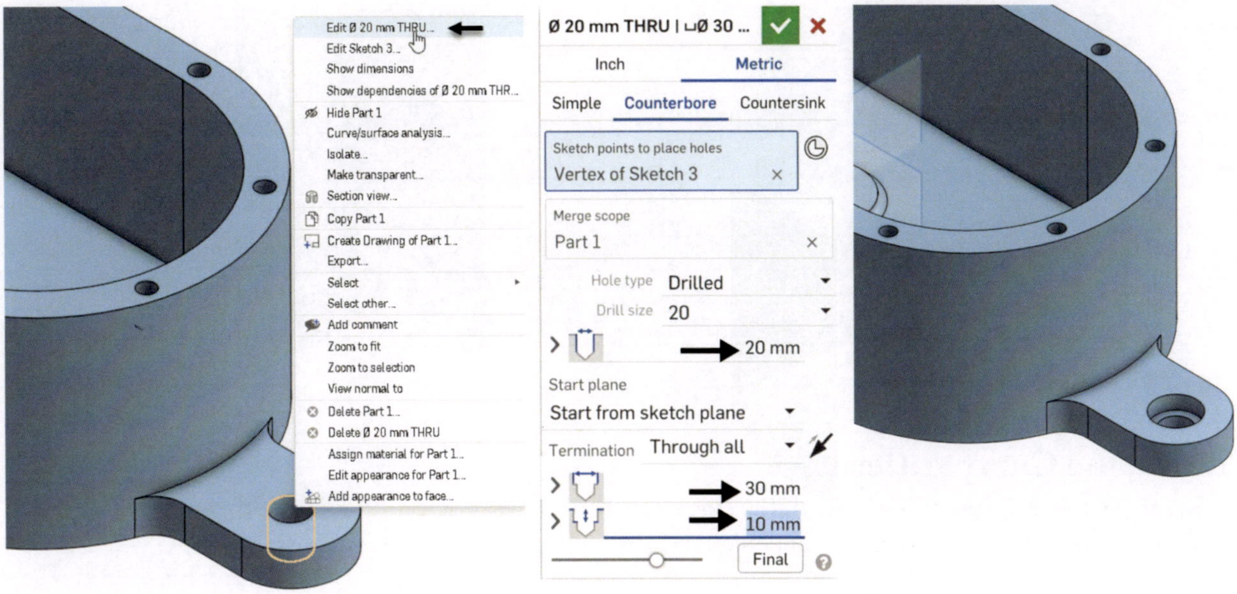

Moving Faces

1. On the Toolbar, click the **Modify Face** drop-down > **Move Face**, and then select **Translate** from the **Move face type** drop-down available on the **Move face 1** dialog.
2. Click on the round faces of the counterbore hole. Next, the cylindrical face concentric to it.
3. Click the **Direction** selection button on the dialog. Next, select the edge of the extruded feature, as shown.

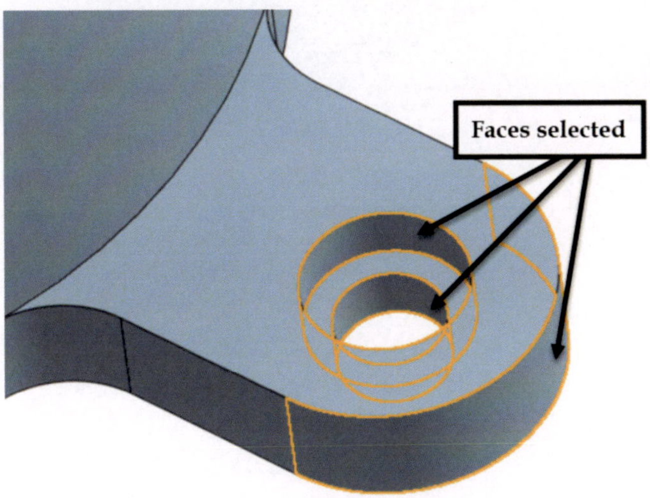

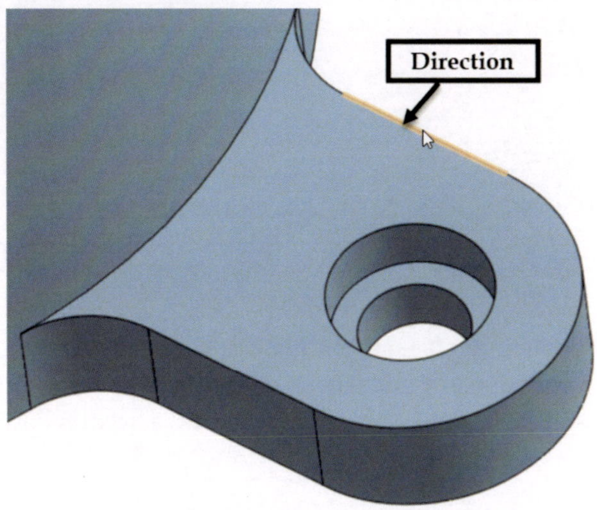

4. Type **20** in the **Distance** box and click the green check on the **Move face 1** dialog.

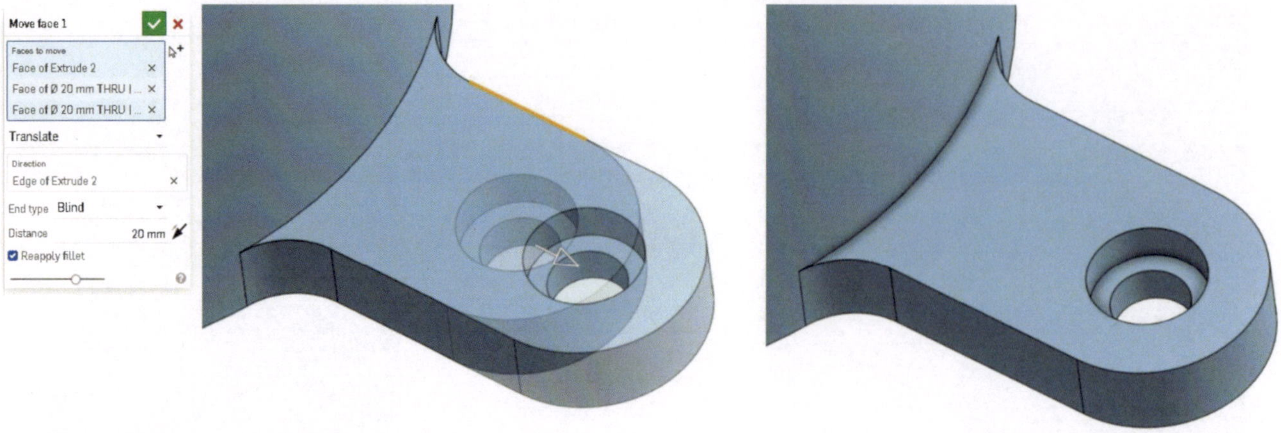

Editing the Curve pattern

1. Right click on any one of the holes of the curve pattern, and then select **Edit Curve pattern 1**.
2. Type 14 in the **Instance count** box and click the green check to update the pattern.

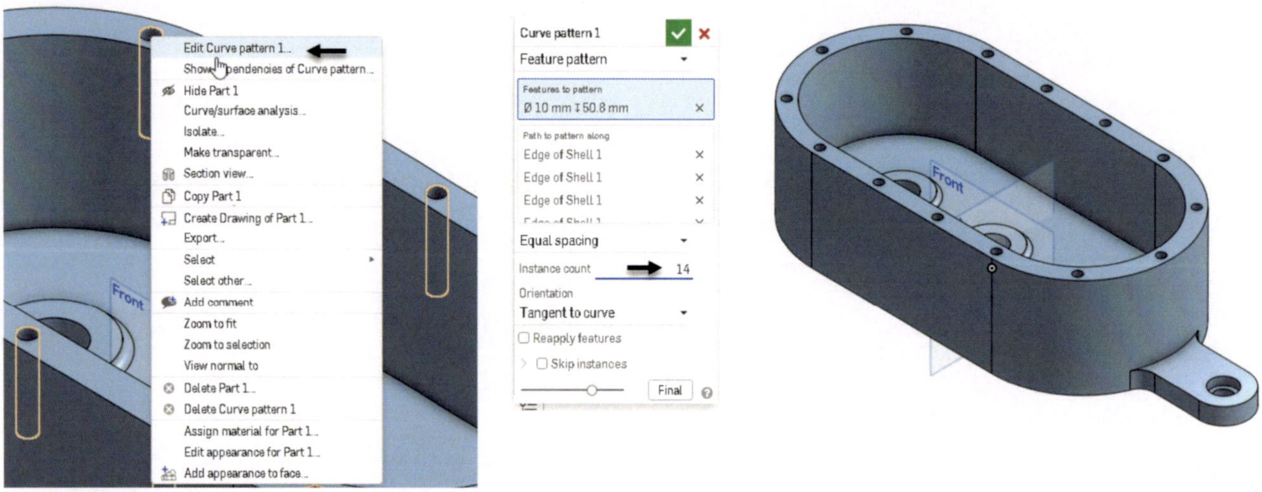

3. On the Toolbar, click the **Move Face** command, and then select **Translate** from the **Move face type** drop-down available on the **Move face 2** dialog.
4. Right-click and select **Select > Create selection** from the shortcut menu. Next, select **Hole** from the drop-down available on the **Create selection** dialog.
5. Select any one of the holes of the curve pattern, and then check the **Select patterns** option from the **Create selection** dialog. Next, click the **Add selection** button and close the **Create selection** dialog.

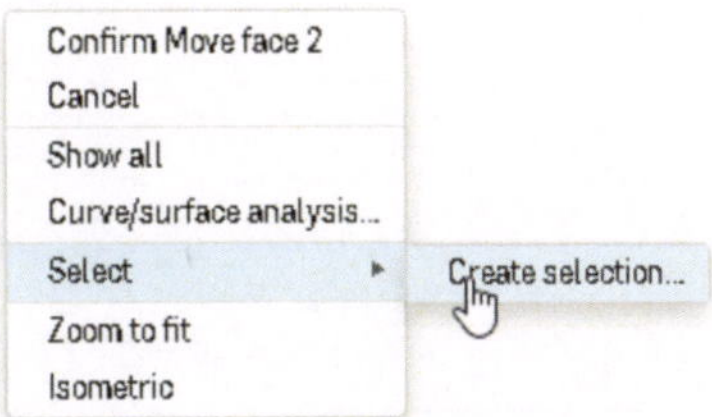

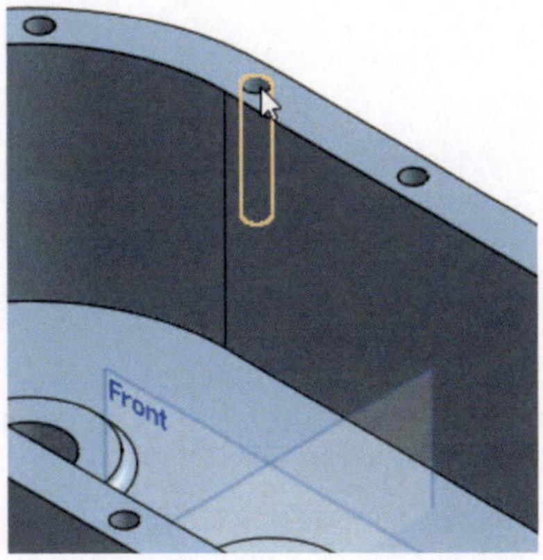

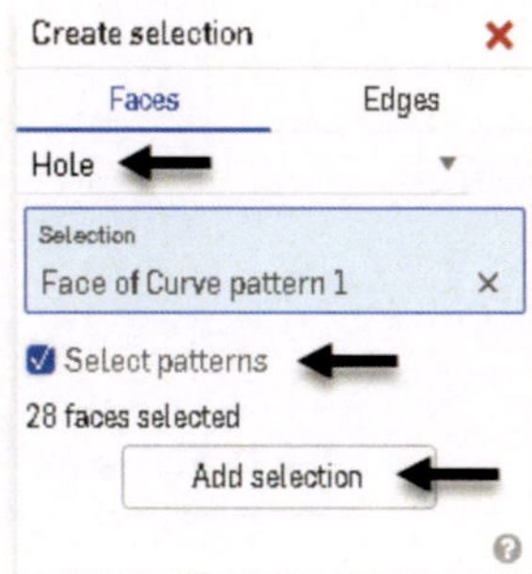

6. Select the top face of the model to add it to the selection.

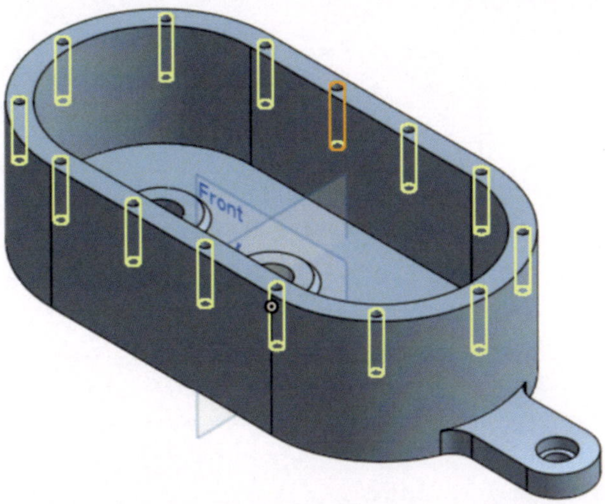

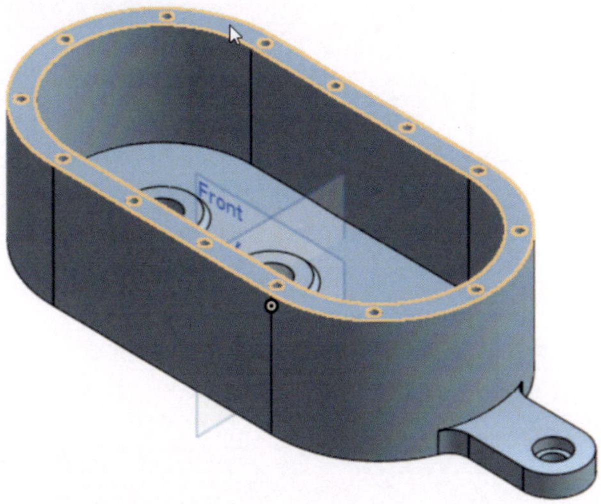

7. Click the **Direction** selection button and select the vertical edge of the model, as shown.

8. Type 40 in the **Distance** box and click the **Reverse direction**  icon next to it.

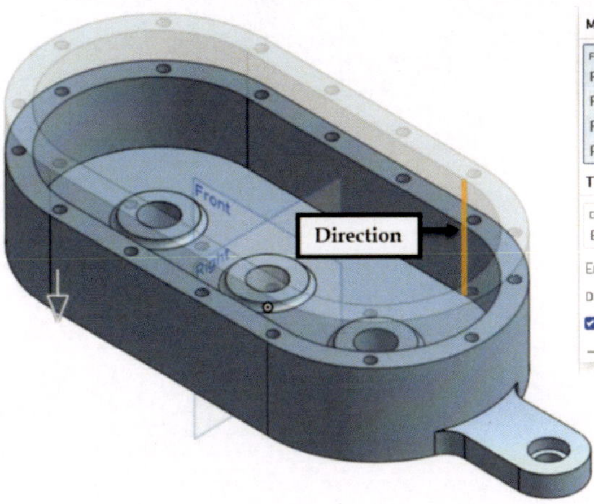

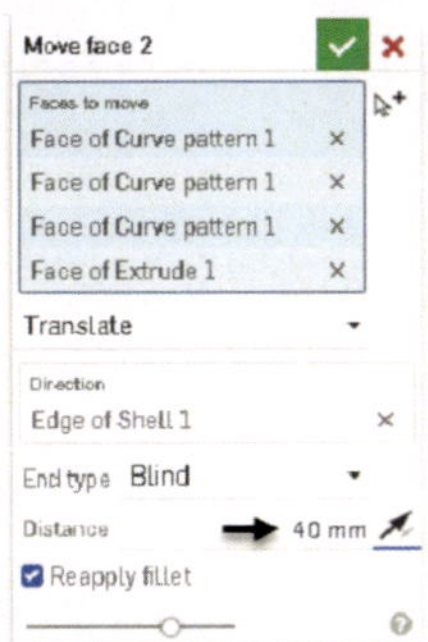

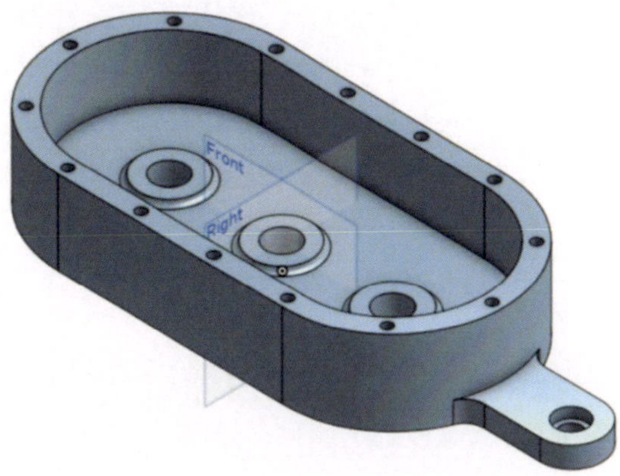

9. Close the document.

Questions

1. How to modify the sketch of a feature?

2. How to modify a feature?
3. How to suppress a feature?

Exercises

Exercise 1

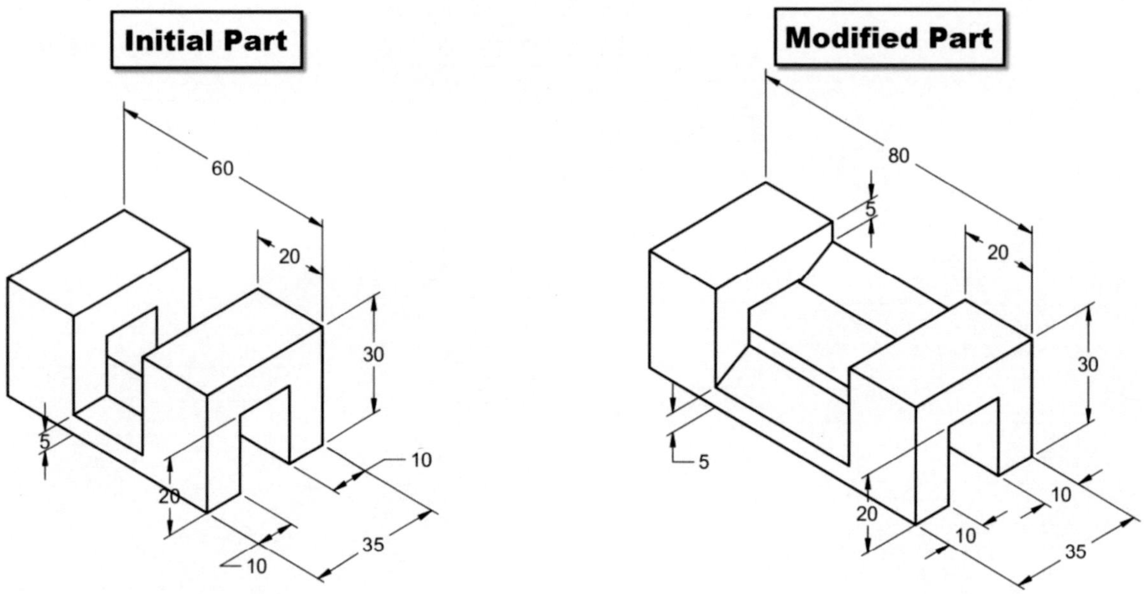

Exercise 2

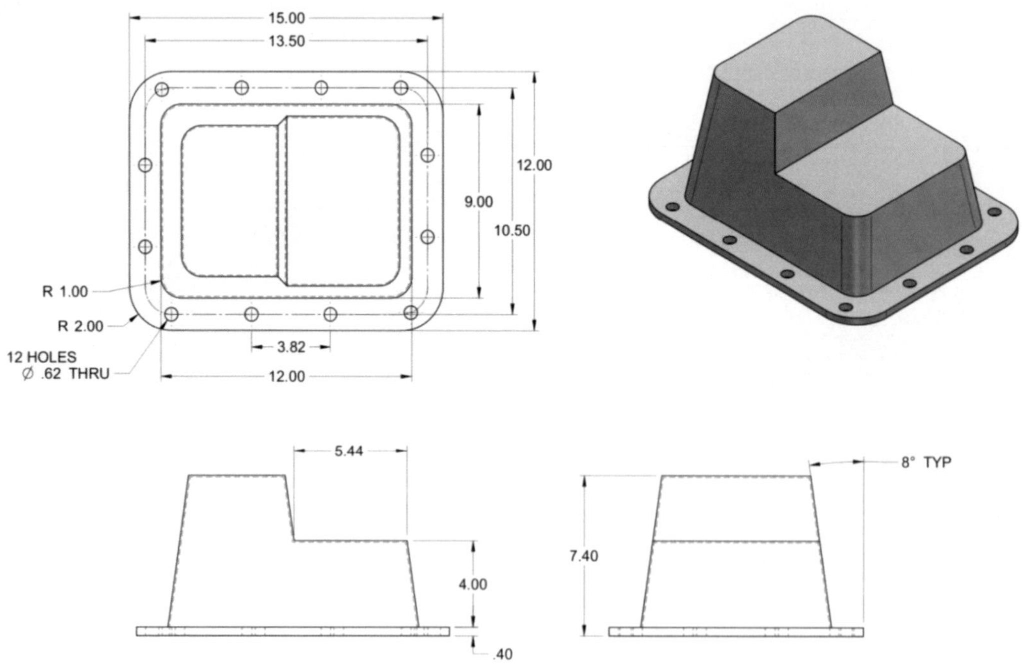

SHEET THICKNESS = 0.079 in

Chapter 10: Assemblies

After creating individual parts, you can bring them together into an assembly. By doing so, it is possible to identify incorrect design problems that may not have been noticeable at the part level. In this chapter, you will learn how to bring parts into the assembly environment and position them.

The topics covered in this chapter are:

- *Starting an assembly*
- *Inserting Parts*
- *Adding Mates*
- *Dragging Parts*
- *Checking Interference*
- *Snap Mode*
- *Editing Assemblies*
- *Replace Parts*
- *Pattern and Mirror Parts*
- *Create Subassemblies*
- *Top-down Assembly Design*
- *Create Exploded Views*

Starting an Assembly

To start an assembly, you can click **Assembly** tab located at the bottom of the screen.

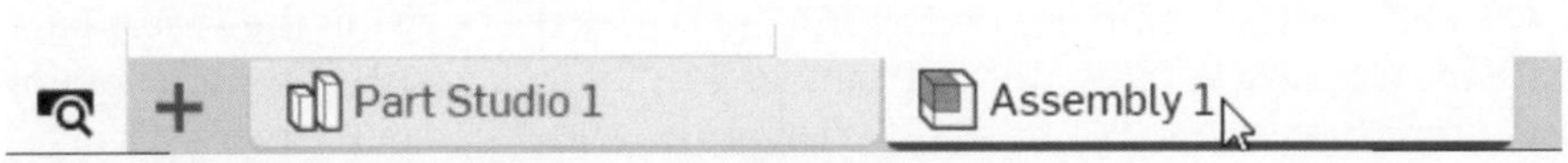

Inserting parts and assemblies

Now, you can insert parts into the assembly by using the **Insert** command. On the Toolbar, click **Insert** command to open the **Insert parts and assemblies** dialog. On this dialog, click the **Current documents** tab to select the part files available in the current document. Click the **Standard content** tab to select the standard components such as nuts, screws, or bolt. Click the **Other documents** tab to select the part file from other documents.

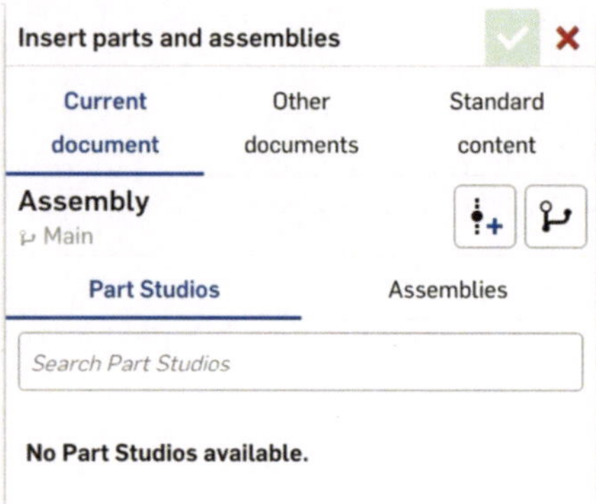

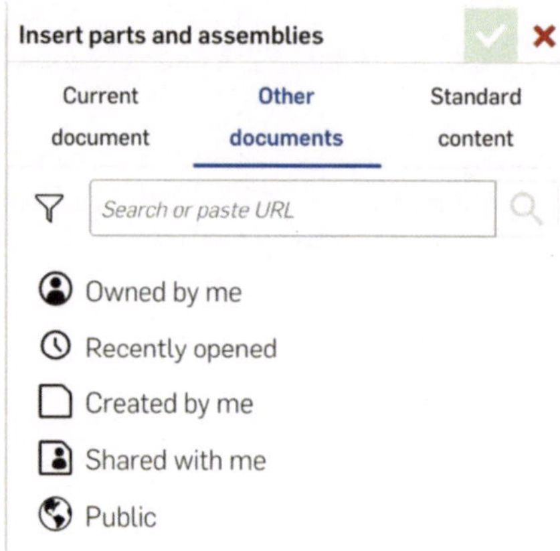

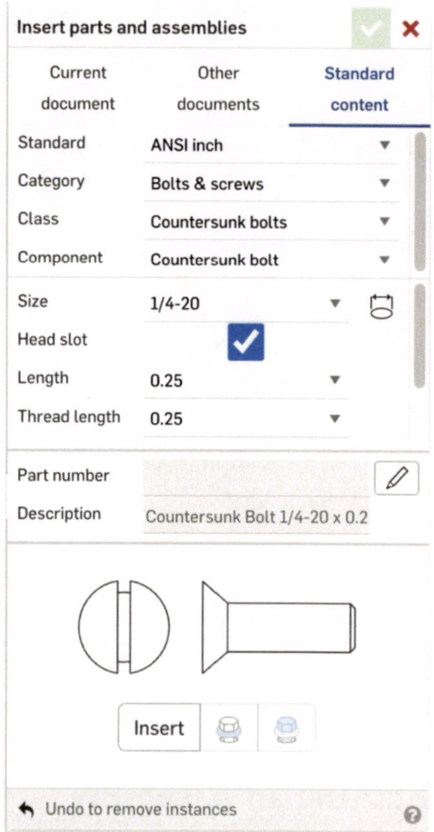

On the Other documents tab, click the **Owned by me** option. Next, go to the folder of the parts on the **Insert parts and assemblies** dialog and select the part; the **Create a version** link appears on the dialog. Click the **Create a version** link to open the **Create a version** dialog. Enter the version **Name** and **Description**, and then click **Create**.

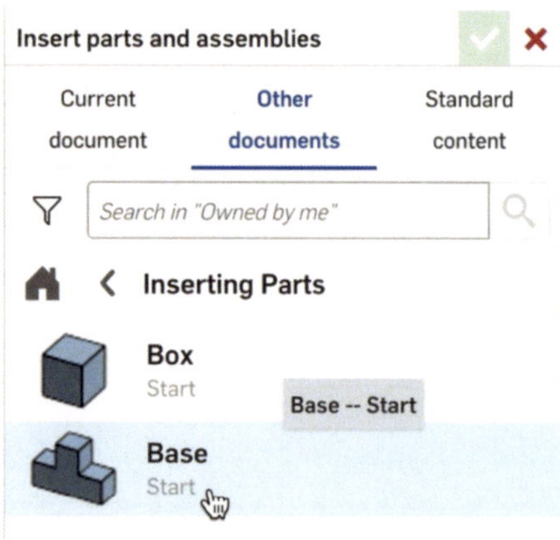

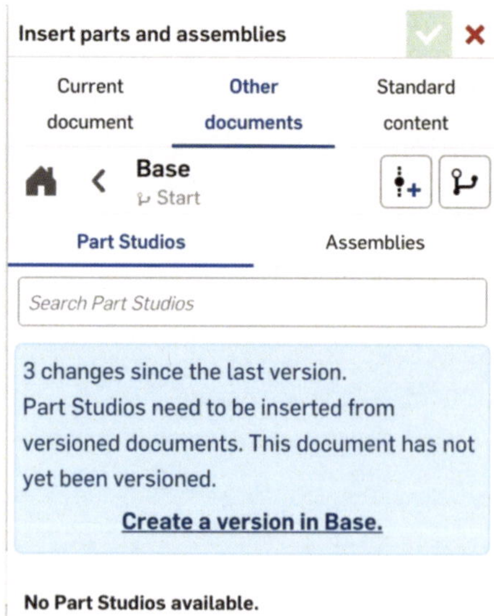

Select the newly created version of the part. Click in the graphics window to place the component at the desired place.

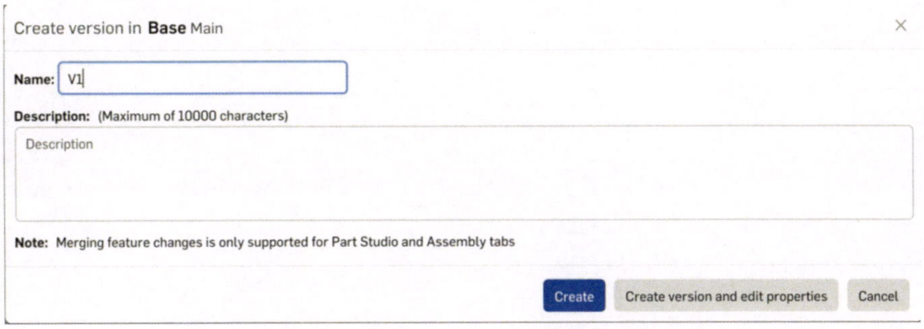

After inserting the first component, right-click on the component and select the **Fix** option to fix the component. As a result, all degrees of freedom of the part will be eliminated.

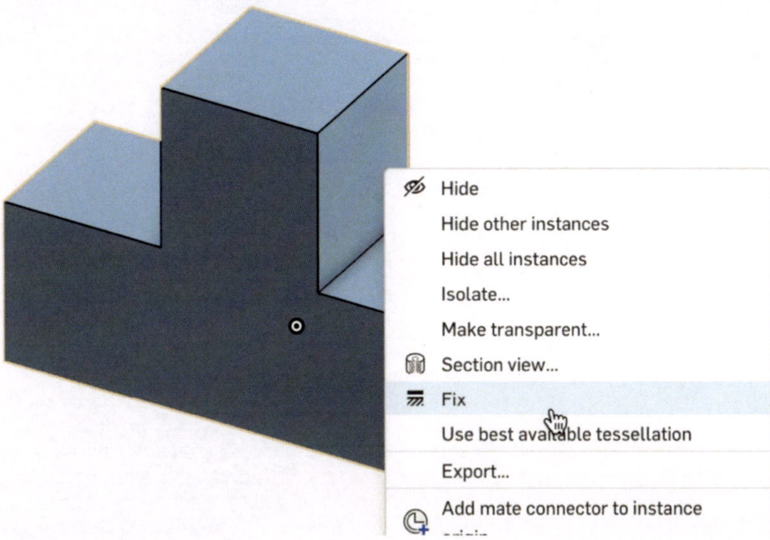

Likewise, insert the second component into the assembly window. Next, click the green check on the dialog to insert the part.

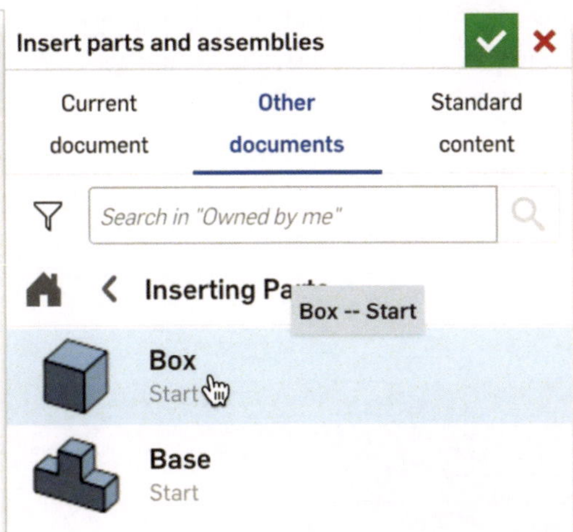

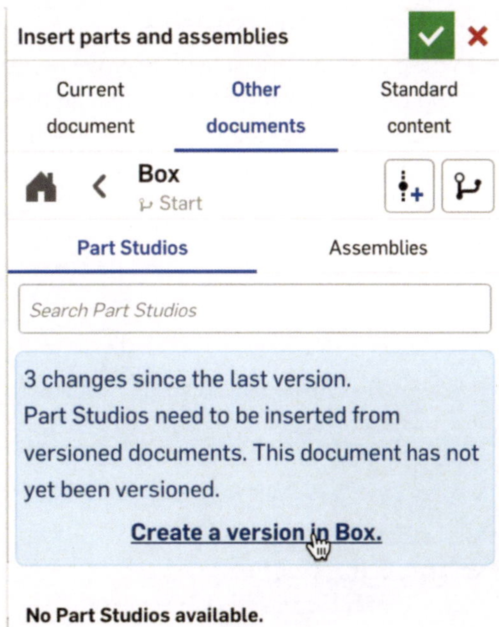

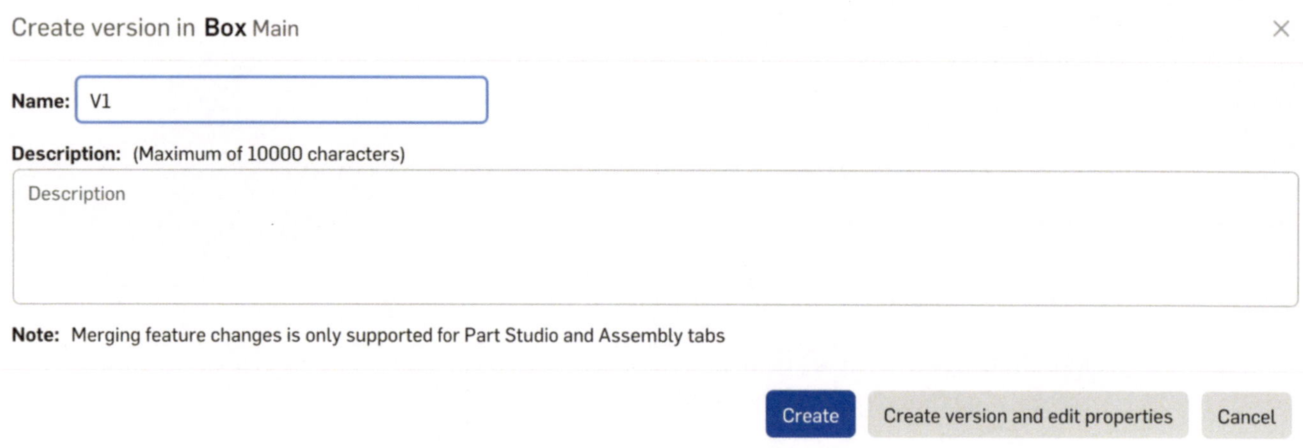

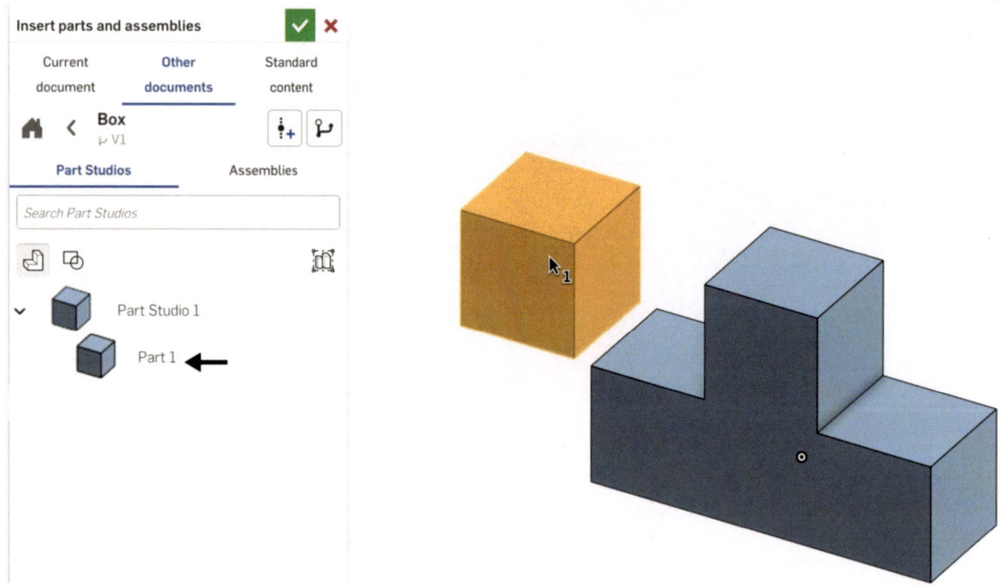

Moving and Rotating Components

Onshape allows you to drag or rotate the selected components if they are under-constrained. You can simply press and hold the left mouse button on the part and drag the cursor. However, you can move or rotate the part in a specific direction. To do this, select the part and notice that a manipulator is displayed. Press and the left mouse button on the X, Y, or Z axes of the manipulator, and then drag the pointer.

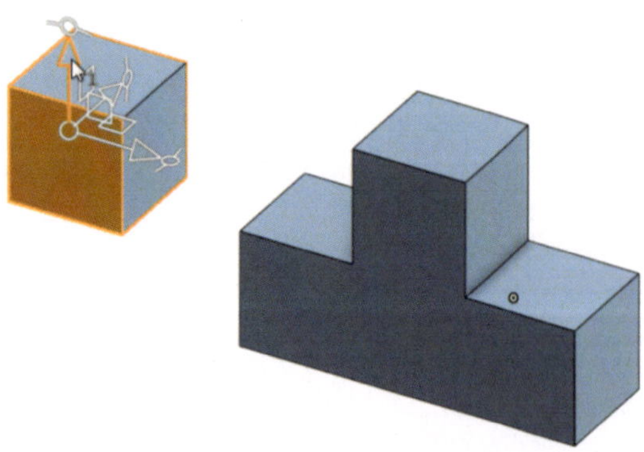

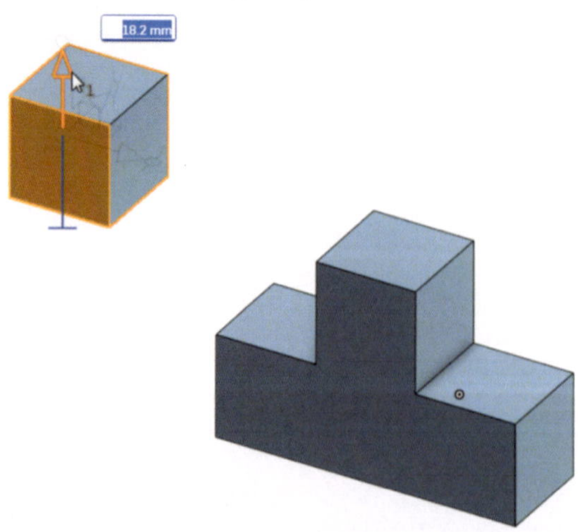

You can move the part in a particular plane by clicking and dragging anyone of the planes of the manipulator. Click and drag anyone of the rotate handles to rotate the part.

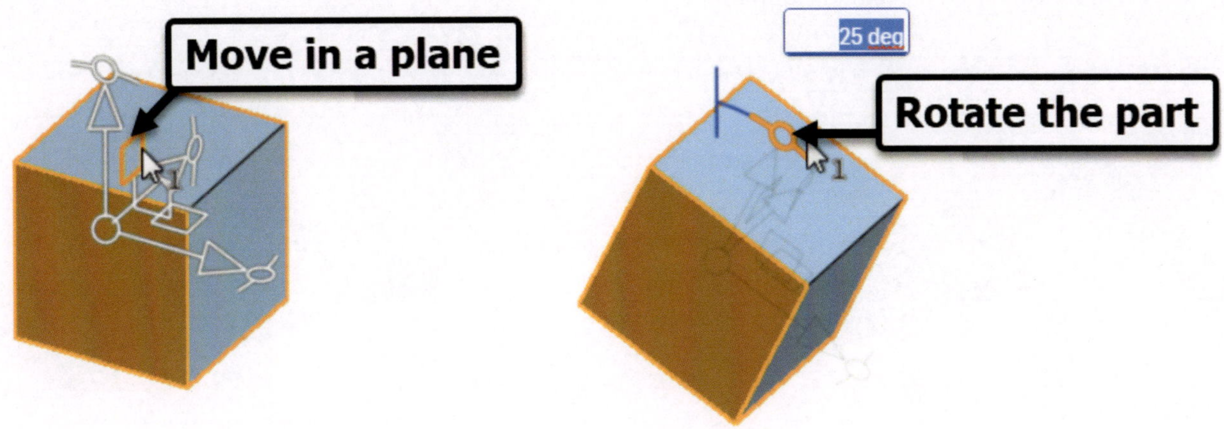

Mates

In an assembly, you need to create mates between the parts which control the position and movement. There are many types of mates available in Onshape: **Fastened mate**, **Revolute mate**, **Slider mate**, **Planar mate**, **Cylindrical mate**, **Pin slot mate**, **Ball mate**, and **Parallel mate**. These mates are explained next:

Ball mate

The **Ball mate** creates a ball joint between two spherical shaped faces. Click the **Ball mate** icon on the toolbar. Next, select the spherical face of the first part. Likewise, select the spherical face of the second part; the ball mate is created between the selected faces.

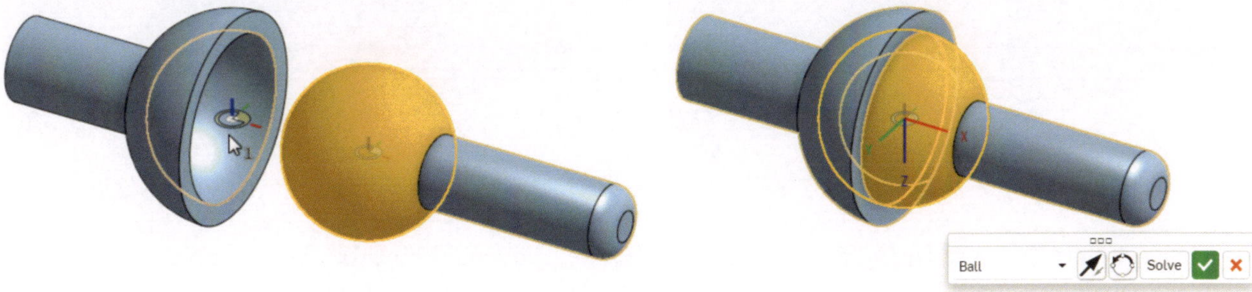

You can click the **Flip primary axis** icon on the **Ball** dialog to flip the second component. To change the alignment direction, click the **Reorient secondary axis** icon on the context toolbar. Click green check to create the ball joint.

Revolute mate

The **Revolute mate** command creates a revolute mate between two cylindrical faces. On creating this mate, all the degrees of freedom of the component are constrained except the rotational movement. First, click the **Revolute mate** icon on the toolbar. Next, place the pointer on the cylindrical face of the first component; you can notice the three mate connectors on the cylindrical face. Select the mate connector on the end face of the cylinder.

Likewise, select the mate connector on the end face of the second cylindrical feature; the two selected mate connectors are aligned, and a revolute mate is created between the cylindrical faces. Click the **Animate mate degree of freedom** icon to view the mate animation.

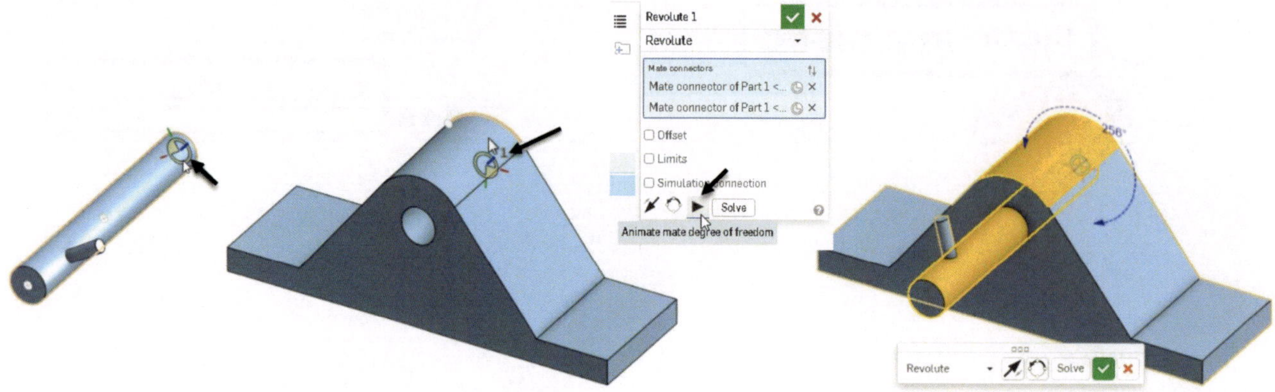

You can use the **Flip primary axis** and **Reorient secondary axis** icon to reverse the component and its alignment, respectively.

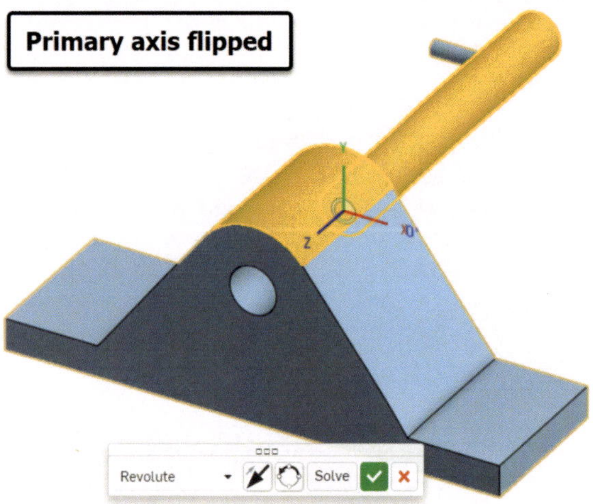

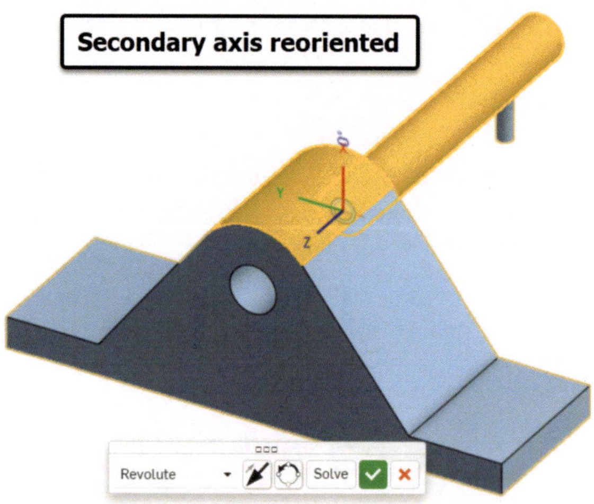

You can check the **Offset** option and type a value in the **Offset Z distance** box; the mate connectors are offset along the Z-direction.

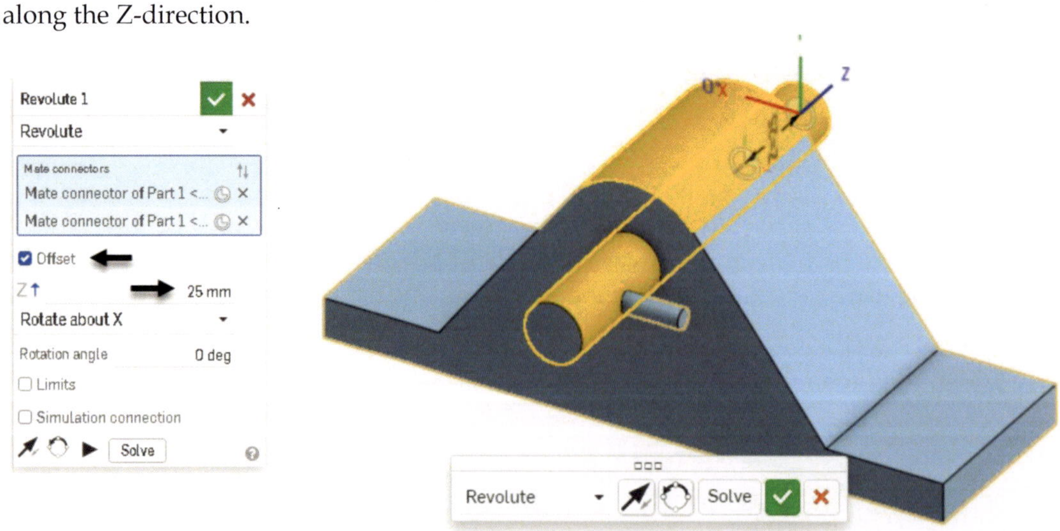

Likewise, check the **Limits** option and specify the minimum and maximum angle values in the **Limit axial Z minimum angle** and **Limit axial Z maximum angle** field, respectively. The inserted component will be rotated within the specified limit values. Click green check to create the revolute mate.

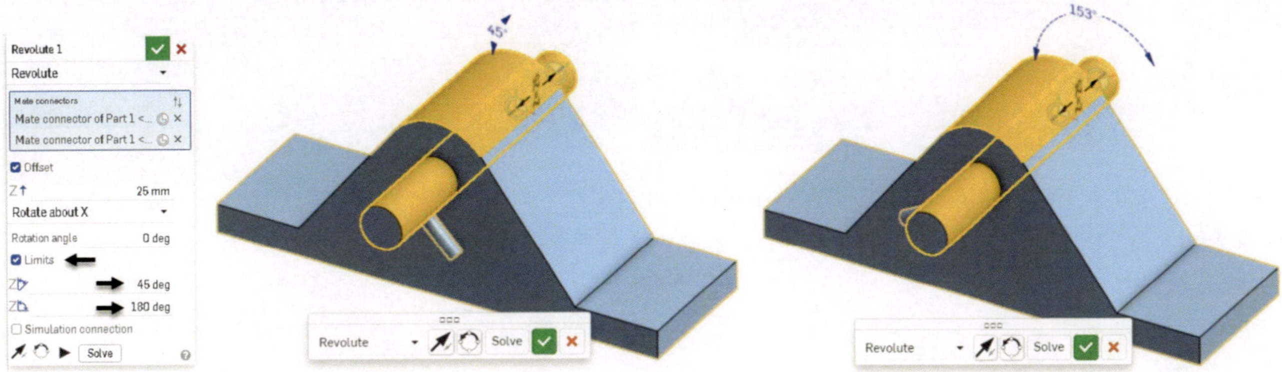

Fastened mate

The **Fastened mate** makes the selected parts to form a rigid set. It mates two parts and removes all the degrees of freedom. As you move a single part of a rigid set, all the other parts will also be moved. Click the **Fastened mate** icon on the toolbar. Select the mate connector from the first part. Likewise, select a mate connector from the target part.

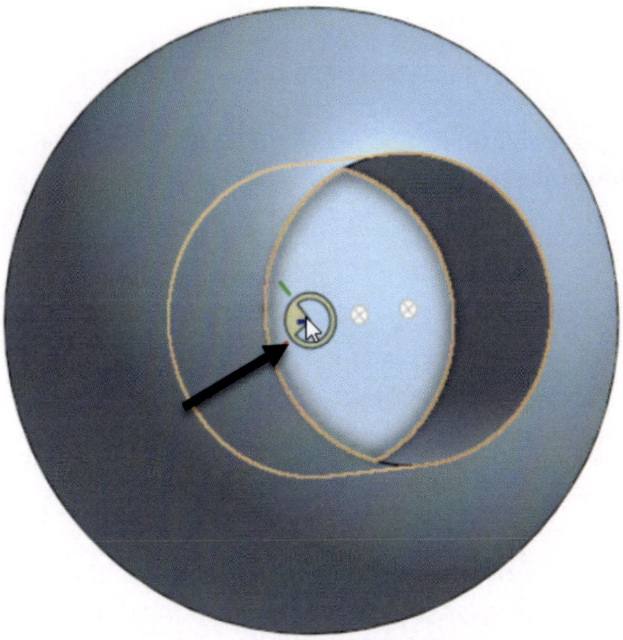

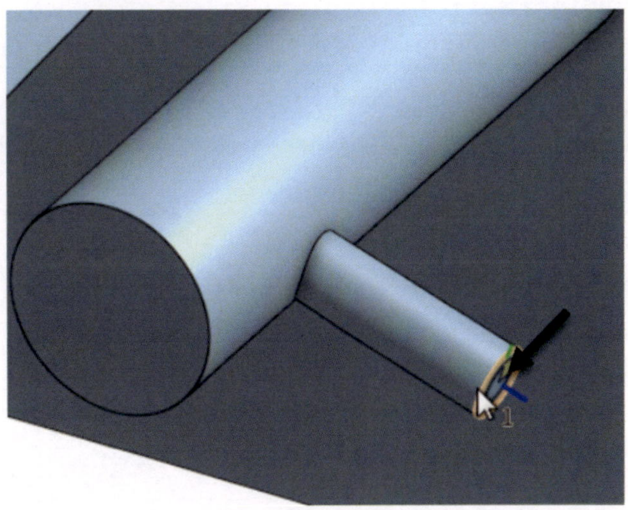

Click the **Flip primary axis** icon to reverse the direction of the component. Click green check to create the fastened mate.

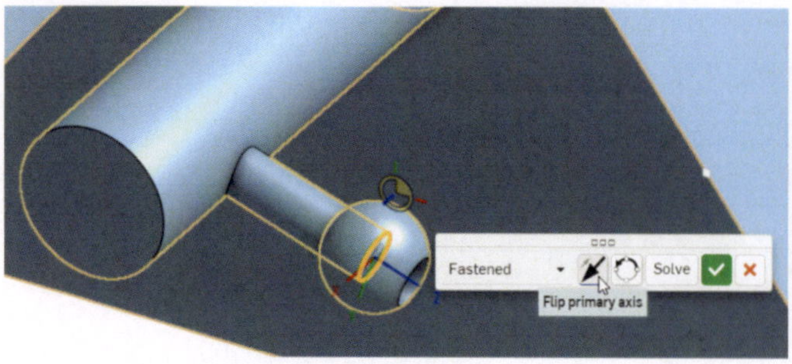

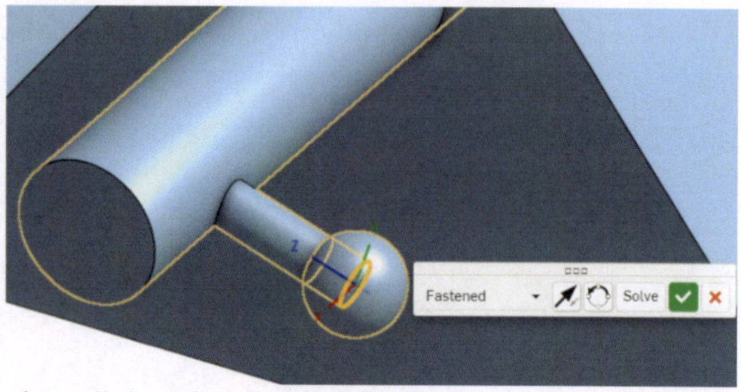

Now, if you change the position or orientation of one part, then all the other parts of the fastened mate will also be affected.

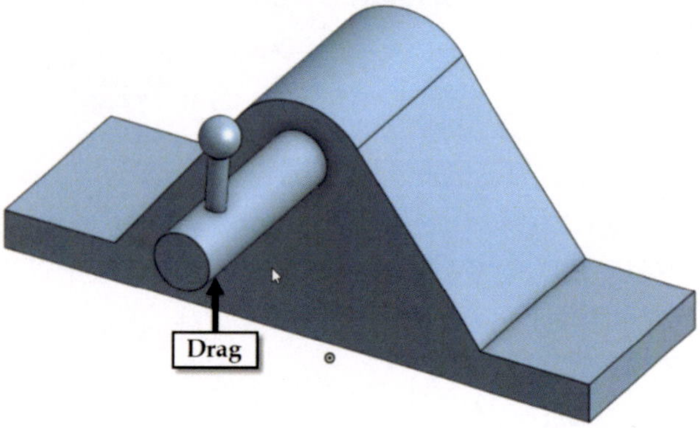

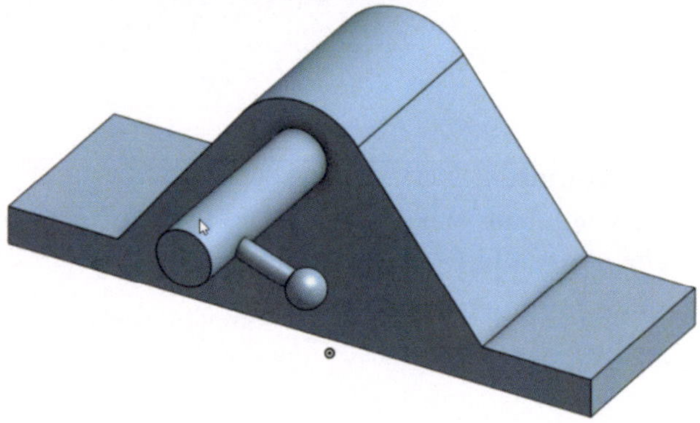

Cylindrical mate

The **Cylindrical mate** command creates a mate with one translational and one rotational degree of freedom. Click the **Cylindrical mate** icon and select the mate connectors from the cylindrical faces of the first and second components. Click **Flip primary axis** to reverse the direction of the component.

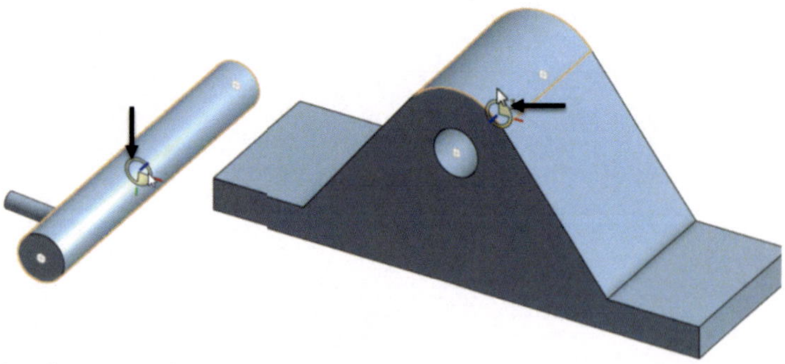

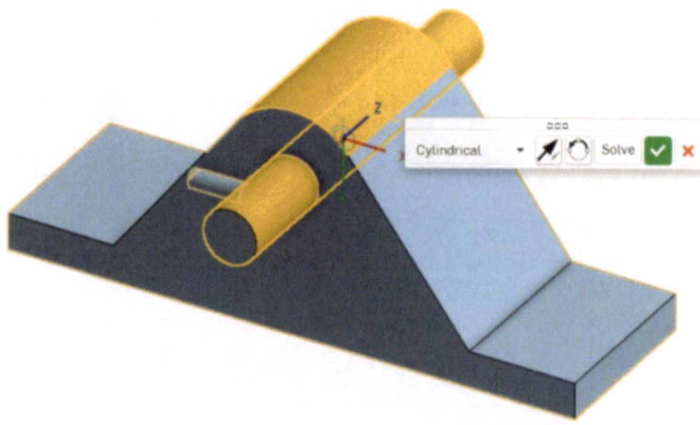

On the **Cylindrical** dialog, check the **Limits** option and specify the minimum and maximum limits for distance and angle. Next, click the **Animate mate degree of freedom** ▶ icon to play an animation of the cylindrical mate. Click green check to create the cylindrical joint. The component can rotate and translate.

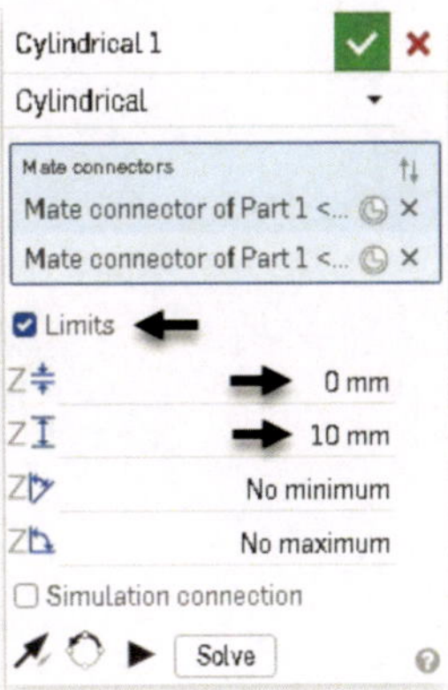

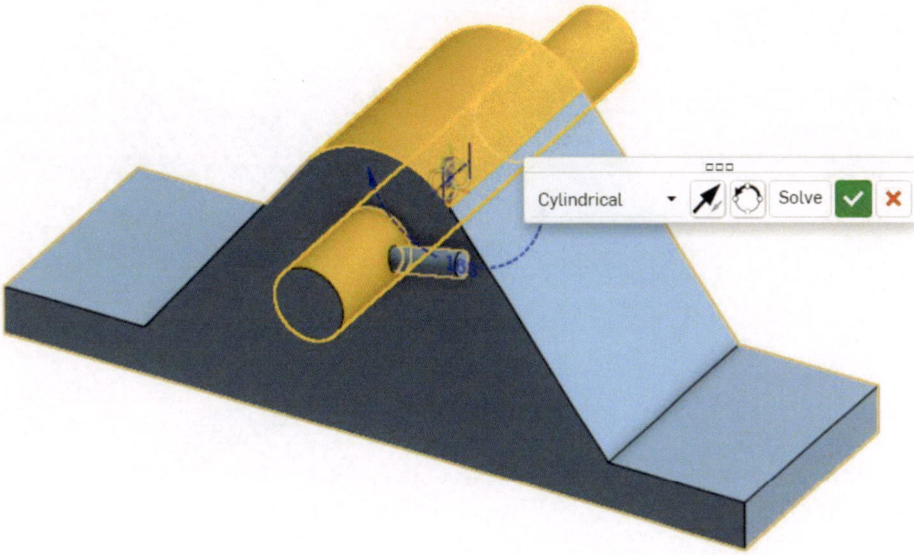

Planar mate

The **Planar mate** makes the two selected planar faces coincident with each other. Also, the placed component has two translational and one rotational movement. Click the **Planar mate** command and select the mate connectors on the planar faces of the first part and target part, respectively. Click **Flip primary axis** to reverse the direction of the component.

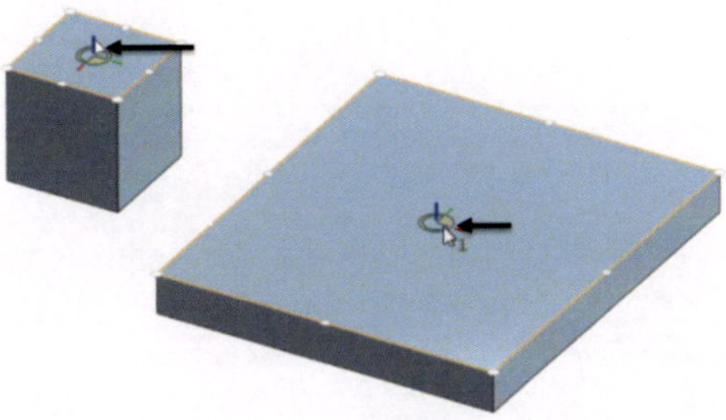

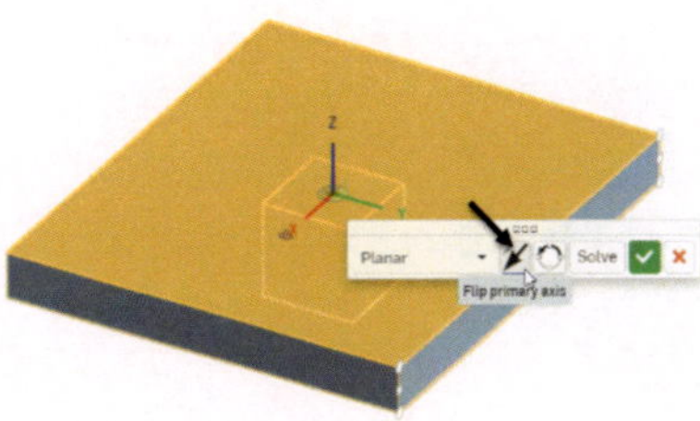

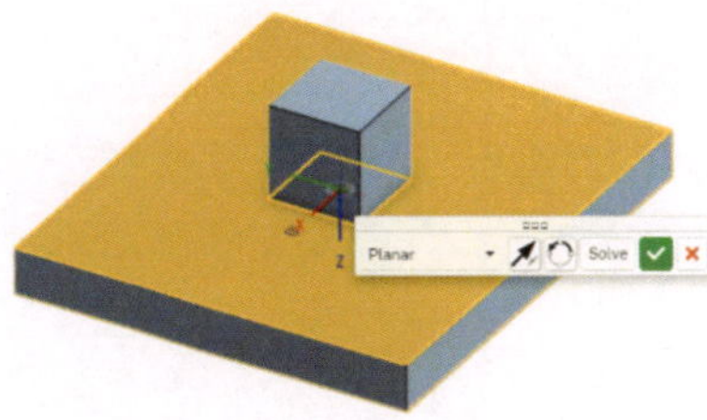

Check the **Offset** option if you want to offset the mate connectors.

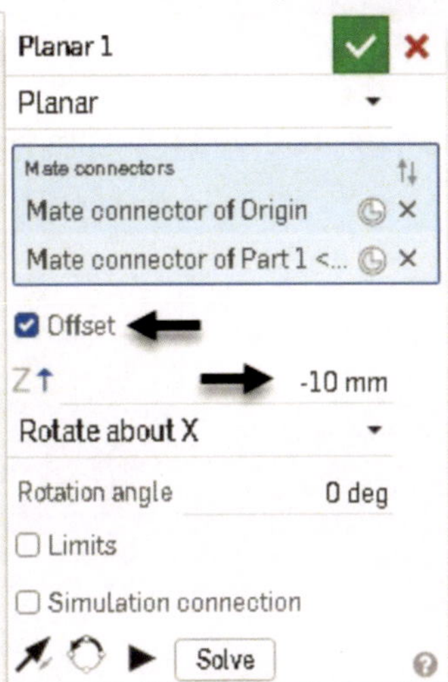

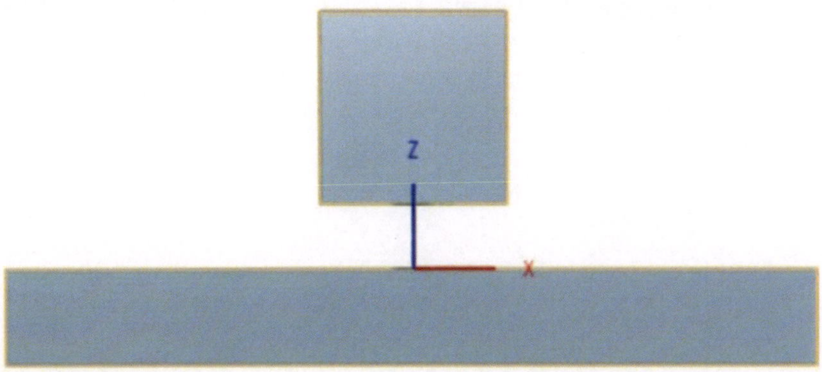

Check the **Limits** option and specify the minimum and maximum limit in the X, Y, and Z directions. Click the **Animate mate degree of freedom** ▶ icon and notice that the component moves within the specified limits.

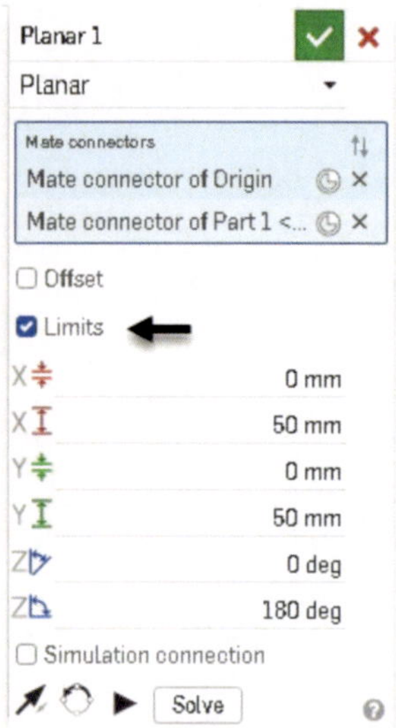

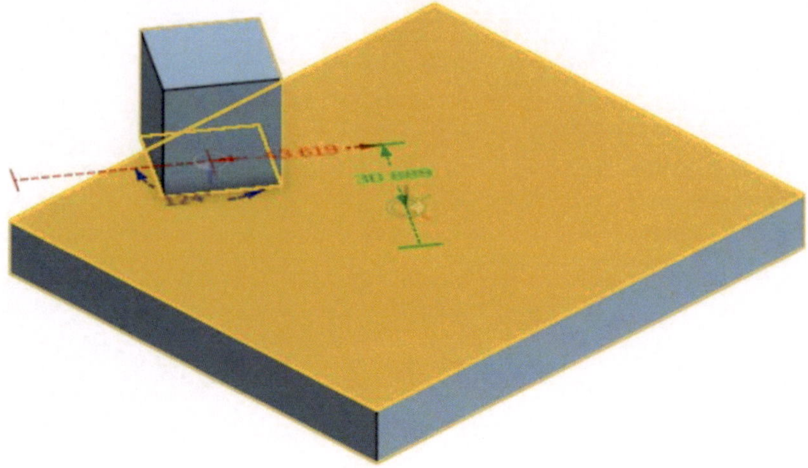

Pin slot mate

The **Pin slot mate** command helps you to insert a cylindrical component into the slot. The cylindrical component will be able to translate along with the slot. In addition to that, it can rotate about its axis. To create this mate, click **Pin slot mate** on the toolbar. Next, select a mate connector of the cylindrical component. Also, select the mate connector of the slot face of the second component.

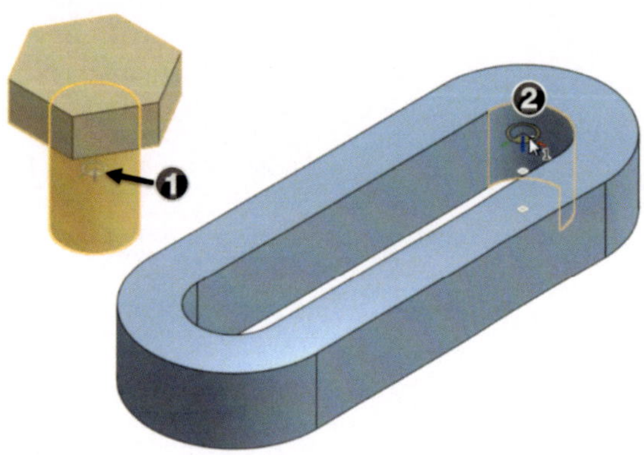

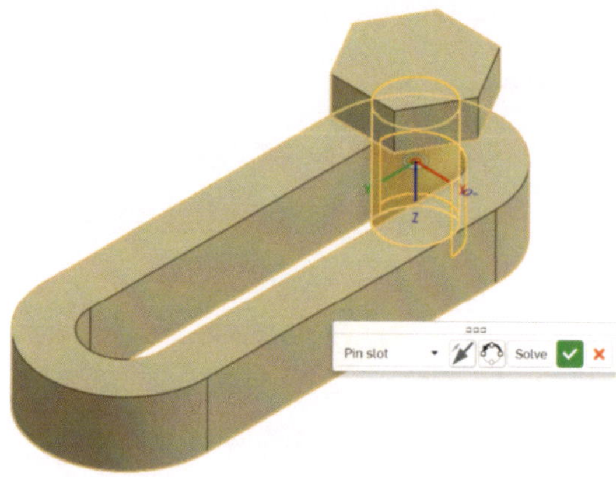

On the **Pin slot** dialog, click the **Animate mate degree of freedom** icon to play the animation of the pin slot mate. You can notice that the first part slides along the X-axis.

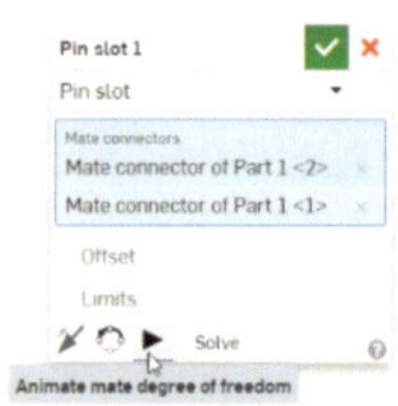

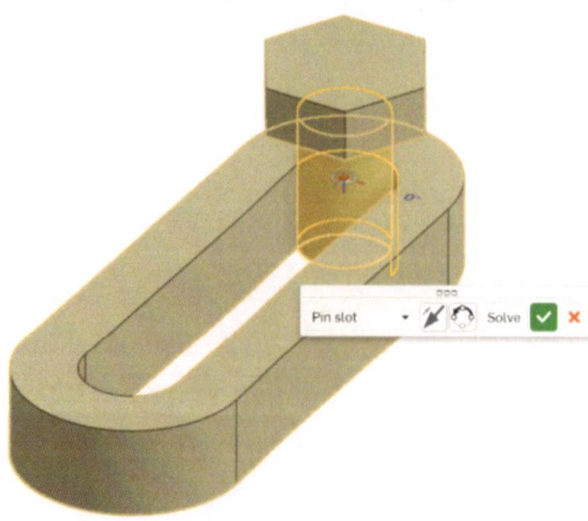

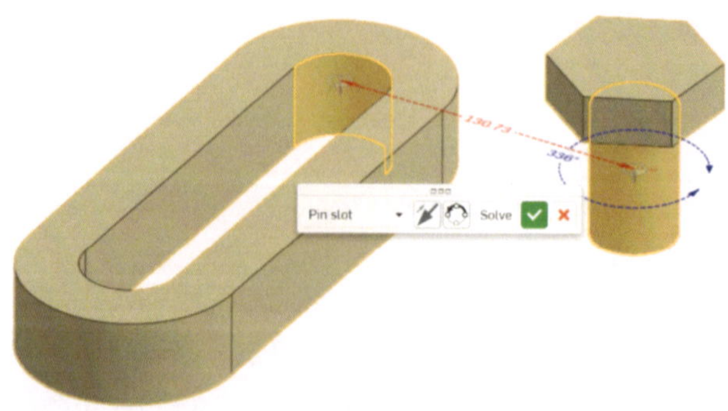

Click the **Reorient secondary axis** icon on the contextual menu. You can view that the first part orients by **90** degrees.

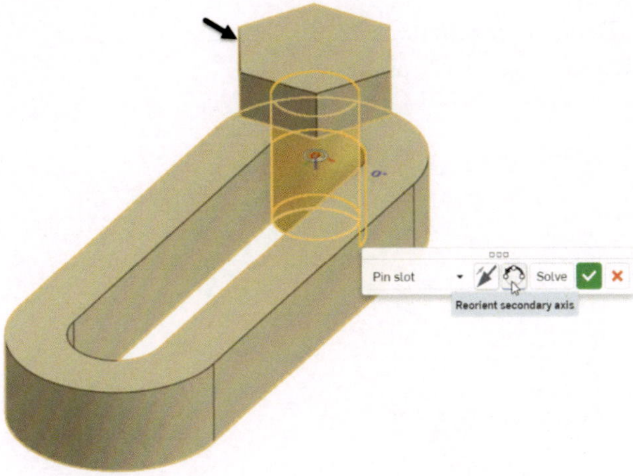

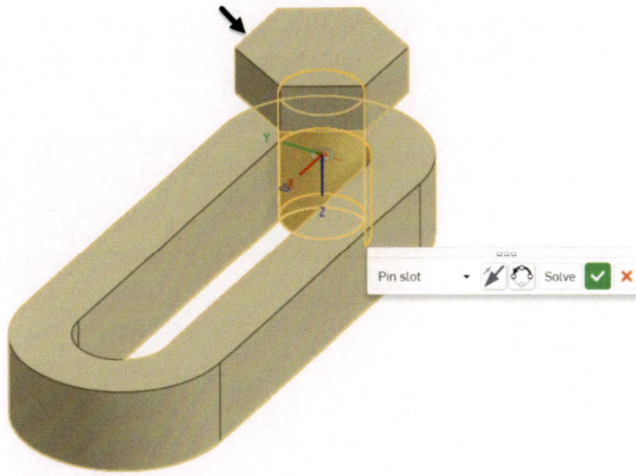

On the **Pin slot** dialog, check the **Limits** option to specify the start and end limits. Now, specify the minimum and maximum limit distance values in the **Limit X minimum distance** and **Limit X maximum distance** fields, respectively. You can also specify the minimum and maximum angle values in the **Limit axial Z minimum angle** and **Limit axial Z maximum angle**, respectively. Click the **Animate mate degree of freedom** icon to check whether the first part slides along the specified axis and distance.

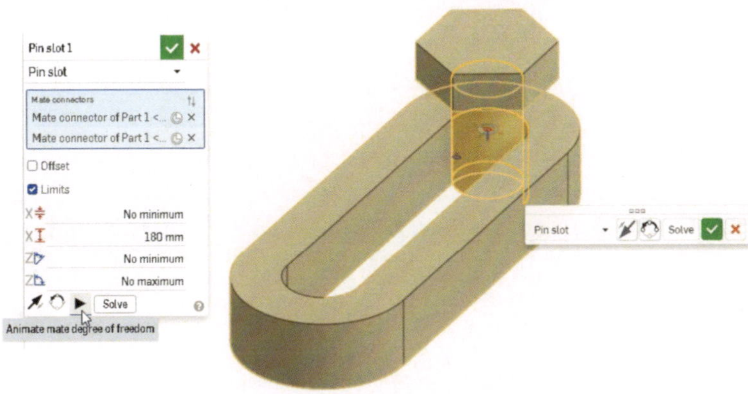

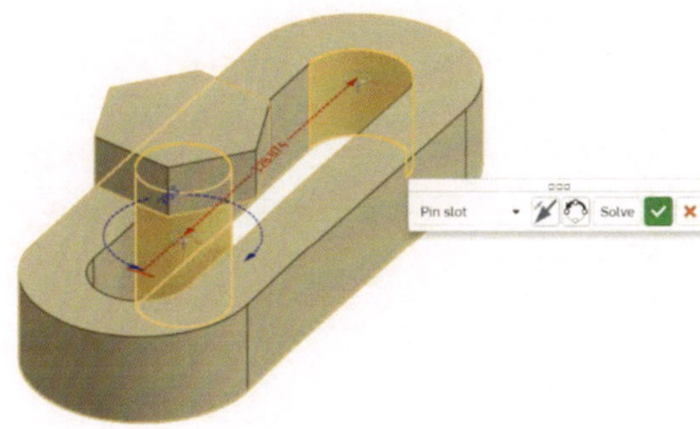

Click green check on the dialog, to create the pin slot mate.

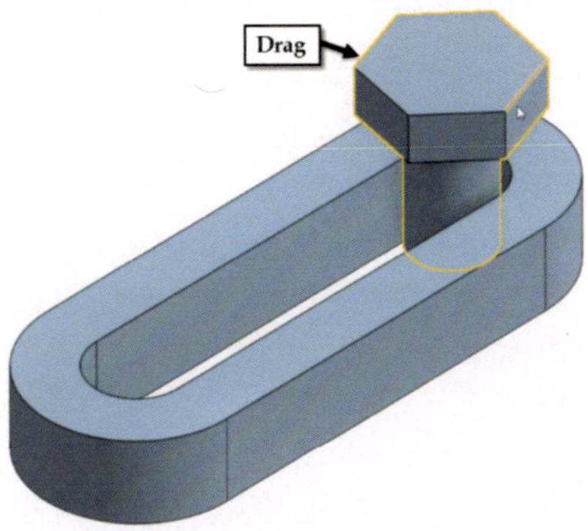

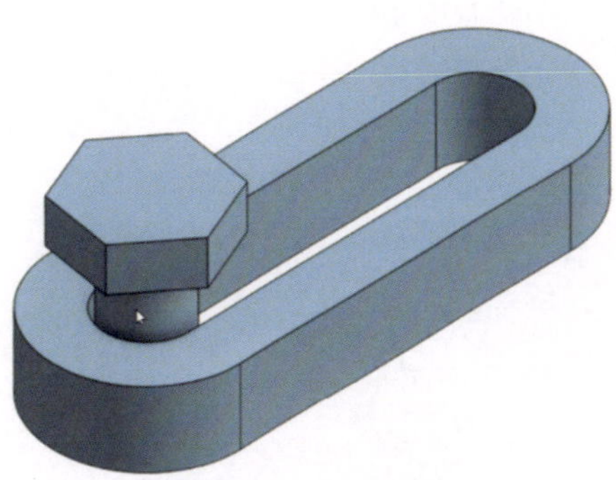

Slider mate

The **Slider mate** creates a slider mate between two components. The inserted component will slide in the target part. The sliding direction is normal to the mate connector. To create this mate, click **Slider mate** on the toolbar. Next, specify the mate connectors on the placement and target parts, as shown.

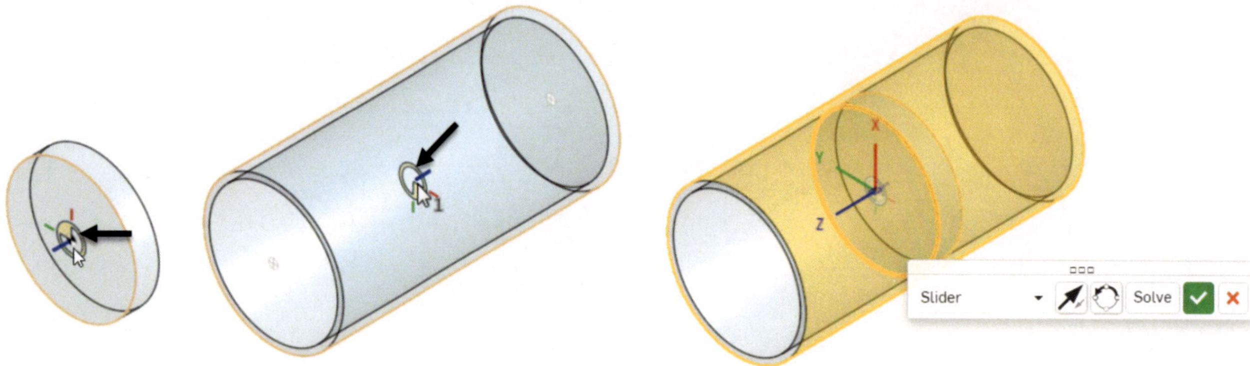

On the **Slider** dialog, check the **Limit** option and specify the minimum and maximum limits along the Z-direction. Next, click the **Animate mate degree of freedom** ▶ icon to view the resultant mate. Click the green check to create the slider mate.

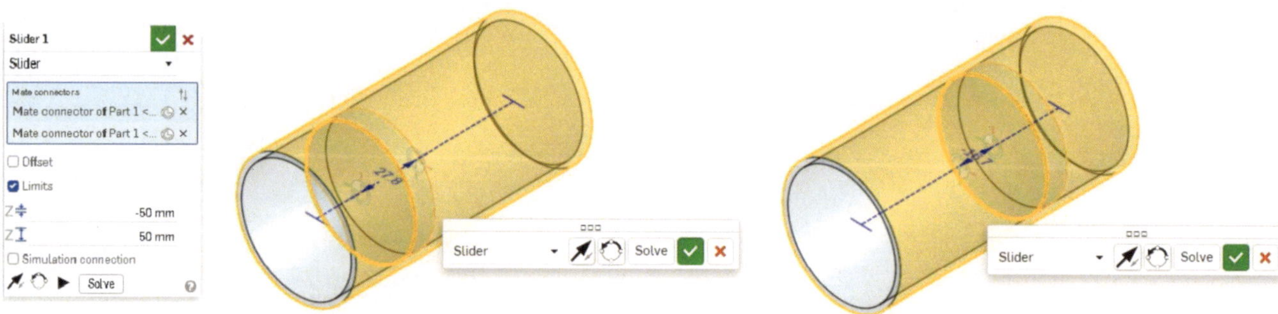

Parallel mate

The **Parallel Mate** makes two faces coincident to each other. To apply this mate, click the **Parallel Mate** icon on the Toolbar. Select a face of the placement part, and then click on a face of the target part. The two selected faces will mate with each other. You can also check the **Limits** option to set distance limits between the selected faces.

You can also click the **Flip primary axis** button to change the orientation of the axis. Click the **Reorient secondary axis** button to rotate the quadrant orientation of the instance by 90 degrees. Click the green check to create the mate.

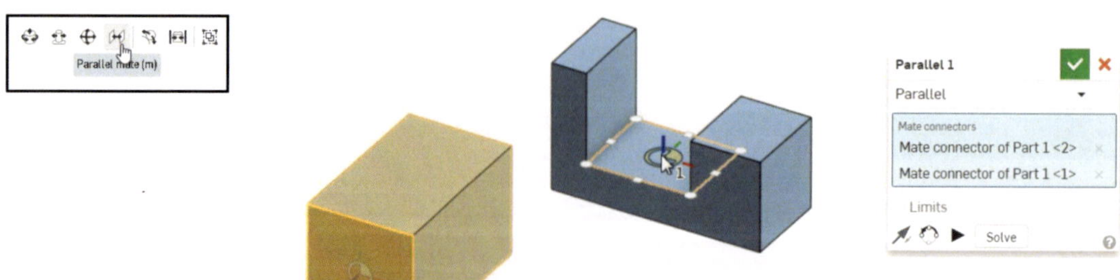

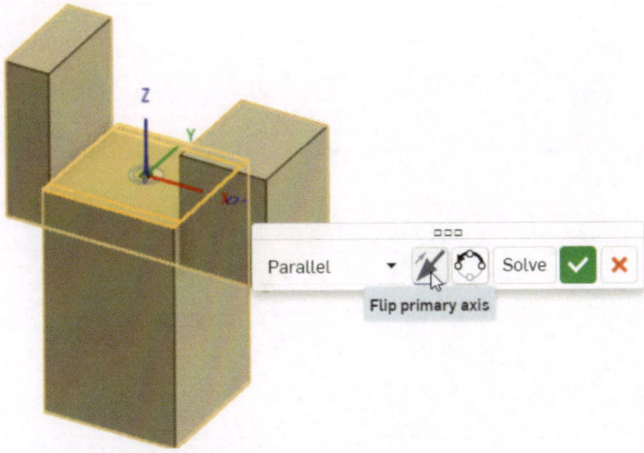

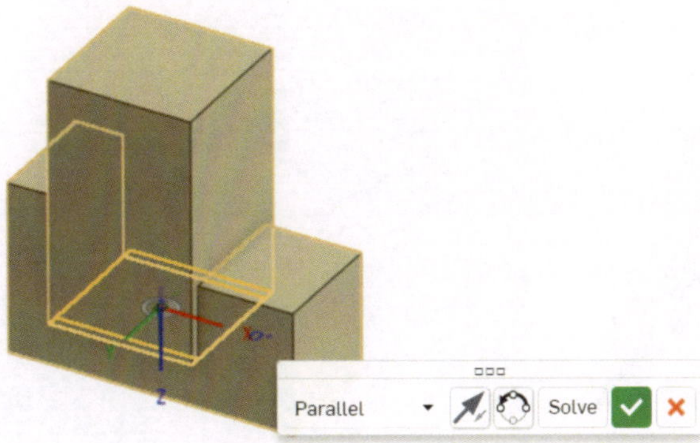

Tangent mate

The **Tangent mate** command is often used when working with cylinders and spears. It causes the geometry to maintain contact at a point of tangency. Click the **Tangent mate** icon on the toolbar. After activating this command, click on the face to be made tangent. Next, click on the tangent face on the target part. The first part will be made tangent to the target part. Use the **Flip primary axis** icon to flip the tangency side.

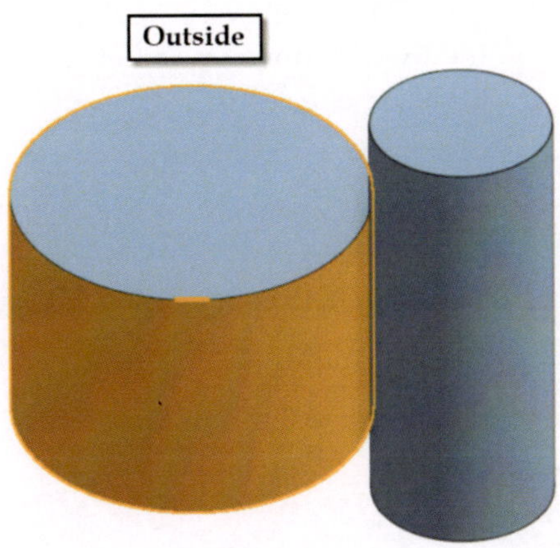

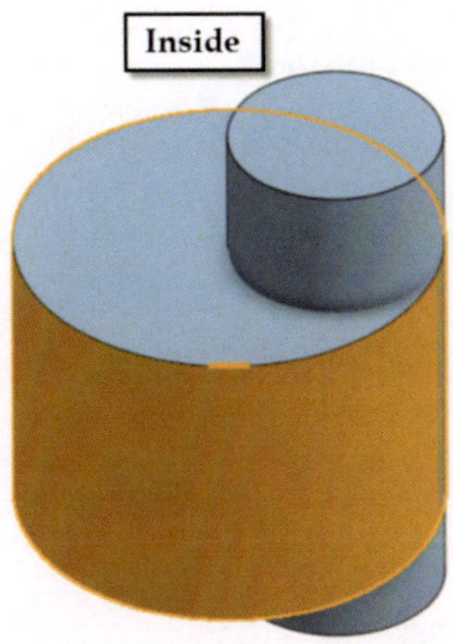

Mate Connectors

Mate Connectors are snapping points on the components that are used to create a mate between two components. For example, activate the **Revolute mate** command and place the pointer on the cylindrical face of the shaft, as shown. You can notice the snap points on the component at both the ends and middle. Select the mate connector displayed at the bottom end. Next, place the pointer on the cylindrical face of the hole; the mate connectors appear. Select the joint origins located inside the hole. Next, click the green check to create the mate.

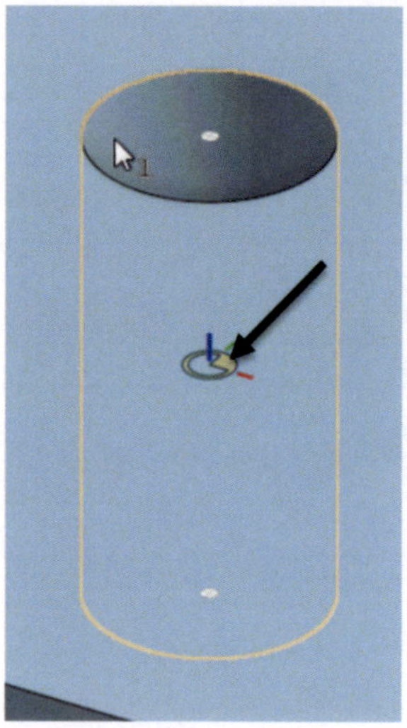

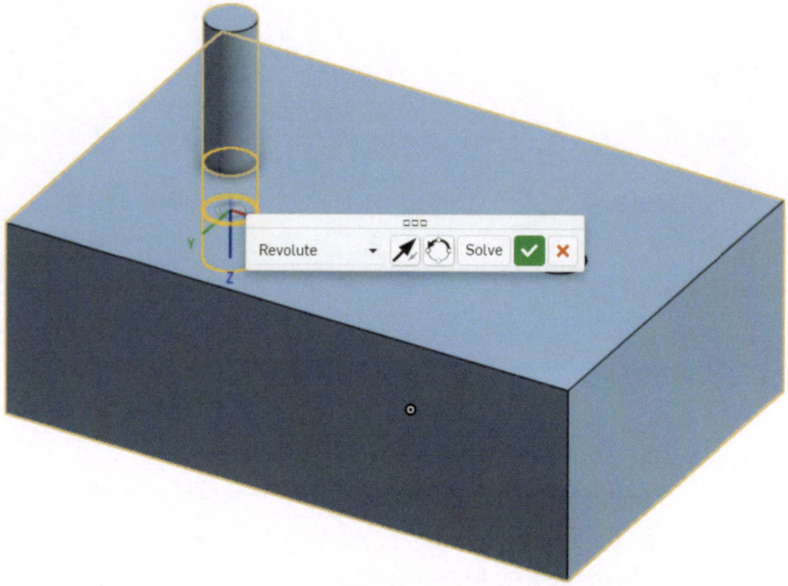

You have noticed that the mate connectors are displayed at the ends and middle of the component. However, you can create a mate connector at the location other than the end and middle of the component. To do this, click **Mate Connector** on the toolbar. Next, select **Origin type > On entity** from the **Mate connector** dialog. Select the mate connector on the bottom end face of the component, as shown. On the **Mate connector** dialog, check the Move option, and then type -15 in the Z box. Next, click the green check on the **Mate connector** dialog.

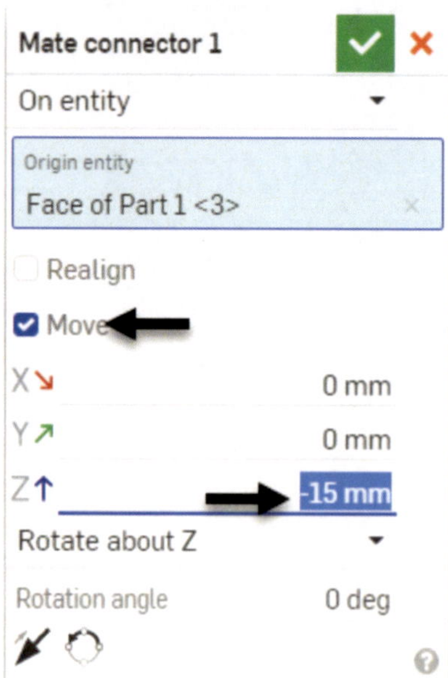

Activate the **Revolute mate** command and select the newly created mate connector. Next, select the mate connector on the top end of the hole, as shown. Click the green check to create the translate mate between the two mate connectors. Now, change the **Visual Style** to **Translucent** and notice that the component is placed in the hole without any intersection.

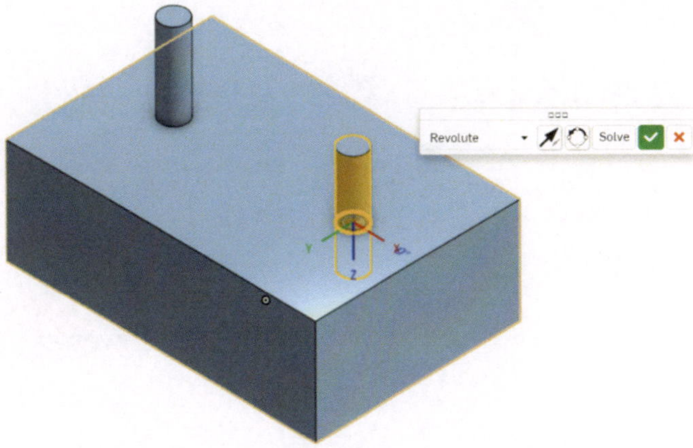

Snap Mode

The **Snap Mode** command makes it easy to assemble components by merely dragging closer to each other. Start a new assembly file and insert the components into the assembly. Click the **Snap Mode**  icon on the toolbar and place the cursor on an edge or face of the first component; a mate connector is displayed. Press and hold the left mouse button and drag the pointer. Next, release the cursor at the desired location on the second component; the Fastened dialog appears on the screen. Select the desired mate from the **Mate type** drop-down available on the dialog. Specify the Offset and Limits on the dialog, if required. Use the Flip primary axis and Reorient secondary axis icons to align the components. Click the green check to create the mate.

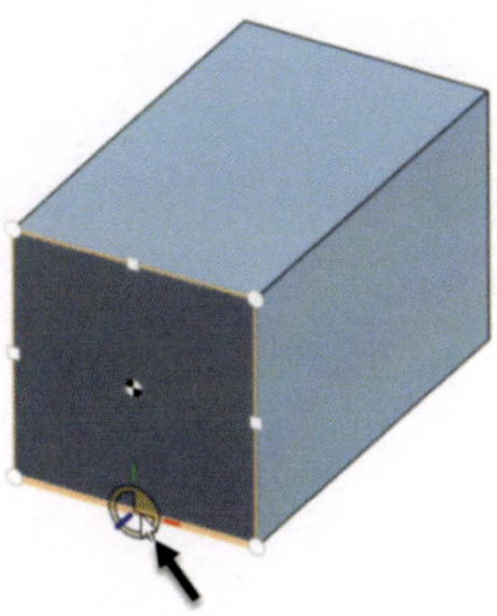

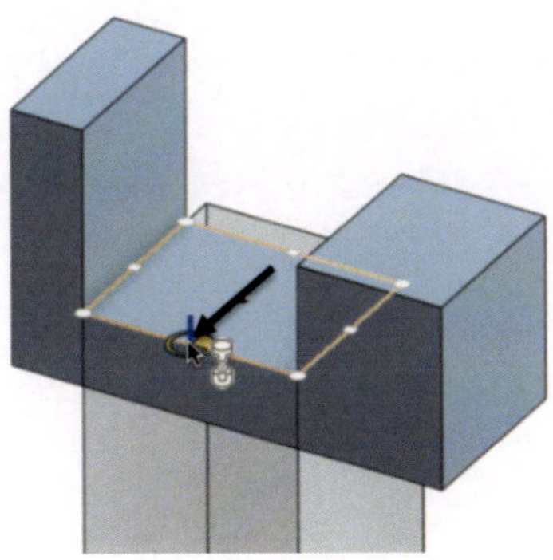

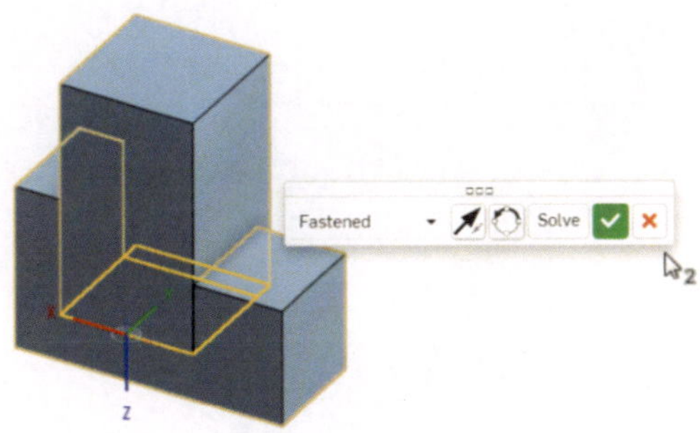

Interference detection

In an assembly, two or more parts may overlap or occupy the same space. However, this would be physically impossible in the real world. When you add relations between parts, Onshape develops real-world contacts and movements between them. However, sometimes interferences can occur. To check such errors, Onshape provides you with a command called **Interference detection**. Click **Show analysis tools** icon on the bottom right corner of the Onshape interface and select **Interference Detection**. Next, select the parts from the graphics window. The interference detected is shown in red color. If there is no interference, the **No interference** message is displayed on the **Interference detection** dialog. Next, close the **Interference detection** dialog.

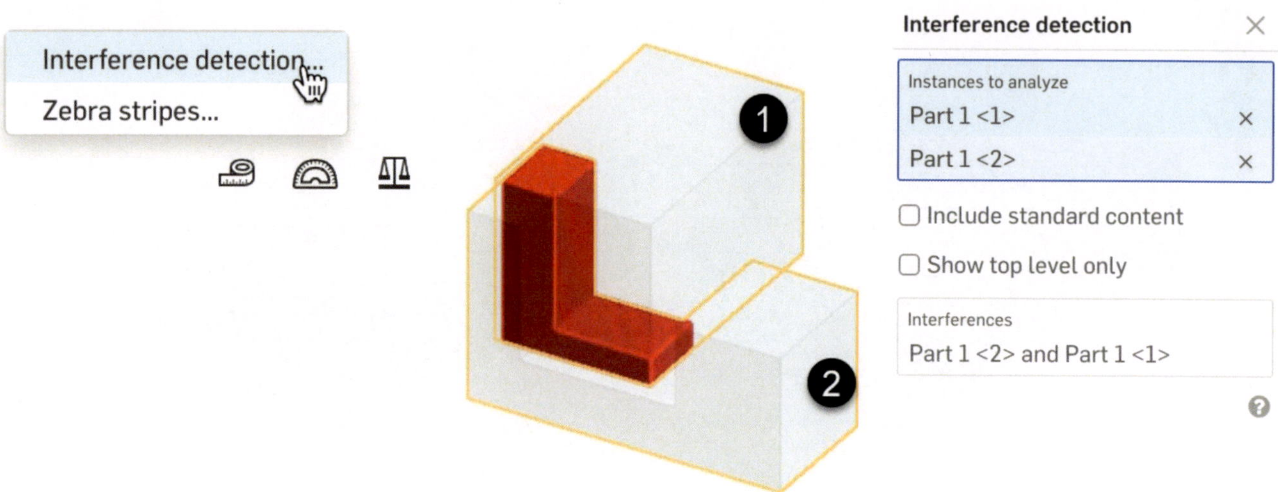

Replicate

If you have an assembly in which you need to assemble the same part multiple times, it would be a tedious process. In such cases, the **Replicate** command will drastically reduce or even eliminate the time used to assemble commonly used parts. To use this command, first mate the two components. For example, create the *Base* component along with holes on it and *Screw* component, as shown. Next, apply the **Cylindrical mate** to the circular edge of the screw and circular edge of the hole.

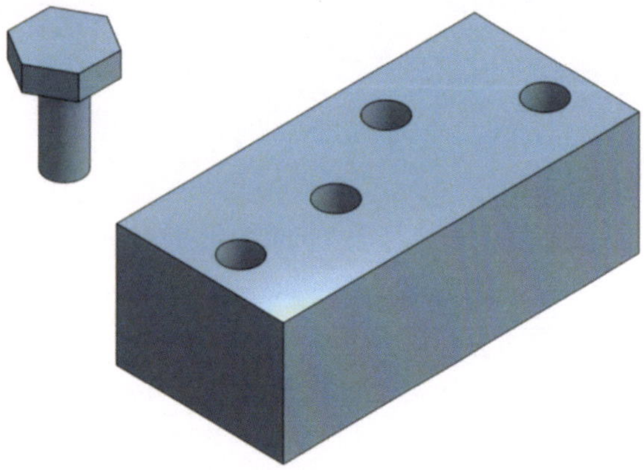

Click the **Cylindrical mate** icon on the Toolbar and select the mate connector displayed on the top circular edge of the screw. Next, select the mate connector displayed on circular edge of the hole, as shown. Click the green check to create the cylindrical mate.

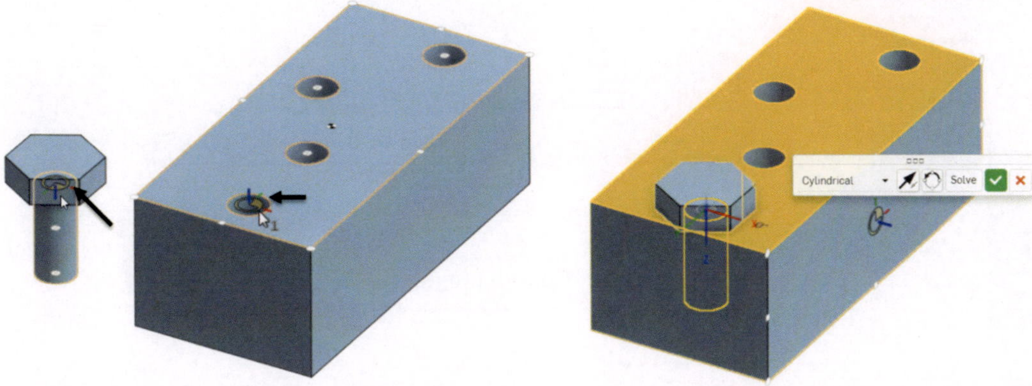

0Click the **Replicate** icon on the Toolbar. Select the *Screw* component. Next, click **Face to find match in** and select the top face of the *Base* component, as shown in the figure.

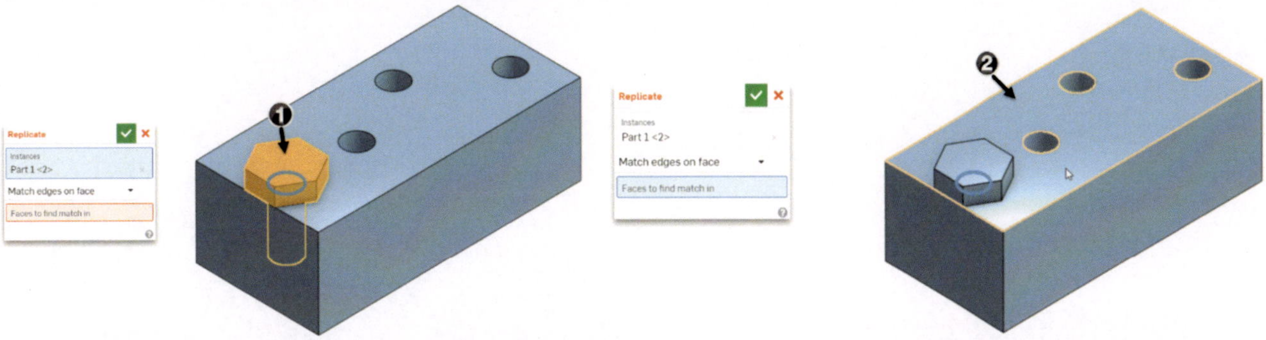

You can notice that the screw is inserted into all the remaining holes. Click green check to close the **Replicate** dialog.

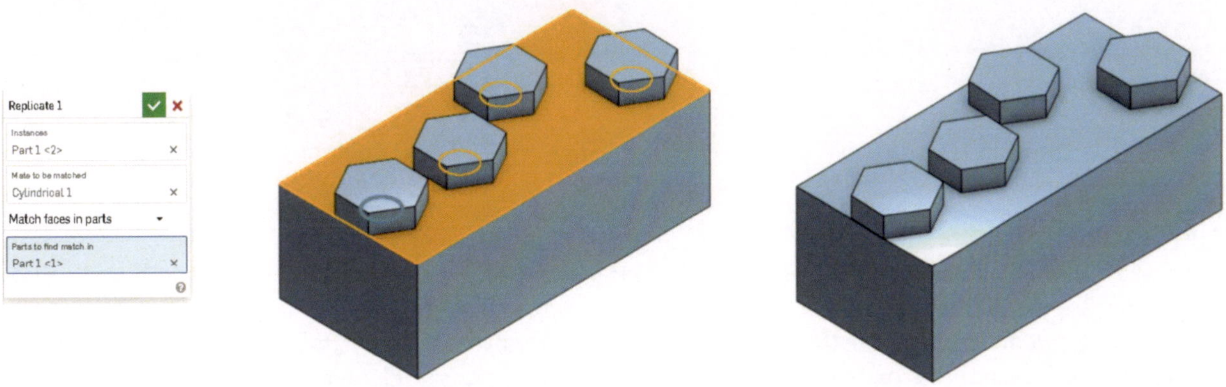

Editing and Updating Assemblies

During the design process, the correct design is not achieved on the first attempt. There is always a need to go back and make modifications. Onshape allows you to accomplish this process very easily. To modify a part in an assembly, right-click on it and click **Edit in context**; the Part Studio will be activated. Make changes to the part and click **Create version and update in Assembly**; the Assembly studio will be activated.

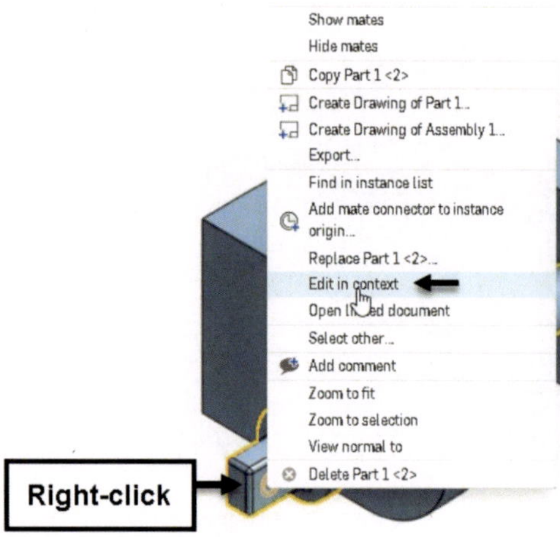

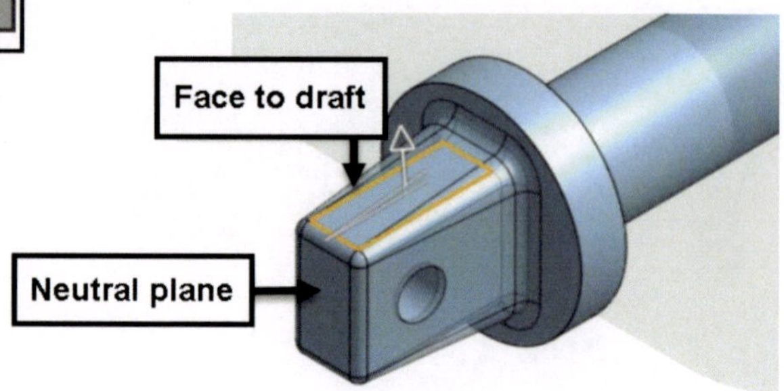

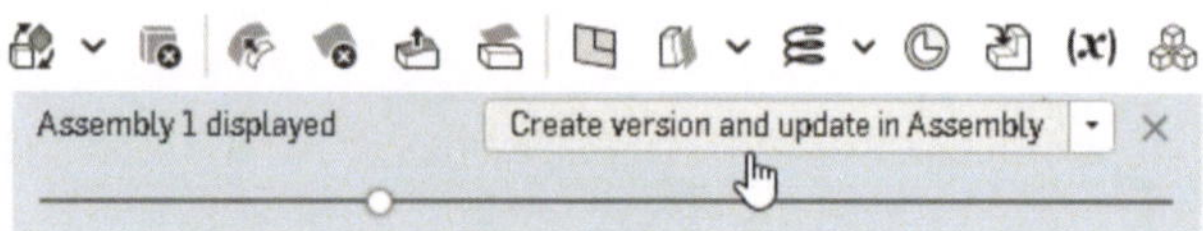

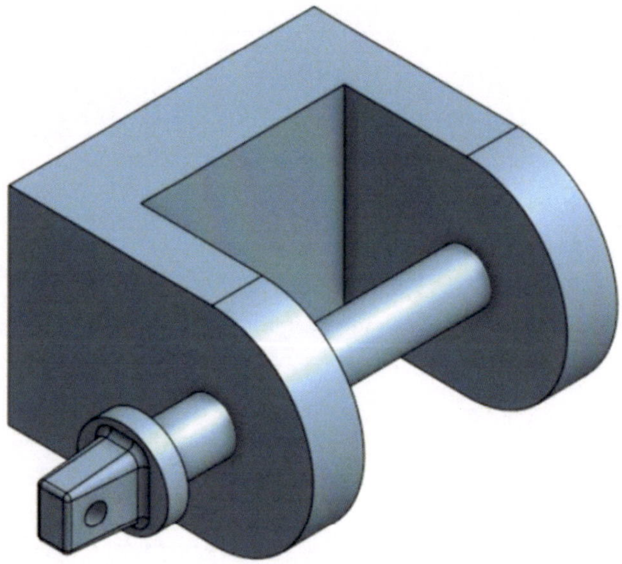

Editing Mates

You can also edit mates in an assembly. Select a part from the graphics window. Next, right click and select **Show mates**; the mates applied to the part appear on the assembly. Click the right mouse button on a particular mate to display the shortcut menu. You can use this menu to delete, suppress, animate, or edit mate. If you select **Edit**, the dialog related to the mate appears on the screen. You can redefine the faces or elements between which the mate is applied. For example, if you want to edit the **Cylindrical mate**, right-click on it and select **Edit Cylindrical**. On the **Cylindrical** dialog, clear the selections in the **Mate connectors** section, and then click on a face of the placement part. Next, select the face of the target part. Click the green check to apply the mate.

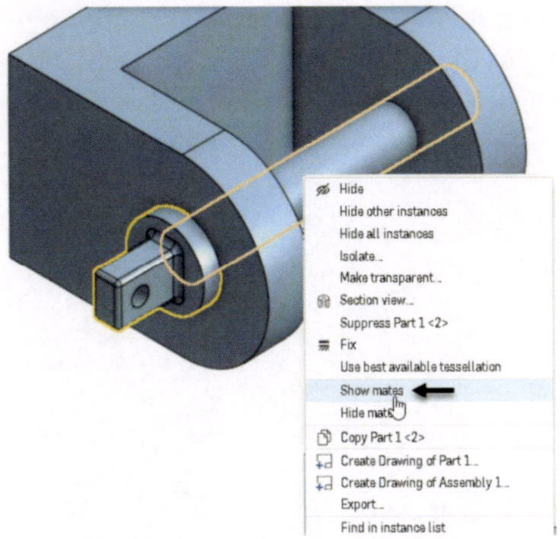

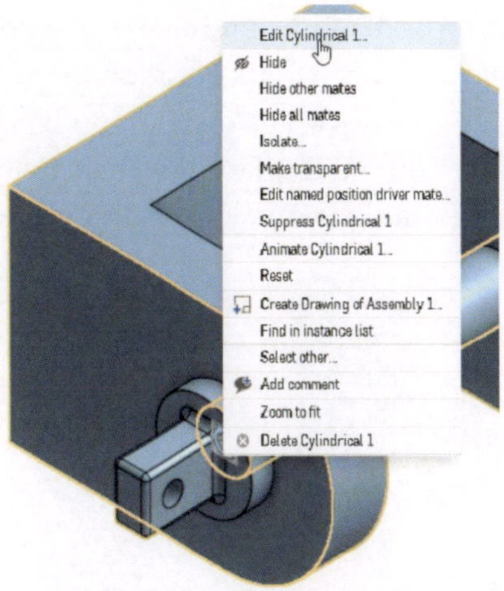

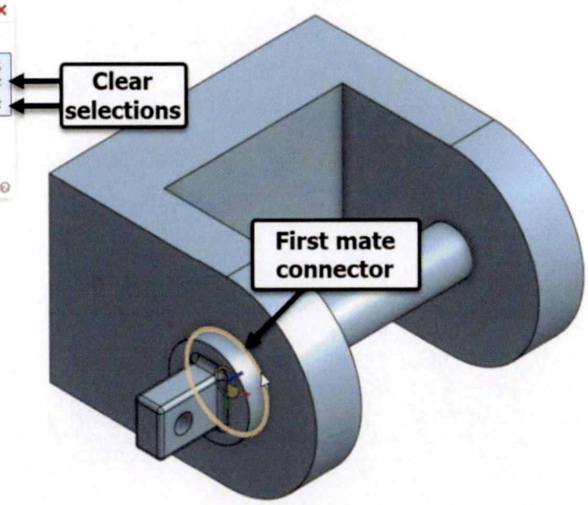

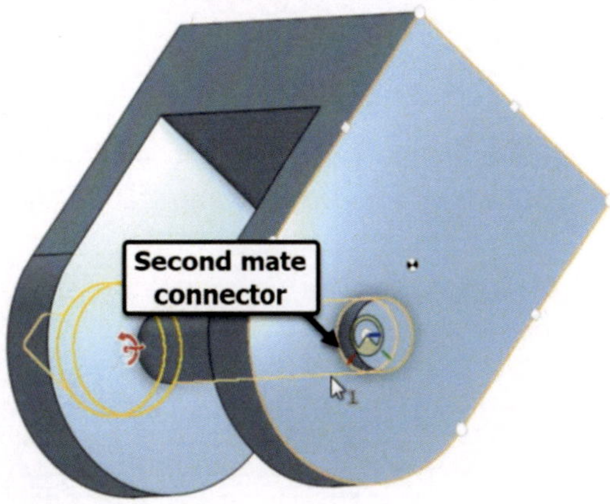

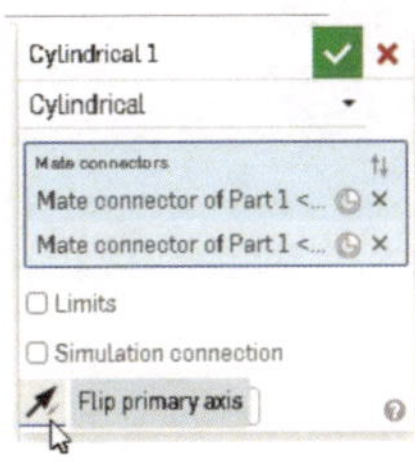

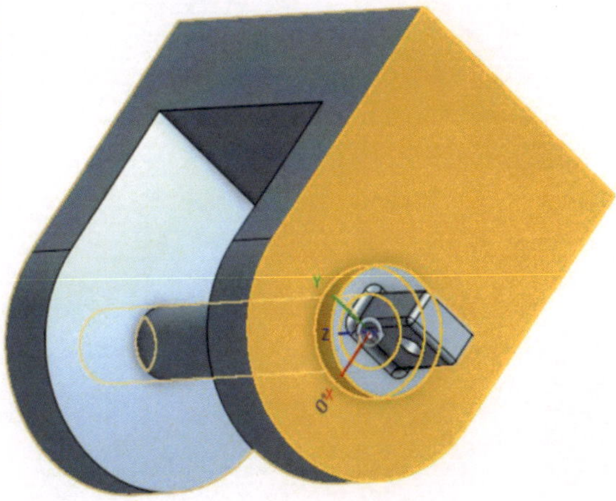

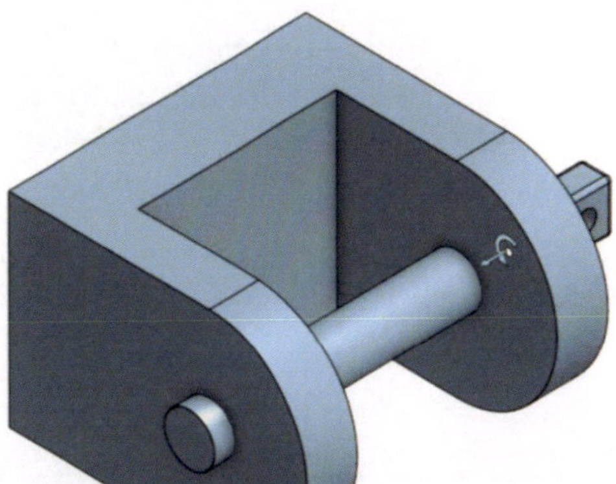

Replace instances

Onshape allows you to replace any component in an assembly. To do this, go to the **Features** window and click the right mouse button on the component to replace. Select **Replace instances** to open the **Replace instance** dialog. You can also click the **Replace instances** icon on the Toolbar. On the **Replace instance** dialog, click the

Select replacement component selection box; the **Select replacement component** dialog appears on the screen. On this dialog, go to the location of the replacement part and select the component. As you select the component, the dialog closes on its own. If you have more than one instance of the part in the assembly. Check the **Replace all instances** on the **Replace instance** dialog, to replace all of the instances. Click green check on the **Replace instance** dialog. Now, you can redefine the existing mates or delete them and define new mates.

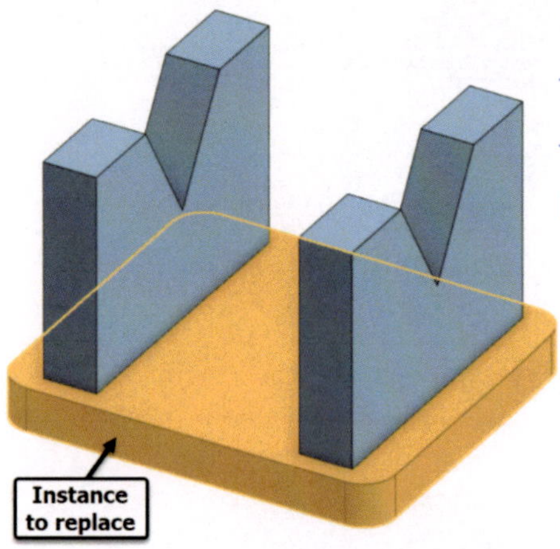

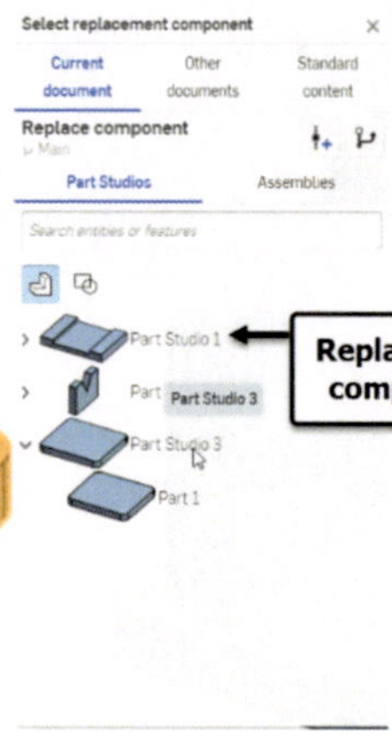

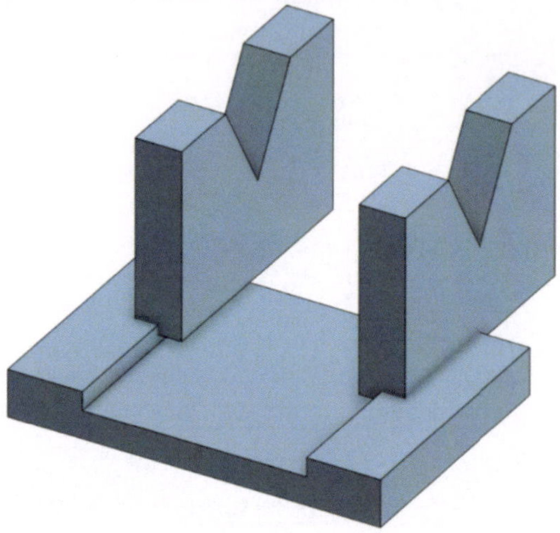

To redefine the mate of the replacement part, right click on mates with error symbol, and then select **Edit**. Select new mate connectors from the model and click the green check.

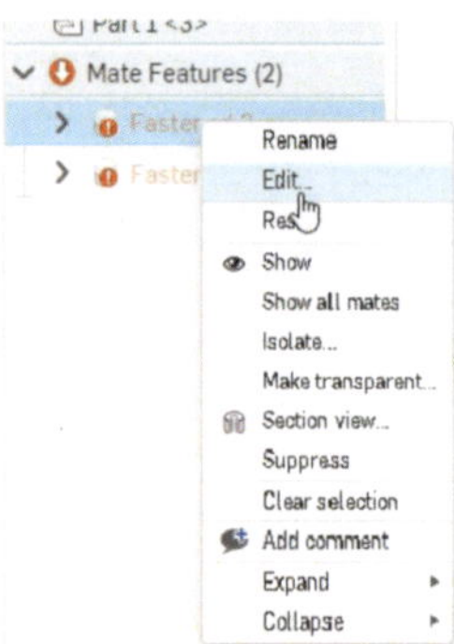

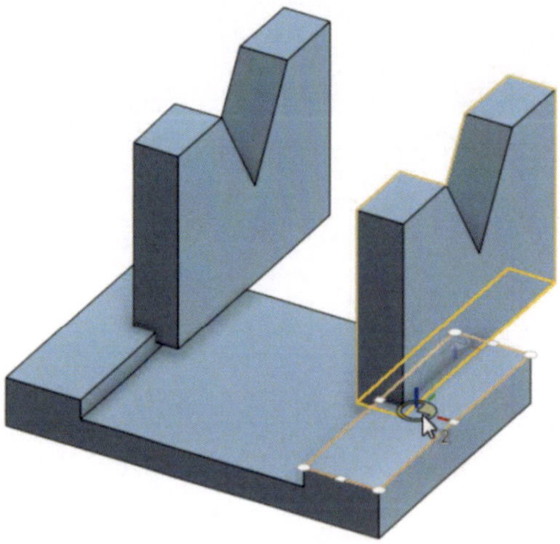

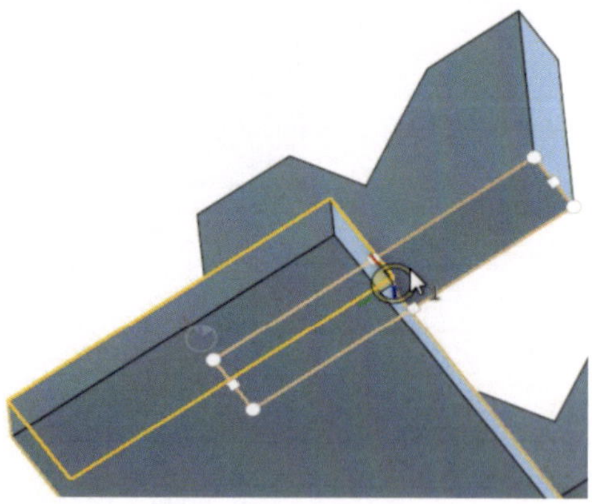

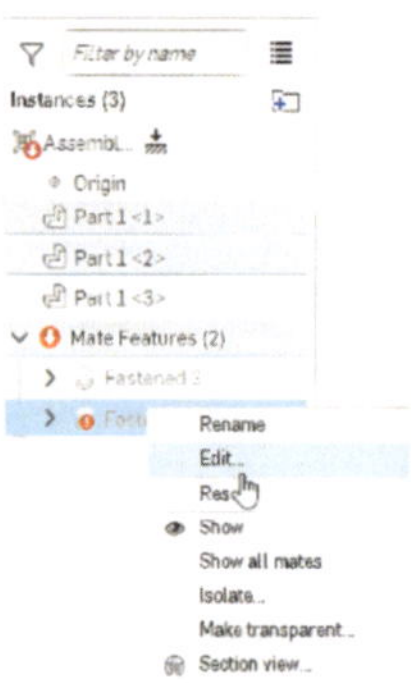

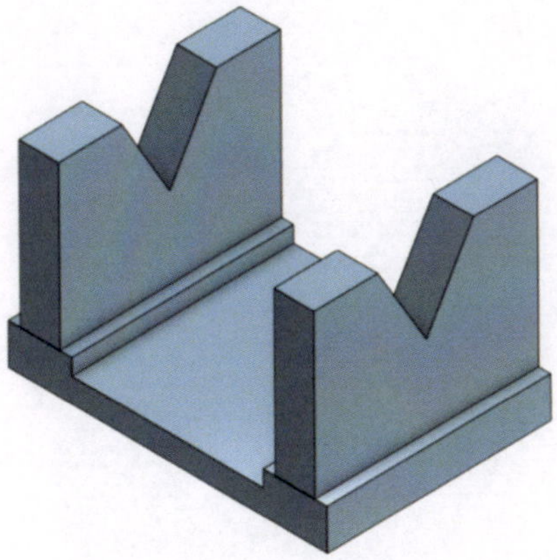

Assembly Circular Pattern

The **Assembly circular pattern** command allows you to replicate individual parts in an assembly about an axis. First, position the screw in one hole using the **Cylindrical mate** command. To do this, activate the **Cylindrical mate** command and click on the circular edge of the screw. Next, select the circular edge of the hole, as shown. Click green check on the **Cylindrical** dialog to mate the screw in one of the holes.

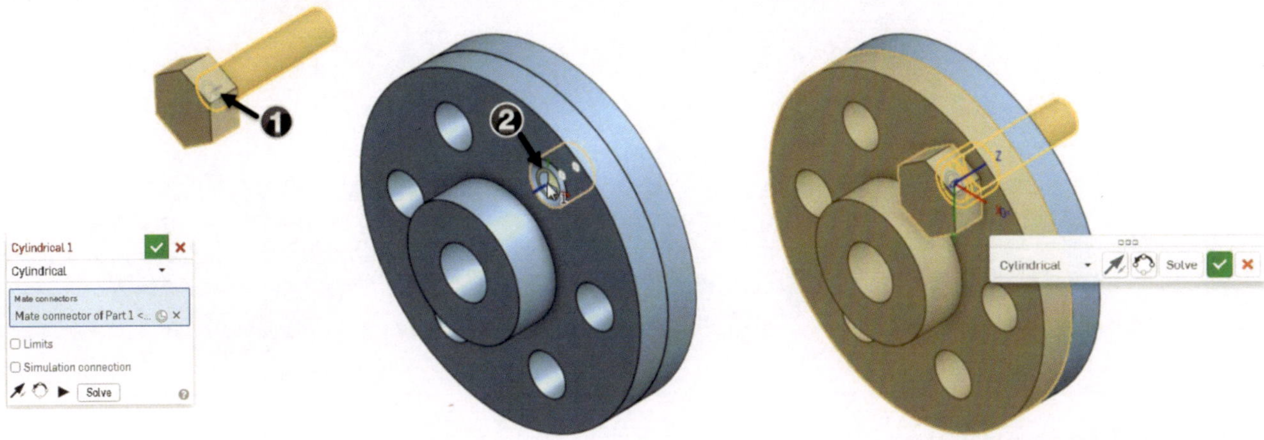

Next, click the **Assembly circular pattern** icon on the Toolbar and click on the part (In this case, screw) to include in the pattern. On the **Circular pattern** dialog, click the **Axis of pattern** selection box and select the outer circular edge of the second component. The default angle value is **360** degrees. You can change the angle value in the **Angle** field. Specify the number of instances in the **Instance count** field. Click green check to create the *Assembly circular pattern*.

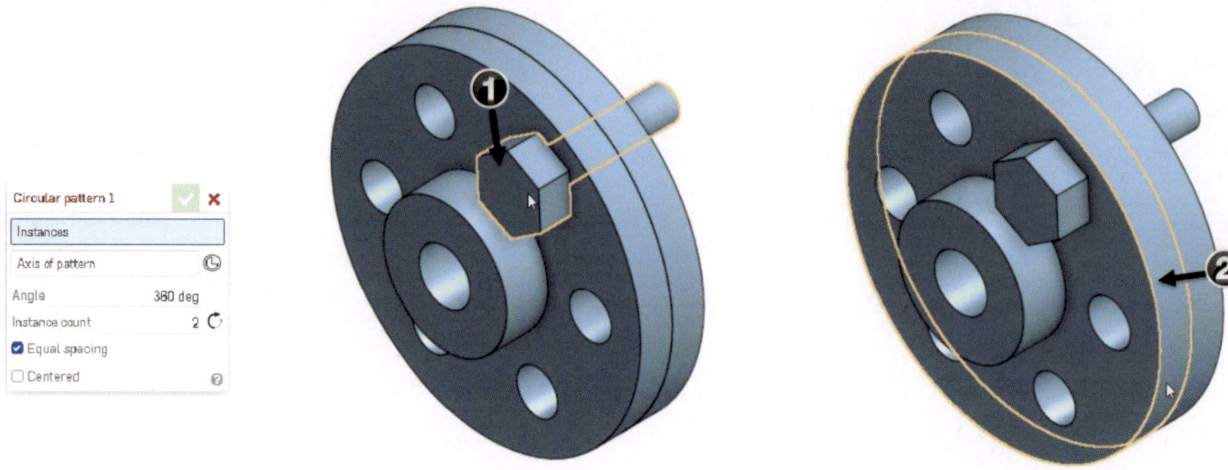

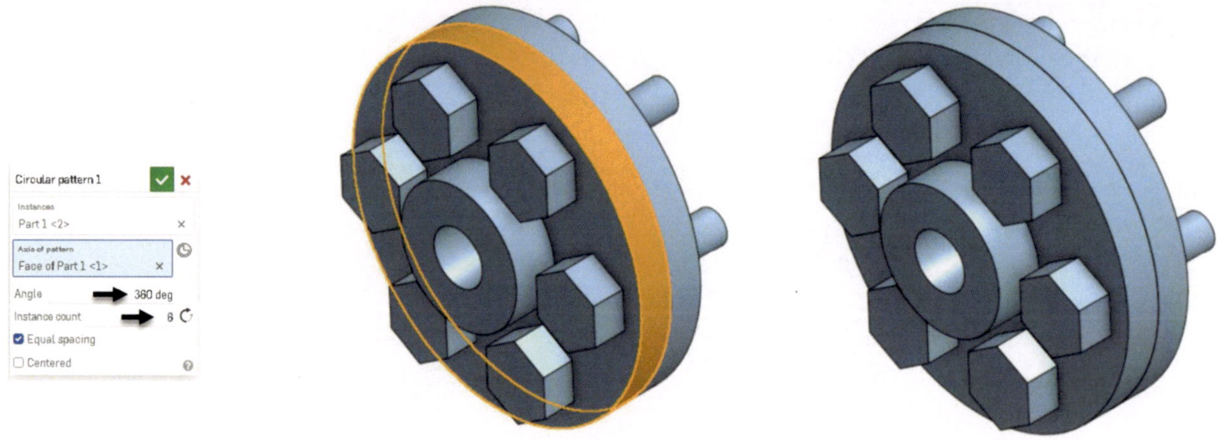

Assembly Linear pattern

The **Assembly Linear pattern** command allows you to replicate the individual parts in a linear fashion. First, position the screw in one hole using the **Cylindrical mate** command. To do this, activate the **Cylindrical mate** command and click on the circular edge of the screw. Next, select the circular edge of the hole, as shown. Click green check on the **Cylindrical** dialog to mate the screw in one hole.

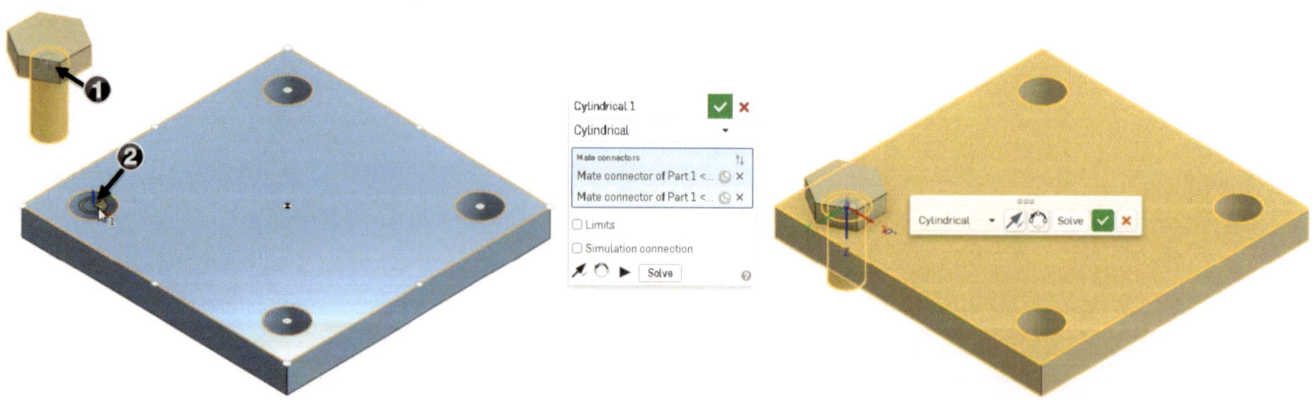

Next, click the **Assembly Linear pattern** icon on the Toolbar and click on the part (In this case, screw) to include in the pattern. On the **Linear pattern** dialog, click the **Direction** selection box and select the top edge of the second component, as shown. Change the distance value in the **Distance** field. Specify the number of instances in the **Instance count** field. You can also change the direction by clicking the **Opposite direction** icon.

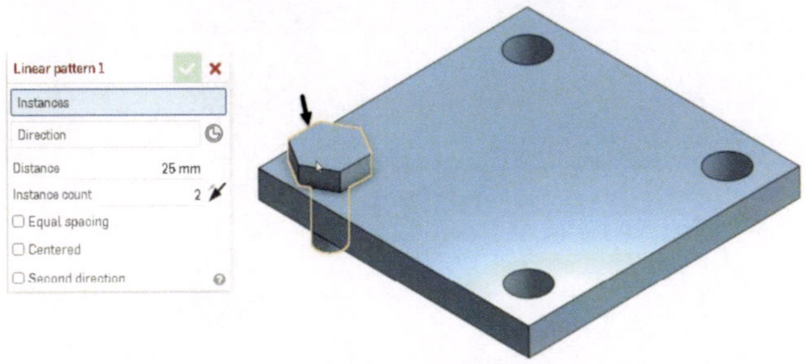

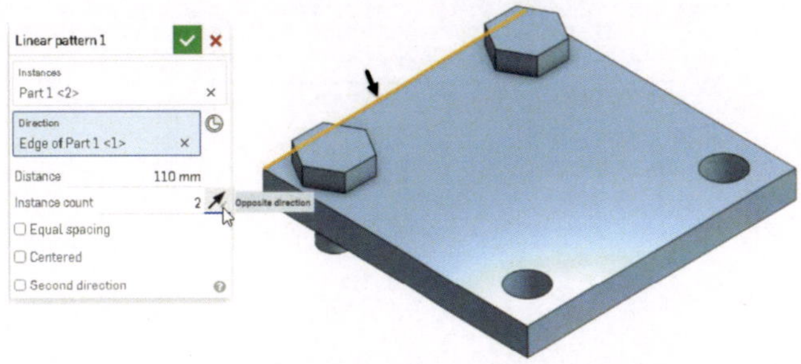

Check the **Second direction** option, if you want to pattern the component in the other direction also. Select the front edge of the second component, as shown. Change the distance value in the **Distance** field. Specify the number of instances in the **Instance count** field. Click green check to create the *Assembly Linear pattern*.

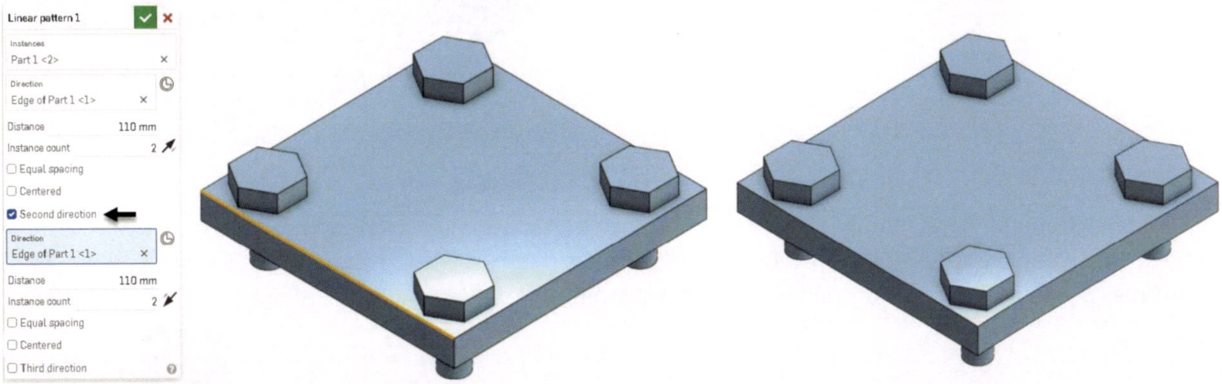

Sub-assemblies

The use of sub-assemblies has many advantages in Onshape. Sub-assemblies make large assemblies easier to manage. They make it easy for multiple users to collaborate on a single large assembly design. They can also affect the way you document a large assembly design in 2D drawings. For these reasons, it is important for you to create sub-assemblies in a variety of ways. The easiest way to create a sub-assembly is to insert an existing assembly into another assembly. To do this, click the **Insert parts and assemblies** icon on the toolbar. Next, click the **Other documents** tab on the **Insert parts and assemblies** dialog. Click the **Assemblies** tab and select the assembly to be inserted. Click in the graphics window and click the green check.

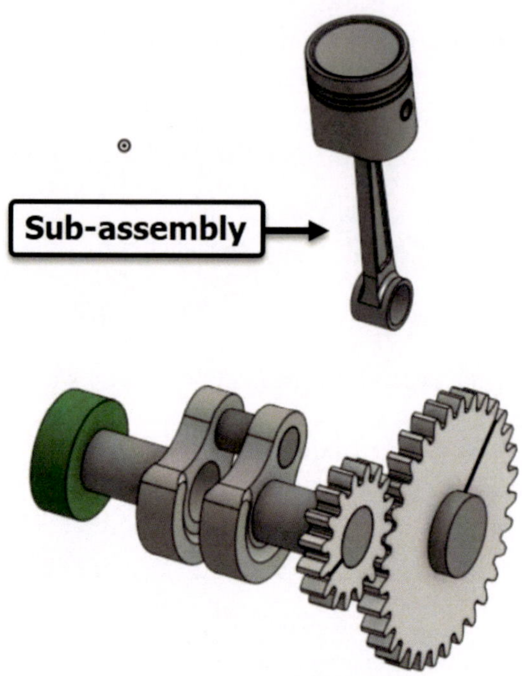

Next, apply mates to mate the assembly. The process of applying mates is very simple. You are required to apply mates between only one part of a sub-assembly and a part of the main assembly. In addition to that, you can easily hide or suppress a group of parts with the help of sub-assemblies.

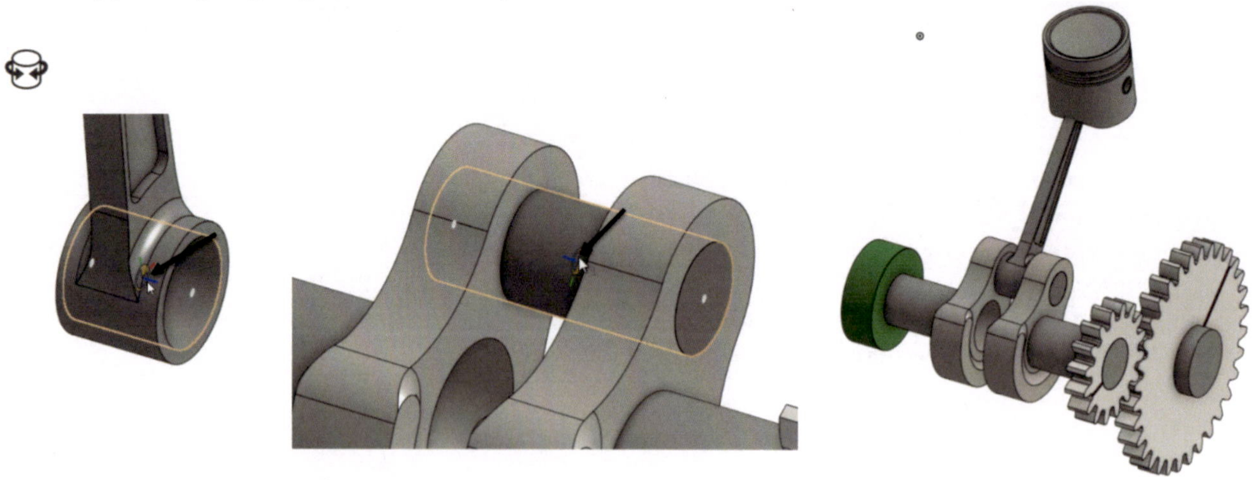

Creating a sub-assembly from parts

In addition to creating sub-assemblies and inserting them into another assembly, you can also take individual parts that already exist in an assembly and make them into a sub-assembly. To do this, select the parts from the assembly. Next, right click and select **Move to new subassembly**; the parts are moved to the new subassembly.

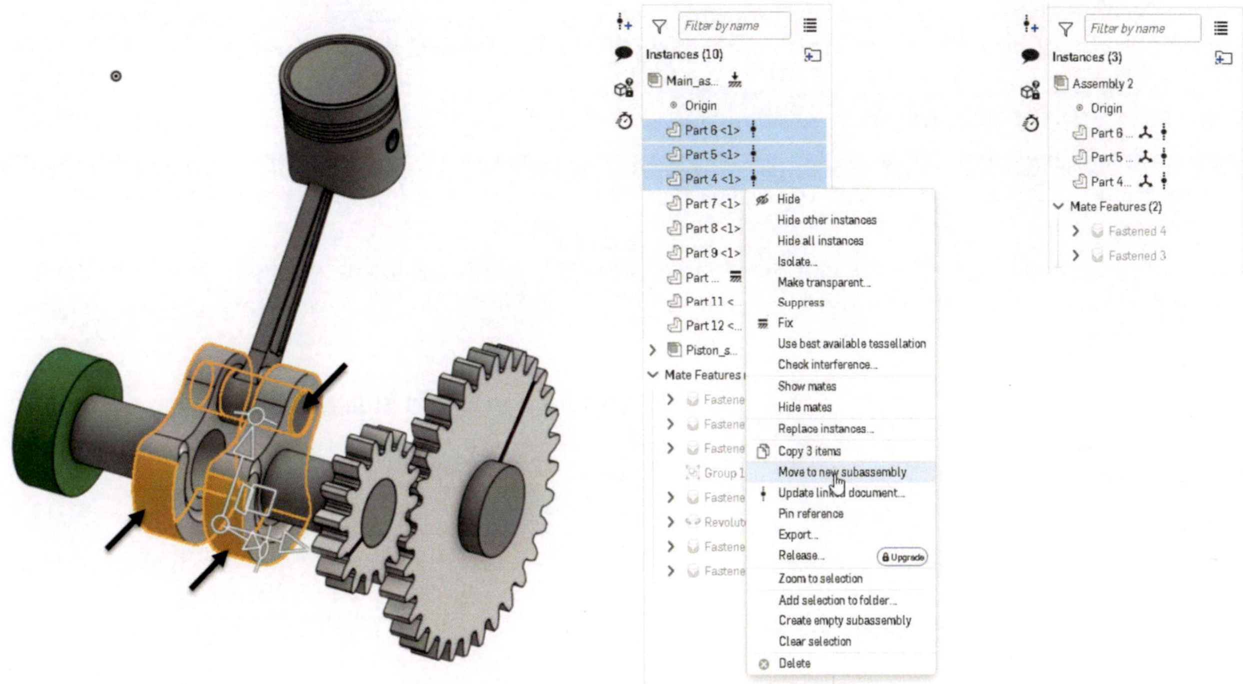

Moving the Parts from Sub-assembly to Main assembly

After inserting subassemblies, you may require to disperse them into individual parts. In the **Assembly** list, expand the subassembly and select the part to be dispersed. Next, click and drag the part under the sub-assembly into the main assembly.

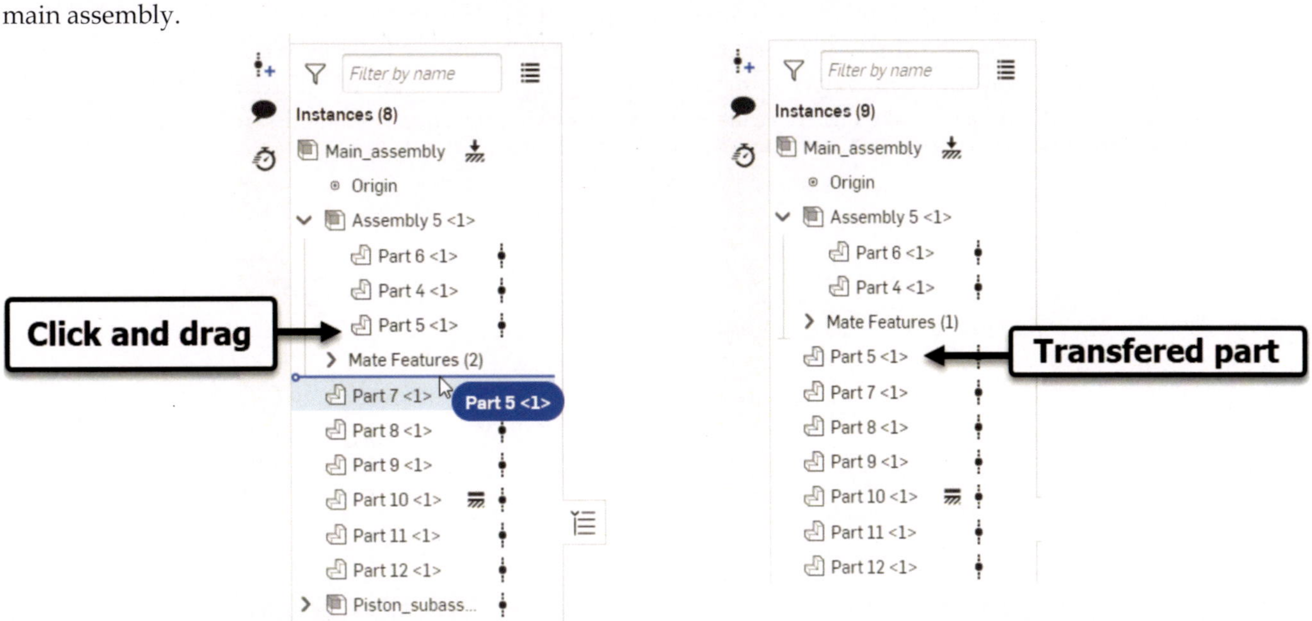

Top-Down Assembly Design

In Onshape, there are two methods to create an assembly. The first method is to create individual parts, and then insert them into an assembly. This method is known as Bottom-Up Assembly Design. The second method is called Top Down Assembly Design. In this method, you will create individual parts within the assembly environment. This allows you to design an individual part while considering how it will interact with other parts in an assembly.

There are several advantages in Top-Down Assembly Design. As you design a part within the assembly, you can be sure that it will fit properly. You can also use the edge from the other parts as a reference.

Create Part Studio in context

Top-down assembly design can be used to add new parts to an already existing assembly. You can also use it to create assemblies that are entirely new. To create a part using the Top Down Design approach in the existing assembly, right-click **Origin > Create Part Studio in context**  in the **Instances** window. Next, click the green check on the **Origin of new Part Studio** dialog; Part Studio is activated. Now, you can draw a sketch and create the part features.

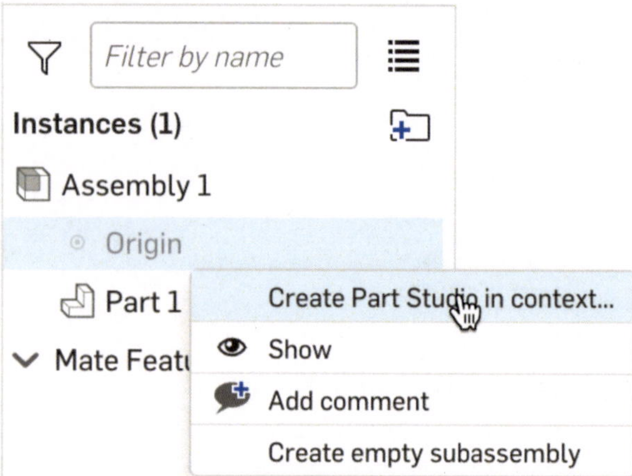

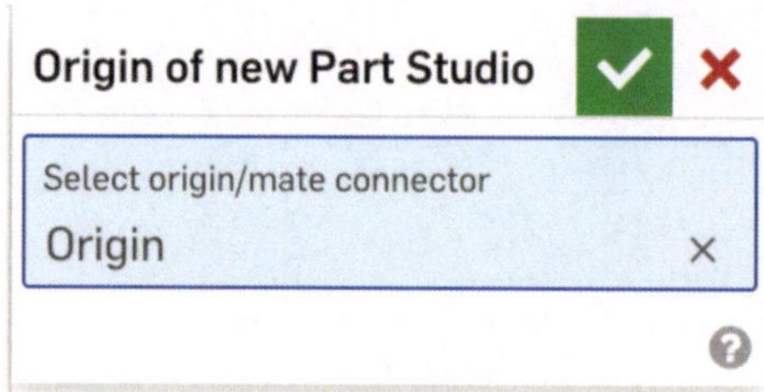

Click **Sketch** icon on the toolbar and select a face on the first part; the part is created and opened in the Part environment. Now, create the features of the part, and then close and return to the assembly. In the example given in the figure, the **Use(project/convert)** command is used to project the edges of the existing part to create a sketch. Next, extrude the projected sketch. This makes it easy to create a part using the edges of the existing part.

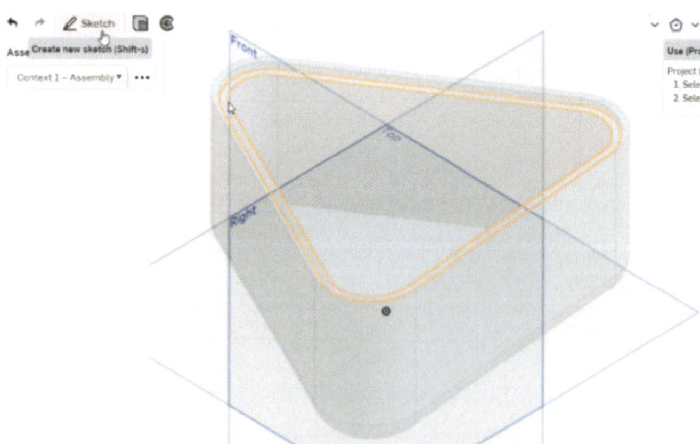

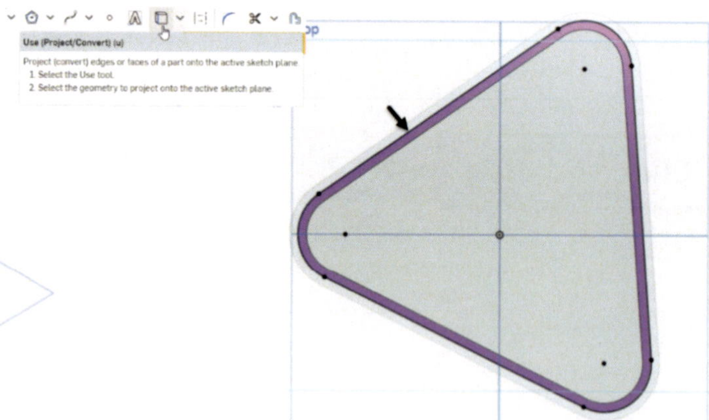

A contextual toolbar is displayed in the graphics window in orange color. It has two options: **Insert and go to Assembly** and **Go to Assembly**. Click the **Insert and go to Assembly** option to insert the created part into the assembly. Click the **Go to Assembly** option to switch to the Assembly studio without inserting the created part. Next, click green check on the **Select items to insert** dialog to confirm inserting the part into the assembly.

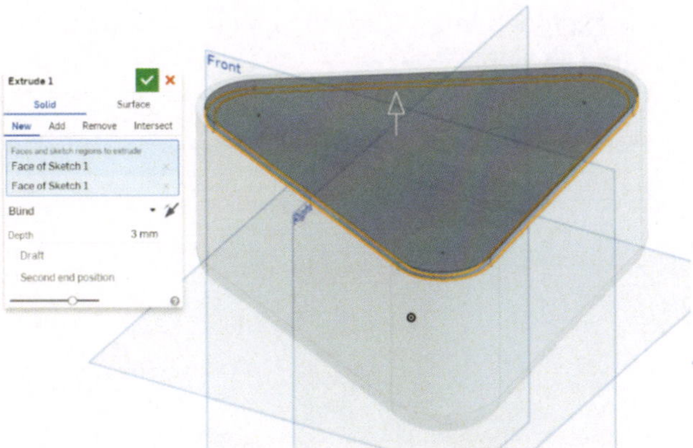

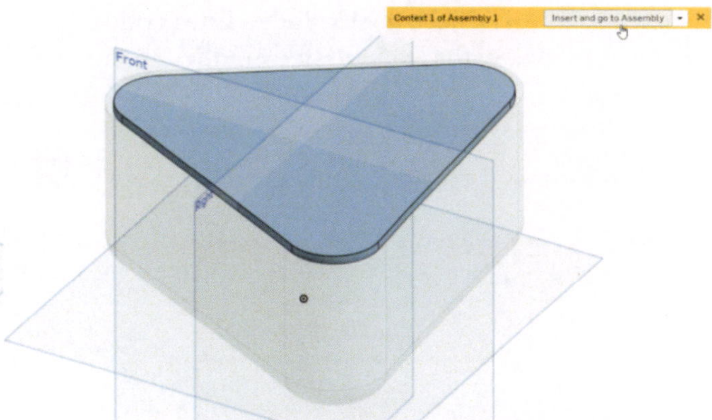

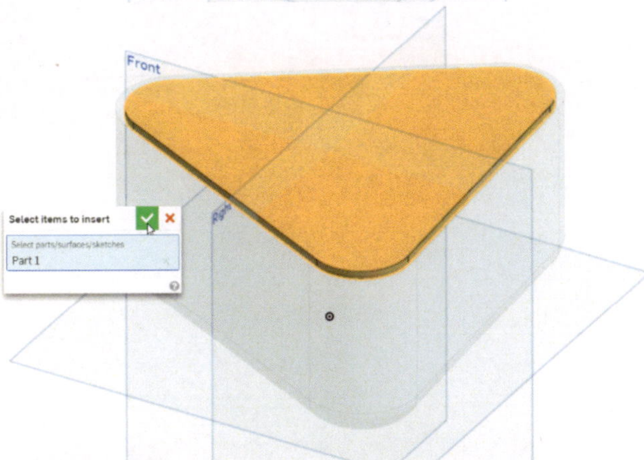

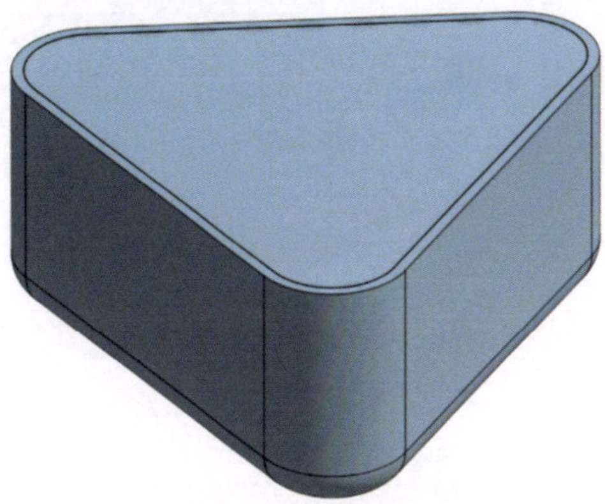

Now, if you change the parameters of the base component, the linked component will also change, automatically. To update the linked component manually, right-click on the linked component in the **Assembly** list and select **Update context > Context 1**.

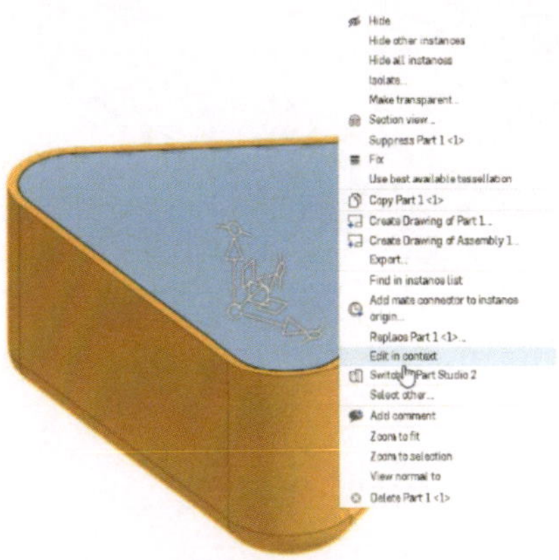

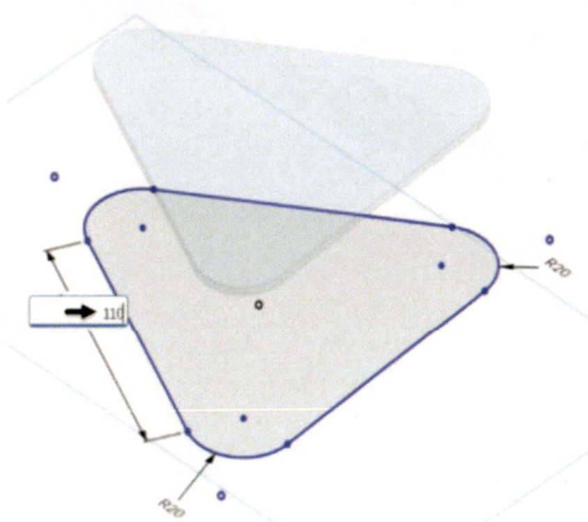

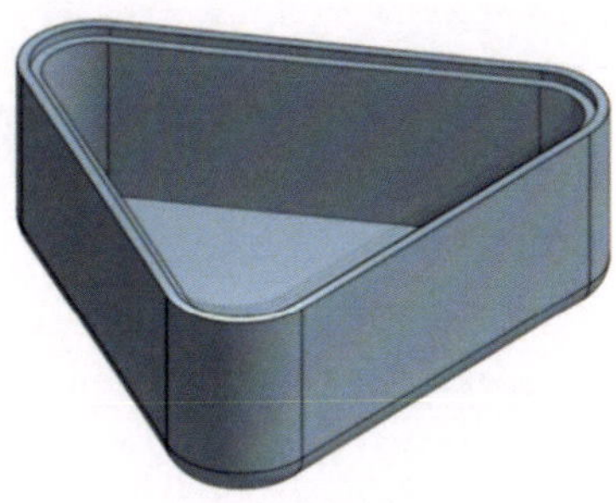

Exploding Assemblies

To document an assembly design properly, it is very common to create an exploded view. In an exploded view, the parts of an assembly are pulled apart to show how they were assembled. To create an exploded view, click the **Exploded views** tab located at the right-side of the window; the **Exploded views** panel appears. Click the **Add exploded view** button on the Exploded views panel. Next, select the component(s) to be exploded; the manipulator appears on the selected component(s). Select any one of the arrows of the manipulator to define the explosion direction. Next, press and hold the left mouse button on the selected arrow, and then drag it. Next, release the mouse button; the **Explode step** dialog appears. You can specify the exact explode distance in the

Distance box. Next, check the **Exploded lines** option to create the exploded lines. Click the green check on the Explode step dialog; the explode step is added to the **Exploded Step** section.

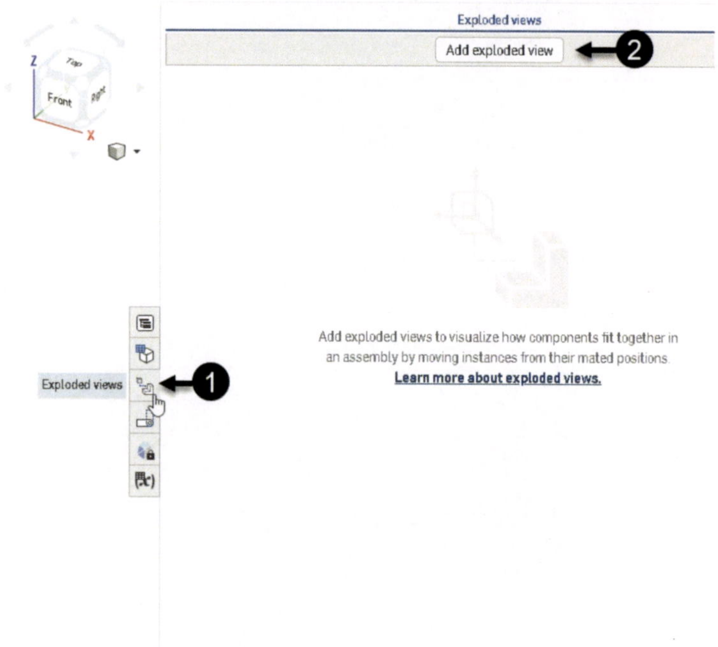

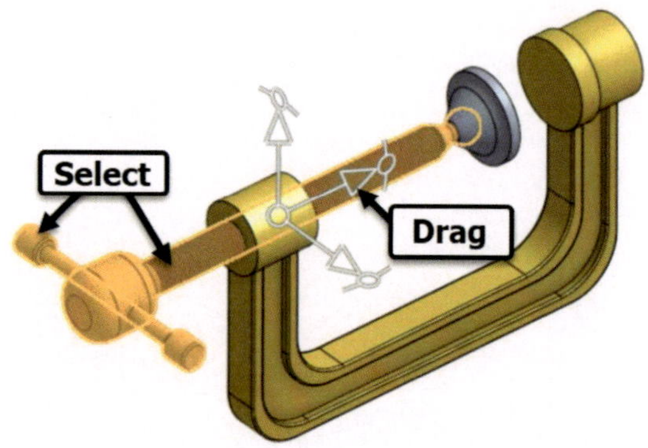

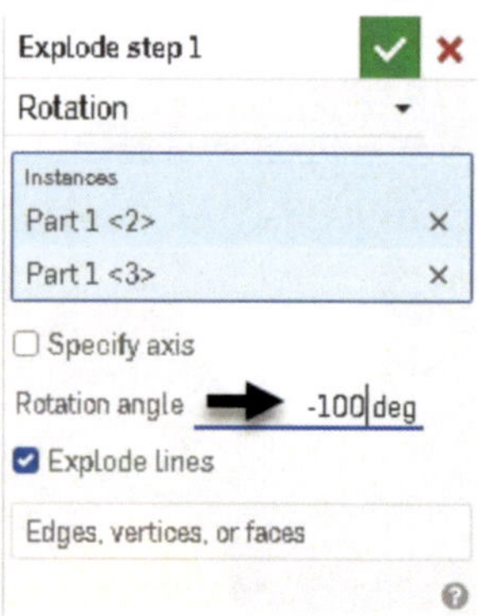

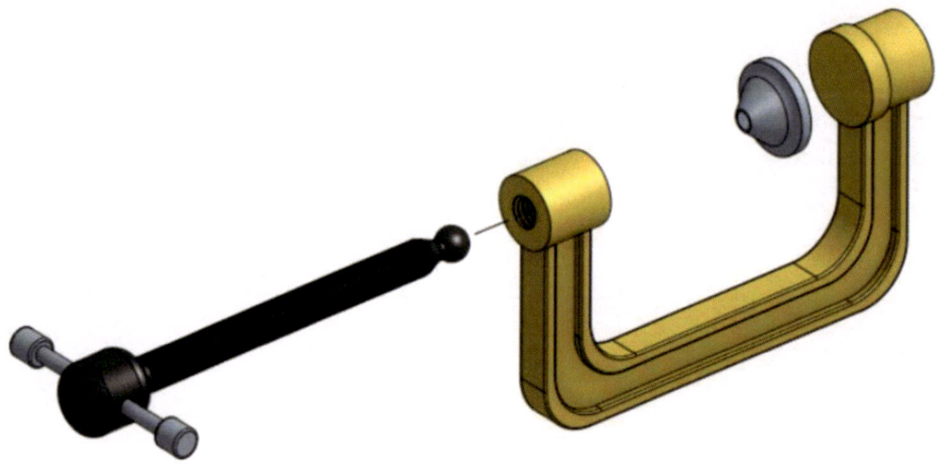

Likewise, explode the other component, and then click **Done**.

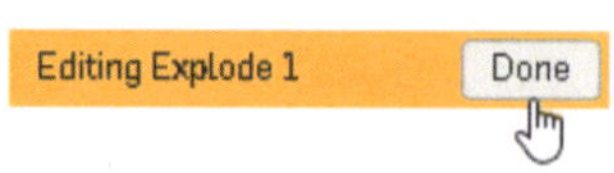

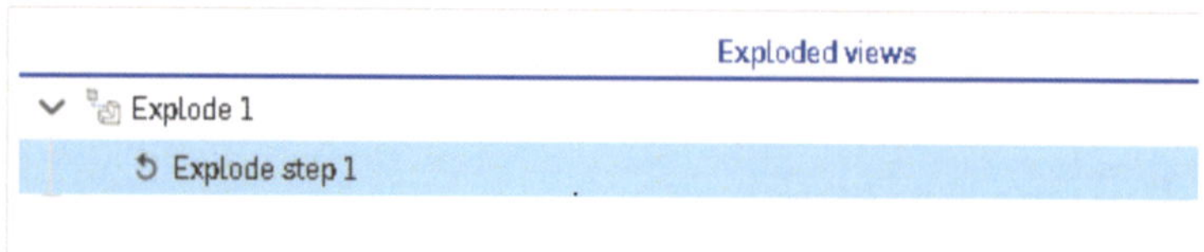

Tutorial 1 (Bottom-Up Assembly)

In this example, you create the assembly shown below.

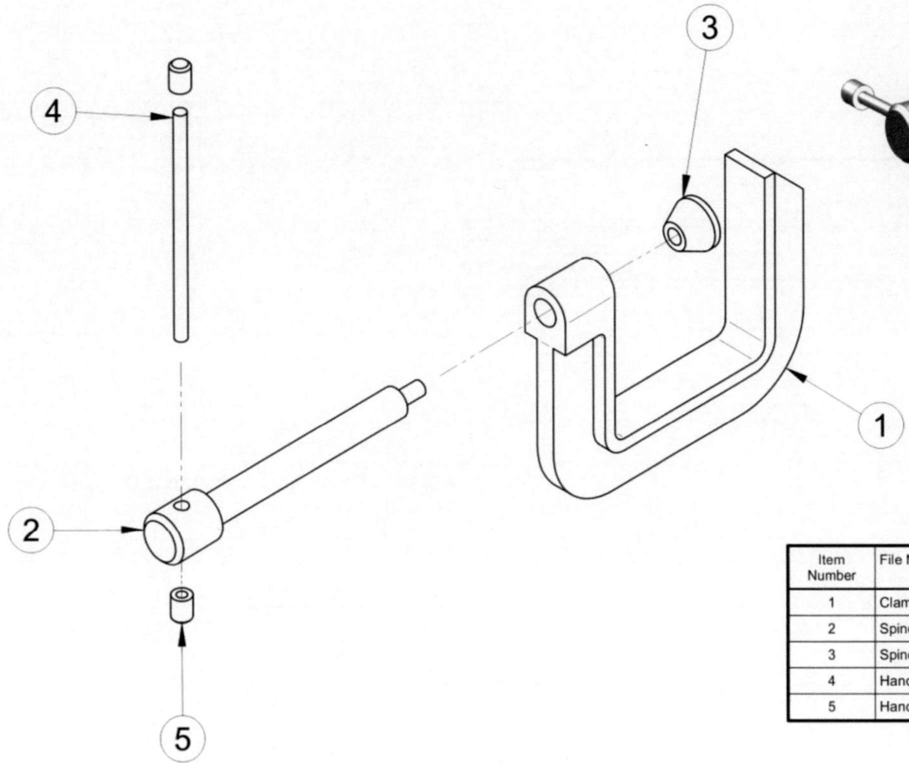

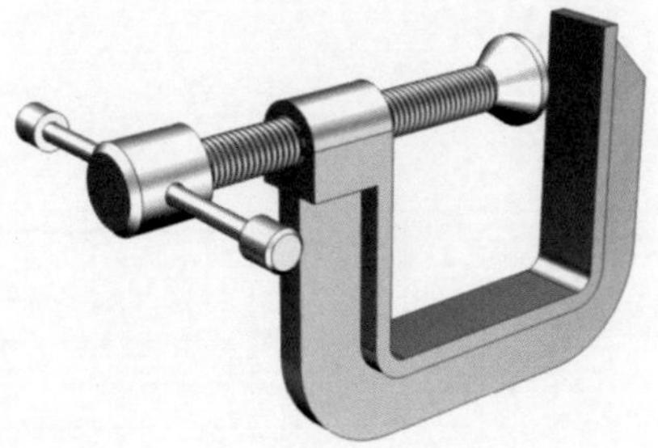

Item Number	File Name (no extension)	Quantity
1	Clamp Jaw	1
2	Spindle	1
3	Spindle Cap	1
4	Handle	1
5	Handle Cap	2

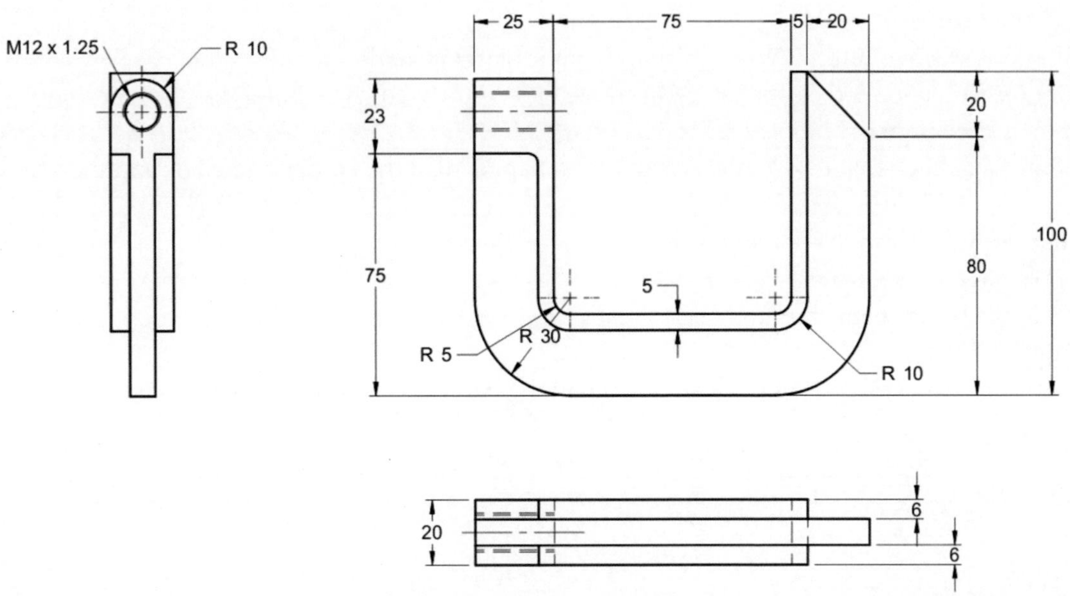

CLAMP JAW

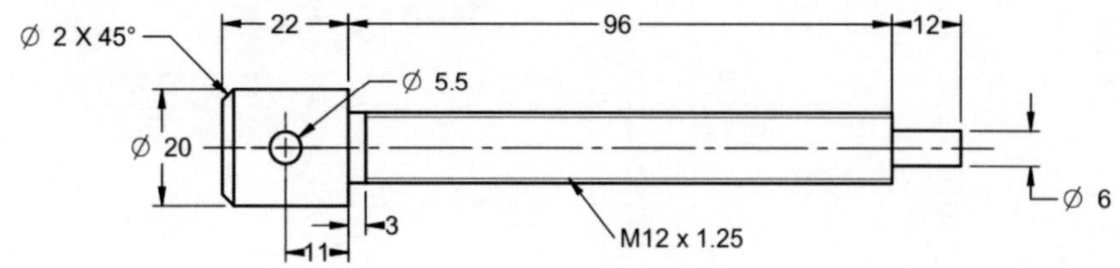

SPINDLE

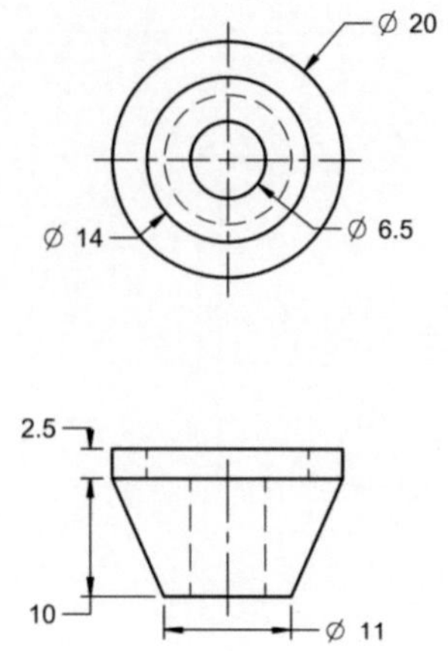

SPINDLE CAP

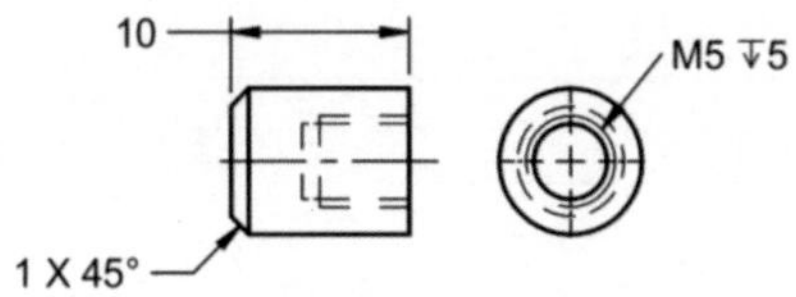

HANDLE CAP

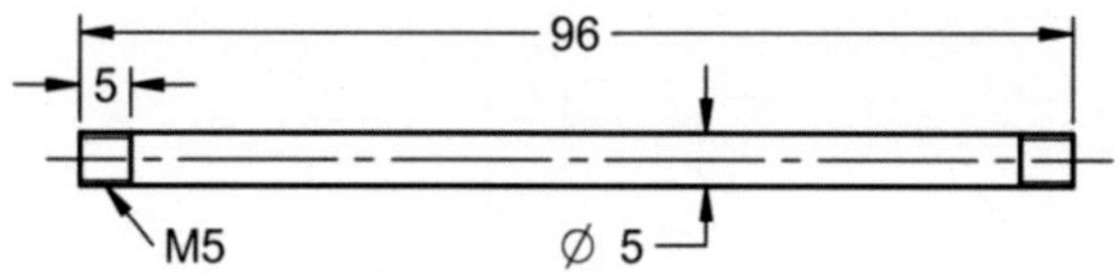

HANDLE

Creating the Part files

1. In your Internet Browser, go to https://www.onshape.com to start Onshape.
2. Next, click **SIGN IN** button located on the top right corner side of the web page. Enter the username and password, and then, click **Sign in**.
3. On the Documents page, click **Create > Folder**. Next, type Chapter 10 in the **Folder name** box and then click **Create**.
4. Click on the **Chapter 10** folder in the **Folders** section.
5. On the Documents page, click **Create > Folder**.
6. Enter **Tutorial 1** in the **Folder name** box and click **Create**.
7. Click on the **Tutorial 1** folder.
8. Create all the parts of the assembly. You can also download the part files from the companion website.

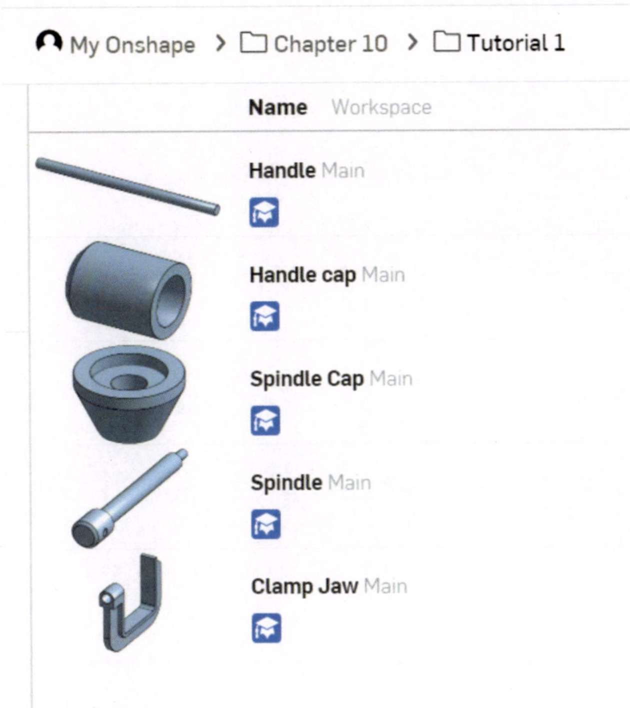

9. On the **Documents** page, click **Create > Document**; the **New document** dialog appears on the screen.
10. Enter **Tutorial 1** in the **Document name** box and click **Create public document**.
11. Click the **Document menu** located at the top left corner of the window and select **Workspace Units**; the **Workspace Units** dialog appears on the screen.
12. On the Workspace Units dialog, select **Length default unit> Millimeter** from **Length** section.
13. Select **Mass default unit > Gram** from the **Mechanical** section.
14. Leave the other default settings and click the green check.

Inserting part files in the Assemblies

1. Click the **Assembly 1** tab at the bottom of the graphics area.
2. On the toolbar, click **Insert parts and assemblies** command; the **Insert parts and assemblies** dialog appears.
3. On the **Insert parts and assemblies** dialog, click the **Other documents** tab and select **My Onshape**.
4. Expand **Chapter 10** and then click the **Tutorial 1** folder.
5. Select the **Clamp Jaw** part file from the list; a message appears that the part is not versioned.
6. Click the **Create a version in Clamp Jaw** link, and then click the **Create** button; a new version of the **Clamp Jaw** part file is created.
7. Likewise, create version files for the remaining parts, as shown.

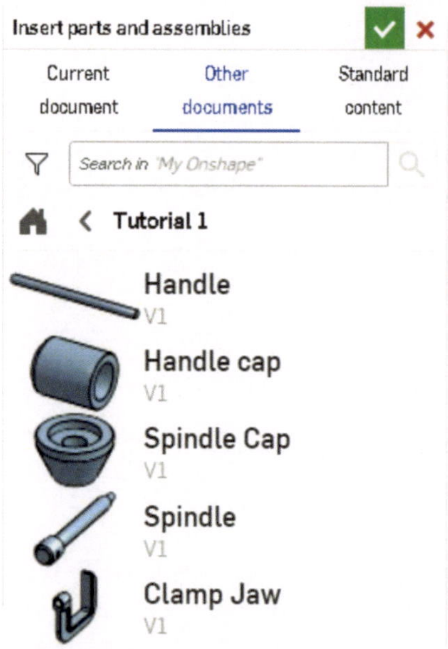

8. Select the **Clamp Jaw** file and select **Part Studio 1**. Next, click in the graphics area to place the clamp jaw.
9. Next, right click on the **Clamp jaw** in the graphics area and select **Fix**; the part is fixed at its position.

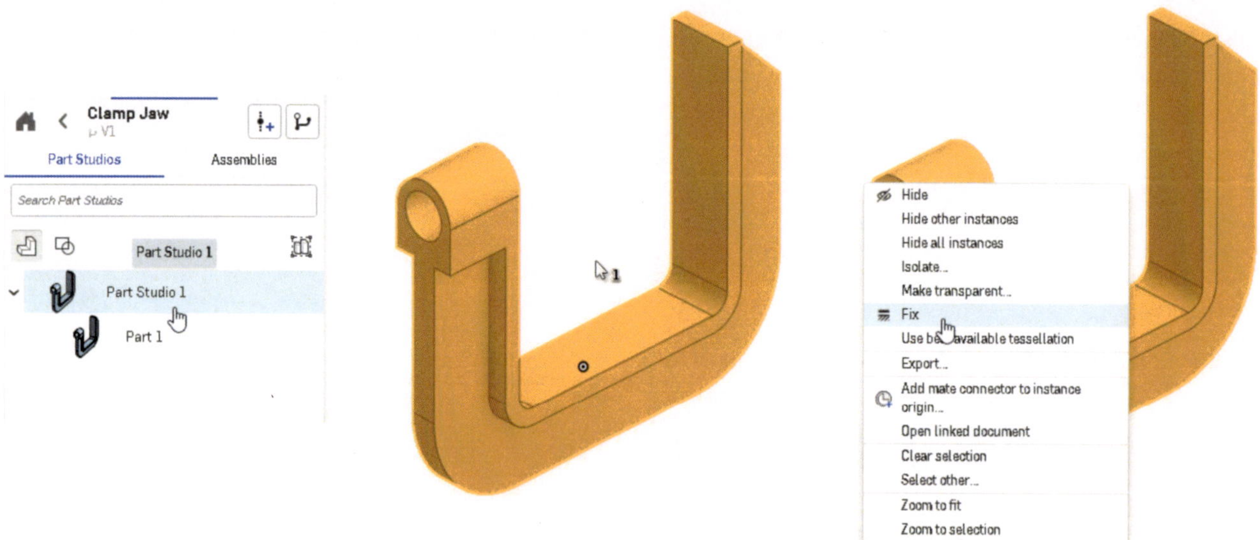

10. On the **Insert part and assemblies** dialog, click the arrow button next to Clamp Jaw.
11. On the **Insert parts and assemblies** dialog, click *Spindle*, and then click **Part Studio 1**. Click in the graphics area to place the component.

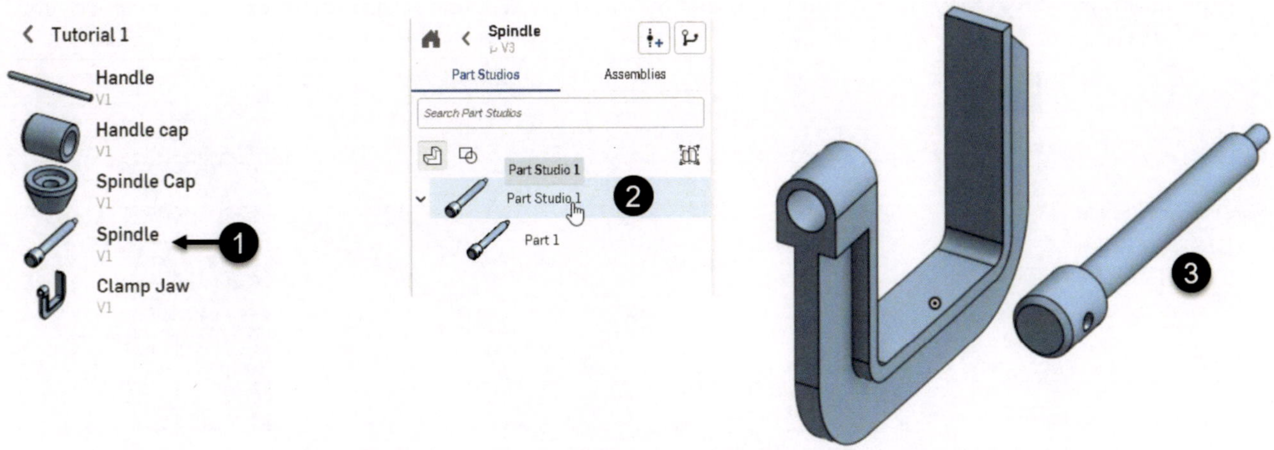

12. Likewise insert the *Spindle Cap, Handle,* and two instances of *Handle Caps*. Next, click the green check on the **Insert parts and assemblies** dialog.

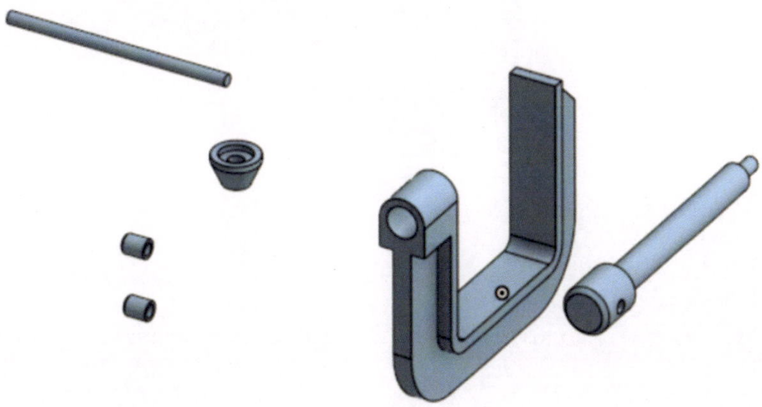

Adding the Cylindrical mate

1. On the toolbar, click the **Cylindrical mate** command.
2. Select the circular edge of the *Spindle* and the *Clamp Jaw*.

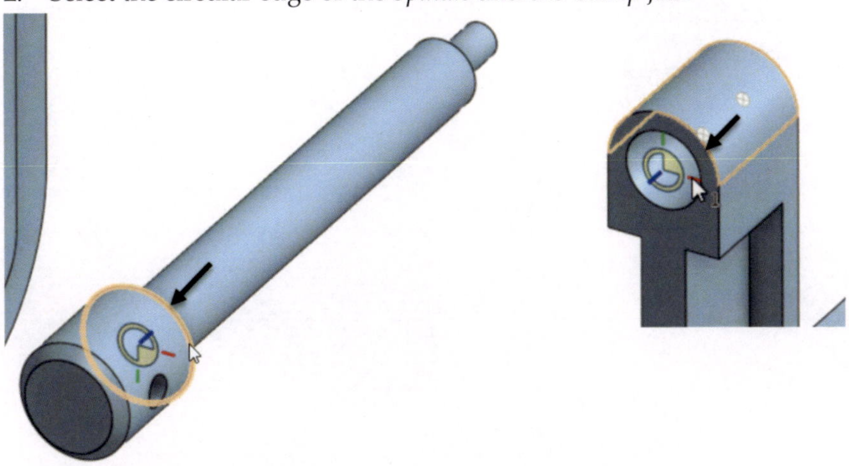

3. On the **Cylindrical 1** dialog, check the **Limit** option.

4. Type-in **-31** and **-16** in the **Limit Z minimum distance** and **Limit Z maximum distance** boxes, respectively. Next, click the green check on the dialog.

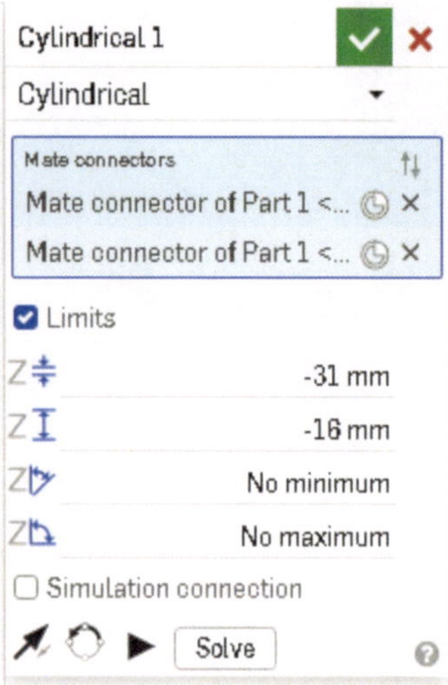

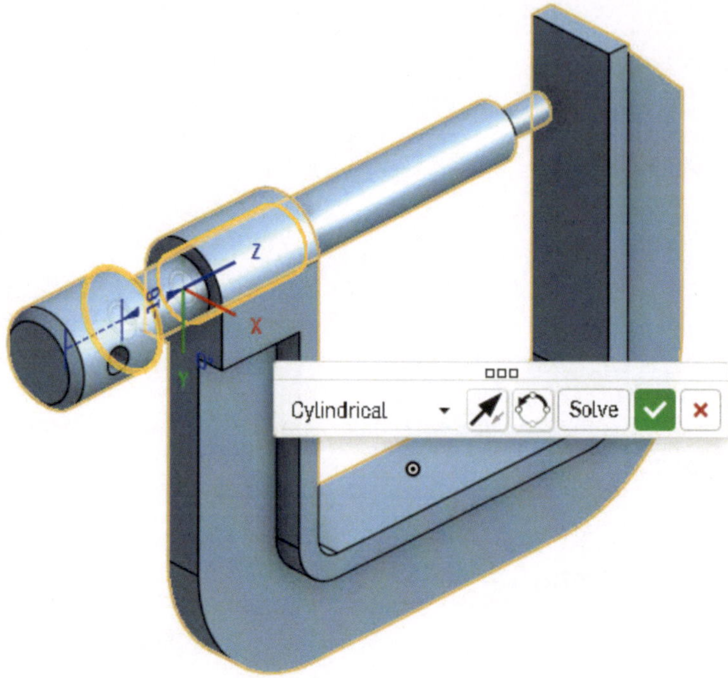

Adding the Fastened mate

1. Click the **Fastened mate** command on the toolbar.
2. Click on the circular edge of the *Spindle Cap* hole, as shown.
3. Click on the circular edge of the *Spindle*, as shown; the *Spindle* and *Spindle Cap* are axially aligned and positioned opposite to each other.
4. Click the green check on the **Fastened 1** dialog.

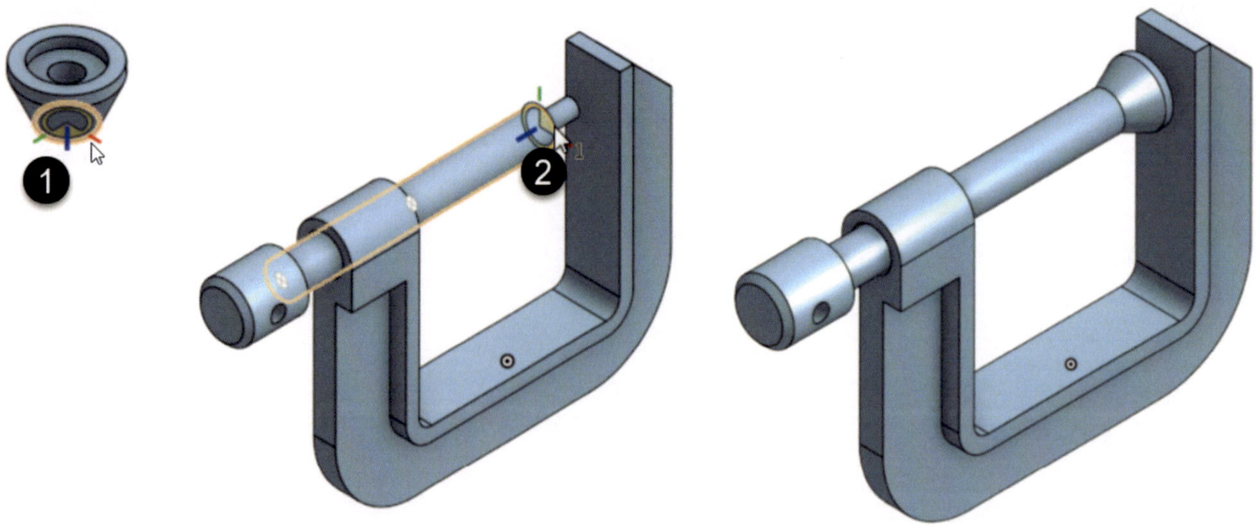

Adding the Slide mate

1. On the toolbar, click the **Slide mate** command.

2. Place the pointer at the midpoint of the *Handle* and select the Mate connector located at the midpoint.
3. Zoom-in to the hole of the *Spindle* and place the pointer on the hole. Next, move the pointer to the midpoint of the hole, and then select the Mate connector located at the midpoint.

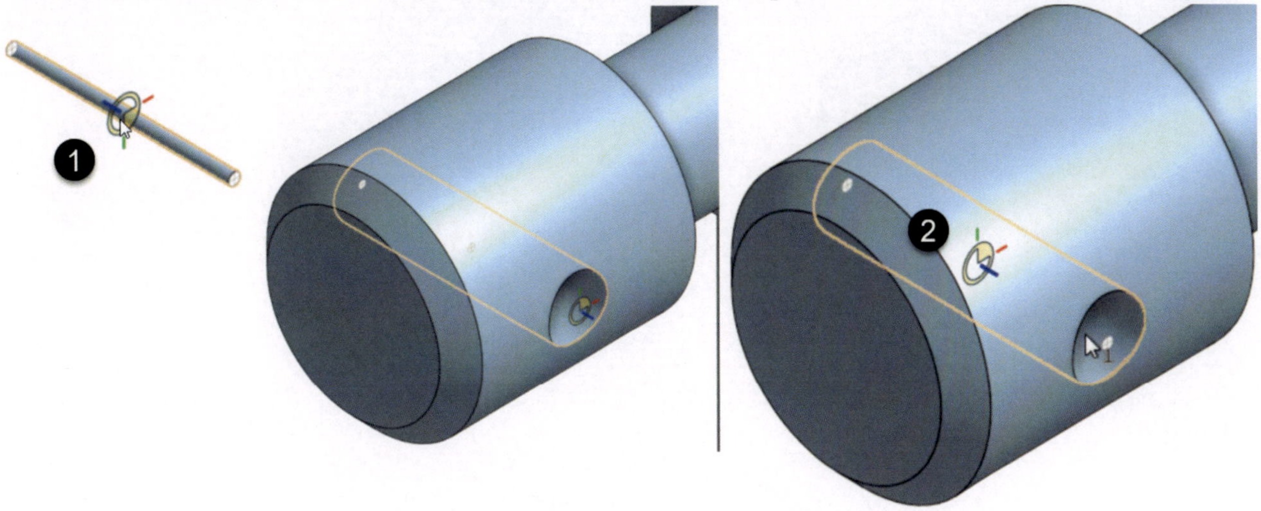

4. On the **Slider 1** dialog, check the **Limit** option.
5. Type-in **-32** and **32** in the **Limit Z minimum distance** and **Limit Z maximum distance** boxes, respectively.
6. Click the **Animate mate degrees of freedom** ▶ icon located at the bottom of the **Slider 1** dialog. Next, click the green check on the dialog.

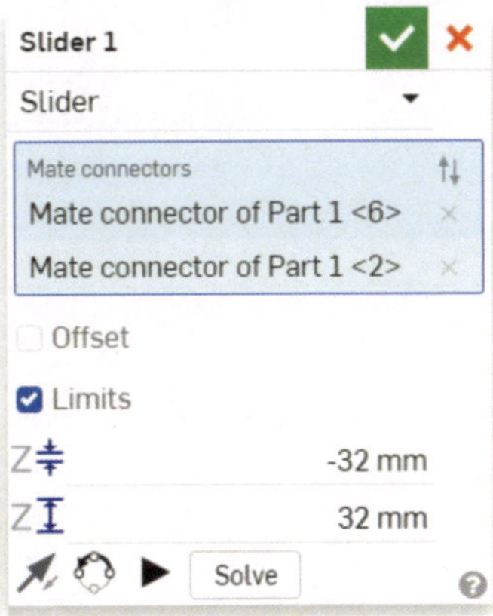

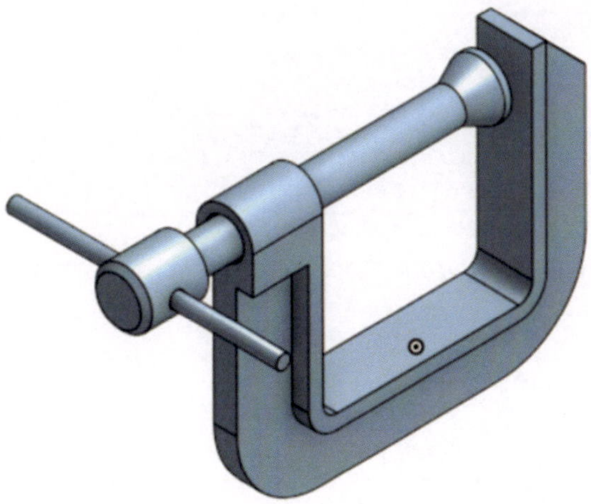

Adding the Revolute mate

1. On the toolbar, click the **Revolute mate** command.
2. Zoom to the hole of the *Handle Cap*, and then place the pointer on the hole. Next, move the pointer and select the Mate connector located at the bottom edge of the hole, as shown.

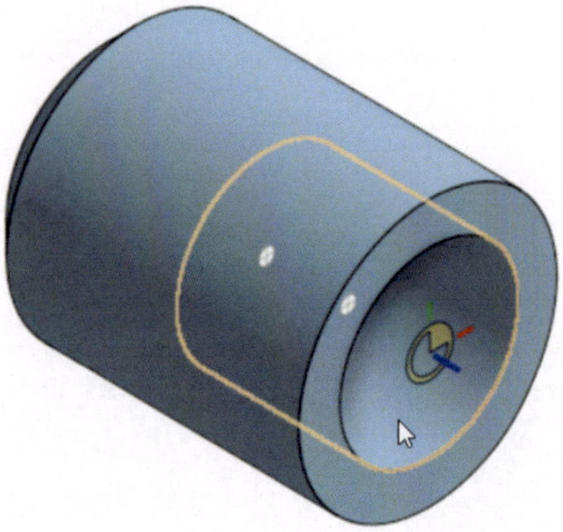

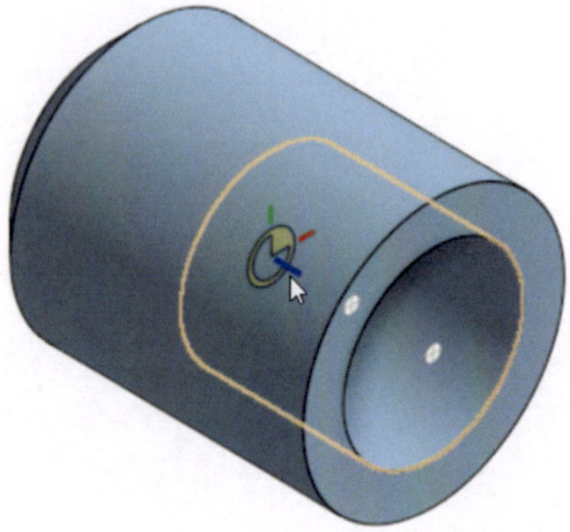

3. Select the circular edge of the *Handle*, as shown. Next, click the **Flip primary axis** icon on the **Revolute 1** dialog.

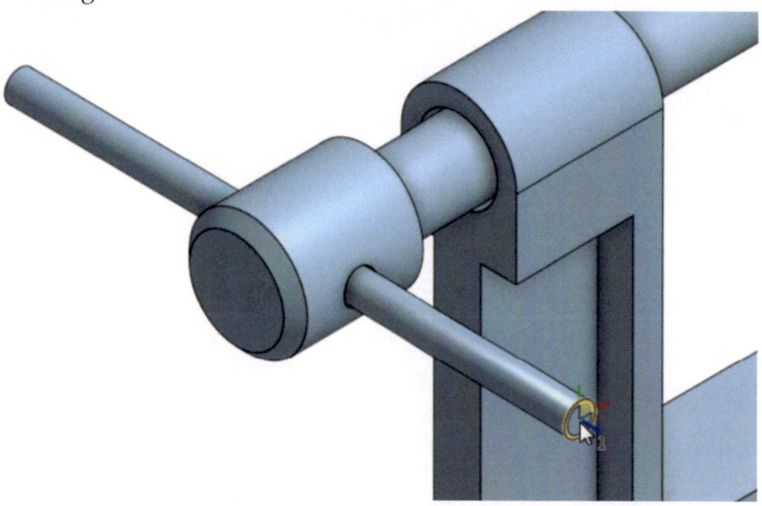

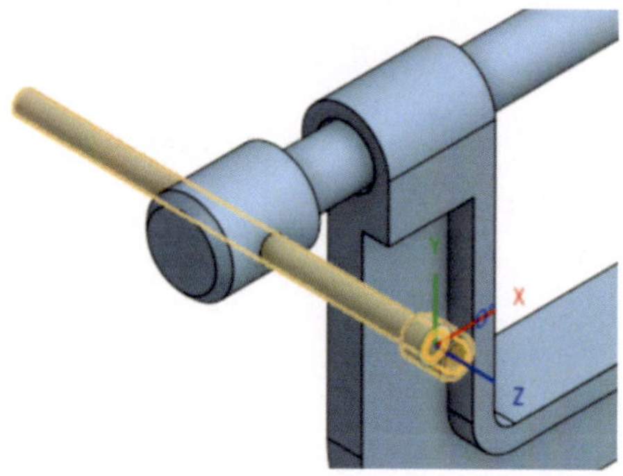

4. Click the **Animate mate degrees of freedom** ▶ icon located at the bottom of the **Revolute 1** dialog. Next, click the green check on the dialog.

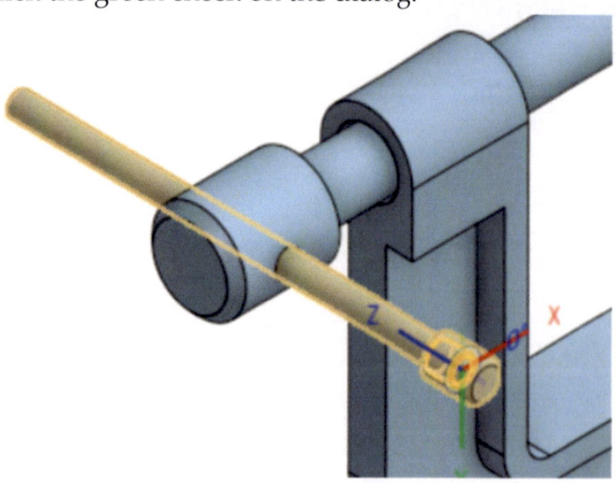

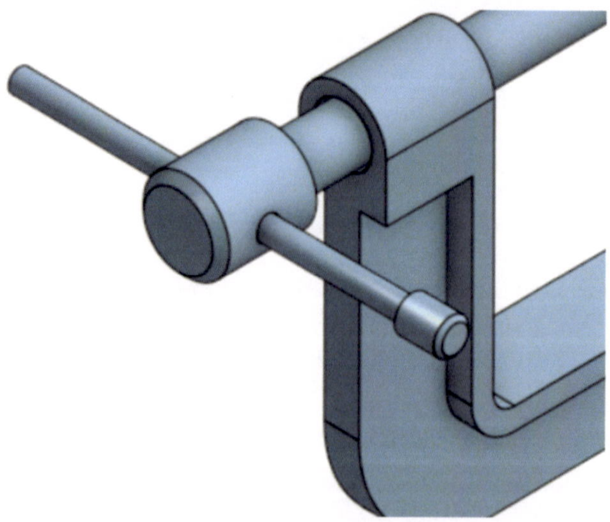

5. Likewise, insert and joint *Handle Cap* on the other side of the *Handle*.

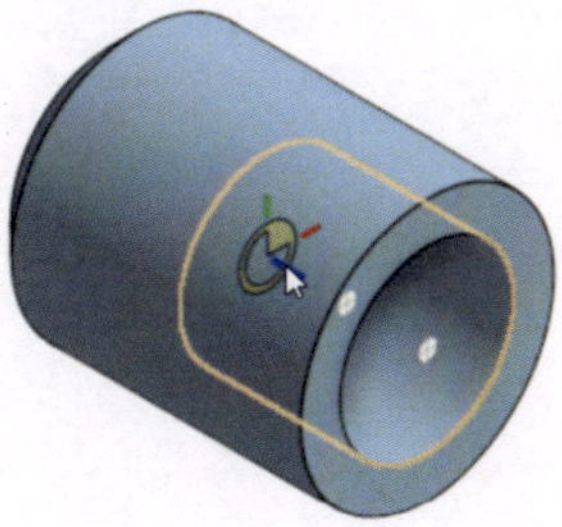 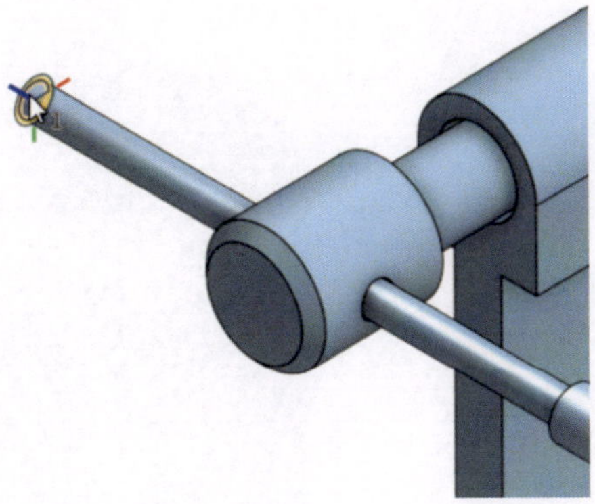 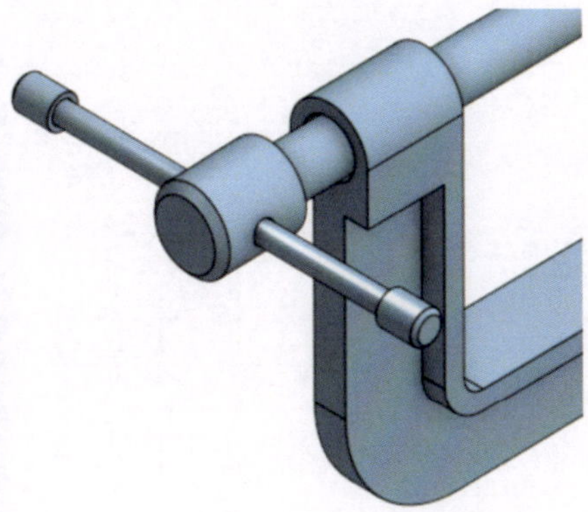

6. Close the assembly file.

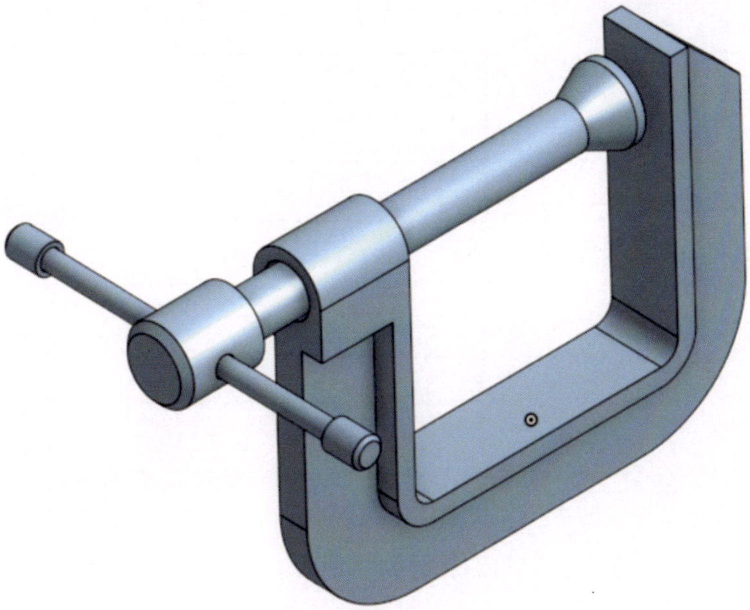

Tutorial 2 (Top-Down Assembly)

In this example, you create the assembly shown below.

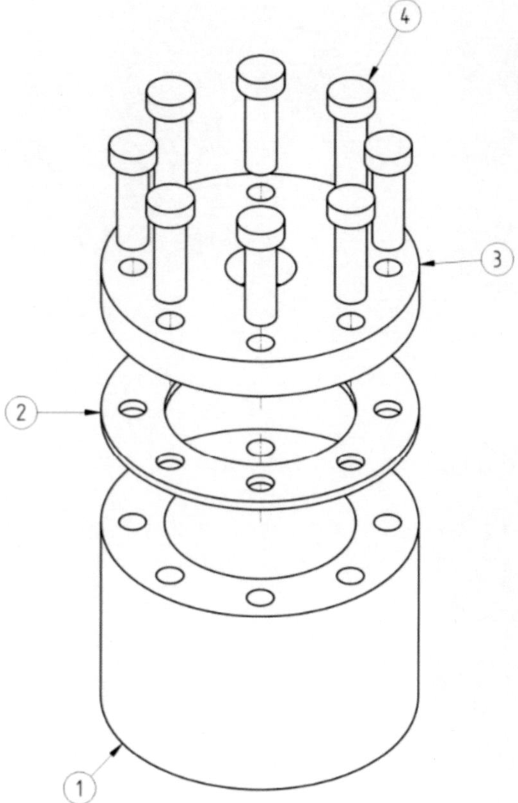

Item Number	File Name (no extension)	Quantity
1	Cylinder base	1
2	Gasket	1
3	Cover plate	1
4	Screw	8

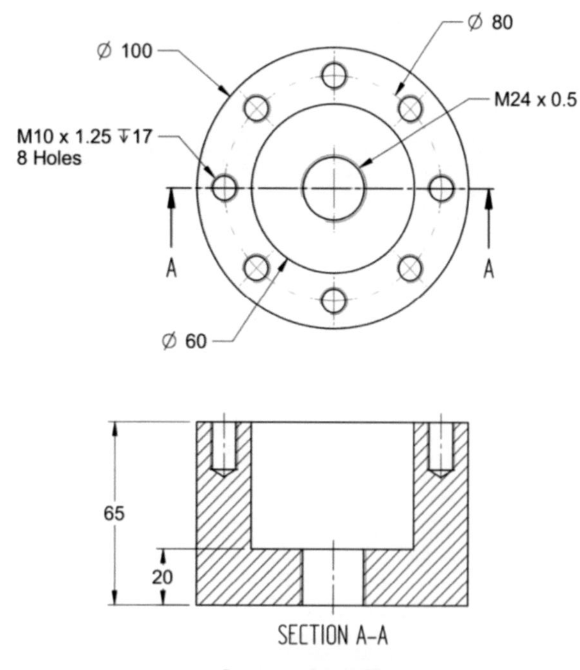

Cylinder Base

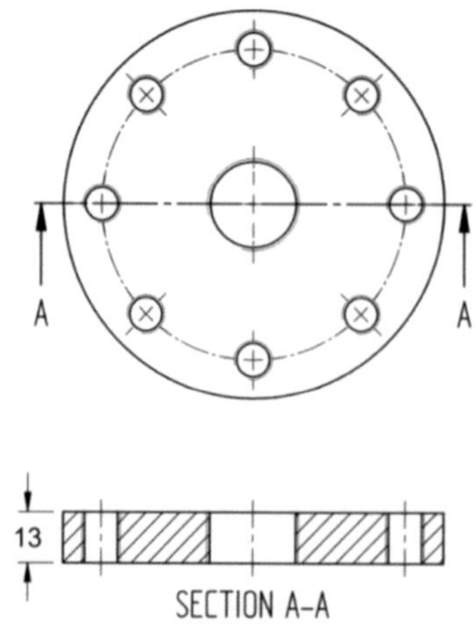

Cover Plate

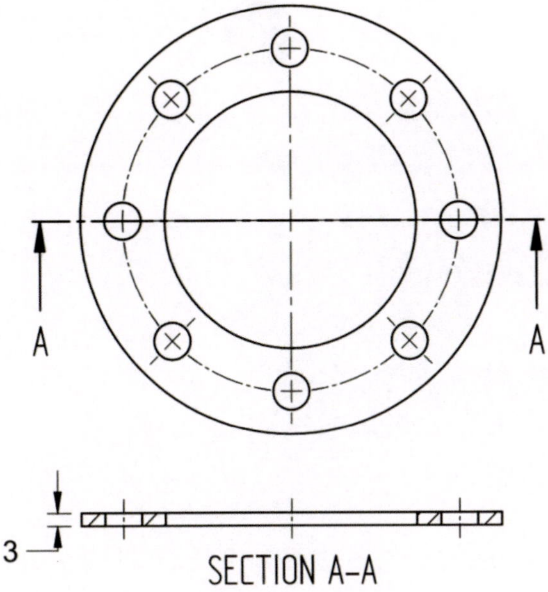

Gasket

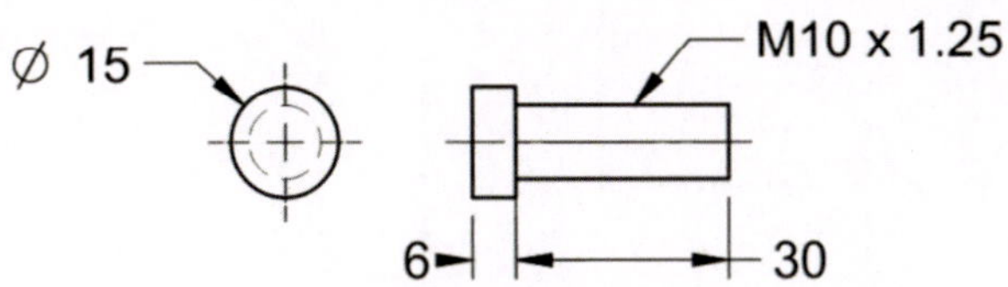

Screw

Creating a New document

1. In your Internet Browser, go to https://www.onshape.com to start Onshape.
2. Next, click the **SIGN IN** button located on the top right corner side of the web page. Enter the username and password, and then, click **Sign in**.
3. Click on the **Chapter 10** folder in the **Folders** section.
4. On the Documents page, click **Create > Folder**.
5. Enter **Tutorial 2** in the **Folder name** box and click **Create**.
6. Click on the **Tutorial 2** folder.
7. On the Documents page, click **Create > Document**; the **New document** dialog appears on the screen.
8. Enter *Pressure Cylinder* in the **Document name** box and click **Create public document**; a new document appears.
9. Click the **Document menu** located at the top left corner of the window and select **Workspace Units**; the **Workspace Units** dialog appears on the screen.
10. On the **Workspace Units** dialog, select **Length default unit> Millimeter** from **Length** section.
11. Select **Mass default unit > Gram** from the **Mechanical** section.
12. Leave the other default settings and click the green check ✓.
13. Click the **Part Studio 1** tab at the bottom of the graphics area.
14. Create a *Cylinder Base* by following the steps illustrated in the figure.

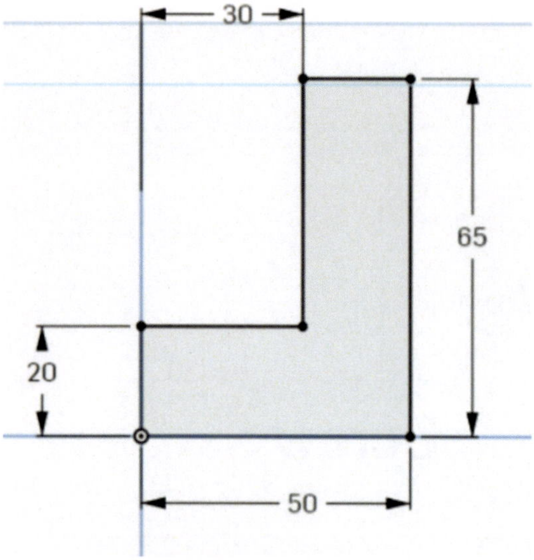
30
65
20
50

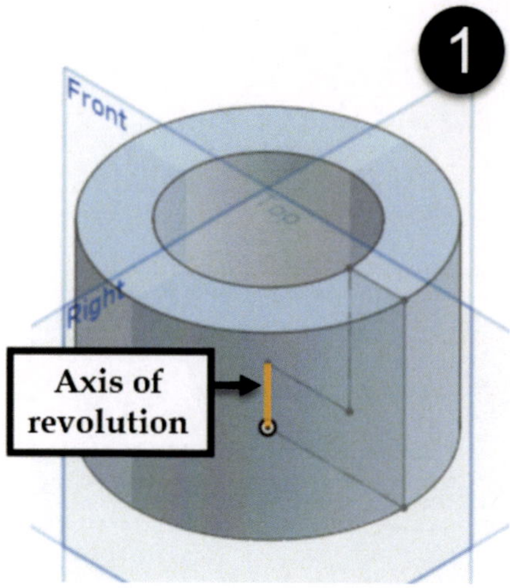
1
Front
Right
Axis of revolution

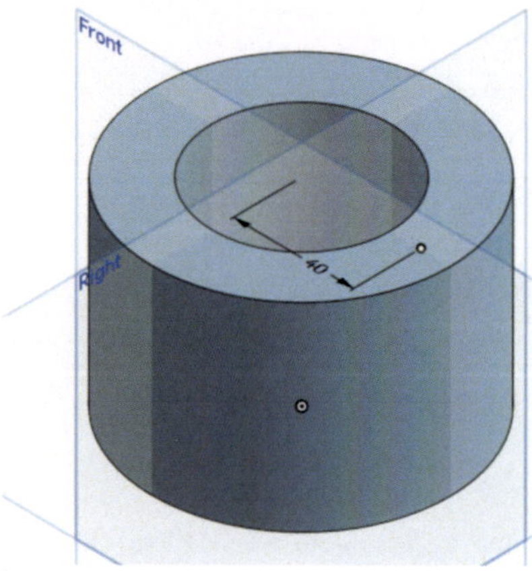
Front
Right
40

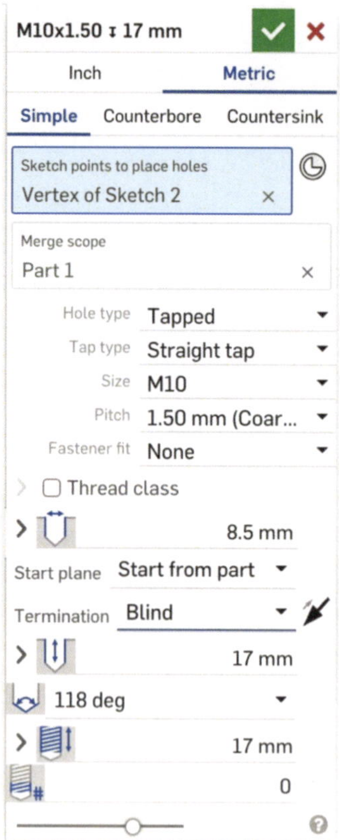
M10x1.50 ↧ 17 mm
Inch
Metric
Simple
Counterbore
Countersink
Sketch points to place holes
Vertex of Sketch 2
Merge scope
Part 1
Hole type Tapped
Tap type Straight tap
Size M10
Pitch 1.50 mm (Coar...
Fastener fit None
Thread class
8.5 mm
Start plane Start from part
Termination Blind
17 mm
118 deg
17 mm
0

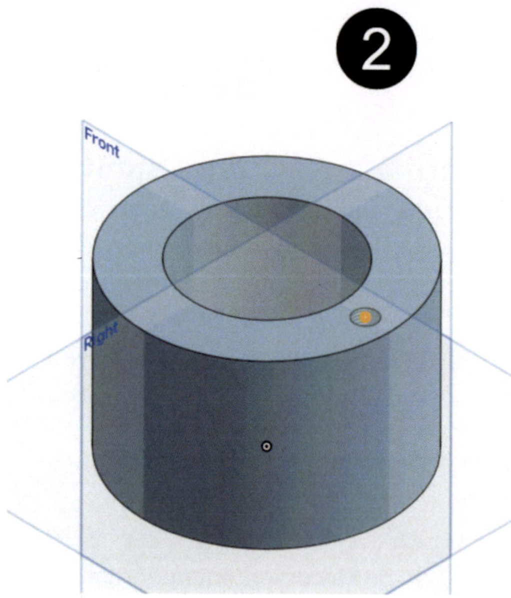
2
Front
Right

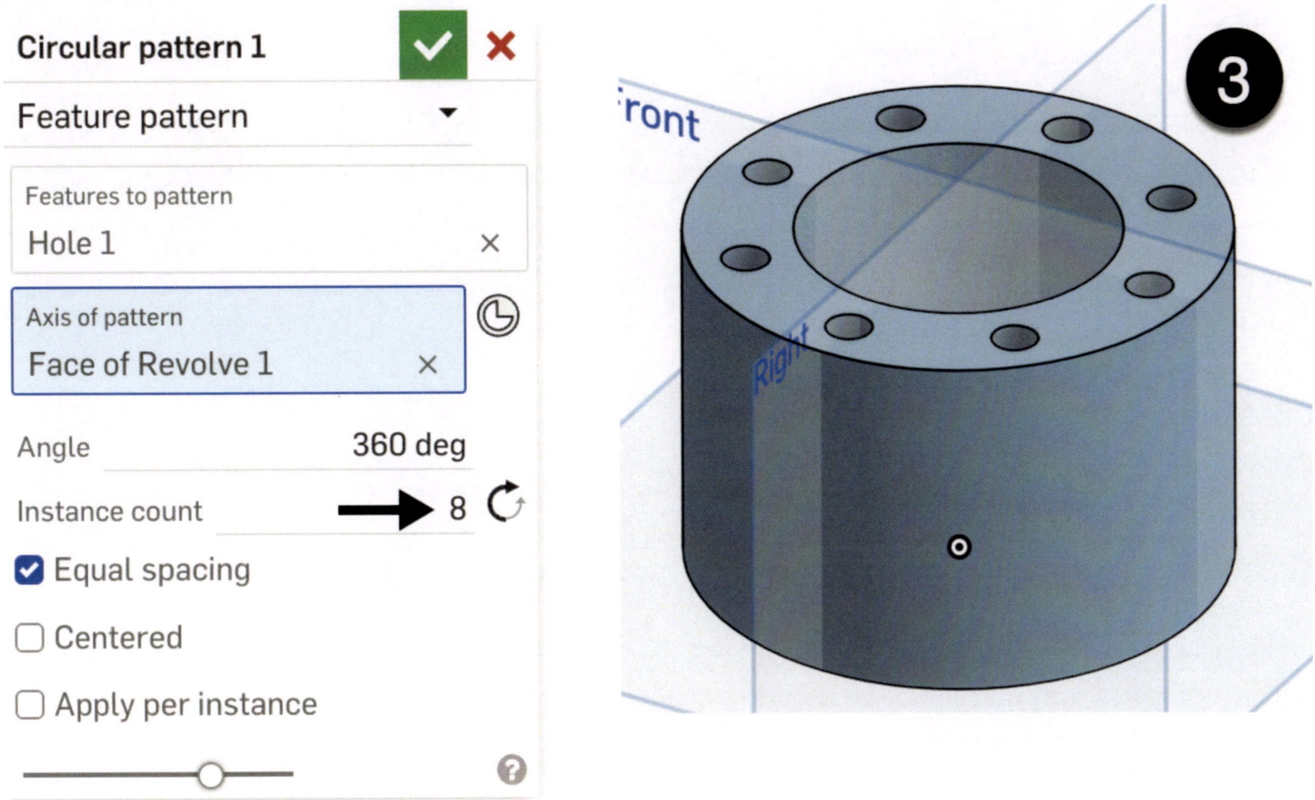

15. Create an offset plane 20 mm above the Top plane. Start a new sketch on this plane, place a point at its center, and use that point to make another hole.

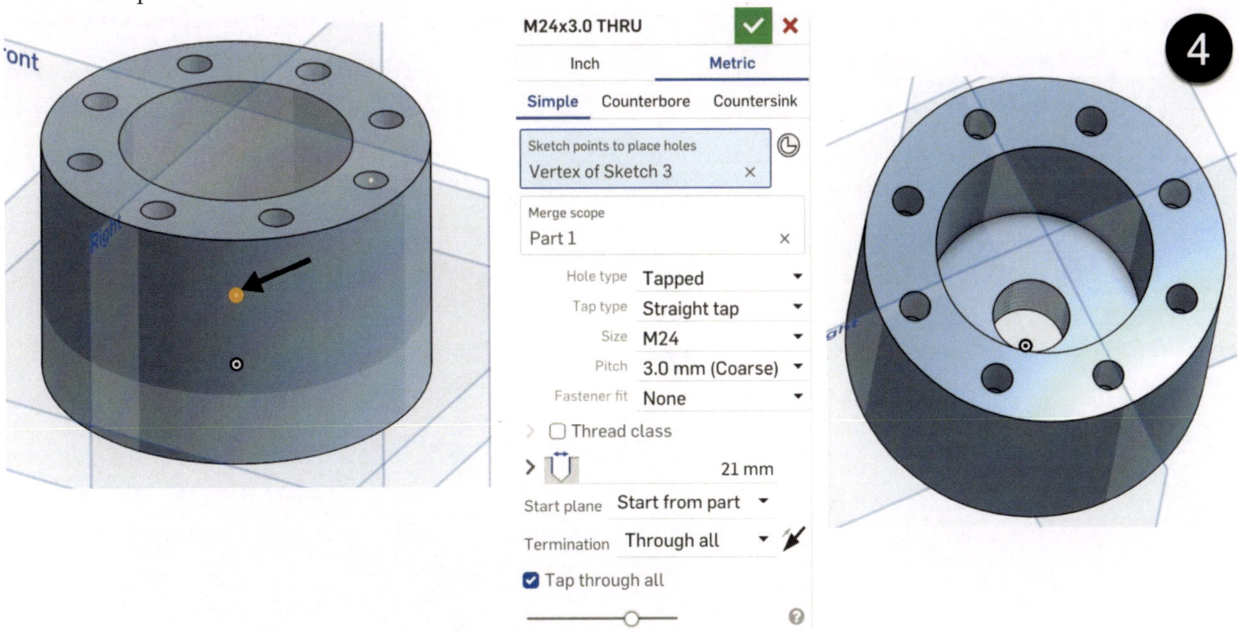

16. Right click on **Part 1** located at the bottom of the **Instances** window, and then select **Rename**.
17. Type **Cylinder Base** in the **Rename** dialog and click the green check.

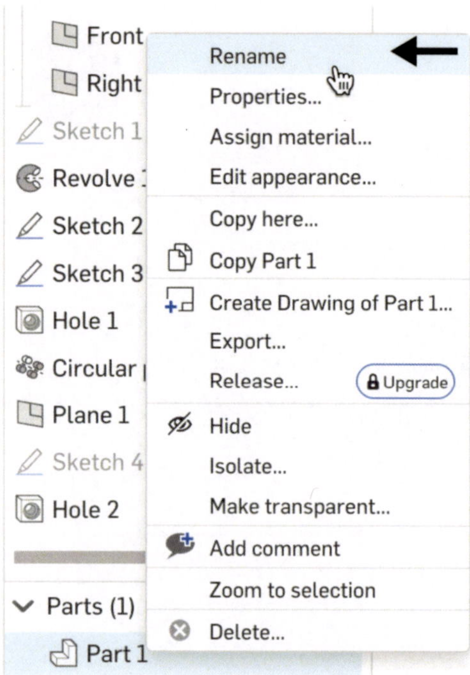

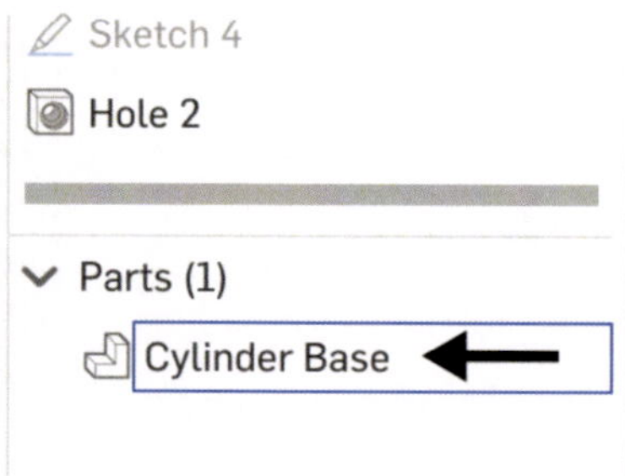

Inserting the Part into the Assembly

1. Click the **Assembly 1** tab at the bottom of the graphics area.
2. Click the **Insert parts and assemblies** command on the toolbar. Next, click the **Current document** tab on the **Insert parts and assemblies** dialog.
3. Expand **Part Studio 1** from the list, and then select Cylinder Base. Next, click the green check on the dialog.

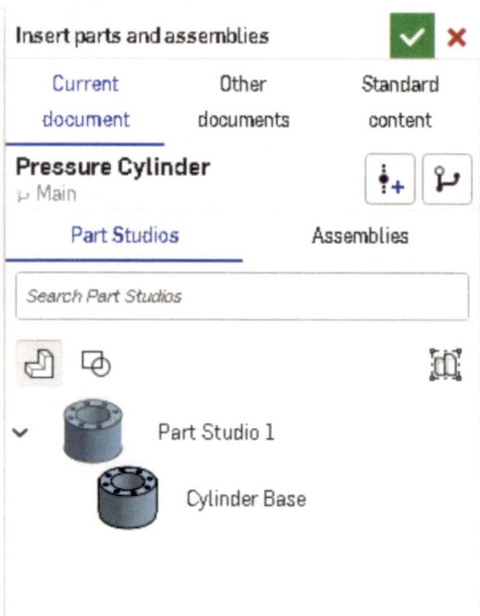

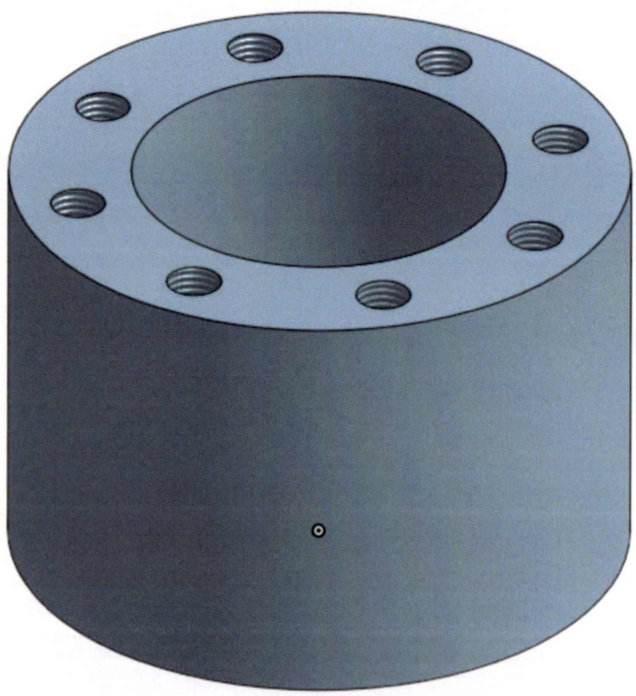

4. Right-click on the Cylinder Base and select **Fix**; the *Cylinder base* is fixed at the same place.

Creating the Mate connector

1. Click the **Mate connector** command on the toolbar and select the center point of the top face of the model, as shown.
2. Click the green check on the **Mate connector 1** dialog to create the mate connector.

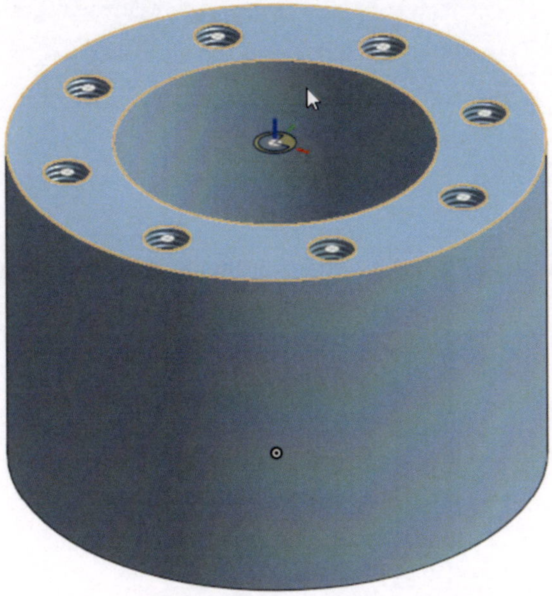

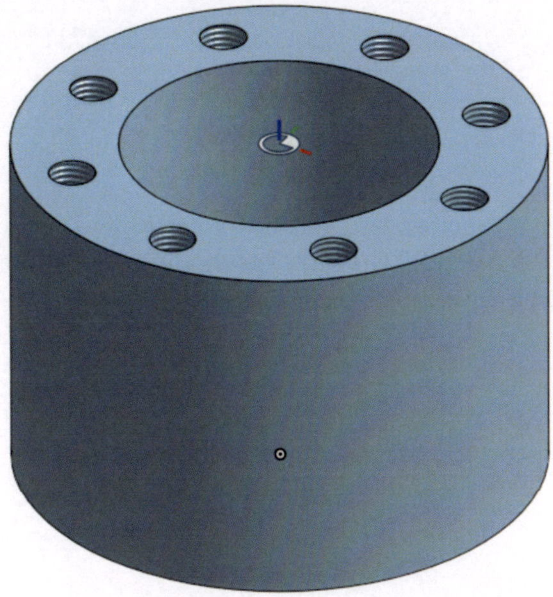

Creating Part Studios in context to the Assembly

1. Click the **Create Part Studio in context** command on the toolbar.
2. Select the newly created mate connector and click the green check on the **Origin of new Part Studio** dialog; the **Part Studio** environment appears.

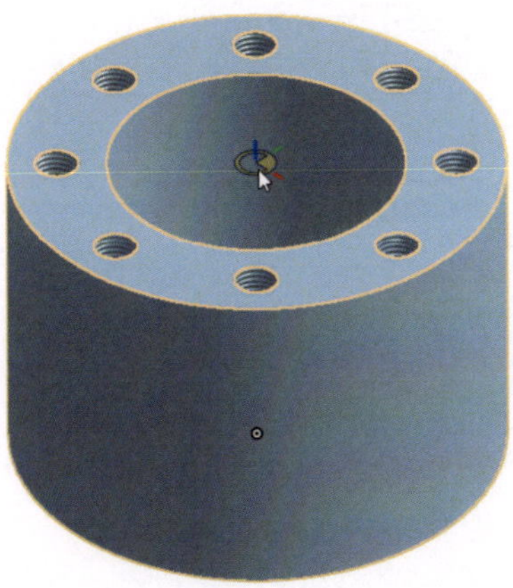

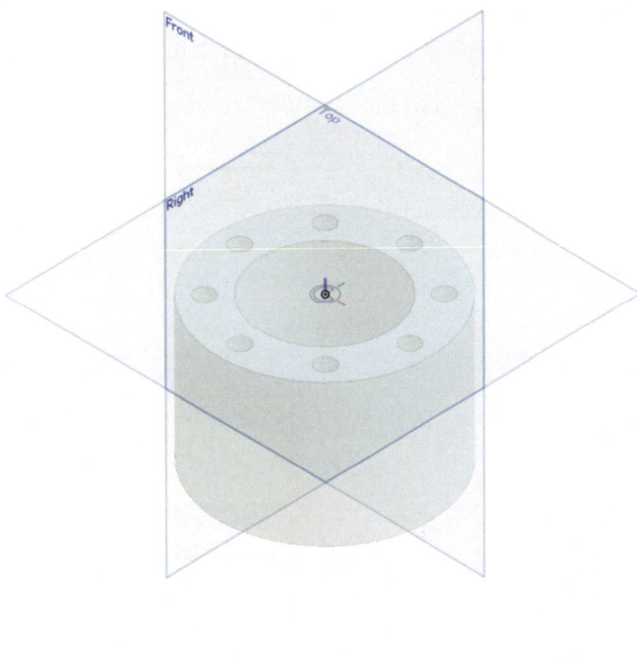

3. On the Toolbar, click the **Sketch** command. Next, select the Top face of the *Cylinder Base*.

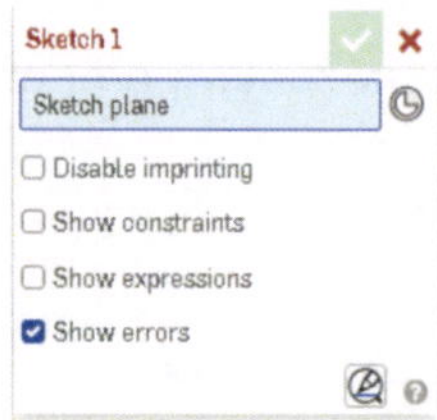

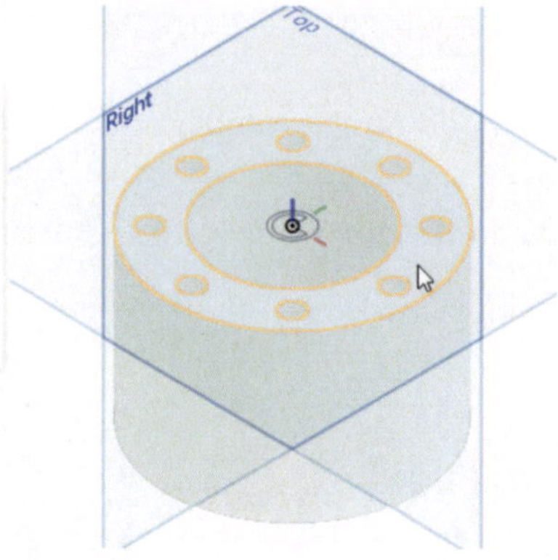

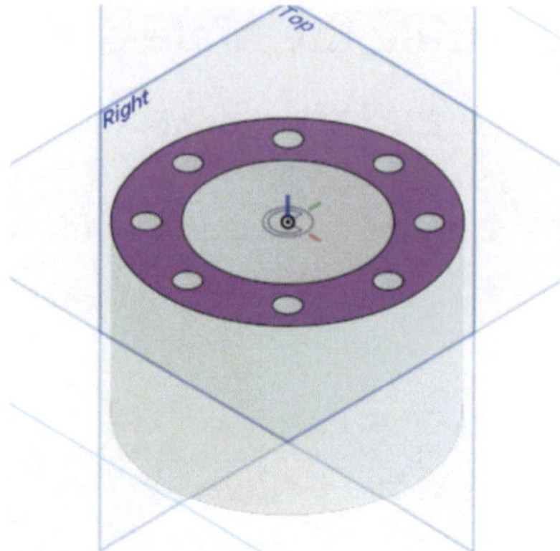

4. On the toolbar, click the **Use(project/convert)** command.
5. Click on the all circular edges on the top face of the *Cylinder Base*. The edges are projected to the sketch plane.
6. Click the green check on the **Sketch1** dialog.

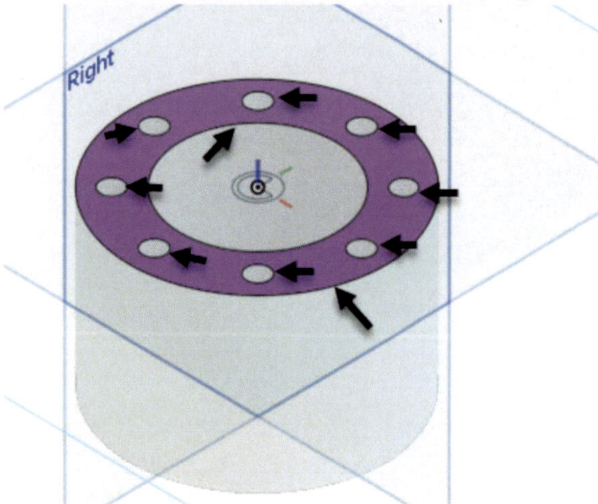

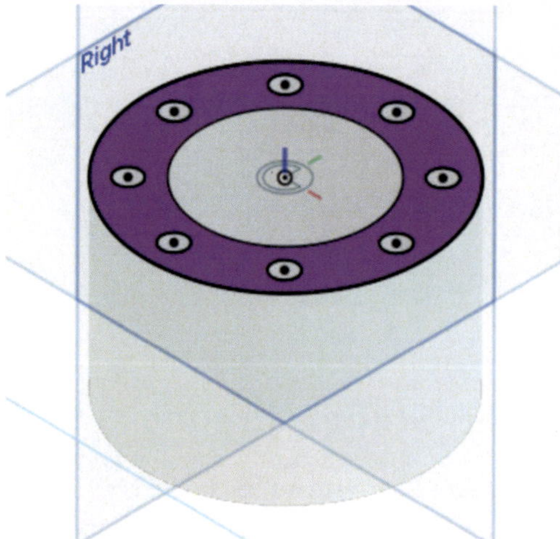

7. Activate the **Extrude** command and click on the region enclosed by the sketch.
8. On the **Extrude** dialog, click the **New** tab.
9. Select **End type > Blind**. Type 3 mm in the **Depth** field. Click the green check to create the *Extruded* feature.

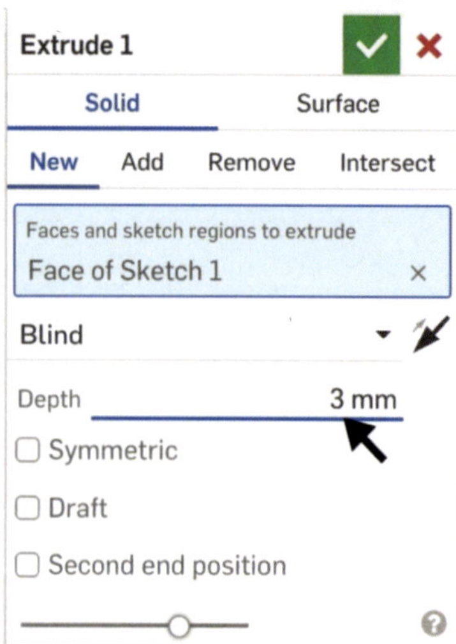

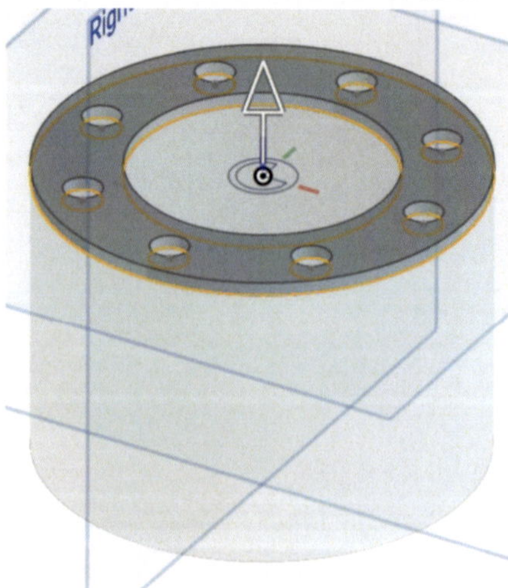

10. Right click on **Part 1** located at the bottom of the **Parts** window, and then select **Rename**.
11. Type **Gasket** and press ENTER.
12. In the graphics area, click the **Context 1 of Assembly 1** drop-down and select **Insert and go to assembly** option. Next, click the green check on the **Select items to insert** dialog to switch to Assembly environment.

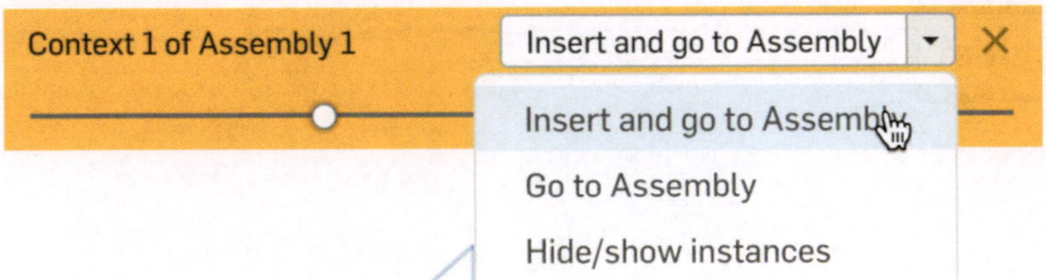

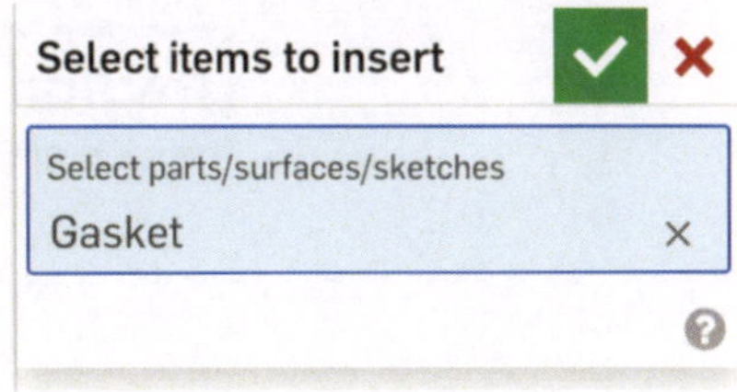

13. Click the **Mate connector** command on the toolbar and select the center point of the top face of the model, as shown.
14. Click the green check on the **Mate connector 2** dialog to create the mate connector.
15. Click the **Create Part Studio in context** command on the toolbar.
16. Select the newly created mate connector and click the green check on the **Origin of new Part Studio** dialog; the **Part Studio** environment appears.

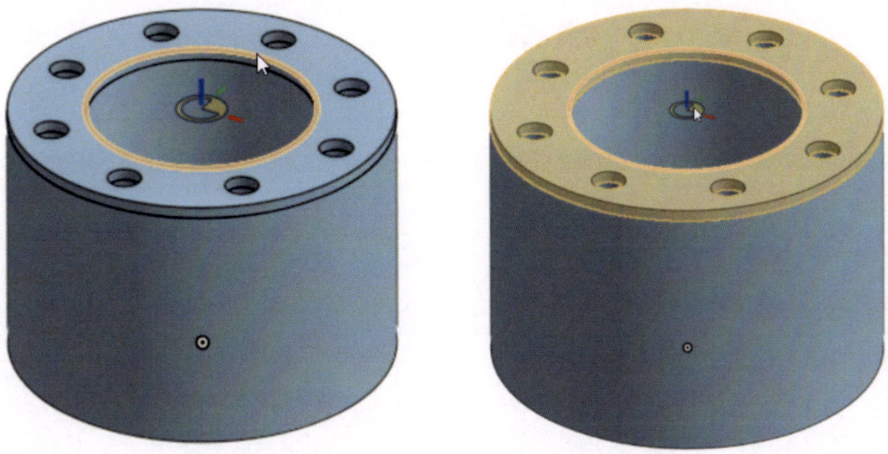

17. Activate the **Sketch** command and click on the top face of the *Gasket*.
18. On the toolbar, click the **Use(project/convert)** command.
19. Click on the outer and small circular edges of the *Gasket*; the edges are projected to the sketch plane.

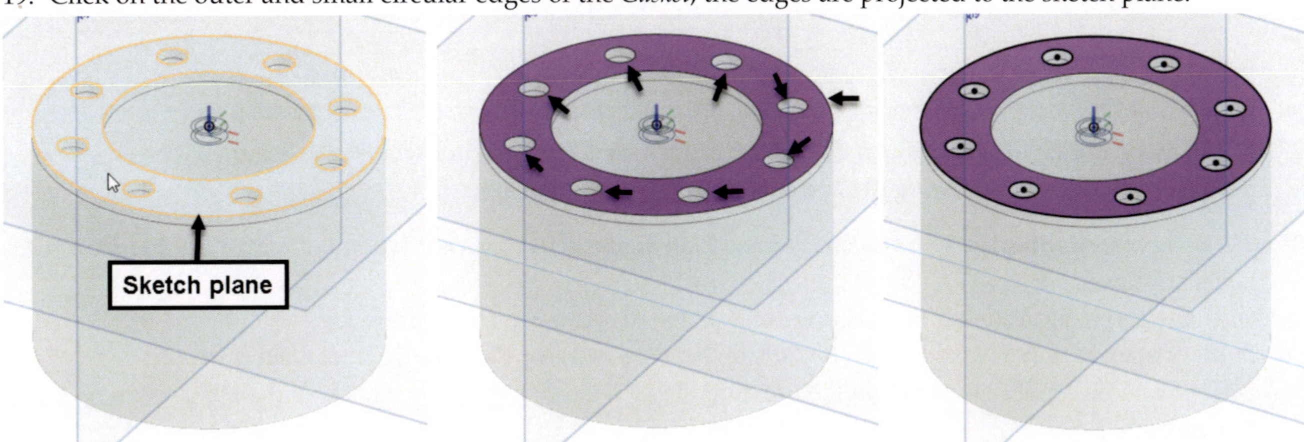

20. Click the green check on the **Sketch** dialog to confirm the sketch.
21. Click the **Extrude** command on the toolbar and click the regions enclosed by the sketch, as shown.
22. Type 13 in the **Depth** box and click the green check on the **Extrude 1** dialog.

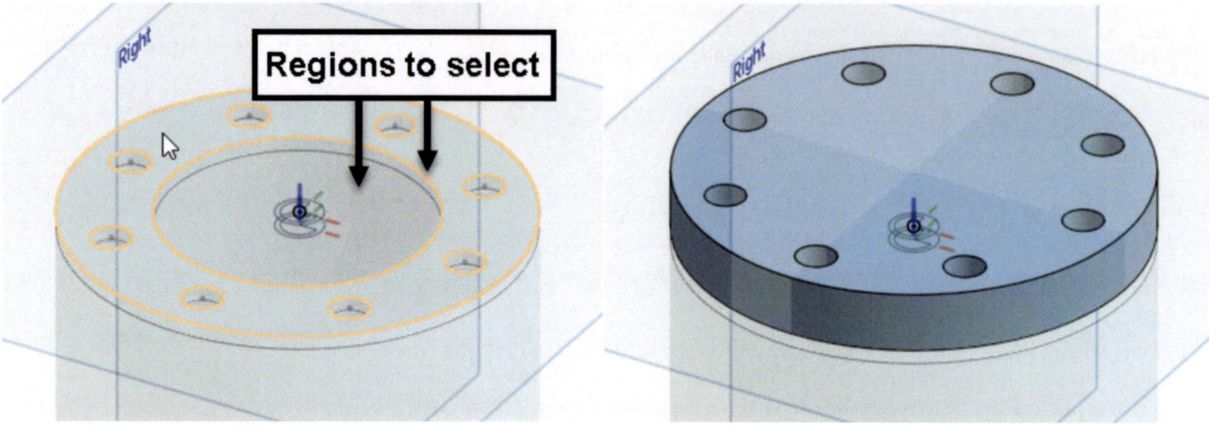

23. Start a sketch on the top face of the Cover plate, and then place a point at its center.
24. Create a hole in the center point of the *Cover plate*, as shown.

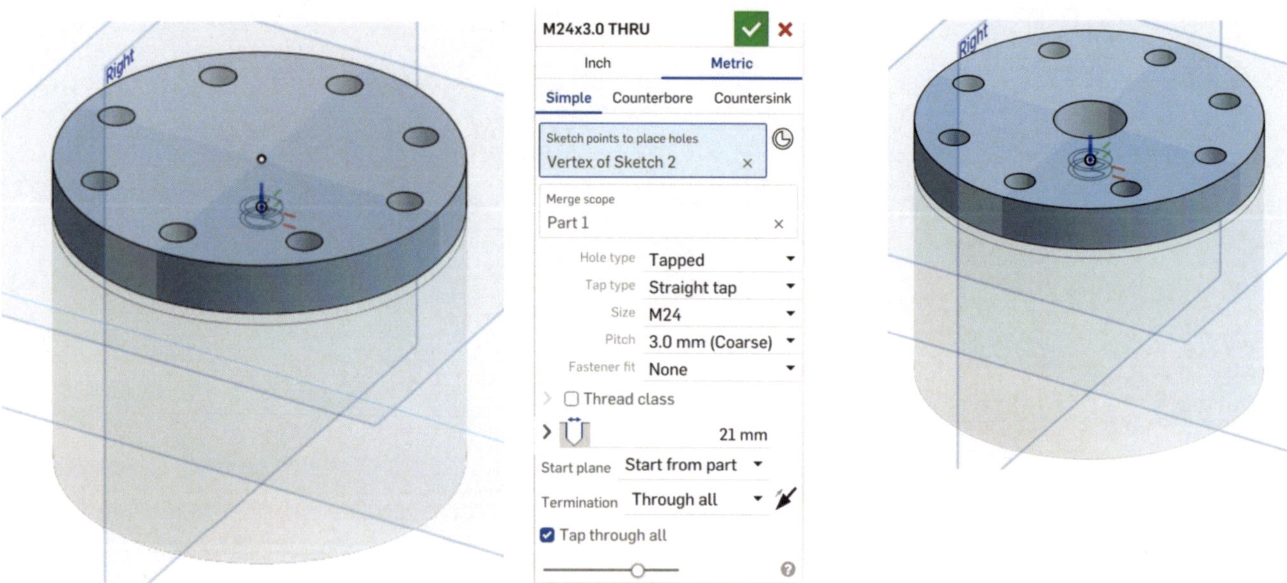

25. Right click on **Part 1** located at the bottom of the **Parts** window, and then select **Rename**.
26. Type **Cover Plate** and press ENTER.
27. Click **Insert and go to assembly** on the **Context 1 of Assembly1** drop-down. Next, click the green check on the **Select items to insert** dialog to switch to Assembly environment.
28. Click the **Mate connector** command on the toolbar and select the center point of any one of the small holes, as shown.
29. Click the green check on the **Mate connector 3** dialog to create the mate connector
30. In the **Instances** window, right-click on **Origin** and select **Create Part Studio in context**.
31. Select the mate connector created in the previous step. Next, click the green check on the **Origin of new Part Studio** dialog.

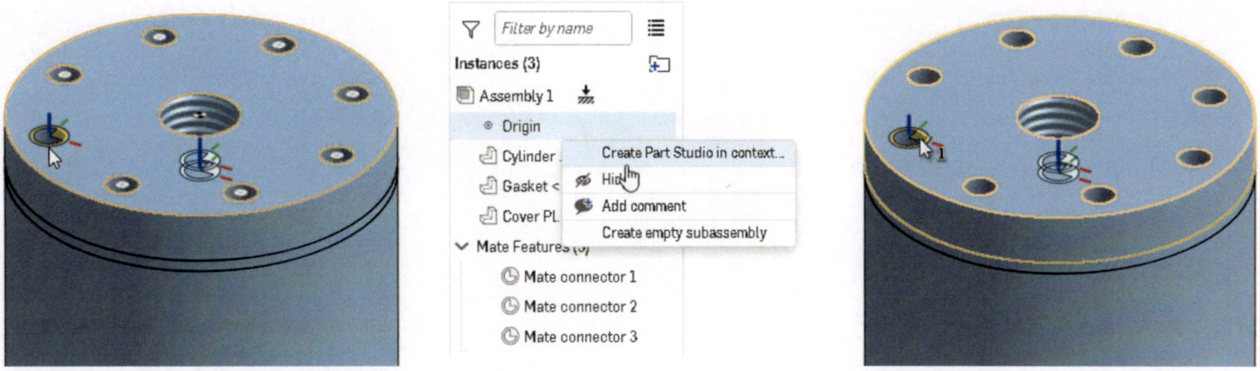

32. On the toolbar, click the **Sketch** command and click on the top face of the *Cover Plate*.
33. On the toolbar, click the **Use(project/convert)** command and select any one of the circular edges of the holes. Click the green check on the **Sketch** dialog.

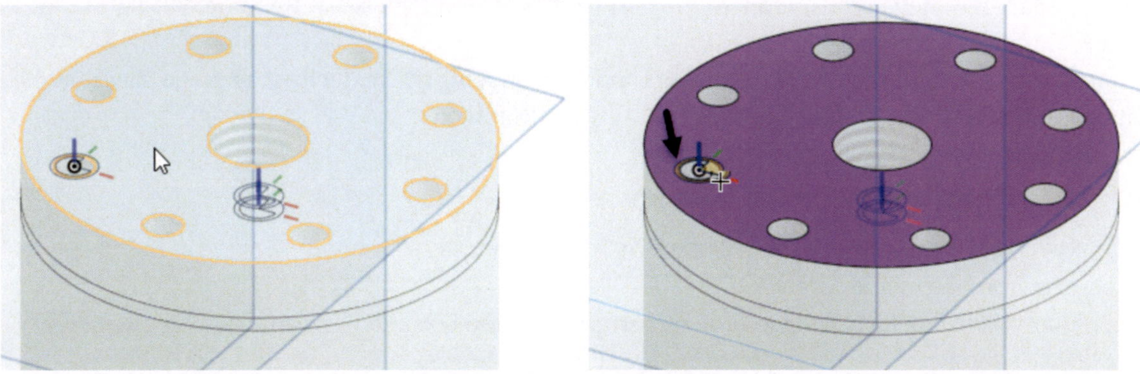

34. Use the sketch and create an *Extrude* feature of 30 mm depth. The direction of extrusion should be downward.

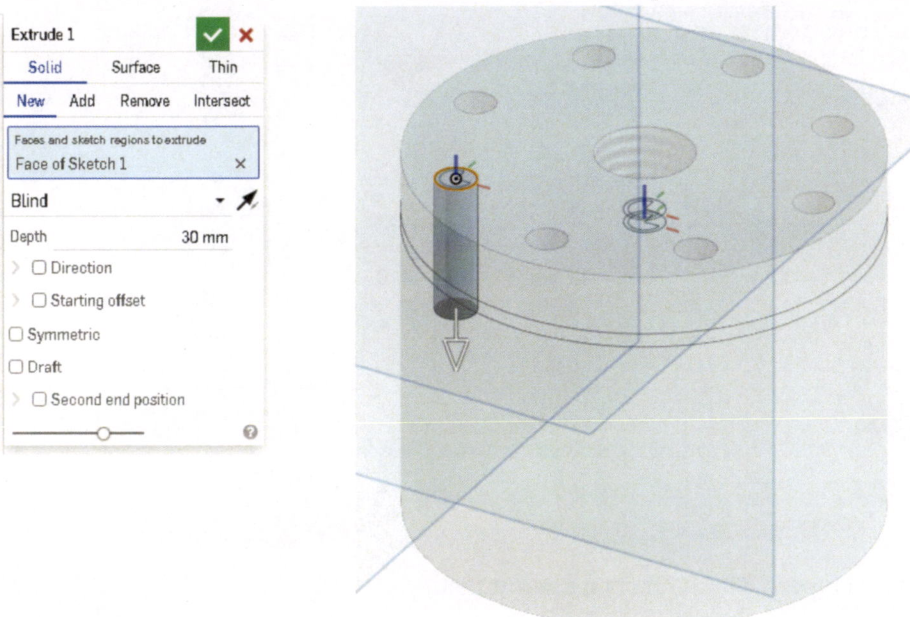

35. Activate the **Sketch** command and click on the top face of the newly created *Extruded* feature.
36. Draw a circle of 15 mm diameter and make it concentric to the circular edge of the *Extrude* feature. Click the green check on the **Sketch 2** dialog.
37. Extrude the circle in the upward direction. The extrude depth is 6 mm.

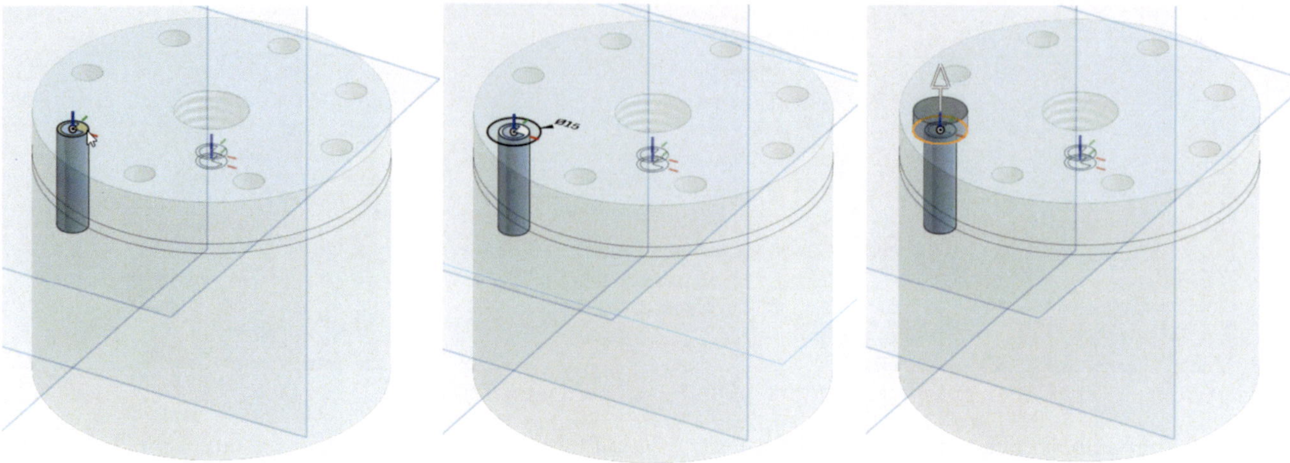

38. Right click on **Part 1** located at the bottom of the **Parts** window, and then select **Rename**.
39. Type **Screw** and press ENTER.
40. Click **Context 1 of Assembly** drop-down > **Insert and go to assembly**. Next, click the green check on the **Select items to insert** dialog to switch to the Assembly environment.

Creating the Assembly circular pattern

1. On the Toolbar, click the **Assembly circular pattern** command.
2. Select the *Screw* from the model geometry.
3. On the **Circular pattern** dialog, click the **Axis of pattern** selection box and click on the outer circular face of the *Cover Plate*, as shown.

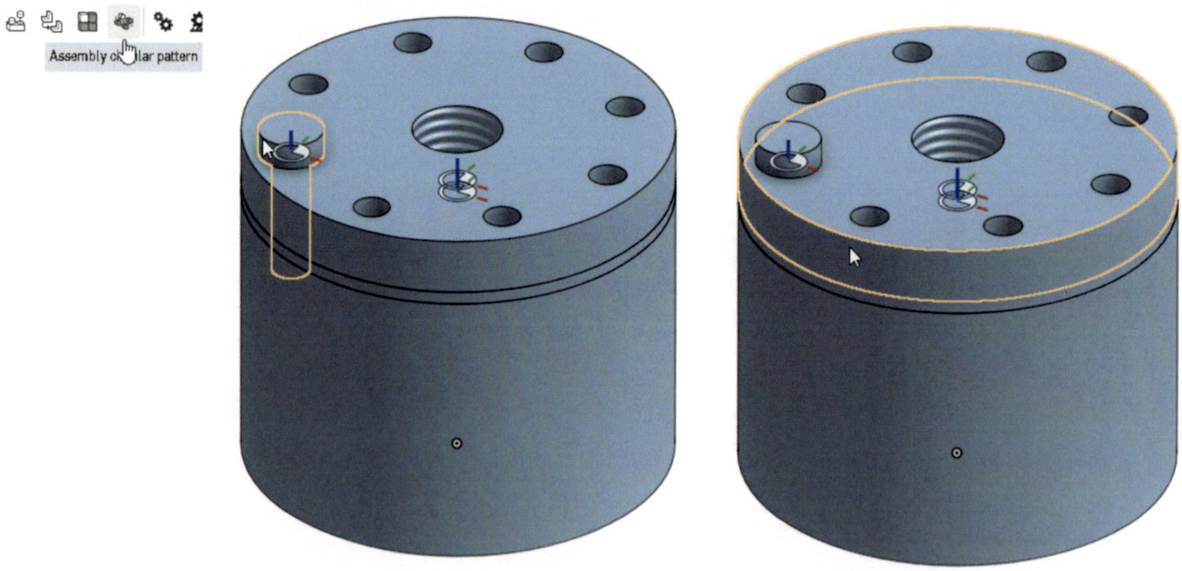

4. Type **360** in the **Angle** field and type in **8** in the **Instance count** field.
5. Click the green check to create the circular pattern of screws.

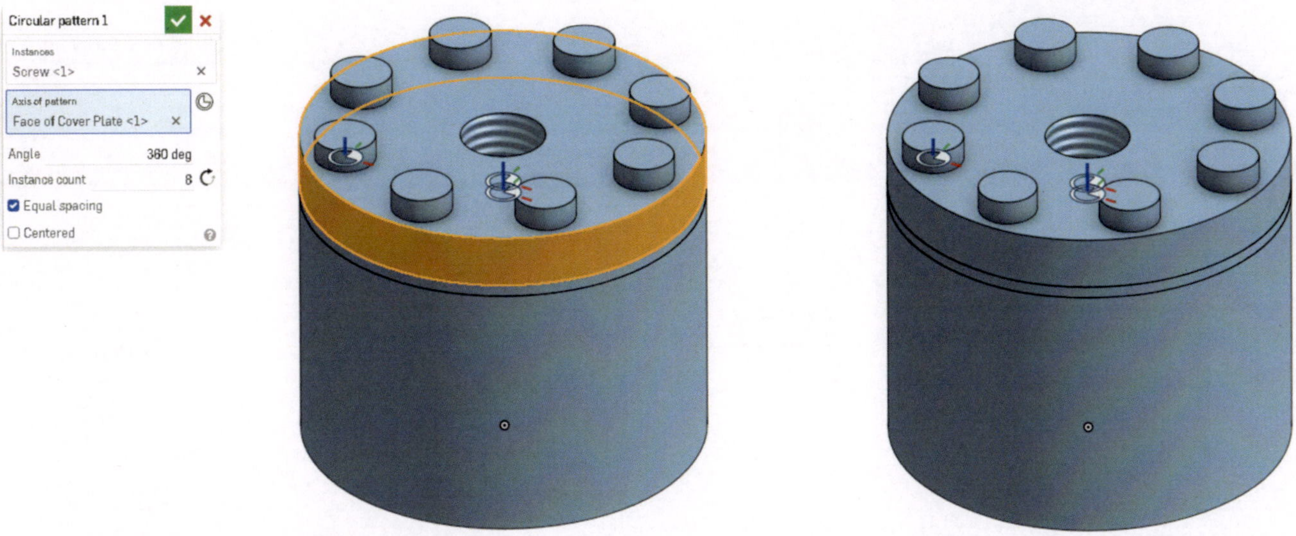

Creating the Named Positions

1. On the right-side panel, click the **Named position** tab. Next, click the **Add named position** button and type **Assembled View** in the *Name* box; a new named position is created.
2. Right-click on the **Assembly View** and select **Apply named position.**

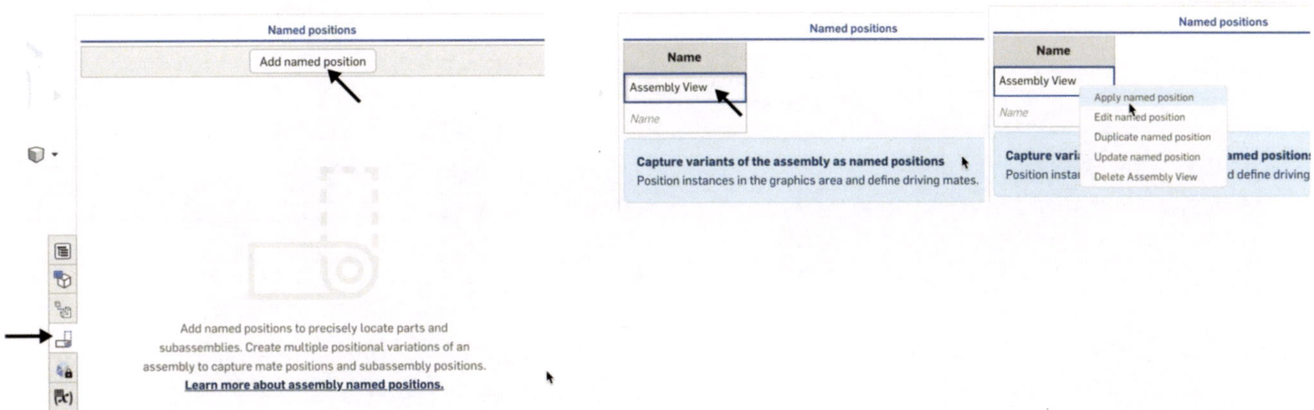

3. Type **Exploded view** in the second *Name* box , and then press ENTER. Next, select the **Exploded view** position right-click and select **Apply named position.**

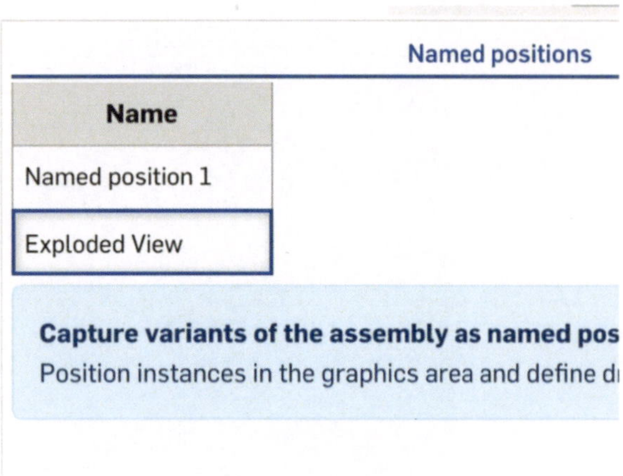

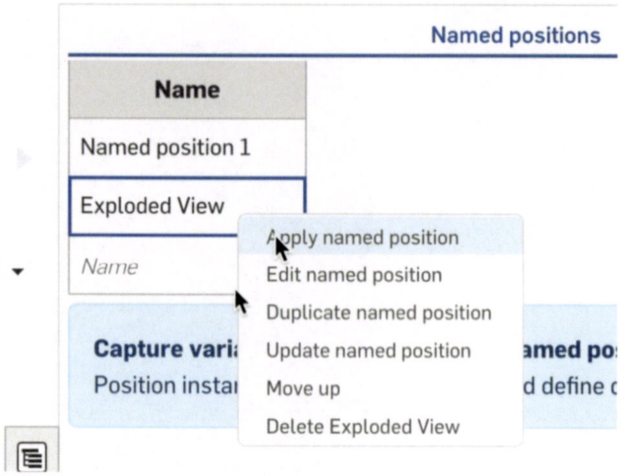

4. Click **Named positions** on the right panel to close.
5. Select the anyone of the screws from the assembly; the move triad appears on the selection.
6. Click on the axis pointing in the upward direction. Next, press and hold the left mouse button, drag it upward, and then release.
7. Type **100** in the **Distance** box that appears on the screen. Next, press Enter to move all the screws to the specified distance.

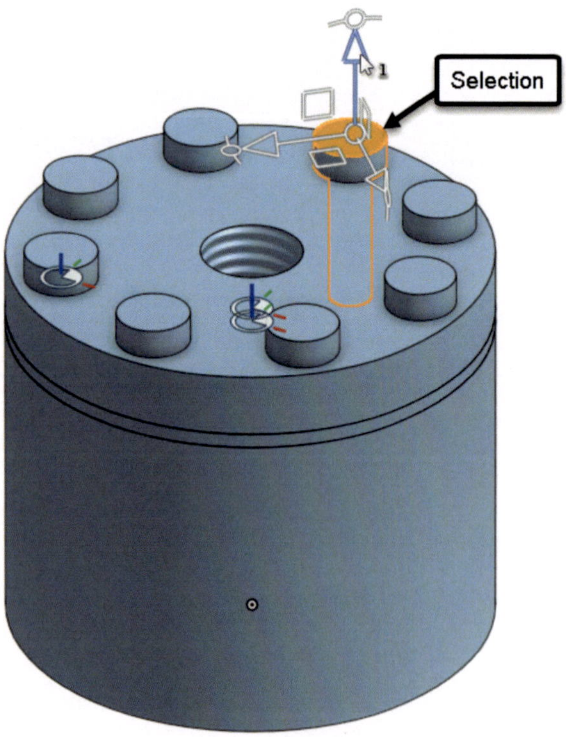

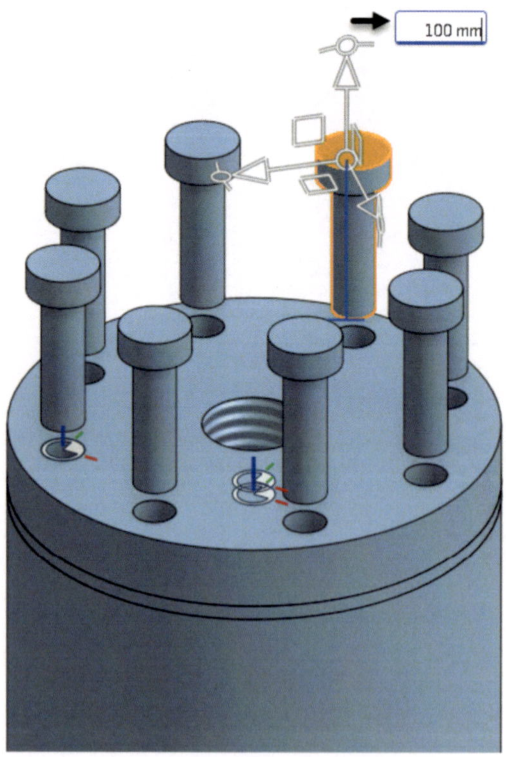

8. Click in the graphics area to deactivate the **Move** command.
9. Likewise, move the Cover plate and Gasket up to a distance of 50 and 25, respectively.

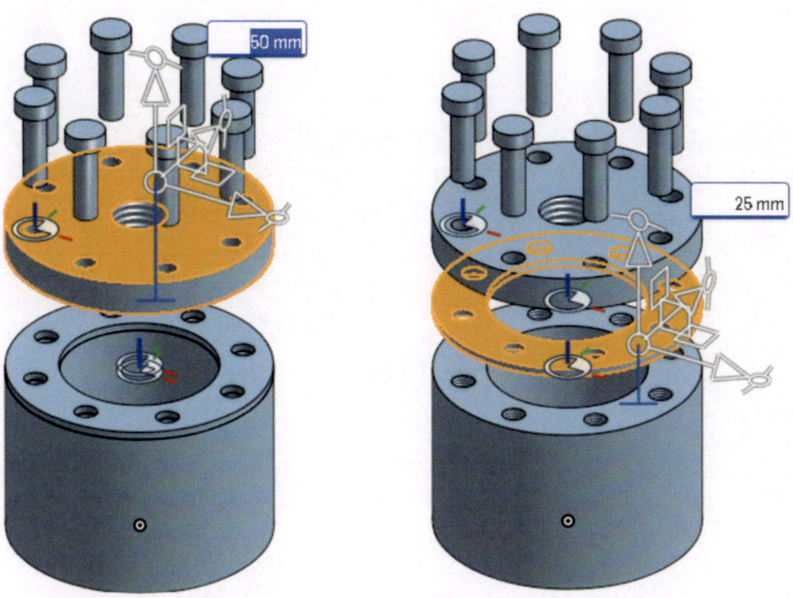

10. Click the **Done** button on the **Editing Assembly View** toolbar displayed in the graphics window.

11. Click the **Named positions** button located at the right side of the graphics area.
12. Select the **Assembly view** position right-click and select **Apply named position**; the assembly is collapsed.

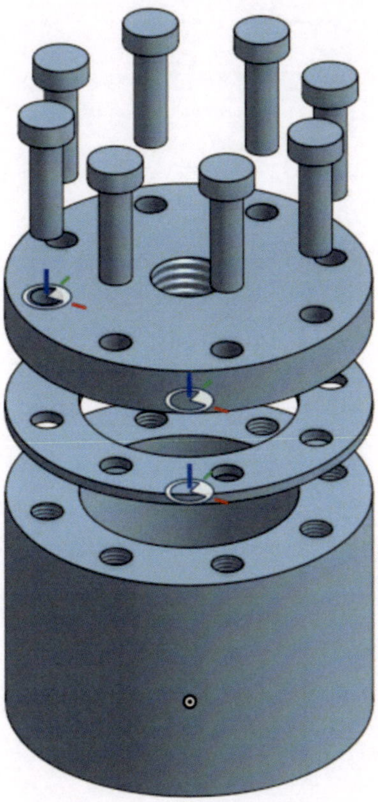

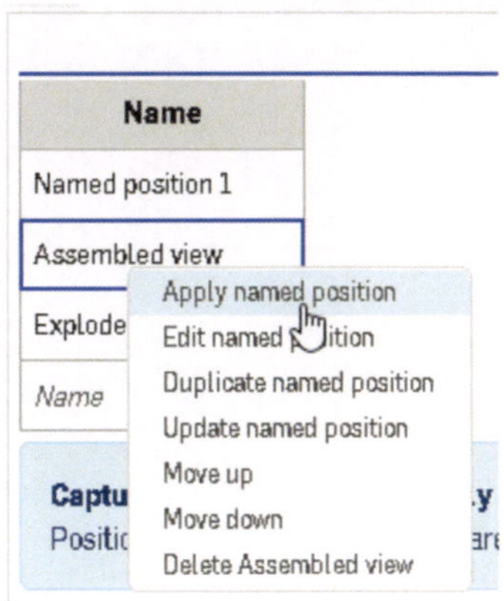

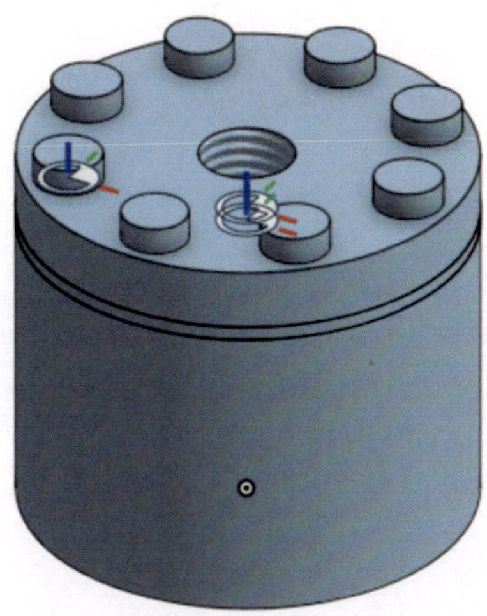

13. Click **Named positions** on the right panel to close.

Configuring the BOM Table

1. Click the **BOM Table** button located at the right side of the graphics area; the **Bill of materials** table appears.
2. On the **Bill of materials** table, right click on the **Part number** column. Next, select **Remove column; the Part number** column is removed.

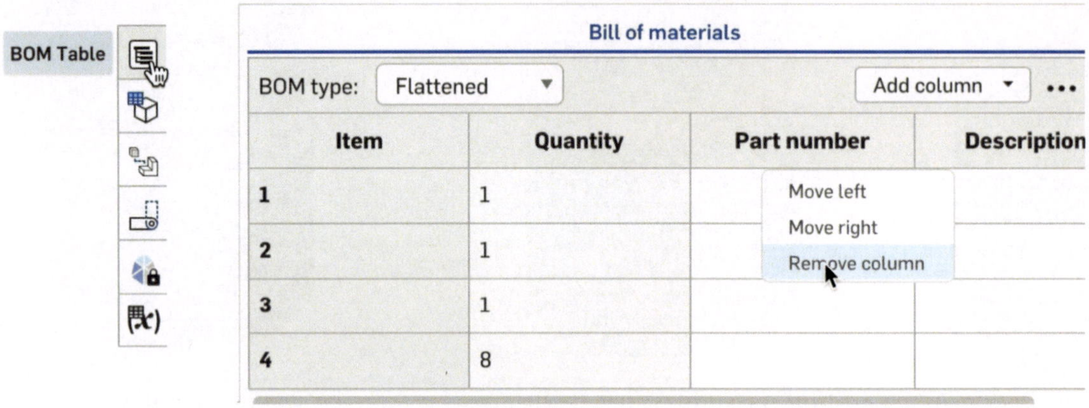

3. Click the **Add column** drop-down and select **Name**; the **Name** column is added to the table.
4. Right click on the **Name** column and select **Move left**.
5. Click the **BOM Table** button to hide the **Bill of materials** table.

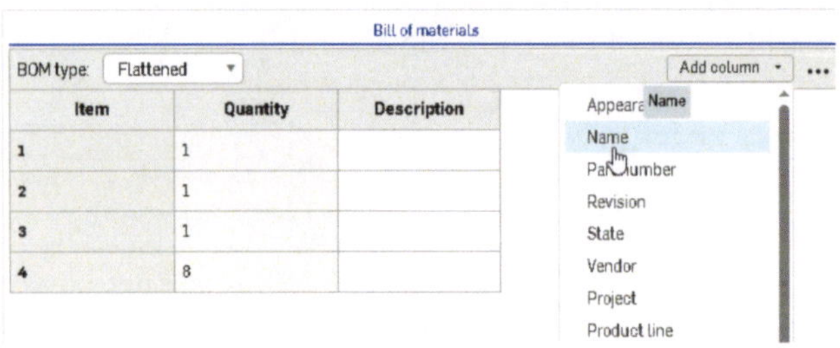

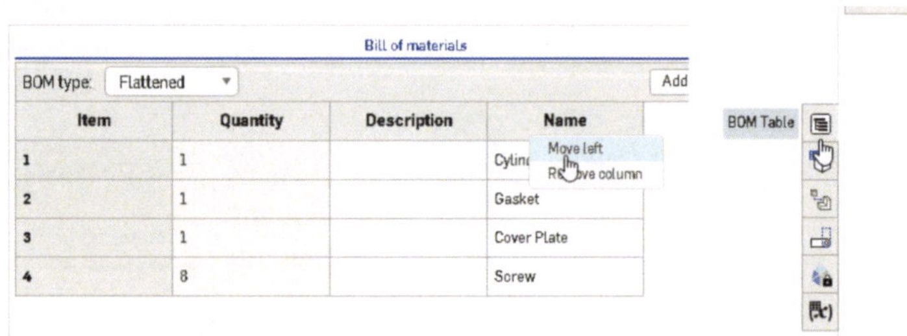

6. Close the document.

Questions

1. How do you start an assembly?
2. What is the use of the **Mate Connectors** command?
3. List the advantages of Top-down assembly approach.
4. What is a fixed part?
5. What is the use of the **Snap Mode** command?
6. How do you create a sub-assembly in the assembly environment?
7. Briefly explain the **Create Part Studio in context** command.
8. How to detect any interference between the parts?
9. What is the difference between **Revolute** and **Cylindrical** mate?
10. How to mirror a component?

Exercises

Exercise 1

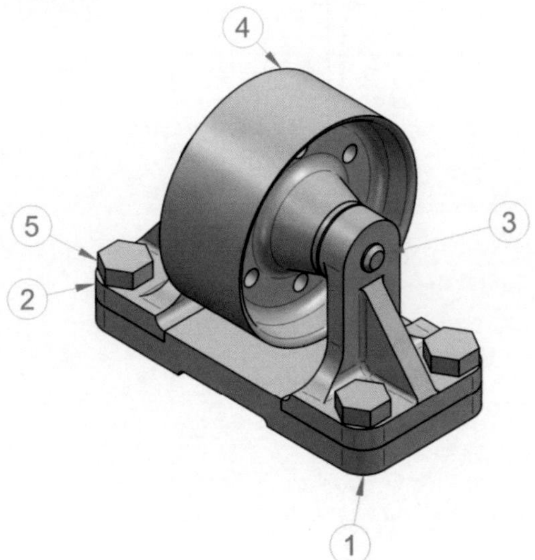

Item Number	File Name (no extension)	Quantity
1	Base	1
2	Bracket	2
3	Spindle	1
4	Roller-Bush assembly	1
5	Bolt	4

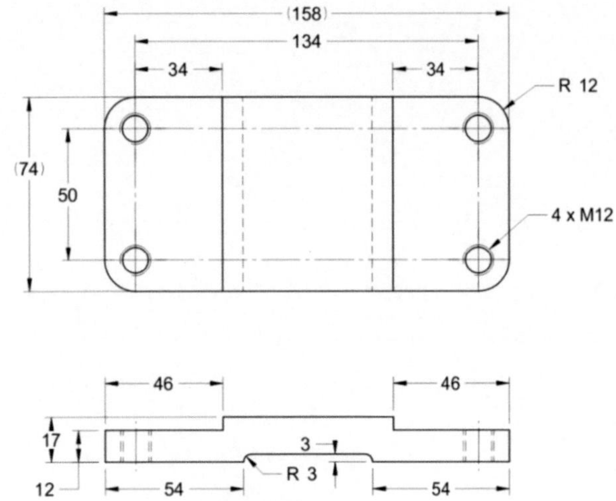

Base

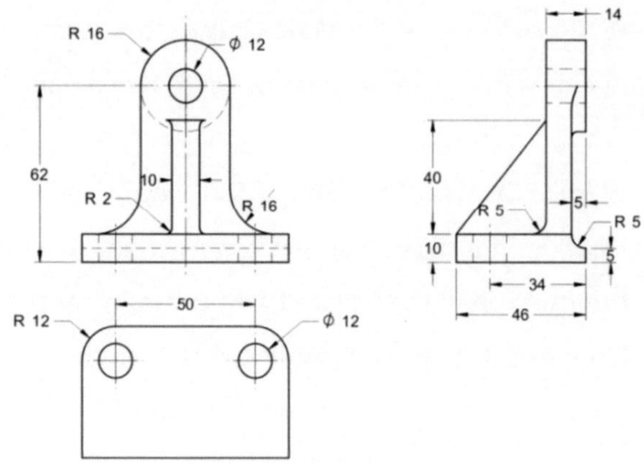

Bracket

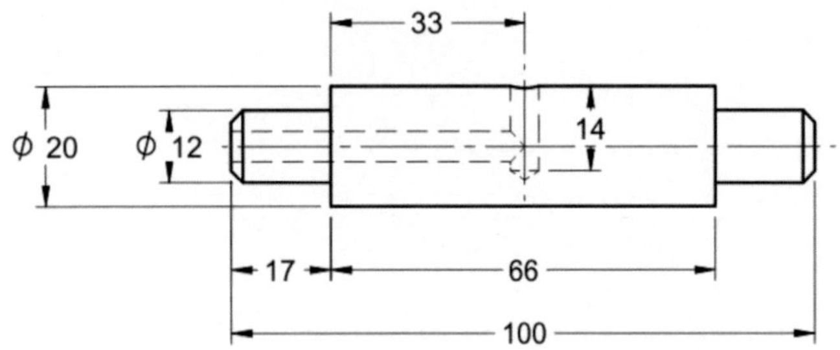

SPINDLE

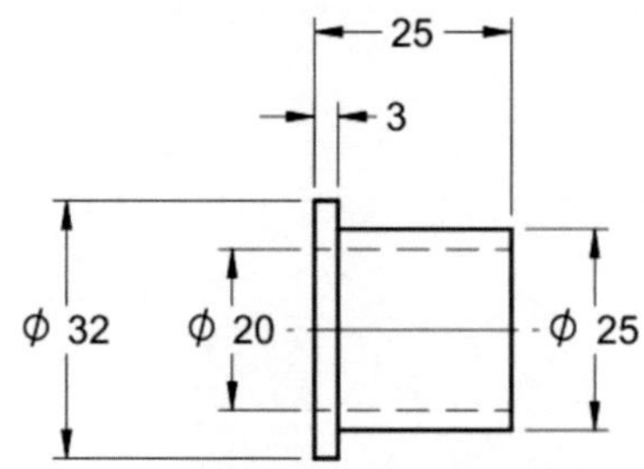

BUSH

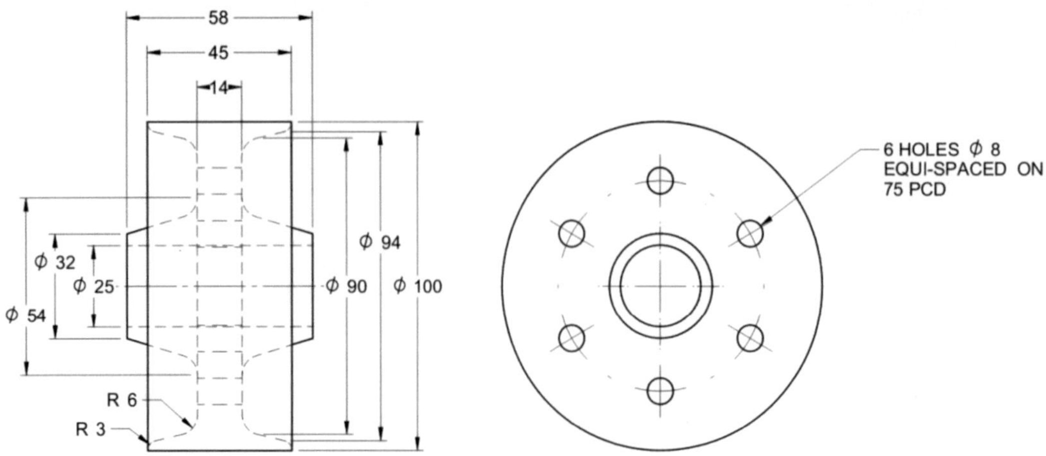

Roller

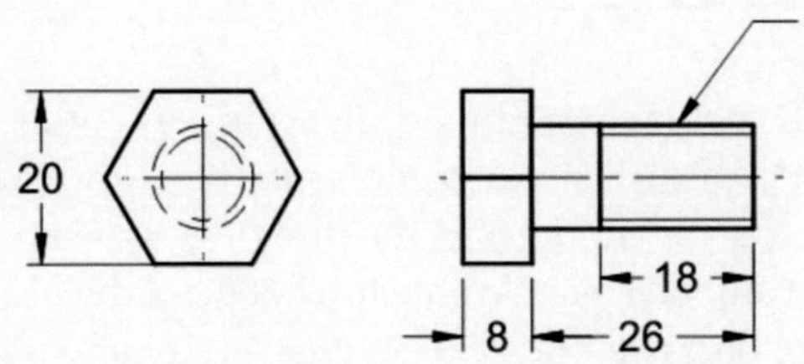

Bolt

Chapter 11: Drawings

Drawings are used to document your 3D models in the traditional 2D format including dimensions and other instructions useful for manufacturing purpose. In Onshape, you first create 3D models and assemblies and then use them to generate drawings. There is a direct association between the 3D model and the drawing. When changes are made to the model, every view in the drawing will be updated. This relationship between the 3D model and the drawing makes the drawing process fast and accurate. Because the 2D drawings are widely used in the mechanical industry, drawings are one of the three main file types you can create in Onshape.

The topics covered in this chapter are:

- *Create Base Views*
- *Projected views*
- *Auxiliary views*
- *Section views*
- *Detail views*
- *Break-Out views*
- *Break a View*
- *Display Options*
- *View Alignment*
- *Parts List and Balloons*
- *Dimensions*
- *Ordinate Dimensions*
- *Center Marks*
- *Centerlines*
- *Hole Callout*

Starting a Drawing

To start a new drawing, on the taskbar click **Insert new element** and select **Create Drawing**. Next, select the required template from the **Existing templates** tab of the **Create Drawing** dialog

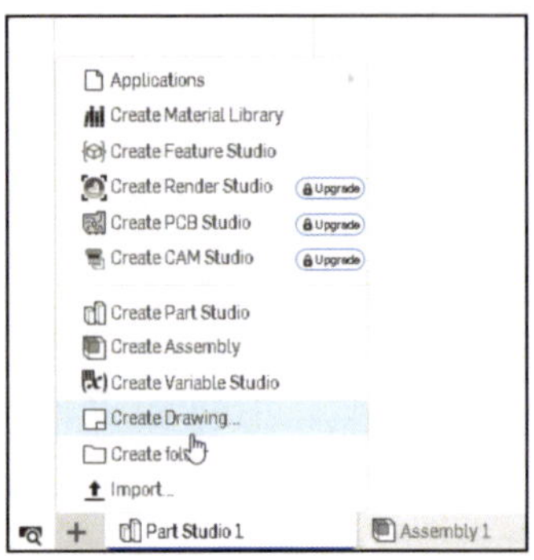

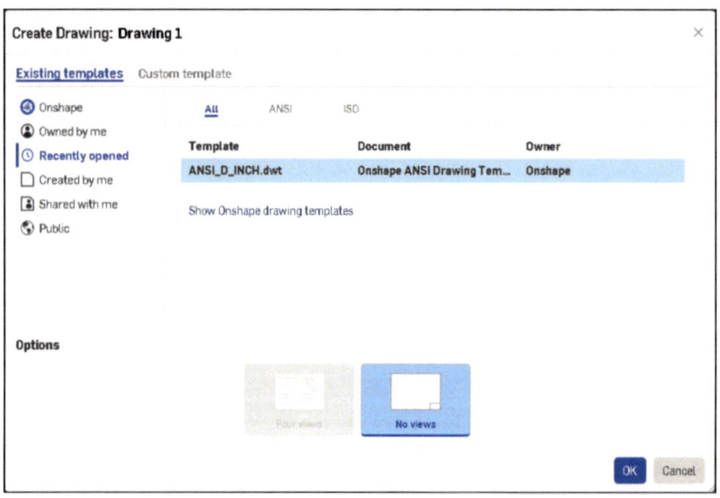

If you want to create a new template, click the **Custom template** tab on the **Create Drawing** dialog. Next, specify the **Standard, Size, Units, Decimal separator**, and **Projection**. Next, specify the options in the Border section or leave the default settings. Click **OK** to create a new drawing.

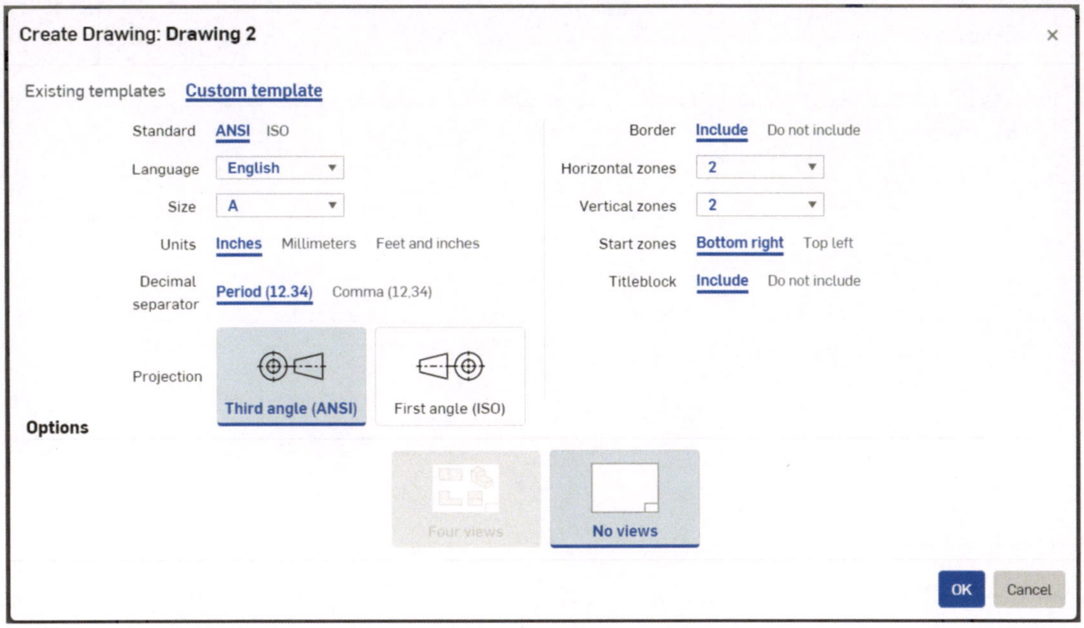

Inserting Views

There are different standard views available in a 3D part: front, right, top, and isometric. In Onshape, you can create these views using the **Insert view** command. This command is activated automatically if you have created a drawing from an already opened part. If it is not activated, click **Insert view** on the Toolbar; the **Select part or assembly** dialog appears. If the part is available in the opened document, then it will be listed in the **Current documents** tab. If the document is not available in the opened document, then click the **Other documents** tab on the dialog and browse to the location of the part or assembly and select it. Use the **View** drop-down on the **Insert view** dialog to change the orientation of the view. Use the **View scale** to change the scale factor and adjust the size of the view. Next, click to place the view in the drawing sheet.

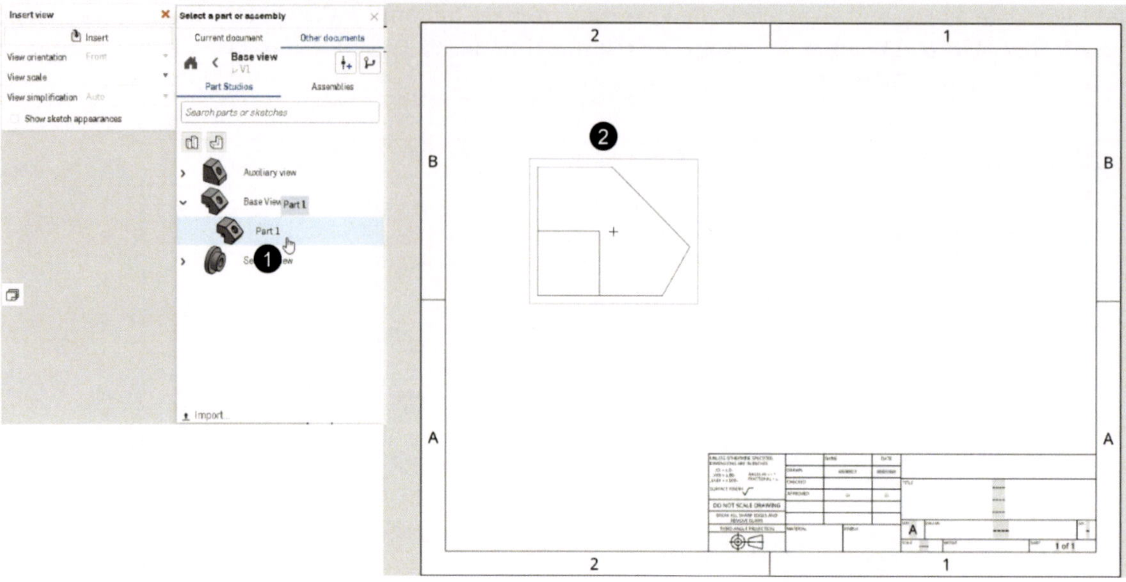

Projected View

After you have created the first view in your drawing, a projected view is one of the simplest views to create. Click **Projected View** on the Toolbar and select a view you wish to project from. Next, move the pointer in the direction you wish to have the view to be projected. Next, click on the sheet to specify the location. Press **Esc** to deactivate the **Projected view**.

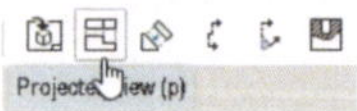

Auxiliary View

Most of the parts are represented by using orthographic views (front, top and/or side views). However, many parts have features located on inclined faces. You cannot get the true shape and size for these features by using the orthographic views. To see an accurate size and shape of the inclined features, you need to create an auxiliary view. An auxiliary view is created by projecting the part onto a plane other than horizontal, front or side planes. To create an auxiliary view, click **Auxiliary View** on the Toolbar. Next, the **Normal** tab on the **Auxiliary View** dialog. Click the angled edge of the model to establish the direction of the auxiliary view. Next, move the pointer and notice that the movement is locked in the direction normal to the selected edge. Click at the desired location and click to locate the view.

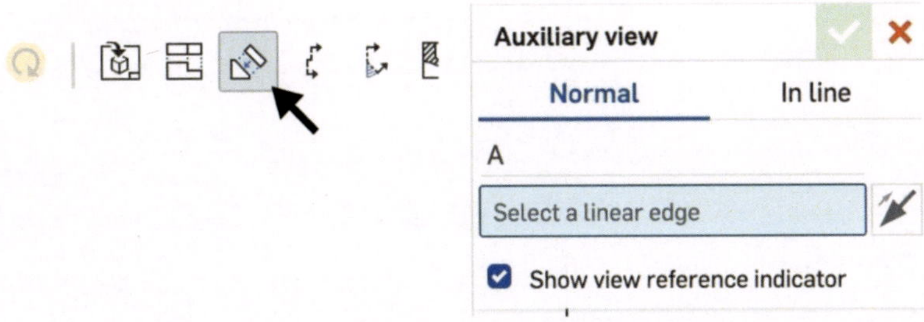

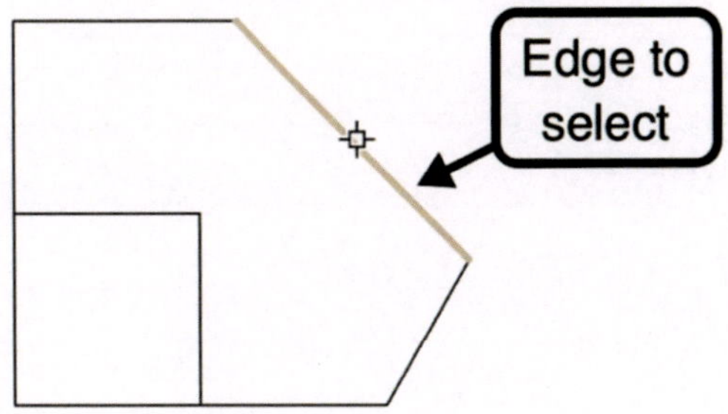

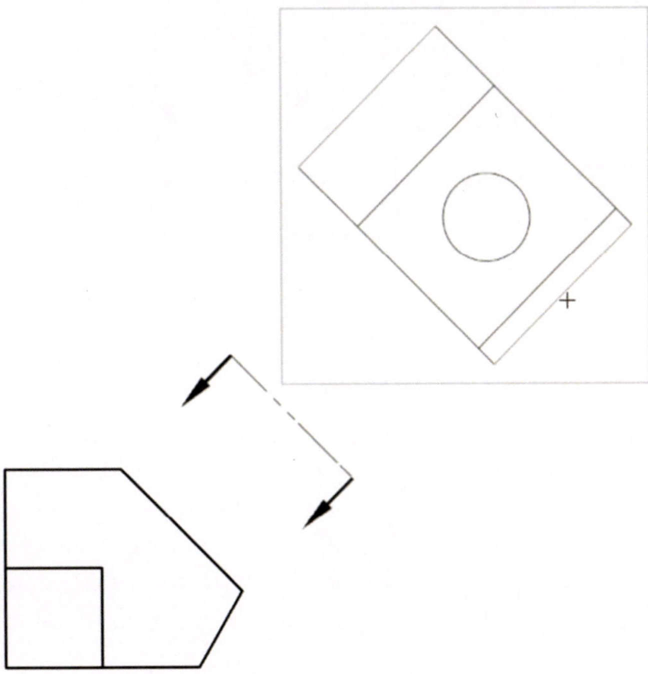

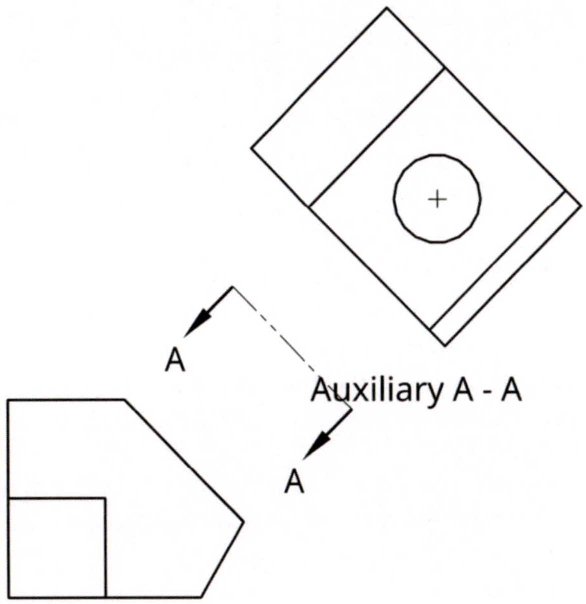

In-line Auxiliary View

To create an in-line auxiliary view, click the **In line** tab on the **Auxiliary View** dialog and select a specific edge on the base view. Next, move the pointer and notice that movement is locked along the selected edge. Click to specify the location of the auxiliary view; Onshape generates the auxiliary view by projecting the model's geometry along the direction of the edge you selected.

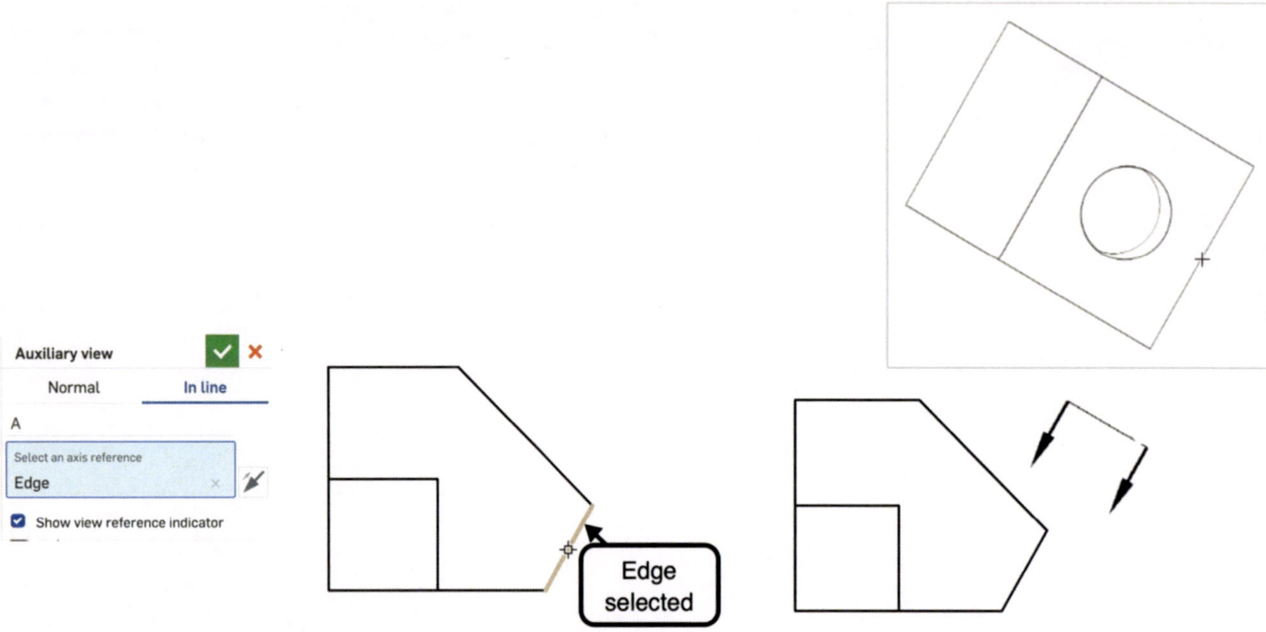

Section View

One of the most common views used in 2D drawings is the section view. Creating a section view in Onshape is very simple. Once a view is placed on the drawing sheet, you need to draw a line where you want to section the drawing view. Click **Section View** on the toolbar and select the center of the drawing view; the centreline appears. Move the pointer on either side of the cutting place to indicate the view direction. Next, click to position the section view.

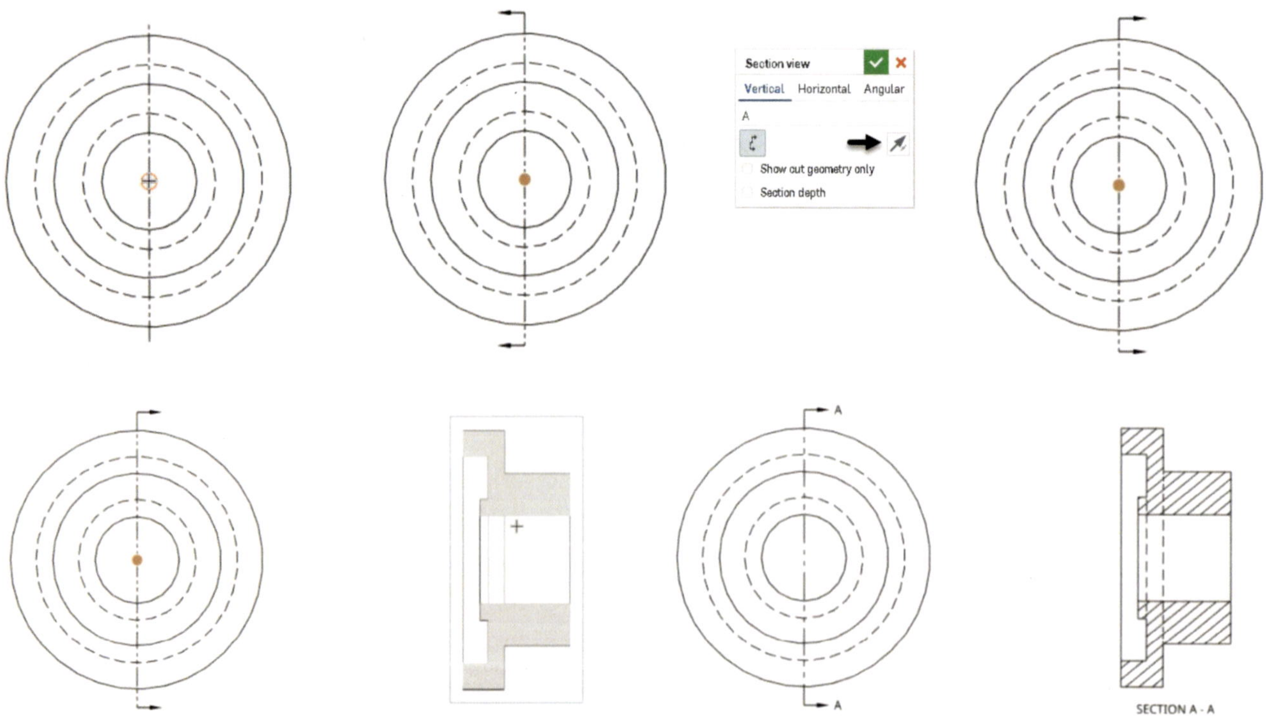

You can also use a multi-segment cutting line to create a section view. To do this, click the Vertical or Horizontal tab on the Section view dialog. Next, select the multiple points on the drawing view; a cutting plane is created passing through the selected points. Move the pointer and click to position the section view.

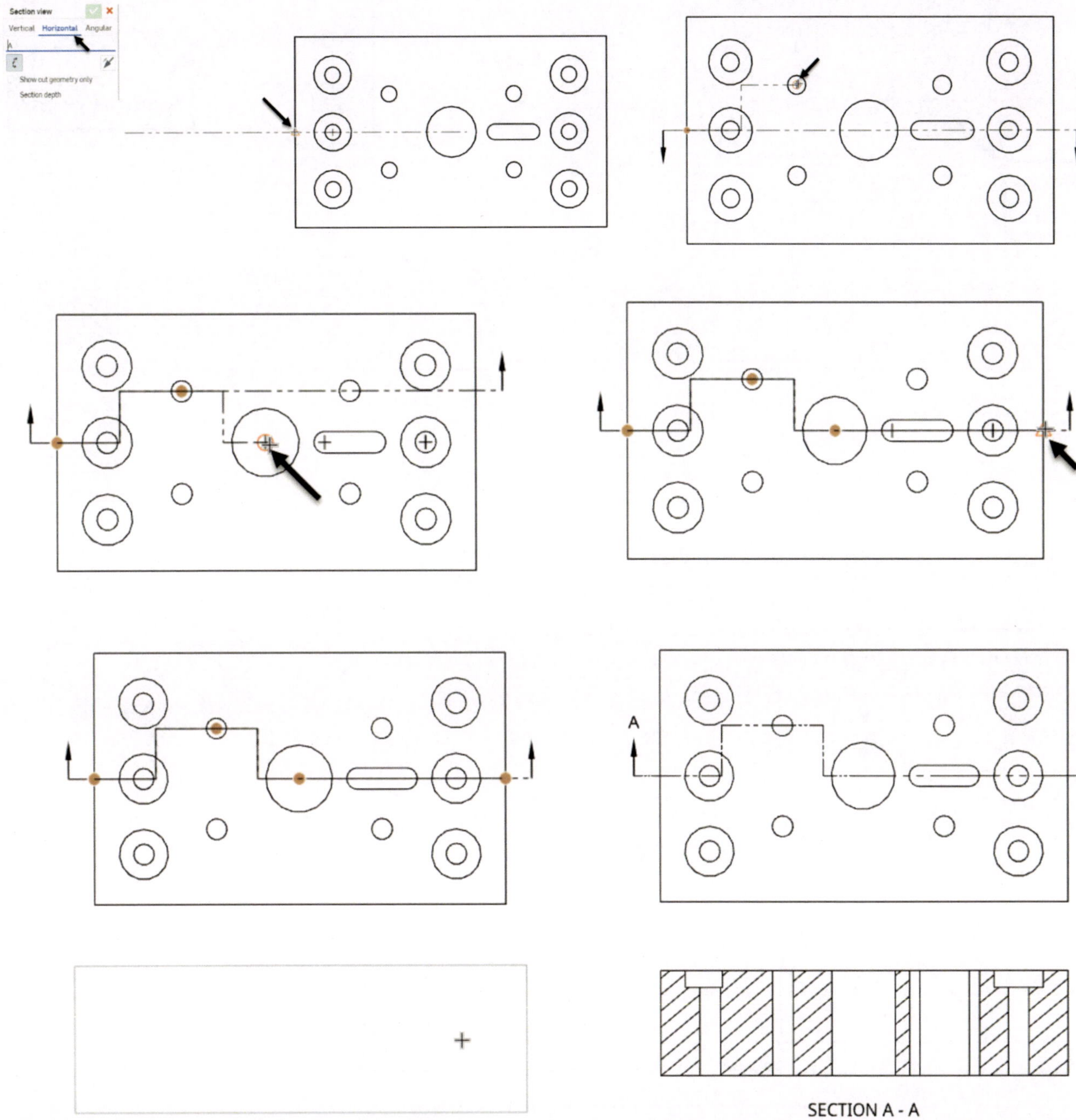

You can also use the **Section depth** option to create a multi-segment section line. To do this, activate the **Section view** command and specify the first point of the section line. Next, check the **Section depth** option and select the **Up to entity** option from the **End type** drop-down. Select the second point on the drawing view. Next, move the pointer and click to position the section view.

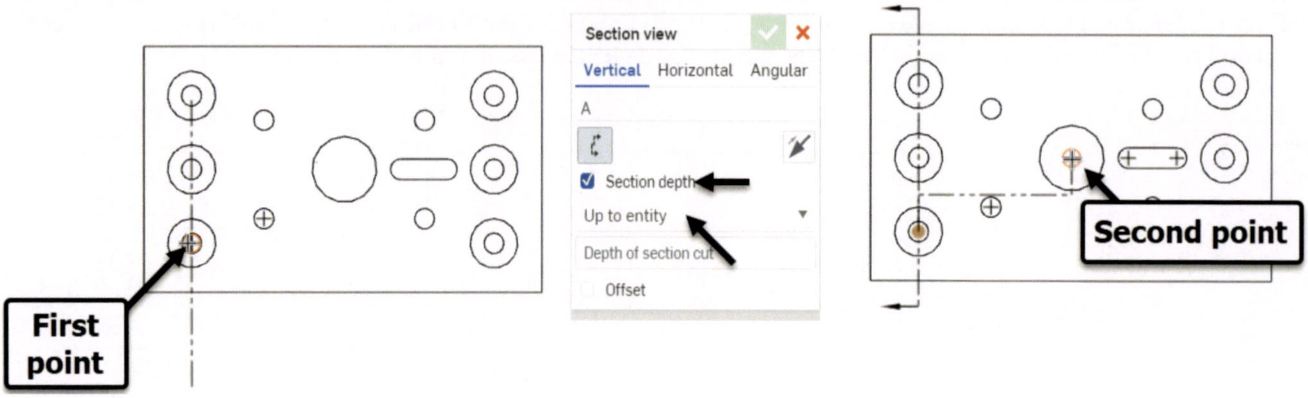

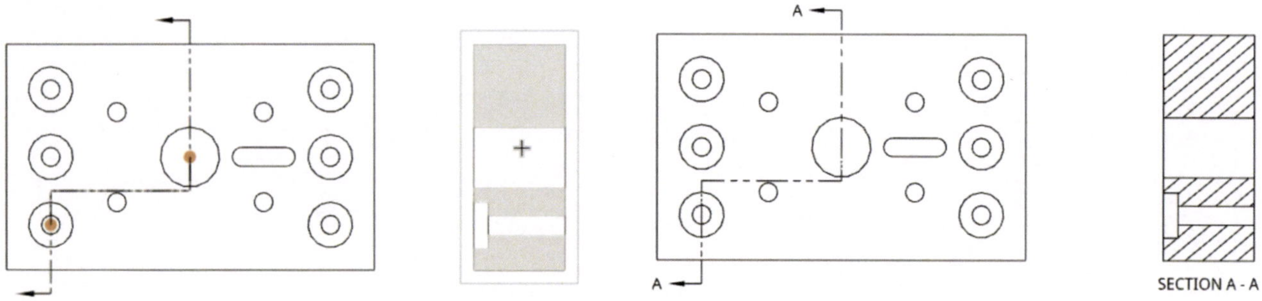

Use the **Show cut geometry only** option to display only the geometry on the cutting plane.

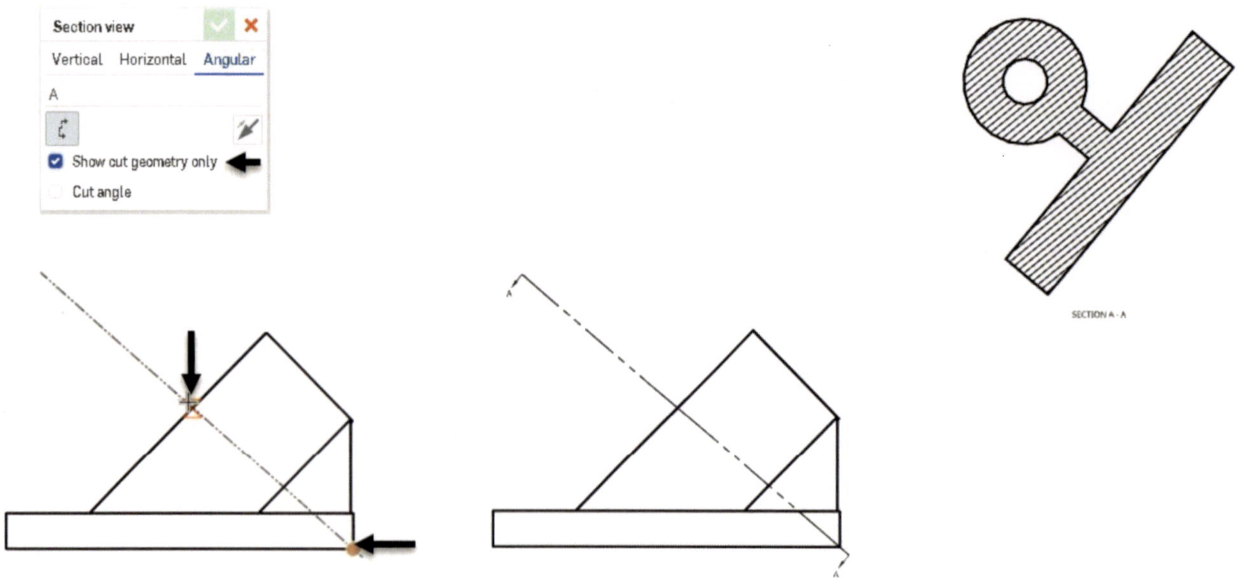

Detail View

If a drawing view contains small features that are difficult to see, a detailed view can be used to zoom in and make things clear. To create a detailed view, click the **Detail View** on the Toolbar. Next, click in the area you wish to enlarge. Click and drag them to define the perimeter of the circle. On the **Detail view** dialog, set the **View Scale** and **View Label**. Next, move the pointer and click to locate the view; the detail view will appear with a label.

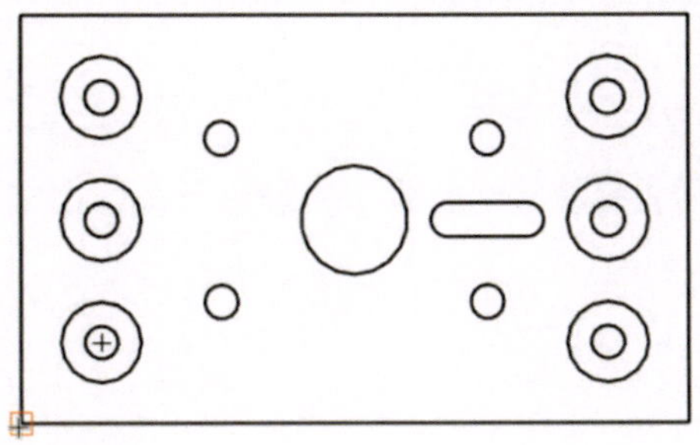

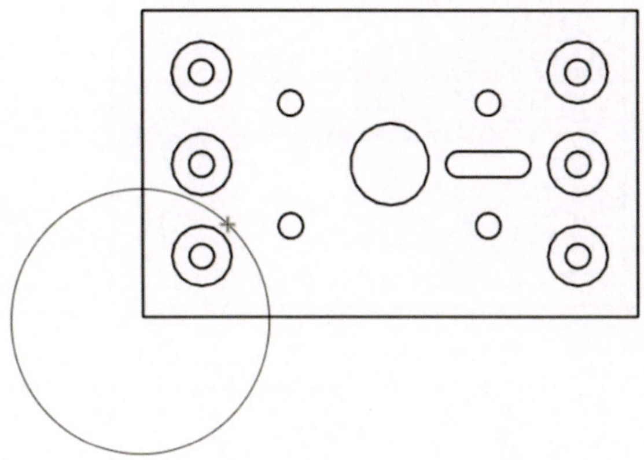

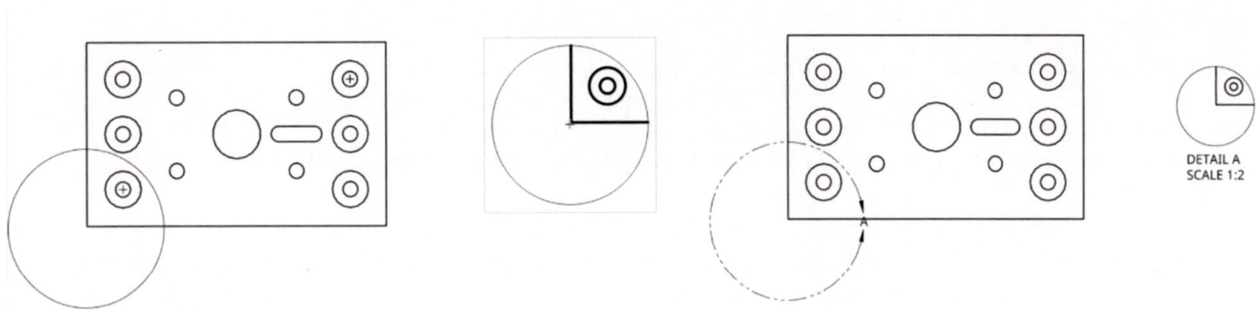

Resizing a Detail view

You can also resize the detailed view in onshape. To resize the detail view, select the circle on the base view. Now, click the grip point between the arrows on the circle. Move the pointer inward or outward to reduce or increase the size of the detailed view.

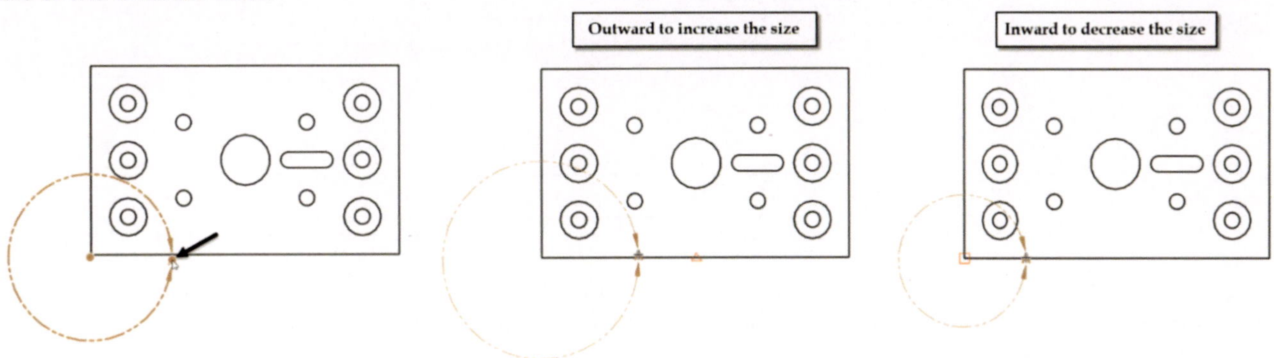

Moving a Detail view

You can also move the detailed view. To do this, select the detailed view circle and click the grip point at the center on the circle. Move the pointer to a new location and click to place the view.

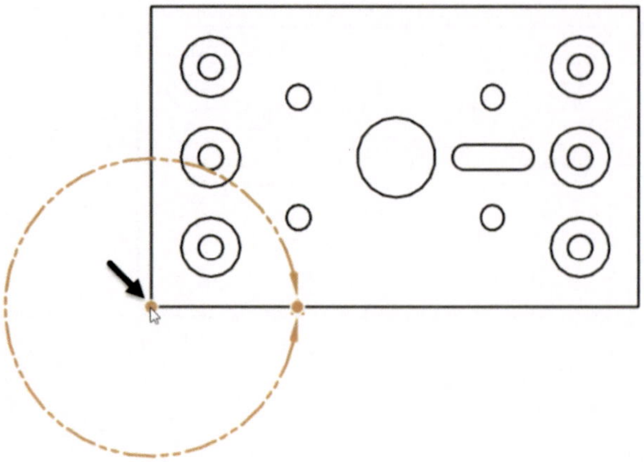

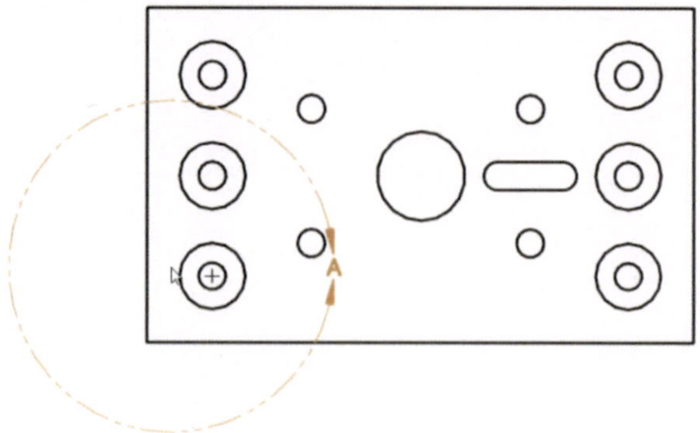

Break View

Break lines are added to a drawing view, which is too large to fit on the drawing sheet. They break the view so that only important details are shown. To break a view, click the **Break view** icon on the Toolbar and select the view; the **Break view** dialog pops up. On this dialog, click the **Vertical** or **Horizontal** tab on the **Break view** dialog.

Select an option from the **Break line type** drop-down **(Zig zag, Small zig zag, Curve, Straight)** to define the break line style. Type-in the desired value in the **Gap distance** box to specify the gap between the break lines.

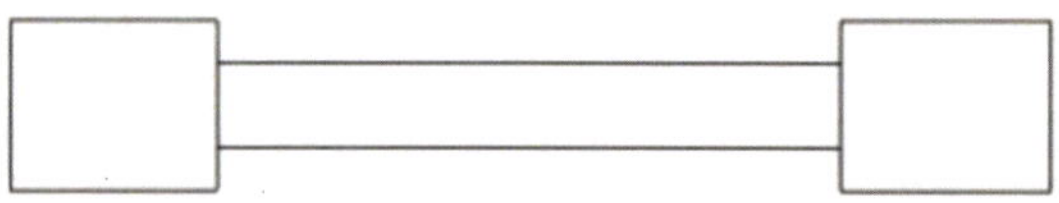

Click once to locate the beginning of the break. Move the pointer and click again to locate the end of the break; the view is automatically broken. Click the green check to confirm the break view.

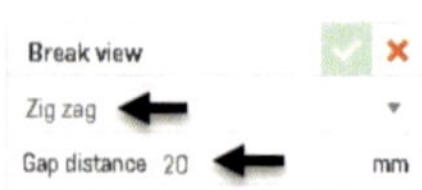

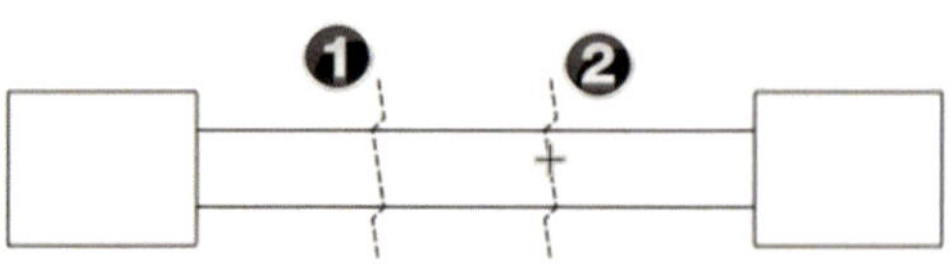

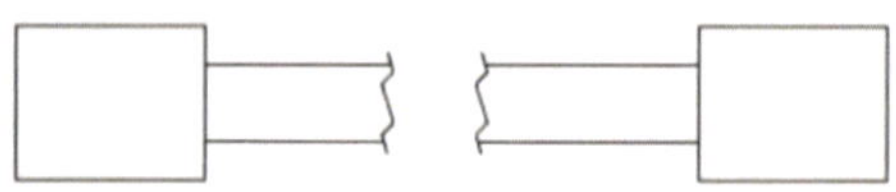

Break out section

The **Break out section** command alters an existing view to show the hidden portion of a part or assembly. This command is very useful to show the parts which are hidden inside an assembly view. You need to have a closed profile to break-out a view. For example, if you want to show the inside portion of a part shown in the figure, click the **Break-out section** icon on the toolbar. Next, draw a closed profile on the drawing view, as shown.

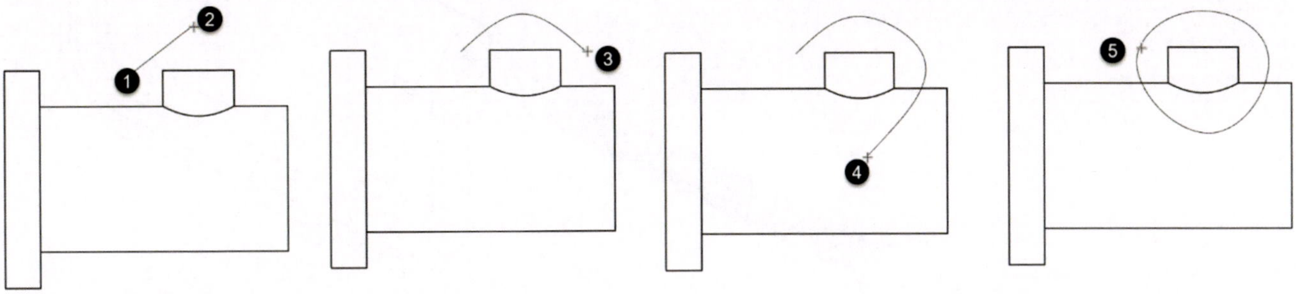

Now, you need to specify the depth of the break out. You can specify the depth using two options available in the **End type** drop-down: **Up to entity**, and **Blind**. Select the **Up to entity** option from the **End type** drop-down, and then specify the start point of the depth on the adjacent view. Next, check the Offset option and specify the offset value, if required.

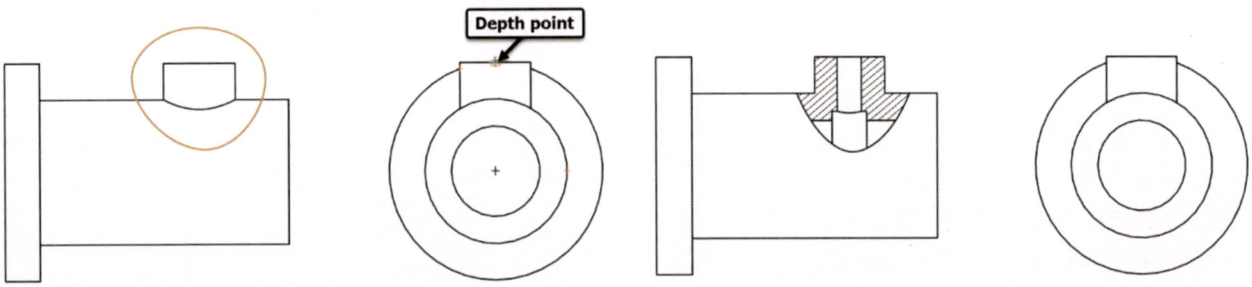

Exploded View

You can display an assembly in an exploded state as long as the assembly already has an exploded view defined in the assembly studio. In addition to that, exploded steps are needed to be created in the Assembly Studio. If you want to add an exploded view to the drawing, activate the **Insert View** command and click the **Insert** button. Next, click the **Assemblies** tab and select the assembly from the **Select a part or assembly** dialog. On the **Insert view** dialog, set the **View Orientation** to **Isometric**. Next, select **Explode/Position > Explode 1**. Click at the desired location on your drawing sheet.

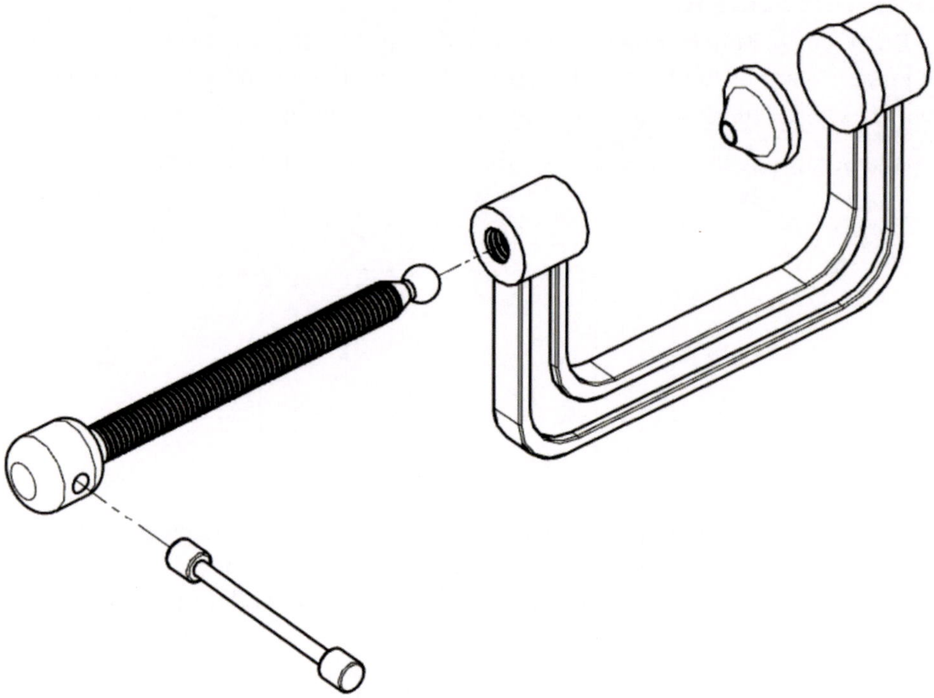

View Style

When working with Onshape drawings, you can control the way a model view is displayed. Select a model view from the drawing sheet, and then right-click and select the **Show/hide** > **Show shaded view** option. The view style of the selected model view is changed.

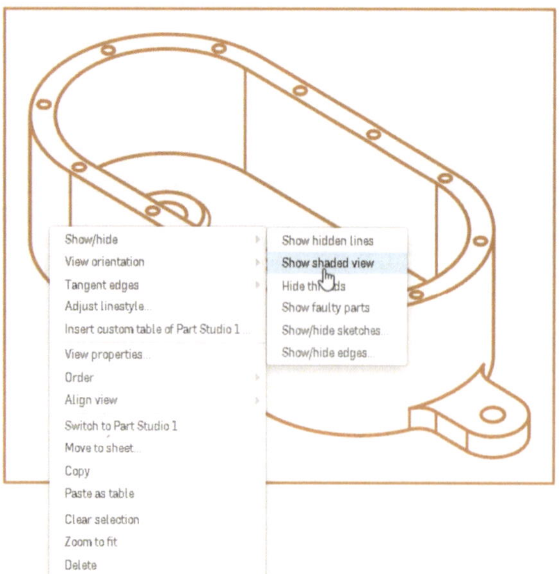

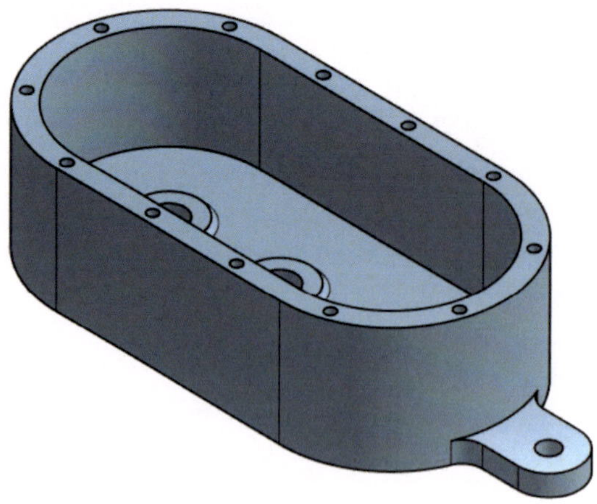

View Alignment

There are several types of views that are automatically aligned to a parent view. These include section views, auxiliary views, and projected views. If you move down a view, the parent view associated with it will also move.

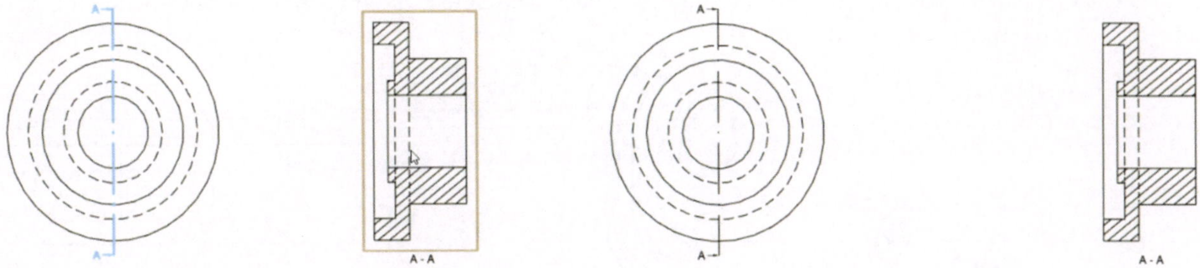

You need to break the alignment between them to move the view separately. Right-click on the section view and click **Suppress alignment with parent**.

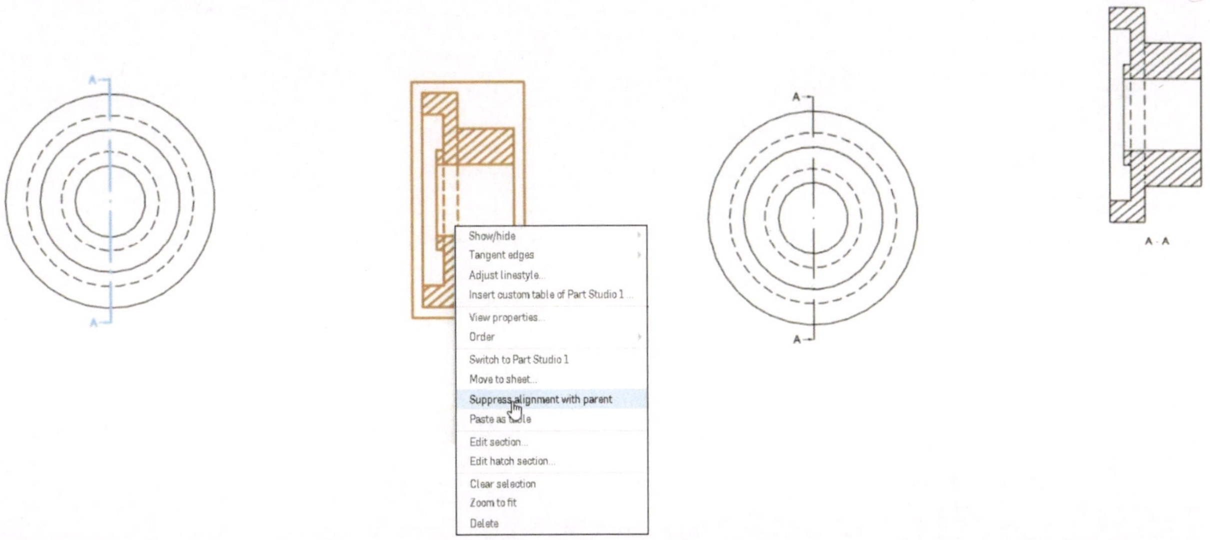

You can also unsuppress the alignment by right-clicking on the section view and selecting the **Unsuppress alignment with parent** option.

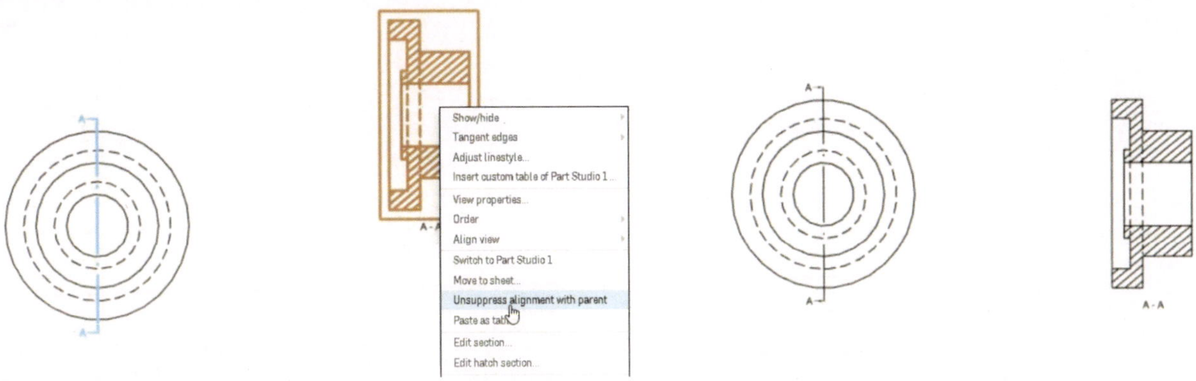

BOM table

Creating an assembly drawing is very similar to creating a part drawing. However, there are few things unique in an assembly drawing. One of them is Bill of materials. A Bill of Materials table list identifies the different components in an assembly. Generating a **BOM** table is very easy in Onshape. First, you need to have a view of the assembly. Next, click on the drawing and then click the **BOM table** icon on the drawing Toolbar; the table appears on the screen. On the **BOM table** dialog, select the **BOM type** from the drop-down, there are three types of BOMs: **Flattened, Structured-Top Level** and **Structured-Multi level**. Next, select an option from the **Order** drop-down, there are two types of orders: **Top to bottom** and **Bottom to top**. Move the pointer to the desired location and click to place the BOM table on the drawing sheet. The **Select fixed corner** options anchor the Bill of Materials (BOM) table by one of its four corners.

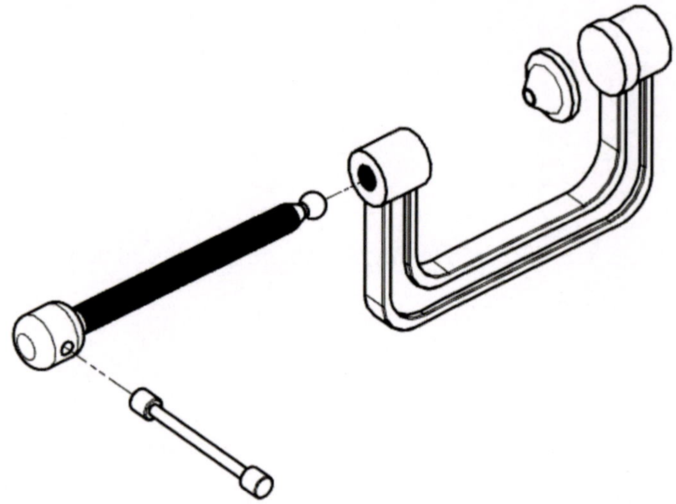

Item	Quantity	Part number	Description
1	1		
2	1		
3	1		
4	1		

Notice that the BOM table is empty. You can edit the table to display the desired data in it. To do this, switch to the **Assembly Studio** by right-clicking on the assembly view and selecting **Switch to Assembly**. Next, click the **BOM Table** tab located at the right-side of the graphics window.

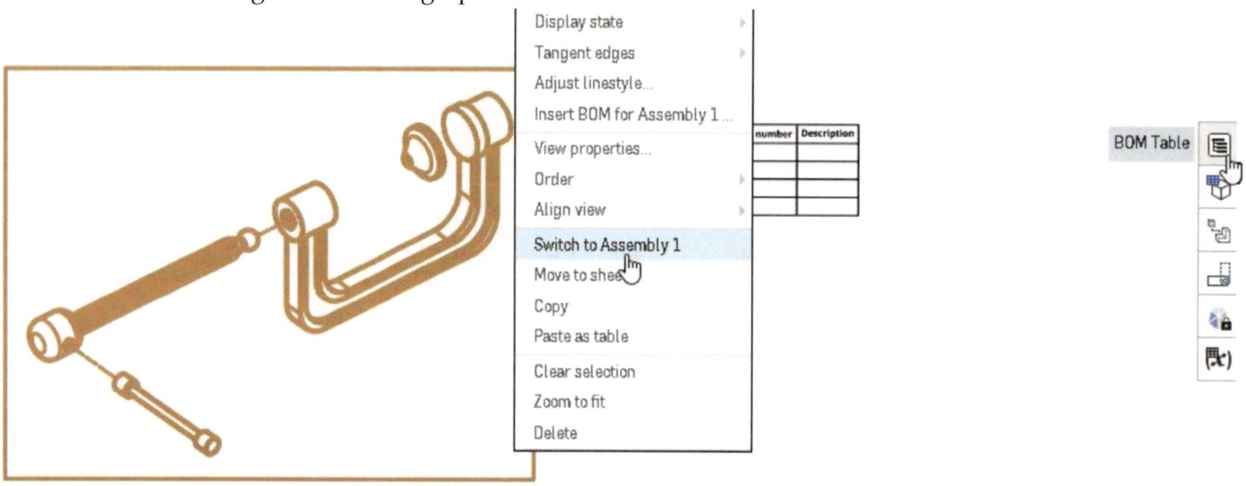

On the **Bill of Materials** panel, right-click on the **Part Number** column and select **Remove Column**. Next, click the **Add column** drop-down and select **Name**.

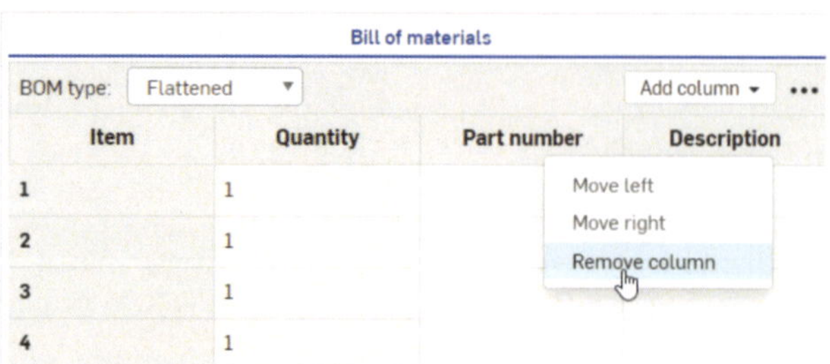

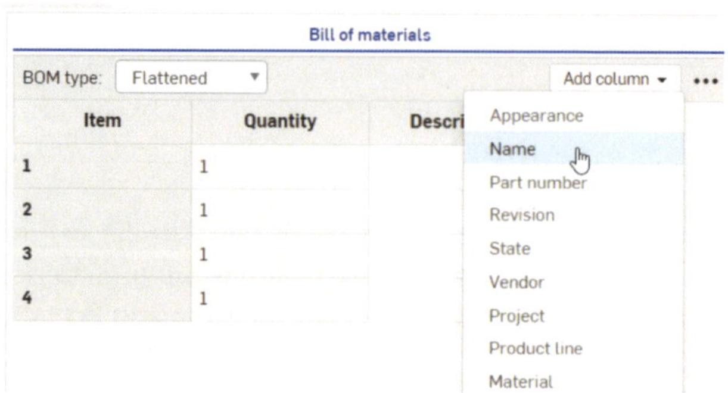

Click the right-mouse button on the **Name** column and select **Move Left**.

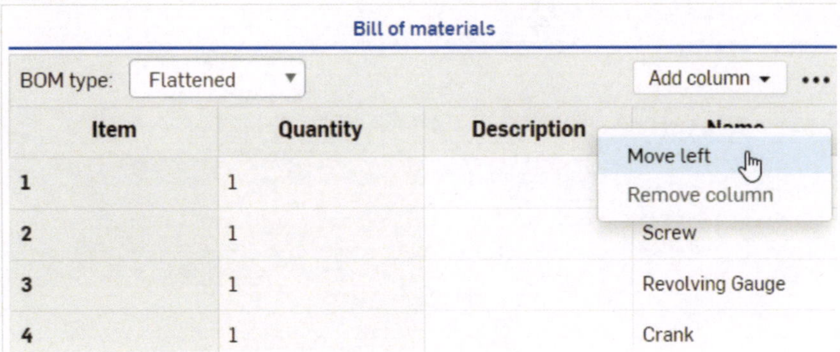

You can fill the **Description** column adding the description to the part files. To do this, right-click on the part file in the **Assembly** list and select the **Properties** option. Next, enter the text in the **Description** box, and then click **Apply** and **Close**. Switch to the drawing by clicking on the **Drawing** tab located at the bottom of the graphics window.

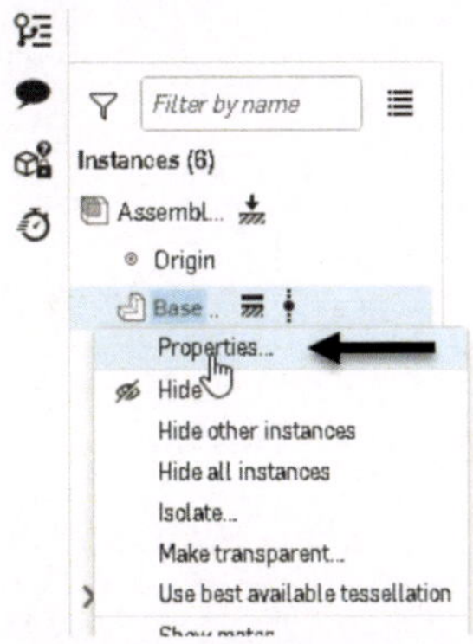

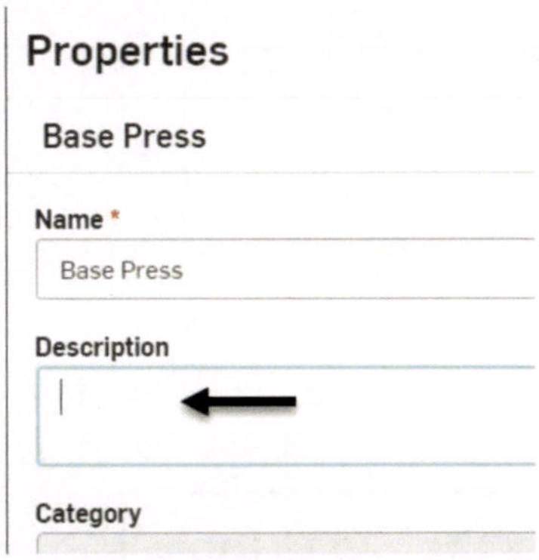

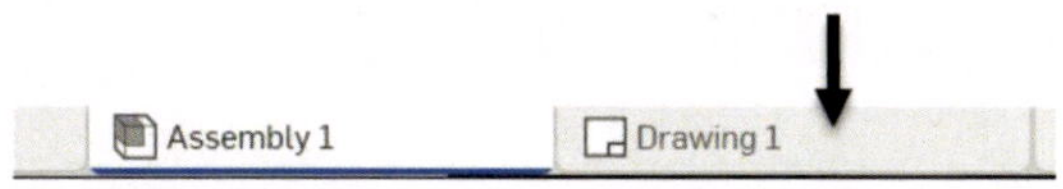

Click the Update from this workspace icon on the toolbar to update the BOM table.

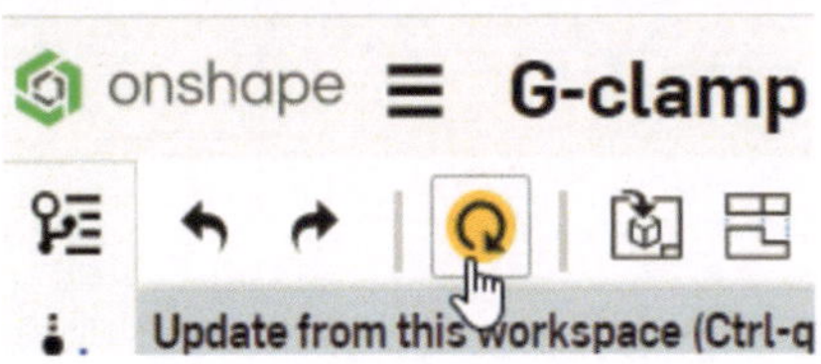

Item	Quantity	Name	Description
1	1	Base Press	
2	1	Screw	
3	1	Revolving Gauge	
4	1	Crank	

You can also edit the BOM table, by right-clicking on the table and selecting the **BOM table properties** option; the **BOM table properties** dialog appears. In this dialog, you can modify various settings for your Bill of Materials. You have the ability to change the table's Template, choose a BOM type like **Flattened**, and set the display Order of the components, such as **Top to bottom**. Additionally, the dialog shows the source **Document** and **Reference assembly**. You can also use the **Select fixed corner** options to define the table's anchor point, controlling the direction in which it expands as items are added or removed.

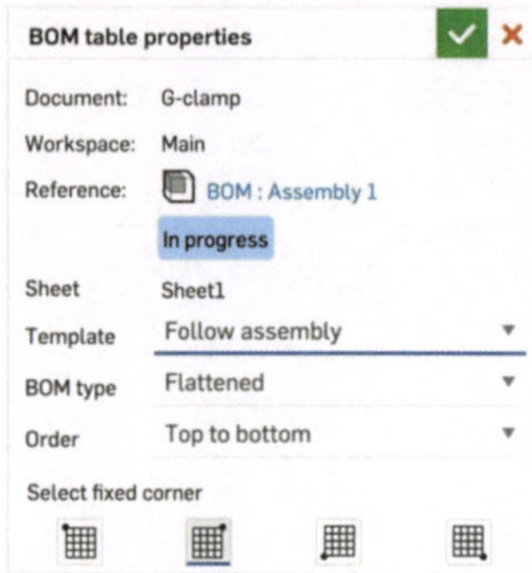

To delete the BOM table, select the entire table and right-click and select the **Delete** option (or) press Delete on the keyboard.

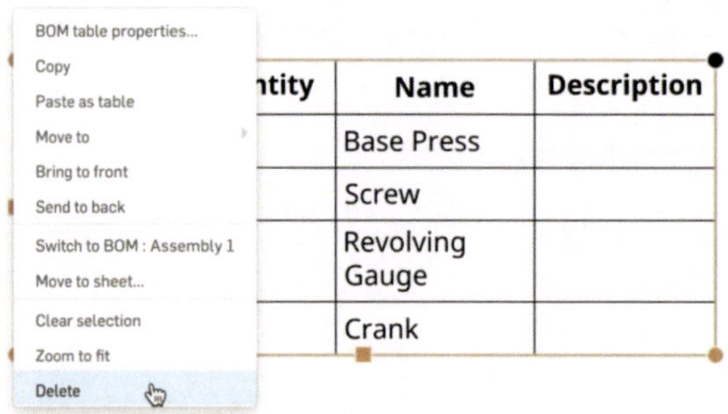

To move the BOM table, click and drag the corner grip of the table. Next, move the pointer and click to reposition in the desired location.

Moving the BOM table

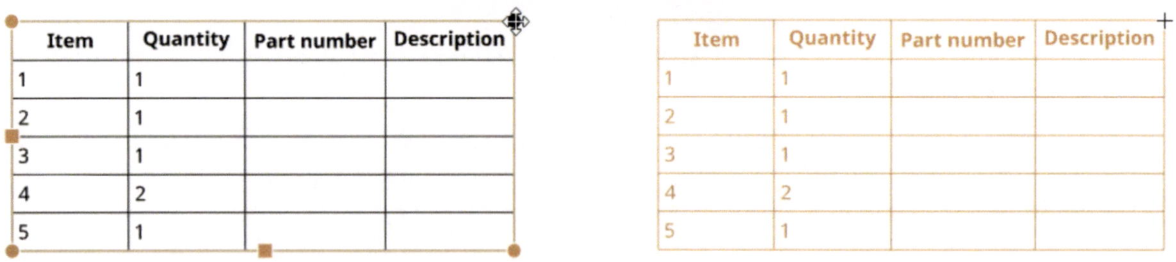

To resize the BOM table, select the entire table and click and drag on the middle grip of the table edges.

Resizing the BOM table

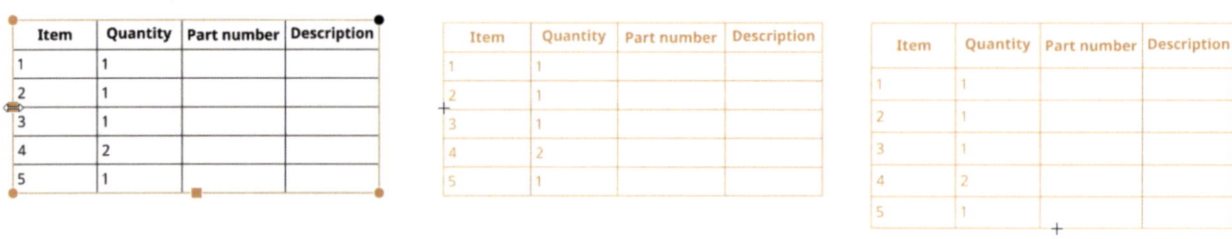

Adding Callouts

Click the **Callout** icon on the Drawing Toolbar. On the Callout dialog, specify the Table property and Part property options. By default, the Table property is set to **Item No**. It helps you to add balloons with item numbers in them. The **Part property** drop-down helps you to add additional information to the balloon such as Name, Description, and Part Number. Next, change the border shape from the **Border shape** drop-down. The different types of borders: *Circle, Diamond, Double Circle, Flag, Hexagon, Octagon, Rectangle, Split Circle, Square Circle, Triangle,* and *Underline*. Set the height of the text using the **Text height** drop-down. You can also add additional text in the text boxes displayed on the dialog.

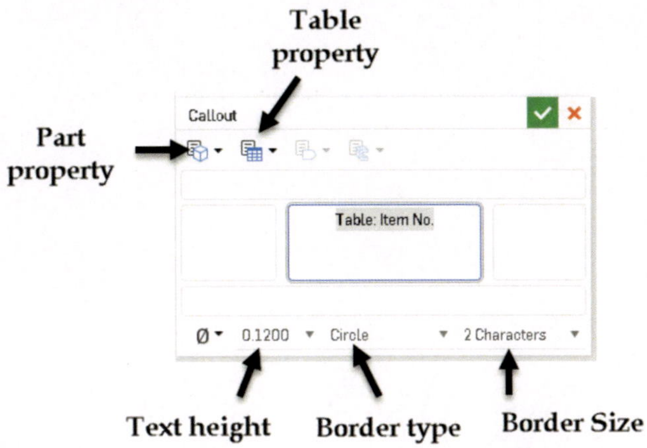

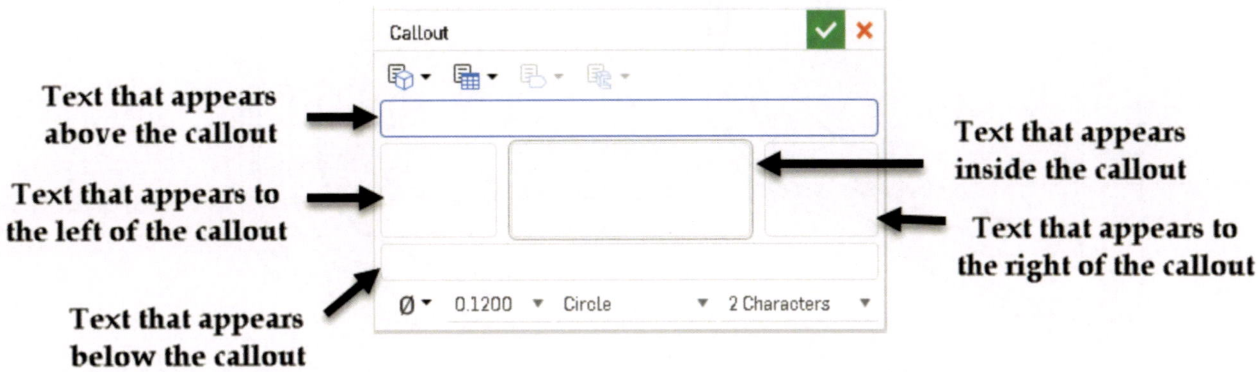

Next, select the part to add a callout. Move the pointer and click to locate the callouts. Likewise, select the other parts on the view to add other callouts and move and place the callouts. Click the green check to add the callout.

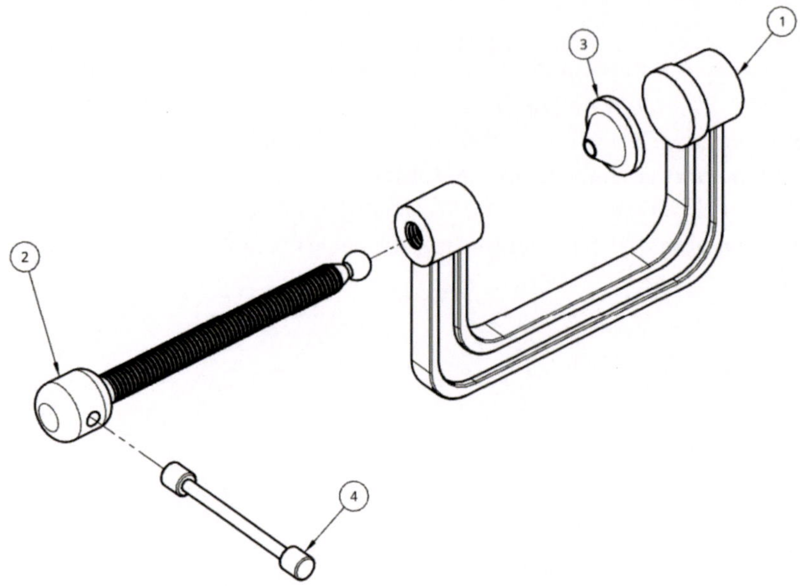

Item	Quantity	Name	Description
1	1	Base Press	
2	1	Screw	
3	1	Revolving Gauge	
4	1	Crank	

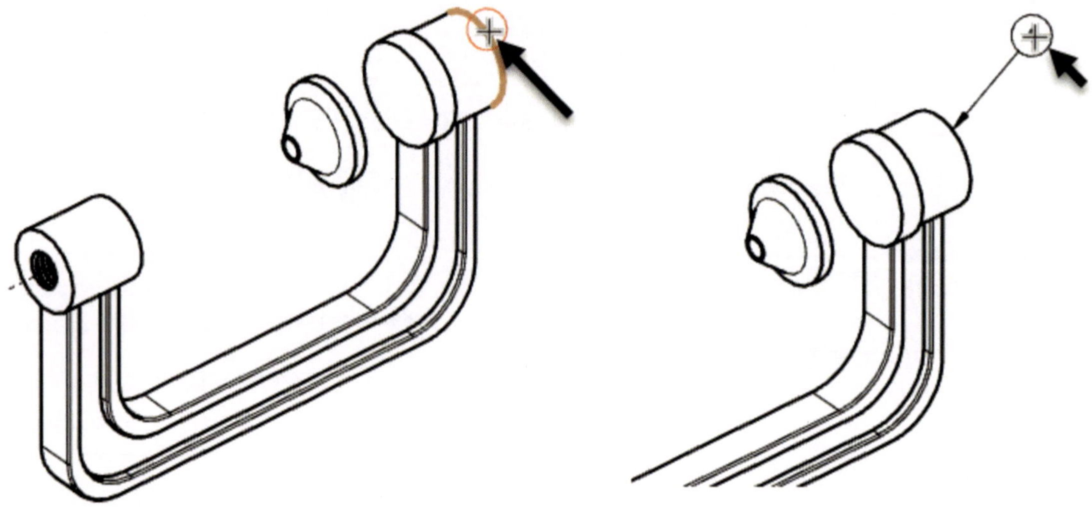

Dimensions

The **Dimensions** command helps you to create different types of dimensions based on the entity that you select. This command was explained in Chapter 2: Sketch Techniques. The remaining commands in the Drawing environment are explained next.

Maximum or minimum dimension

The **Maximum or minimum dimension** command allows you to create the dimension between the two selected circles or arcs. On the toolbar, click **Dimension** drop-down > **Maximum or minimum dimension** . Next, click on the outer portions of the circles or arc; a dimension is created between the outer portions of the circles. The dimension will be the maximum distance between the circles or arcs. Likewise, a dimension will be created between the inner portions of the circles, if you click on their inner portions.

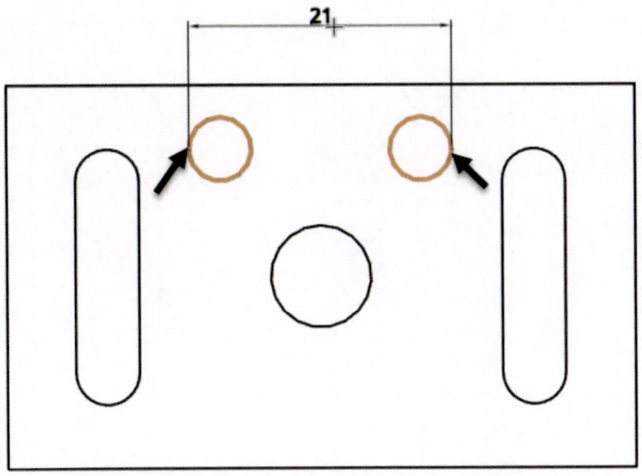

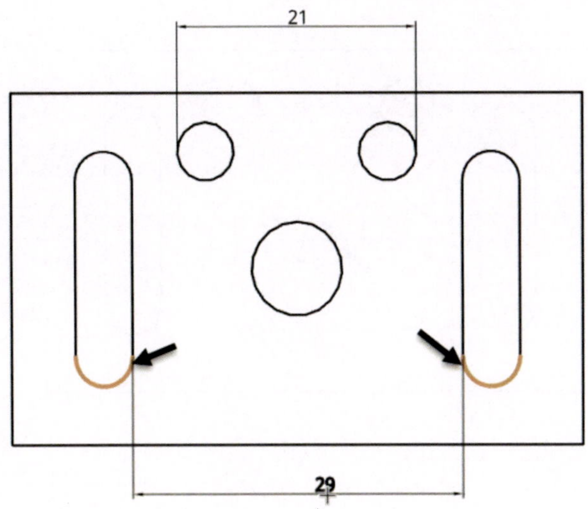

2 point Linear Dimension

The **2 point linear dimension** command allows you to create the dimension between the two selected points. You can create the vertical or horizontal or rotated linear dimensions using the two selected points. Click **Dimension > 2 point linear dimension** on the Toolbar. Next, select two points from the drawing view. Move the pointer and click to position the dimension.

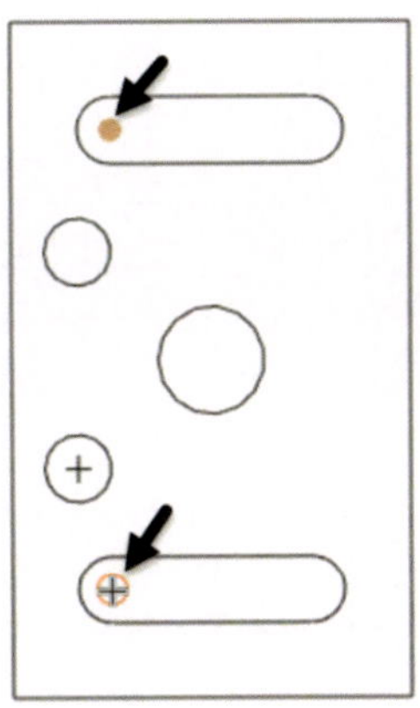

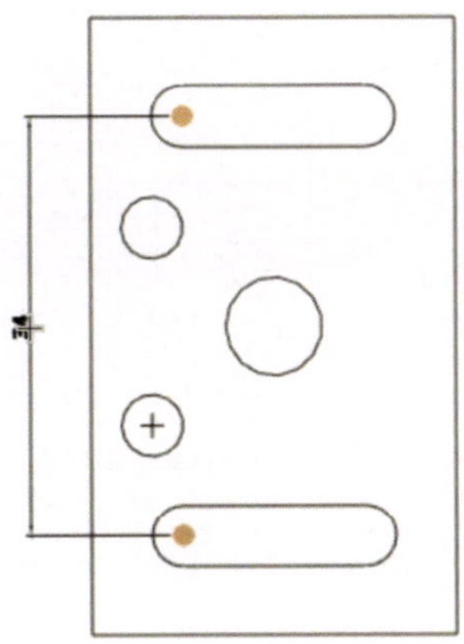

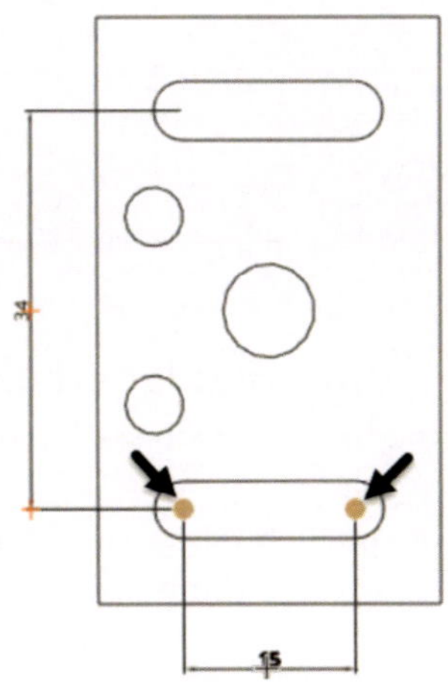

Point to Line Dimension

The **Point to line dimension** command allows you to create a dimension between a point and a line. You can create the vertical or horizontal or rotated dimensions using a point and a line. Click **Dimension > Point to line dimension** on the Toolbar. Next, select a point and line. Move the pointer and specify the dimension location.

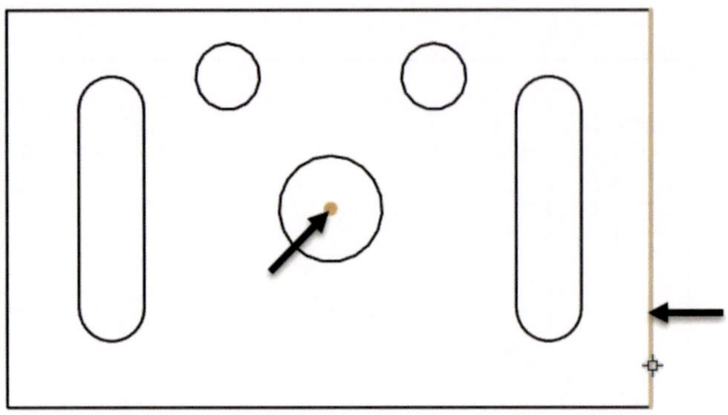

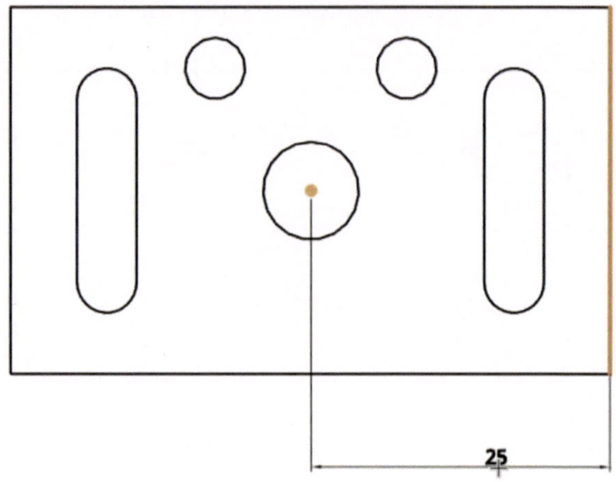

Line to line dimension

The **Line to line dimension** command allows you to measure the distance between the two parallel lines. On the Toolbar, click **Dimension > Line to line dimension**. Next, select two lines from the drawing view. Move the pointer and click to specify the dimension location.

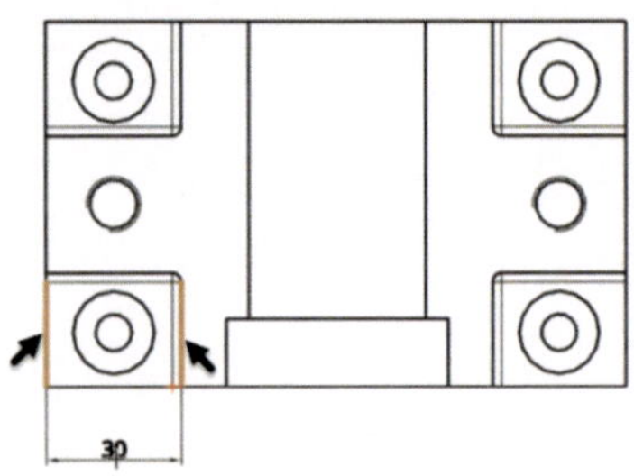

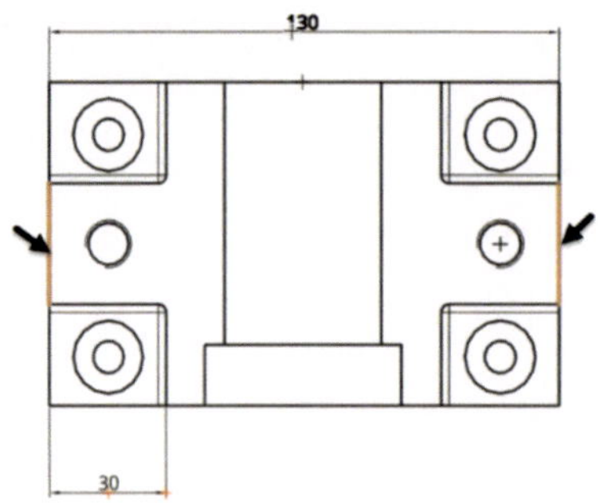

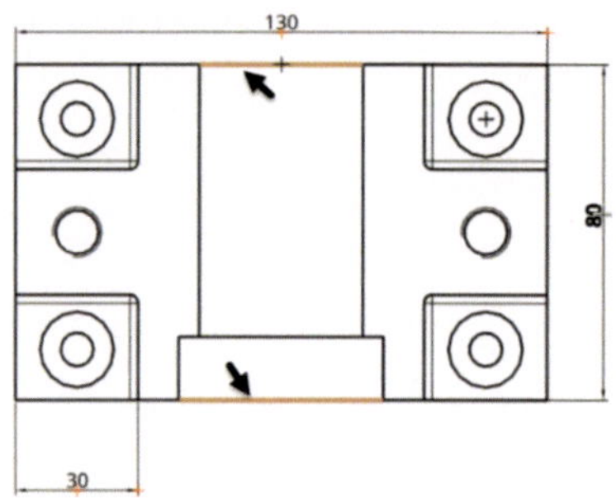

Line to line angular dimension

The **Line to line angular dimension** command allows you to create an angular dimension between two lines. On the toolbar, click **Dimension > Line to line angular dimension** and select two lines. Move the pointer and click to place the dimension.

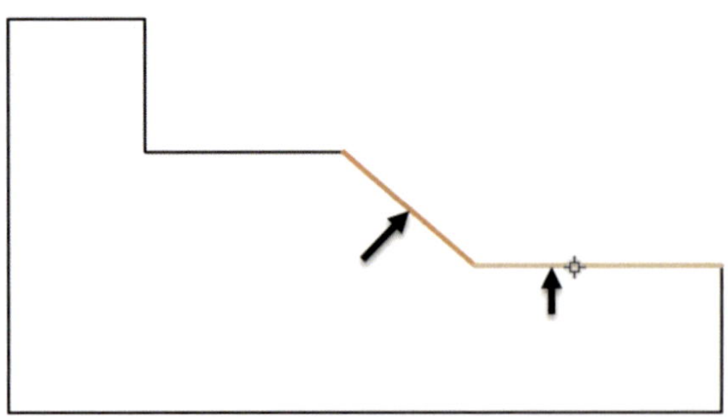

SCALE 1:1

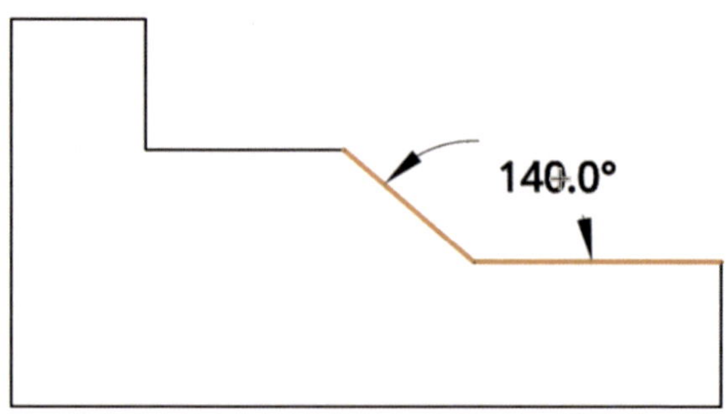

SCALE 1:1

3 Point angular dimension

The **3 Point angular dimension** command allows you to create an angular dimension between three points. On the Toolbar, click **Dimension > 3 Point angular dimension** and select the first point. Next, select the other two points; the angle dimension appears on the screen. Move the pointer and click to place the dimension.

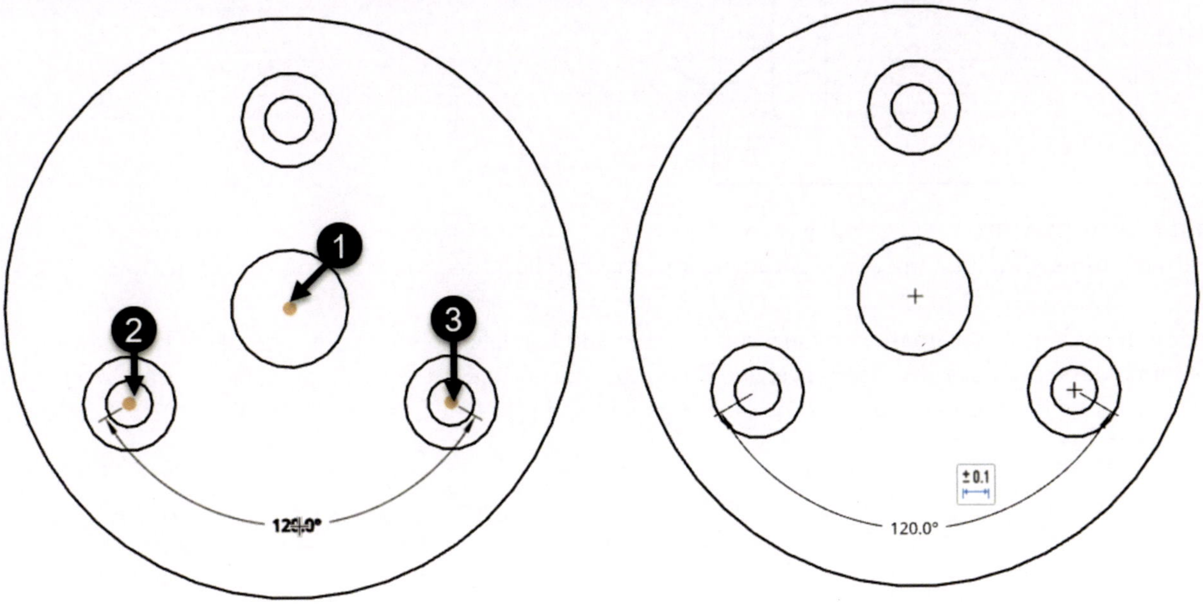

Radial Dimension

The **Radial dimension** command allows you to add a radial dimension to a circle or arc. On the Toolbar, click **Dimension > Radial dimension** and select the circle or an arc. Move the pointer and click to place the radial dimension.

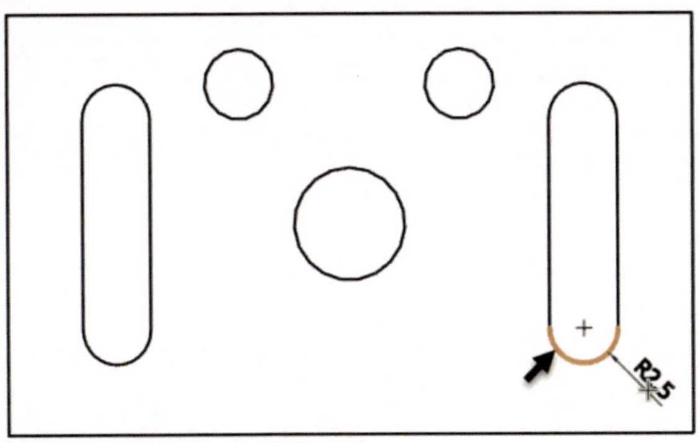

Diameter Dimension

The **Diameter dimension** command allows you to add a diameter dimension to the circle or arc. On the Toolbar, click **Dimension > Diameter dimension** and select the circle or an arc. Next, click to place the diameter dimension.

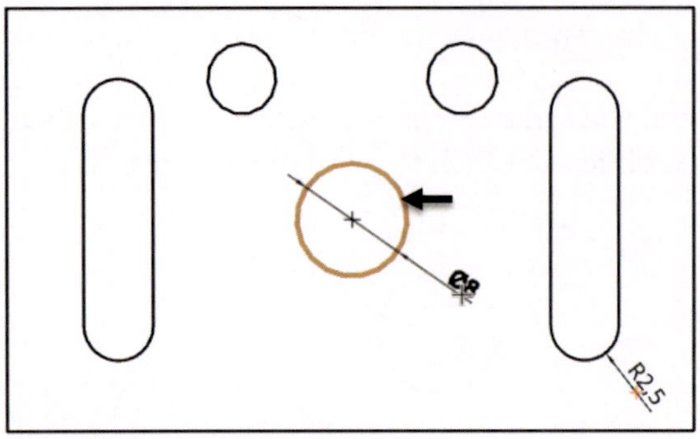

Ordinate Dimension

The **Ordinate dimension** is another type of dimensions that can be added to a drawing. To create them, click **Dimension** drop-down **> Ordinate Dimension** on the Toolbar. Click on the point or edge of the drawing view to define the ordinate or zero reference, and then move the pointer in the horizontal or vertical direction and click. Now, click on the points or edges of the drawing view and place the ordinate dimensions.

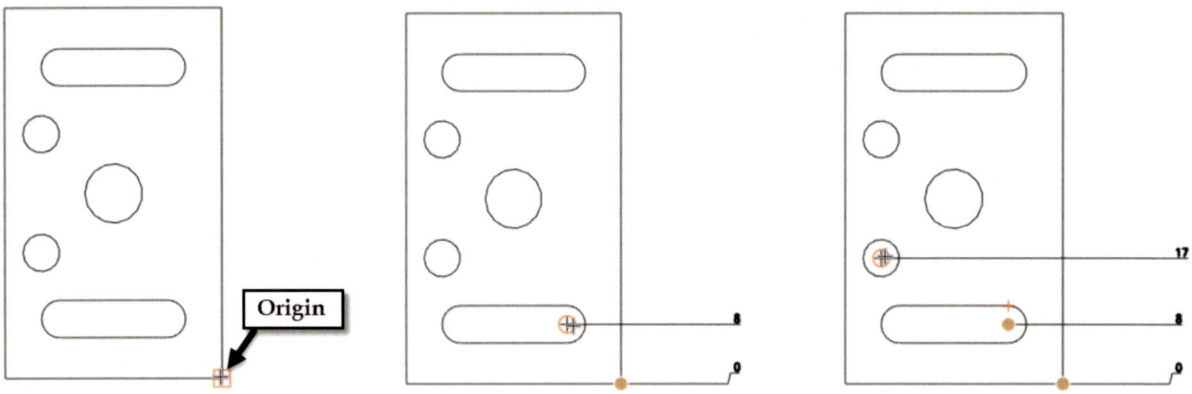

Likewise, select the remaining edges or points to create ordinate dimensions. Press **Esc** after you have finished creating the ordinate dimensions.

Chamfer Dimension

The **Chamfer Dimension** command dimensions the beveled edges created in the Part Studio. Click **Dimension > Chamfer Dimension** on the toolbar and select the chamfered edge. Next, select the reference edge, move the pointer, and click to position the chamfer dimensions.

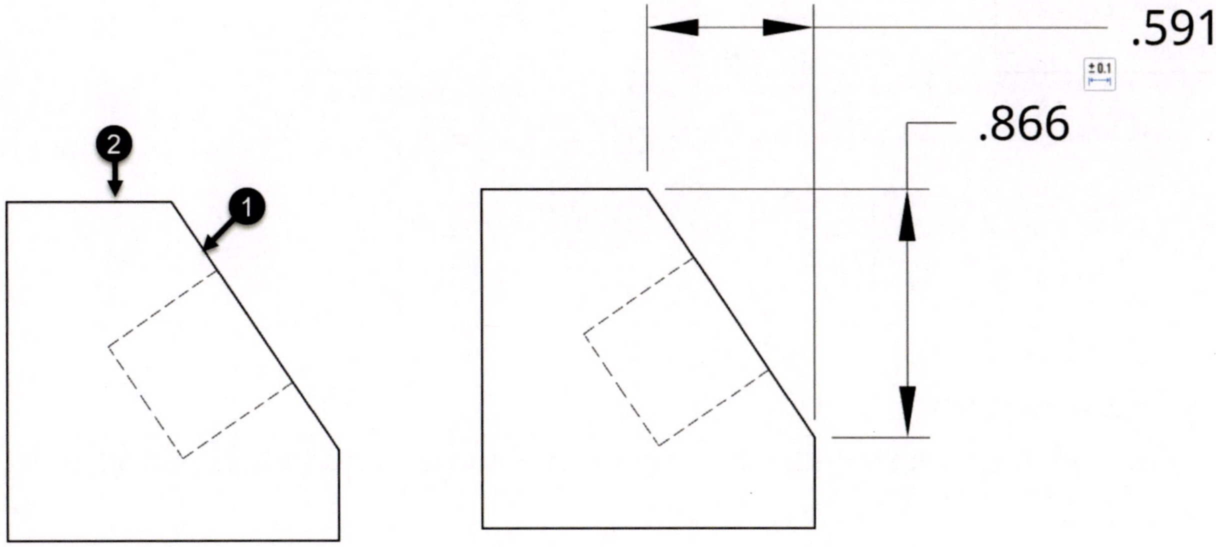

Hole Callout

The **Hole Callout** command allows you to add a note to a simple or threaded hole. Click **Hole callout** ⌀↧ on the toolbar and select a hole; the note is attached to the pointer. Notice that the **Hole callout** command captures the information of the hole from the 3D model. It displays detailed information of the hole only when you have created the hole using the **Hole** command rather than the **Extrude** or **Revolve** command. Move the pointer and position the hole callout. Likewise, you can add a thread note to the threaded hole or external thread. Press **Esc** to deactivate the command.

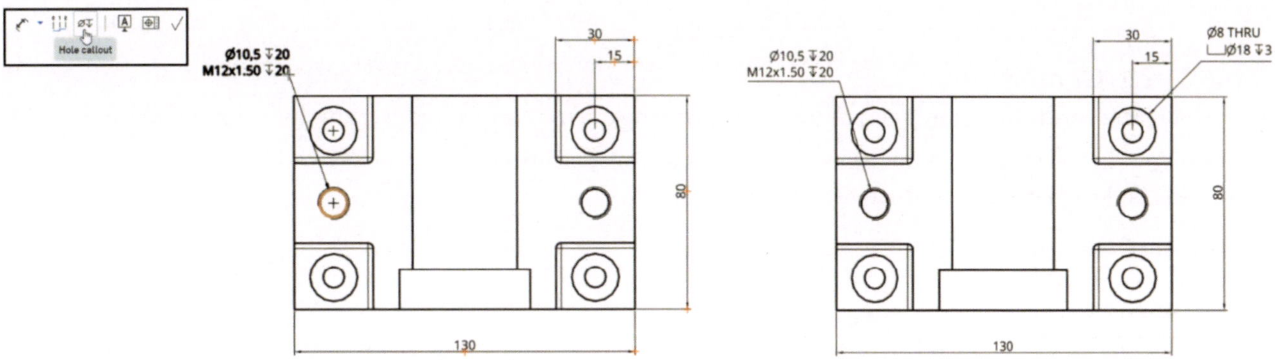

Center Marks and Centerlines

Centerlines and Centermarks are used in engineering drawings to denote hole centers and lines. The commands to create center marks and centerlines are explained next.

2 Point Centerline

The **2 point centreline** command is used to create a linear centreline using two points on the drawing view. Click the **2 point centreline** icon on the Toolbar. Next, select the two points on the drawing view.

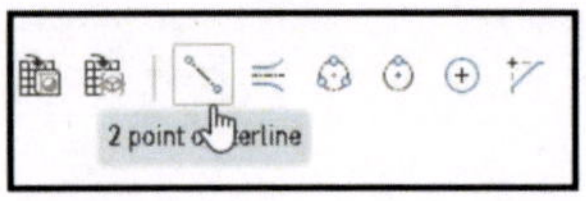

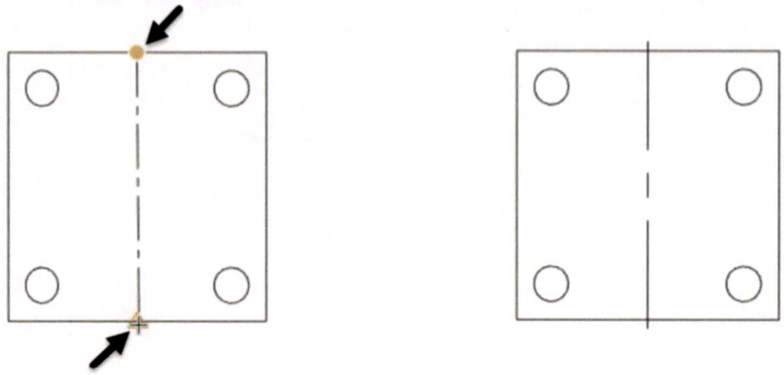

Edge-to-edge centerline

On the Toolbar, click **Edge to edge centreline** , and then click on two edges of the drawing view. A centerline will be created between the two lines.

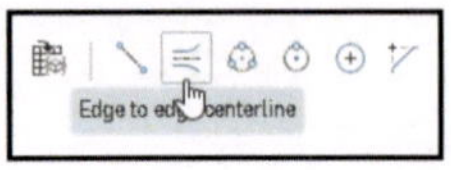

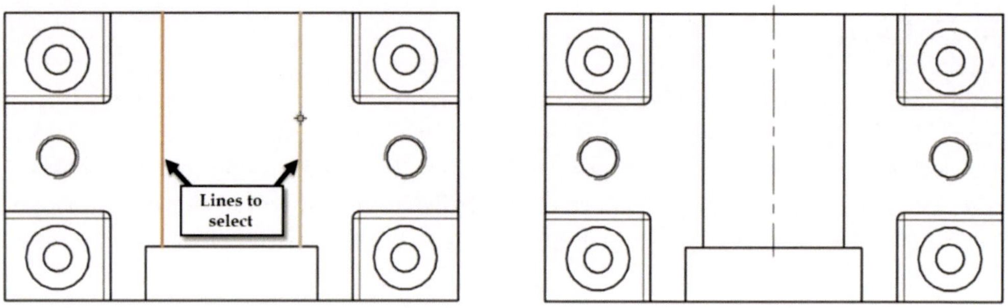

3 Point Circle Centerline

The **3 Point circle centreline** command allows you to create circular centreline passing through the centers of the circles arranged in a circular fashion. Click the **3 Point circle centreline** icon on the toolbar. Click on the center points of the circles. Press Esc to deactivate the command.

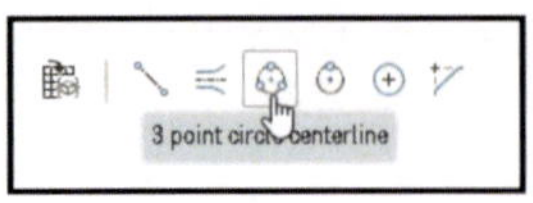

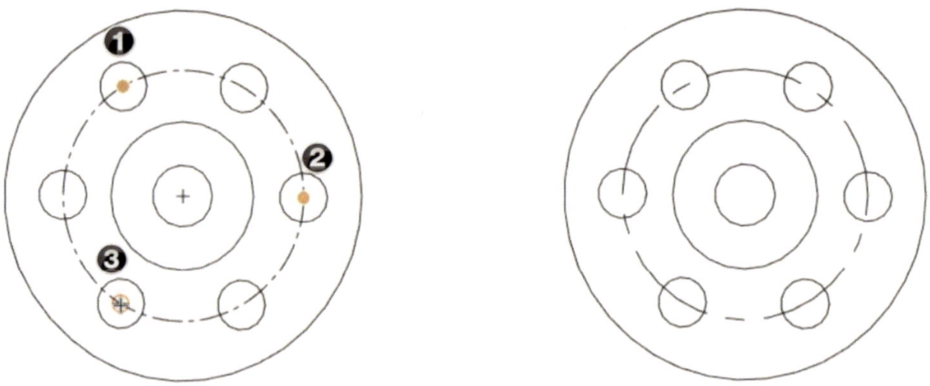

Two Point Circle Centerline

The **Two point circle centreline** command is used to create a circular centreline by specifying its center and radius point. To add circular centreline, click the **Two point circle centreline** icon on the Toolbar. Next, specify the center and radius point of the circular centerlines. Press Esc to deactivate the command.

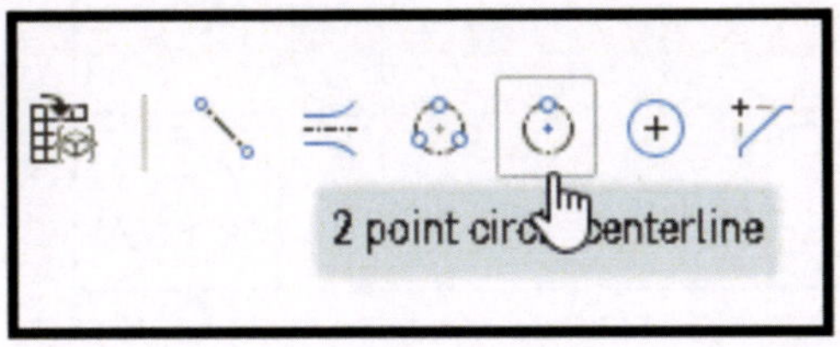

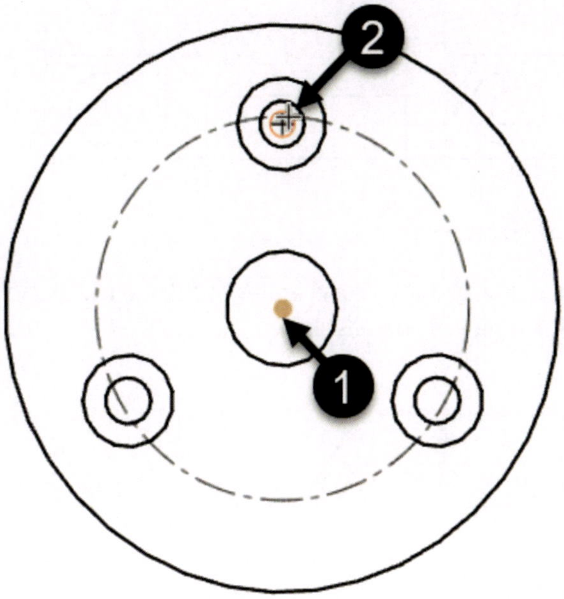

Centermark

To add center marks to holes, click the **Centermark** icon on the Toolbar and select the hole circle. Press **Esc** to deactivate the command.

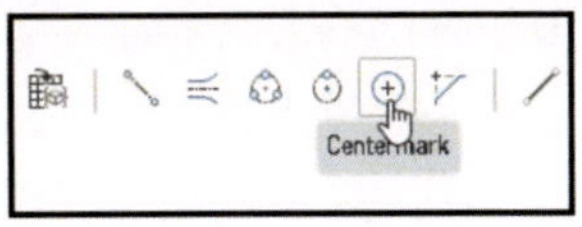

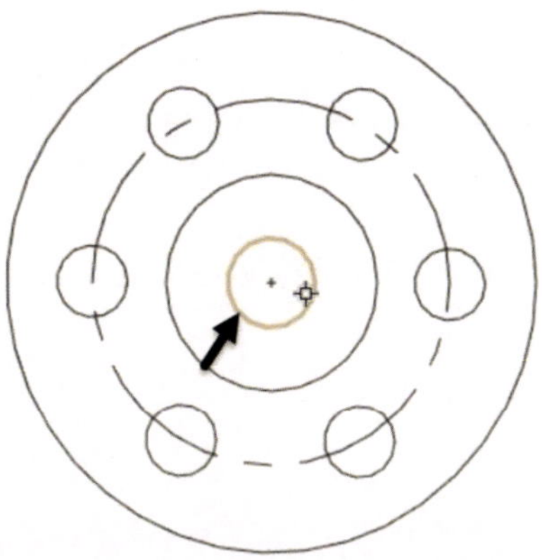

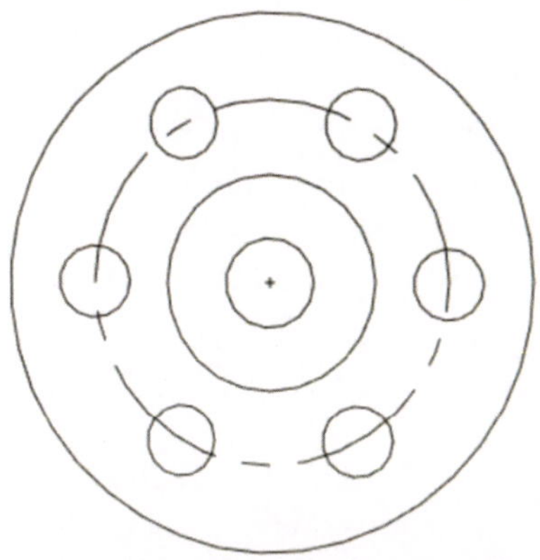

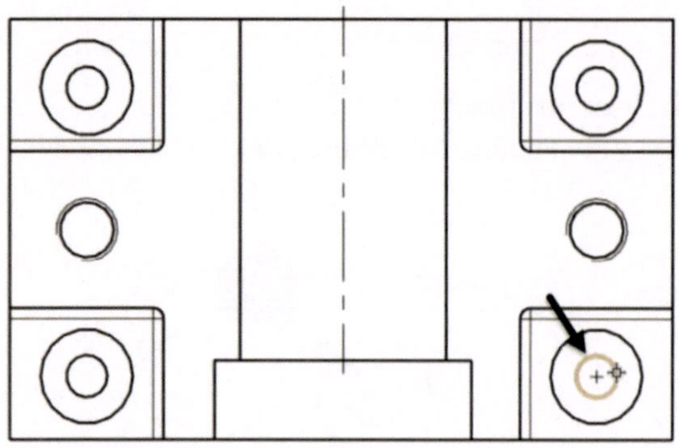

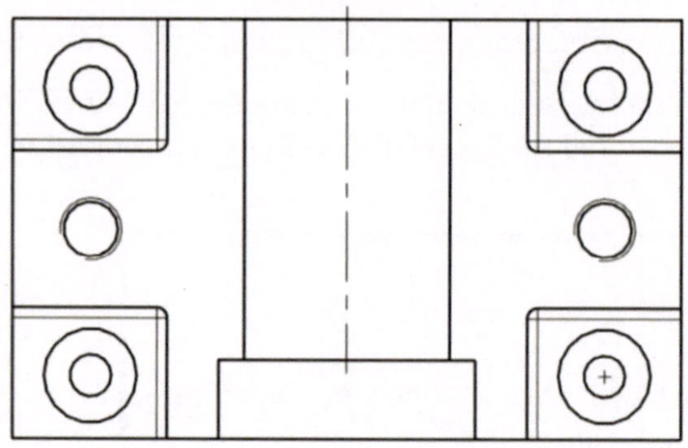

Virtual Sharp

To add a virtual sharp to a chamfer or fillet, click the **Virtual Sharp** icon on the Toolbar and select two linear edges forming a corner, as shown.

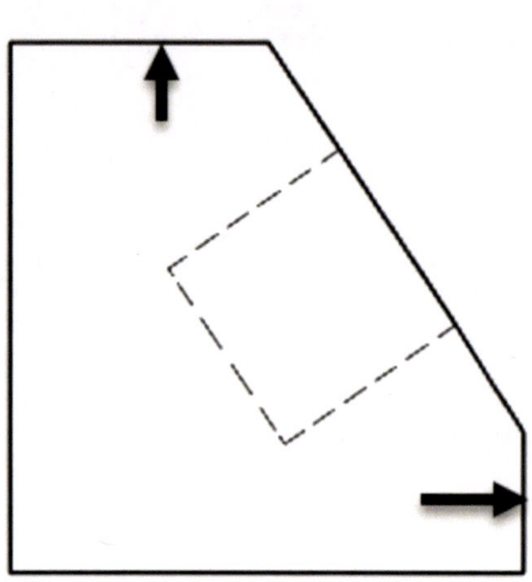

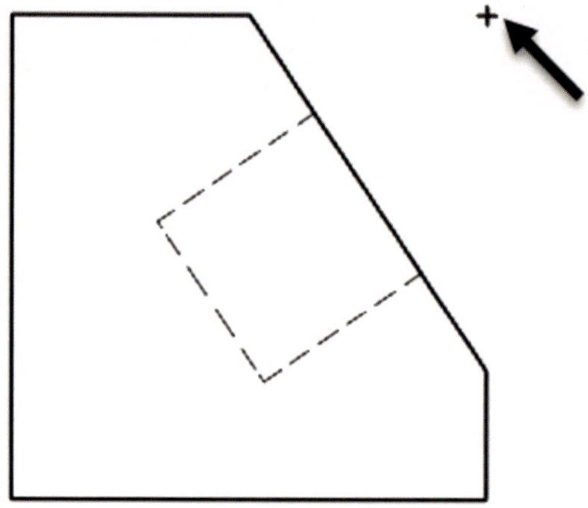

Note

Notes are an important part of a drawing. You add notes to provide additional details, which cannot be done using dimensions and annotations. To add a note or text, click **Note** on the Toolbar. Click on the drawing sheet to specify the note location. On the **Note** dialog, select the **Font** and **Text height**. Type in a text in the text box. You can use the symbols from the **Insert symbol** drop-down on the **Note** dialog. On the dialog, click the green check to add a note.

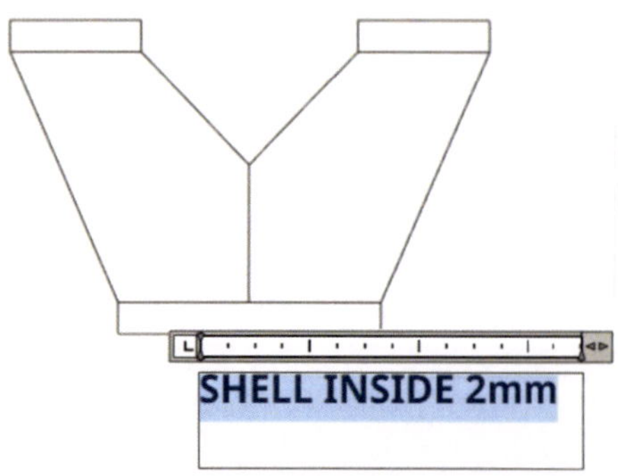

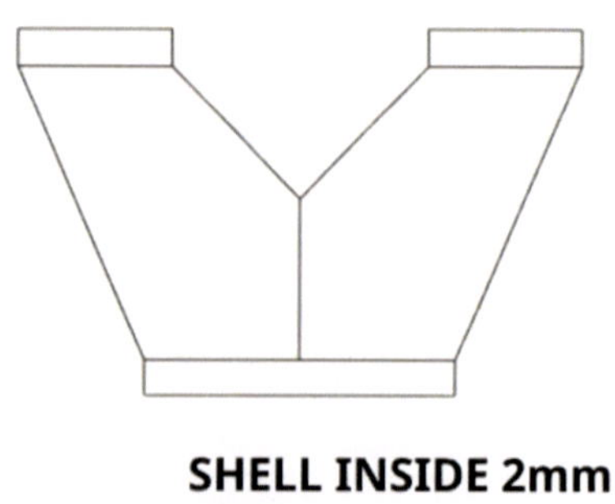

Tutorial 1

In this example, you create the 2D drawing of the part shown below.

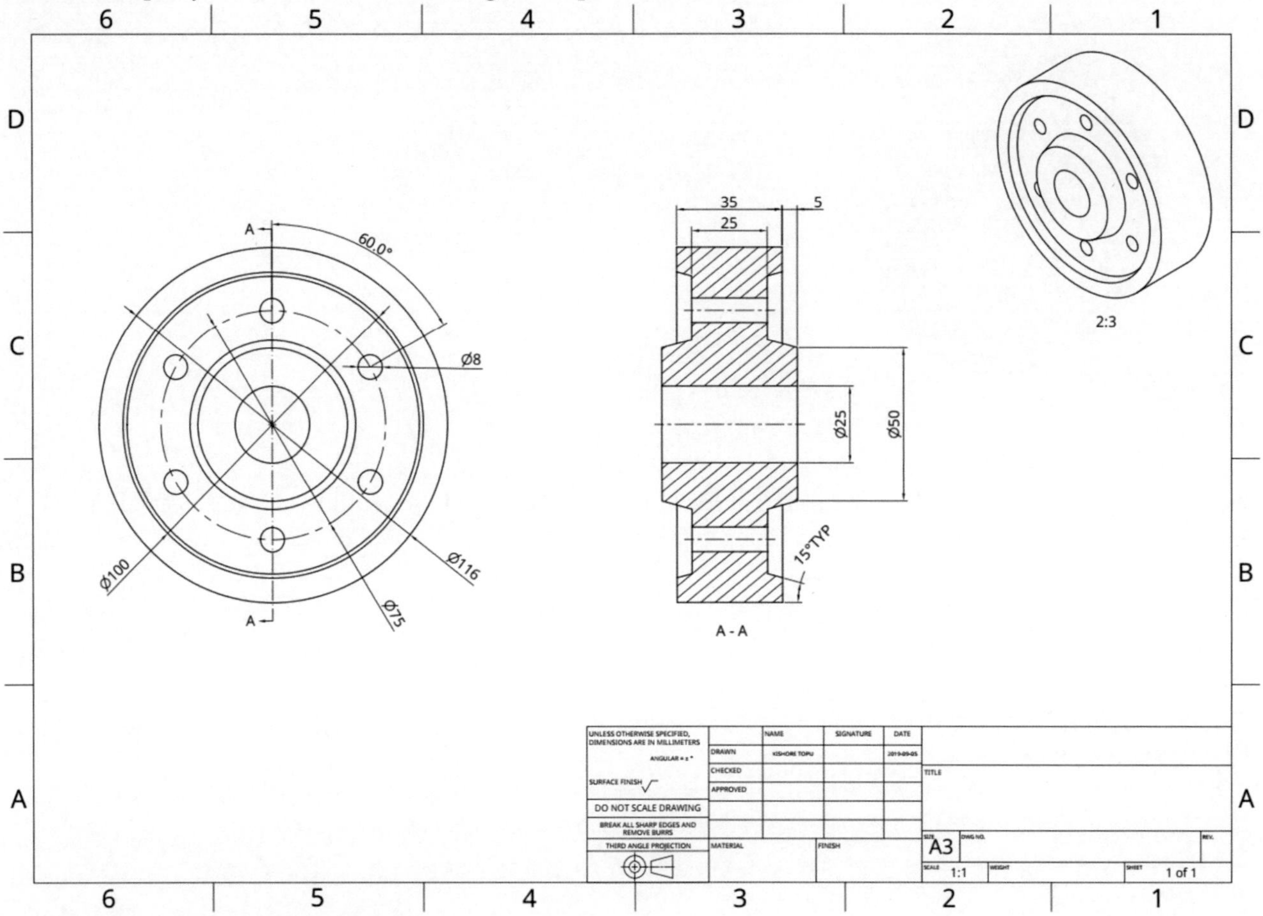

Creating a New Drawing

1. Download the **Chapter 11** part files from the companion website. Next, extract the zip file.
2. In your Internet Browser, go to https://www.onshape.com to start Onshape.
3. Next, click the **SIGN IN** button located on the top right corner side of the web page. Enter the username and password, and then, click **Sign in**.
4. On the Documents page, click **Create > Folder**. Next, type Chapter 11 in the **Folder name** box and then click **Create**.
5. Double-click on the **Chapter 11** folder in the **Folders** section.
6. On the Documents page, Click **Create > Import Files** and select the **Tutorial 1** part file from the extracted zip folder. Next, click **Open** to import the selected file.
7. Double click on the imported document to open it.

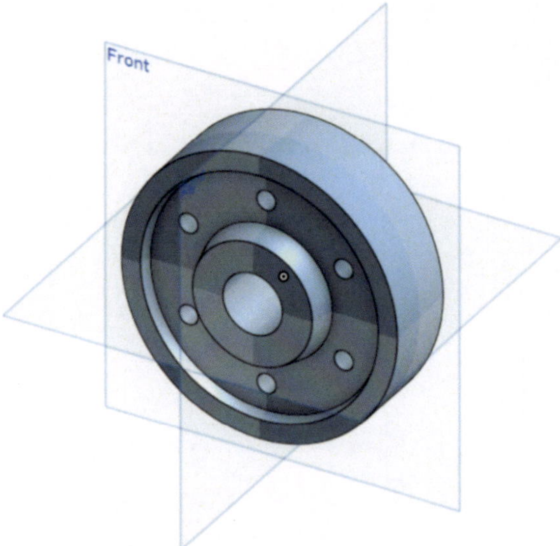

8. Click the **Insert new element** button located at the bottom left corner of the window. Next, select **Create Drawing** from the menu.

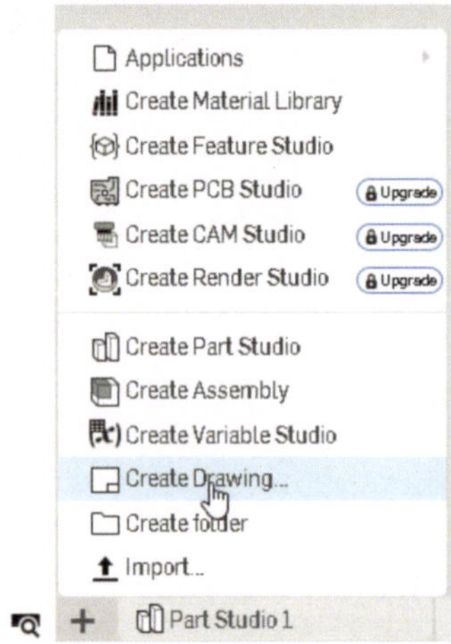

9. On the **Create Drawing** dialog, click the **Custom template** tab to create a custom template.
10. Select the **Standard > ISO** and then select **Size > A3**.
11. Select the **Units > Millimeters** and then select **Decimal separator > Period (12.34)**.
12. Select **Projection > Third angle (ANSI)**.
13. In the **Borders** section on the right side of the dialog, click **Include** option to include the border in the drawing sheet.
14. Select **Horizontal zones > 6** and **Vertical zones > 4**.
15. Click **Start zones > Bottom right** and **Titleblock > Include**.
16. Click **OK** to create a custom template and start a new drawing file.

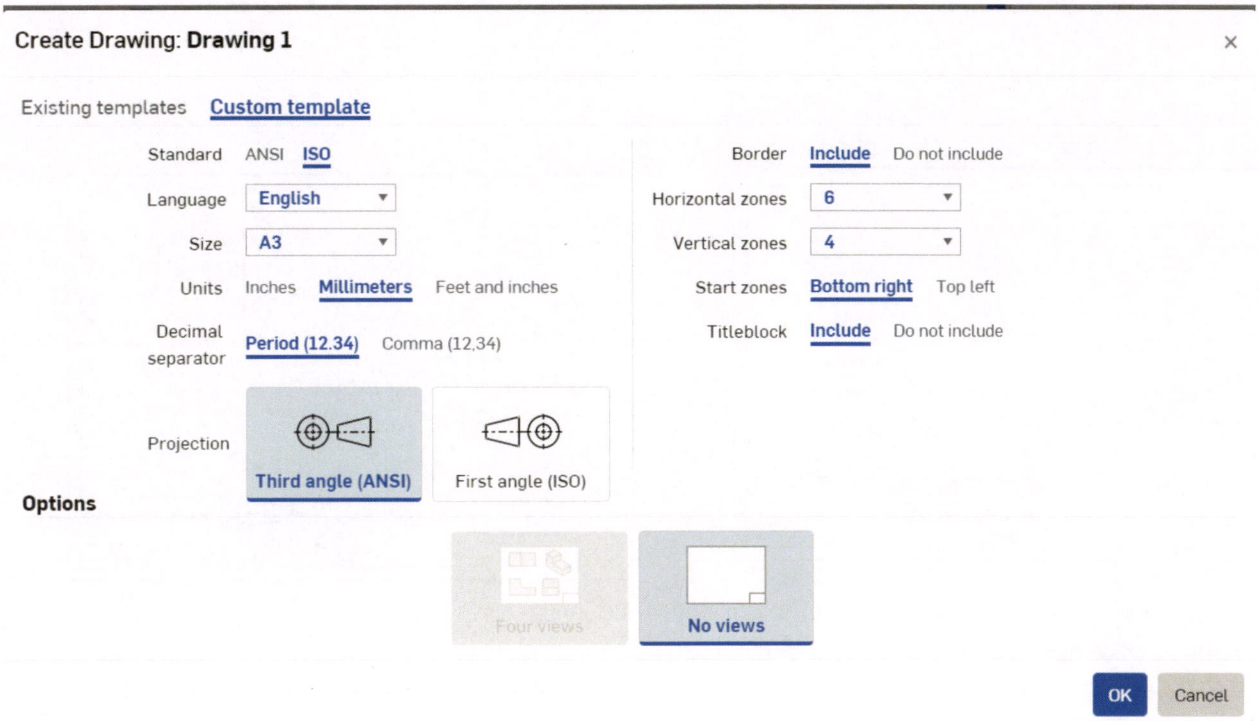

17. Select **Part 1** from the **Select a part or assembly** dialog.

Inserting Drawing Views

1. On the **Insert view** dialog, select **View > Front**. Next, select **View scale > 1:1**.
2. Click on the drawing sheet at the location, as shown.

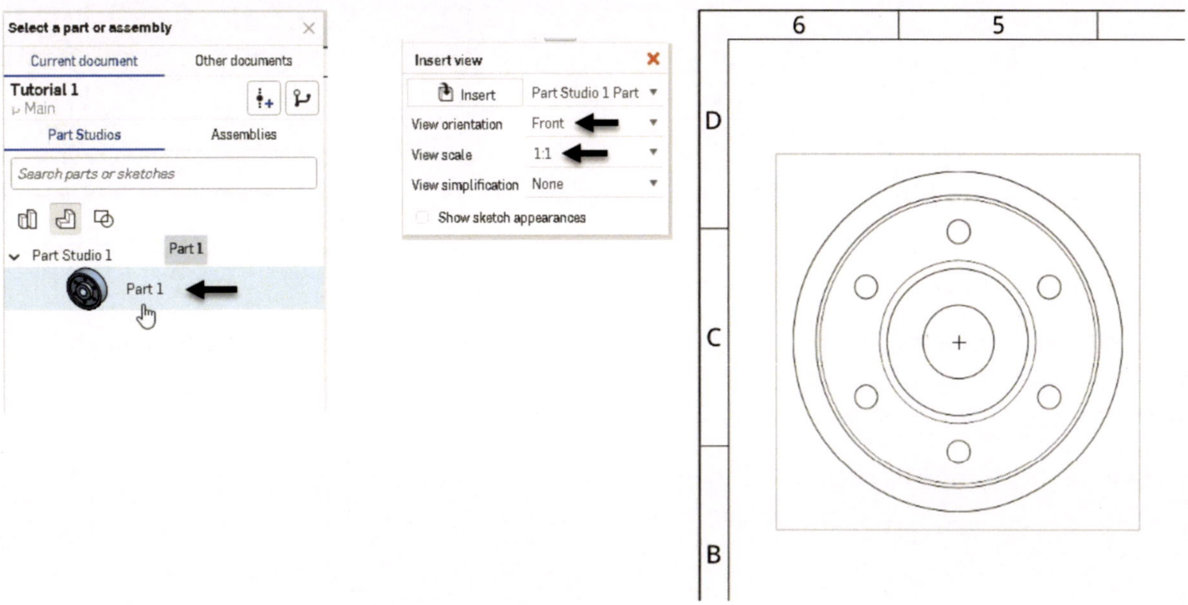

3. Move the pointer toward top right corner and click to position the isometric view, as shown.
4. Press Esc to deactivate the **Projected view** command.
5. Click and drag the Isometric view to the location, as shown.

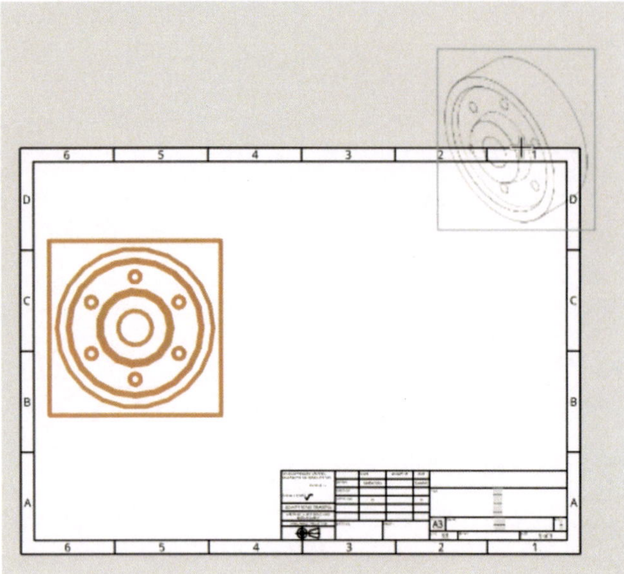

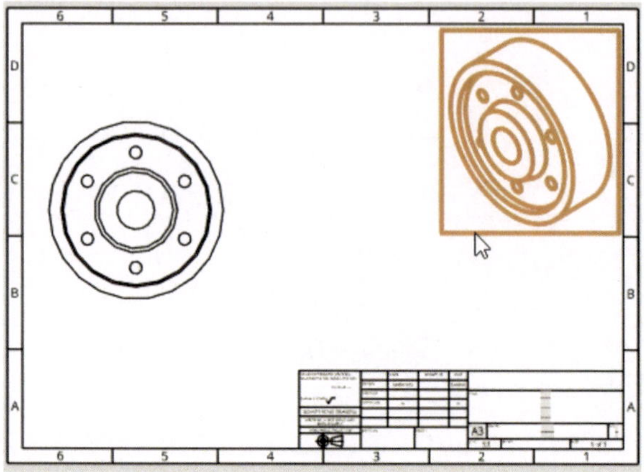

6. Double-click on the Isometric view; the **View properties** dialog appears.
7. On the **View properties** dialog, type **2:3** in the **Scale** box and click the green check.

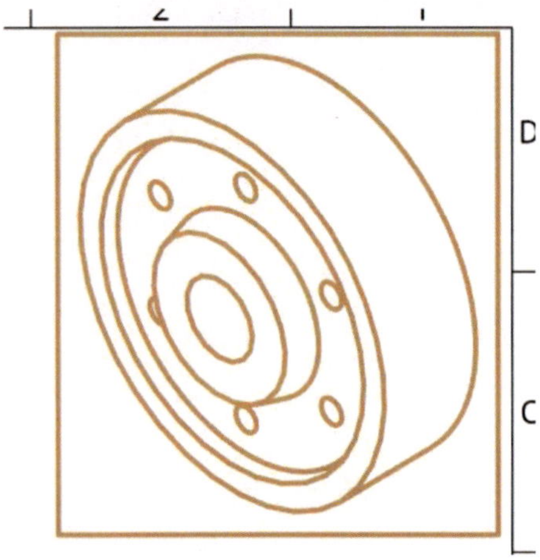

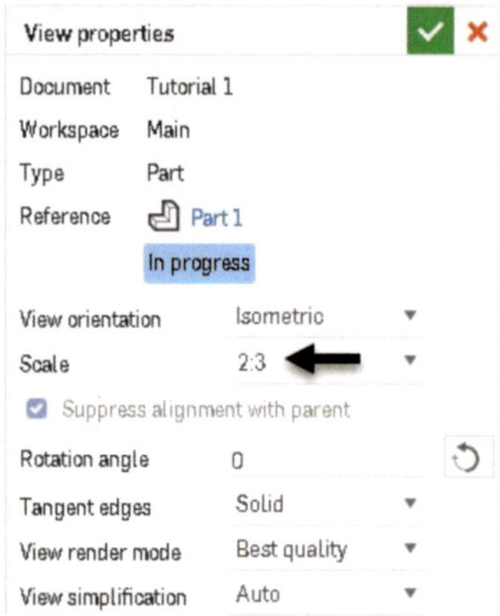

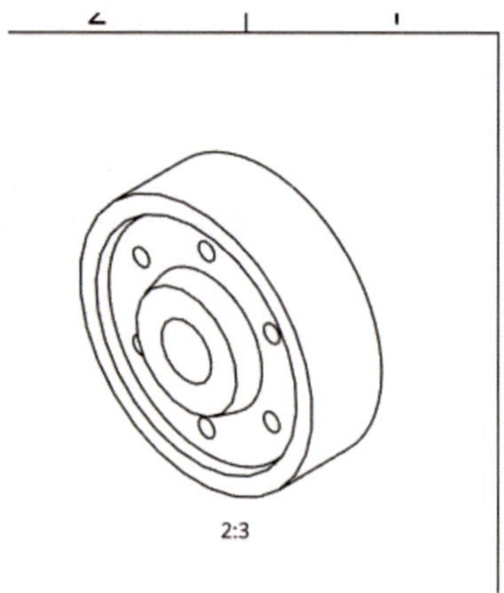

Creating the Section view

1. Activate the **Section view** command (click the **Section view** icon on the Toolbar) and click the **Vertical** tab on the **Section View** dialog.
2. Select the center point of the front view. Next, click the **Opposite direction** button on the **Section view** dialog.
3. Move the mouse pointer towards the right and click to position the section view.

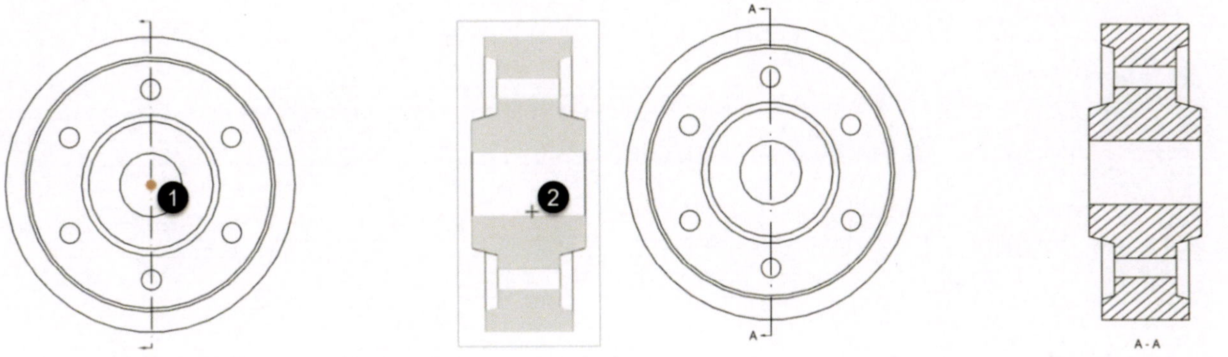

4. Activate the **Edge to edge centerline** command (click the **Edge to edge centreline** icon on the toolbar).
5. Select the two edges on the section view, as shown. The centreline is created between the two selected edges.
6. Likewise, create two more centrelines, as shown.

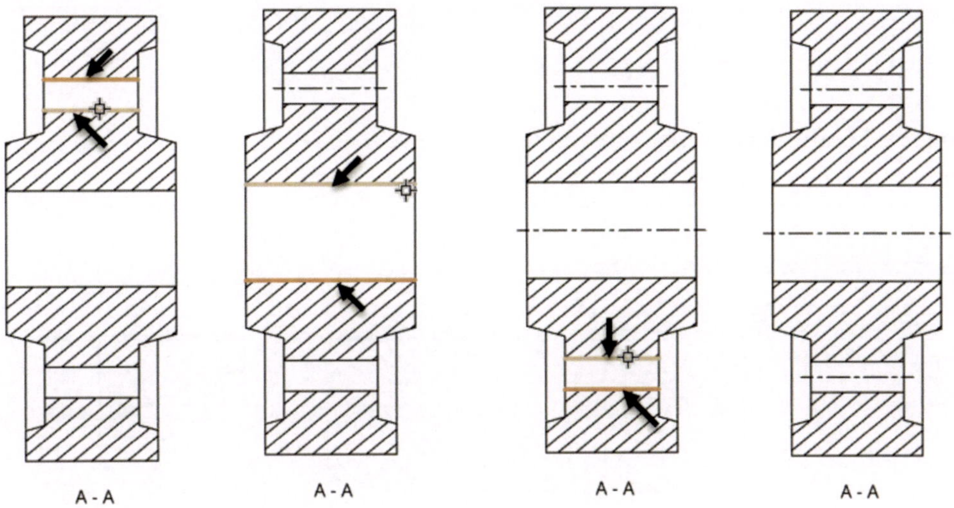

7. Activate the **3 point circle centerline** command (click the **3 point circle centreline** icon on the Toolbar) and click on the center point of the small hole at the top.
8. Likewise, select the remaining two center points of the small holes, as shown. The centreline is created between the three selected holes.

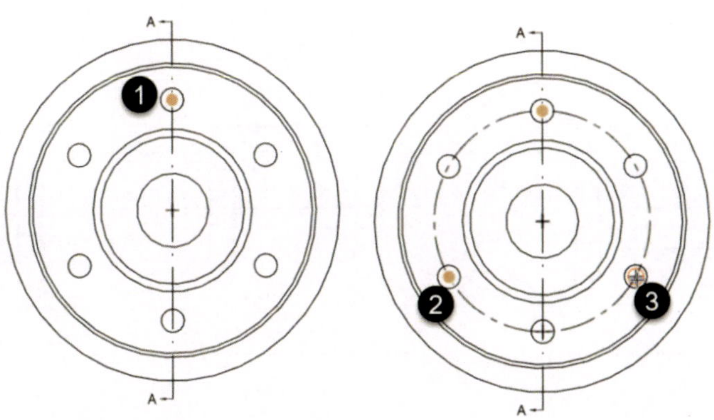

9. Click the **Centermark** command on the toolbar and select the inner circular edge of the front view.

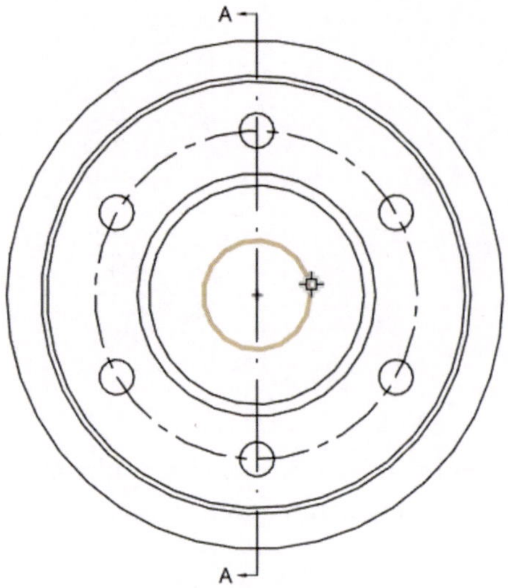

Adding Dimensions

Now, you add the dimensions to the drawing views.

1. Click **Dimension** drop-down > **2 point linear dimension** on the Toolbar.
2. Select the two points of the section view, as shown. Next, move the pointer upwards and click to add dimension.

3. Click **Dimension** drop-down > **Point to line dimension** on the toolbar.
4. Select the corner point and the line of the section view, as shown. Next, move the pointer and place the dimension, as shown.

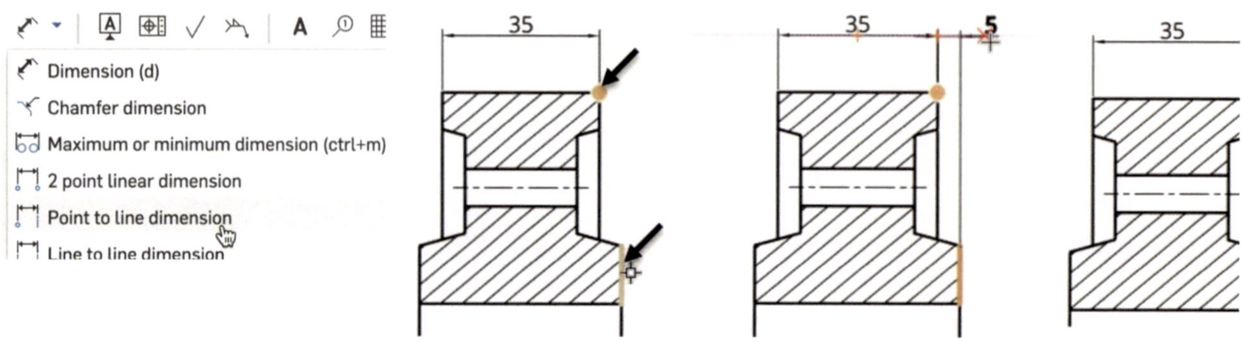

5. Click **Dimension** drop-down > **Line to line dimension** on the toolbar.

6. Select the two parallel edges of the section view, as shown. Next, move the pointer upward and click to position the dimension.

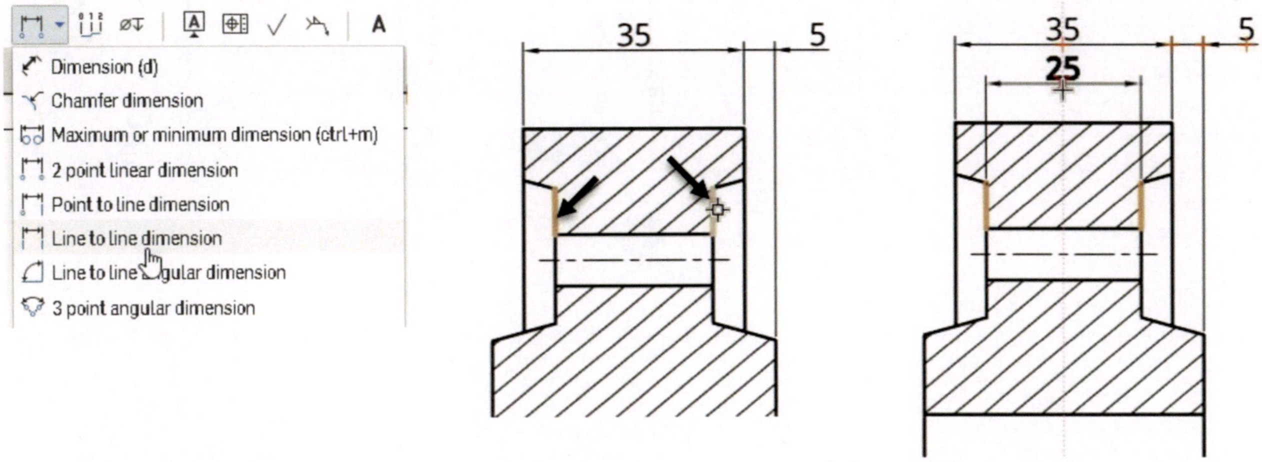

7. Click the **Dimension** command on the toolbar and select the two horizontal edges of the section view, as shown.
8. Move the pointer toward the right and click to position the dimension.
9. Place the pointer on the tolerance button that appears next to the dimension. Next, click the Insert symbol drop-down and select the diameter symbol.
10. Click in the graphics area.

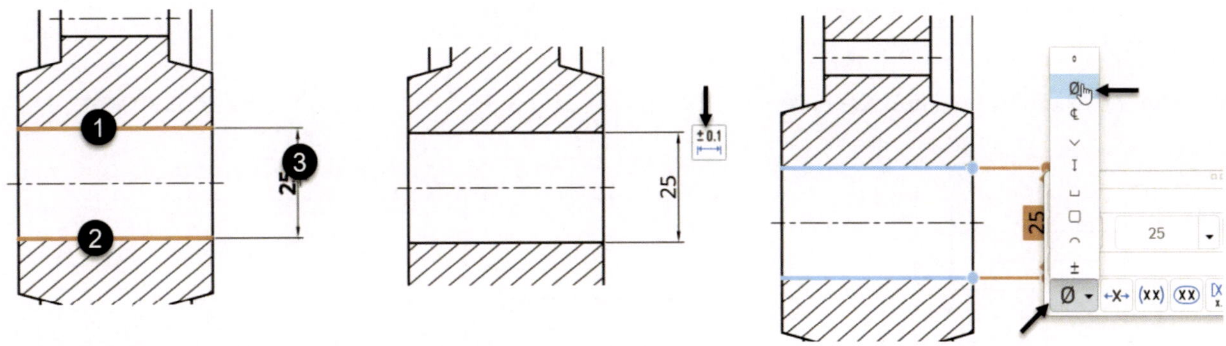

11. Likewise, add another dimension to the section view, as shown.

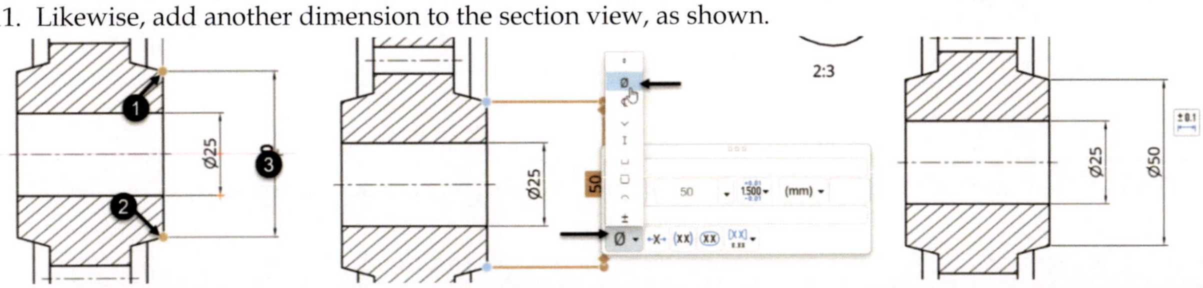

12. Click **Dimension** drop-down > **Line to line angular dimension** on the toolbar. Next, select the two edges of the section view, as shown.
13. Move the pointer toward the right and click to position the angular dimension. Next, click the tolerance button that appears next to the dimension.

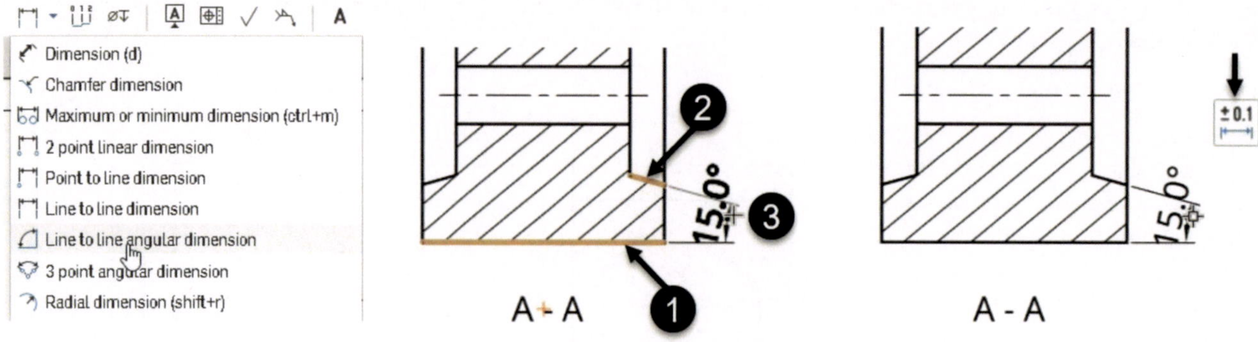

14. Click the **Precision** drop-down and select 0. Next, type **TYP** in the box next to the **Precision** drop-down.

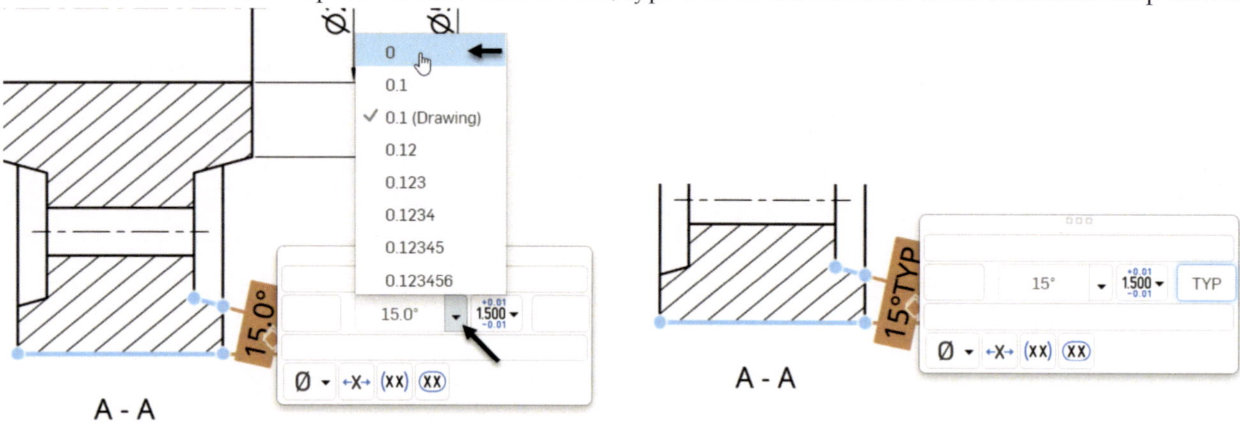

15. Click in the graphics area, and then press Esc. Next, click and drag the angular dimension, as shown.

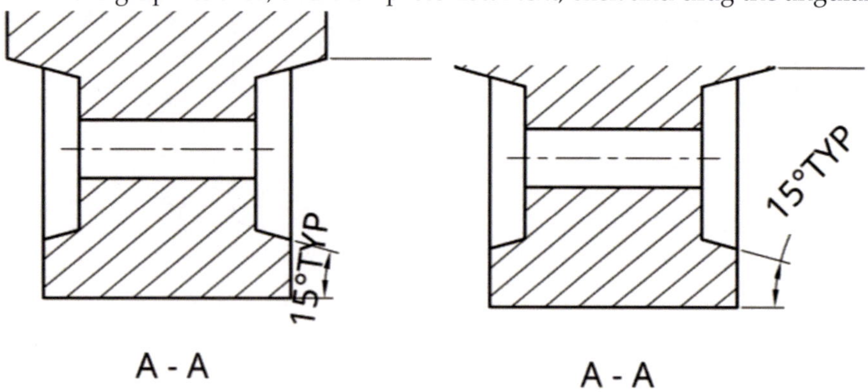

16. Click **Dimension** drop-down > **Diameter dimension** on the toolbar. Next, select the outer circular edge, as shown.
17. Move the pointer and click to position the dimension at the location, as shown.
18. Likewise, create another diameter dimension, as shown.

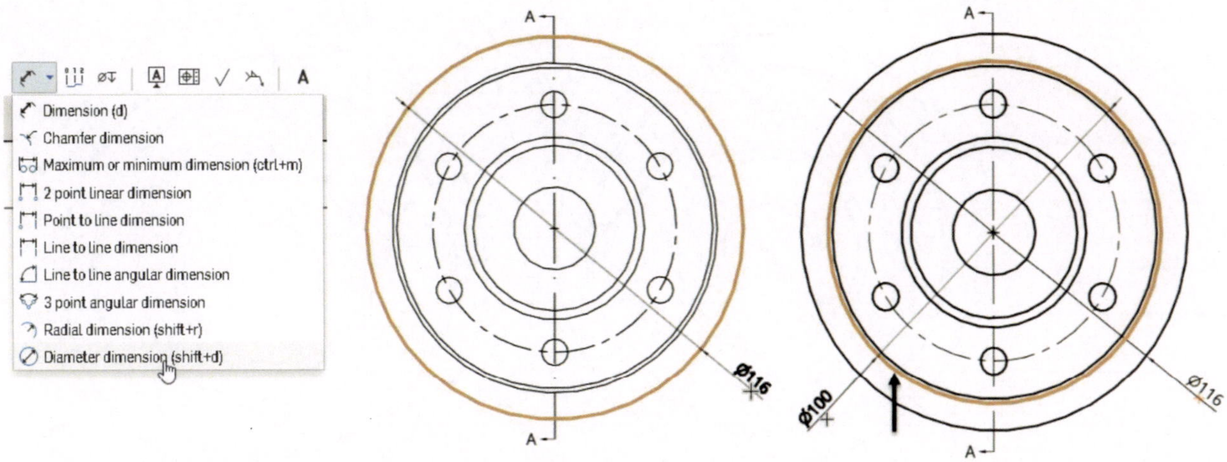

19. Activate the **Dimension** command (click the **Dimension** icon on the toolbar) and select the small hole on the front view, as shown.
20. Move the pointer diagonally and click to place the diameter dimension.
21. Likewise, apply the diameter dimension to the centerline passing through the small holes.

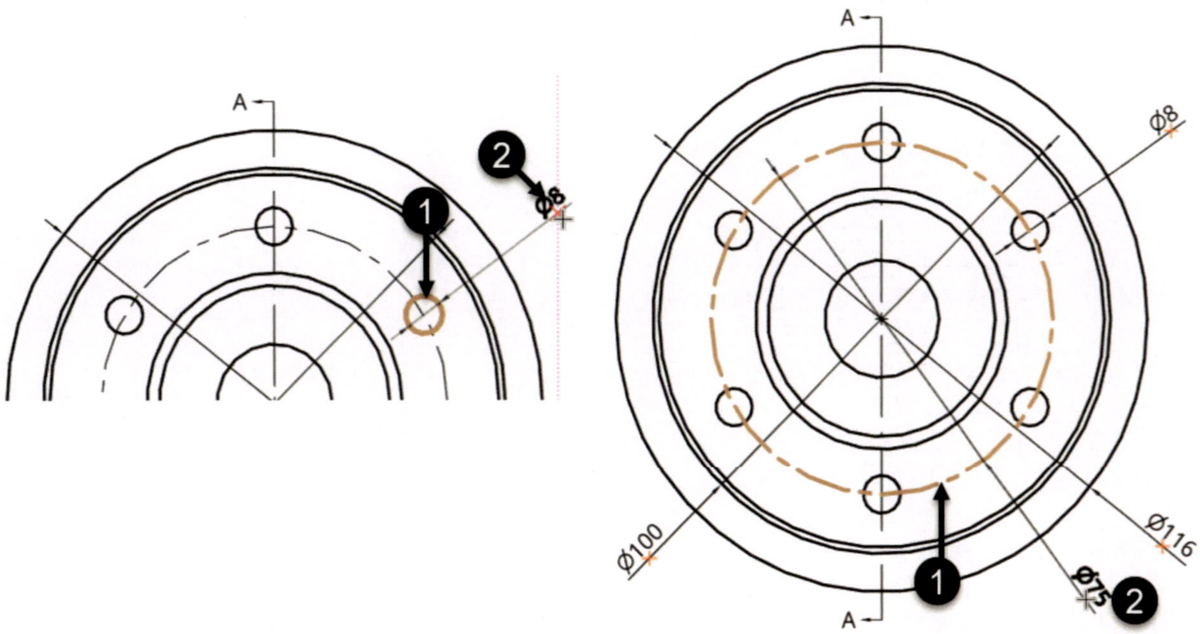

22. Click **Dimension** drop-down > **3 point angular dimension** on the toolbar. Next, select the centerpoint of the circle located at the center of the front view.
23. Select the center points of the two circles, as shown. Next, move the pointer outward and click to position the angular dimension.

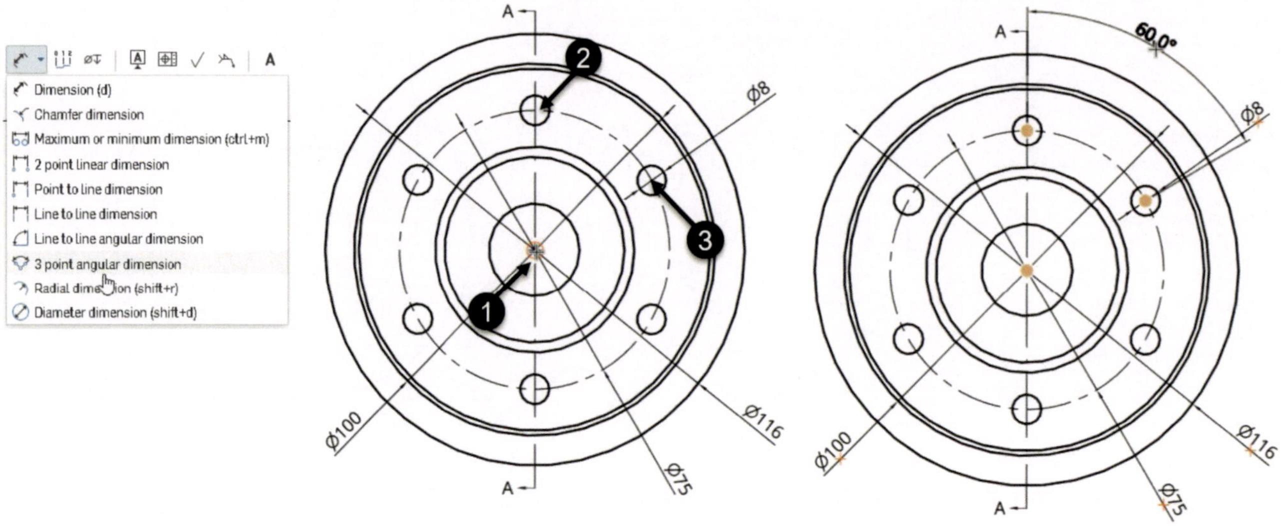

24. Click the **Document menu** located at the top left corner of the graphics area and select **Close document** to close the document.

Tutorial 2

In this example, you create an assembly drawing shown below.

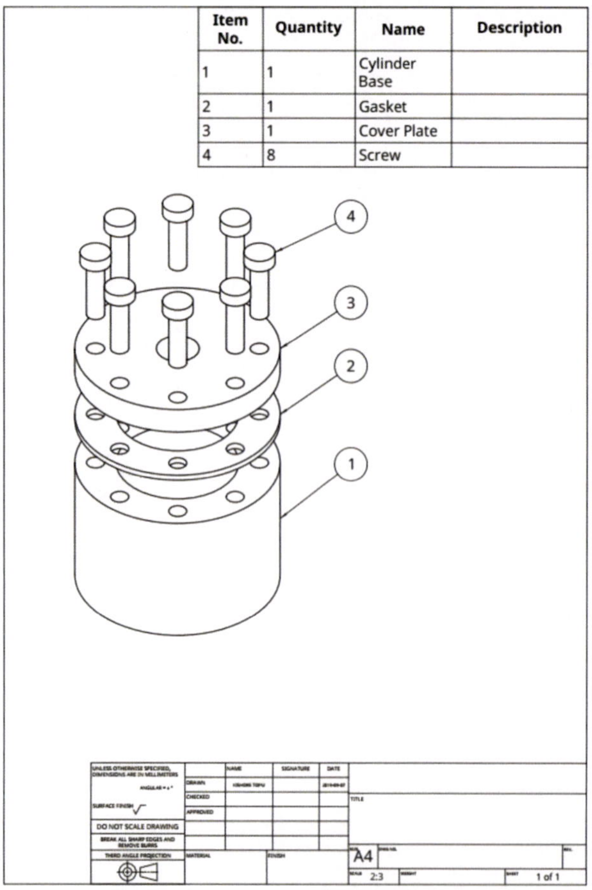

Item No.	Quantity	Name	Description
1	1	Cylinder Base	
2	1	Gasket	
3	1	Cover Plate	
4	8	Screw	

Creating a New Drawing

1. In your Internet Browser, go to https://www.onshape.com to start Onshape.
2. Next, click **SIGN IN** button located on the top right corner side of the web page. Enter the username and password, and then, click **Sign in**.
3. Double-click on the **Chapter 11** folder in the **Folders** section.
4. On the Documents page, Click **Create > Import Files** and select the **Tutorial 2** part file from the extracted Chapter 11 zip folder. Next, click **Open** to import the selected file.
5. Double click on the imported document to open it.

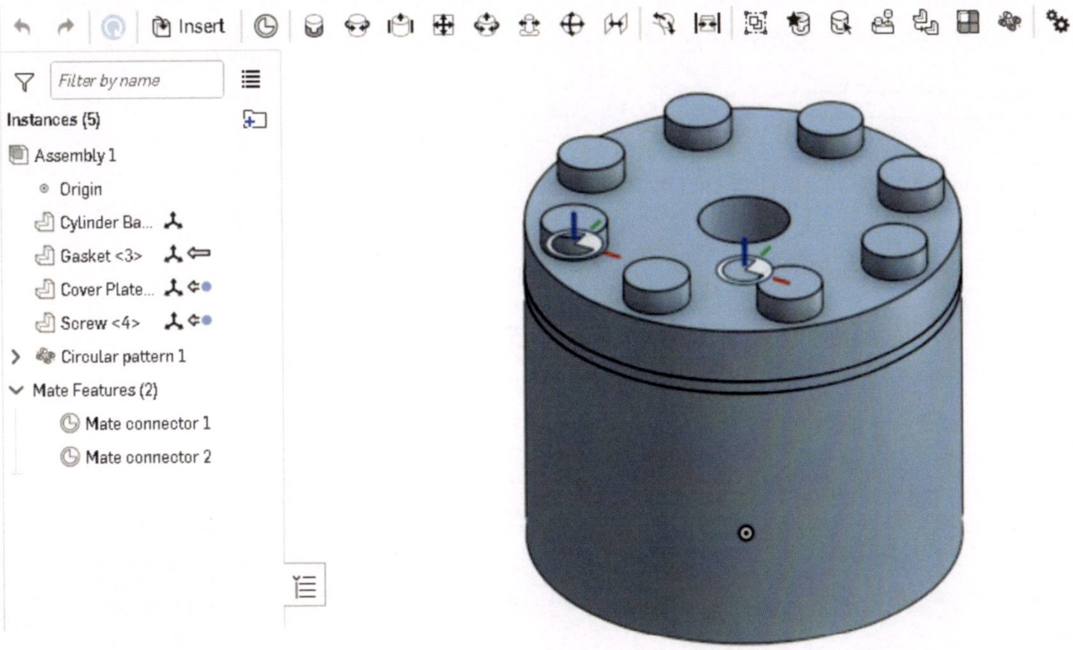

6. Select the **Exploded view** position from the drop-down located at the bottom of the **Named positions** dialog; the assembly is exploded.
7. Close the **Named positions** dialog.
8. Click the **Insert new element** button located at the bottom left corner of the window. Next, select **Create Drawing** from the menu.

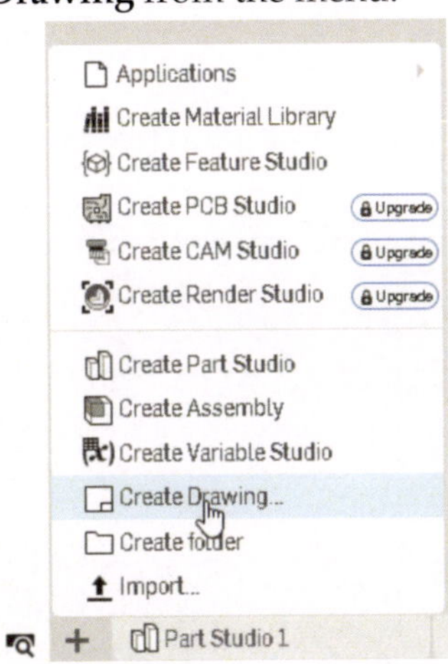

9. On the **Create Drawing** dialog, click the **Custom template** tab to create a custom template.
10. Select the **Standard > ISO** and then select **Size > A4 Portrait**.
11. Select the **Units > Millimeters** and then select **Decimal separator > Period (12.34)**.
12. Select **Projection > Third angle (ANSI)**.
13. In the **Borders** section on the right side of the dialog, click **Include** option to include the border in the drawing sheet.
14. Click **OK** to create a custom template and start a new drawing file.
15. Click on the **Assemblies** tab and select the **Assembly 1** from the **Select a part or assembly** dialog.
16. On the **Insert view** dialog, select **View > Isometric**. Next, type **2:3** in the **View scale** box.
17. Click on the drawing sheet at the location, as shown.
18. Press Esc to deactivate the **Projected View** command.

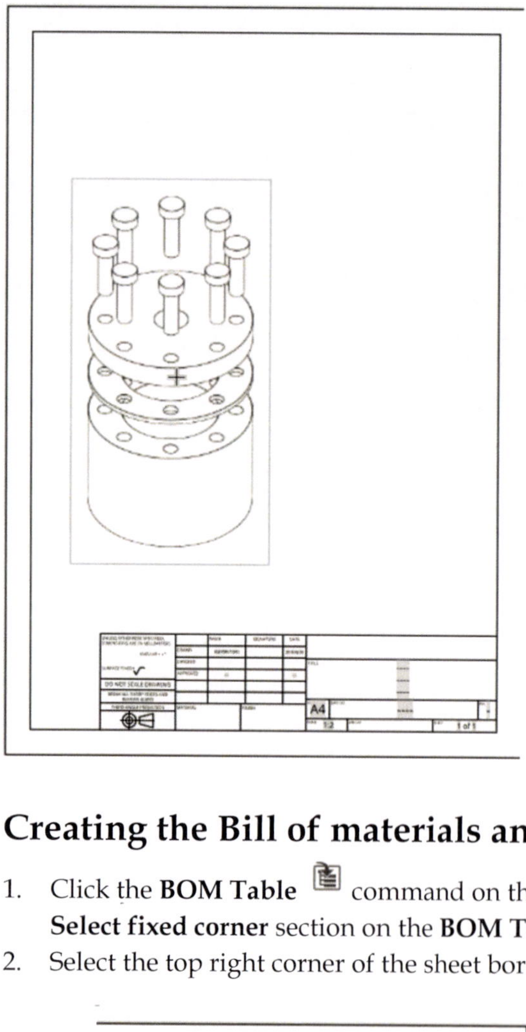

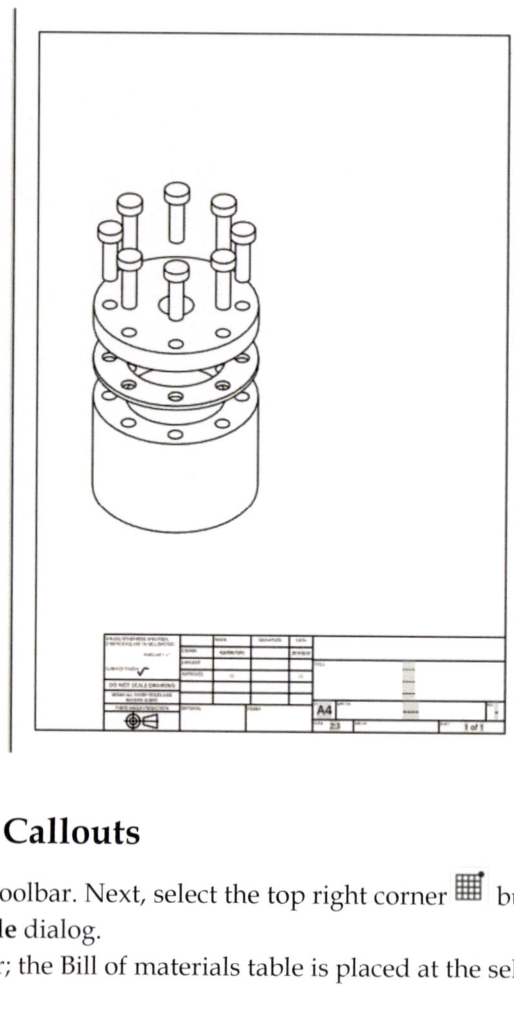

Creating the Bill of materials and Callouts

1. Click the **BOM Table** command on the toolbar. Next, select the top right corner button from the **Select fixed corner** section on the **BOM Table** dialog.
2. Select the top right corner of the sheet border; the Bill of materials table is placed at the selected point.

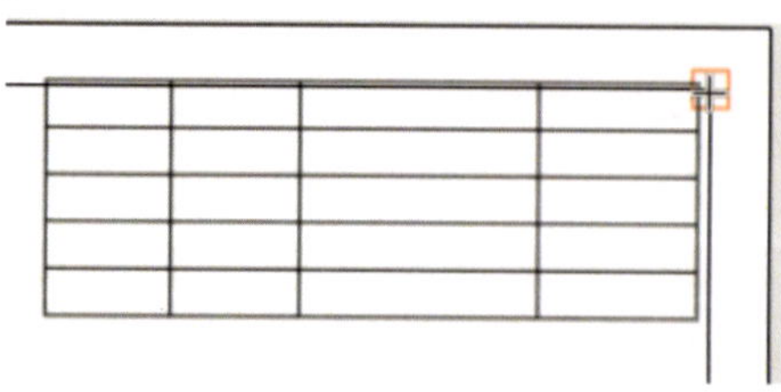

Item No.	Quantity	Name	Description
1	1	Pressure Cylinder	
2	1	Gasket	
3	1	Cover Plate	
4	8	Screw	

3. Place the pointer on the column edge of the **Description** column.
4. Press and hold the left mouse button and drag the pointer toward left; the **Description** column width is changed.

Item No.	Quantit y	Name	Descriptio n
1	1	Pressure Cylinder	
2	1	Gasket	
3	1	Cover Plate	
4	8	Screw	

Item No.	Quantit y	Name	Description
1	1	Pressure Cylinder	
2	1	Gasket	
3	1	Cover Plate	
4	8	Screw	

5. Likewise, change the column width of the **Quantity** column.

Item No.	Quantit y	Name	Description
1	1	Pressure Cylinder	
2	1	Gasket	
3	1	Cover Plate	
4	8	Screw	

Item No.	Quantity	Name	Description
1	1	Pressure Cylinder	
2	1	Gasket	
3	1	Cover Plate	
4	8	Screw	

6. On the toolbar, click the **Callouts** command.
7. On the **Callout** dialog, select **Table property** drop-down > **Item No.**
8. Select the midpoint of the vertical edge of the cylinder base to define the start point of the callout.
9. Move the pointer diagonally toward the right and click to define the balloon location.

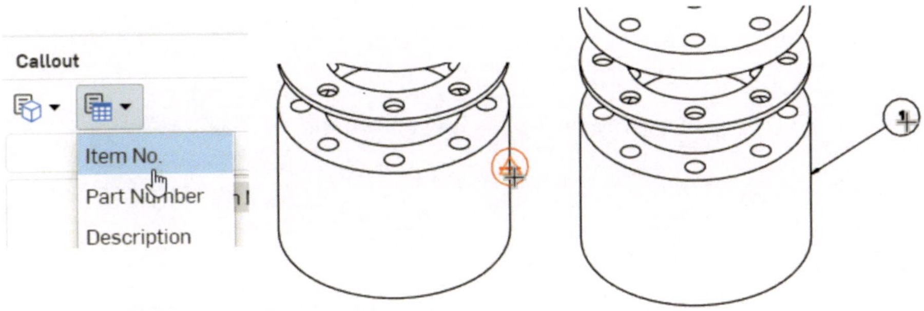

10. Select the quadrant point of the circular edge of the gasket. Next, move the pointer until a vertical traceline appears from the first balloon.
11. Click to position the balloon.
12. Likewise, add a callout to the cover plate and screw. Next, click the green check on the **Callout** dialog.

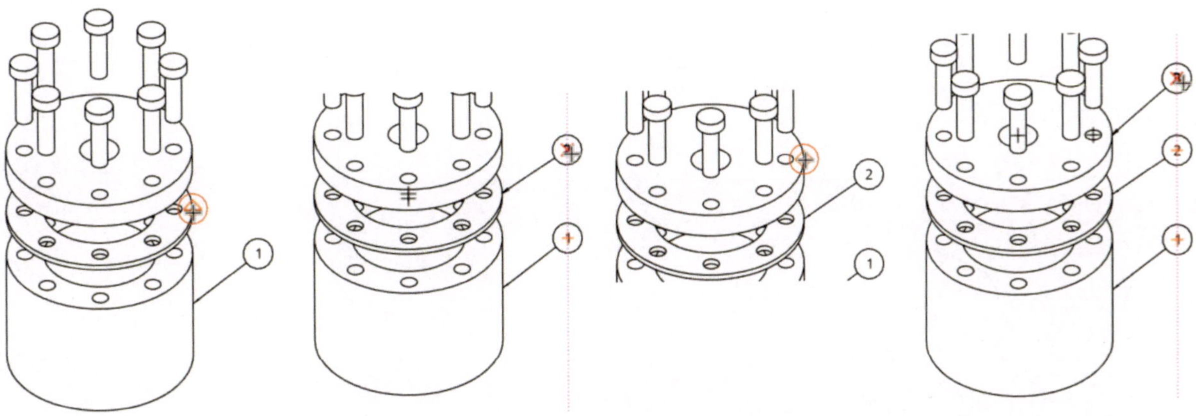

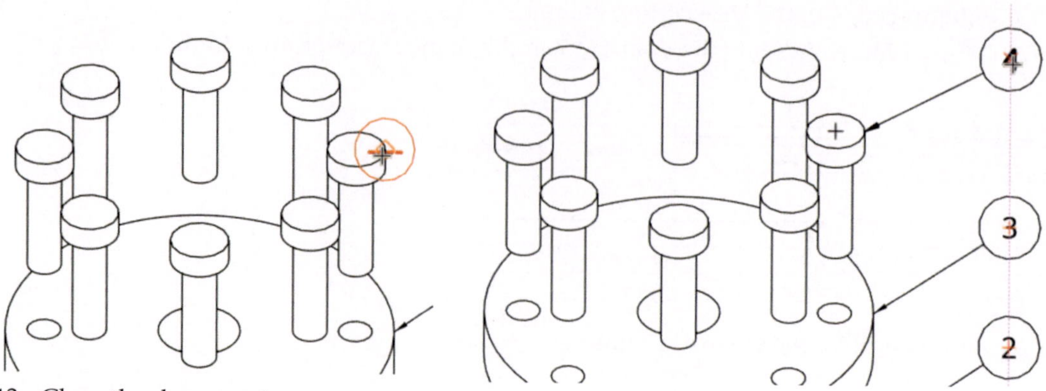

13. Close the document.

Questions

1. How to create drawing views from an existing part or assembly file?
2. How to change the display style of a drawing view?
3. List the commands used to create centerlines and center marks.
4. How to add symbols and texts to a dimension?
5. How to add break lines to a drawing view?
6. How to create revolved section views?
7. How to create an exploded view of an assembly?
8. How to edit a BOM table?
9. List the types of section views that can be created using the **Section View** command.

Exercises

Exercise 1

Create orthographic views of the part model shown below. Add dimensions and annotations to the drawing.

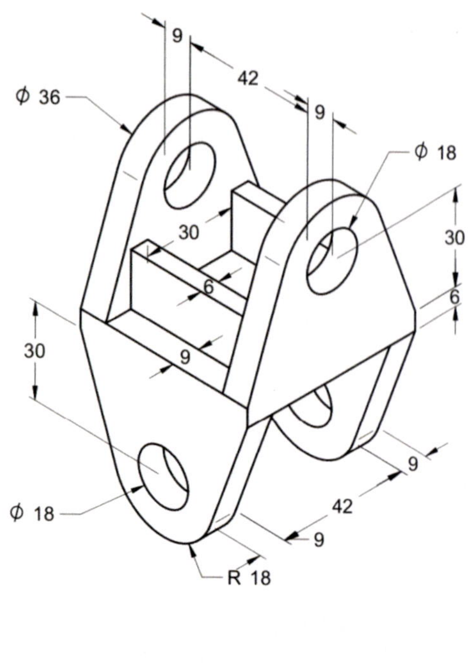

Exercise 2

Create orthographic views and an auxiliary view of the part model shown below. Add dimensions and annotations to the drawing.

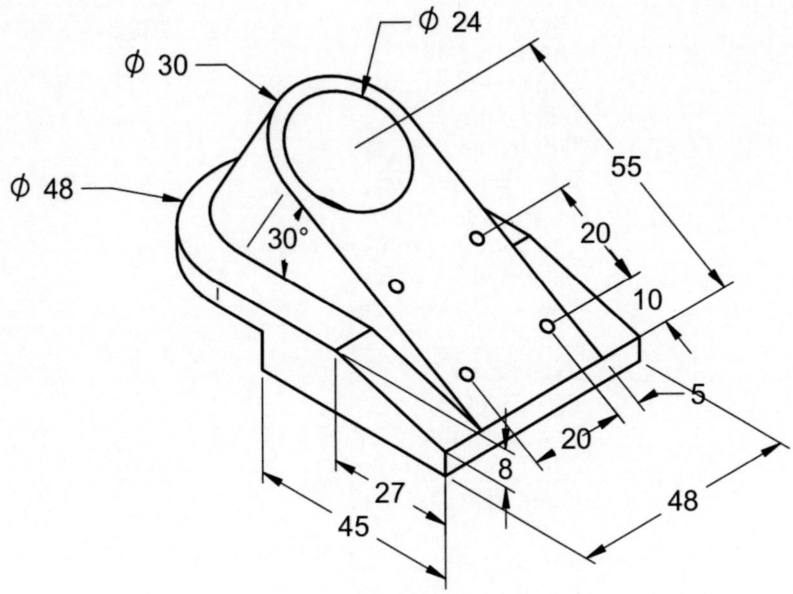

Index

9 788199 428911

Printed at Repro India Ltd.